Enterprise and Small Business
Principles, Practice and Policy

We work with leading authors to develop the
strongest educational materials in business, bringing
cutting-edge thinking and best learning practice
to a global market.

Under a range of well-known imprints, including
Financial Times Prentice Hall, we craft high quality
print and electronic publications which help
readers to understand and apply their content,
whether studying or at work.

To find out more about the complete range of our
publishing please visit us on the World Wide Web at
www.pearsoneduc.com

Enterprise and Small Business

Principles, Practice and Policy

Edited by

Sara Carter and Dylan Jones-Evans

An imprint of **Pearson Education**

Harlow, England · London · New York · Reading, Massachusetts · San Francisco · Toronto · Don Mills, Ontario · Sydney
Tokyo · Singapore · Hong Kong · Seoul · Taipei · Cape Town · Madrid · Mexico City · Amsterdam · Munich · Paris · Milan

'To Harri and Ben – entrepreneurs of the future.'

Pearson Education Limited

Edinburgh Gate
Harlow
Essex CM20 2JE
England

and Associated Companies around the world

Visit us on the World Wide Web at
www.pearsoneduc.com

First published in Great Britain in 2000

Copyright © Pearson Education Limited 2000

ISBN 0 201 39852 4

British Library Cataloguing-in-Publication Data
A CIP catalogue record for this book can be obtained from the British Library.

10 9 8 7 6 5 4 3 2 1
04 03 02 01 00

Typeset by 42 in 10/12 Sabon
Printed by Ashford Colour Press Ltd., Gosport

Contents

8 The psychology of the entrepreneur 132

Frédéric Delmar

9 Family and enterprise 155

Denise Fletcher

10 Gender and enterprise 166

Sara Carter

11 Ethnicity and enterprise 182

Monder Ram and Giles Barrett

12 Franchising and enterprise

John Stanworth and David Purdy

13 Technical entrepreneurship

Sarah Cooper

14 Intrapreneurship

Dylan Jones-Evans

15   Entrepreneurship in transitional economies   259
Milford Bateman and Lester Lloyd-Reason

Section III   MANAGEMENT AND THE SMALL FIRM   281

16   Strategy and the small firm   283
Colm O'Gorman

17   People and the small firm   300
Susan Marlow

Contents

List of figures

List of tables

List of contributors

Giles Barrett is a Lecturer in Human Geography at Liverpool John Moores University.

Milford Bateman is Head of the Local Economic Development in Transition Economies Unit at the University of Wolverhampton.

Jürgen Kai-Uwe Brock is a Doctoral Researcher at the Department of Marketing, University of Strathclyde.

David Brooksbank is a Principal Lecturer in Economics at the Welsh Enterprise Institute, University of Glamorgan.

Sara Carter is a Senior Research Fellow in the Department of Marketing, University of Strathclyde.

Stephen Conway is a Lecturer in Innovation at Aston University.

Sarah Cooper is a Lecturer in Strategic Management at the Department of Business Organisation at Heriot-Watt University, Edinburgh.

David Deakins is Professor and Director of the Paisley Enterprise Research Centre at the University of Paisley.

Frédéric Delmar is Assistant Professor at the Entrepreneurship and Small Business Research Institute (ESBRI), Stockholm.

Denise Fletcher is a Senior Lecturer at the Centre for Growing Businesses, Nottingham Trent University.

Kevin Ibeh is a Lecturer in the Department of Marketing, University of Strathclyde.

Robin Jarvis is Professor of Accounting and Finance at Kingston University.

Anne Jenkins is a Senior Research Associate at the Foresight Research Centre, University of Durham Business School.

Steve Johnson is a Research Consultant at the Centre for Enterprise and Economic Development Research, Middlesex University Business School.

Dylan Jones-Evans is Professor of Entrepreneurship and Small Business Management at the Welsh Enterprise Institute, University of Glamorgan.

Lester Lloyd-Reason is a Senior Lecturer in Business at Anglia Business School.

Susan Marlow is a Lecturer at the Department of Human Resource Management, De Montfort University.

Harry Matlay is a Reader in Entrepreneurship at the University of Central England Business School.

Alison Morrison is a Senior Lecturer at the Scottish Hotel School, University of Strathclyde.

Colm O'Gorman is a Lecturer in the Michael Smurfit Graduate School of Business, University College Dublin.

David Purdy is Deputy Director of the International Franchise Research Centre at the University of Westminster.

Monder Ram is Professor of Small Business at the Department of Corporate Strategy at De Montfort University Business School.

Richard Scase is Visiting Professor at the Institute for Economic and Social Research at the University of Essex.

Leigh Sear is a Research Associate at the Small Business Centre, University of Durham Business School.

Eleanor Shaw is a Lecturer in the Department of Marketing, University of Strathclyde.

David Smallbone is Professor of Small and Medium Enterprise and Head of Centre for Enterprise and Economic Development at Middlesex University Business School.

Alan Southern is a Lecturer in the Management of Economic Development at the University of Durham Business School.

John Stanworth is Professor and Director of the International Franchise Research Centre at the University of Westminster.

David Stokes is a Research Fellow in Small Business Studies at the Small Business Research Centre, Kingston University.

Geoff Whittam is a Lecturer in Economics at the University of Paisley.

Peter Wyer is a Reader in Small Business Management at De Montfort University Business School.

Acknowledgements

We are grateful to the following for permission to reproduce copyright material:

Table 2.1 from Labour Market Trends 1997, Office for National Statistics © Crown Copyright 1999; Table 2.2 from N. Meager, 'Self-employment in the United Kingdom', *IMS Report* No. 205, 1991, Institute of Manpower Studies; Figure 2.2, Figure 2.3 from DTI SME Statistics Unit 1997, reprinted with permission from Her Majesty's Stationary Office; Table 2.3 and Table 2.4 from M. Daly, 'The 1980s: a decade of growth in enterprise', *Employment Gazette*, March 1991, Office for National Statistics © Crown Copyright 1999; Table 2.5 from Labour Force Survey 1995, Office for National Statistics © Crown Copyright 1999; Table 2.6 from Labour Force Survey 1991, in M. Campbell and M. Daly, 'Self-employment in the 1990s', *Employment Gazette*, June 1992, Office for National Statistics © Crown Copyright 1999; Table 2.8, Table 2.9, Table 2.10 and Table 2.11 from DTI SME Statistics Unit 1997, reprinted with permission from Her Majesty's Stationary Office; Figure 5.1 from J. Painter, 'Regulation, regime, and practice in urban politics', in Lauria, M. (ed) *Reconstructing Urban Regime Theory: Regulating Urban Politics in a Global Economy*, copyright © 1997, reprinted by permission of Sage Publications, Inc; Table 10.1 from Labour Force Survey 1997, Office for National Statistics © Crown Copyright 1999; Figure 11.1 from *Employment Gazette*, June 1992, Office for National Statistics © Crown Copyright 1999; Figure 12.3 from A. Felstead, *The Corporate Paradox – Power and Control in the Business Franchise*, copyright © 1993, reprinted by permission of Routledge; Figure 22.1 abbreviated from L.G. Tesler, 'Networked computing in the 1990s', *Scientific American*, Special Issue 1995, 6 (1), 'The Computer in the 21st Century', reprinted from the September 1991 issue; Figure 22.2 adapted from R. Boaden and G. Lockett, 'Information technology, information systems and information management: definition and development', *European Journal of Information Systems*, 1 (1) 1991, reproduced with permission from Macmillan Press Limited; Figure 22.4 from Department of Trade and Industry 1998, reprinted with permission from Her Majesty's Stationary Office; Figure 23.1 based on Figure 5.1, in D. Storey, *Understanding the Small Business Sector*, copyright © 1994, reprinted by permission of Routledge; Figure 24.1 from R. Luostarinen, *Internationalisation of the Firm*, published by the Helsinki School of Economics 1980; Table 24.1 from OECD, *Globalisation and Small and Medium Enterprises (SMEs)*, vol. 1, copyright © OECD 1997.

Whilst every effort has been made to trace the owners of copyright material, in a few cases this has proved impossible and we take this opportunity to offer our apologies to any copyright holders whose rights we may have unwittingly infringed.

SECTION I

The small business environment

CHAPTER 1

Introduction

Sara Carter and Dylan Jones-Evans

1.1 Background

During the last twenty years, society's attitudes towards entrepreneurship have changed considerably. Gone are the days when the entrepreneur would be seen as the 'deviant' individual on the margins of society. In today's society, individuals such as Richard Branson and Bill Gates, who have single-handedly built up business empires from relatively humble beginnings, are revered as role models that many wish to emulate.

In the same way that entrepreneurs have become an accepted part of everyday life, the influence of the small firm has also grown considerably. Whilst this has been driven by various factors – such as the decline of large businesses, the development of an 'enterprise culture' and opportunities for niches arising from structural changes such as the information revolution – awareness of the existence of small firms has increased mainly because of the significant roles they have played within the economies around the world throughout much of the twentieth century.

As this book will demonstrate, perhaps their greatest contribution during the last twenty years has been in the creation of employment. Whilst it has been argued that a small firm, because of its size, can make only a minor contribution to the economy, as there are so many small firms their collective contribution is substantial. For example, in the European Union, large firms experienced employment loss in nearly every member state, whilst employment by small firms grew considerably. According to data from the European Observatory (ENSR 1997), SMEs (small and medium-sized enterprises, employing up to 250 people) accounted for 68 million jobs in the European Union in 1995, with large firms employing approximately 35 million. In particular, they have been vital to the success of many countries on the continents of Asia and Africa, and, more recently, in the restructuring of the former Soviet bloc countries of Eastern Europe.

Apart from creating jobs in the economy, small firms also play a variety of other roles. For example, whilst the economies of scale in production and distribution enable large firms to make a significant contribution to the economy, many of them could not survive without the existence of small companies, who sell direct to the public most of the products made by large manufacturers as well as providing them with many of the services and supplies they require to run a competitive business. Small firms have also introduced many products and services to the consumer, especially in specialised markets that are too small for larger companies to consider worthwhile. Finally, small businesses also provide an outlet for entrepreneurial individuals, many of whom would have found it almost impossible to work for a large organisation.

1.2 Why this book?

The increased importance of entrepreneurs and the small-firm sector has led to considerable growth in interest in such individuals and the companies they establish and grow. Whilst it can be argued that the economists of the eighteenth century established the first understanding of this area, the field has grown considerably during the twentieth century to encompass disciplines as varied as sociology, psychology, management studies and anthropology. Indeed, the chapters within this book draw on various approaches to explain issues such as the enterprise culture, technological entrepreneurship, finance in the small firm, and the psychology of the entrepreneur. Therefore, the field of small business and entrepreneurship studies has always been diverse.

Contemporary interest in the subject essentially dates from the early 1970s, when a number of critical events saw both a loss of confidence in large-scale industry and growing popular and governmental interest in small businesses. Even before this period, however, there had been research analysing the small-firm sector from historical, geographical and socio-economic perspectives. What changed in the 1970s was both the volume of research undertaken and its direct role in influencing national economic policy. For the first time also, academics researching the field from within different disciplines formed associations, held international conferences to advance research in the area, and established a number of university-based centres focusing on the study of small business and entrepreneurship. These early initiatives have developed considerably. Many of the annual colloquia, such as the UK Small Firms Policy and Research Conference and the United States Association of Small Business and Entrepreneurship, have now entered their third decade. The range of scholarly journals focusing on the small firm has increased substantially, as has their specialisation. The number of university-based small business and enterprise research centres has also increased. Importantly, many of these centres have increasingly sought to disseminate their work within the mainstream university curricula by offering courses to undergraduate and postgraduate students. At the same time, there has been an increasing number of business schools around the world that now offer small business and entrepreneurship as a legitimate subject within their studies. However, whilst this sort of course is commonplace within the USA, it is still only beginning to be accepted by business schools in Europe, albeit in increasing numbers, especially as many students now expect this area to be an integral part of their management degree.

Despite these developments, small-firm research is often regarded as a new area. Clearly, this is no longer the case. As each of the contributions in this volume demonstrates, research undertaken over the past three decades has led to substantial theoretical and methodological advances. The field is far from exhausted, however. Each chapter within this volume demonstrates the extent, and also the incompleteness, of our understanding of many issues surrounding the small-business sector. The development of the subject has not been confined to research, and can also be seen in the teaching of small business studies. The growing trend to include small business studies as part of mainstream university curricula reflects both popular interest in small firms and their importance in economic development. Like many management subjects, small business studies draws from a range of disciplinary sources including, among others, economics, sociology, psychology, history and geography. We have tried to reflect the broad base of the subject in the breadth of the themes covered in this volume.

The initial idea for this book was raised at a seminar for small business researchers held at the University of Glamorgan in September 1997, and developed in further seminars held at the universities of Durham, Strathclyde and Nottingham Trent. The wide range of research interests within even this small group of people appeared to reflect the growing diversity of research themes which make up the small business and enterprise field. As the small business research field has grown and diversified over the past thirty years, so too have the number and content of small business courses taught in universities and colleges throughout the world. However, there is no single textbook that encapsulates the range of small business themes in the depth required for undergraduate and postgraduate work. This book has been designed specifically to address the need for a single reference point for the growing number of students undertaking courses in small business and entrepreneurial studies.

In determining the themes to be included in this book, guidance was taken from the syllabuses of several university and college courses. Many of the initial small business courses taught in universities and colleges, such as the Graduate Enterprise Programme, were designed to encourage and enable students to actually start an enterprise. Increasingly, however, courses are designed to provide students with a more comprehensive insight into the small-business sector. This reflects not only the need to encourage students to perhaps start in business for themselves, but also that an increasing number of graduates will be employed within the small-business sector or in occupations that directly or indirectly support that sector. Today, courses in small business studies are taught by a range of subject departments, including business and management, social sciences, arts and humanities. By including a broad range of themes in the required depth, we hope that this book will satisfy all students of the subject, irrespective of departmental affiliation.

This book contains 24 chapters from 30 contributors. One of the difficulties of editing such a large number of contributions is to ensure a degree of standardisation with regard to focus and remit. When writing their chapters, authors were asked to present an overview of the specific body of work and explain how the field had developed over time. Even in such a large volume as this, not all issues can be explained in the depth which may be required; however, we believe that each chapter amply fulfils the criterion of providing a starting-point for students. One of the advantages of an edited collection of work is the ability to draw on acknowledged subject experts to provide specialised accounts of their specific research areas. We would like to thank each contributor not only for their chapter contributions, but also for giving their time and enthusiasm so freely. Collectively, this book represents a substantial body of knowledge, written by subject experts, which we hope will provide an excellent reference point for students, researchers and teachers alike.

1.3 Structure of the book

The book is divided into three main sections that essentially reflect the three areas that concern the small firm today. These are the environment in which it operates, the various types of individuals who start and subsequently manage the venture, and finally the various functions which have to be managed within the firm in order for it to succeed. As you will see when reading the various chapters, there are often no distinct boundaries between the issues discussed within chapters and so, where possible, we have linked the relevant sections to other chapters within the book.

The first section examines the small business environment, and begins with an overview of self-employment and business ownership within the overall economy. Subsequent chapters in this section build upon this initial overview to examine the social, political and cultural environment of small firms.

The second section concentrates on entrepreneurship within the small firm. We begin by examining the cultural influences that enable entrepreneurship to be initiated within different societies (Chapter 6). The next chapter then considers the act of new-venture creation through analysing the specific factors that lead to business start-up. A great deal of research interest has focused on the distinctive personality characteristics of the entrepreneur and their relationship with business success. Frédéric Delmar's chapter explores the various approaches to the psychology of the entrepreneur. The next five chapters in this section each examine distinctive types of entrepreneur – family, female, ethnic, franchised and technological – each demonstrating specific characteristics which differentiate them from other types of owner-manager. The remaining two chapters in this section examine two emerging themes within the entrepreneurship research literature, namely that of creating an entrepreneurial environment within a large organisation, and that of stimulating entrepreneurial development within transitional economies.

The final section focuses on specific management functions within the small business. Mainstream management subjects such as strategy, human resource management (HRM), training, finance and marketing are discussed from the specific viewpoint of the small firm and its stakeholders. In addition, specific challenges to the future development of the small firm – such as networking, information and communication technologies, growth and development, and internationalisation – are explored to highlight the potential for further expansion that exists within the sector.

CHAPTER 2

Self-employment and small firms

David Brooksbank

2.1 Learning objectives

There are three learning objectives in this chapter:

1 To appreciate the numbers of individuals involved in self-employment and small firm activity in the UK and their importance to the economy.
2 To be aware of the major trends and changes to the stock of self-employed and small firms over the past two decades.
3 To link the important themes, covered elsewhere in the text, to the baseline data.

Key concepts

- self-employment   ▪ small businesses   ▪ statistical profiles
- personal characteristics

2.2 Introduction

This chapter provides a general introduction to the core statistical data on the self-employed and small firms in the UK. The chapter starts by providing an overview of the self-employed, who they are, why they enter self-employment, their personal characteristics, their jobs and the industrial sectors that they enter. The chapter then goes on to discuss the small-firm sector. After providing some official definitions of small firms, the chapter goes on to highlight some of the key trends in the numbers of small firms, industry patterns and regional differences. A key feature discussed in this chapter is the growth in self-employment and small business activity over the past twenty years. Although this chapter concentrates on the UK situation, this trend has been apparent in many other countries.

2.3 The self-employed

Detailed and comprehensive analysis of the self-employed received very little attention from the economics profession prior to the 1980s. Set against a background of declining numbers stemming from the days of the industrial revolution, this is hardly surprising. However, during that decade something new happened to self-employment in the UK: the numbers of self-employed rose by approximately 60% to 3.4 million, forming almost 13% of the workforce. This dramatic rise has caused a well-deserved resurgence of interest. The increases in self-employment in the 1980s and the subsequent fall during the recession at the start of the 1990s have given rise to a lively debate about the types of people tempted to give self-employment a try.

The first part of this chapter presents the data on these people and will allow you to link themes and trends to the rest of the text. Research undertaken by Meager *et al.* (1996) studied the income distribution of the self-employed – both male and female. (Other authors have also added interesting material to this debate, including Jenkins (1994) and S. Parker (1997).) On average, the self-employed earn as much as wage earners but there is a significant dispersion, with one group of very high earners at one end of the spectrum (usually male) and at the other a large and growing group of poor self-employed. To elaborate, a self-employed person has more than three times the chance of falling into the bottom 10% of the income distribution as does a comparable type of employee (i.e. earning approximately £40–£50 per week). Meager *et al.* also comment that self-employment, even if it forms only part of a working career, can put people's future financial security at risk. If a person has a 'punctuated' work history with periods of employment, unemployment and self-employment, then they are more likely to be pushed into the poorer group of self-employed workers in later life because they are less likely to have a stable occupational pension and less likely to have a significant volume of savings. This in turn implies a greater dependency upon the state pension in later life. The increased heterogeneity of the self-employed population means that those at the bottom end of the earnings spectrum cannot expect things to improve dramatically over the next few years.

There is no automatic link between self-employment and poverty, although equally there is no such link between self-employment and success. Storey (1994) believes that it is important for the self-employed to have a realistic understanding of what they are undertaking. He has discovered instances where people have entered self-employment and then run up considerable personal debt. They survive in business only by working very long hours at low rates of pay (although in some cases this provides them with not only employment, but a certain status within society).

If self-employment risks leading to debt and poverty, then why are so many people choosing it? Anecdotal evidence suggests that some of the new self-employed have been actively forced into it by their companies. Citizens' Advice Bureaux across the country have noticed that for the last five or six years an increasing number of people are coming to them with problems associated with self-employment. One major problem is that self-employment status has been imposed upon them. Employers see the advantages, in a short-term sense, of having a self-employed workforce. The rights of these people are then adversely affected by this when the company is no longer liable for pension contributions and employer's National Insurance contributions. It is hard to determine how many of these types of people there are among the total self-employed, but such reluctant entrepreneurs should be kept in mind.

A larger group who have entered self-employment are those who were previously unemployed. The encouragement of the unemployed to become their own bosses has been a constant of government policy since the early 1980s. There has been a succession of initiatives: the Enterprise Allowance Scheme (EAS), the Business Start-Up scheme and the Enterprise Support Programme. These schemes all require a moderate amount of capital to be injected prior to registration, and often banks are reluctant to lend to people who have previously been unemployed. Lack of capital or assets to act as collateral is a major problem which has been studied by Anup Shah. His research, which is supported by the findings of many other studies (including that of Black, De Meza and Jeffreys (1996)), has shown that house price inflation and financial liberalisation in the 1980s permitted people to borrow and start up on their own far more easily than was previously and is now the case. The illiquid wealth stored in houses could be freed as a result of this financial liberalisation. A deliberate focus of government policy was, therefore, to allow people the chance of entrepreneurship after years of being stuck with few liquid funds. More recently, Martin Robson (1996a) has thrown some doubt on the role played by housing collateral in his informative study of business start-ups. The differing results make this an interesting area for future work.

Meager et al. (1996) have also undertaken research that has convinced the authors that the necessary attributes for success in self-employment cannot easily be inculcated by training. They believe that entrepreneurs are more likely to be born with these attributes, and one of the best predictors of someone becoming self-employed and succeeding is whether either or both of their parents have been self-employed.

The sorts of people who come from a family tradition of self-employment (a small business culture wherein can be found appreciation of the essentials for success, like knowledge of contracts and the need to save in the form of a pension for old age) are more likely to stay in business. However, a picture is also emerging of many people entering from other backgrounds. Many have been employees all their lives, as have their parents, and after redundancy they set up on their own but are less likely to have the skills and attributes which are a good predictor of success. This is likely to be one of the explanations of why these people fall disproportionately into the low-income sector of the self-employed.

Storey (1994) takes the analysis further by emphasising that self-employment for the unemployed (including those made redundant) is no guarantee of an entrepreneurial society. There is a notion that if somehow the unemployed can be transformed into self-employed, this has a number of advantages: first, that these people are no longer registered as unemployed and, secondly, that some additional output *must* be created. In reality, however, the unemployed enter the more casual industries (e.g. window cleaning, hairdressing or vehicle repair) and create unwelcome competition for people already there. These people may then enter unemployment with possible adverse social consequences for themselves. There is a circularity of moving from self-employment into unemployment and back again, with no consequent impact upon aggregate employment or on wealth creation.

The numbers of those becoming self-employed are rising again after levelling off during the depths of the recession in the early 1990s. However, the new evidence suggests that a significant number of these people will be reluctant entrepreneurs. Without prospects of a secure job, people are being forced to give self-employment a try.

2.4 Who are the self-employed and what do they do?

This section begins by finding out what the aggregate data say about the self-employed: how many are there? Which jobs do they do? Where do they live? How have these factors changed over time? The major source of data is the Labour Force Survey (LFS) for Great Britain, and updates of the analysis of self-employment figures in it by Martin Campbell and Michael Daly (1992) for the Employment Department provide the basis for the review that follows.

2.4.1 Aggregate data

In Great Britain the total number of self-employed persons (calculated using the grossing-up procedures adopted for the Labour Force Survey) was some 3,247,000 in 1997. This represents an increase of 1,046,000 (47.5%) since 1981. The figure rose steadily throughout the 1980s and only declined as the recession of 1990 took effect. This remarkable rise is illustrated in Figure 2.1.

A more detailed analysis of the rise during the last decade is shown in Table 2.1, which also provides a breakdown by gender. The figures are for Great Britain only.

Table 2.1 Numbers self-employed, by gender (thousands)

	All persons	Male	Female
1979	1,778	1,442	336
1981	2,201	1,745	456
1983	2,301	1,751	550
1984	2,616	1,980	636
1985	2,713	2,032	681
1986	2,729	2,050	679
1987	2,969	2,224	745
1988	3,148	2,369	779
1989	3,441	2,621	820
1990	3,482	2,641	841
1991	3,330	2,528	802
1992	3,147	2,370	777
1993	3,108	2,316	792
1994	3,216	2,407	809
1995	3,269	2,471	798
1996	3,205	2,392	813
1997	3,247	2,402	845
% increases			
1981–1990	59	52	85
1990–1991	–4	–4	–5
1991–1992	–6	–6	–3
1981–1997	47	38	86

Source: Labour Market Trends (1997), Office for National Statistics © Crown Copyright 1999

Figure 2.1 Self-employment (thousands)

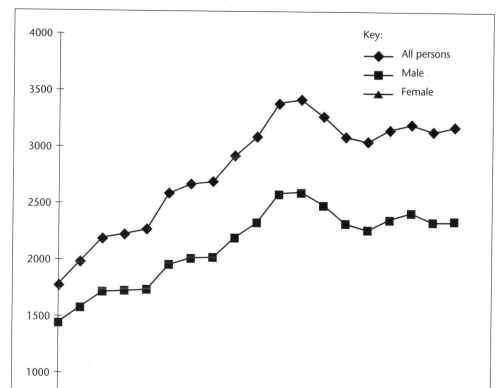

The share of the self-employed in total employment increased from under 9% in 1981 to over 12% in 1991. However, whilst the increase in absolute numbers of self-employed continued in the second half of the 1980s, during this period they increased their share of the total labour force at a slightly lower rate than at the start of the decade. This was matched by a corresponding increase in the rate of growth in the number of employees.

Meager (1991) produced an analysis of the flows into and out of self-employment for the two pairs of years 1983–4 and 1986–7. The results of this analysis are shown in Table 2.2. The flows are very small in relation to the overall stocks of self-employed. The inflow was, however, larger than the outflow in both periods, although the gap narrows over time. Meager attributes this to a lag effect of business failures following a period of rapid growth in new small firms.

Table 2.2 Changes in employment status

Status	1983–1984 (thousands)	1986–1987 (thousands)
Employed both years	18,592.7	18,870.7
Self-employed both years	2,241.4	2,598.1
Inflow to self-employment during year	432.6	435.6
Of which:		
Employment previously	204.3	231.2
Unemployed previously (inc. govt schemes)	87.7	103.4
Other (economically inactive) previously	140.7	101.0
Outflow from self-employment during year	209.4	253.0
Of which:		
Employment subsequently	82.6	114.0
Other (unemployed/inactive) subsequently	126.6	138.9
Total	21,476.1	22,157.4

Source: Meager (1991)

A prominent concern recently has been the growth in part-time employment (self-employment). In 1987, 2,464,000 (83%) were full-time self-employed and 503,000 (17%) were part-time self-employed. In 1997, 2,570,000 (79%) were full-time and 677,000 (21%) were part-time. There is no discernible pattern or split between the proportion of male or female self-employed moving to part-time work over the period. This is not the case for employees where there has been a noticeable shift towards female part-time as the main form of employment.

Meager's analysis was prompted by the work of Hakim (1988b), who noted that the statistics generally did not support the popular view that unemployment pushes people into self-employment. Only 20% of the 1984 inflow and 24% of that in 1987 came from the ranks of the unemployed. Government schemes, such as the EAS, account for some of the new entrepreneurial activity, but by no means all of it. However, the flow of unemployed into self-employment is proportionately higher than the representation of the unemployed within the workforce as a whole would suggest.

Research that has tried to measure the impact of the EAS has shown that many participants were not unemployed for over a year. They may not, therefore, have been included within the unemployment totals for the year prior to the survey dates and so the LFS, from which Meager (1991) takes his data, could be a poor indicator of the impact of this particular policy.

Daly (1991a) also considered the aggregate flows into and out of self-employment. He noted that changes in self-employment rates are likely to follow changes in total employment. Between 1981 and 1987 the rise in self-employment was primarily caused specifically by increases in the proportion of people who were self-employed. After that date, total employment itself increases rapidly, which accounted for most of the increases in self-employment rates. Additional research by Abell, Khalif and Smeaton (1995), using LFS data for 1975–1991, studies flows into and out of self-employment from other states of the labour market. The LFS devoted part of its questionnaire to employment state one year prior to the interview and from this it is possible to analyse transitions between alternative states. The conclusion they reach is that much of the apparent increase in self-employment between 1979 and 1989 (with entries greater than exits during this time) can be explained by wage employees becoming self-employed.

The rest of this review concentrates upon the empirical patterns of self-employment in a number of key areas. These are:

■ the role of personal characteristics in the determination of employment status;

■ important characteristics of the jobs that the self-employed choose to do;

■ the flows into and out of self-employment.

A distinctive feature of self-employment is that it involves taking risks which entail the possibility of failure (see Chapter 8). Once a self-employed person establishes a business, some risks decline, but they never disappear. The penalties of failure vary with the degree of personal commitment, the availability of alternative wage employment or self-employment, and the extent of a social safety net, but they usually involve high personal cost. An employee may be made redundant but there is often some financial compensation, perhaps guaranteed by the state, and there is a social concern that offers at least nominal encouragement. However, the bankrupt self-employed person (who may not be able to take advantage of any bankruptcy protection) has less of a safety net, and he (and even his family) may be deprived of all financial assets. While the risks are inherent, self-employment would be more attractive if fewer of those who entered were likely to fail. If the standard of entrants were higher, the survival rate would be higher. If that were achieved by more rigorous screening rather than an upgrading of human resources, less labour would enter the sector and the government's programmes for encouraging the sector would be more effective.

The self-employed are concentrated mainly in industries and trades where there are many producers, where entry is relatively easy and competition vigorous. The resultant crowding can lead to market saturation, and the self-employed often operate close to the margin. When times are difficult (in general, or in their particular trade), they drive themselves and their families harder; when circumstances are easier, they reap the benefits. Hakim (1988b) notes that the self-employed exhibit a tendency to increase their hours and effort during tough times rather than cut staff. In better times they then cut hours and effort rather than strive only for financial reward. It is largely a personal question of how badly or how well they treat themselves in terms of hours and conditions of work. For those with employees, the danger is that they will expect the employees to accept the same treatment that they themselves tolerate, or worse. As a consequence, the self-employed are sometimes seen as bad employers. They are concentrated in service trades where many employees are paid low wages; these wages may be further reduced when the employer's earnings fall. Employers may also be tempted to extend hours of work and neglect safety conditions, and there is little guarantee that in good times the gains of self-employment will be shared with the employees.

In many trades where self-employment is extensive the enterprises are too small for there to be any real likelihood that trade unions can organise the employees. Moreover, where trade unions endeavour to do so, small employers and often their employees as well may resist these efforts. Trade unions tend, therefore, to be suspicious of self-employment. Laws and regulations may not apply or may be difficult to enforce. Employment terms accepted by employees of very small-scale employers may be seen as a threat to the terms which trade unions negotiate in larger firms. Employees in trades where the self-employed are a significant element may find their terms and conditions of work constrained. Their employers may argue that they have to face competition from very small firms and thus cannot afford 'excessive' labour costs. Poor employment conditions of employees in some very small firms, although at the margin of an industry, may have a wider depressing effect on wages and working conditions. Trade unions may believe that it is the owners of micro-enterprises with whom they cannot negotiate who weaken their bargaining power in other enterprises where they are organised.

2.5 Personal characteristics of the self-employed

2.5.1 Gender

Table 2.1 showed that males make up a significantly greater proportion of the self-employed than do females. They have continued to do so throughout the period covered by the table and there appears to be no reason to suspect that this will change dramatically over the next few years. However, it is also clear that female self-employment has grown over the total period by twice as much as has male self-employment. This phenomenon has been debated recently in the literature. Some commentators have argued that the role of 'the female entrepreneur' has become steadily greater as the preconceptions of society about the role of women in the workplace have changed (see, for example, Carter and Cannon (1988) and Hakim (1988a)). Other writers have argued that the figures obtained from the LFS exaggerate the true picture. Curran and Burrows (1989) use the General Household Survey (GHS) to show that the ratio of male to female self-employment has remained relatively constant over the years.

The two distinct arguments are resolved when one decomposes the relative changes into two segments. In the first half of the 1980s there was a very rapid increase in female self-employment relative to male. In later years the increases have been similar in proportionate terms. The absolute rise in female self-employment is partly caused by the overall increase in the number of women in the labour market as a whole. Over the period 1979–92 the female self-employment rate has changed very little, from approximately 5% in 1979 to just over 7% in 1992. Daly (1991a) reports that almost all of the increase for females, in the late 1980s, was due to the increasing numbers in total employment, not as a result of an increase in the self-employment rate.

Analysis of the flows into and out of self-employment by gender reveals that the inflow of females was relatively higher than the outflow and higher than the inflow for males over the early part of the 1980s. After 1987 this trend, whilst still applicable to the inflow data, does not hold for the outflow. There was a definite increase in the numbers of women leaving self-employment in the late 1980s. This could be due to differing success rates between sexes or, as Meager (1991) suggests, simply a 'statistical phenomenon' caused by the rapid rise in female self-employment in the earlier period. This issue is discussed further in Chapter 10.

2.5.2 Age

Table 2.3 shows the numbers of self-employed by age and also splits the data by gender. Examining the information contained in Table 2.3, it is clear that self-employment becomes an increasingly inviting option as one nears middle age. This may be due to a potential entrepreneur reaching a capital threshold and being able to afford the start-up costs of a new venture. Alternatively, the former employee may have accumulated sufficient knowledge or experience of a certain trade to try going into business alone. One factor explaining the increased prevalence of middle-aged self-employed could be that this is the vulnerable age for redundancies in times of recession. Experienced and motivated managers and workers made redundant may well be tempted to try their hand in their own enterprise.

Another feature of the table is the increase in the participation of the over-65s. This reflects a number of key points. Firstly, if the business was the creation of the

Table 2.3 Age profile of the self-employed

	1981		1991		
	Thousands	Percentage of total employment	Thousands	Percentage of total employment	Percentage increase 1981–91
Male					
16–24	108	4.2	198	7.9	82
25–44	884	13.8	1291	17.9	46
45–54	387	14.4	591	21.6	52
55–59	149	11.7	201	19.5	35
60–64	107	13.1	130	19.9	21
65+	90	28.0	100	32.3	12
All	1726	12.2	2511	17.4	45
Female					
16–24	26	1.2	48	2.2	88
25–44	236	5.9	441	8.0	87
45–54	103	5.2	195	8.8	89
55–59	38	4.7	59	8.0	54
60–64	24	7.0	30	9.2	27
65+	24	13.8	31	20.1	26
All	451	4.7	805	7.2	78
All persons					
16–24	134	2.8	246	5.2	83
25–44	1120	10.7	1733	13.6	55
45–54	491	10.5	786	15.8	60
55–59	187	8.9	260	14.7	39
60–64	131	11.3	160	16.3	22
65+	141	23.0	131	30.4	15
All	2177	9.2	3316	13.0	52

Source: Daly (1991a), Office for National Statistics © Crown Copyright 1999

entrepreneur, there may be considerable reluctance to retire. The self-employed can adjust their hours and effort to cope with the effects of old age and can, therefore, stay on much longer. Secondly, the self-employed may well not be covered by pension arrangements as adequately as much of the employed sector. They may have to rely on only a state pension and it could very well be that, to some extent, the self-employed cannot afford to retire. Thirdly, many occupations require that their workforce retire at some statutory age and in recent years many firms have actively used an early retirement policy to rationalise the workforce. A good example of this is the local government sector; as councils are merged it has been important to shed employees. Compulsory dismissals would be unpopular in what is a highly unionised sector.

The comparatively low levels of self-employment among the younger age groups reflect the difficulty of establishing any enterprise without sufficient funds or experience. Meager (1991) poses the question: how great is the effect on economic activity rates of the distinct growth in the 65+ group, as growing numbers of people reach normal retirement age? If people are being pushed into self-employment because of redundancy or other factors (and the growth is not coming from the traditional 'petit bourgeoisie') then are the financial structures which society has designed to deal with 'ordinary retired employees' adequate for this new class of older entrepreneur?

The age distribution for the self-employed is roughly similar for both sexes. Meager (1991), however, illustrates that the propensity for males to enter self-employment at an early age is almost four times that of similarly aged females. The ratio falls to about 2:1 in middle age and then rises again amongst the oldest age groups. Family commitments and other social factors can explain the mid-range figures. However, it is not at all clear why young women should be so small a proportion of those entering self-employment. The pattern of overall self-employment rates is similar across the range of ages, with some tendency for the increases to be concentrated among the very young and the much older age groups. This does not imply, however, that the average age of the self-employed has increased over the period. The explanation for the growing self-employment rates in the older age range lies in the changes which took place over the same period in the number of employees. Overall, the number of employees grew slightly until 1991, but this growth was particularly rapid amongst the 20–44-year-old age groups, more than offsetting the significant decline in the 45+ age ranges. Given this latter decline, therefore, the self-employed accounted for a growing proportion of all those in work in these older age ranges.

The age profile of the self-employed did change over the 1980s. In particular the average age of the sector fell over the period, although analysis of the flows shows that this was not primarily due to new entrants being younger. Instead, the phenomenon appears to have been caused by the rapid increase in new entrants, who are, by definition, younger than those who comprise the existing stock. Splitting the decade in half, it appears also that the increase in numbers of young entrants in the first half is offset by an increase in outflow of these people in the second.

2.5.3 Marital status

Daly (1991a) analyses the marital status of the self-employed in some detail. The self-employment rate is much lower for single people than it is for people in other categories (such as married, widowed, divorced or separated). This reflects, in part, the fact that people below the age of 25 are less likely to be married than those in the older age categories. However, it also appears that single people of whatever age are less likely to be self-employed. Marriage seems to provide support in establishing a successful enterprise, and spouses are often partners in such schemes. Meager (1991) notes that it is often assumed that the female partner plays the role of 'housewife' whilst her husband goes out to run his own business. Women should therefore be seen to have less of an impact on the self-employment data if they are married because of this minor role. In fact, the financial support of a spouse may actually be equally (or more) important. If the spouse is already employed, and providing a steady and stable income, there is every reason to expect that this will be of benefit to the potential entrepreneur. This factor can work equally well for women as for men.

There are a few differences to note between the sexes. Divorced men have higher self-employment rates than divorced women. This is probably caused by the fact that in many of the family business partnerships the man plays a fairly dominant role and he is likely to continue running the business after a divorce or separation. Widowed women have a higher self-employment rate than all other categories. This may be because they inherit such businesses from their deceased husbands. Some will have been partners of the firm before the death, but a large number may well have been ordinary employees elsewhere.

Daly (1991a) stresses the importance of dependent children in determining self-employment rates. Over all age groups there is little difference between men with and those without dependent children. Disaggregating by age group shows that self-employment rates are far higher amongst men with dependent children in the age brackets 25–34 and 45–54. Men aged 35–44 showed no difference, whilst there was a large difference in the opposite direction for those aged 16–24. Further effects of children are also identified. Women with dependent children are more likely to be self-employed, but they are then less likely to employ others. For men, the opposite is true. LFS data also point to the fact that a large proportion of married people who are both self-employed are partners in the same firm, although responses to the LFS questionnaire do not show this directly. It is possible to show, however, that most respondents placed themselves in the same industrial category and it seems reasonable to conclude that this implies some sort of partnership. Further evidence for this is that almost one-third of self-employed couples are in the hotel and catering industries where partnership is the norm.

2.5.4 Ethnic group

The ethnic minority population in the UK tends to be concentrated in fairly distinct geographical regions. Communities appear to stick together, where cultural traditions can be observed and family businesses established. Curran and Burrows (1989) used the GHS to examine 'ethnicity' and found that self-employment was high among the Asian population, whilst it was much lower (relative to whites) among those of West Indian origin. They qualify their arguments by stating that 86% of Asians still work for someone else. Those people who are of Mediterranean background (Cyprus, Malta and Gibraltar) were found to be over twice as likely to be self-employed as those of

Asian background and over four times as likely as whites. However, according to the GHS, ethnic minority groups comprised only 7% of the whole self-employed sample and so the arguments about higher propensities among these groups must be kept in perspective. It is true to say that this proportion is higher than their proportion in the working population as a whole, which in 1992 was about 4.5%.

The only group of workers to experience a consistent upward trend over much of the 1980s was the 'white' sector. The West Indian group did not share in the overall increases of the decade, whilst the rest did grow in absolute terms (although this growth was not a consistent trend). It appears that whilst certain ethnic groups have experienced an increase in self-employment participation rates, care should be taken when analysing the significance of these sectors. Traditional beliefs about the 'corner shop' family businesses associated with certain ethnic groups are not disproved by the research. However, the relative size of these minorities must be stressed before conclusions can be reached about their role in influencing economy-wide self-employment rates.

Clark and Drinkwater (1998) use GHS and Census of Population data to examine how both 'push' and 'pull' factors may lead members of the non-white, ethnic minority groups to enter self-employment. They claim as motivation for their work the evidence of Metcalfe *et al.* (1996), who found that the desire to avoid labour market discrimination in the form of low-paid jobs was a principal explanation for the entry of minorities into self-employment. Clark and Drinkwater find that there is substantial variation between ethnic minority groups in self-employment, but in general they earn less than whites – even whites with similar characteristics. They conclude that any analysis of ethnic self-employment must take into account differences in ethnicity within the minority groups and must avoid amalgamating a particularly heterogeneous sector. The issue of ethnicity and enterprise is discussed further in Chapter 11.

2.5.5 Levels of education

The level of education achieved by the potential entrepreneur has long been seen as a crucial factor in determining both the actual entry into self-employment and, thereafter, the longer-term success of the venture. There have been a number of attempts to analyse these factors over the past few years. The results of the studies have thrown up an interesting inconsistency. Curran and Burrows (1989) used GHS data to show that self-employed men are less qualified than men in wage employment. Men in self-employment with employees are more likely to have formal qualifications than those in self-employment without employees. For women, however, those in self-employment with employees are less well qualified than their male counterparts, whilst those without employees are better qualified than their male counterparts and women wage employees generally. They are, however, less well qualified than male wage employees. The paper concludes that the self-employed appear to have a lower level of educational attainment than wage earners, although there is some overlap between the two groups.

Daly (1991a) and Meager (1991) used the LFS to analyse the issue. They both found that, generally, the self-employed appear to have a higher level of educational achievement than employees. Also, the higher the level of the qualification, the higher the likelihood of the individual being self-employed. Table 2.4 shows the movement over the

Table 2.4 Qualifications of employees and the self-employed

	1981			1991		
	Employees (%)	Self-employed (%)	Self-employed with employees (%)	Employees (%)	Self-employed (%)	Self-employed with employees (%)
Degree or equivalent	7.8	10.5	16.1	10.2	11.3	16.5
Higher education below degree level	6.0	3.2	3.6	7.4	3.8	4.4
A-level or equivalent	22.4	31.9	30.5	26.9	38.1	34.8
O-level or equivalent	13.6	8.8	9.4	19.9	12.7	12.4
CSE below grade 1	4.9	2.0	1.3	4.2	2.5	1.5
Other qualification	4.1	4.3	4.0	6.3	5.6	4.8
No qualification	41.1	39.4	35.1	25.1	25.9	25.7
All	100.0	100.0	100.0	100.0	100.0	100.0

Source: Daly (1991a), Office for National Statistics © Crown Copyright 1999

last decade and is based upon LFS data. The highest rates of self-employment are amongst those with their highest qualification being A-levels or equivalent. The lowest rates are among those with higher education below degree level. These qualifications are typically courses associated with a vocational career and include banking exams and nursing diplomas. The most noticeable change between 1981 and 1991 is the rise in the educational achievements of employees, and there does appear to be some narrowing of the gap between employees and the self-employed.

The inconsistency between the findings of Curran and Burrows (1989) with their GHS data and those of Daly (1991a) has received some attention. Meager (1992) suggests that some of the difference could be accounted for by looking at the definitions of self-employment used by the two sets of authors. Unlike Daly, Curran and Burrows exclude the 'professional self-employed' from their data set. This group will include those who are likely to be better qualified on average than the self-employed population as a whole. The work of both of these authors does indicate that the educational level of the self-employed is increasing over time and this is consistent with the analysis of flows into and out of self-employment below.

There is clearly a complex relationship between educational qualifications and participation rates for the self-employed. That relationship depends critically upon the definitions used in defining the data sets and, indeed, upon which survey is used to compile those data. Meager (1991) reports that preliminary multivariate analysis using the LFS has confirmed the findings of Daly (1991a), whilst Burrows (1990) again finds a negative relationship between educational qualifications and entry into self-employment using more recent GHS data.

Turning to the flows into and out of self-employment, there appears to be an overall increase in the qualifications of the sector over time. This is particularly shown at the extremes of the qualification ladder. The number of people with degree or equivalent shows a larger inflow than outflow and the proportion within this inflow is higher than that in the stock of self-employed. A similar pattern is seen for those entering the sector with GCSE or equivalent. There are a number of reasons why one might expect a swing towards more highly qualified entrants. Firstly, the data suggest that women in self-employment are, in general, more qualified than men. Since the data also show a higher entrance rate for women, a higher general level of education should result. Secondly, as time passes and more young people enter the sector the average level of qualifications will rise because the educational standards of the younger, newly available, workforce are higher than those of the already self-employed. The final factor may be linked to the increase in the number of schemes that have promoted self-employment over the past few years. The ability of young entrepreneurs to start their own businesses, either by an easing of credit conditions or by direct policy intervention, has meant a larger number of graduates and other highly qualified people being attracted into self-employment.

2.6 The jobs of the self-employed

2.6.1 Industrial division

The responses that make up the LFS allow the researcher to place the self-employed into various standard industrial categories. Intuitively, one would expect most respondents to fall into sectors that are traditionally associated with entrepreneurial or family enterprise. Daly (1991a) illustrates that this is indeed the case. There are high rates of participation in sectors such as agriculture, construction and private-sector services, whilst there are low participation rates in areas such as manufacturing and those sectors that are dominated by the public sector. Table 2.5 shows the way in which the self-employed make up the major industrial sectors. The main feature is that the self-employed are very highly specialised and are concentrated in a few sectors.

Table 2.5 Self-employment rates by industrial sector, 1995

Industry division	Males (%)	Females (%)	All (%)
0 Agriculture	52.8	34.5	48.9
1 Energy and water supply	*	*	*
2 Minerals extraction, etc.	2.8	*	2.9
3 Metal goods and engineering	4.3	2.1	3.8
4 Other manufacturing	8.8	6.4	7.9
5 Construction	37.7	11.5	35.2
6 Distribution, hotels and repairs	24.2	10.7	16.9
7 Transport and communication	13.0	3.9	11.0
8 Banking, finance, etc.	19.6	6.9	13.6
9 Other services	9.5	6.3	7.5
All	16.3	7.5	12.6

* Indicates cell sizes too small for estimates to be made.
Source: Labour Force Survey, Office for National Statistics © Crown Copyright 1999

The sectors in which self-employment has a foothold are those (with the exception of agriculture) which have experienced higher than average employment growth during the 1980s. The sectors which have been in decline are those in which the option of self-employment appears to be less feasible. Agriculture employs approximately 49% of the self-employed, but only accounts for about 2% of total employment.

The recent patterns of self-employment propensities exhibited by an analysis of the changes over the last two decades prompt an important question. Is the recent – and unusual – growth in self-employment caused by structural change in the economy, with a growth in the service sector and a decline in manufacturing, or is it also heavily influenced by an increase within individual sectors? Research has been performed using 'shift-share' analysis. This decomposes the changes over time into that change which would have occurred had the self-employment rates within each industry remained unchanged over the period and a residual growth element comprising the growth within sectors over time. Both Meager (1991) and Daly (1991a) illustrate that the sectoral component of growth over the 1980s was much smaller than that associated with the within-sector growth. This does not follow the pattern established by OECD (1986). In six OECD countries (excluding Great Britain) most of the increase in self-employment over the first half of the 1980s was attributed to a sectoral shift. Meager (1991) notes that it is this feature – of rapid within-sector growth – that distinguishes the changes in self-employment in Great Britain from those changes that occurred elsewhere. Hakim (1989a) draws these points out in some detail. There appears to have been a change in the attitudes of employers to using subcontracted labour both in the construction industry and elsewhere. This 'demand-side' effect is not easy to distinguish from supply-side influences because in most cases it has not been possible to work at a sufficiently disaggregated level. Such details would probably show a larger industry shift component, but at the moment it remains unlikely that such effects could account for more than a small proportion of the total change.

The analysis of flow data for industries is interesting. The pattern of inflow and outflow is broadly similar to the raw data for stocks. However, certain industrial categories do show greater growth rates than others. In particular, the construction industry has a much larger inflow in the early years than outflow, which is consistent with a higher degree of subcontractor use in the sector. Also, the banking sector shows rapid growth commensurate with the establishment of a great many financial services companies. The recession at the end of the decade is highlighted by a very large outflow from many of these sectors which experienced such growth earlier on. Indeed, a large part of the fall in the recession of the early 1990s appears to be accounted for by a substantial fall in the numbers employed in the construction industry in the South-East.

2.6.2 Regional differences

Table 2.6 illustrates the self-employment rate by region in 1991. The highest rate in Great Britain is the South-West (an area hit particularly hard during the recession at the end of the 1980s and beginning of the 1990s) and the lowest rate is the North at 9.1% in 1992.

Table 2.6 Self-employment by region: a shift-share analysis for 1991

	Self-employment rate (actual)	Standardised self-employment rate
South-East	13.0	14.2
East Anglia	14.1	13.8
South-West	18.4	16.4
West Midlands	11.4	12.4
East Midlands	12.8	13.3
Yorkshire and Humberside	11.5	11.8
North-West	11.7	12.2
North	9.1	9.9
Wales	13.3	13.1
Scotland	10.0	9.7

Source: Labour Force Survey; Campbell and Daly (1992), Office for National Statistics © Crown Copyright 1999

The regional variations in self-employment rates are not as pronounced as those for the sectoral differences. However, the strong influence of industry type on these propensities suggests that regions where, for example, there is a majority of manufacturing firms may well have a lower than average self-employment rate. This can be seen in the cases of the North, where there is a concentration of manufacturing, and the South-East, which relies heavily on construction and services. This industrial effect can explain some of the variation across regions, but not all of it. To help to decompose the effects of industrial concentration a shift-share analysis is used.

The shift-share analysis of Table 2.6 calculates a standardised self-employment rate for each region. This is the overall regional self-employment rate which would have been obtained if the industry structure in each region were identical to the national average but the propensity for self-employment within a given industry in a region were as observed. The table shows the effect of variations in the basic mix of industries.

Another important area that is covered by an analysis of the regional factors associated with self-employment is that concerned with the correlation between regional unemployment and self-employment. Creigh *et al.* (1986) failed to find any positive relationship between the variables. They argued that the conventional wisdom that states that unemployment pushes people into self-employment does not appear to hold. Furthermore, the depressed conditions that are associated with regional unemployment mean that conditions are not suitable for positive entrepreneurial activity and therefore any 'push' effect will be cancelled out by these depressed circumstances. Meager (1991), however, does find a positive correlation between unemployment and self-employment for certain regions (the exceptions being Northern Ireland, which had the highest unemployment rate, and the East Midlands, which had a rate slightly below the national average). Blanchflower and Oswald (1991) also found a positive relationship at the regional level, but their model did not include an industrial structure variable.

There is then some debate as to the major factors that determine differences in self-employment rates across regions. There is an industrial factor and there is a labour market factor. However, it is not clear what else influences the propensities. Creigh *et al.* (1986) put the explanation down to an unspecified bundle of 'other factors', whilst Blanchflower and Oswald (1991) offer no further guidance. Curran and Burrows (1989) do identify longstanding historical factors as one major influence. They claim that the industrial structure among former generations has a significant impact today. This might suggest that policies aimed at promoting self-employment should be targeted at regions that have a history of such entrepreneurial activity, rather than, perhaps, giving block assistance to every region.

It also suggests that differences across regions may well persist even if the other factors – such as industrial mix and the labour market – change over time. Analysis of flow data also shows that regional differences appear to be maintained over time. There are proportional representations in the flows similar to those in the figures available for the stocks.

2.6.3 Occupations of the self-employed

The section above analysed the self-employed in terms of industrial sectors. It is also possible to examine more carefully the occupational categories into which these people fall. A common problem is the urge for most self-employed persons to classify themselves as managers. There is, therefore, a need to compare these responses carefully with those that make up the industrial category decomposition. Such a review is carried out in Meager (1991). The article concludes that female self-employment is much higher than male self-employment in the 'managerial' categories. This result is consistent with the findings described above, which showed that better-qualified women had a relatively higher self-employment rate. One possible explanation for this, put forward by Meager (1991), is that labour market rigidities (perhaps even in the form of positive sex discrimination) prevent these well-qualified women achieving in the employee sector. They are then pushed into self-employment in order to fulfil their ambitions.

The flow data given by the LFS reinforce these ideas. Large net inflows are apparent in those sectors that, primarily, cover the service industries. One notable feature is that the construction occupation does appear to have a relatively larger outflow than inflow towards the end of the decade. This is consistent with the idea that construction work may be very sensitive to the business cycle.

2.6.4 Other factors associated with self-employment

There are a number of supplementary factors. These include hours of work, employees and the temporary nature of some self-employment jobs. The self-employed report themselves as working longer hours, in general, than ordinary employees. Self-employment is typically characterised as a very demanding role and, whilst there may be some degree of over-reporting, over 60% of respondents to the LFS throughout the 1980s said that they worked more than 40 hours per week. This compares to less than 40% of employees. The differential is even greater for those claiming to work more than 60 hours per week. The self-employed with employees tend to work longer hours than those without. This finding is supported by Creigh *et al.* (1986) and by Curran and Burrows (1989).

r (1991) reports that two-thirds of the self-employed have no employees of
1. Most of the rest have fewer than 25 employees. Hakim (1988b) stresses
...t the self-classification of individuals responding for the LFS may lead some small
business owners to label themselves as employees rather than as self-employed. This
could mean that the figures for those self-employed with employees are underestimated. Turning finally to the classification of employment as full- or part-time, it
appears that there is a lower rate of part-time working amongst the self-employed.
This is probably explained by the under-representation of women in the self-employed
group.

2.7 Small firms – the data

This section examines the data available on small firms in the UK. Key to this is to
define what is meant by a small business.

2.7.1 Definitions

There is no single definition of a small firm, mainly because of the wide diversity
of businesses carried out in the UK. The most well-known attempt to provide a
description of the key characteristics of a small firm was that made by the Bolton
Committee in its 1971 *Report... on Small Firms*. This stated that a small firm is an
independent business, managed by its owner or part-owners and having a small
market share.

The Bolton Report (1971) also adopted a number of different statistical definitions.
It recognised that size is relevant to sector – i.e. a firm of a given size could be small in
relation to one sector where the market is large and there are many competitors;
whereas a firm of similar proportions could be considered large in another sector with
fewer players and/or generally smaller firms within it. Similarly, it recognised that it
may be more appropriate to define size by the number of employees in some sectors
but more appropriate to use turnover in others. Across government, it is most usual to
measure size according to numbers of full-time employees or their equivalent. However, as Storey (1994) points out, the Bolton Report 'employed a hotchpotch of different definitions of a small firm' which made comparisons over time or country almost
impossible.

Small businesses are also defined in law. Section 249 of the Companies Act of 1985
states that a company is 'small' if it satisfies at least two of the following criteria:

- a turnover of not more than £2.8 million;
- a balance sheet total of not more than £1.4 million;
- not more than 50 employees.

A medium-sized company must satisfy at least two of the following criteria:

- a turnover of not more than £11.2 million;
- a balance sheet total of not more than £5.6 million;
- not more than 250 employees.

Table 2.7 European Commission definition of SMEs

Criterion	Micro	Small	Medium
Max. number of employees	10	50	250
Max. annual turnover	–	7m ecu	40m ecu
Max. annual balance sheet total	–	5m ecu	27m ecu
Max. % owned by one, or jointly by several, enterprise(s) not satisfying the same criteria	–	25%	25%

Note: To qualify as an SME, both the employee and the independence criteria must be satisfied and either the turnover or the balance sheet total criteria.

For statistical purposes, the Department of Trade and Industry (DTI) usually uses the following definitions:

- micro firm: 0–9 employees;
- small firm: 0–49 employees (includes micro);
- medium firm: 50–249 employees;
- large firm: over 250 employees.

However, in practice, schemes which are nominally targeted at small firms adopt a variety of working definitions depending on their particular objectives.

In February 1996, the European Commission adopted a communication setting out a single definition of SMEs and applied this across EU programmes and proposals with effect from 1 January 1998. The details are set out in Table 2.7. The communication also includes a (non-binding) recommendation to Member States, the European Investment Bank and the European Investment Fund encouraging them to adopt the same definitions for their programmes. The communication permits them to use lower threshold figures, if desired.

2.7.2 Small businesses in the UK: numbers and trends

There were an estimated 3.7 million active businesses in the UK at the start of 1997, according to the Statistical Bulletin *Small and Medium Enterprise (SME) Statistics for the UK, 1997*. This contains a size breakdown of the number of businesses in the UK, from small traders with no employees to those with 500 or more employees. It also shows the contribution to employment and turnover made by businesses of different sizes, industry by industry.

Of the 3.7 million businesses in 1997, over 2.5 million were 'size class zero' businesses – those made up of sole traders or partners without employees (see Table 2.8). ·

Of the entire business population of 3.7 million enterprises only 25,000 are medium sized (50 to 249 employees) and only 7,000 are large (250 or more employees). Small businesses, including those without employees, account for over 99% of businesses, 45% of non-government employment and (excluding the finance sector) 40% of turnover. In contrast, the 7,000 largest businesses account for 43% of non-government employment and 46% of turnover (see Figure 2.2).

Table 2.8 Number of businesses, employment and turnover by size of enterprise, 1997

Size (number of employees)	Number			Percentage		
	Businesses (000s)	Employment (000s)	Turnover[1] (£millions)	Businesses	Employment	Turnover
0	2,524	2,866	86,706	68.1	13.6	4.8
1–4	803	2,106	215,110	21.7	10.0	12.0
5–9	192	1,396	112,403	5.2	6.6	6.3
10–19	107	1,511	142,295	2.9	7.2	7.9
20–49	50	1,539	152,559	1.3	7.3	8.5
50–99	15	1,071	105,087	0.4	5.1	5.8
100–199	8	1,121	112,913	0.2	5.3	6.3
200–249	2	352	38,550	–	1.7	2.1
250–499	3	1,118	142,789	0.1	5.3	7.9
500+	3	7,993	688,751	0.1	37.9	38.3
All	3,708	21,073	1,797,164	100.0	100.0	100.0

[1]Excluding VAT. Finance sector turnover excluded from turnover totals.
Source: DTI SME Statistics Unit

Figure 2.2 Proportion of businesses, employment and turnover in small, medium and large firms at start of 1997

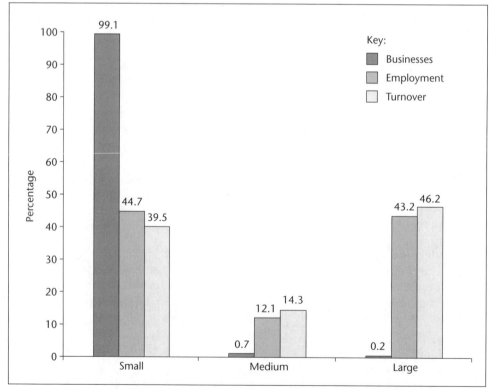

Source: DTI SME Statistics Unit

Table 2.9 SME share of businesses, employment and turnover by industry, 1997

| | Businesses | | Employment | | Turnover |
	Total number (000s)	SME percentage share	Total employment (000s)	SME percentage share	SME percentage share
All industries[1]	3,708	99.8	21,073	56.8	53.8
A, B: Agriculture, forestry and fishing	221	100.0	532	98.3	96.0
C: Mining/quarrying	5	98.9	87	33.5	29.6
D: Manufacturing	322	99.2	4,466	49.7	46.4
E: Electricity, gas, water supply	0.3	83.7	161	2.5	2.4
F: Construction	829	100.0	1,587	87.2	75.2
G: Wholesale, retail and repairs	526	99.8	4,269	53.6	47.2
H: Hotels and restaurants	149	99.8	1,484	57.7	56.8
I: Transport, storage and communication	212	99.8	1,456	39.9	29.6
J: Financial intermediation	52	99.3	981	22.5	19.2
K: Real estate, renting and business activities	707	99.9	2,812	71.0	63.6
M: Education	109	99.9	241	86.5	72.6
N: Health/social work	218	99.7	1,982	43.8	37.6
O: Other community, social/personal	356	99.9	1,014	77.0	65.1

[1]Finance sector excluded from turnover totals.
Source: DTI SME Statistics Unit

2.7.3 Industry patterns

At the start of 1997, at least 99% of businesses in all but the electricity, gas and water supply and mining/quarrying sectors were SMEs. The share of employment provided by SMEs varies greatly from one industry to the next. In construction 87% of employment is accounted for by SMEs, while in finance it is only 23%. Table 2.9 shows the difference between sectors in more detail. Employment is particularly reliant on small businesses in areas as diverse as veterinary services, recycling, computing and salt production.

2.7.4 Regional analysis

Small and medium enterprises account for over 99% of businesses in all regions. The share of employment in SMEs is highest for those based in Northern Ireland and lowest for those based in London. The share of turnover in SMEs was also highest in Northern Ireland, but was lowest in the West Midlands.

2.8 Business start-ups and closures

The most widely used measure of business start-ups and closures by industry sector is the register of VAT registrations and de-registrations. Coverage is almost complete among businesses operating above the turnover threshold for VAT registration (£48,000 in 1997) and, unlike the number of incorporations, registrations cover both companies and self-employed businesses. Also, unlike the number of insolvencies, de-registrations include closures that do not involve unpaid debt. However, obviously the register excludes many of the very smallest one-person businesses that trade below the registration threshold. The data presented in Table 2.10 examine the trends for 1997, when there were 182,600 registrations in the UK. In the same year there were 164,500 de-registrations, giving a net gain of 18,100 registered enterprises. This means that there were 39 registrations for every 10,000 people aged 16 or over and 35 de-registrations for the same population proportion. To make the figures as comparable as possible over time, a number of adjustments are made by the government. The figures for recent years are increased slightly to allow for the small number of registra-tions and de-registrations that take more than a few months to be reported. The fig-ures are also adjusted to allow for periodic changes to the VAT system. Robson (1996b) uses these data to examine the macro-economic factors that have a major impact upon the birth and death of small firms in the UK.

In 1997, 61,000 registrations, or one in three of the UK total, were in the business services sector, which includes consultancy, legal, accounting and computer services. There were 37,200 registrations in London, the largest number of any region. In Lon-don there were 66 registrations for every 10,000 residents aged 16 or over, compared with 27 in Wales and 20 in the North-East. The number of registrations rose by 14,400 between 1996 and 1997, to its highest level for four years. In contrast the number of de-registrations fell by 600, to its lowest level for four years. The net gain of 18,100 enterprises during 1997 follows a small net gain of 3,100 enterprises during 1996 and net losses in each year from 1991 to 1995. Details of the main sectoral data are given in Table 2.11. Many factors influence the pattern of business start-ups. Among the most important are economic growth (encouraging new ventures and cre-ating demand for business and personal services), the level of industrial restructuring and contracting out, and the stock of people with management or small business experience.

Table 2.10 Stock, start-ups and closures: UK VAT registrations and de-registrations, 1994–7

	1994	1995	1996r	1997
Start-year stock of registered enterprises	1,629,235	1,609,335	1,600,065	1,603,200
Net change in stock	–19,900	–9,270	3,135	18,115
Registrations				
Number	168,240	163,960	168,200	182,570
Per 10,000 people aged 16+	36	35	36	39
De-registrations				
Number	188,140	173,230	165,065	164,455
P er 10,000 people aged 16+	40	37	35	35

r: de-registrations and net change revised.
Source: DTI SME Statistics Unit

Table 2.11 Registrations and de-registrations by sector, 1997

	Registrations	De-registrations
All sectors	182,570	164,455
Agriculture, fishing (A, B)	4,565	5,745
Mining, energy (C, E)	195	235
Manufacturing (D)	13,540	14,755
Construction (F)	18,645	20,535
Wholesale, retail (G)	37,030	44,155
Hotels, restaurants (H)	16,540	16,340
Transport (I)	9,190	8,410
Finance (J)	1,745	1,730
Business services (K)	60,980	35,305
Education, health (M, N)	2,045	3,025
Other services (L, O)	18,095	14,220

Source: DTI SME Statistics Unit

Figure 2.3 Registrations and de-registrations by country and region, 1997
(rate per 10,000 residents aged 16 or over)

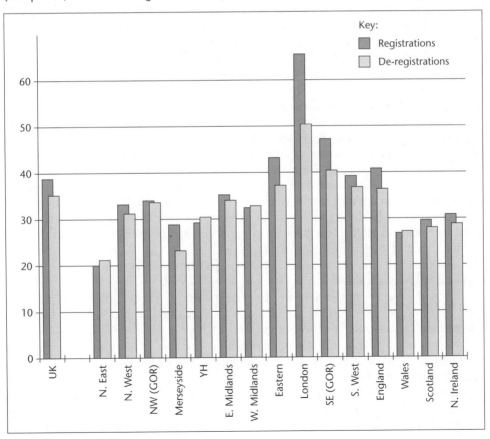

Source: DTI SME Statistics Unit

2.8.1 Business start-ups and failures in the regions

Examining the data for 1997 shows that the highest rates of business start-ups were concentrated in London and the South-East. The smallest rates were in the North-East, Wales and Northern Ireland (see Figure 2.3).

There were net gains in the stock of registered enterprises in Northern Ireland, in Scotland, and in six of the English regions in 1997, including the North-West (1,000), the East Midlands (500) and the South-West (900). In contrast, only Northern Ireland and London had experienced net gains two years previously. The differences in registration rates have widened between 1994 and 1997. For example, the rate in the Eastern region rose from 38 to 43 while the rate in Scotland rose from 28 to 30 and the rate in Wales remained at 27. Regions with a consistently high registration rate also tend to have a high de-registration rate. This reflects the short lifespan of many new enterprises.

2.9 Chapter summary

This chapter has reviewed the data on the incidence of self-employment and small-firm activity in the UK. Central to the first part was the rise in self-employment from 1979 to 1990. In particular, male self-employment rose from 1,442,000 to 2,641,000 over the period in the UK – a rise of 63%. The predominant flow into self-employment was from wage employment and the flow was concentrated in industries that favoured the sector, e.g. construction, distribution and services. The decade was also characterised by extensive financial liberalisation, when access to loans became easier, and by explicit government policies aimed at promoting new enterprise.

The major question, of course, is how one interprets all of this evidence to put together a story about the rise in self-employment. There is now clear evidence that it was caused by the coincidence of a number of factors which had not previously been combined in such a setting. The economic recession caused a large number of manufacturing workers to become unemployed, many of whom had redundancy funds to act as collateral in starting new businesses. This inflow was boosted further by government schemes such as the Enterprise Allowance Scheme and Small Firms' Loan Guarantee Scheme and later in the decade by unprecedented financial liberalisation. Loans from banks and institutions became simple to obtain and, coupled with a government drive to create an 'enterprise culture', business start-ups accelerated.

Outflows from the sector still took place, many of which were new small businesses set up by the inexperienced. However, the inflow exceeded the outflow and the numbers continued to rise. Further stimulus was also provided as existing (and surviving) large employers started to subcontract much of their non-core work. This was done for reasons of taxation and (presumably) to allow for ease of lay-off. Employment (or 'self-employment') of this type became the norm in construction, as well as in other manufacturing processes.

When the recession hit at the end of the decade the position was rapidly reversed. Loans became very hard to obtain and repossessions and calling-in of debt became commonplace. Business confidence started to fail, followed immediately by a greater outflow than inflow in the small self-employed business sector. Whilst the 1979–80 recession hit manufacturing (in particular in the North and the West Midlands) and thus provided a pool of willing potential entrepreneurs, the early 1990s recession hit those industries favouring self-employment and for the first time had a big effect on the South-East and London. The demand for the services provided by the self-employed fell and this caused unemployment of these workers in the construction, distribution and services sectors. Only as the economy has started to pull out of the recession has the position started to improve. The continued problems in the housing market have meant that recovery via construction industry recruitment has been extremely slow.

Prospects for the self-employed were alluded to briefly at the start of this chapter. Many commentators believe that entry to self-employment in the future will be at the margins: entry as a wealthy entrepreneur (the 'pull' hypothesis) mixed with entry as reluctant entrepreneurs at the other end of the income spectrum (the 'push' hypothesis).

The overarching conclusion from the review of small firm data is that they make up by far the largest number of businesses in the UK. Whilst it is important to be consistent with the definition used to define the sector, small firms are vitally important to the economic success of the nation and make a major contribution to GDP in almost every industrial setting.

Questions

1 What factors influence the decision to become self-employed and start new businesses?

2 Using the empirical data on patterns of self-employment, describe the personal characteristics of the self-employed.

3 What are the future prospects for the numbers of self-employed people in the UK?

CHAPTER 3

The enterprise culture: the socio-economic context of small firms

Richard Scase

3.1 Learning objectives

There are five learning objectives in this chapter:

1 To understand the origins of the enterprise culture in Britain.
2 To recognise the importance of socio-cultural factors in encouraging entrepreneurship.
3 To appreciate some of the structural forces leading to the increasing significance of entrepreneurship and small businesses in a modern economy.
4 To obtain an overview of trends in the emerging information economy that will reinforce the importance of small and medium-sized enterprises.
5 To understand some of the outcomes of entrepreneurship for lifestyles, attitudes and future social structures.

Key concepts

■ enterprise culture ■ corporate change ■ state intervention
■ employment patterns

3.2 Introduction

The purpose of this chapter is to outline some of the major features of the 'enterprise culture'. It does this by first discussing the reasons for the term's emergent use in the vocabulary of policy-makers, politicians and academic social scientists in the 1970s. It then proceeds to explore some of the socio-economic and structural forces that have led to the development of an enterprise culture over the past two decades. This is then followed by a review of how the state and large business corporations have responded to these forces. After this, the focus will shift to the consequences of the enterprise culture for personal careers as well as for work and employment patterns. The discussion is then concluded with an appraisal of how the enterprise culture is likely to be affected by the coming of the information age.

3.3 The origins of the enterprise culture

'Enterprise culture' became a term in political and academic debate in Britain and the United States in the late 1970s. Of course it was often used before then but it was not until this time that it came to the forefront of political discussion and was regarded as a topic of serious academic analysis (Goss 1991). It was not to become relevant in political discussion until much later in the rest of Europe. What were the forces that brought this about?

The 1960s and 1970s were the era of what has been variously described as 'corporatism', 'collectivism' and 'tripartism'. In their different ways, each of these reflected a number of common assumptions. The first was that the state should be both directly and actively involved in the management of the economy. Its function was not only to provide a suitable economic, fiscal and political context for economic growth, but also to be directly engaged in planning processes that would regulate, for example, wage increases offered by companies, corporate investment plans and labour relations. The role of government was to be interventionist at both the macro- and micro-economic levels and, through this means, national economic growth could rise at a higher rate than in the past. The attempt in Britain was to emulate the experience of the Scandinavian countries and, to a lesser extent, that of Japan with their traditions of state interventionism. This was particularly the view of Labour regimes in the 1960s and 1970s which promised improvements in education, health and welfare, all of which were to be funded by greater economic growth. Within this scenario, entrepreneurship and small businesses were seen to have virtually no role since they were regarded as part of a legacy of an earlier economic era which was characterised by poor technology, archaic working practices and outdated business attitudes (Boswell 1973).

This leads to a second assumption of the era. This was that economic growth and national competitive advantage could only be achieved by the economics of large-scale production; in other words, through the rationalisation of medium-sized business units and their concentration in large corporations. It was the era of 'Big Business'. Hence, one of the objectives of economic policy pursued by successive governments – both Labour and Conservative – was to encourage corporate mergers and acquisitions. Indeed, this was often encouraged by the offer of financial incentives as well as by governments investing in businesses, or by 'bailing out' those facing failure, so that the private sector could be rationalised into larger, 'more efficient' economic units. It should, of course, be borne in mind that at this time the British economy was heavily dependent upon manufacturing, which accounted for almost 40% of all employment. The aim of governments, therefore, was to focus upon the rationalisation of this sector of the economy in order to protect employment levels as well as to generate job opportunities. These policies were also pursued on the assumption that it was necessary for a modern economy to have a large and, indeed, expanding manufacturing base.

With the creation of 'Big Business', it was assumed that the modern large-scale corporation provided the appropriate context for the application of the most advanced techniques of modern management. This was because of a number of factors. Firstly, the large workplace was seen to be favourable for the implementation of the principles of 'Scientific Management' (Friedman 1977). Work processes could be subject to detailed scrutiny and, on the basis of this, organised according to rational criteria. This entailed the development of job specialisation within a tightly controlled and co-ordinated division of labour. In this way, employee productivity could be greatly improved because the design of work enabled piece-rate reward systems to be implemented. Secondly, there could be the application of rational management practices which could replace the traditional 'custom and practice' methodologies that characterised British management in the 1960s. It was alongside this attempt to modernise management that the first two business schools – London and Manchester – were established. Thirdly, the large corporation was seen to offer an environment in which research and innovation could be encouraged. It was only in this way that there would be sufficient resources to allow invention and innovation to be co-ordinated and then converted into the development and manufacture of profitable products. Indeed, this required there to be a fully integrated work process in which these different activities could be undertaken. This needed the large firm since, without this, there would be neither the economies of scale nor the 'critical mass' of R&D to allow this process to operate effectively.

If the cultures of both government and management encouraged close collaboration in order to generate a high-performing, competitive national economy, this could only be achieved with the full co-operation of organised labour. Hence, a further assumption of 'corporatism' was that government, Big Business and labour should collaborate in both national macro-economic and micro-enterprise planning. Within corporations, trade unions were encouraged to abandon their conflictual attitudes towards management and instead to co-operate with it in attempts to improve productivity and efficiency. This required the exercise of wage restraint and the end of shopfloor industrial militancy. In return, wage increases would be negotiated with management, paid for out of productivity and according to national economic planning targets. Accordingly, trade unions were to be regarded as partners by both government and business in a 'tripartite' system of national economic planning (Winkler 1977).

In all of these debates in the 1960s and 1970s, the roles of small businesses and of enterprise were seen to be of almost no relevance. They were regarded as relics of a bygone era with little to contribute to national economic regeneration and wealth creation. This was to be the era of planning in which the economies of scale would predominate and in which the strategies of business would be the outcome of bargaining with organised labour and geared to the attainment of government-determined national economic targets.

It was the under-realisation – or indeed the failure – of these ambitions that directly led to debates which sowed the seeds for the growth of an enterprise culture in Britain during the late 1970s. It became increasingly recognised that there were heavy costs associated with the economies of large-scale production. Not only were there issues of environmental pollution but there was also debate as to whether the economies of scale were as profound in practice as they were supposed to be in principle. It became apparent that large companies were not particularly innovative and that their growth rates were not greater than the small and medium-sized enterprises of the past. They did not appear to be creating additional jobs, and government economic targets were not being achieved. Further, the implementation of corporatist institutions did not appear to be solving Britain's industrial relations problems with its high incidence of strikes and industrial disputes. At the same time, the experience of work in factories with assembly-line technology seemed to be creating worker alienation. This became reflected not only in high strike rates but also in absenteeism, labour turnover and the manufacture of poor-quality products. Certainly, by the end of the 1970s it was clear that rather than solving many of Britain's economic problems, the emphasis upon tri-partism, planning and the rationalisation of large-scale manufacturing enterprises was probably making matters worse (Rainnie 1989).

It is within this context that the enterprise culture was born. By the end of the dec-ade, debates about 'what is wrong with the economy' were leading to a return to an interest in classical liberal economic theory amongst an ascendant sector within the Conservative Party (in opposition at the time) as well as a renewed interest in 'laissez-faire' capitalism and entrepreneurship. Conservative politicians were searching for a new agenda, often inspired by developments in the nature of political debate in the United States. By this time, it was becoming recognised that there was a role for small firms in a modern economy and that these could be a force for economic renewal through job creation as well as through the development of innovative products and services. Indeed, the potential of small firms was also becoming acknowledged through the work of some academic social scientists (Burrows 1991b).

Although regarded by their colleagues as working outside the 'accepted assumptions of social science debate', they were beginning to argue the case for a small-firm revival (Curran, Stanworth and Watkins 1986). This was as a result of evidence which dem-onstrated that small businesses played a key role in the success of both the German and Japanese economies. They were also able to show that this sector was significant within the other economies of Europe as a source of employment. This, together with the election of a Conservative government in Britain in 1979 with Margaret Thatcher as Prime Minister, brought the potential of an enterprise culture to the very forefront of political discussion. But no longer was such a culture associated solely with the regeneration of the small business sector, it came to be more broadly defined to incor-porate a set of principles that would shape almost all spheres of economic and social policies over the next decade. These were to become the drivers for the privatisation of state-owned industries and for the reform of the health and welfare systems as well as for the restructuring of large privately owned businesses. 'Thatcherism' became identified with these changes and a term used to describe the shift from a corporatist economy to one in which the state was to withdraw from direct intervention in micro-economic management. At best, the rightful role of the state was seen to be to provide a facilitative framework within which companies could grow unfettered by either gov-ernment or trade union interference. However, it should be borne in mind that although politicians may shape the development of social structures, they are also guided by them. There were, in fact, also other forces emerging which would lead to the generation of an enterprise culture by the early 1980s.

3.4 Forces for entrepreneurship

The failure of corporatism to produce improved economic results led not only to the pursuit of alternative policies by the newly elected Conservative government, but also to a reappraisal by companies of their corporate strategies. Corporate leaders saw the election of a new administration as an opportunity to develop a more 'unfettered' management style whereby they would be able to manage their businesses without the 'interference' of either government or trade unions. They were further encouraged to do this by the ideas that were being espoused by management 'gurus' in the United States, who were pressing for not only a deregulated economy but also the restructuring of internal business processes. More specifically, they were arguing for the abandonment of bureaucracy and for the implementation of entrepreneurial principles at the very core of internal corporate activities. By the mid 1980s, a number of books had appeared arguing the case for the post-bureaucratic organisation (Peters and Waterman 1982). The implementation of these principles, within the context of an increasingly deregulated labour market in Britain, was to have far-reaching effects for the growth of small firms and the enterprise culture.

Essentially, the post-bureaucratic organisation was to be structured according to principles that were diametrically opposite to those that typified traditional forms of organisation design. According to classical theories of bureaucracies, organisations should consist of clearly defined work roles which are hierarchically structured within precisely determined authority relationships. Accountabilities are explicit and laid down in formally prescribed protocols and operating procedures. The hierarchical nature of the organisation assumes that policies are formulated at the top and then communicated 'down the line' to be executed by those vested with the appropriate authority. The whole process is co-ordinated by a hierarchical system of supervision and control whereby individual performance is monitored.

It is as a result of these organisational attributes that bureaucracies are characterised by a number of features which were seen to be dysfunctional by those arguing for their displacement by post-bureaucratic forms. It was held that their emphasis upon procedures and protocols made them inappropriate for responding to more dynamic market conditions. The careers and relatively secure jobs which they offer lead to conservatism and complacency among staff and encourage conformity rather than risk-taking. They are also conducive to a preoccupation with organisational means rather than ends. If these are geared to the delivery of customer or client services, then these suffer because internal organisational processes are viewed as more important than these organisational objectives. In other words, the opinion of managers is viewed as more important than that of clients – hardly surprising in view of the internal promotion processes of traditional bureaucracies (Kanter 1983).

Hence, it was argued by management gurus in the early 1980s that both private- and public-sector organisations needed to restructure if they were to fully realise the opportunities created by more deregulated labour markets in the United States and in Britain. This was imperative if companies were to compete against Japanese and South-East Asian businesses in both domestic and world markets. Accordingly, they put the case that organisations needed to operate in terms of a post-bureaucratic paradigm: in other words as entrepreneurial businesses. These are seen as having a number of key features:

- They should operate with 'flat', decentralised structures. In these, managers should be encouraged to feel that they are running their own businesses. Hence, they must have the authority to develop their own strategic plans and be responsible for their implementation.

- The organisational means that they use to achieve their business goals should be left to their own discretion, including the cost structures according to which they operate.

- How staff are recruited and rewarded is left to them. Generally, the rewards should be in terms of performance-related criteria rather than in terms of length of service as is the case in traditional bureaucracies. All that matters is that profit targets, as pre-negotiated with senior corporate management, are achieved.

- There should also be the generation of a culture that puts customers and clients first through the implementation of various 'formal' and 'informal' feedback mechanisms (Goffee and Scase 1995).

The application of these ideas within large-scale organisations is an attempt to make them more 'enterprising' and, therefore, more innovative and market-driven (a more detailed account of this type of corporate entrepreneurship or 'intrapreneurship' is described in Chapter 14). However, even with hindsight and twenty years after these ideas were first espoused, it is difficult to assess whether the adoption of post-bureaucratic principles has had a major impact upon the way most companies operate. Without doubt, these organisational ideals, as embedded in the post-bureaucratic paradigm, have had a major impact upon predominant management assumptions in both private and public sector organisations. In the public sector, they have been a major driver for the provision of services according to purchaser–provider relations. In the private sector, they have been a major force nurturing the formation and growth of small firms. In short, they have been a major factor accounting for the growing importance of small businesses in present-day economies.

As soon as corporate managers are made responsible for the operating costs of their devolved units, there is a tendency for them to focus upon two major issues: firstly, how to generate additional revenues either through leveraging sales from existing product portfolios or by developing new products; secondly, how to reduce operating costs. In addition to paying only the minimum for labour and materials in terms of what the market will bear, the other means – in terms of transaction costs analysis – is to determine which activities to 'keep in house' and which to externalise; in other words, to shift fixed costs to variable costs – unless, that is, the commodity or work task can be provided more cheaply 'in-house'. The analysis of internal cost structures led many managers responsible for newly devolved operating units to 'externalise' many of their functions so that they became variable costs; in other words – to use the language of practising managers – to 'strategically outsource' and to establish 'strategic alliances' (Hammer and Champy 1993). The outcome of this has been the growth of small firms as the providers of specialist products and services that would previously have been provided in-house. The process first began with the provision of support services – such as catering and facilities management – but increasingly this is occurring in relation to many core management activities. In many companies, functions such as information technology, human resource management and accountancy are outsourced in this way. Even teams of senior managers can be 'bought in' on a short-term basis to restructure a business and to develop and implement a new corporate strategy.

Often these services will be provided by small businesses established by those who have previously worked in the hiring company, but since their services are only purchased on a short-term, fixed-contract basis, the costs of these to the hiring company are much lower (assuming the quality of service and the level of commitment remain the same). However, the outcome is that the provider of these services often has spare capacity to do work for other businesses. Indeed, in order to reduce their market vulnerability, subcontractors offering products and services of whatever type have a vested interest in creating a diverse client base and, to ensure that the requirements of a variety of customers are met, it is often necessary to recruit staff and to expand their businesses. It is for this reason that many specialist subcontracting businesses are 'forced' to grow.

As larger organisations restructure to become 'confederations of semi-autonomous business units' the tendency to outsource services is reinforced. Indeed, in the extreme instance, there is the emergence of the virtual organisation (Goffee and Scase 1995), consisting of no more than a co-ordinating mechanism of a diverse range of service providers (see Chapter 22 for other examples). However, it is this process of corporate change that is a major driver of business start-up in the advanced post-industrial economies. This is being reinforced by many large companies deciding that they can only compete effectively if they focus upon a particular core competence, leading them to 'slim down' and often divest some of their business activities to concentrate upon leveraging the sales of products and services derived from the exercise of particular corporate skills (Scase 1998a). The outcome of this process has been the creation of small and medium-sized enterprises through the break-up of many corporate conglomerates and the divestment of business units through either management buy-outs or buy-ins. With the former, teams of managers purchase parts of the business from their employing organisation while with the latter, consortia of managers will acquire parts of the company. In both cases, City institutions, such as venture capitalists, are crucial as the providers of finance (see Chapter 19).

If corporate change is a major structural force leading to the formation and growth of small firms, there is also a range of market-driven factors that are significant in this process. Increasing global, regional and national competition is forcing businesses to be more efficient in their manufacture and delivery of goods and services. This not only leads to a tendency to specialisation, but also allows greater opportunities for smaller firms to compete. Many consumer markets have become more fragmented, with niche markets appearing in what were once regarded as relatively undifferentiated mass markets (see Chapter 20 for a further discussion). This has occurred in spheres ranging from financial services to personal consumption and leisure, recreation, travel and sport. As lifestyles become more differentiated, personal preferences and needs in society become more varied. These, in turn, offer opportunities for entrepreneurship and business start-up in the provision of services to meet these needs (Storey 1994). A couple of examples will suffice to illustrate this point.

Thirty years ago, holidays abroad were a relatively novel experience. As a result consumers were content to pay for package holidays for the security and the convenience which they offered. Tour operators met all their needs and, in return, those buying these services were prepared to forgo individuality for the convenience provided. Today, that market still exists and there is still a large demand for such holidays, but alongside this, there are also niches of consumers who, in return for paying higher prices, want to purchase more personalised itineraries. This offers opportunities for business start-ups in providing such services. Indeed, larger companies either are unable to compete or choose not to do so because their cost structures are geared to low profit margins and high volume turnover.

The finance sector offers another example. One of the outcomes of the Thatcher government's goal to create an enterprise culture was to deregulate the financial services industry. This allowed greater competition between businesses already in this sector as well as allowing others to set up companies to compete against them. This led to the start-up of a number of companies that decided to focus upon the provision of specialist services geared to specific niches of customer. Many of these were 'direct line' telephone-based services that were able to undercut the more established mass providers. Through focused marketing they have been able to generate a high level of customer loyalty and, along the way, a number of entrepreneurs have become multi-millionaires.

If there are various structural forces that have provided the material basis for the creation of an entrepreneurial culture, a number of psychological factors have also been significant. Many of these are, indeed, a function of this same culture. From what has already been discussed, it is evident that employees working in large organisations have to operate in a much more entrepreneurial manner. Without the offer of life-long secure jobs, they have to prove their contribution through performance-related reward systems. However, within these more insecure corporate environments, the risks of quitting the corporate umbrella and establishing their own businesses appear to be that much lower. Indeed, many choose to do so often in partnership with work colleagues. This is usually in those sectors of the economy where businesses can be established on the basis of personal talents and skills, which may be of a technical, scientific, creative or interpersonal nature. But the common factor is that large sums of money are not required for the purposes of business start-up (see Chapter 7). The emergence of the information society, and the related decline of manufacturing, are reinforcing this process (Scase 1998b).

The greater psychological capacity to take risks is leading to more entrepreneurship because of a further feature (see Chapter 8 for a detailed discussion of this issue). The personality make-up of those who are highly qualified and who possess different creative and expert skills may lead them to resent control relationships (Chell, Haworth and Brearley 1991). Working in large organisations almost inevitably requires an ability to conform and to adhere to stipulated rules and procedures. However, business start-up offers an alternative to this by providing a source of remuneration and the opportunity for personal growth, without the need to obey the commands of others. With increasing numbers of young people attending universities and then obtaining work-related skills that offer the basis for entrepreneurship, it would be surprising if this trend did not continue in the future. This is often particularly the case for women, who can be subject to corporate pressures that restrict their career opportunities (see Chapter 10). As research has shown, women are less likely to be promoted to senior management positions and those that are, have often had to out-perform their male colleagues. It is necessary for them to prove that they possess exceptional skills in the execution of their tasks as well as an almost excessive degree of corporate commitment. By setting up their own businesses, these women are able to avoid these corporate pressures (Carter and Cannon 1988). Often they will pool their financial and intellectual resources with other female colleagues who are subject to similar experiences with the result that the businesses which they start are often established as partnerships. In this way, there is a degree of psychological and material support which those who set up as sole traders are unable to enjoy. This can offer the potential for greater 'success' at the initial stage of business trading, but these partnerships can often face problems later. These can arise through each of the partners having conflicting objectives as to the future direction of the business in terms of, for example, whether or not it should grow.

The motives for business start-up among professional and managerial men and women demonstrate that the enterprise culture is not solely about people wanting to make money (see Chapter 6). Of course, this can be the case for some but it is not the most commonly stated reason. Among both men and women, academic studies have produced findings that suggest that there is a variety of factors which underpin the motivation for setting up businesses. These can range from the need to escape the control relationships of large firms to such factors as the desire to exercise more fully a personal talent or skill, the need to generate a stream of earnings compatible with a particular lifestyle, or the attempt to overcome an experience of disadvantage in the educational system or the labour market. Each of these factors has been shown to be a driver of entrepreneurship in the modern economy.

Many large companies – despite their claims to the contrary – fail to encourage innovation and the creative talent of their staff, and appear to be incapable of tolerating nonconformity and originality in their talented employees. Any suggestions for product or service innovation are therefore interpreted by senior managers as 'criticism' rather than as contributions to innovation (Kanter 1983). Business start-up offers an opt-out route for these employees. Similarly, there are others who become entrepreneurs because of lifestyle reasons. They possess particular intellectual, creative or expert skills that can be used for trading purposes outside of the confines of the large enterprise. Indeed, with the development of information and communication technologies, it is possible for many of these skills to be exercised in even the most remote parts of the world (see Chapter 22). Thus, the attraction of entrepreneurship for many is the ability to make money in ways that are compatible with other lifestyle preferences. There may be no commitment to business growth but, instead, simply to generate enough trade to provide a level of income to sustain a particular material standard of living (see Chapter 23). As a result, small business advisers often misunderstand this motive in their attempts to force such 'lifestyle' entrepreneurs to grow. Equally, there are others who, for one reason or another, are unable to be upwardly mobile within the conventional labour market. Because of their lack of qualifications, they are unlikely to be appointed to the more highly paid corporate positions or to become professional employees in the public sector. A traditional role of entrepreneurship has been to offer 'alternative' paths of success for such people. In Britain, this has been the route taken by members of ethnic minority groups, women and underqualified men (Goffee and Scase 1985b). They have succeeded in all sectors of the economy (but particularly in retailing, leisure and entertainment, and personal services) and often it is in those sectors where little capital funding is needed. Their businesses often have to be self-financing because they are perceived by banks and other financial institutions as constituting a high risk. It is these entrepreneurs, when they do become outstandingly successful, who are often presented as the role models of 'personal ambition', typifying the values of the enterprise culture – for a further discussion, see Chapters 10 and 11. Certainly, they personify the 'openness' of capitalist society and the extent to which personal disadvantage, of whatever kind, can be overcome. The fact that this is an experience enjoyed by only a very small number of people, and which does little to improve the condition of the overwhelming majority, is irrelevant. What is significant is the fact that their personal success sustains an ideology of 'openness' and a rhetoric of 'equal opportunity'. As such, their biographies act as an inspiration to others and, thereby, reinforce the attractions of an enterprise culture (Branson 1998). But if personal enterprise has been traditionally associated with the 'free market', the state has been directly involved in nurturing this since at least the early 1980s.

3.5 The state and enterprise

In a fully developed enterprise culture, it would be expected that the state would play a relatively minor role because the free market would lead to the creation of businesses. This, however, has not been the case. First with the Conservative governments of the 1980s and the early 1990s, and then with the subsequent Labour administration, the state has been positively involved in encouraging business start-up (see Chapter 4). This is because of a number of factors, including the recognition of the need to respond to those structural and psychological forces mentioned above. Governments have appreciated that the structure of the economy is changing, with national competitive advantage being driven by the need to become an information society in which the key assets are personal creativity and intellectual capital (Scase 1999). In such a society, there is likely to occur the demise of the large manufacturing enterprise and the growth of small firms. It is, then, the task of government to encourage this process of structural change. This can be done by encouraging those with the relevant expert skills to obtain the technical and psychological competences required for business start-up. Hence, there has been a variety of government-sponsored initiatives for school-leavers and university graduates as well as for those who have been made redundant or taken early retirement (see Chapter 18). The purpose has been to create and expand small businesses in high technology, electronics, the bio-sciences and other allegedly future-orientated sectors of the economy (see Chapter 13).

Alongside such training measures, there have been collaborative ventures between the state, local government and business organisations to provide infrastructural support for start-up ventures. These include the creation of science parks, enterprise centres and 'incubators' in which those who are running their own businesses can have access to technical support and various kinds of expertise. Often the motive is to encourage these entrepreneurs to expand so that job opportunities are created. Indeed, a further motive of state initiatives has been to encourage business start-up as an integral policy of reducing levels of unemployment. As manufacturing industry has declined as an employer of labour, entrepreneurship has been presented by successive governments as the self-help solution to the processes of structural change that have created high levels of unemployment (Storey 1994).

But there has been a further means whereby the state has embodied the ideals of enterprise. This has been in terms of its own functions and how it has reshaped its role in the economy. There has, of course, been the privatisation of many of its post-war activities. In areas ranging from health and transport to telecommunications and atomic energy, publicly owned utilities have been turned over to private ownership. This has not only increased the capitalisation of the London stock market but changed the whole culture of business in Britain. Directors in the newly privatised companies have been able to introduce huge wage differentials which have then become 'models' for practice in other businesses. On the basis of allegedly performance-related criteria and by reference to world market demand for their services, they have awarded themselves salary increases that created a new culture of rewards in large businesses in general. A further outcome has been a growing pattern of social and economic inequality in society as a whole. The fact that the justification for these rewards is often unable to stand up to scientific scrutiny has highlighted the presence of inequity as an inevitable ingredient of the enterprise culture.

The state has also imposed a model of the market and of enterprise within its own continuing functions (Keen and Scase 1998). Many central government tasks are now undertaken by agencies which are expected to operate as privately owned businesses in services such as highways, customs and excise, and tax collection. Local authorities have been encouraged to operate as enabling bodies, purchasing their services from various competing firms providing such services, for example, for the care of the old, the infirm and children. As stated earlier, this process of outsourcing has been a major factor encouraging the growth of small firms and of 'service-provider' entrepreneurship. Equally, schools, universities and hospitals are expected to operate as businesses with budgets, strategic plans and mission statements, with patients, pupils and students treated as 'customers' whose wishes the professional providers are expected to serve. The election of a Labour government within the UK in May 1997 had little impact in changing these assumptions and the new government has pursued policies on the basis that an enterprise culture should be sustained and that it will continue in the future.

3.6 Big business and the enterprise culture

Big business has responded to the enterprise culture by exploiting its ideals and values to rid itself of government and trade union interference, and has also taken advantage of these to redefine the employment relationship. With the decline of organised labour and collective bargaining, there has been the emergence of individually negotiated contracts and the introduction of performance-related reward systems (Edwards 1995). But equally as important has been the imposition of an employment relation between employer and employee which is defined solely in instrumental and contractual terms (see Chapter 17). High-trust cultures have become superseded by those of low trust, and obligations and reciprocities have been eroded, to be replaced by a focus upon short-term, profit-maximising opportunities. Whether this is to the longer-term benefit of companies remains an unanswered question. The extent to which this 'enterprise culture' within large corporations is appropriate for nurturing the commitment and hence the creativity of employees, upon which future competitive advantage depends, is debatable. Within this high-risk, performance-related work environment, employees are encouraged to be self-reliant and to plan their own career strategies. Such work cultures are likely to encourage employees to think of themselves as becoming self-employed, as freelancers and as consultants, as well as setting up their own businesses. Within this context, entrepreneurship offers security in contrast to the insecurity of employment in the large corporation. This, then, leads to changing patterns of work and employment in an enterprise culture.

3.7 Patterns of employment in an enterprise culture

The various patterns of organisational change that have occurred in both private- and public-sector organisations have had important ramifications for personal work and career experiences. For a start, individuals need to possess greater diversities of skills. No longer can they expect long-term careers and to be employed by, perhaps, no more than two or three large companies during the course of their working lives. Instead, there is the need to possess both specialist as well as general skills that are appropriate for a variety of work environments. In terms of the former, competences in information and computer technology are becoming imperative as companies compete on the basis of various kinds of information which they use for product and service development. But alongside these, it is necessary to be able to adapt to the changes created by a continuously shifting occupational structure. Skills rapidly become obsolete as individuals move from one organisation to the next. To remain employable requires individuals to constantly adapt their competences for new employment opportunities. Sometimes these arise in large corporations while on other occasions they are available within the confines of small businesses. In short, each person's work experiences are characterised by a far greater degree of unpredictability and risk than in the past (Brown and Scase 1994).

Within these work patterns, self-employment and business proprietorship become more pronounced. In the early 1980s, approximately 4% of the labour force was self-employed, although by the late 1990s this had increased to about 15% (see Chapter 2). Projections for the labour force into the 21st century suggest that this trend will continue as Britain becomes a service-based, information economy, and within certain growth sectors – such as the entertainment and media industries – the self-employed already constitute a higher proportion than these figures suggest. These are sectors of the economy in which intellectual capital is a tradable asset which individuals can sell to any potential employer. Thus, the production of goods and services is being undertaken through market rather than employment relationships.

Indeed, such a trend is reinforcing the permanence of an enterprise culture as one in which individuals have to be self-reliant in the organisation of their work patterns as well as in their broader lifestyles. To be self-employed requires more than simply the exercise of a particular set of expert or technical skills. This can be illustrated by comparing freelance television producers with those who are on the payroll of a company. Both groups will have similar work tasks in terms of how they manage the creation and manufacture of television programmes. But alongside this there will be major differences between them. The former will need to market themselves to the potential purchasers of their services. They will need to negotiate contracts in terms of the price and the time-spans of particular programme projects. Business plans will have to be prepared and, within these, staff costs will have to be calculated. The preparation of programmes will require the collaboration of a number of specialists (camera opera-tors, sound engineers, performers), all of whom will have their various 'charge-out' rates as well as other possible work commitments. To engage such a diverse range of people will require considerable negotiation and planning. At the same time, costs will have to be managed and kept within budgets, with loans often having to be negotiated to fund projects as producers may not receive full payments from commissioning broadcasting companies until the completed products have been accepted.

In contrast, producers who are engaged by companies as full-time employees have few of these pressures. There may be various internal organisational issues to handle and the programmes may have to be completed within budgets, but there is not the same need to rely upon open market mechanisms as in the case of the freelance pro-ducers. It is these demands that require the self-employed to acquire additional skills in order to complete their tasks at hand. The same is true of any other sector of the self-employed, whether they are computer programmers, engineers, accountants, or what-ever. Indeed, it is the failure to appreciate that to be self-employed requires the ability to negotiate prices for services rendered, to be able to market these services, and to manage the costs and finances associated with the sale of these in the marketplace, that leads to so many of the self-employed going out of business in their initial periods of trading. It is for this reason that some policy-makers argue for the need for changes in the higher education system so that university graduates are better equipped to cope with the experiences of self-employment which they are likely to face as part-and-parcel of their future career portfolios in an information age (Brown and Scase 1994).

The consequences of self-employment extend beyond the world of work as it makes it more difficult for people to plan their futures. Unlike those from long-term career jobs in large companies, earnings are difficult to predict. As a result, personal financial planning is more problematic and a more cautious approach has to be adopted towards making substantial commitments. The career bureaucrat could commit her/himself to mortgages and other large loans because security of employment was rea-sonably assured. This is not the case for the self-employed. Furthermore, the latter have to make provision for periods of ill health as well as for their retirement. The fact that so many fail to do so could be a major problem for social services in the 21st cen-tury. When retired, many of those previously self-employed may have insufficient means to support themselves. In other words, the emergence of an economy containing a growing proportion of those who are self-employed and small business owners has major macro-economic effects. These trends will shape the central direction of govern-ment policy and cease to be merely of peripheral significance.

3.8 The information age and the enterprise culture

The revolution in information and communications technology is the major factor bringing about the break-up of large organisations and their fragmentation into devolved, decentralised operating structures (see Chapter 22). It is this that is enabling large firms to operate as confederations of small businesses. At the same time, this rev-olution is leading to the restructuring of supply chains and the relationship between firms (see Chapter 21). Manufacturers, distributors and retailers are able to collaborate in the design, development, manufacture, distribution and sale of products and services (Tapscott and Caston 1993). But if in the past this operated on a limited scale within generally constrained geographical locations, this is no longer the case. The development of intranet and internet technologies allows these relationships to operate on a global basis (Tapscott 1995). This is leading to, in other words, the 'death of distance', and this is having a major impact upon the nature of the economies of Europe. Companies are increasingly finding themselves competing in a global market where there are 'world prices' not only for commodities but also for labour. Businesses in Britain now have to compete 'head-on' with those in South-East Asia and the rest of the world (see Chapter 24). There are at least three outcomes that appear to be emerging from this trend:

- the social wage and other overhead costs have to be kept to a minimum if companies in Europe are to compete. In other words, the material conditions of an enterprise economy are a functional necessity that mitigate against the return of corporatism or tripartism in a global economy;
- there is the emergence of an international division of labour, with the economies of Europe and the United States becoming information-based as manufacturing shifts to other lower-cost parts of the world;
- the business environment of small firms is becoming increasingly international, integrated as they are within global supply chains, and as they take greater advantage of the trading benefits of information technology. Even the smallest of businesses located, for example, in the South Pacific can now market their products and compete in a global economy. Traditional craft businesses in India now sell their products, via the Internet, to customers in the United States. Small software companies in Argentina have developed market sectors in Spain and other parts of southern Europe.

In other words, the capabilities of information technology have made size and geographical location of businesses irrelevant for the purposes of global trading. The economies of scale no longer prevail, being superseded by competitive advantage derived from knowledge and business intelligence.

Electronic commerce is likely to reinforce these trends in consumer markets. Although the dominance of supermarkets and the growth of shopping malls are likely to continue, interactive electronic shopping may soon appear as a significant market niche. This offers trading opportunities for small firms across national borders. Although perhaps trading as single-person businesses, ventures such as record stores, bookshops, travel bureaux and computer outlets can operate in this way. As far as customers are concerned, the size of the businesses from which they purchase goods and services is irrelevant. All that matters is price, quality of service and convenience. Therefore, electronic commerce enables small firms to offer these and also to undercut larger companies. It is already possible to purchase CDs from the United States via the Internet, and cheaper than to buy them from a local store in Britain. Purchasing products in a global electronic marketplace will become increasingly the pattern as consumers become aware of the capabilities of information technology, and in this future, the role of small businesses will become even more pronounced.

3.9 Chapter summary

Many of the trends regarding the enterprise culture discussed in this chapter have yet to be the subject of detailed empirical enquiry. There has been a tendency to focus upon traditional small firms and to consider the nature of the enterprise culture in these terms. What is now needed is a broader frame of reference which views the dynamics of small-business formation and growth as driven by a range of global, structural and technological imperatives and not solely by a political rhetoric that was ascendant in the early 1980s. Indeed, as stated earlier, this was as much a response to these broader changes as a major cause of them.

However, if the small-business agenda is to be taken seriously, it is necessary to shift the focus to emerging rather than traditional forms of small business. More research is needed into the dynamics of those small firms that trade on the basis of knowledge, expertise, creativity and intelligence, to answer such questions as: How are customer relations established? What is the role of small businesses in global supply chains? How far are they realising the opportunities being created by the Internet and other developments in information and communication technologies? What are the social relations of these firms? How are creative and highly educated employees managed?

If the principles of line management are inappropriate for reasons to do with both the size of small businesses as well as the psychology of employees, how are harmonious and productive working relations to be established? A possible solution is the setting up of businesses as partnerships so that everyone has a stake in the ownership and the rewards. But how are decisions taken in these businesses and according to what principles are authority relations established among those who are (legally) co-owners? How is growth managed in such firms and how is 'employee autonomy' protected in the face of the need to develop organisational co-ordinating mechanisms?

If these are issues that warrant attention at the 'micro' enterprise level, there are other 'macro' economic topics that require further debate and enquiry. What, for example, are the implications of a rapidly growing small-business sector for the management of a modern economy? To what extent can prices, wage increases and tendencies to inflation be monitored in an economy that is dependent upon services produced by a large small-business sector? How is the care of the old to be financed if the self-employed – constituting perhaps 25% of the labour force – make inadequate provision for themselves? How is cross-border trading by small firms to be regulated for the purposes of tax collection and customs and excise? Equally, how far are education systems (as they are presently structured) appropriate for preparing highly qualified people for participation in the future enterprise economy – that is, for being capable of setting up and managing their own businesses either as partners or as sole proprietors? In the discussion of such issues it becomes clear that the enterprise culture is here to stay, driven as it is by a range of structural, technological, global and even psychological factors. The aim of this chapter has been to provide a review of some of the more important of these.

Questions

1 What factors account for the growing importance of small firms in Britain?

2 What employment experiences are likely to encourage men and women to start their own businesses?

3 What qualities are needed to be a successful entrepreneur?

4 How will the development of the Internet and the growth of the information economy affect the opportunities for business start-up?

CHAPTER 4

Small-business policy, support and governance

Steve Johnson, Leigh Sear and Anne Jenkins

4.1 Learning objectives

There are four learning objectives in this chapter:

1 To explore the key trends and issues associated with small-firms policy.
2 To unpack the key trends in small-business support structures and governance.
3 To examine the key actors within the small-business policy community and their activities in the UK.
4 To explore future patterns of governance and support within the small-business policy community.

Key concepts

■ support structures and organisations ■ policy initiatives ■ Business Links
■ TECs/LECs ■ local enterprise agencies

4.2 Introduction

Studies from commentators such as Birch (1979) and Storey and Johnson (1987) have stressed the importance of small firms to job and wealth creation and economic regeneration. Over the last 15 years, policy-makers have used the findings of such studies as the rationale for providing a range of small-business support programmes, which have attempted to assist the development of the small-business sector. However, in many European countries, there has never been a small firms 'White Paper', providing a conceptual framework for this flurry of activity, and a number of agencies and initiatives have come and gone from the institutional landscape. Therefore, there are a number of concerns with the effectiveness of small-business support, and whether small firms are the panacea to the economic ills of many economies. This chapter unpacks some of the key issues and trends surrounding small-business policy and support structures, with specific reference to the situation in the UK, and provides a number of scenarios as to the future direction for policy and support.

should be ready to consider at this point is: how does the term 'enterprise culture' actually capture such a profound set of changes and their effects on the small firm?

5.4.2 Enterprise culture – the metaphor for the small firm

As enterprise culture in the 1980s came to represent a break with the past, it became correlated with a rise in attention directed towards the activities of the small firm. Or put another way, the small firm became a representation for the way in which the competitive nature of the UK economy could be recast. This is still the case. Policy-makers, when speaking about small firms, use language concerned with growth, large firms talk in terms of small firms' spending power and purchasing patterns, and often academics wonder about the causes of small-firm growth and death. This tangled association of enterprise culture, the small firm and competitiveness has provided an incremental knowledge of the subject which has focused on the performance of the small firm as a metaphor for the performance of the economy as a whole.

Apart from this placing an impossible burden on the small-firm sector (expected to drag the UK out of the recessions of the past two decades), it fails to recognise other important changes which have taken place in society. Deeper shifts in culture have involved the emergence of a wide range of new political, economic and social trends (see, for example, Hall, Held and McGrew 1992). While enterprise culture is clearly too limited a notion to make sense of all these sorts of change, there does need to be some way of recognising how they have had important consequences on the way the small firm fits into society. As Schwengel (1991: 136) suggests, 'If you think of enterprise culture only in economic terms, or as a business ideology, then although everything does indeed "begin with the economy", you miss the changes in political leadership that enterprise culture implies ... you do not recognise it as a process that will still be important even when many British people may have forgotten that once there was a seemingly irresistible blue tide of conservatism.'

To put this another way, in our investigations on the small firm we need to be able to evaluate the many different trends and changes which have affected society over the past two decades, and which have therefore influenced the way small firms operate. The idea of an enterprise culture does not really help in this. In fact, it causes more ambiguity than it explains because those early ideas on enterprise culture misled the debate on the relevance of the small firm in society – suggesting, almost, that the small firm was a panacea for many of the UK's social and economic ills. The notion of an enterprise culture, then, has been problematic. It has not helped our understanding of the small firm in the UK as we approach the end of the twentieth century.

5.4.3 Enterprise culture as a contested concept

As this notion of enterprise culture is problematic and is limited in helping us to understand the small firm, in recent years there has been a growing literature that has developed a critical stance towards the concept. One such critique has been provided by Ritchie (1991: 24), who introduced something of a relativist approach to the term. Ritchie positions the idea of enterprise culture held by the owner-manager alongside the view held by others interested in the small firm. He suggests enterprise culture is a self-descriptive notion from the perspective of the owner-manager. This contrasts with the view held by policy-makers, politicians and small-firm advisers who see the term as something of an article of faith in the small firm. He then suggests that from the eyes of the sceptic, enterprise culture is seen as a euphemistic myth, something with no grounding in reality. Finally, Ritchie considers how academics and other analysts view the notion of an enterprise culture, and he believes that this group sees it as a carefully attested concept, which needs to be handled with some caution. Ritchie's work is useful because it shows how the idea of an enterprise culture cannot be easily confined to one interpretation.

Burrows (1991b) is also critical of the term 'enterprise culture' although he offers a different view from Ritchie. Burrows argues that the idea of an enterprise culture provides 'a wide ranging semiotic rationale' for the role of the small-firm sector in the industrial restructuring processes faced by the UK economy (p. 5). What Burrows is suggesting is that in some way a consistent understanding forms around the meaning of the term whenever it is used. So, although enterprise culture is used by different people and in different contexts, a common meaning takes shape associating the term with efforts and new attempts to restructure the economy. In addition, this consistency is often based on vague ideas on the relationship of enterprise and small firms with culture. Burrows, then, is hinting at the weak foundations of the term to explain the role of the small firm in bigger issues of economic and business development, and at the very heart of this is a positioning of the small firm which relates enterprise and culture with more generic shifts in the nature of society.

So where does this leave the reader when faced with the term 'enterprise culture'? For example, how can this section add to the work outlined by Richard Scase in Chapter 3 of this book? The points made by Ritchie and Burrows provide a critique on the notion of enterprise culture and begin to indicate that it is too restrictive a term; it is a term which cannot capture the myriad of social relations which exist in and around small firms. One way the student may think about this is to consider how contagious the idea of enterprise culture is as it is used in many different contexts, and then to question whether this provides a good understanding of what is being discussed. However, the main message from this section is that the student should recognise the limitations of the idea of an enterprise culture. When it is used, questions should be asked about what other types of conceptual framework are necessary to explain the more meaningful changes that the small firm has experienced and is still experiencing. It is a problematic term which does not help to explain the relevance of the small firm today.

5.5 The small firm and its environment: the role of actors and structures

In this section, the student is encouraged to look at the small firm and ask about how the owner-manager interacts with the business environment. What happens, for instance, when an article of government legislation comes into force: how does the owner-manager shape this legislation, or react to it? Rather than look in detail at particular events like this, the roles of actors and structures are outlined so the student can begin to question how the two relate and comprehend how complex the small-firm world is.

Many business textbooks look at the way in which the small firm interacts with its environment, and it is regarded as a necessary condition when thinking about the strategic orientation of firms. For example, the work of Michael Porter (1990) considers the competitive economic environment in which firms operate, identifying such issues as innovation, rivalry and supply-chain linkages. However, this section provides a different perspective of the small firm and its environment. It looks specifically at the role of small-firm actors, like the owner-manager, employees and even small-firm advisers, and the role of structures, such as government policy or other institutional strategies (for instance, large-firm strategy), and how these might be useful in explaining the way small firms behave. This is an important area, not least because of the way the small firm is regularly situated in the middle of a complex web of interactions.

5.5.1 What are small-firm actors and structures?

When the term 'small-firm actor' is used, it refers to those key individuals who have some effect on the way things are organised in the small-business domain. When the term 'structures' is used, it refers to the conditions in which small firms exist. Structures operate in and around the small firm in such a way that they enable certain things to take place, but at the same time they impose some form of constraint on what can actually take place. When in business literature the student comes across the term 'driving forces', it is often a reference to structures. Structures might be political, economic, social or cultural (see Hall *et al.* 1992). Also, it is common in studies on the small firm to see structures described as very determinant features. When structures (or driving forces) are regarded as impacting in some way on small firms, then usually actors are considered to be quite passive. Alternatively, some see the role of actors to be the main feature of small-firm behaviour. If this is the case, then it usually means that structures are an outcome of the aggregate behaviour of many individual actors, who, it is often felt, behave in completely rational ways, pursuing well-thought-out strategies. The student should be careful when thinking about the idea of actors and structures in the small-firm world.

If we concentrate too much on actors, there is the danger of seeing what happens in the small firm as being the sole outcome of motives and intentions of key people in the business. This view would give the impression that the composition of the small-firm sector and its surroundings is an outcome of all the individual activities of owner-managers and their equivalents. This would also demonstrate the notion that some form of order can be achieved in the small-firm world through the outcome of individual behaviour. By way of illustration, it would presume that availability and take-up of finance to fund small-firm start-up and development was an outcome of a rational decision-making process, whereby the owner-manager and the financier have at their disposal 'perfect' information on which to make a choice. This analysis would pay less attention to the effects of global financial shifts, for instance. On the other hand, accounts which pay attention only to structures will assume that all behaviour is an outcome of forces beyond the control of any individual. Often, this is seen as deterministic, paying too little attention to the choices and decisions carried out by small-firm actors. For example, it might be argued that government policies distort the market for certain types of private-sector services, and that these structural features will have an adverse affect on small-firm behaviour overall (see Bennett, Wicks and McCoshan 1994). This analysis would pay less attention to the choices individuals can make to determine the behaviour of the small firm.

The debate on actors and structures raises important issues about how we explain what happens in small firms. Are events and behaviour in the small-firm world an outcome of the decisions made by actors, or the outcome of a set (or series) of driving forces? To provide a response to this we can paraphrase Roy Bhaskar (1986: 123), a social philosopher, who has spent some considerable time thinking about actors and structures. His argument suggests that if the behaviour of the small firm is an outcome of the owner-manager and employees, then the behaviour of the owner-manager and employees is equally an outcome of the small firm.

What Bhaskar is saying is that there is a dual relationship between structures and actors and the two should be thought of in this way. Through this duality we can understand how the small firm is a continually reproduced outcome of its environment and of the people who work in and around it. This is a dynamic relationship between the two and not a case of competing tendencies. The owner-manager is important, but so too are the employees, the adviser, the bank manager and then also other small firms, the government and the policies they set, as are larger multinational firms, international currency markets, global consumption trends and so on.

5.5.2 Examples of the interaction between small-firm structures and actors

To digress for a moment, we can consider a couple of examples of how this might operate in practice. Recently, one major driving force impacting on the small firm has been the decision by the UK government to give the Bank of England autonomy in setting the interest rate for borrowing. Subsequently the level of interest rates has risen, causing much concern for businesses and for business pressure groups like the CBI (the Confederation of British Industry). Small businesses, it is claimed, are suffering because of increasing costs due to the high rate of borrowing. Also, because interest rates are high this has a causal impact on the high value of UK sterling in relation to other currencies. This is also damaging business because it means UK exports are less attractive, while it encourages more foreign imports. It would appear, then, that these economic structures are having an adverse effect on small businesses. However, at the same time small-business owner-managers through their actions influence the trajectory of the economy. Their spending contributes to inflation trends and to the demands for lending. They can also act and respond to the levels of interest rates within the confines of their own business. At an extreme level they can decide that business has become too costly and decide to stop trading altogether. Taking a less extreme approach, they can decide to make reductions in spending in other areas, perhaps cutting back on training as they feel the squeeze on their profit margins. Whatever the structures and however the actors contribute to these structures, there is a dual process going on here.

Another case concerns the actions of large multinational companies. Consider the strategy adopted by many larger firms over the past few years to reduce the number of smaller firms who provide them with all sorts of goods and services. Here, the structures of globalisation have an effect on the small firm (see Chapter 24). For example, a large steel company would be looking to exploit new global markets to bring in raw materials of sand and coal. Previously this may have been sourced on a much more local basis but because of global driving forces, the steel company has to search out the most attractive markets. It is cheaper, in some instances, to import raw materials from another part of the world than to purchase them locally. As the steel company realises the benefits it can gain because of the globalised economy, it looks to source other goods from afar as well, such as machinery and scrap. The small firm begins to feel the consequences of these global driving forces as it is squeezed out of the supply chain. What is happening in such an instance is that the structures of globalisation, the political and economic policies adopted by large companies, governments and financial institutions, impact on the small firm. The actors in the small firm are able to respond to this, however. Small firms are encouraged to be part of the global marketplace and to consider exporting to other parts of the world to maintain their levels of output. Or alternatively, they are encouraged to become more efficient so they can compete with companies from afar who can offer their products more cheaply. Again, there is an interaction of structures with actors which determines small-firm behaviour.

By using this perspective of structures and actors we can see how the idea that the small firm interacts with its environment takes hold. Small firms are outcomes of the people in and around them *plus* the environment in which they are situated. This is a complex relationship. Studies on small firms which presume that actors shape the behaviour of the business, or that driving forces do so, tend to marginalise one or the other. The student will find that this is a common feature in business studies. That this is the case should not be too surprising because understanding the dual relationship between structures and actors is a very difficult thing to attain. One of the key messages that the student should take away from this section is that they should recognise the complex interaction between key actors in the small firm (such as owner-managers) and the structures around the small firm, as reports and advice are given on business operations. The small firm does not operate outside this duality of social relations.

5.6 The small firm, stakeholders and the idea of habitus

This third section looks at the position of the small firm with respect to its many stakeholders. This section will be a challenging read because it introduces Pierre Bourdieu's (1984; 1990) notion of habitus. The student should see this as a framework for taking account of the different motives stakeholders have as they work in the small-firm world. It would also be useful if the student and teacher could raise questions about how useful this concept is. Many other chapters in this book are concerned with the behaviour and practices of owner-managers and their stakeholders, and once again the student should read this section alongside the viewpoints adopted by other authors in this book.

As the previous section indicated, there are many actors in the small-firm world. They may be part of the small firm itself, or may well be in other organisations, working in the public sector (in the UK's Training and Enterprise Councils and Business Links for instance), in the private sector, in banks, as accountants, or as consultants, in other firms – whether large, medium or small businesses – or even in the families of an owner-manager. Another way of referring to these actors is through the phrase 'stakeholders', a common term which has pervaded the language of business in recent years. In this section, the term 'stakeholders' is used in an interchangeable way with the word 'actors'. However, this section looks at small-firm actors in a different way and begins to question what it is that differentiates the behaviour of the many stakeholders. To help with this, the notion of *habitus* is introduced. Habitus is a difficult concept drawn from the work of Bourdieu (1984; 1990), who worked mainly in sociological and cultural studies. The student or teacher will not therefore find the notion of habitus used often in small-firm studies and here it is used only in an exploratory fashion.

5.6.1 What is meant by habitus and what is its relevance here?

To dispel some of the anxiety in dealing with the idea of habitus, it can be explained as the concept which is used to mediate between what we recognise as structures and how behaviour takes place (for an introduction to habitus see the work of Miller 1987a; Chaney 1996; and Painter 1997). Habitus helps to draw out points concerning difference. While the relationship between structures and actors explains the small firm in its environment, habitus helps to explain the sorts of thing which *motivate the different practices we find in and around the small firm*. Habitus is only a theory and the student should treat it as such, taking into account what sort of value it has to offer and looking to see where it can be applied further.

Bourdieu's initial work considered habitus with respect to difference between classes, and he used it to suggest something which was a generator of behaviour and an outcome of behaviour. He arrived at this point by raising some fundamental questions of what people mean as they investigate what is real and what is felt to exist. For example, if we think about a small firm, what can we claim is objective knowledge? We might say that it is a real entity and point to some type of actual built workplace. Bourdieu (1990) identified this type of thinking as *objectivism*. Of course, not all firms have such workplaces. Some operate from a virtual address, such as a PO Box number or a World Wide Web page – a self-employed business may operate from a front room in a domestic house. However, when we use the term 'small firm' we all construct an image in our heads of what we mean and this image is open to interpretation from many different quarters. What the owner-manager interprets as a small firm may not be the same as the small-firm researcher believes such a firm to be. This sort of thinking was identified by Bourdieu as *subjectivism*. For Bourdieu, neither of these was an adequate way of explaining what an entity is. In this case, neither objective knowledge nor subjective knowledge can, on its own, explain what a small firm is and what it does.

As objective and subjective knowledge were inadequate ways of explaining the social world for Bourdieu, he put forward a theory of practice. In this theory of practice the concept of structure remains central, but so too does the idea that there are 'principles which generate and organize practices and representations that can be objectively adapted to their outcomes without presupposing a conscious aiming at ends or an express mastery of the operations necessary in order to attain them' (Bourdieu, cited in Painter 1997, p. 136).

Trying to put this simply, we can say that habitus is the path from structures to practice. If we use the previous example concerning large companies and their small-firm suppliers, we can say that the processes of globalisation form part of the structure of economies, and that habitus is the path owner-managers follow to make sense of what globalisation means for their business. The owner-manager then behaves accordingly and – an important point – differently to many other owner-managers experiencing the same problems. This does not presuppose behaviour as a considered, rationalised strategy, but it does suggest an approach used by an owner-manager in terms of ways of knowing about the business, and ways of doing things which support the business.

5.6.2 Grounding the habitus of small-firm stakeholders

Thinking about habitus should force the student and teacher to stand back and to develop some level of critique about what goes on in and around the small firm. We can consider this further by looking at the habitus of small-firm stakeholders. Stakeholders also have ways of knowing and ways of doing when they work with small firms. These are based on the different forms of knowledge they possess about the operations of the small firm: the bank manager has ways of knowing about the financial management of the small firm; the customer has ways of knowing about the product or service of the small firm; the employee has ways of knowing about the working procedure operated by the owner-manager in the small firm, and so on. In fact, while many people have pointed to the small-firm sector as being diverse, it is important to understand that small-firm stakeholders are also diverse, covering many different groups.

Drawing on Painter's (1997) innovative use of habitus to explain urban governance, we can say that different ways of knowing are very important in helping stakeholders to decide whether to step into – or step out of – the small-firm world. Painter (1997: 137) suggests that the habitus knowledge appears to be instinctive and natural. 'It is labelled common sense and determines the actors' view of the field and of the prospects associated with particular courses of action.' This means the habitus acts to instruct how stakeholders should behave in their dealings with the small firm. What is important for each of the different stakeholder groups is the way in which the habitus is grounded in some form of knowledge. Figure 5.1 provides an initial outline of this.

Ways of knowing and ways of doing are grounded in different habitus and we need to consider this when understanding what happens in the small-firm world. It is important to note that we are not simply talking about context here: habitus is shaped by, and is a shaper of, behaviour. Because the habituses of small-firm stakeholders are grounded differently, it is likely that each of the stakeholder groups will form distinct sets of values which motivate their ways of doing and knowing in the small-firm world. An important point from this is that stakeholder groups are not united, and do not act in some uniform way for the benefit of the small-firm sector. The different grounding of the small-firm stakeholder habitus means that we will see different types of small-firm stakeholder behaviour.

Habitus is simply a theoretical tool which can be used to help us think about the behaviour and practices pertinent to small-firm activity. Many other authors in this book are concerned with the same subjects but think about them in different ways. Denise Fletcher, for instance, talks about how the practice of business is entwined with family (Chapter 9); Monder Ram and Giles Barrett note the influence of race and

Figure 5.1 The habitus of small-firm stakeholders

Small-firm stakeholder	The Habitus of the stakeholder
Owner-manager	Endures a process of socialisation through doing business, being successful, having informal rules of (own) employment; looks to develop trust with customers and suppliers; has a sound concept of what the 'business world' is; will use profit for his/her wage and for reinvestment; connects to 'local' networks; holds values of the same kind as other similar owner-manager types.
Self-employed	Has a process of socialisation very similar to the owner-manager; often family situation is a high consideration and there may be little separation between work life and home life; internalises many business processes rather than having them as formal procedures; can feel a sense of isolation at key business moments.
Small-firm employee	Influenced by formal rules of employment; the wage relation is very important as is the (often loose) division of labour which determines his or her work schedule; clear separation of work from home; not likely to hold the same values as the employer.
Public-sector support agency (TEC, Business Link, local authority etc.)	Expected to work to codes of profession; will seek to demonstrate entrepreneurial credibility; will try to integrate knowledge of the public sector into the work with the private sector to leverage new opportunities; will work within spatial constraints (i.e. the 'local economy'); will hold some values concerning accountability.
Private-sector consultant	Has an entrepreneurial language which they consider to be sympathetic with the small firm, looking to guide the business in a mutually beneficial manner; advocate of good, common-sense business practices which piece bits of the business process together; will look for business 'progress'; will consider themselves to share many of the values of the owner-manager.
Large-firm manager	Influenced by the hierarchical structure of the large organisation; works to a set of rules, codes and norms geared towards the efficiency (and 'bottom line') of the large firm; may regard the small firm as a 'little' big firm; will be convinced that he or she is sympathetic to the problems experienced by the small firm but actions may not be interpreted by others in this way.
Financial adviser (such as in banks)	Will also be influenced by degree of formality based on organisational rules and hierarchy which are often unsympathetic to the small firm; will look for formal business plans and strategies of doing business; will look to develop an empathy with the business; likely to hold values determined by the organisation which may differ from those of the owner-manager.
Policy-maker (such as politician or civil servant)	Socialised through high levels of bureaucratic knowledge; respectful of hierarchy, organisational structure and record-keeping; political elements will be socialised through party line, concerned with values of accountability.

Source: adapted from Painter (1997: 138) copyright © 1997 Sage Publications, reprinted by permission of Sage Publications, Inc.

ethnicity on business practice (Chapter 11); while Sara Carter juxtaposes gender relations and business practice (Chapter 10). We might ask what grounds the habitus of owner-managers in ethnic or in family businesses, or of women in business? In addition, how is the habitus of the stakeholders in ethnic businesses grounded differently to the stakeholders in family businesses? In each case, we will see that the habitus is grounded differently and we will find difference in the motivations for being involved in the small-firm domain.

As long as the student is not frightened off by the complicated appearance of habitus, he or she might be able to address such questions. Nonetheless, the key message for the reader from this section is that stakeholders do make an important contribution to the day-to-day activities of small firms. Stakeholders have their own distinct ways of knowing about the small firm, and their behaviour will be led by this. Stakeholder groups are diverse and we cannot presume that their intentions will conform to what the owner-manager feels is in the best interests of the small firm.

5.7 Small-firm embeddedness

The fourth section of the chapter looks at the way small firms become 'embedded' in their environment. If the concept of habitus relies on a structuralist view, the notion of embeddedness has a (neo-)Weberian starting-point. 'Embeddedness' refers to the actions an owner-manager will take to support the day-to-day activities of running a business, but which cannot be defined solely as economic activities. For instance, as the owner-manager tries to win trade, he or she needs to build up relations of trust which become central to the process of trade transaction. Aspects of small-business activity such as this have been considered elsewhere (see Curran and Blackburn 1994). In this section the student is encouraged to develop a framework from which to understand this and to consider how all small-firm business has a social and cultural element. Putting it simply, embedding is pivotal for small businesses because it enables trust – required in economic activity in all advanced economies – to be established. There would be no small-business activity, no transactions between owner-managers and their suppliers and customers, if business was not embedded.

5.7.1 Embedding economic activity

Granovetter's (1985) starting-point for embeddedness is a critique of the idea that rational, self-interested behaviour in business is effected minimally by social relations. He suggests that developing trust in business activity is essential. Being aware of the development of malfeasance (the opposite of building up trust) is equally as important. There are a number of points relevant to the small firm which Granovetter sets out.

On the idea of trust and malfeasance Granovetter provides an illustration of the way this is shaped. He considers the case of an economist who, despite all notions of rational behaviour, leaves a tip for a waiter in a restaurant which he has never previously visited. Granovetter (1985: 490) suggests that such a transaction has three simple characteristics:

■ the two actors involved in the transaction are previously unacquainted;

- they are not likely to transact again;
- it is unlikely that information about the activities of either will reach other people with whom they might transact in the future.

The point we can deduce from this is that some element of trust must operate in an economic transaction, as, left to a market-based explanation, we cannot provide an adequate reason for leaving a tip. This is even more apparent when transaction occurs between people who have prior knowledge of each other. It happens this way precisely because the embeddedness concept stresses 'the role of concrete personal relations and structures (or "networks") of such relations in generating trust and discouraging malfeasance' (Granovetter 1985: 490).

Thus, when a small-business owner-manager or a self-employed person has had prior business dealings with a customer, he or she holds a certain knowledge about the method and practicalities of doing business with them, and this will be an important feature of enabling future business to be done. Precisely because the owner-manager places some degree of trust in the knowledge they hold of the previous transaction, then he or she can consider how that previous transaction left the way open for future business. This can 'oil' the business relationship, paying particular attention to the social content that carries expectations of trust and abstention from opportunism. If it does not exist, then efforts are made to create trust, via networking, learning about potential customers, and by generally building up relationships of credibility.

At this point it is worth stopping for a moment and spending some time to reflect on how a typical small business (if there is such a thing) develops different levels of embeddedness. The following case study provides a qualitative snapshot of a small firm and is introduced to illustrate the way an owner-manager seeks to embed his day-to-day business activities in a number of different networks for different purposes. The details of this process cannot all be included here due to obvious constraints, but a picture of embeddedness can be built up which covers the spatial environment of the business, the main markets in which the business operates, and the public-sector support networks the owner-manager felt it was worth discussing.

5.7.2 A case study of embeddedness

This case study is not entirely fictitious and is based on research undertaken a few years ago. It is related to a factual account on small firms but the facts have been stretched a little to give some points more salience. Rather than representing any specific small firm, the study is a composite drawn from a number of small firms interviewed during a previous investigation (see Sadler and Southern 1995).

Case study 5.1

Karl is the owner-manager of a modest small business established in 1987. The business, located in the North-East of England, is in an area with a longstanding association with traditional industries. Recent local economic restructuring has meant unemployment has risen and structural unemployment is a problem. In this business there are five people employed full-time including Karl. There is also one additional part-time employee. The firm operates in the metal manufacturing sector, with the main product being aluminium ingots used in die-casting by many different manufacturers, such as large steel companies. Turnover for this small firm is in the region of £500,000 per annum. Mainly because the sector overall is subject to peaks and troughs, the business is prone to alternating periods of high and low demand for its products. At its most recent peak there were eight people employed including the owner-manager, although it was not too long ago that everyone was laid off.

The owner-manager, Karl, operates in a number of personal networks mostly on an informal and casual basis for the benefit of his business. For the recruitment of labour he speaks to people in his trade known to him and with whom he has dealt before, such as other owner-managers. In the past he has also contacted previous employees who he knows can do a good job for him. Only rarely does he have to go via formal channels for new employees, such as the local Job Centre. As the work falls mainly into two classifications (skilled and unskilled) Karl feels that there are few problems to be encountered in recruitment. He associates this with the knowledge he has of the local area, concerning problems of unemployment, and contacts he is sure and confident of.

The majority of the market for this business is in Europe, accounting for approximately 60% of all custom. While this is a little unusual because many other similar firms in the same locality have markets much closer to home, the work won in countries such as Germany and Switzerland has been in regions with which Karl is familiar. Of the remaining 40% of trade, most of this is with other businesses in the North-East. The business has recently been under some pressure because of the high value of UK sterling and Karl has tried to maintain business through a number of overseas connections which he has cultivated during the last ten years. Some of these are from networks he was involved with prior to moving to the UK.

When Karl deals with potential and existing customers he tries to foster a feeling of reliability, showing that his firm can deliver on his promises. On reflection, he feels he neglected an important relationship in the past when a major steel company became a customer for part of a year, taking ten tonnes of aluminium ingots per month. They subsequently took their custom to another local company without providing a full explanation. Karl feels, in part, responsible for losing this trade and during the business transaction he never felt that he held the confidence of the purchasing manager, who was his main contact in the large firm.

When Karl deals with new and existing suppliers he attempts to keep a good (but different type of) relationship with them. Most of these are needed to provide the business with aluminium castings, steel scrap, oil (energy for the furnace which is oil-based) and day-to-day consumables. He knows that local suppliers can be quick to demand payment and if customers are a little slower in paying for goods, then a problem of cash flow can be encountered. Because of this, Karl looks to work up a relationship of empathy with local suppliers so they can understand his

Case study 5.1 *continued*

cash-flow problems when they occur, while at the same time demonstrating to his customers that his products are of value, and his business is reliable and worthwhile. He has also been able to nurse new business contacts in Europe which may be beneficial, but it is notable that he has some concern about this, and his confidence of bringing these to fruition is dampened by the high value of the pound sterling and high UK interest rates.

Karl is quick to see a potential benefit of local public-sector support services. Some of these have been proactive in developing a relationship with the business, and Karl is receptive to this. His feeling is that at least they are trying to understand his business. One contact in a nation-wide quango was particularly keen to help him identify future growth, and encouraged Karl to employ people he wouldn't otherwise have considered. This has led the two parties (the business and the public-sector support agency) to develop a mutual trust and, as part of this, some financial support has been given for training purposes. Further advice on how to replace the oil-based furnace was also provided, and the business was able to progress a little based on this. In addition, Karl was able to use these connections to develop other contacts with people from the local authority, the local TEC and the local City Challenge project for support on matters such as security, accountancy and training. Overall, Karl feels that his experience of one support group was such that he is prepared to trust others.

5.7.3 Some of the main points concerning small-firm embeddedness

While this case shows the student some particular aspects of small business in practice, it also draws out some relevant points with respect to the processes of embedding that any particular small business goes through. The first of these is that we can say that the embedded nature of this particular business is not simply a property of an economic transaction (between Karl and his clientele) but of the concrete social relations which are built up between the two (Granovetter 1985). A second point is that the owner-manager has to work on the relationship between himself and his contacts in Germany or Switzerland (or wherever they may be) prior to any form of economic transaction taking place. If there are pre-existing relationships, both parties bring elements of trust, worthiness or even some malfeasance to bear, as could well have been the situation when the business lost work.

In essence, the trust which is built up by the owner-manager is 'an essential public good in economic interaction and concerns both competence and honesty; [social and] cultural norms reduce doubts about both through their moral content and through providing familiar and reassuring systems of signs – particularly the forms of acceptable address and redress – which reduce uncertainty' (Sayer 1997: 19).

Thus, another point to draw out from this is that small-business processes cannot be simply reduced to the pursuit of some form of rational self-interest. In other words, the search for business will always contain some element which has a social and cultural dimension.

Fourthly, we can point to the vagaries of the environment and consider that while social relations are strongly associated with the build-up of trust, since they will pervade Karl's world on an irregular basis (as his trade cannot be guaranteed) the absence of distrust, opportunism and disorder is by no means certain. This means that attempts to embed the business can, in fact, result in malfeasance. A final point is that while this case is a snapshot bounded both temporally and spatially, and we are concerned with only one business in a manufacturing sector, the behaviour of the owner-manager will be closely embedded in a range of interpersonal relationships. Thus, the 'thickness' of the network of social relations can overlay the day-to-day economic activities of the small firm which act to underpin the very existence of the business. As we saw, the owner-manager was very much aware of economic pressures but continued to build up trust within business contacts.

The idea of small-firm embeddedness has already taken hold in small-business research. One recent feature is the investigation of high-technology networks, clusters and supplier relationships and the idea of multi-firm co-operation in industrial districts (cf. Grabher 1993; Keeble and Lawson 1997). If the student or small-firm researcher is interested in this aspect then bear in mind the ideas introduced here about embeddedness. You might even read the chapter by Sarah Cooper in this book, in light of these ideas (see Chapter 13). The main message for the student to draw out from this section is that all business transactions have social and cultural elements embedded in them. This is best thought about in terms of the networks the owner-manager deals in, as he or she pursues the business, and how in these networks there is a development of the relationships between transactors (see Chapter 21).

5.8 Chapter summary

This chapter has introduced the student to different ways of understanding what the small firm does and how it interacts with the rest of society. Too often, analyses of the small firm are underpinned solely by an economic rationale. Such an understanding is vital to comprehend what the small firm does but on its own can provide a restrictive view of why and how small firms and their stakeholders act in the ways that they do. Simply by presenting an analysis of the small firm from four different perspectives we can see that there is still much to understand about the way this subject connects with other parts of the business and non-business world.

Each of the perspectives outlined here contains an important learning message. The first of these came from the view on the small firm which considered the notion of an enterprise culture. The main message for students from this was to question the accuracy and value of this term when it is applied to small firms. Enterprise culture is not able to explain wide-ranging changes in society of which the small firm is an important part. Those who use the term may say it was never intended to be utilised in this way. However, the notion of enterprise culture has placed unrealistic expectations on the small firm and, all too often, the small business is seen as a metaphor for a new type of economic activity simply because it is felt to represent something called an 'enterprise culture'.

The second perspective introduced the student to the ideas of structure and actors in the small-firm world. This is often considered in business studies, by examining the small firm in its environment, or the driving forces which affect small firms. The key message for the student from this section was that he or she should take account of the duality between people in the firm and the structures around the firm when analysing small-firm behaviour. Rather than looking to attribute business activity as an outcome of structures *or* actors the student should recognise the complex dynamic *between* the two which shapes the activities of the small firm.

Structures and behaviour were examined further as the notion of habitus was introduced. Habitus is a rich theory which was used originally in an analysis of the differences in class. In this chapter, the idea of habitus was tested out in an exploratory manner to see if it was useful in understanding the motives behind small-firm stakeholders. It was suggested that this concept can be seen as the mediation processes between the structures in and around the small firm and the practices of small-firm stakeholders. Thus, habitus helps us to think about the differences in the motivation, practice and behaviour of all those interested in the small firm. One important point from this section is that the habituses of small-firm stakeholders are grounded differently and are not universal; therefore the practices and behaviour of small-firm stakeholders differ. Thus, when small-firm stakeholder behaviour is identified as being contradictory, habitus provides one way of explaining why this might be.

The fourth perspective used in this chapter examined the idea of small-firm embeddedness. A main message from this section was that all economic activity has a social and cultural aspect to it. Owner-managers of small firms look to embed their business through a process of building up relationships of trust and credibility within many different networks. All transactions operate with some degree of this. It is also important to note that as owner-managers build up such relationships there is no guarantee that trust is an automatic outcome. Developing the relationships between the small firm and its suppliers and customers can result in the opposite of trust and credibility being established. The processes of embeddedness are social and cultural and are also integral to economic activity.

Obviously, with each of these perspectives there is much more to debate. They are only presented here as a simple introduction to encourage the reader to view the small firm in different ways. Business does not operate outside of the realms of social, cultural, economic and political processes. For the teacher, researcher and student, there is still much work to be done to understand the small firm with respect to a holistic view of these processes.

Questions

1 How general can theories, concepts and ideas be on a sector that is renowned for its diversity?

2 How can such theories be relevant across such a complex subject?

3 Describe the way that different stakeholders can make an important contribution to the development of small firms.

SECTION II

Entrepreneurship and the small firm

CHAPTER 6

Initiating entrepreneurship

Alison Morrison

6.1 Learning objectives

There are four learning objectives in this chapter:

1 To develop an understanding and awareness of the cultural and societal factors which contribute to stimulation and/or stifling of entrepreneurship initiation.

2 To recognise the relevance of these factors within specific societies and geographic sub-regions.

3 To instigate a shift in thinking from universal generalisations to a deeper understanding of the relationship between entrepreneurship and culture.

4 To identify implications for policy-makers and practitioners.

Key concepts

■ cultural specificity   ■ enterprise triggers   ■ characteristics of society
■ entrepreneurial motivations

6.2 Introduction

It is apparent that there exists no such thing as one identifiable and universal entrepreneurial culture. Furthermore, the key to initiating the process of entrepreneurship lies within the individual members of society, and the degree to which a spirit of enterprise exists, or can be stimulated. The key question is: what triggers the release of this invaluable enterprising spirit? This chapter seeks to make a contribution towards an explanation by focusing on one aspect – the relationship of certain cultural and societal factors. It is argued that there is a significant relationship between entrepreneurship and cultural specificity. This has been progressed through a cross-country study that involved nine countries (see below). Following a review of the variables that contribute to culture in general and entrepreneurial culture in particular, findings from the study are integrated to illustrate key categories of analysis. This approach provides an 'umbrella' framework within which entrepreneurship at a geographic sub-region level can be understood. It also facilitates the identification of each issue which will be investigated in greater depth in the following chapters. However, it is acknowledged that even this particularistic approach is in danger of being overly generalistic. Furthermore, as Hofstede (1991) warns, it is important not to perpetrate a 'reserve ecological fallacy'. Thus, any explanation of what triggers the release of the spirit of enterprise leading to the initiation of entrepreneurship must work from an understanding of the collectives generally accepted as characteristics of certain societies and must respect and acknowledge the individuality and uniqueness of members of such societies who are motivated to act entrepreneurially.

6.3 Initiating entrepreneurship

It has been proposed that the process of entrepreneurship initiation has its foundations in person and intuition, and society and culture. As a result, this process is much more holistic than simply an economic function, and represents a composite of material and immaterial, pragmatism and idealism. The essence of entrepreneurship is therefore the application of innovatory processes and the acceptance of a risk-bearing function, directed at bringing about change of both a social and economic nature. Ideally – but not necessarily – the outcomes will have positive consequences.

The key to initiating the process of entrepreneurship lies within the individual members of society, and the degree to which a spirit of enterprise exists, or can be stimulated. In this respect Kirzner (1979) believes the source to be within the human spirit, which will flourish in response to uncertainty and competition. Gilder (1971: 258) describes this enterprising spirit in inspirational terms as 'welling up' from the history of the West, 'infusing' the most modern of technological adventures and 'joining the old and new frontiers'. As such it 'asserts a firm hierarchy of values and demands a hard discipline. It requires a life of labor and listening, aspiration and courage. But it is the source of all we are and can become, the saving grace of democratic politics and free men, the hope of the poor and the obligation of the fortunate, the redemption of an oppressed and desperate world.'

In this scenario, the key question is: What triggers the release of this invaluable enterprising spirit which leads to the initiation of entrepreneurship? This chapter makes a contribution towards an explanation by focusing on one aspect – the relationship of certain cultural and societal factors to the initiation of entrepreneurship. At the same time it is recognised that non-cultural and contextual factors will undoubtedly play a significant role in shaping entrepreneurial behaviour and action, and these are addressed throughout this chapter.

It is argued that there is a significant relationship between entrepreneurship and cultural specificity. This is progressed through the presentation of findings from a cross-country study (Morrison 1998) that involved nine countries (Kenya, Slovenia, Scotland, North America, Mexico, Finland, Australia, Singapore and South Africa). The chapter reviews the variables that contribute firstly to culture and then to entrepreneurial culture. The findings are then integrated to illustrate key categories of analysis. The aim is to instigate the consideration of a shift in thinking from universal generalisations relative to entrepreneurship. For as Joynt and Warner (1996: 3) propose, 'If the world is to survive and flourish, we all need to know more about the differences rather than concentrating on the similarities.'

6.4 Defining culture

Tayeb (1988: 42) presents a definition of culture and its scope as 'A set of historically evolved learned values, attitudes and meanings shared by the members of a given community that influence that material and non-material way of life. Members of the community learn these shared characteristics through different stages of the socialisation processes of their lives in institutions, such as family, religion, formal education, and society as a whole.' However, Garrison (1996) suggests that such attempts at definition are problematic due to culture's amorphous, shifting nature. This is further compounded by its multiple representation within such elements as:

- different levels (national, regional, business, individual);
- layers of society (gender, age, social class, occupation, family, religion);
- varying context of life (individual, group, community).

Culture therefore represents a complex phenomenon. It is a shared, collective, way groups of people understand and interpret the world, a largely ethereal phenomenon aptly described by Trompenaars (1993: 21) using the following metaphor: 'A fish only discovers its need for water when it is no longer in it. Our own culture is like water to a fish. It sustains us. We live and breathe through it. What one culture may regard as essential, a certain level of material wealth for example, may not be so vital to other cultures.' Hofstede (1994) attributes this ethereality to a form of mental – or cultural – programming that starts in the environment in which a young child grows up (usually a family of some form) and continues throughout school and into adult working life. Politics and the relationships between citizens and authorities are extensions of the relationships found in the family, at school and at work, and in their turn they affect these other spheres of life. Religious beliefs, secular ideologies and scientific theories are extensions of 'mental software' demonstrated in the family, the school, at work and in government relations, and they reinforce the dominant patterns of thinking, feeling and acting in the other spheres.

Hall (1959) provides a simple explanation of culture as the pattern of taken-for-granted assumptions about how a given set of people should think, act and feel as they go about their daily affairs. Thus, societies can be distinguished from each other by the differences in the shared meanings they expect and attribute to their environment. Hofstede (1991) differentiates between cultures by introducing a framework containing five dimensions:

- level of power distance;
- individualism;
- masculinity;
- uncertainty avoidance;
- long-term versus short-term orientation.

These will now be discussed and the findings from the cross-country study (as referred to earlier) will be integrated to illustrate the relevance of each to entrepreneurial behaviour.

6.4.1 Level of power distance

'Power distance' is the degree of inequality among the people, which the population of a country considers normal. Impressionistically, Hofstede (1996) asserts that dependence on the power of others in a large part of our world has been reduced over the past two generations. Most of us feel less dependent than we assume our parents and grandparents to have been. This is the case for the 'Coloured' community of South Africa which found itself in a socially marginalised position, both during the days of apartheid and subsequent to the democratic election of a new government. For the majority of the community this impacted negatively on entrepreneurial characteristics such as initiative and self-confidence. For others, with a strong desire to attain personal control, such oppression actually stimulated entrepreneurial behaviour.

6.4.2 Individualism

This means the degree to which people in a country prefer to act as individuals rather than collectively as members of groups. In individualist societies, the concept of 'self' prevails over the interests of the group, and individuals are practically or psychologically independent. In most collectivist societies the extended family is dominant, with members exhibiting strong practical and psychological dependence relationships. The strong relationship between national wealth and individualism is undeniable. Countries which have achieved fast economic development have experienced a shift towards individualism. This is illustrated in Australian and North American economies. The high proportion of migrants in the populations has resulted in a history of individualism among settlers. This continues to be the case, and it significantly contributes to high levels of immigrant activity in the small-business sector which makes a vital contribution to these nations' economic and social welfare.

6.4.3 Masculinity

This refers to the degree to which 'masculine' values – such as assertiveness, competition and success – are emphasised, as opposed to 'female' values such as quality of life, warm personal relationships and service. The behaviours which are considered 'feminine' or 'masculine' differ not only among traditional but also among modern societies. This is most evident in the distribution of men and women over certain professions, commonly accepted gender roles within certain societies, and the mental programming effect this has for future generations. For example, masculine values are clearly illustrated within the values of North American entrepreneurs which include competitive spirit, aggressive selling skills, dogged determination, deviousness, symbolism of material wealth, and resilience against considerable adversity. However, in Kenya and Finland, entrepreneurs exhibit much more feminine values concerned with the quality of life, and welfare of the community over materialistic gain (Morrison 1998).

6.4.4 Uncertainty avoidance

This is the degree to which people in a country prefer structured over unstructured situations. Ways of handling uncertainty are part-and-parcel of any human institution in any country. The essence of uncertainty is that it is a subjective experience, but may be partly shared with other members of one's society and is acquired and learned. Those feelings and the ways of coping with them belong to the cultural heritage of societies and are transferred and reinforced through basic institutions like the family, school and state. They are reflected in the collectively held values of the members of a particular society. For example, Singaporean society has experienced a situation of full employment with comfortable remuneration levels. In addition, the Singaporean government-controlled Central Provident Fund saving scheme provides employees with a 'nest egg' for retirement. These two factors combine with a societal low tolerance for failure. This results in a population which is moved to avoid the uncertainty and lack of structure generally associated with entrepreneurial behaviour.

6.4.5 Long-term versus short-term orientation

Long-term orientation stands for the fostering of virtues orientated towards future rewards, in particular perseverance and thrift. In contrast, short-term orientation refers to the nurturing of virtues related to the past and present, in particular respect for tradition, preservation of 'face' and fulfilling social obligation. For example, by nature the Finnish are cautious and conservative. They have a need to adopt a long-term orientation, planning and saving for the future in order to avoid any uncertainty which might damage their welfare. The converse is the Kenyan society, which as a whole does not prioritise the creation of savings for the future, being content to enjoy life as it is now. They retain a village, communal and rural mentality, with short-term planning horizons. Both these orientations have significance relative to start-up funding and the strategic development of business.

6.4.6 The impact of culture

Therefore, these five dimensions provide a useful tool which has the potential to categorise certain important aspects of culture. Certainly in the case of more developed cultures, such as that of North America, it is possible to form a cultural profile which rates low on power distance, long-term orientation and uncertainty avoidance, and high on individualism and masculinity. However, in less developed and transitional countries the complete set of dimensions is less clear-cut. Consequently, it is more difficult to administer to any satisfactory level of validity, although certain individual dimensions can be extracted.

Furthermore, Tayeb (1988) and Van der Horst (1996) emphasise that not all individual members of a society need necessarily be assumed to follow all the dimensions of their cultures in every aspect of their lives, and there will be those persons who are moved to deviate from the cultural norm. Thus, Hofstede (1994) proposes that a person's behaviour is only partially predetermined by their mental programmes. They have a basic ability to deviate from them and to react in ways that are new, creative, destructive or unexpected – for example, entrepreneurially. However, Lessem and Neubauer (1994) caution that excessive deviation can weaken individual cultures; conversely, it is also apparent that cultural differences generate options, the integration of which may be beneficial to societies.

This perspective of culture emphasises the importance of developing a social action approach, which recognises that most human beings do not see the world through the same rational, ordered form as policy-makers and academics. Their world is intuitively shaped and interpreted (Weber 1976) through their own attitudes, attributes, behaviours and values, at the interpersonal level (Parker *et al.* 1972). Thus, culture is made by people interacting, and at the same time determining future interaction (Trompenaars 1993). In this manner, social valuables such as knowledge and status are exchanged, in the negotiation of a self-identity, which may be partly innate (albeit modified by culture) and partly acquired from culture (Argyle 1969). In addition, as almost everyone belongs to a number of different cultural levels, layers and contexts at the same time, people will inevitably behave in different ways, corresponding to the categories in society to which they may belong simultaneously. In modern society, these are not necessarily in harmony (Hofstede 1996).

6.5 Entrepreneurial cultures

Given the influence of culture on people's lives, it is proposed that the culture of societies and the characteristics of people living in these societies, impacted by certain innate personality traits (see Chapter 8), will influence the degree to which entrepreneurship is initiated. Clearly, culture is important in any discussion of entrepreneurship because it determines the attitudes of individuals towards the initiation of entrepreneurship (Vernon-Wortzel and Wortzel 1997). Over the years, entrepreneurship has become linked to the development of economies, cultures, social structures, and sectors of industry and technology in specific eras differently (Hoselitz 1951; Haahti 1987). Each era produces its own model of entrepreneurship according to the specific needs of the host society. However, it has been described consistently using terms such as innovative, holistic, risk-taking and co-ordinating ways of behaviour. Furthermore, Drucker (1985), Kirchhoff (1991) and Hornaday (1992) argue that entrepreneurship refers to the ability of organisations in general to create innovation and enterprise, irrespective of size (see Chapter 14). Tan (1998) progresses this debate in suggesting that this approach could be applied at a national level, where many members of the population are involved in the process of entrepreneurship as more widely defined. For example, the label 'Singapore Inc.' has been applied to Singapore where government-linked companies managed by civil servants are considered as representing 'state entrepreneurship' (Lee and Low 1990).

Fass and Scothorne (1990) incorporate a human dimension into the process of entrepreneurship by the identification that it is driven by the motivations of individuals, who are seeking to satisfy their personal goals. The entrepreneur is motivated to create a venture, which reflects their vision and ambitions, and is prepared to re-view and re-organise their social environment to materialise it. However, the reality of why persons initiate entrepreneurship should be questioned. Such persons are in fact 'buying' personal independence and control through the process of venture creation or acquisition. In this respect, entrepreneurship may be seen as an aspect of the theory of choice (Reid and Jacobsen 1988). But to what extent does this represent freedom of choice? The truth is that in a situation of high unemployment, and/or other deprivations of a social or economic nature, persons are frequently forced to choose entrepreneurship as the only alternative to no job and no income. In this scenario individuals may be 'pushed' into entrepreneurship. This moves discussion of entrepreneurship into a choice between earning money or not earning – eating or starving. Thus, it is important to recognise that the routes towards entrepreneurship may be various – a response to a crisis situation, exploitation of a market opportunity, or both.

Currently, the term 'entrepreneurial culture' (see Chapters 3 and 5) has become popular and widely accepted internationally, and is an expression of and attitude towards commerce at a business level. It can be described as one in which a positive social attitude towards personal enterprise is prevalent, enabling and supporting entrepreneurial activity. According to Bateman (1997), those economies and regions which have flourished in the late 20th century have in common a business culture which can be broadly described as 'entrepreneurial'. It is attuned to the needs of a changing market economy and receptive to changing demands, innovations, products, opportunities and technologies. An entrepreneurial culture grows partly out of the current business environment of a country. Yet, as previously identified in this chapter, it is a much broader concept because alongside figure the historical experiences, beliefs, attitudes and values of the host society (Gordon 1996). Thus, of equal significance for entrepreneurial culture are the future hopes and aspirations not only of business but of society at large in a given country.

Internationally, it would appear that there exists a wide range and diversity of entrepreneurial cultures, each of which enables and supports entrepreneurial behaviour to varying degrees. According to Timmons (1994: 9), what is needed is a favourable environment which combines social, political and educational attributes. In particular it requires 'A culture that prizes entrepreneurship, an imperative to educate our population so that our entrepreneurial potential is second to none; and a government that generously supports pure and applied science, fosters entrepreneurship with enlightened policies, and enables schools to produce the best educated students in the world'.

Throughout history, entrepreneurship has been found to be important and meaningful in society at points of transition: for example, traditional to modern, modern to post-modern, and state-controlled economies to free markets. At each of these points, entrepreneurship is harnessed by societies as a common approach to solving dilemmas, to break old, stable and hierarchical traditions and institutions and to introduce new, innovative ways of behaviour. According to Schumpeter (Kilby 1971), entrepreneurship is an instrument which can be applied to change and improve economies and societies, through assembling production factors into a new combination; he called this a process of creative destruction. However, Bagby (1988) question whether the process of entrepreneurship creates change, is created from change, or both. This debate suggests that there is a link between entrepreneurship and change which has the potential to significantly impact the culture of an era.

In this respect, entrepreneurs have the potential to challenge directly many of the aspects associated with cultural tradition, continuity and stability in their countries. Indeed, a new entrepreneurial orientation may pull a country in contradictory directions. It often involves the devaluation of tradition and heritage. For societies, this represents a shift from a world of stable and continuous reference points. The comforts of tradition are fundamentally challenged by the imperatives to forge a new self-interpretation based upon the responsibilities of cultural transition (Corner and

103

Harvey 1991). Furthermore, it would be delusory to accept that all outcomes from the process of entrepreneurship will be positive, even if it is hoped that any 'destruction' (in Schumpeterian (1934) terms) will be creative. However, changes in a culture generally happen because people realise that certain old ways of doing things no longer work. In this respect, Joynt and Warner (1996) argue that it is not difficult to change culture when people are aware that the survival of the society is at stake, that is, where survival is considered desirable.

As such, entrepreneurship has a pervasive effect on the societies it serves and from which it draws resources. It affects the physical environment and values, and purposively attempts to influence the society in which it is located. If the culture contains pro-entrepreneurial values, it serves as an incubator in the entrepreneurship initiation process (Johannisson 1987a). Furthermore, history has proven that societies nurture individuals who enhance their communities in original ways (Joynt and Warner 1996). The converse is also true. In societies where entrepreneurship has become tainted with charges of profiteering, speculation, violence and criminality, it has not been well received. This has been evidenced in the likes of the Chicago of the 1930s, and in a number of the transition economies of Eastern Europe (see Chapter 15) in the 1990s. This negativity could be an inevitable stage of transitional development (Bateman 1997), but it may also foster strong and durable anti-entrepreneurial values.

6.6 Cultural specificity in enterprise

From the foregoing, it would appear that the relationship of certain cultural and societal factors to the initiation of entrepreneurship is significant. At a macro-level, it can be accepted that people belonging to a certain country tend to exhibit collective cultural similarities. However, at a micro-level an individual's cultural orientation may indicate differences. The social institutional framework provides a construct within which the socialisation process mentally programmes members of that society. This results in shared sets of characteristics, attitudes, behaviours and values. Through continuous social interaction, the meanings and values associated with social and economic relationships are interpreted and shaped.

However, it has been recognised that individual members of society are free to negotiate a self-identity and to deviate from cultural norms. One way in which this may exhibit itself is through the initiation of change using the process of entrepreneurship, the outcomes of which may be creative and/or destructive. The degree to which members of society will support such change will be dependent upon their interpretation of the incremental benefit which will arise in the long term. Furthermore, the multiple representations of members of society within the different levels, layers and contexts may support and/or inhibit the initiation of entrepreneurship to differing degrees.

According to Tayeb (1988), the major strength in applying a cultural perspective to any phenomenon is the recognition of:

- the role it plays in shaping work-related values, attitudes and behaviours of individual members of various societies;
- the fact that cultural values and attitudes are different in degree from one society to another;

■ the way that different cultural groups behave differently under similar circumstances because of differences in underlying values and attitudes.

All of these features are considered of significance in the development of an understanding of the triggers involved in the initiation of entrepreneurship internationally.

Haggett (1983) argues that if we are searching for a single organisational unit in humanity's organisation of the world today, there would seem to be simple and persuasive reasons for using the country as this basic unit. However, as Hofstede (1996) points out, the invention of 'nations' is a recent phenomenon in human history. It was only introduced world-wide in the mid 20th century. Therefore, he warns that nations should not be equated to societies. Historically, societies are organically developed forms of social organisation, and the concept of a common culture applies, strictly speaking, more to societies than to nations. Furthermore, to apply national norms to a specific group of individuals would be to perpetrate the 'reserve ecological fallacy' (Hofstede 1991).

Within countries, factors such as social class, regional characteristics, ethnic grouping and religion have interacted historically, and will continue to do so. This results in layers of sub-cultures, which mitigate against thinking of culture in macro-terms – such as persons being categorised as stereotypical American, African, British, etc. (Joynt and Warner 1996). In most cases, plural cultures live under the one encompassing title of the host country. Yet a country is often the only feasible criterion for classification, and while micro-level differences are accepted, at the same time these people, groups and nations do tend to exhibit certain similarities. For example, Hampden-Turner and Trompenaars (1994) argue that people from the same country will generally try to resolve dilemmas in the same way, as cultural cohesion is a prerequisite for stability in a society. Clearly, when researching culture, nationality should be used with care.

Figure 6.1 presents a tentative attempt at summarising the findings from literature and cross-country research undertaken (Morrison 1998). The model represents an open (social action) system that recognises that culture is no more fixed than the histories and circumstances which contribute to it. Societies, cultures and mentalities are in a continual state of development and change. There are, of course, 'constants' – collective experiences and collective memories and the mythology that they generate – but even their permanence should not be overestimated (Van der Horst 1996). As advocated by McClelland (1961), it is important to recognise that culture is not a static, but a dynamic variable, which has the potential to be modified to the benefit of future generations. This model is used to structure discussion and illustration through the presentation of the findings from the cross-country study (Morrison 1998); and identifies the key features associated with culture that may impact upon the degree to which entrepreneurship is initiated and sustained, including inputs, societal constructs and the evidence of entrepreneurial behaviour.

6.6.1 Inputs

The initiation of entrepreneurship starts at the 'grass-roots' level where a range of inputs commences the mental and social conditioning of the populace. These include the following.

Figure 6.1 Summary model – key features associated with entrepreneurship initiation

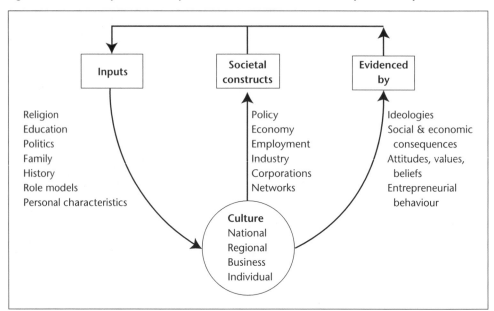

Religion

According to Heelas and Morris (1992), it seems to be a common assumption among advocates of the values of the enterprise culture that there is no inherent opposition between individualistic entrepreneurship and religion, at least as far as Judaism and Christianity are concerned. Indeed, Weber (1976) showed that there are grounds for giving credit to Judaism and Christianity for providing some of the ethical motivation and commitment, as well as habits of self-discipline. However, the relationship is more complex. Religion informs the relation between individual economic activity and community values. This includes the morality of the methods adopted to create wealth and the extent to which wealth creation takes precedence over other forms of activity and identity. Furthermore, it impacts on the formal education system to which the young are exposed, and reinforces traditional gender divisions of domestic and economic activity in the home (Deacon 1992). In Kenya, the majority of the population attend church on a regular basis. The religious leaders condemn wealth creation and give the impression that a rich individual equates to a corrupt person who has obtained riches through devious means. In addition, the belief in the will and power of God is dominant. These two factors combine to promote a culture which lacks enterprise and innovation, and acceptance of responsibility for self. At the other extreme is North America where the historical roots of entrepreneurship are embedded in the Protestant ethic based on Calvinism. This introduced new patterns of individualism stressing qualities such as diligence, responsibility, self-reliance and personal drive.

Education

The manner in which the young are conditioned from an early age through the formal education system, and the fact that dominant approaches are frequently reinforced within family life, play a significant role in the initiation of characteristics generally associated with entrepreneurial behaviour (Gibb 1996). In particular, the formal education system has been recognised as a strong influence in the development of conformist, anti-entrepreneurial behaviour in Kenya, South Africa, Singapore, Finland and Slovenia. This has resulted in population masses ambivalent towards entrepreneurship as a consequence of their educational conditioning. Current examples of direct intervention within the formal education systems, designed to promote an entrepreneurial culture, were evidenced in North America, Scotland and Mexico.

Politics

Given the direct involvement of the state in all aspects of social and economic life (see Chapters 3 and 4), it has a dominant power base which will undoubtedly influence the culture of a nation (Deacon 1992). This was found to be particularly relevant relative to the extent to which structures have historically been designed to enable individualism or communitarianism, and equality or hierarchy. In general, the historic political systems within Slovenia, South Africa, Kenya and Finland have, to differing degrees, served to promote an anti-entrepreneurial culture due to the dependency on, or control of, the populace by the state which decreased the propensity for private enterprise. This has resulted in a significant power distance in society that has served to divide the population with the majority being 'ruled', either formally or informally, by an elite group. This serves to produce persons who are lacking in the personal attributes generally associated with entrepreneurs, in particular leadership, creativity, self-reliance and self-confidence. However, in the more egalitarian and democratic societies of North America and Australia these qualities are fostered, thus stimulating entrepreneurial behaviour.

Family

It has been identified that a characteristic of entrepreneurship is that it tends to pervade family life (see Chapter 9), with the entrepreneur being unable to divorce business from social living (Deakins 1996). In this respect, family background plays a role in two ways. Firstly, if entrepreneurs have previous experience of the effect of entrepreneurship from a family member they are more prepared for the consequences of their own activities. Secondly, family support of entrepreneurship can make a positive contribution to its sustenance. For all the entrepreneurs represented in the study, positive immediate family support for their entrepreneurial behaviour had played an important part in its sustenance. What was also identified as of significance was the role of the extended family in enabling access to funds and markets to support individual entrepreneurs in the creation and development of their businesses. This was particularly emphasised in the findings from Kenya, South Africa, Australia and North America.

History

One of the reasons for the considerable variance in the responses of populations to entrepreneurship is as a consequence of the history and resultant characteristics of their country (Haggett 1983). At different times the following countries have been dominated by foreign governments: Kenya, Singapore and North America were colonised by Britain; and Slovenia and Finland were governed by foreign powers. Their reactions on release differ. Kenya appears unable to alter the established colonial order of society, dominated by 'seniors' and 'juniors'. Singapore drew on the opportunistic trait exhibited by early entrepreneurs to promote the benefits of entrepreneurship to the population. North America emerged rebelling against tradition and engaging in the struggle to counteract authoritarianism. Substantial historic subordination by external powers and state control has left Slovenia making a very slow transition towards the development of entrepreneurial behaviour. The complex historical development of Finland resulted in a political climate and environment which was formerly not supportive of entrepreneurship. Clearly, the historical conditioning of these countries has impacted upon the extent to which entrepreneurial characteristics exist within the population and the degree to which entrepreneurship is accepted as socially legitimate.

Role models

It has been found that the degree to which an entrepreneurial culture has been, and currently is, embedded in a country will affect the volume of practising and historic entrepreneurs who can be identified as role models for future generations (Anderson 1995). From analysis of the entrepreneurs in the study, no direct link to role models was apparent. At one extreme was the female Kenyan entrepreneur, who is unique in her time and has few (if any) intergenerational role models to which to refer. At the other extreme was the North American entrepreneur, who has an abundance of role models. However, it would appear that the entrepreneurs represented within the study were less concerned with role models, and more interested in being entrepreneurial.

Personal characteristics

Each entrepreneur brings their own unique set of personal characteristics (see Chapter 8) to interact with their specific host society and business environment, which may then translate into entrepreneurial activities and behaviour. Furthermore, the different roles which entrepreneurs play are interwoven. Private and professional codes of conduct merge, social and commercial concerns mix (Johannisson 1987b). However, it is possible to identify common characteristics and behaviours (McClelland 1961). The following emerged relative to all the entrepreneurs in the study: they bring intelligence and sound analytical skills to bear on risk management; they are all in some respect deviants from the social norms within their countries; to differing degrees they exhibit strong moral, work and business ethics; irrespective of industry sector a strong 'trader's' instinct is apparent; they are committed to life-long learning through both formal and informal mechanisms; and extensive use is made of both informal and formal networks. In the cases of Finland, Australia and Kenya the characteristics and behaviours are of a more implicit, 'low-key' nature rather than aggressively explicit.

6.6.2 Societal constructs

Certain social, economic and institutional constructs surround the socially developed entrepreneur. Within them, entrepreneurs may assess the degree to which they are sufficiently robust to support the initiation of entrepreneurship.

Policy

Over recent decades, there has been an attempt by policy-makers (see Chapter 4) to directly effect a change in the motives and values of subsequent generations. In this way, they aim to establish a regime whereby the individual, rather than the state apparatus, can flourish in recognition of the value, qualities and contributions of entrepreneurs (Heelas and Morris 1992). This is particularly apparent in countries experiencing transition (see Chapter 15). However, the effects of political intervention have been mixed. In a number of countries, such as Slovenia, it has been inconsistently applied which has resulted in limited impact on the level of entrepreneurial behaviour. In the case of Finland, an example of start-up funding was provided which was deemed to have been moderately successful in the stimulation of new venture creation. The approaches adopted in Mexico, America and Scotland were evaluated as being relatively considered, strategic and effective. However, in Kenya early attempts at intervention led to a dependency culture. This brings into question the degree to which the state should intervene to contrive what is essentially a natural expression of personal enterprise, self-sufficiency and initiative.

Economy

In general, recognition of the distinctive contribution of the individual in the process of economic restructuring has ensured that entrepreneurship is supported by policy-makers internationally (Pearce 1980). The trigger of this recognition has usually been born out of adverse economic conditions; however, it has also been a response to a desire to enhance already strong economies. Each of the countries in this study has experienced different degrees of volatility within its economy, and various causes of the problems faced. They are perhaps best depicted on a continuum moving from severe, transitional, moderate, to strong. First is Mexico, which has experienced profound economic recessionary problems, with many persons living on an average of $1 a day. Within this context entrepreneurship represents a means by which the economy – and the population – can be saved from yet further degeneration. Second is Slovenia, which has only evolved into an independent state, and been in a position to create an autonomous economic system, since 1991. Thus, economic restructuring is still in a transitional phase, within which the encouragement of entrepreneurship is of high importance. Thirdly, Scotland and Finland have experienced moderate economic recession, and policy-makers have directed their efforts at expanding the pool of latent entrepreneurial talent to become agents in economic regeneration. Finally, Singapore has sustained high economic growth within which small and medium-sized enterprises (SMEs) play a key role, benefiting from their profusion and activity.

Employment

In most countries internationally, the nature of work is changing, and the proportion of populations who have full-time and permanent work is falling. A job for life, with its planned career structure, is rare. This has led policy-makers to focus on increasing the number of persons who create new ventures and/or enter into self-employment (see Chapter 2), as a means of bringing more members of the population into economic productivity (Chell *et al.* 1991). Furthermore, individuals have responded to these employment patterns by taking personal control of their own career through entrepreneurship.

However, there are examples of countries which are exceptions to these general employment patterns, and which generate their own distinct approaches to employment practices. At one extreme Mexico was identified, where heightened entrepreneurship as a means of creating employment opportunities (particularly for the young) is an explicit strategy within a country suffering from economic crisis, widespread poverty, low levels of educational attainment and high unemployment. In sharp contrast is Singapore which has experienced high and sustained economic growth in recent years, and has a situation of nearly full employment. These factors act as a deterrent against entrepreneurship in that country. An employment practice of particular interest was highlighted, linked to a strong tribal, clan or ethnic group identification, in a number of countries such as South Africa, Kenya and Australia. This leads to inter-group employment practices, favouring family and tribe, which can result in protracted decision-making procedures and diminishes the potential for business performance.

Industry

In the majority of countries represented in this cross-country research project, the small firm is statistically dominant in the industry structure, in terms of operating units (see Chapter 2). This is particularly true in the service sector, where SMEs make up the majority of firms, often located at service points close to the customer (Storey 1994). Increasingly, a strong, indigenous small-firm sector is being seen as a vehicle for regional economic development internationally. Statistically, the small firm dominates the industry structure in Mexico, Scotland, Australia and Finland. Within the remaining countries the recognition of the social and economic significance of a strong, indigenous small-firm sector is constantly strengthening. This is particularly true in the case of Singapore where it represents a means of providing insulation from the volatile activities of multinational companies (MNCs).

Corporations

Current terminology associated with the strategies of large corporations includes 'downsizing', 'delayering', 'outsourcing', and 're-engineering' (see Chapter 14). This has arisen through recognition of the importance of the ability to focus on core activities, adapting quickly and innovating within specific specialised markets (Goffee and Scase 1995). It has the potential to generate significant entrepreneurial opportunity, and is seen as a major contributor to new business growth within the small-business sector. Australia represents an example of one country where the workplace is undergoing major reform, as corporations streamline their operations and outsource non-core activities to effect savings and to achieve strategic goals. From such activity, the Australian, Scottish, Finnish and Slovenian entrepreneurs identified entrepreneurial opportunities in the form of acting as subcontractors to large corporations who had decided to outsource a number of their activities. In contrast, the South African and Mexican entrepreneurs found themselves in a position where they contracted out a number of their own activities, thus spreading the level of participation in entrepreneurial activity to self-employed craftspersons. A further example of changes in corporate organisation was provided by Singapore, where a partnership relation has developed between local enterprises and MNCs to assist small-firm contractors to improve operating and process efficiency, and to widen their product ranges.

Networks

The development and maintenance of effective informal and formal networks (see Chapter 21) is recognised as a central feature of successful entrepreneurial activity. This is particularly true regarding those of an informal nature (Curran and Blackburn 1994). Within the study, examples of informal and formal entrepreneurial networks are numerous: in Kenya the informal, tribal network provided support and facilitated market development in an urban setting; immigrants to Australia used the networks which evolved from their ethnic association to develop export markets; in Finland a strong national and local entrepreneurs' association network provided significant informal peer support, advice and motivation; the flea market traders in South Africa facilitated a valuable experiential learning network; and in Mexico the network established by the educational institute ITESM gave entrepreneurs in training access to support and advice from the business community and provided an international showcase for their products. With respect to formal networks, Australia operates within a highly formalised official environment which requires entrepreneurs to understand and learn to operate within this network in order to achieve business success.

6.6.3 Evidence of entrepreneurial behaviour

Inputs and social constructs combine to provide the evidence – negative and/or positive – of entrepreneurial behaviour. These will in turn impact on the extent to which a society values the behaviour and will nurture or stifle it in the future. This is evidenced through the following factors.

Ideologies

The ideological practices of a population refer to the pattern of thinking which is most characteristic (Burrows 1991b). This was specifically evidenced in relation to the manner in which failure is viewed. Singaporeans, Slovenians, the Finnish, and to a certain extent the Scottish, appear to have a low tolerance to failure which tends to leave a durable stigma. However, in more open societies, such as North America and Australia, entrepreneurial behaviour is applauded. Failure has few associated negative connotations, with the significance and value of having applied personal initiative and enterprise (albeit unsuccessfully) viewed as positive.

Social consequences

There is a belief that entrepreneurship has the potential to improve the fabric of society through the balancing of economic wealth creation with social responsibility to the community, sensitive to a country's cultural, historical and social values (Timmons 1994). Thus, positive and/or negative social consequences will combine to shape societal responses to entrepreneurship (Gilder 1971). In Slovenia the historical perspective was that entrepreneurship was intertwined with capitalist greed for material gains through the exploitation of others. In other countries, such as Scotland, Kenya and South Africa, those members of society who deviated from the social norm of 'ordinary' employees to be successful entrepreneurs were frowned upon as being 'upstarts' daring to be successful; whereas entrepreneurship for material gain is recognised as socially legitimate in North America. The importance of positive social outcomes was particularly emphasised in the findings from Mexico, Finland and Australia. For example, the mission statement of ITESM in Mexico explicitly states that it wishes to form entrepreneurial professionals who are committed to the development of their communities, respect human dignity, and appreciate the cultural, historical and social values of their community. It is proposed that societies will not permit entrepreneurship to be sustained if social amelioration is not one of the major objectives. The alternative is a society which destroys itself through greed and exploitation. Provided the outcomes of entrepreneurship become recognised, on balance, as positive, societal responses will become gradually more pro-entrepreneurship, effecting incremental cultural change.

Economic consequences

Pearce (1980) proposes that entrepreneurs are the first among equals in the process of wealth creation. This can be interpreted at an individual, business, regional and national level. If successful, through the personal endeavour of individuals within society, economic consequences (as measured by the personal wealth of the entrepreneur, sustained economic performance of the business, new job opportunities and economic multiplier effects, and improved gross domestic product) will be generated, rippling out to the economic benefit of society as a whole. Real economic benefits as a consequence of entrepreneurship have already been proved in Scotland, Australia and North America. In Finland, Mexico, South Africa and Slovenia the transition to an entrepreneurial culture is still in progress, and as such the evidence is less conducive. However, in the case of Kenya there remains considerable doubt that the populace will ever be persuaded to participate in entrepreneurship; thus the economic consequences of the current low level of entrepreneurship initiation are insignificant.

Attitudes, values and beliefs

The dominant cultural attitudes, values and beliefs of a population at one particular point in time will result in a particular common mindset relative to the degree to which entrepreneurship is supported by society (Gilder 1971). In particular, the extent to which these values are communal or individual has been identified as significant for entrepreneurship. Societies that predominantly hold strong communal and collective values, such as Kenya, Slovenia and South Africa, do not support individualistic wealth creation through entrepreneurship, while those with strong individualistic values, such as North America and Australia, generally do. Furthermore, in those countries where there is a moral obligation to provide for the community, the priority for income earned is to support kin as opposed to investment in private enterprise.

Entrepreneurial behaviour

Ideologies, social and economic consequences, and attitudes, values and beliefs, combine to either promote or inhibit future entrepreneurial behaviour (Scase and Goffee 1980). Within North America, Australia and Scotland the positive impact experienced regarding entrepreneurship sows the seeds from which future entrepreneurial behaviour will be propagated. Conversely, the early examples of Slovenian entrepreneurship – which exhibited negative features such as poor employment practices, high failure rates, and evidence of crude profiteering and general exploitation – meant that the

seeds of entrepreneurship fell on infertile ground. Thus, it is clear that the degree to which entrepreneurship takes root and flourishes will be influenced by the host society's evaluation of entrepreneurial behaviour as culturally acceptable, beneficial, or otherwise.

6.7 Chapter summary

The immense intricacy and complexity of human and entrepreneurial cultures must be recognised, as must the fact that the relationship of entrepreneurs to their environment is not just a matter of demography and economics. The key features identified throughout this chapter enable us to understand the manner in which entrepreneurship, culture, politics, society, the economy and business development and management are interwoven within the institutional structure of society. A distinctive cross-country cultural variety has been highlighted, in which beliefs and dreams, traditions and taboos all have their place, alongside government-driven policies and economies. It appears that there is a significant relationship between entrepreneurship and cultural specificity, combined with an intuitive response by individual members of society, albeit part innate and part cultural conditioning. Certainly, the cultural context in which persons are rooted and socially developed plays an influencing role in shaping and making entrepreneurs, and in the degree to which they consider entrepreneurial behaviour to be desirable.

Specific cultural dimensions that are significant for whether entrepreneurial behaviour is supported by a society have been identified as: communal versus individual; conformist versus divergent; and equal versus elitist. Furthermore, the role of the family (immediate and extended) is recognised as having the potential to make a positive contribution towards entrepreneurial behaviour through the provision of intergenerational role models, and as a tangible and intangible support provider. The profile of an entrepreneur which emerges through the study is one who is intelligent and analytical; is an effective risk-manager and networker; possesses a strong set of moral, social and business ethics; exhibits a basic trader's instinct; and is dedicated to life-long learning in its many forms.

Despite intensified interventions by policy-makers to strengthen factors designed to enable and mobilise entrepreneurial intent, it would appear that they have resulted in variable degrees of success. Specifically, it seems that any attempt at political intervention requires the achievement a balance between support directed at increasing self-sufficiency of entrepreneurs, while at the same time reducing dependency upon the state. This is particularly the case in addressing the important issues of financial resource scarcity, without entrepreneurs having to resort to a dependency upon the state as the main source. Furthermore, in certain countries there has been policy intervention with regard to entrepreneurship education and training provision. This has been made available to potential and existing entrepreneurs with the commendable aim of creating a critical mass of professional entrepreneurs which will perpetuate a gradual transition towards a sustainable entrepreneurial culture.

In a number of the countries represented within this study, societal response towards entrepreneurship is showing an incremental change, coming more into the mainstream of ideologies, cultural attitudes, values and beliefs. However, Hofstede (1994) reminds us that such changes are peripheral and do not affect the major dimensions. Support for future entrepreneurial behaviour will be dependent on a society's interpretation of the peripheral worth of entrepreneurship as a tool in economic restructuring, and as a generator of both immaterial and material social outcomes. Entrepreneurship will not necessarily have the power to reach the innermost psyche of a society.

It is concluded that approaches to defining what makes and/or shapes an entrepreneur must work from a consolidation of understanding relative to a wide range of factors at work in society and the economy which influence entrepreneurial behaviour. They should not be driven by the prevailing attitudes of business monitors and governments at any particular point in time. Thus, it is proposed that entrepreneurship be recognised to represent an innovative value-adding social and economic activity. Fundamentally, it is a very basic human act, practised by ordinary – but at the same time exceptional – members of society, which can be applied to enhance human endeavour in all spheres of life – economic and material, social and immaterial.

Questions

1 To what extent does a person's cultural background influence entrepreneurial behaviour?

2 Identify the manner in which family support for entrepreneurship may influence a person initiating entrepreneurship.

3 In what ways can policy-makers effectively change a society's attitude towards entrepreneurship?

CHAPTER 7

Business start-up: theory, practice and policy

David Deakins and Geoff Whittam

7.1 Learning objectives

There are five learning objectives in this chapter:

1 To relate theory to practice in the process of business start-up.
2 To describe and identify elements of the business start-up process.
3 To discuss theoretical developments in the area of funding new-start entrepreneurial ventures.
4 To describe the possible benefits of mentoring support to new-start entrepreneurs.
5 To argue the case for and against policy interventions in business start-up.

Key concepts

- human capital and entrepreneurship ■ serendipity and the start-up process
- mentoring and entrepreneurship ■ small-business support policies

7.2 Introduction

This chapter examines the theory, practice and policy of small-business start-up. It is argued that the start-up process is characterised by uncertainty and, although theoretical development is limited, nevertheless insights can be gained by the application of theory to explain some results observed in practice. In addition, theoretical underpinnings can also help to guide interventions and policy in this area. Despite some academic controversy, the application of mentoring principles can justify policies, such as those announced in a recent White Paper, which encourage and support new small-business and entrepreneurial development.

7.3 Small-business start-up: theory, practice and policy

Despite the increased attention given to entrepreneurship and entrepreneurial phenomena, the process of entrepreneurial start-up is characterised by both uncertainty (in terms of outcomes, success, failure, survival) and lack of knowledge and understanding in much of the literature. For example, Reynolds and White (1997: 1) comment that 'there is little known about the initial phases of the process [entrepreneurship]. The conception, birth and early development of new ventures are very much an uncharted territory.'

Thus, because of this lack of knowledge, in attempting to write about the initial phase of entrepreneurship, the subject has to be treated with a great deal of caution. In order to provide a framework, however, where knowledge is scarce, it is useful to draw upon theory. Therefore this chapter is organised under headings of theory, practice and policy. Policy is included as a heading because, despite the lack of knowledge, entrepreneurial start-up is an area that has attracted prescriptive advice and policy. To begin with, however, relevant theory on the entrepreneurial start-up process is reviewed, start-up in practice is examined and the relevance of policy and its potential impact on this process is considered.

7.4 Start-up theory

One of the problems with theoretical developments in business start-up is that they can often contain unrealistic assumptions, for example on new entrepreneur motivations, on objectives and on entry strategies. Thus, it is arguable that there is little *relevant* theoretical development that may underpin our limited understanding of the start-up process. For example, Reynolds and White (1997: 2) comment in their review that 'the result [of theoretical developments] has been a series of assumptions about the workings of new and small firms that are not only poor representations of the reality of modern economies – but may actually be misleading'. Hence, there is a need to exercise the caution remarked upon in the introduction. Nevertheless, there are a number of areas from which relevant theoretical developments can be used, including:

- human capital approaches;
- finance;
- motivations;
- networks.

7.4.1 Human capital approaches

The formation of business ideas and the ability to start successful businesses will be affected by a nascent entrepreneur's past experience, training, education and skill development. This accumulation of knowledge, skills and experience is termed 'human capital' – a concept used particularly in the context of labour markets by economists following the pioneering work of Gary Becker (1962). Formulation of business ideas may be influenced by work experience, by individual training and by recognition that a particular product or process 'could be done better'. Recognising that a process or product could be done in a superior and different way has been the spur behind many new businesses. Development of this human capital approach has been undertaken by Cressy (1996) in his research with a database of start-up businesses from customers of the NatWest Bank. Cressy has argued that human capital is an important determining factor in new business creation. The importance of human capital tends to be reinforced by external financial institutions: previous research has shown that bank managers rate employment experience as an important factor in lending to new-venture entrepreneurs (Deakins and Hussain 1994a).

For younger entrepreneurs, who will have limited human capital, it can be argued that education can have an important role in providing a conducive environment for idea formulation. It has been suggested that younger entrepreneurs (below the age of 30) are under-represented in entrepreneurship because of limited personal capital and limited access to finance (Gavron *et al.* 1998). However, the limited scope for idea formulation will also be a constraint, and the limited experience (or human capital) that potential entrepreneurs, in this age range, can draw upon will limit the potential opportunities for developing ideas. Idea formulation here will be affected by educational experience and early training. It is arguable that education should provide scenarios that encourage creativity, lateral thinking and problem-solving. However, there can be a conflict in providing sufficient scope within a curriculum for the development of such transferable and 'core' skills. There are indications that greater importance is being placed on 'enterprise' abilities including problem-solving, group work and idea generation. Education systems are important in the development of creativity and idea formulation. For example, Timmons (1994: 43) comments: 'The notion that creativity can be learned or enhanced holds important implications for entrepreneurs who need to be creative in their thinking.' Thus, education is an important conditioning experience. Creative thinking can be enhanced or constrained by the education system: this will affect the way opportunities are viewed, not just in our formative years but later in life as well.

7.4.2 Finance

The economics of information suggests that asymmetric information will play an important role when an entrepreneur tries to obtain start-up finance. As Cressy (1996) has pointed out, the majority of new-start entrepreneurs do not set out to raise external finance; for those that attempt to (whose numbers greatly exceed those that succeed), their ability will be affected by the information supplied to the potential funder.

The problems that exist theoretically can be analysed using theory from the economics of information. When conditions of uncertainty combine with asymmetric information (where providers and borrowers have different sets of information), for the funders there are problems of selection (choosing profitable and successful new ventures) and moral hazard (monitoring what the new entrepreneur does with the funding). Start-up entrepreneurs face disadvantages because they have no trading track record, and funders may not have sufficient information to make risk assessments. In addition to supply-side finance theory, in terms of demand, the Pecking Order Hypothesis (POH) (Myers 1984) also suggests that (new) entrepreneurs prefer to avoid raising external finance (see Chapter 19).

7.4.3 Motivations

Motivations of new entrepreneurs are associated, theoretically, with either 'positive' or 'negative' factors. Positive factors are those associated with the desire for 'entrepreneurial aspirations' on the part of the nascent entrepreneur – for example, a desire to be independent, to be their 'own boss' and to achieve a growth business. Negative factors are associated with discrimination in alternative employment opportunities. Being an entrepreneur is not a first choice and entry may arise because of a lack of alternative job opportunities, or insufficient income from alternative employment. Theoretically, it is expected that such negative motivational factors are more important with entrepreneurs drawn from certain groups in society that may face discrimination, such as ethnic minority groups, younger age groups and women.

Indeed, attempts to explain the importance of ethnic minority entrepreneurs concentrate on the relative primacy of 'negative' or 'positive' factors in the motivations and development of ethnic minority small-firm owners (for example, Ward and Jenkins 1984). The debate surrounds whether or not the discriminatory factors faced by ethnic minorities in the labour market were the predominant motivating factors in business ownership and entrepreneurship or whether positive entrepreneurial factors such as a group's background experience of business ownership were more important in the motivation decision. Although Curran and Blackburn (1993) have indicated that motivational factors such as 'independence' were significant in entry to entrepreneurship, there is little doubt that a history of disadvantage and discrimination has led to the concentration of ethnic minority firms and entrepreneurs in marginal areas of economic activity.

Curran and Blackburn (1993) surveyed 76 ethnic minority entrepreneurs from three groups in three different localities. The three groups were African-Caribbeans, Bangladeshis and Greek-Cypriots and were selected from London, Sheffield and Leeds. On motivation, perhaps surprisingly, Curran and Blackburn found that positive factors associated with the desire to be independent were higher than expected and they claim that this was on similar levels to white-owned businesses. To some extent, the strong motivational factors were confirmed by research with African-Caribbean entrepreneurs and (later) with Asian entrepreneurs in Scotland (Ram and Deakins 1995; Deakins *et al.* 1997b). For example, over 80% of African-Caribbean and Asian entrepreneurs agreed with positive statements concerning ambition and control of their environment. Yet, for a significant minority, negative factors associated with the lack of opportunity elsewhere were also important. For example, over 40% (for both these groups) agreed that they had faced discrimination in previous employment (see Chapter 11). In such circumstances, discrimination and the lack of opportunities in the labour market are significant 'push' factors.

7.4.4 Networks

The benefits which can accrue to new firms operating in partnerships/networks/clusters are the potential advantages of economies of scale. Services and inputs (such as advertising, training, access to loan finance at advantageous rates, consultancy advice, financial services, for example) – items which a single firm cannot easily afford or secure, when operating independently – can be secured when operating as part of a larger group. Whilst the organisational structure of firms operating in some kind of cohesive way may be given the title 'networking', firms producing in any economy take on some of the attributes of a networking structure. For example, by engaging in production and trade a firm deals with suppliers and customers, which necessitates a degree of co-operation and trust, factors which are regarded as essential attributes to the successful functioning of a network.

Similarly, however, there is also an element of risk and uncertainty within any business relationship. Trust arises in response to the threat of risk and uncertainty. When trust exists it minimises the potential risk and opportunism. 'Co-operation is more secure and robust when agents have a trust because of the reputation of themselves and other agents in the network for honesty and consistency' (Thompson 1993: 58). Risk and opportunism can also be reduced via contracting but, as Macaulay (1963) notes, whilst detailed clauses are often written into contracts they are seldom used: 'contract and contract law are often thought unnecessary because there are many non-legal sanctions. Two norms are widely accepted. (1) Commitments are to be honoured in almost all situations; ... (2) One ought to produce a good product and stand behind it' (Macaulay 1963: 63). In other words an environment can develop where implicit contracting ensures a degree of trust and co-operation. In other, more established networks, relationships can develop beyond those of a purely contractual kind. Sako (1992) identifies two other kinds of trust: competence trust, being the belief that a trading partner will fulfil a particular task; and goodwill trust, which occurs in situations where initiatives are undertaken beyond the specific remit of a contract: 'the role of goodwill trust extends beyond existing relations and includes the transfer of new ideas and new technology' (Burchell and Wilkinson 1997: 218).

Whilst trust and co-operation have been identified as two attributes of a networking organisation, it is important to identify how these attributes can be strengthened to ensure the efficient operation of the network. In other words, how can contractual trust be developed into goodwill trust? Economists using a game theoretical framework have demonstrated that where firms attach sufficient weight to future interactions, then punishment strategies can be employed to secure co-operation. In situations of joining a formal organisation, such as a network, then defectors and uncooperative players can be excluded. The problem with over-reliance on punishment strategies is that it could lead to distrust which would threaten co-operation – e.g., if you trust me, why are you monitoring my behaviour? The work of Axelrod (1981) suggests that co-operation can evolve over a period of time as firms gradually learn rules and norms of behaviour leading to co-operation. In other words, through continual interaction, and the belief of further interaction, the temptation to cheat diminishes. The firms build up reputations for co-operation and these reputations have to be protected (see Chapter 21 for a detailed discussion of networking concepts).

7.5 Start-up practice

The business start-up process can be broken down into a number of stages:

- the formation of the idea;
- opportunity recognition;
- pre-start planning and preparation including pilot testing;

■ entry into entrepreneurship launch;

■ subsequent development (including management buy-outs and buy-ins).

Each of these stages will have a number of factors that will impinge on the process; these may either encourage further development or have a negative influence, perhaps causing the individual nascent entrepreneur to terminate the process. A representation and suggested paradigm of this process, including the nature of the local environment, culture, access to finance and enterprise, is illustrated in Figure 7.1. For the sake of simplicity the representation abstracts from reality; in practice a host of factors may affect each stage, including factors such as individual entrepreneur's – their mental processes and personal characteristics, such as tenacity and perseverance in overcoming obstacles and barriers.

7.5.1 Idea formulation

It is worth bearing in mind that the start-up and development process can occur over a considerable period of time. Initial business ideas take time to formulate and research, the entrepreneur may have to raise funding and find partners, and initial ideas may be considerably refined before the launch of the business. Every business start-up is a unique event – circumstances that contribute to success are intangible and may be different for each individual entrepreneur; thus there is a need to be careful about suggesting that there are any recommended 'paths to success' – what may work for one entrepreneur may not for another. However, intervention and support still have a role in the start-up process. Later in this chapter, we will look at research examining start-up entrepreneurs and the impact of the provision of business development start-up support which suggests that such intervention and support can achieve an impact on survival and performance of new business start-ups.

7.5.2 Opportunity recognition

Converting an idea into a business opportunity is the key element of the process of business creation. Moving from the idea stage to the exploitation of the opportunity requires many elements to be in place. The economic environment has to be conducive, the culture must be appropriate for risk-taking and the nascent entrepreneur must have the confidence to take an idea through to the fulfilment suggested by the opportunity. Opportunities are generated by change. Change may be political, economic, social, demographic or technical. For example, economic change may be characterised by a period of economic growth and expanding demand, which may create opportunities for new business ideas that take advantage of increased affluence, leisure time and spending power of the population. The growth in the leisure industry has spawned many new developments, opening niche markets in areas such as sports, holidays and travel. The increased pace of technical change has created the opportunities for new business ventures in new technologies, in new developments in information technology such as the Internet, in new applications in biotechnology. Social and demographic change may provide opportunities through changing attitudes or through creation of new markets in ageing population structures. These factors are the engines of change,

Figure 7.1 Business creation and the start-up process: a suggested paradigm

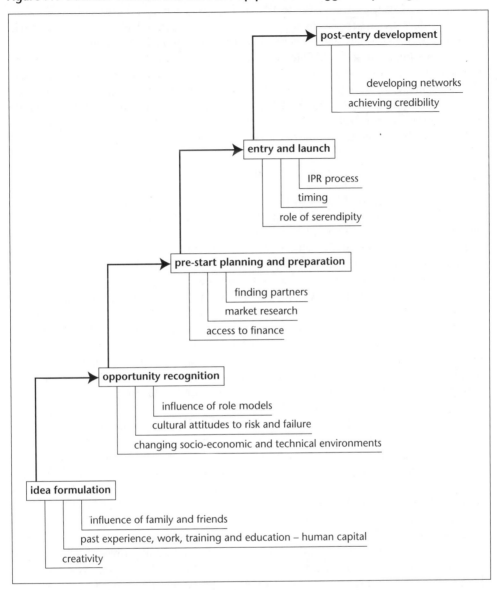

but harnessing such change to create new business ventures requires new entrepreneurs to formulate ideas and fit them to the opportunity. It is this combination that is important.

Cultural attitudes to risk and failure affect this process. For example, it has been suggested that, in the UK, there are lower tolerance levels for failure than in other nations such as the USA (Birley and Macmillan 1995) and different attitudes to risk-taking. Cultural factors are obviously intangible and difficult to gauge, but they help to determine whether the entrepreneur who has a business idea and has recognised an opportunity will be encouraged or discouraged from attempting to exploit that opportunity. If failure is heavily punished, as it is in the UK, then fear of failure may act as a significant constraint on this process (Reynolds and White 1997). The existence (or otherwise) of role models will also affect such a process. In Scotland a deliberate attempt has been made to provide more role models of new and recently successful entrepreneurs through the publication of the most important as 'Local Heroes' (Scottish Enterprise 1997). Other developments to provide more role models and 'surface' examples of under-represented groups have also been made in the UK, e.g. with successful black, female entrepreneurs (Wanogho 1997). The purpose of such role models is to remove one of the barriers in the process of new business creation: role models help to identify with success, with encouraging the next step of developing the business idea and identifying the right opportunity.

7.5.3 Pre-start planning and preparation

A further combination of factors will be important to the eventual success of new business creation. Among the most important are research, obtaining information (to determine entry strategy) and raising sufficient finance.

The depth and time of the search activity will depend on the opportunity and the characteristics of the new venture. If formal venture capital is required, raising such finance may take some time, because of due diligence procedures (12 months), as well as research and preparation. Recent research with entrepreneurs using non-executive directors produced a number of cases where the entrepreneurs had spent some time researching opportunities in preparation for a management buy-in (MBI) (Deakins *et al*. 1998). In these cases the entrepreneurs had researched a large number of potential candidate companies (up to 100) as a target for an MBI. If informal (or 'business angel') finance is sought this will still involve a search and matching process by the entrepreneur before a suitable investor may be found (Mason and Harrison 1995). Even raising bank finance can involve a search procedure and time to find sufficient bank finance and the best terms and conditions (Deakins and Hussain 1994b).

Preparation may also involve getting the right management team with complementary skills. Evidence on team starts suggests that teams have advantages over individual entrepreneurs because of the match of skills brought together with the team (Vyakarnaram *et al*. 1997). However, the evidence is far from conclusive; for example, Oakey (1995) found with small firms exploiting new technology that the best performers were those with a single founder. Team starts have been the focus of policy 'best practice' (DTI 1996b), but it must be remembered that it is important to get the right 'mix' of skills in the proposed entrepreneurial team. Involving a friend who has been privy to the development of a new business idea may not work unless each person involved is able to bring knowledge or skill that is required in the business. The research with entrepreneurs that had appointed non-executive directors demonstrated that the matching process was crucial to the success of the relationship and impact on the growth and performance of the firm (Deakins *et al*. 1999).

7.5.4 Entry and launch

It has been suggested above that the timing of entry is important. While advantages exist to first movers, moving too early can result in insufficient customers to make large investment worthwhile. The issue of timing becomes more important if the protection of intellectual property rights (IPR) is involved. The entrepreneur with a new product or process needs to decide whether and when to patent. Patents are expensive and time-consuming to acquire but they may be a necessary prerequisite for formal or informal venture capital. Developing the entry strategy is an important part of the launch of the new business; attention will need to be paid to developing a marketing strategy, a factor that is sometimes neglected by a technology-based entrepreneur (Oakey 1995).

The role of serendipity is often an underplayed factor in the start-up and business-creation process. For example, to the casual observer, the entrepreneurial and marketing strategies developed in start-up firms may appear to contain a strong element of chance, yet precursor developments can be highly important as preparation for exploitation of the business opportunity. The role of serendipity has scarcely been acknowledged – let alone researched – in entrepreneurial development and strategies (Martello 1994), yet evidence suggests that chance is only one element: the entrepreneur must be prepared to exploit opportunities and be able to recognise and take advantage of them.

7.5.5 Post-entry development

Early-stage development is a crucial phase for the novice entrepreneur. At this stage, the entrepreneur is naïve and must learn quickly to understand customers, suppliers, cash flow and dealing with other stakeholders in the new business, which may include the bank manager or other financiers. For businesses involved in a team start, it is the post-entry stage which leads to the testing of relationships between individuals, confirmation of their role, and the value that each individual can bring. One of the most important issues that a new business faces is credibility. Being new – especially if markets are competitive – means that customers have to take quality on trust, that suppliers will be unwilling to give trade credit and that banks will be unwilling to extend significant credit facilities. One strategy that can overcome this lack of credibility is to include an experienced entrepreneur as a part-time director in early-stage development. For example, from the research with small companies that employed non-executive directors, a sub-sample of start-up companies was isolated; in this sub-sample the most important reason for employing a non-executive director was to achieve credibility (Deakins *et al.* 1999). Alternatively, the use of an experienced entrepreneur as a mentor may also lead to introductions to key customers and to achieving credibility with suppliers, as well as bringing invaluable experience that overcomes the relative naïveté of the start-up entrepreneur. A discussion of the value of mentoring support is given later in this chapter. Additionally, the new firm may gain credibility by belonging to a network which would vouch for the new entrant's viability. The benefits of networks have been discussed briefly, earlier in this chapter. The roles of networking and more spatially specific collaboration through clustering are highlighted in the recent White Paper (Department of Trade and Industry 1998). Whilst many of the measures regarding networking in the White Paper are not exclusively for SMEs, it can be argued that they are intended to assist the creation of an entrepreneurial economy.

7.5.6 Management buy-outs and management buy-ins

Neither management buy-outs (MBOs) nor management buy-ins (MBIs) have been regarded, traditionally, as examples of entrepreneurship and business creation (see Chapter 14 for other examples of corporate entrepreneurship or intrapreneurship). MBOs involve the buy-out of the equity of a company by the existing management team, often funded by a venture capital institution. Although this can lead to changes in management style and strategy, it can be argued that little new is created. MBIs involve an outside entrepreneur or management team buying into the equity of an existing company, again often funded by a venture capital institution. As stated before, our research with small companies that employed non-executive directors revealed that MBIs involving a single outside entrepreneur often entailed the processes of new business creation, with considerable pre-MBI planning, research and search activity.

MBOs, by their nature, do not lead to new business creation *per se* and have been regarded as very different from new-start business creation. This may well be the case where an existing management team is given an opportunity to 'buy out' the equity of previous owners, a situation which does not necessarily lead to new business creation. However, some MBOs can be much closer to entrepreneurship, where either a team or an individual can virtually transform an old company and its associated way of doing business. In addition, where an MBO is undertaken by an individual – rather than, say, the previous management team – this can be virtually equivalent to new business creation.

7.6 Start-up policy

The recent White Paper on competitiveness (Department of Trade and Industry 1998) states that 'Developing an entrepreneurial culture in the UK is at the heart of the White Paper ... And when entrepreneurs, at whatever age are ready to make a start, Government will be there to offer them help and advice ... there is much it [the Government] can do to encourage innovative start-ups in their early years.' This represents a remarkable turn-around in government policy for start-up business development support, which, during the early 1990s, had gradually abandoned start-up assistance. As Chapter 4 describes, Business Links from 1992 onwards had been established to target business development support at *existing* firms employing more than 20 people, with potential to grow. By contrast, in October 1998, the Secretary of State for Trade and Industry announced that 'within three years he wanted Business Link partnerships to be providing high quality tailored services to 10,000 innovative, high growth potential start-ups per annum' (DTI 1998).

Whether governments should support new entrepreneurial activity has been subject to some academic debate (Storey 1993) – see Chapter 4. Despite the acceptance that a significant proportion of jobs are created via new-firm formation (although perhaps not on so grandiose a scale as Birch (1979) claimed), business start-up support has been the subject of academic criticism in the literature. This is partly because it is acknowledged that only a very few new firms grow and create these jobs (Storey 1994). Similarly, it is recognised that a large proportion of new firms do not survive. According to Stanworth and Gray (1991: 11), 36% of all VAT registered businesses fail within three years of registration. Additionally, the policy of subsidising firm start-up has been difficult to justify, due partly to the problems associated with turbulence and the nature of a substantial proportion of new firms. Storey and Strange (1992: 67) established that 'more than one-quarter of wholly new firms in Cleveland in the 1980s were either hairdressers or in the car-related trades ... This would not seem to be a strong basis for the long-term development of the country's economy.' In order to attempt to overcome these problems identified with new-firm formation there has been an increased emphasis on policy initiatives aimed at established firms coupled with targeted support at potential new growth companies.

There is strong evidence that, due to known high levels of turbulence in birth and death rates in new-firm formation, providing business start-up support can be counter-productive. For example, Cressy and Storey (1996) have shown that new-venture failure rates are very high. Less than 30% of their sample survived longer than six years from their database of new-venture starts over the period 1988–94. These figures, and the associated high degree of turbulence, are similar to officially recorded new-firm failure rates (DTI 1996b). These high new-firm failure rates give ammunition to supporters of the Storey (1993) view, that support agencies should concentrate on supporting growth firms that can be identified after the first 2–3-year trading record. There is a lot of power in an argument which effectively abandons start-up support, because it is impossible to discriminate before the first 2–3-year trading period, when the evidence on new-firm failure rates is so striking. Investing public money in supporting new-firm formation has become markedly less popular as this argument has gained ground.

Thus, developing and delivering start-up business support can be seen to be 'against the grain' of current academic thinking. In an often-quoted analogy, Storey (1993: 16) has compared the provision of start-up support to 'a lottery in which the odds of winning are not good'. The basis for this view has been that the blanket coverage of start-up support programmes such as the Enterprise Allowance Scheme (EAS) has not resulted in a noticeable impact on the quality of firm starts and may have encouraged low-quality firm start-ups (even though Storey considered the EAS to be one of the 'better schemes'). The vast majority of new-firm starts are known to be poor job creators (Storey 1994). Thus, it has been argued that the opportunity cost of such start-up support is high, since the careful targeting of public funds (in the form of enterprise support) at the small number of high-performing growth firms that are new starters should result in a more cost-effective way of supporting new-venture development.

It is probably worth expanding the analogy of a lottery in the same vein as Storey's article (1993). Storey takes this analogy further by comparing public-sector start-up business support to backing horses at the start of a race, where the odds (of survival/growth) are unknown. Taking the analogy literally, it would be better to back horses after a significant number of hurdles. That is, provide business support after the start-up period, when the high number of failures associated with that period have materialised; the high-growing firms will also have materialised and such successful new businesses can easily be targeted for support. Storey suggests that this should be after the first 3-year trading period. Until the recent White Paper, policy was geared to post-start-up support, as delivered through Business Links. Despite this policy, one review of business start-up support concluded that there is a clear case for supporting start-ups

(Atherton *et al.* 1996). That case is stronger in regions where the business start-up rate is considered too low to maintain vitality in local economic development, i.e. in regions such as the North, Wales or Scotland. The remainder of this chapter draws upon the results of a study undertaken in one such region, in the West of Scotland.

7.7 Using mentors to provide support: evidence from Scotland

Intervention at the pre-start and start-up stages should be beneficial by reducing the known high failure rates. One of the problems in the UK has not been *when* interventions have taken place but *how* those interventions have taken place. The impact – on the small firm and the ability of the entrepreneur to learn from mistakes and experience – of the relationship between the 'new' entrepreneur and business adviser – whether the adviser is agency employed or operating as a private consultant – is poorly understood. Yet, theoretically, in the early stages of business development, such intervention should have a major impact. Case-study research undertaken into the learning process with start-up entrepreneurs (Deakins and Freel 1997) has revealed that the learning process in SMEs is a crucial part of their evolution. The entrepreneur, through experience, acquires the ability to learn. Rarely is this learning process planned, but is rather the result of a series of reactions to critical events, in which the entrepreneur learns to process information, adjust strategy and take decisions. The implications for policy are that interventions must be based on helping the entrepreneur to learn rather than imposing prescribed solutions and 'expert' consultancy.

In the context of this, recent research has examined one support initiative that has involved the mentoring principle employed by one local business start-up programme. Mentoring involves principles drawn from experiential and cyclical approaches to learning: the entrepreneur learns from experience but, with the mentor, learns 'how to learn' from that experience. Cox and Jennings (1995) suggest that it is this ability to learn from mistakes that makes successful entrepreneurs. While they found that entrepreneurs who had started their own businesses and built them into large corporations did not appear to identify any one individual who had acted as a 'mentor', they nonetheless could relate to the importance of learning from experience from critical incidents. They were in fact 'individuals who had to make their own way in the world, the process [of becoming innovative] seems to start early in their childhood. Successfully coping with extreme difficulties while very young seems to set a pattern of resilience and ability not only to cope with, but also to learn from, adversity. It is this ability to learn from their experience which is the key attribute of these successful individuals.'

The notion of mentoring, however, is problematic. For example, Mumford (1995) points out that differences in learning styles affect the mentor relationship. This implies that attention needs to be given to matching individual mentor styles to new entrepreneur clients if the relationship is to be managed effectively.

The first-stage study (Deakins *et al.* 1997b) found that some clients on the support programme put forward a view that there may be scope for greater matching of mentor to client – either through the mentor's sectoral experience, or gender. In addition, the evidence suggested that interpersonal relationships with advisers had changed over time – an indication that as entrepreneurs develop they require different skills or assistance from the mentor (Clutterbuck 1991). There is, therefore, some debate on the required characteristics of mentors at varying stages in the entrepreneurs' development and the client/mentor matching process. While some argue that there is a need to match mentor and client to take account of both the 'career/technical' and psychosocial functions, there is also an argument that the influence of 'personal chemistry' between the two individuals is of prime significance. Unless some form of, say, psychometric testing takes place to match the two it will largely be through trial and error that effective relationships will be formed. In this scenario perhaps the needs of the client and indeed the 'personal chemistry' required in the relationship may alter as the entrepreneur and the enterprise develop. There is an argument for matching on one hand, but on the other, since the personal chemistry between the two individuals is so important, then any attempt to pre-select or force a mentor–client relationship is likely to be unsuccessful. Such a view is taken by Kram (1986) who states that 'Assigned relationships through formal programmes were found to be problematical'.

For the study reported here (Deakins *et al.* 1997b), the impact of the mentor on knowledge, skills and attitude of the client is examined. Such impacts are measured in two main ways:

- through rank order of the significance of intervention and how this changes;
- through impact of the mentor on area and style of intervention.

7.7.1 Perceptions of mentor support

The first-stage findings (which examined start-up–mentoring relationships) indicated that the mentor was the most important source of advice for new-start entrepreneurs when compared to other sources such as accountants or bank managers (Deakins *et al.* 1998). It was expected that the importance of such advice would decline as the novice entrepreneurs become established and deal more frequently with such external bodies. A related issue is the extent of networking, which was found, at the first stage, to be undeveloped. It was expected that the value of networking with other entrepreneurs/firms would be rated higher. The change in importance of these sources of advice is shown in Table 7.1.

The change is actually greater than that shown in the table: for example, the accountant was rated considerably behind the mentor at the first stage. Obviously, as the business becomes established, so the importance of such advice increases. The relative decline in the importance of the mentor is probably a desirable outcome for the support agency.

Table 7.1 Changes in importance of sources of advice (rank order)

Source of advice	1st-stage importance	2nd-stage importance	Change in rank order
Business adviser/mentor	1	2	−1
Accountant	2	1	+1
Family	3	3	0
Bank manager	4	4	0
Friends	5	6	−1
Other	6	5	+1

Table 7.2 Significance of intervention (rank order)

Difference to:	1st-stage rank order	2nd-stage rank order	Change in rank order	Mentor ranking
Achieving objectives	1	1	0	1
Ability to learn	3	2	+1	7
Ability to cope with problems	2	3	−1	3
Profitability	7	4	+3	5
Ability to manage	4	5	−1	8
Ability to cope with change	5	6	−1	2
Turnover	6	7	−1	6
Employment	8	8	0	4
No. of firms/sample	45	28		10

The impact of mentoring on knowledge and skills of the clients was assessed. Table 7.2 compares rank orders of the impact of the mentor: the impact on ability to learn and to achieve objectives were rated more important than the impact on 'hard' measures such as turnover and employment at both the first and second stages of the research. This was regarded as an important finding at the first stage and reinforces the view that the impact of the mentor is important for the novice entrepreneurs as they learn to establish their business, to manage and to overcome problems. Interestingly, it also appears that the mentors have an impact on forcing the novice entrepreneurs to focus on profit, rather than just on turnover.

Apart from the ability to learn, there is quite a close correlation between the client rankings on impact and impact as perceived by the mentor/adviser. This could be because the mentor does not perceive their impact on the ability to learn as directly as does the client. The strong correlation, however, on the impact on achieving objectives and coping with problems indicates that the mentor is having a strong impact on the client by influencing them to focus on objectives; the client also sees the value of this focus, and furthermore believes that they learn from this process.

The impact on attitudes of clients was also investigated through the mentor relationship and actions undertaken by the mentors. Mentors were former and existing entrepreneurs themselves, and as such they are likely to have strong personalities, they may wish to intervene and to take a hands-on role – in some cases there may even be a clash of personalities; issues which have been discussed in our review of the mentoring literature. The first stage revealed that 69% of entrepreneurs reported a very good relationship with their mentor. There was a small deterioration in reported relationships, which may reflect a gradual disengagement of the mentor relationship, but 68% still reported the relationship as good or better.

The most important actions from a prepared list as perceived by both the client and the mentor are given in Table 7.3. From the perspective of the novice entrepreneurs, the most important actions that the mentor undertook were concerned with providing constructive criticism, being a friend and providing guidance and support. By contrast, mentors saw their role as being concerned with encouragement and motivation, and guidance and support. Being a friend was an action or role that was not rated by the

Table 7.3 Client and mentor perspectives of most important actions

Action	Client mean score	Mentor ranking*
Most important five		
1 Being a friend	4.0	not ranked
2 Constructive criticism	4.0	5
3 Encouragement and motivation	3.9	1
4 Guidance and support	3.9	2
5 Feedback	3.6	not ranked
Least important five		
14 Relating concepts (to practice)	2.5	not ranked
15 Emotional support	2.5	not ranked
16 Administration	2.4	9
17 Technical assistance	1.8	not ranked
18 Other action or none	0.7	not ranked

* The mentor was presented with the same list, but not asked to score, merely to rank the five most important actions; consequently, where an action is not ranked this means that none of the mentors ranked it in the top five actions.

mentor, despite being seen as important by the client. For completeness, other actions which were also ranked by the mentors included structuring tasks (given a low rating of 2.7 by the clients) and discussing alternative solutions to problems (scored at 3.3 by the clients).

The table indicates that the novice entrepreneur clients actually perceive more value in the relationship than do the mentors. The clients value encouragement, motivation, guidance and support which were also ranked highly by the mentors. There are some implications from the table concerning induction of both entrepreneurs and mentors. For the mentors it can be seen that clients value highly constructive criticism and their role as someone to call on 'as a friend'; possibly indicating the lack of networking activity by such novice entrepreneurs. The relatively low ranking given to constructive criticism by the mentors, yet high ranking accorded by the clients means that encouraging mentors to give more criticism may yield benefits and be welcomed by the clients. By contrast, mentors focus more on encouragement and motivation; our analysis suggests that this could be better balanced, with possibly more feedback by the mentors – something that was highly valued by the clients. Obviously, as the mentors themselves pointed out, different styles (of intervention) may be needed with different clients, but each mentor had a different approach. This can be an advantage if the programme is well managed and different mentors are matched with different clients; however, any matching attempts appeared to be haphazard.

7.8 Chapter summary

This chapter has examined both the theory and the practice of business start-up. While theoretical development in this area has been limited, nevertheless the application of mentoring principles to a business start-up support programme was found to provide some beneficial results. Our study of one programme of mentoring support showed that such support was highly valued by the clients. In particular, the main areas of value added by the mentoring support were shown to be:

- clients had a clearer focus on achieving objectives;
- clients were more likely to use business planning;
- clients focused on profitability rather than just turnover or cash;
- new-start entrepreneurs were helped to learn, manage their businesses and cope with change.

The value added by such impacts cannot be measured precisely, but the start-up programme will have results in terms of better performance of new-start businesses, better competitiveness and hence better survival rates. Mentors were allocated to individual start-up clients for the first 18-month trading period. There was some evidence that the intervention of the mentor was particularly important to clients at the initial start-up stage as a source of advice. This gradually declined, with the result that clients were using other forms of external advice (possibly encouraged by the mentors) by the end of the relationship. This is probably a desirable outcome of the programme, since there is the issue of where the client can seek advice following the end of the mentoring relationship.

Some of the most positive outcomes lay in the value of the intervention by the mentor. A good correlation existed between the impact of the intervention perceived by the client and that perceived by the mentor. Intervention was clearly focused on achieving objectives. However, the clients did rate the impact on ability to learn as more important than did the mentors, indicating that mentoring support did achieve the aim of fostering the ability of clients to learn from problems and to incorporate changes into their management.

Finally, three areas of support were identified which could additionally be developed by support agencies wishing to implement a similar programme. In maximising the effectiveness of mentoring support, there is a clear role for support agencies to undertake the following three functions:

- Selective matching of client to mentor after initial screening and interview of the client. For example, different clients will suit different mentor styles.
- Induction of clients to increase the effectiveness of the mentor relationship. There is an onus on the client to make use of the mentor at appropriate times, and induction will help to achieve this.
- Training of both clients and mentors. In the support programme staff development was undertaken with the mentors, but this needs to be continuous and can help the mentors to reflect on their own style of intervention and learning.

There were also issues concerning the continuation of support after the mentor period was completed. In the local area programme, clients were expected to move on to an entirely different style of support programme. Mentoring was replaced with part-funded short-term consultancy. This left a 'gap' and a step change in support after the 18-month mentoring support. Yet the start-up support programme provided an ideal way for the fast-growth firms to be identified and supported over a longer time period than the 18-month mentoring programme. For carefully selected firms, non-executive directors (NEDs) should provide a close model of the mentor relationship for small, growing firms. Such selected firms could be encouraged to take on a mentor/NED on a purely commercial basis. Development agencies could support the creation of a list of appropriate people to be NEDs in such growing small firms. In addition, since such firms would have to be companies, this may also increase the likelihood of raising external equity finance (an issue not reported in the paper was the low take-up of such finance).

There are some similarities in the NED role to that of the mentor, especially for fast-growth small firms. A parallel study (Deakins *et al.* 1998), undertaken with entre-preneurs in growth firms using a mentor, indicated that the most important role of the mentor was perceived as guiding, advising and counselling. The greater networking ability of such entrepreneurs meant that networking and contacts were rated quite low in importance. Some clients indicated a willingness to pay for the mentor role – a role that could easily be converted to that of a NED.

If the government wishes to promote high-value, growth-based start-ups as identi-fied in the 1998 Competitiveness White Paper (Department of Trade and Industry 1998), then the experience of Scotland suggests that this can be achieved successfully, through carefully targeted support. However, our evidence also suggests that interven-tion needs to be carefully promoted, with attention being paid to induction, training, networking and matching of mentors or start-up business advisers.

Questions

1 Argue the case either for *or* against the intervention of the government in the small-business start-up support process.

2 You have been given the task, as Business Development Director of a government-funded agency, of designing support for new small-business start-ups. Explain what measures you would like to introduce and what guiding principles you would use.

3 Why has the subject of *extent* of entrepreneurial behaviour in our society become the focus of government policy? How would you improve it?

CHAPTER 8

The psychology of the entrepreneur

Frédéric Delmar

8.1 Learning objectives

There are six learning objectives in this chapter:

1 To explore the development of the field.
2 To examine why the trait approach has been adopted to study the entrepreneur.
3 To understand why the trait approach has failed in understanding entrepreneurial behaviour.
4 To define and explore the major theoretical schools of the psychology of the entrepreneur.
5 To understand the practical as well as theoretical advantages of cognitive models.
6 To understand how entrepreneurship can be promoted from a psychology perspective.

Key concepts

■ personality characteristics ■ proximal and distal processes ■ cognition ■ motivation ■ entrepreneurial behaviour

8.2 Introduction

In this chapter, evidence on the entrepreneurial personality and behaviour is reviewed. The chapter begins by describing how this area has evolved, concentrating on different problems and criticisms related to the subject. Thereafter, entrepreneurial traits are reviewed, such as the need for achievement, locus of control and risk-taking propensity. The chapter then continues with an overview of current research and results about entrepreneurial behaviour, with a focus on cognitive motivation models which have the ability to address individual differences in entrepreneurial behaviour and performance. The chapter also addresses the training and education of potential entrepreneurs.

8.3 The entrepreneurial personality

The personality of the entrepreneur is often perceived by students and practitioners as one of the most fascinating topics in the field of entrepreneurship. The reason for this is the human tendency to attribute great performances to a person's individual characteristics rather than to situational constraints. That is, there is a general tendency to explain the behaviour of others as a consequence of their personalities rather than as a consequence of what the situation has to offer. This is often referred to as the 'fundamental attribution error', which suggests that it is often believed that a successful entrepreneur is the result of a special set of personal abilities and characteristics, rather than the result of either being in a favourable situation or pure chance.

As a natural consequence of this belief, the psychological perspective in entrepreneurship research has, until recently, concentrated on discovering stable individual characteristics such as personality traits. It is, as pointed out earlier, an attractive explanation, and of direct practical relevance as most parties having a financial interest in entrepreneurship would like to find an easy test which could identify potential successful entrepreneurs.

As will be explained, psychology cannot offer (at the present time) such a valid test, but enterprises are run by men and women and there is a need to understand how they behave. The entrepreneur (and his or her ideas) often represents the only information that various stakeholders – such as venture capitalists, bankers or policy-makers – have available to make the decision of whether or not to grant finance to that individual or to create an infrastructure promoting entrepreneurship. In order to make such decisions, these parties need to have information about what characterises entrepreneurial behaviour and how it can be understood.

Personality traits cannot explain more than a minor share of entrepreneurial behaviour and differences in business performance. As will be seen, these disappointing results can be explained by theoretical as well as methodological problems characterising the perspective (Carsrud and Johnson 1989; Chell, Haworth and Brearley 1991; Delmar 1996; Gartner 1988; Herron and Robinson 1993; Sexton and Bowman 1985). The research field of entrepreneurial behaviour has instead turned its attention towards more sophisticated models where, instead of personality traits, people's cognition and motivations are the explanatory factors behind entrepreneurial behaviour.

8.4 The development of the field of entrepreneurial personality and behaviour

Figure 8.1 illustrates the complexity and the inherent problems associated with the psychological perspective. It is composed of four boxes, each containing a basic question related to the research field and numbered from 1 to 4. The numbers represent the approximate historical evolution of the field. In short, research first began by trying to find a personality profile describing entrepreneurs (Box 1), although it became clear that more conceptual work was needed to define what an entrepreneur really is and what task(s) s/he is performing (Box 2). This conceptual work led to a greater

Figure 8.1 The field of applied psychology in entrepreneurship

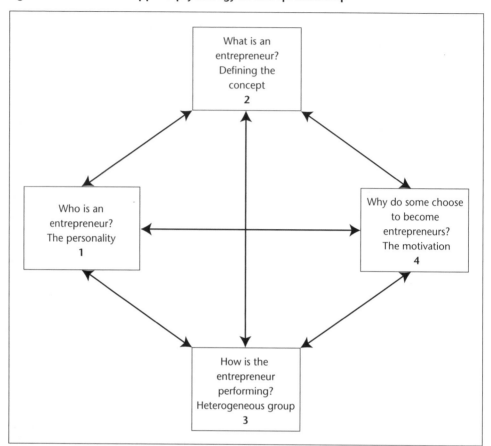

awareness that entrepreneurs act at different stages in business development. Research then focused to relate different personality traits to performance of the firm (Box 3). However, traits theories were proven not to be a viable alternative in explaining entrepreneurial behaviour, and cognitive motivation models have been adopted instead (Box 4). It is worth noting that the boxes are interrelated and that any one question cannot be answered without taking the other questions into consideration.

8.4.1 Who is an entrepreneur? Understanding the concept of personality

Personality is often loosely defined in terms of regularities in action, feelings and thoughts that are characteristics of the individual (Snyder and Cantor 1998). In other words, there is supposed to be a set of characteristics or traits that is stable across situation and time. This means that one hopes to find an entrepreneurial personality profile that can help to better understand which characteristics lead to success, and which lead to failure. If it were possible to identify such personality characteristics, the financial risk exposure of venture capitalists and bankers could be limited by giving them an effective selection instrument. Furthermore, it would be possible to encourage those with winning personalities to engage in an entrepreneurial career and discourage those with failing personalities. However, the search for the entrepreneurial personality has stumbled upon several problems.

Inconsistency

The first problem of the perspective is the inconsistency of such an approach due to the large number and variants of traits. Furthermore, researchers have not reached consensus on the relevance of these individual characteristics, their importance, and how they vary in different situations. For example, Hornaday (1982) identified more than 40 traits that have been associated with entrepreneurs, and the most popular identified by previous research include the need for achievement, internal locus of control, risk-taking propensity, tolerance for ambiguity, over-optimism and the need for autonomy. Thus, there is a rich abundance of different characteristics that are attributed to the entrepreneur, which will be explained in greater detail later in this chapter. For the moment, it is important just to remember that it is difficult to reach a common frame of reference because of the large number of characteristics and their definitions.

The static nature of entrepreneurial characteristics

The second problem is the assumption that the variables characterising the entrepreneur and the environment are static. However, it is clear to all that the environment changes constantly, and traits or characteristics alone have very little ability to explain behaviour. Thus, the external validity of the psychological trait approach can be questioned.

Obsolescence of current theory

The third problem is that the theory and methods in use are, in relation to modern psychological research, obsolete. The concept of personality is not one-dimensional (and measured with only one trait) but multidimensional. An individual's personality is now mainly measured in five broad dimensions called the 'Big Five' (cf. Goldberg 1993; Hogan 1991; Hogan, Hogan and Roberts 1996). Hence, when measuring personality, the measures should include at least these five dimensions of interpersonal evaluation.

Furthermore, it is not possible to unambiguously state that differences are due to predispositions (i.e. not yet having managed a venture) or are the results of having entrepreneurial expertise (i.e. already managing a venture) (Mitchell and Seawright 1995). In other words, the fact that entrepreneurs exhibit certain characteristics does not necessarily mean that they had them from the very beginning. These characteristics could have been developed during the time they have been entrepreneurs. It is therefore difficult to state clearly if the characteristics exhibited by entrepreneurs are caused by previous life experiences or are the result of being an entrepreneur.

American bias

Finally, there is the problem that the research is mainly based on US samples. As a result, it has been argued that many of these characteristics (especially the need for achievement) are culturally dependent, and as a consequence lacking of predictive power in other cultures (Spence 1985). As Chapter 6 demonstrates, research findings about entrepreneurs' attitudes in different countries give some support to this argument, at least when the USA is compared to Asian countries (Stimpson, Robinson, Waranusuntikule and Zheng 1990).

The inability to handle these five problems in the field of entrepreneurship has led to the abandonment of the attempts to identify a single trait. Instead, researchers have attempted to adopt increasingly complex approaches in the hope of more fruitful results. More specifically, social psychological models incorporating individual characteristics and social contexts have been proposed to better understand the psychology of the entrepreneur (Herron and Robinson 1993; Katz 1992; Krueger and Brazeal 1994; Starr and Fondas 1992). In addition, researchers are now increasingly developing studies which attempt to understand what entrepreneurship really is and how it can be better measured, i.e. defining entrepreneurship and understanding how an entrepreneur performs.

8.4.2 What is an entrepreneur? Defining the concept

Whilst defining an entrepreneur is beyond the scope of this chapter, it is enough to remind the reader of the diversity in definitions and the fact that there is no general agreement of what is and what is not entrepreneurship. However, the characteristics associated with entrepreneurship have mainly been examined by concentrating on differences between entrepreneurs and other groups (Low and MacMillan 1988). Thus, previous research has tried to link the state of being defined as an entrepreneur to different personality traits. This is problematic as it assumes that entrepreneurs are a homogeneous group. However, it is clear that this is not the case as individuals will start businesses for different reasons. Whilst some are only interested in having an extra income besides their regular jobs, others only want to create a business large enough to support them and their families. In addition, there are a few individuals who want to create a fast-growing, expanding business.

One of the first studies to specifically differentiate amongst entrepreneurs was the work of Smith (1967), who examined the differences between the type of entrepreneur and the type of firm created by the entrepreneur, with the basic assumption that the way the firm was organised and performed was reflected by the personality of the entrepreneur. He identified two types of entrepreneur:

- the craftsman-entrepreneur;
- the opportunistic entrepreneur.

It was assumed that the craftsman type had a lower education, preferred manual work and wanted a stable income to support the family. On the other hand, the opportunist had a higher education, and was more prone to be a leader and to expand the business. Even if this may now seem an overly naïve conception of entrepreneurship, it has the important advantage of highlighting the difference between entrepreneurs themselves. Therefore, it is a serious flaw of research not to acknowledge that entrepreneurs have totally different personal goals and, as a result of these, very different business goals.

It is therefore more accurate to assume heterogeneity and thus focus on the differences between different types of entrepreneur. More precisely, research has become more aware of the problem of defining entrepreneurship and now pays more attention to problems of definition and the need to examine entrepreneurship at different points of the dynamic process of business creation and expansion.

8.4.3 How do different entrepreneurs perform?

The previous two sections have described the development of the field from a simple assumption that entrepreneurs are all alike (but different from other people), to a more complex picture where entrepreneurship can be studied at various stages of a firm's development and in which entrepreneurs as a group are very heterogeneous. One consequence of this is that research has moved towards trying to explain the performance of the firm by examining the link between different personality characteristics of the entrepreneur and contingency variables such as firm age, industry affiliation and organisational structure (e.g. Miller 1987b; Miller and Toulouse 1986). However, even though the models had evolved from simple trait-states models (as described previously) to more complex models taking into account the characteristics of the firm as well as the characteristics of the entrepreneur, the results were still weak. Two main explanations of this can be identified, namely the definition of performance and the link between personality characteristics, entrepreneurial behaviour and business performance.

To start with, what is meant by 'performance' in this case? Three different measures are most often associated with the concept of performance:

■ survival of the firm – what factors influence the long-term survival of the firm?

■ firm growth – what factors affect the expansion of the firm?

■ firm profitability – what factors influence the firm's ability to generate profits?

These performance measures can then, in turn, be operationalised in a number of ways, thus adding to the confusion (Delmar 1997; Murphy, Trailer and Hill 1996). However, this is not the main problem, which remains one of linking traits to behaviour and then linking behaviour to business performance. When modelling behaviour and subsequent performance, psychologists tend to make a distinction between distal and proximal factors affecting behaviour (Ackerman and Humphreys 1990).

A distal factor is one that may explain general behaviours (such as eating, sex drives and sleeping) but which has little ability to explain how individuals act in a specific situation. For example, individuals have the need to eat and the explanation is that they have to refuel energy supplies in order to survive. However, the explanation that behaviour is driven by needs will not explain why one may have a preference to eat hamburgers instead of an à la carte dinner.

A proximal explanation looks at factors defining the situation in which individuals find themselves when choosing to go to a restaurant instead of a hamburger bar: for example, it is Friday night, they have just received a pay cheque and want to impress someone. Therefore they choose to go to a fancy restaurant to eat instead of choosing a hamburger bar. The actual behaviour is then better explained by proximal factors (task characteristics) than by distal factors (traits and needs). Traits are, in general, distal factors and they therefore have little ability explaining actual behaviour, and even less business performance.

Furthermore, the entrepreneurial venture can be characterised as highly complex, i.e. the demands on an individual in undertaking simple tasks such as playing pinball are very different to those of starting and maintaining a business. Campbell (1988) suggests business venturing is an example of one of the highest degrees of complexity, and these so-called 'fuzzy tasks' (characterised by the presence of both multiple desired end-states and multiple ways of attaining each of the desired outcomes) are also characterised by uncertainty and conflicting interdependence. In such a case, the relation between behaviour and performance is weakened by the interactive effects between motivational processes, cognitive abilities and environmental factors. Not acknowledging this lack of correspondence between behaviour and performance has serious consequences for understanding the effects of motivation on entrepreneurial performance. For example, whilst motivation can yield high levels of cognitive effort, if it is misdirected then there will be a failure in performance (Kanfer 1991). Thus, as McCloy, Campbell and Cudeck (1994) suggest, a successful entrepreneur will have to:

- possess the prerequisite knowledge;
- master the prerequisite skills;
- actually choose to work on the job tasks for some period of time at some level of effort.

To sum up, research examining the different traits or other psychological factors characterising the entrepreneur needs to take into account the complexity of the situation of the entrepreneur. This is because trait theories are not sophisticated enough to account for the complexity of entrepreneurial behaviour. Therefore, research has evolved towards explanations where entrepreneurial behaviour and business performance are explained by more proximal psychological theories and where the effect of the situation is better controlled for.

8.4.4 Why become an entrepreneur? The cognitive approach

The studies examined so far have concluded that the trait approach has not given insight of great value. The assumptions behind entrepreneurial behaviour have been far too simplistic by trying to relate a trait to the state of being an entrepreneur or to the performance of the firm. It is therefore impossible to say that entrepreneurs are characterised by traits predestining them to engage in business activities. Entrepreneurs are not, to a large degree, different from people in general. However, this does not explain why certain individuals still choose to undertake an entrepreneurial career. The answer probably lies in the fact that the same situation is perceived differently by different people depending on their previous experiences. Simple trait theories cannot account for that, and the research field has now turned its attention towards theories that help us to understand how people perceive and comprehend the world and how it affects their behaviour. Theories trying to explain behaviour by individuals perceiving and interpreting the information around them are called cognitive theories.

Paralleling the development of social psychology, entrepreneurship research has moved from simple trait theories towards more cognitive theories that are better able to explain the complexity inherent in entrepreneurial behaviour. Cognitive theories assume that individuals do not possess a perfect knowledge of the world because there simply is too much information out there to handle. As a consequence, they have to select information and interpret it; thus, based on their previous experience, they tend to see and know the world differently (Taylor 1998). For example, what is seen as a business opportunity by one person is viewed as an enormous problem impossible to solve by another. In short, individuals are actively involved in the construction of their own realities.

The use of cognitive theories enables a better understanding of why people engage in entrepreneurial behaviour. The contribution of these theories is that they make it possible to better understand the interaction between the characteristics of the situation and the characteristics of the entrepreneur. In other words, there is a movement from studying the personality of the entrepreneur to studying the situations that lead to entrepreneurial behaviour (Baron 1998; Carsrud and Johnson 1989; Shaver and Scott 1991). Behaviour is heavily based on how individuals perceive the situation or environment and how it is presented to them.

In other words, behavioural patterns are the products of two psychological processes. The first process operates through the selection of environments, and the second through the production of environments. When people have gained certain preferences and standards of behaviour, they tend to choose activities and individuals who share the same set of preferences, thereby mutually reinforcing pre-existing personal inclinations and fixed courses of action (Bandura 1982; Deci 1992a). More precisely, the individual characteristics leading to an entrepreneurial career are only activated when exposed to a favourable socialisation process, where an entrepreneurial career is seen as a viable possibility among others. Thus the social environment is of primary importance in fostering future entrepreneurs. The general idea is that individual characteristics are precursor traits and, in the context of a given 'cafeteria of experiences', help to determine both how experiences are weighted or attended to and how the individual reacts to those experiences. That is, individuals will only activate their entrepreneurial potential if they have:

- a certain specific ability and sensitivity;
- environmental possibilities;
- social support.

These three prerequisites must be fulfilled if actions are to be taken to become an entrepreneur. Thus the relation between intentions to act in a certain direction, the current situation and experience forms the base used to better understand human – and, of course, entrepreneurial – behaviour (some of these issues and the importance of mentoring to this process are discussed in Chapter 7).

Thus, two questions arise from this section and the previous one on the characteristics of the entrepreneurial situation:

- How do people come to choose an entrepreneurial career?
- What does the entrepreneur need to do in order to perform satisfactorily?

These are questions that cannot easily be answered without taking into account the complexity of human nature based on previous experience, abilities and intentions to act. The research field of entrepreneurial behaviour has, as a consequence, come to rely more and more on complex cognitive models – and especially cognitive motivation models – in order to better understand and explain the functioning of entrepreneurial behaviour, and the next step of linking actual behaviour to business performance. This is a very positive development, because the use of more sophisticated psychological models enables the research to make better sense of findings in other fields of entrepreneurship.

Motivation theories provide a good support for understanding the choices made by entrepreneurs and why they persist in doing what they do. They are easy to operationalise and have proven validity. Thus there is a good and reliable understanding of what motivates entrepreneurs. However, there are still problems in understanding the link between the intention to do something and the actual behaviour because these theories focus on volitional behaviour, and a large part of entrepreneurial behaviour is dependent on available resources, the co-operation of others and skill.

8.4.5 The development of research in entrepreneurial behaviour

This section has shown so far that this research area has been dominated by four different basic research questions:

- Who is the entrepreneur?
- What is an entrepreneur?
- How does an entrepreneur perform?
- Why does an individual become an entrepreneur?

It was suggested that the elaboration of these four questions could explain the development of the research field from a simple quest of trying to link single traits to the state of entrepreneurship to complex cognitive models taking into account the heterogeneity of entrepreneurial behaviour. In other words, the field has developed from examining personality traits in isolation to examining the interaction between the entrepreneur's perception, intention and ability and the characteristics of the situation. Thus, the research field in general does not offer an easy answer to the question of who is an entrepreneur. Instead, it has evolved towards acknowledging entrepreneurship as a process which is created by entrepreneurs in co-operation with others. In short, entrepreneurial behaviour should be regarded as the consequence of person–situation interactions.

8.5 Individual characteristics of entrepreneurs

This section describes some of the individual characteristics which are supposedly related to entrepreneurs and the intention to pursue an entrepreneurial career:

- risk-taking propensity;
- need for achievement;
- locus of control;

- over-optimism;
- desire for autonomy.

The first four concepts are closely related to each other as they affect our decision-making under risk and uncertainty (Mellers, Schwartz and Cooke 1998). The fifth concept is closely related to the choice of becoming an entrepreneur, as autonomy and freedom are often quoted as among the most important reasons to start a business. Whilst these five characteristics are often seen as positive characteristics of entrepreneurs, some research has also been undertaken on the more negative entrepreneurial characteristics, and the section is concluded by an overview of the 'entrepreneur's dark side'.

8.5.1 Risk-taking propensity

According to economic theory, one of the important roles of the entrepreneur is that of economic risk-taker or risk-bearer of the economic system (Buchanan and Di Pierro 1980; Knight 1921). Can it therefore be assumed that the entrepreneur is attracted to risk-taking more than others are? The answer is clearly no, as a number of studies have found no significant differences between entrepreneurs and others when measuring general risk propensity (Brockhaus 1980; Masters and Meier 1988; Peacock 1986). Scheré (1982) found, when examining tolerance for ambiguity (which is a concept related to risk-taking), that entrepreneurs have a somewhat greater degree of tolerance than managers. Tolerance of ambiguity is an emotional reaction to such ambiguity and uncertainty, and low tolerance results in stress and unpleasantness in a complex situation. Individuals with high tolerance, on the contrary, find such situations desirable and challenging. Therefore, individuals with high tolerance would expose themselves to higher risks than individuals with low tolerance, who prefer well-understood situations.

Whilst these studies assume that risk-taking is independent of the situation, it has been found that risk-taking is extremely dependent on either a perception of the situation (Hogarth 1987; Mellers *et al.* 1998) or the perception by decision-makers of themselves as experts in the field (Heath and Tversky 1991). One of the most well-known studies in the field of decision-making under risk is the work of Kahneman and Tversky (1979). In their 'prospect theory', they suggest that a person's willingness to take risks is dependent on the perception of the situation. Individuals will be risk-averse if they perceive themselves in a win situation, but will be risk-seeking in a loss situation. Heath and Tversky (1991) have also suggested that individuals take considerably more risks in situations in which they feel competent.

Studies in entrepreneurship taking the context into consideration have found that risk-taking was dependent on the entrepreneur's age, motivation, business experience, number of years in business, and education (Schwer and Yucelt 1984). In similar studies, Ray (1986; 1994) found that entrepreneurs are able to give up job security and take specific risks because they have the confidence that they will succeed. To sum up, results from research on risks and entrepreneurs are mixed, but apparently the perceived context (knowledge and situational characteristics) is a more important determinant of risk-taking than personality.

Dickson and Giglierano (1986) propose another perspective on entrepreneurial risk-taking. In their conceptual work they argue that the concept of risk can be divided into two separate components, namely the likelihood of a new venture failing and the likelihood of missing out on a strategic opportunity. According to this research, management and marketing research has mainly focused on the likelihood of failing and not on the search for new opportunities to explore. However, entrepreneurs may give more weight to the likelihood of missing out on a strategic opportunity than to the likelihood of a new venture failing. Das and Teng (1997) have also proposed a more detailed view on risk behaviour by proposing that risk is closely related to the time perspective, and an entrepreneur has to balance short-term risks against long-term risks. This has been empirically tested by Tsur, Sternberg and Hochman (1990) who found that risk-averse individuals were prepared to accept great risk in the short term if they believed it would minimise their long-term risk exposure. In other words, an entrepreneur will accept the risk of launching a new venture, if it is believed that the venture will minimise long-term risks (e.g. being unemployed and not having a satisfactory income).

8.5.2 Need for achievement

One of the most popular characteristics associated with entrepreneurs is McClelland's 'Need for Achievement' (1961; McClelland and Winter 1969). This characteristic is also closely related to risk-taking as it takes into account the perceived risk of the situation as well as the perceived level of competence. According to McClelland, entrepreneurs are individuals who have a high need for achievement, and that characteristic makes them especially suitable to create ventures. McClelland's theory identifies the situations preferred by individuals high in need for achievement, and which situations arouse the achievement motivation. Individuals who are high achievers will choose a situation characterised by:

- individual responsibility;
- moderate risk-taking as a function of skill;
- knowledge of results of decisions;
- novel instrumental activity;
- anticipation of future possibilities.

It is the prospect of achievement satisfaction, not money, which drives the entrepreneur. Money is important primarily as a measure of how well one is doing in business. McClelland's theory has received consistent empirical support suggesting that there is a relationship between entrepreneurship and achievement motivation (Begley and Boyd 1987; Bellu 1988; Davidsson 1989a; Delmar 1996; B. Johnson 1990; McClelland 1961; Perry, MacArthur, Meredith and Cunnington 1986).

Recently Miner and his associates have developed McClelland's achievement motivation theory by developing five motive patterns instead of the single achievement motive. This task motivation theory suggests that it is not possible to predict behaviour or performance on the basis of a single value, as in the case of need for achievement, but that performance can be predicted by a complex set of values or motive patterns. Miner's five motive patterns form an overall index of task motivation:

- self-achievement;
- risk-taking;
- feedback of results;
- personal innovation;
- planning for the future.

Results show that the 'Miner scales' have consistent validity, in that scores (especially total score on all scales combined) correlate significantly with entrepreneurial perform-ance, particularly growth (Bellu 1993; Bellu and Sherman 1995; Miner, Crane and Vandenberg 1994; Miner, Smith and Bracker 1989; Miner, Smith and Bracker 1992).

8.5.3 Locus of control

The concept of 'locus of control' can be traced back to Rotter's social learning theory (Rotter 1966) of how individuals' perception of control affects their behaviour. The theory assumes that individuals categorise events and situations based on their under-lying, shared properties. One such category concerns whether a potential end or goal can be attained through one's actions or follows from luck or other uncontrolled exter-nal factors. A person believing that the achievement of a goal is dependent on his or her own behaviour or individual characteristics believes in internal control. If, on the other hand, a person believes that an achievement is the result of luck and external factors, s/he believes in external control. Therefore, locus of control is conceived as one determinant of the expectancy of success (Weiner 1992).

To date, some empirical results have found a low to moderate positive correlation between internal control and entrepreneurs, and there is a weak tendency that a high internal orientation is associated with better performance (Brockhaus 1982; Miller and Toulouse 1986). However, a number of studies have reported no significant differ-ences between entrepreneurs and managers with respect to locus of control (Sexton and Bowman 1985). In psychology, the concept and measurement of locus of control have been heavily criticised (Furnham and Steele 1993), and the concept has been more or less abandoned in favour of attribution theory which has a more complex view on causality orientation (Anderson and Strigel 1981; Weiner 1985). As a result, locus of control is a concept which should probably not be included in future empirical research on entrepreneurial behaviour.

8.5.4 Over-optimism

Over-optimism is closely related to locus of control, because both are related to expectancy of success. Cooper, Dunkelberg and Woo (1986) have studied entrepre-neurs' perceived chances of success shortly after they became business-owners. Their responses were then compared to the actual success rate in the respective industries. When asked about the chances for a business resembling their own to survive, most of the entrepreneurs were optimistic (78% considered the chances of survival as 50:50 or higher). When asked about their own success chances, the entrepreneurs were extremely optimistic (81% considered the chances of survival to be 70:30 or higher).

Egge (1987) also found that a majority of entrepreneurs were over-optimistic about their success rates.

This can be compared to the research undertaken on personal and general risk. Personal risk is defined as ratings made by the respondents of a risk as pertaining to themselves. On the other hand, ratings of a risk pertaining to people in general are called general risk ratings. Personal risks are often rated as lower than general risks as individuals have a tendency to believe that a risk (such as being hit by a car or abusing alcohol) is larger for others than for themselves. The difference between these two types of risk is related to perceived control (Sjöberg 1993). Consequently, these differences between personal and general risk perception are of a general nature and not unique to entrepreneurship and the business setting.

8.5.5 Desire for autonomy

Entrepreneurs have been found to have a high need for autonomy (Sexton and Bowman 1985) and fear of external control (Smith 1967). Entrepreneurs value individualism and freedom (i.e. the possibility to make a difference for oneself) more than do the general public or managers, even if those values imply some inequalities in society (Fagenson 1993; McGrath, MacMillan and Scheinberg 1992). This desire to manage one's own business is a central feature of entrepreneurship, but it is difficult to explain the causal order. That is, do individuals with a high desire for autonomy start a venture because they want autonomy, or do they want autonomy because they do not want others to take control of what they have created? Differently stated, desire for autonomy can result in venture creation, but can also be a result of having created a business.

8.5.6 The dark side of entrepreneurship

Any review of the psychological approach would be incomplete without mentioning the contribution of Kets de Vries (1977) on the dark side of the entrepreneur. The reason Kets de Vries is included in this chapter is his psycho-analytic approach to entrepreneurship, despite the fact that the study was undertaken more than 20 years ago. When most researchers see entrepreneurial behaviour as the result of positive characteristics or drives, Kets de Vries takes an opposite standpoint. According to him, entrepreneurial behaviour is the result of negative characteristics and drives and its financial benefits do not always lead to personal satisfaction and happiness. On the contrary, the entrepreneur is 'an anxious individual, a non-conformist poorly organized and not a stranger to self-destructive behaviour' (Kets de Vries 1977: 41).

Furthermore, he suggests that financial success is often followed by personal crises, and even poverty. Basically, what goes up must come down. This behavioural pattern is explained by experiences related to a troublesome and very disturbed childhood where the father is often absent. As a consequence, the entrepreneur becomes a person with low self-esteem and lacks self-critical reflections, always dreaming of becoming a person in total control and independent of everything and everyone. This would then explain why entrepreneurs become engaged in high-risk situations and choose to create their own organisation instead of working within an established one.

144

However, there are doubts about this research. Entrepreneurs are no more troubled than anyone else, and there is substantial evidence that entrepreneurs come from financially and emotionally stable families. For example, a substantial number of studies have pointed out that positive role models – and especially parents – are of central importance for fostering future entrepreneurs (Aldrich, Renzulli and Laughton 1997; Matthews and Moser 1995; Scherer, Brodzinski and Wiebe 1991), which is obviously in conflict with Kets de Vries' study. His main contribution is the acknowledgement that entrepreneurs are not some kind of superhuman heroes, but that they are people like the rest of us with faults and merits, and that their behaviour can be explained by more or less noble goals. Furthermore, Kets de Vries points at the fact that entrepreneurs encounter problems that they cannot solve and that they may therefore fail. Therefore, it is clear that the psychological perspective has been far too interested in success, and that behaviour in crisis and failure situations is an under-researched field.

8.5.7 Summing up individual characteristics of entrepreneurs

A large number of traits or characteristics have been proposed to describe entrepreneurs. With the exception of the need for achievement, the results have been poor and it has been difficult to link any specific traits to entrepreneurial behaviour. The reasons for this are complex but what can be seen is that these traits now seem to collapse into broader areas – risk-taking, need for achievement, locus of control and over-optimism are all closely related to decision-making under risk. Therefore, those researchers still interested in risk and entrepreneurship tend to rely more and more on cognitive decision theories. However, the problem with such theories is that they do not take into account individual differences, and this is still the main objective of the field. There is still a need to understand why some engage in entrepreneurial behaviour and others not. Cognitive motivation models offer the ability to explain both highly complex behaviour and differences in choices and performances. The next part of this chapter will discuss the most recent advances in the field.

8.6 Cognitive models of entrepreneurial behaviour

There is a need for an understanding on an individual level of the processes leading to entrepreneurial behaviour which has not been met by studies of individual traits. Research, as stated earlier, has evolved towards more integrated and complex models that take into account not only psychological characteristics of entrepreneurs, but also situational variables and personal background (e.g. age, sex). These models can be divided into two groups depending on their focus. As they are models of human behaviour they overlap, but they focus on different theoretical explanations of human behaviour.

The first group is mainly interested in how our attitudes to entrepreneurship (i.e. starting a business or expanding a business) shape our behaviour. This group is labelled 'attitude-based models'. The second group is concerned with motivation in achievement contexts. That is, why do individuals engage and behave in situations where they have to compete with others and therefore risk failure? This group is labelled 'achievement context models'.

8.6.1 Attitude-based models

Attitude is one of the major concepts in motivation theories. An attitude is a valuation of an object or a concept, i.e. the extent to which an object or concept is judged as good or bad (Eagly and Chaiken 1993). In psychological language, traits such as 'locus of control' or 'over-optimism' are distal, i.e. weak determinants of specific behaviours. Attitudes on the other hand are proximal, i.e. more specific, and because of their specificity, they are considered to be important determinants of behaviour. Furthermore, attitudes are interesting because of their applied relevance. It is believed that attitudes have an impact on behaviour; it is therefore interesting to understand how attitudes can be changed. Consequently, the impact of attitudes on entrepreneurial behaviour is worthy of closer examination because they are supposed to have a directive influence on behaviour and are much easier to change than personality and other, more distal traits or characteristics. This would mean that if the attitudes characterising entrepreneurs starting a new business were known, other people could be influenced to adopt these attitudes and, as a result, increase the number of people starting a business.

The drawbacks concern the accuracy of attitudes in actually predicting behaviours and explaining when or why a specific action is engaged. The importance of attitudes in predicting behaviour has been much debated, but recent research has now shown that attitudes can predict behaviour if certain conditions are met (Bagozzi and Warshaw 1992; Doll and Ajzen 1992; Kim and Hunter 1993). Attitudes are tendencies or dispositions to behave in a generally favourable or unfavourable way toward the object of the attitude. For example, this means that it is difficult to say if a person *will* start a business just because his or her attitudes are positive to the act of starting a business. It is only known that this person will act in a way that is in accordance with his or her attitudes. In this example, it means that this person will behave favourably to everything that is connected to business start-ups, such as encouraging a friend or relative to start a business, financing a start-up effort, or even individually establishing their own business. A shortcoming of attitude theories is that they give no information about how an individual's evaluations of a concept are translated into action and outcomes. Differently stated, attitude theories help us understand how choices are made and why, but they give little guidance about the chosen level of effort and persistence (Locke 1991).

Nevertheless, the advantages override the disadvantages. The possibility to examine closely attitudes towards different facets of entrepreneurship and the ability to communicate the results easily to a wider audience (such as policy-makers) are strong arguments. Furthermore, even if attitudes are not perfect predictors of behaviours, they are still much better than distal personality characteristics. As a consequence, attitude theories have received a fair share of attention within the field of entrepreneurship. Two attitude concepts have been predominantly researched, namely attitudes to becoming self-employed or starting a business, and attitudes to business growth. The research around these concepts is based either on formal attitude theory or on finding simple relationships among attitudes and the concept. The model most used is Ajzen's (1991) theory of planned behaviour, or adapted versions of it. Researchers such as Krueger and colleagues (Krueger and Brazeal 1994; Krueger and Carsrud 1993) have proposed the theory as a possible venue for explaining entrepreneurial behaviour, and especially the engagement in the start-up of a business.

The purpose of the theory of planned behaviour is to explain behaviour when a person is not acting under complete behavioural control – that is, when actions are dependent on something or someone else outside one's control. Starting a business is an example of when actions are dependent on necessary resources and knowing the right people. The basic assumption is that people carefully assess the information they have about the behaviour and form beliefs about it, and then try to act in accordance with these beliefs or attitudes. The theory postulates that the tendency to engage in a particular behaviour is determined by the individual's intention to do so. These behavioural intentions mediate the effect of attitudes on behaviour (Ajzen 1995). This means that a person will start a business if they have:

- enough information to form an opinion;
- an opinion favourable to the behaviour of starting a business;
- the intention to start a business.

Thus, behaviour is determined directly by one's intention to act, and intention in turn is influenced by attitudes. This is the first factor of the theory of planned behaviour.

The second factor is subjective or social norms which, in combination with attitudes toward the behaviour, determine intention and consequently actual behaviour. Social norms as a concept are defined as the perceived social pressures (what others think the individual should do) to perform or not to perform the behaviour (Bagozzi and Kimmel 1995). To continue the business start-up example, this means that a person will only try to start a business if s/he feels that people around him or her encourage or support that kind of behaviour.

However, these two factors (attitudes and subjective norms) are by themselves not enough to explain why people engage in specific behaviour when it is not under full behavioural control. Hence, a third factor is introduced in order to predict intentions and behaviour, namely perceived behavioural control. This is a concept of central importance for explaining entrepreneurial behaviour and is defined as the perceived ease or difficulty of performing the behaviour. Furthermore, it is supposed to reflect anticipated problems and obstacles as well as past experiences. Assuming somewhat favourable subjective norms and attitudes to a behaviour, a person's intention to perform the behaviour will increase with perceived behavioural control. Furthermore, if perceived behavioural control is in accordance with actual behavioural control, they can help to predict the likelihood that intentions will be realised as behaviour (Ajzen 1991; 1995).

How does this theory then help to better understand entrepreneurial intentions? First of all, it is a theory taking into account the complexity of human behaviour and it points out a central wisdom: 'You are not born an entrepreneur, you are made an entrepreneur'. That is, attitude models such as the theory of planned behaviour give us valuable instruments to understand how to change people's feelings and beliefs towards entrepreneurship, and consequently to create a more supportive environment for entrepreneurship. Thus, the theory of planned behaviour is often cited in entrepreneurship research, but few have actually tested the model. Most research is based only on measurement between the three different factors (attitudes, subjective norms and perceived behavioural control) and intentions. The link between intentions and actual behaviour is still an uncharted area. Nevertheless, valuable results have emerged.

Whether business start-ups (Davidsson 1995; Kolvereid 1996a; 1996b; Krueger 1993) or growth (Davidsson 1989a; Kolvereid 1992; Kolvereid and Bullvag 1996; Wiklund 1998; Wiklund, Davidsson, Delmar and Aronsson 1997) are examined, the same results tend to be repeated. Firstly, attitudes have by themselves little ability to predict the intention to expand a business or to start one. Secondly, subjective norms have an even weaker predictive power. What others believe or feel to be important does not particularly affect the entrepreneur's intentions. However, what is important and stands out as the strongest predictor is perceived behavioural control. In other words, people in general are rather positive towards entrepreneurship (starting or expanding a business), which means that perceived behavioural control does not discriminate especially well between those that engage in a particular behaviour and those that are just favourable. What stands out instead is whether people feel that entrepreneurship is a feasible option for themselves. In other words, a person will try to start a business if s/he believes that s/he can do it in terms of possessing the ability and knowledge required to carry it out. Thus, perceived behavioural control or perceived feasibility is the key component in explaining when a person will engage in entrepreneurial behaviour. Davidsson (1995) studied intentions to start a business amongst people in Sweden and found that men and women differed little in their attitudes, but women were low on perceived behavioural control. This could then explain why women are under-represented among entrepreneurs. They do not have enough confidence in their own ability and in their know-how to start and operate a business, and therefore they abstain from doing so (this will be explored further in Chapter 10).

To sum up, research on attitudes and entrepreneurship has yielded consistent findings. A number of studies found that perceived behavioural control was the single most important predictor of intentions. Both attitudes and subjective norms played a relatively minor role. However, attitude models such as the theory of planned behaviour offer little information as to how and why a certain behaviour is chosen by an individual.

8.6.2 Cognitive motivation models and entrepreneurship

This next section will review two cognitive motivation models of human behaviour and how they have been applied to the field of entrepreneurship. The common denominator of these models and the one presented above is the search for control. That is, individuals try to organise their lives in ways that give a level of perceived control. However, the following two models go a step further by incorporating moods and emotions. The theory of planned behaviour is concerned with preferences (what is and what is not important) rather than emotions (what we find enjoyable, boring or stressful to do), but human behaviour is dictated to a large extent by our moods and feelings. Furthermore, these models deal with both behaviour and actual performance. Therefore they are referred to as 'achievement context models'.

Perceived self-efficacy

It was seen above that perceived behavioural control is an important determinant of entrepreneurial behaviour. A closely related concept is the concept of perceived self-efficacy. It is a concept 'concerned with people's beliefs about their capabilities to produce performances that influence events affecting their lives' (Bandura 1995: 434). In other words, it is about a person's beliefs in his or her capabilities to mobilise the motivation, cognitive resources and courses of action needed to control events in his or her life. Hence, it is concerned with how individuals' beliefs about their own capabilities shape the perceived control of their levels of functioning and over the events of their lives. A person's beliefs in his or her efficacy influence the decisions s/he makes, the level of aspirations, how much effort is mobilised in a given situation, how long s/he persists at the task in the face of difficulties and setbacks, and whether his or her thought patterns are self-hindering or self-aiding.

Perceived self-efficacy has been proposed as a central concept in entrepreneurship (Boyd and Vozikis 1994) because it is proximal in nature and has been proven to be associated with initiating and persisting in achievement-related behaviours, such as in business settings (Wood and Bandura 1989). The perceived self-efficacy of entrepreneurs has been proven to affect the strategies and performance of their businesses (Westerberg 1998), and it was found that entrepreneurs high in perceived self-efficacy in general achieved a higher performance for their firms than those low in perceived self-efficacy. Performance was here measured as profitability, customer satisfaction and ability to survive. Perceived self-efficacy is also positively related to the intention of starting one's own business and exploring new opportunities (Chen, Gene Greene and Crick 1998; Krueger and Dickson 1993; 1994).

The roots of self-efficacy can be traced back to the concept of locus of control discussed earlier – although there is one large difference. Whilst an individual's self-efficacy depends on the situation, locus of control can be seen as generalised self-efficacy. In other words, self-efficacy is closely related to a situation or to an object, which means that we can have high self-efficacy in one situation and low self-efficacy in another. For example, individuals may perceive themselves as highly capable rock climbers, but with low capabilities in business matters, even if the two situations involve considerable risk-taking.

Furthermore, perceived self-efficacy is part of a larger theory called the social cognitive theory of self-regulation (Bandura 1986; 1991; Wood and Bandura 1989). The aim of this theory is to explain goal-directed behaviour and it assumes that most behaviours have a purpose regulated by forethought. More precisely, individuals tend to form beliefs about what they can do, they anticipate the likely consequences of prospective actions, they set goals for themselves, and plan courses of action that are likely to produce the desired outcome. In this theory, perceived self-efficacy is one of the most central mechanisms as it is the key to understanding how individuals function when setting up goals and carrying out the actions needed to fulfil them. In comparison to the theory of planned behaviour (which focuses on predicting behaviour), it is more relevant for explaining the functioning of perceived control and its effect on both behaviour and performance.

People with a high level of self-efficacy (i.e. with high assurance in their capabilities) approach difficult tasks as challenges to be mastered rather than issues to be avoided. They set themselves challenging goals and maintain strong commitment to them. They are persistent even in the face of failure, and they maintain an analytical distance that guides effective performance. They also tend to attribute failure to insufficient effort and poor knowledge. On the other hand, people with a low level of self-efficacy shy away from difficult tasks, which are perceived as personal threats. They have a low level of aspiration and commitment to the goals they have chosen to pursue, do not maintain any analytical focus, and they give up easily. Failure is attributed to external obstacles and personal deficiencies. As a consequence they rapidly lose faith in their own capabilities. A person's level of self-efficacy is often the result of previous successful or unsuccessful experiences (either personal experiences or those of role models). Therefore, self-efficacy has the tendency to form the pattern of a positive or negative circle – success breeds success and failure breeds failure. In other words, if one has observed successful entrepreneurs or had personal positive experience there is a high probability that one might engage in the same behaviour again and be successful in it again. In the same manner, a person with low self-efficacy will not tend to engage in a specific behaviour, and if that person does still engage in this behaviour s/he has a high probability of failure. However, a negative pattern due to low self-efficacy can be broken and self-efficacy enhanced through proper training (Bandura 1986; Westerberg 1998).

To conclude, self-efficacy is related to perceived behavioural control, but the concept focuses more on the actual functioning of perceived capabilities: that is, how belief in one's capabilities to mobilise the motivation, cognitive resources and courses of action needed to control events in one's life (such as starting and managing a business) affect one's behaviour and subsequent performance. The role of self-efficacy has been researched within the field of entrepreneurship and has received support. Self-efficacy is a proximal concept and is closely related to a person's feeling towards a behaviour. This means that self-efficacy is malleable, and (as with the rest of the cognitive models) it means that self-efficacy can be enhanced through proper training. The training and development of cognitive resources such as self-efficacy will be discussed separately when the impact of cognitive models on our understanding of entrepreneurial behaviour is summarised. The next model is also related to the relationship between motivation, behaviour and performance, and focuses specifically on one of the positive effects of high self-efficacy: the feeling of intrinsic motivation.

Intrinsic motivation

Intrinsic motivation is closely connected to or even equated with interest and enjoyment. Intrinsic motivation is often determined as an action engaged for its own sake, contrary to extrinsic motivation where external motivators play a central role to motivate behaviour (e.g. acting to get a reward, and not because the task itself is attractive) (Amabile, Hill, Hennesey and Tighe 1994; Deci 1992b). In other words, intrinsically motivated behaviours are ones for which there is no apparent reward except for the activity itself. On the other hand, extrinsically motivated behaviours refer to those behaviours where an external controlling variable can be readily identified by the persons acting. People focusing more on behaviours for their extrinsic benefits tend to perform less well than those who focus on behaviours for their intrinsic benefits. Compared to perceived self-efficacy which focuses on one's representation of capabilities and control of behaviour, theories of intrinsic motivation focus on one's representation of what one finds enjoyable (and self-fulfilling) and control of behaviour. However, these are different aspects of the same coin, and Bandura (1991; 1995) points out himself that intrinsic motivation is both an antecedent and a consequence of high self-efficacy.

Theories about intrinsic motivation or task interests have the capacity to integrate attitudes, goals and emotions. Interest is closely connected to the emotion of enjoyment, and it is an important factor in achievement settings. Attitudes differ from interests, where the latter refers to what the individual likes/dislikes and the former to what the individual finds important/unimportant. Thus, certain events can be considered important, but not interesting, and vice versa. Together, attitudes and interests can be assumed to form a set of preferences that guides our choices between different alternatives in decision-making. Preferences are used when, through rank-ordering, assessments are made of the alternatives in choice situations. Interests, attitudes, and preferences therefore reflect the emotional value of the cognitive representations of reality.

Interest functions primarily as an important positive emotion motivating cognitive and motor search and exploratory behaviour, and is a significant determinant of selective attention and hence of the contents of perception and cognition. It determines not only the choices made, but also the intensity and strength of an experience. The direction of interest is highly personal and varies strongly between different individuals. It probably has its background in personal development, and is connected to an inborn ability and sensitivity and the possibilities and support given by the environment. Interest is a function of challenge and ability, which in its turn determines what is a moderately difficult challenge. It is therefore important that the challenge can stimulate a person to an activity where the individual has a good chance, but is not certain to succeed. Interest is also a prerequisite condition for a really creative contribution, as creativity on a high level demands great devotion to a certain kind of activity which one may be unwilling to undertake if one does not feel great interest (Csikszentmihalyi 1992; Izard 1984).

Task or job interests have been shown to predict entrepreneurial behaviour (measured as business growth and profitability) and how it is manifested (Delmar 1996). Interest plays a central role in entrepreneurial behaviour as it is closely connected to central entrepreneurial concepts such as achievement, autonomy and creation. Interest can also be assumed to be central to the entrepreneurial process, since an entrepreneur has, in some sense, to be interested in (or attracted to) some aspect of entrepreneurship. The entrepreneur's interests are important because they are related to which goals are chosen and how much effort will be made in order to achieve them.

The relation between goal-setting and interest and enjoyment is based on the fact that when people are engaged in interesting activities, they often have goals they want to accomplish (Elliot and Harackiewicz 1994; Epstein and Harackiewicz 1992; Harackiewicz and Elliot 1993). For example, an entrepreneur might start a business to expand into a larger business, find a pleasurable professional activity, or escape unemployment. An entrepreneur may generate such goals on their own, or the goals may be implicit in a particular situation. An achievement-orientated entrepreneur may strive to expand the venture in any situation, or the situation itself may be structured to elicit achievement (e.g. a highly competitive industry, such as the computer hardware industry). These goals could also be influenced by other people – family, friends or capital providers who try to prompt the adoption of particular goals for performance. What is important is that when the entrepreneur's personal interests coincide with business goals such as expansion, the entrepreneur becomes more effective and successful in operating the business.

To sum up, the emotion of interest and its effect on entrepreneurial behaviour has been discussed. It was found that an entrepreneur's task interest (i.e. what kind of task s/he most enjoys working at) affected the development of the business, measured in terms of profitability and growth. Entrepreneurs more interested in marketing-related questions were more growth-oriented and had more profitable businesses. The explanation is that interest is a significant determinant of selective attention and hence of the contents of perception and cognition. Thus, when the entrepreneur's interest coincides with achievement goals such as business profitability and growth, s/he will have an easier and more enjoyable time, and behave in a way that results in higher performance compared with entrepreneurs not interested in the same things. In short, interest leads to higher attention, better decision-making and a feeling of enjoyment.

8.6.3 Summing up cognitive models

This section has reviewed three different cognitive models or concepts (attitude models, perceived self-efficacy and intrinsic motivation) that have greatly enhanced our understanding of entrepreneurial behaviour. The theoretical value of cognitive models is that they offer a sophisticated theoretical frame of reference which incorporates the complexity of entrepreneurial behaviour, and enables the actual test of the model. They are, in nature, more proximal than the more distal traits or personality characteristics. This leads to a higher explanatory power as we have to get closer to the core of entrepreneurial behaviour. Finally, research can offer better explanations on how entrepreneurs behave because we are focusing on their cognition, i.e. how they organise and come to understand the information around them. This also leads to a number of practical consequences.

By focusing more on how people think and react than on who they are, there has been a shift in attention from stable traits that are not easily changeable, to more flexible cognitive processes. Thus the practical value of this research is that an understanding has been reached of how people become entrepreneurs, and this knowledge can be used to educate and train potential entrepreneurs. That is, in order to develop an environment where more businesses are created and expanded we need to have favourable attitudes and feelings towards this objective. However, what leads to actual behaviour is individuals' feelings of control and their enjoyment of what they are doing. More precisely, an individual will engage in an entrepreneurial act if s/he believes that s/he knows how to do it and that such behaviour is intrinsically rewarding. This knowledge and feeling can, according to Bandura (1995), be obtained in four different ways:

- mastery experiences – personal experience;
- vicarious experiences – experience by observing others;
- social persuasion;
- reduction of negative emotions towards the behaviour.

Mastery of experience is the most effective way of accomplishing a high feeling of control. The reason is that personal experience offers the authentic evidence that one can muster what it takes to succeed. Successes tend to build a strong belief in one's personal capabilities, and failures tend to undermine it, especially if they occur before a strong sense of one's capabilities has been rooted. The second way of creating and enhancing beliefs of capability and control is through vicarious experiences observing role models. Seeing people similar to oneself succeed by sustained effort raises an individual's beliefs about his or her own capabilities; observing others fail despite high effort lowers an individual's beliefs about his or her own capabilities. For the experience to be effective, it is important that the individual can identify him or herself with the role model. A third way – but less effective than the two previous ones – is through social persuasion (i.e. convincing people that they have what it takes to succeed). The last way of modifying people's feeling of control towards a specific behaviour is to reduce the negative emotions such as stress and anxiety. The reason is that people rely to a large extent on their somatic and emotional state (such as having a gut feeling, nervousness, fatigue) in judging their capabilities. As a result, negative feelings are interpreted as meaning low capabilities.

Hence, it can be concluded that cognitive models such as the one presented here have several advantages compared to previous trait-based models. Instead of talking about a set of non-changeable traits, cognitive functions that can be altered should be discussed. Cognitive models both possess greater power to explain entrepreneurial behaviour and offer practical advice on how to train and educate future entrepreneurs.

8.7 Chapter summary

In attempting to present a review of research on entrepreneurial personality and behaviour this chapter has been divided into three major parts. The first part covered the development of the field up to the present, whilst the second part examined the early research related to traits and personality characteristics that dominated the field for a long time. Due to the inability to explain entrepreneurial behaviour, this was abandoned in favour of more complex models taking into account the situation and the person's perception of the situation; these are known as cognitive models.

The development of the field from individual trait theories to cognitive models also represents a shift in how entrepreneurial behaviour can be understood and how knowledge can be utilised. Traits are supposedly stable over time, and can only offer grounds for selection of potential entrepreneurs. Cognitive models (such as those reviewed here) conceive human behaviour as directed by goals and motivation and perception of control. As a consequence, their practical value is that they are better at explaining entrepreneurial behaviour and can create instruments to better educate and train potential entrepreneurs.

However, the careful reader will notice that relatively little research has been undertaken using models based on cognitive theories. There have been several conceptual papers advocating cognitive theories, but little empirical research has actually been carried out whereby different models have been systematically tested. Hence, much more work is still needed in order to fully understand the complexity of entrepreneurial behaviour.

Questions

1 Discuss the trait approach to the entrepreneurial personality and the reasons why it fails to properly predict the behaviour of entrepreneurs.

2 Discuss the differences between the major theoretical schools of the psychology of the entrepreneur.

3 What are the theoretical and practical advantages of the cognitive model in describing the behaviour of entrepreneurs?

CHAPTER 9

Family and enterprise

Denise Fletcher

9.1 Learning objectives

There are five learning objectives in this chapter:

1 To enable identification and analysis of the key antecedents shaping definitions and studies of the family firm.
2 To enable students to 'map' their way through the literature.
3 To critically evaluate the different approaches which can be adopted to study the relationship between organisation of the small-business workplace and family issues.
4 To introduce an interpretive view of 'family' and provoke discussion on the ways in which this contributes to an understanding of family and enterprise.
5 To encourage reflection and discussion on how one might investigate the dynamics of family issues and their impact on the organisation of the small-business workplace.

Key concepts
■ family business ■ workplace ■ social embeddedness ■ interpretive relationships

9.2 Introduction

This chapter is concerned with examining the relationship between the concept of 'family' and organisation of the small-business workplace. In reviewing the relevant literature definitional issues are outlined and a broader view of 'family and enterprise' is proposed. As such, a stronger link is made between the dynamics of family and the workplace. It is also suggested that the rationalist assumptions which pervade family business writing and encourage a polarised view of the 'family' and 'enterprise' need to be seriously re-evaluated. Attention is drawn to sociological, anthropological and business history accounts in order to highlight how a singular focus on the 'family business' limits understanding of the dynamics shaping family and workplace issues. At the same time, alternative perspectives also emphasise how small-business enterprise is embedded within a broader social context incorporating family, kinship and personal relations. A 'social embeddedness' perspective, it is suggested, enhances understanding and knowledge of the processes through which small-business principles and practices are enacted within the enterprise. An interpretive approach which highlights how the concept of 'family' is interpreted, understood and 'drawn upon' by individuals working within the small business is also proposed. Finally, it is concluded that an interpretivist view of 'family' provides for dynamic modes of understanding of the ways in which meanings of 'family' are managed, worked and aligned to shape principles, practices and strategies within the small-business enterprise.

9.3 Family and enterprise

This chapter is concerned with examining the relationship between the concept of 'family' and organisation of the small-business workplace. A business and management focus is emphasised. However, other perspectives are drawn into the discussion in order to provide for more sophisticated insights into the relationship between family issues and smaller workplace organisation. The discussion begins by examining definitional issues of family enterprises. This is followed by a critical review of the dominant approaches and antecedents shaping studies of the family business. It is shown how a rational, 'scientific management' perspective has dominated studies of the family firm whereby attempts are made to separate the family and business elements of enterprise so as to achieve organisational efficiency and effectiveness. Reference is made to business history, anthropological and sociological accounts of family enterprises in order to show that historically there is a strong link between family and organisation of the workplace and that by acknowledging (rather than ignoring) this link much deeper insights and understanding of the small enterprise can be achieved. The chapter concludes by presenting an interpretive and social constructionist view of 'family'. This perspective builds on Bourdieu's (1996) view of family as a 'realised category' whereby the concept of family becomes a means through which individuals working in small organisations use the term to help them 'make the reality that they describe' (Bourdieu 1996: 21). Attention is drawn to how concepts and interpretations of 'family' emerge within the smaller enterprise.

9.4 Defining the family firm

In business and management studies the relationship between family and the workplace is usually examined in the context of businesses traditionally defined as 'family firms'. It is estimated that family businesses (large and small) comprise 75% of all businesses in the UK and a substantial literature has evolved over the last 30–40 years concerned with the 'specialness' and 'distinctiveness' of family firms. Many articles have appeared in the mainly US-dominated family business literature concerned with examining strategic issues and dynamics which characterise family firms. For example, many studies have identified the characteristics and processes that strongly differentiate family from non-family firms (Daily and Dollinger 1993; Poutziouris and Chittenden 1996; Westhead 1997). Such studies necessitate clear and concise classifications and definitions of the 'family firm'. The ambiguity and lack of consensus on precise classificatory schemes of what constitutes a family firm perhaps provides some explanation for the contradictory evidence on the performance of family as opposed to non-family firms. For example, previous research between BDO Stoy Hayward and BBC Business Matters in 1992 (see Leach 1994: 11) showed that family firms considerably outperformed non-family firms. However, Poutziouris and Chittenden (1996) and Westhead and Storey (1997) demonstrated that there was no significant difference (statistically and qualitatively) in the performance and effectiveness of family and non-family firms. However, Westhead and Storey (1997) found that there were some differences in the quality of management.

As with studies of small firms, definitions of the family business are also very difficult to reach. However, in studies or research where a strict classificatory scheme is required (for example when comparing matched samples of family versus non-family firms) then clear definitions are crucial. Many studies have focused on this issue. Holland and Boulton (1984: 16) conclude: 'the monolithic concept of "family business" does not adequately describe the complexity of the institution as it exists currently'. They argue that the family–business relationship changes according to the structure and size of the business. They attempt to delineate between the husband-wife and large family business and also make a distinction based on the participation of family members in ownership and day-to-day management (i.e. pre-family, family, adaptive family, post-family). Also, Gersick *et al.* (1997) take this view forward and propose a three-dimensional view of the family firm which takes account of the position of a company in terms of family, ownership and business life-cycles. This framework, they propose, acknowledges the complexity of family firms in their different guises, emphasising said complexity as family firms move through ownership, management and business life-cycles.

Westhead and Storey (1997) also present a useful classificatory scheme for defining the family firm. They propose that family firms conform to three of the following four criteria: those having undergone an inter-generation transition; those having more than 50% of shareholding owned by family group and/or those companies where more than 50% of family members are involved in day-to-day management; and finally where the company speaks of itself as a family firm. This classificatory scheme is considerably more rigorous than the view that family firms include all those organisations involving family members and relationships (Leach 1994) and is particularly useful when conducting studies evaluating the performance of family as opposed to non-family firms. Although it is interesting to note that in Poutziouris and Chittenden's (1996) representative study of the small-business sector, only 25% of firms had more than one generation of family members and 29% of firms were husband/wife teams, it could be argued that the inter-generational transition element is the ultimate challenge and defining feature of the family firm.

The framework presented by Litz (1995) also provides a comprehensive categorisation of different types of family firm. Building on Barry's (1989) categorisations, he identifies nine categories of family firms derived from two structural considerations: ownership and managerial control. Within his typology three categories are identified as family firms. The first type is a more 'pure' definition: firms involving family members in both ownership and management of the company. Other categories include those firms with non-family ownership but with family managers involved in day-to-day management (for example a first-generation company preparing for succession). Thirdly, other categories include the family business that has gone public but where family members are still in senior management positions. What is particularly useful about this typology is that rather than 'fit' family firms into one category, Litz suggests a range of different types of family firm acknowledging that their ownership/management structure is not static and can evolve from one 'type' to another. Litz suggests, therefore, focusing on the 'intentionality' within the business (i.e. to become, remain, erode or displace the family). This framework considerably pushes forward the debate about what constitutes a family firm. It avoids a static perspective of the family firm and furthermore provides a framework for analysing the role of family relationships at different levels and stages within large and small organisations.

In proposing a much broader framework encompassing firms which are becoming, retaining or eroding the family element, this acknowledges that many firms constitute 'family' firms in one way or another. Depending on the aims of the research, a broader view of the family firm is useful in that it emphasises the decision-making, strategic and emotional processes through which family members are brought in/bought out of the company. Broader definitions also facilitate study and analysis of how, for example, small organisations move from one single entrepreneur or husband/wife team to collective family management, and the problems, obstacles and opportunities involved in that process.

Having discussed the definitional issues surrounding the family enterprise, we shall now conduct a review of the literature linking family issues and organisation of the workplace. This is addressed in terms of the approaches and antecedents shaping studies of family and its link with enterprise.

9.5 Approaches and antecedents in studies of family business

In an insightful article, Kanter (1989b) undertakes a critical review of work and family where she examines the link between family and economic life. She argues that the intersections of the institutions of 'economy' and 'family' as 'connected organisers of experience and systems of social relations, are virtually ignored'. Kanter argues that in pre-industrial societies 'family' and 'working' life were highly integrated and the family unit was seen as important for imposing some control over daily tasks. 'The family was an important work unit in city factories in England ... spinners in textile mills chose their wives, children and near relatives as assistants ... children entering the factory at eight or nine worked for their fathers, perpetuating the old system of authority and the traditional values of parents training children for occupations ... it was the family system that made possible the transition from pre-industrial to industrial ways of life' (Kanter 1989b: 79–80, referring to the work of Hareven 1975 and Nelson 1975).

In highlighting that family and work were so intertwined in pre-industrial societies, this infers that close links between the management of work and family evolve naturally as part of daily family and work life. In this sense it is possible to argue that a close link between family and work life does not constitute a 'special' or unique focus of analysis (as many family business studies would claim). However, the separation of family issues from business or work life does.

It was in the early part of the industrial revolution that Kanter (1989b) suggests capitalist owners found it in their interest to break the family's control over work and workers. The need for loyalty from workers and their family networks became less important to employers. At the same time, as industrial capitalism grew and firms became larger, with work becoming less craft-like and more mechanised, and with better-trained workforces and the growth pattern of cities, Kanter (1989b) argues that the worlds of work and family came to be separated. This, she suggests, had important implications for the movement towards systematic or scientific management in that family influence and control were seen as best isolated from the workplace. This way of thinking, Kanter continues, began to influence organisational practices and became more formalised in organisational anti-nepotism laws.

The importance of outlining the historical context against which to review the development of family business studies is that it provides some explanation as to why, in the early family business literature, the family and its role in business were seen in a negative light. Family ties and emotional issues were seen to compete with the demands of the organisation, and commitment to family clashed with the ability to be loyal, efficient and totally committed to the work organisation. As a result, therefore, early studies of family businesses (Donnelley 1964) tend to be highly normative, attempting to prescribe how the emotional issues involved in running a family business could be smoothed away by preventive or corrective strategies. Attempting to separate the 'family' from the 'business' issues was espoused as the guiding principle for developing a successful business. Thus, the dominant approach adopted for studying the family firm was to view the 'family' and the 'business' as two 'systems' competing for power and control within the organisation. These 'rational' and 'systems' views of business, which are relevant to organisation studies more widely, are discussed now in the context of family business studies.

The rational approach, according to Hollander and Elman (1988), sees two organisations co-existing within the family business – the family, non-rational component and the business, rational component – and when the two parts clash the 'business' side (i.e. structure, functions, purpose) loses out to the power, sentiment and emotional issues of the family. They suggest that early writers on family business (Calder 1961; Donnelley 1964; Boswell 1973) 'lamented the fact that family firms were not operated in a more "business-like" way ... and therefore the solution was to excise the family' (Hollander and Elman 1988: 146). Issues such as kinship ties, nepotism, hereditary management and emotionalism were seen to have a detrimental effect on the company in that the needs, goals and demands of the 'family' conflicted with the needs, goals and demands of the 'business'. The desire by early writers to increase rationality within the family business gave rise to the 'business' and the 'family' being separated as two systems competing with each other inside the firm. As a result, the need to separate and overcome the emotional issues of the family was prescribed in order to sustain a tidy and efficient business.

This is particularly apparent in the many discussions about the various needs of the business: to professionalise the business; to manage succession (Dyer 1989; Fox, Nilikant and Hamilton 1996; Kimhi 1997); to manipulate life-cycle changes (Davis and Stern 1988; Gersick *et al.* 1997); and to encourage entrepreneurialism. The assumption that the family business is not always efficient and entrepreneurial has led to a dualist perspective within family business studies: with the family business placed at one end of a continuum and more entrepreneurial firms at the other. This is epitomised in the most-cited contribution to family business studies (Gartner 1990) in which an attempt is made to set up the 'family business' and 'entrepreneurial business' as domains at each end of a continuum. This has led to the 'family business' and 'entrepreneurial business' being seen as separate but overlapping domains, reflecting the assumption that often in family businesses the family interests may conflict with the interests of the business (Hoy and Verser 1994). In addition, Gibb, Dyer and Handler (1994) examine how family and entrepreneurial dynamics intersect in the life of a small business by analysing the role of the family at each stage of the business cycle. Also Daily and Dollinger (1993) in their findings suggest that small family-managed firms tend to differ from non-family-managed firms, in that family-managed firms tend to be smaller, younger, less formalised and growth oriented, and tend towards the 'defender' strategic typology – i.e. not entrepreneurial. They suggest the need to professionalise those family firms seeking growth opportunities whilst still retaining control by the managing family. Dyer (1989) examines the issues, dilemmas and conflicts of bringing in a professional manager into a family business, arguing that some family businesses need professional management in cases where there is a lack of management skill within the business; when business growth is to be achieved; during succession; in order to change norms and values of business; and to make painful changes that paternalistic orientation (values, leadership and culture) prevents them from doing.

Other approaches to family business studies that have contributed to the view that family firms are special or different from non-family firms are those studies influenced by a 'systems' view. A 'systemised' way of conceptualising the family firm is concerned with understanding the interrelationships of the different components which comprise the business. Aspects of the marketplace, industry, technology, stakeholders, task system, founder and family issues interact to form a 'highly complex, open system of interactive elements' (Hollander and Elman 1988: 157). For example, Beckhard and Dyer (1983) suggest a framework for linking together the business, the founder and the family. The joint system operates according to rules which are derived from the separate components of the system but, at the same time, the conflicting needs and demands of the different components are continuously being adapted to the needs of the whole system (Davis 1983). However, in the case of family businesses where the family is the locus of control and power, family issues are seen to have the effect of disabling the efficient working and balancing of the different components of the system. As a result, boundaries are often drawn around the different components of the system in order to locate problems, which need resolving.

During the 1980s a more developmental view of family firms began to emerge. Kepner (1983), Hollander (1984) and Ward (1987), for example, recognise the separate components of the 'business' and 'family' systems but argue that they are permeable. In this way, family influences are not seen as external to the business system (as in the traditional open systems view discussed above), but instead the family is integral to the efficient working of the business system. This perspective clearly offers an important step forward for developing a theoretical framework for understanding the family business. Also, Hollander (1984) proposes a framework incorporating both systemic and developmental processes within the family firm wherein she emphasises the interdependency and permeability of business, family and environmental components.

However, the predominance of a 'systems' view of family businesses still pervades theorising in this area, which limits the opportunity to open up new theoretical perspectives. This weakness was alluded to by Wortman (1994) where he undertakes a comprehensive systematic review of the theoretical foundations for family-owned businesses but concludes that there is no 'unified paradigm for the field'. He argues that many conceptual models have been proposed but that researchers have tended to focus on narrow segments of the field. He goes on to argue that 'too many "armchair articles" have been written and could be characterised as one-time experiences, folklore and stories' (Wortman, 1994: 3). Also, much of the earlier work (Donnelley 1964) tends to be highly descriptive and anecdotal in style, although providing many good examples of the disadvantages and advantages faced by family firms. What is needed then, in order to enhance understanding of the relationship between family and enterprise, is an alternative perspective, which brings together (rather than separates) family issues and the workplace.

9.6 'Family' and 'enterprise'

Riordan and Riordan (1993) are critical of the 'systems' view for its separation of the business/family systems and for the lack of attention given to the human element, the discretion possessed by key decision-makers and how values, beliefs and ideologies may influence decisions. Also the systems view ignores the potential 'ability of the owner/ manager to allocate resources in non-economic ways to fulfil personal family goals' (Riordan and Riordan 1993: 76). Instead they propose the alternative of 'field theory' which focuses on the psychological forces in the life space of the owner-manager. In addition, Daily and Dollinger (1993) offer the alternative of 'agency theory' as a way of attempting to distinguish between family and non-family management styles.

Furthermore, Kepner (1983) argues that whilst the systemic perspective provides some useful ways of conceptualising the family firm, she is also critical of existing models in that they encourage dualism and polarity (i.e. business vs family) and obstruct understanding of their relationship. She suggests the need to look at a co-evolutionary perspective of family/firm as an interactive relationship between family and enterprise. She also makes the important point that the perspective of most family business research is to consider the 'business as family' and she argues for another perspective: 'the family as business'. McCollom (1992) also explores how the family system can perform a key integrating role for the business which at the same time meets the needs of the family. She argues that intervention in family firms without understanding the interdependencies between family and business systems can be dangerous. She sees the relationship as a dynamic one in terms of dominant–subordinate positions (with the family goals as dominant). Emphasising 'the family as business' and focusing on the dynamic relationship between the aspects of family and enterprise provides a valuable framework for examining the relationship between family and enterprise.

The argument that there is a strong relationship between family issues and the organisation of the workplace is not a new one, and many studies have examined this link. However, studies with this emphasis tend to be derived from sociological and anthropological perspectives. For example, many studies emerge in the form of business history accounts of family firms and industries (Hareven 1975; Nelson 1975;

Kanter 1989b; Crossick *et al.* 1996; Grell and Woolf 1996; Muller 1996; Cookson 1997). Also, other studies focus on regions or industries of Europe where family ties and networks have an important regional economic development potential (Lombardini 1996; Muller 1996; Weidenbaum 1996; Brogger and Gilmore 1997; Heuberger and Gutwein 1997). Furthermore, discussed in terms of social capital, gender and family (Whatmore 1991; Rosa 1993; Stafford 1995; Salaff and Hu 1996), other accounts emphasise the important role of women's emotional labour in facilitating enterprise development and also ethnic or immigrant labour (Ram 1994b; Sanders and Nee 1996). Further studies put greater emphasis on the sociology of family, farming and household labour (Whatmore 1991). Finally, industrial sociologists focus on studies of the small-business workplace whereby leadership styles, co-ordinating mechanisms, control strategies (paternal, autocratic and fraternal), job satisfaction, attitudes in the workplace, the employment relationship and the patterning of social relations through feelings of family are closely examined (cf. Newby 1977; Curran and Stanworth 1979a, 1979b, 1981a and 1981b; Rainnie 1989; Scott *et al.* 1989; Ram 1991, 1994a and 1994b; Wheelock 1991; Holliday 1995; Scase 1995).

The important contribution of these studies is their acknowledgement of the embeddedness of small enterprises within a broader social context incorporating family networks and relationships. Writers within the traditional family business literature have been slow to respond to arguments of social embeddedness (Granovetter 1985; Grabher 1993) and are limited in their adherence to rationalist assumptions about the separation of family from business life. As can be seen from the wide range of studies cited above, the link between family issues and the workplace is not a new one. Thus, family firms are not so special. Economic growth and vitality of regions/industries thrive on the social capital provided by family labour of one sort or another. The key issue for small-business research therefore is not to prove how and in what way small, family enterprises are special or distinctive but how aspects of family are realised in entrepreneurial and small-business activity over time. In some ways this has been approached through the network literature where social network contacts (including family linkages) are seen as a 'resource' through which small-business owner-managers get access to information, resources and capital (cf. Mitchell 1969; Boissevain 1974; Tichy, Tushman and Fombrun, 1979; Aldrich and Zimmer 1986; Johannisson 1987c; Butler and Hansen 1991; Curran and Blackburn 1991; Larson 1992; Ibarra 1993; Ram 1994b). The socially embedded view of enterprises paves the way for linking enterprise and family more closely. However, further attention needs to be given to the ways in which family issues are realised and shaped within the small enterprise.

9.7 Towards an interpretive view of 'family' and enterprise

During the 1990s, conceptualisations of 'family' and its relationship with 'business' are moving away from closed and non-problematised views of 'family' (Levin 1993). Instead, Levin (1993) conceptualises the family enterprise in terms of 'mapped realities' and argues for the need to accommodate the more complex issues drawn from the everyday experience and interpretations of family as perceived by family (and non-family) members. Also, from the analysis of fieldwork findings from ethnographic research with a small family business in the North-East of England (Fletcher 1997), it is suggested that the dominant view which has traditionally shaped the study of family business – which views the 'family' and 'business' as two 'systems' competing for power and control within the organisation – is inadequate for analysing the complex contradictions and paradoxes which emerge from conversations with individuals working in a family business. As discussed earlier, many solutions are offered by rational views of family business to excise family issues such as kinship ties, nepotism and emotionalism because they are seen to have a detrimental effect on the business (Calder 1961; Donnelley 1964; Boswell 1973). However, from the analysis of family issues and their influence upon 'business' issues, it is almost impossible to excise the values, emotions, ties, ways of working within an organisation which have been shaped by family roles and relationships. Furthermore, once the organisational members have been involved with and had interactions with their colleagues (whether family or not) then knowledge of these past interactions is always there to shape future interactions. So that even if a firm is no longer a family business, there are still values, knowledge, emotions, hurts and disappointments from past relationships which shape current and future relationships. In addition, Ram and Holliday (1993) suggest that the 'family' contains complexities and contradictions, which mean the dynamics at work will be contingent and negotiated, for example, on aspects of race and gender.

McCollom (1992) also offers an insightful article focusing on 'organisational' stories in the family-owned business. In this she attempts to reveal how family and non-family employees experience membership in a family enterprise. Through the use of organisational stories, she is concerned with how people are made aware of the relationship between the 'family' and 'business' in their daily work lives and how this relationship shapes organisational structures and processes. She concludes that in her case study the dynamics of family business are constructed in daily interactions/conversations and this discourse was dominated by family issues (McCollom 1992: 19).

An alternative conceptualisation of the family business which moves away from rigid rational and systematised views and instead develops a more interpretive approach to examine the concept of 'family' as it is interpreted and constructed by those working in the family business (Levin 1993) is much needed in the study of the small enterprise. Gubrium and Holstein (1990: 14-16) suggest that 'family discourse is not just a mode of communication ... it also assigns meaning to the actions we take on behalf of the social ties designated as familial'. These authors distinguish between 'the family' and 'family', arguing that 'the family' is a static description but because family discourse is multidimensional, it is interpretively dynamic and so the concept of 'family' is more useful: 'Family discourse is active. Used in reference to concrete social relations, it communicates how one intends to look at, how one should understand, or what one intends about what is observed.'

Family discourse therefore can be seen as a way of talking about, assigning meaning to, and making sense of relations with others, and this also provides courses of action. As Ram found in his studies (1991, 1994a; Ram and Holliday 1993), meanings are negotiated within the firm. In referring to ethnic minority firms, he suggests that central to the negotiation of racial constraints which characterised the firms within his study, was the role of family. He comments that whilst internally, family relationships were a flexible source of labour and means of imposing managerial discipline, externally, family roles were important for overcoming racial obstacles in the market

(1994b: 51). He goes on to refer to the concept of 'negotiated paternalism' to draw attention to the way in which meanings are 'managed' through social relations within ethnic firms (1991, 1994a).

What is important therefore is not 'what is family' but in what ways 'family' is a linguistic or conceptual resource for specifying individuals' relations with others (Gubrium and Holstein 1990). This perspective is consistent with Bourdieu (1996: 21) where he argues that family is a 'realised category', and understandings and interpretations of 'family' are socially constructed and 'help to make sense of the reality [i.e. the small enterprise] that they describe'. This provides an important way forward for studies examining the link between family and the small-business workplace.

In proposing an interpretive view of family and enterprise, it is also envisaged that 'family' is a useful concept for analysing non-family (as formally defined) small firms. This view is reflected in Holliday and Letherby's (1993) research where they explored the 'familial analogy' in small firms and attempted to understand why people in small firms refer to themselves as 'one big happy family'. Ram and Holliday (1993: 165) also make the important point that 'family' culture is not simply a product of employing family members and that feelings of 'family' can be cultivated without blood ties. Also, as Kepner (1983: 60) suggests, the glue that holds firms together is the 'complicated inter-personal linkages ... the emotional bondings and affectionate ties that develop between and among its members'. However, complex interpersonal linkages, emotional and affectionate ties predominate in all organisations.

However, from case studies based on longitudinal work with family firms, it is possible to argue that in the case of family firms the 'glue' is thicker, in the sense that there are family relationships being played out in the business which have a long history and which have developed outside of the business in childhood and adolescence. Thus, in firms where family relationships dominate there is a longer history and knowledge of shared experiences and past events which converge, albeit subconsciously, to influence and shape current activities, events and relationships (Fletcher 1998). Thus the inter-personal linkages, emotional bondings and affectionate ties that characterise all firms are possibly more complex and embedded in family firms. But this claim has to be supported with much wider comparative research on family and non-family businesses alike.

9.8 Chapter summary

In summary, this chapter has provided a review of the literature linking the family and organisation of the small-business workplace. In discussing typologies of the family firm, it is proposed that a more helpful approach is to examine family firms as they are embedded within and move between different modes of organisation. In emphasising the 'intentionality' within the business family to reinforce, sustain, erode or enlarge the role of family members (or non-family managers) in day-to-day business activities, it is also suggested that the rationalist assumptions which pervade family business writing and encourage a polarised view of the 'family' and 'enterprise' need to be seriously re-evaluated. In reviewing the literature, definitional issues have been outlined and a broader view of 'family and enterprise' is proposed for studies that are not concerned with comparative performance of family vs non-family firms. In proposing a broader view of family and enterprise, a much stronger link can be made between the dynamics of family and the workplace. Attention is also drawn to sociological, anthropological and business history accounts so as to highlight how a singular focus on the 'family business' (as a unit of analysis) limits understanding of the dynamics shaping family and workplace issues. Also, in emphasising studies from different perspectives this encourages a view of the small-business enterprise as embedded within a broader social context incorporating family, kinship and personal relations. A social embeddedness perspective, it is suggested, enhances understanding and knowledge of the processes through which small-business principles and practices are enacted within the enterprise.

This is further taken forward in terms of an interpretive approach which, instead of separating the elements of business and family, proposes a more integrated view. In this way what is important is how the concept of 'family' is interpreted, understood and 'drawn upon' by organisational members. However, this does not mean that the relationship is a static one: it is continually being shaped, modified and aligned by family and non-family members alike. Family, therefore, becomes a concept for exploring the interactivity of its members and the way in which interactions, dialogues and sense-making processes are shaped by organisational relationships. Finally, it is concluded that an interpretivist view of 'family' provides for dynamic modes of understanding of the ways in which meanings of 'family' are managed, worked and aligned to shape principles, practices and strategies within the small-business enterprise.

Questions

1 Summarise the key antecedents shaping definitions and studies of the family firm. Which do you think are the most (or least) useful?

2 Critically evaluate the different approaches that can be adopted to study the relationship between organisation of the small-business workplace and family issues.

3 In what ways do family issues impact (positively and negatively) on the small-business workplace?

4 To what extent does an interpretive view of 'family' contribute to an understanding of family and enterprise?

5 Imagine you are planning a small research project on this topic:
   – List a range of potential key research questions.
   – What key concepts might shape your theoretical framework?
   – How would you design the research (constructing a sample, gaining access/ response rate, building relationships, conducting interviews)?

CHAPTER 10

Gender and enterprise

Sara Carter

10.1 Learning objectives

There are four learning objectives in this chapter:

1 To describe the personal and business characteristics of female entrepreneurs.
2 To understand the main management constraints which female entrepreneurs face.
3 To understand the key differences in the performance of male-owned and female-owned small firms.
4 To understand the historical development of research investigating female entrepreneurship.

Key concepts

■ women ■ motivations ■ management constraints ■ finance ■ performance

10.2 Introduction

Female participation in self-employment and business ownership has grown substantially over the past twenty years. Although women still constitute a minority of business owners, varying from 25% to 35% in most countries, their share of business ownership is growing. Research investigating female experiences of starting and running businesses suggests that, although their motivations are very similar to those of male entrepreneurs, many of the barriers and constraints that they face are gender-specific. This chapter reviews some of the main research studies which have been conducted into female entrepreneurship and highlights the main themes that have emerged. Specific attention is given to the analyses of the motivations and the personal characteristics of female entrepreneurs, the managerial challenges that they face – for example in the area of business financing – and the impact of gender on small-business performance.

10.3 Gender and enterprise

Research investigating women's ownership of small businesses essentially dates from the middle of the 1980s. Prior to the research studies undertaken then, the contribution women made to the small-firms sector either as business owners in their own right, or more commonly as providers of labour to family-owned firms (see Chapter 9), was largely unrecognised. The growth in interest in the small-business sector, coupled with a sharp rise in the number of women moving into self-employment in the 1980s, triggered a number of important research studies investigating the issue of gender and enterprise. Importantly, the growth in the numbers of women entrepreneurs and the subsequent research interest into issues of gender and enterprise were not confined to the UK, but were seen in many developed economies.

This chapter highlights some of the key themes which have emerged from these studies. Following this introduction, the chapter starts by documenting the increase in the numbers of women entering self-employment and business ownership. This is followed by an overview of the early, exploratory research studies which concentrated on profiling the demographic characteristics of female entrepreneurs and describing their motivations. As the research effort became more established, increasing emphasis was placed on broad issues of management in the female-owned businesses, in particular the relative access to finance for female entrepreneurs and the role of networks in enabling business survival and growth. More recent research has focused on developing and improving the methodological basis of the studies, in particular the sampling strategies that are used in gender research. Increasingly, more recent large-scale studies have moved beyond broad issues of management and have attempted to assess the relative performance of female-owned firms. Despite the increased research interest, many believe that the study of female entrepreneurship remains a neglected area (Baker *et al.* 1997). The reasons for this neglect are considered at the end of this chapter, which concludes with an overview of the likely developments for research into this topic.

10.3.1 The growth of female entrepreneurship

The past two decades have seen a profound increase in the number of women entering into self-employment and business ownership. Between 1979 and 1997 the number of self-employed women in the UK increased by 163%, from 319,000 to 840,000. In the same period the number of self-employed males increased by 67%, from 1,449,000 to 2,421,000 (Table 10.1). Although female self-employment has increased at a much faster rate, women still constitute only a minority (26%) of the total self-employed. Although these figures indicate a rapid and dramatic growth in the participation of women in entrepreneurship, more detailed analysis of the Labour Force Survey (1997) suggests that this interpretation should be treated cautiously. In particular, the absolute rise in female self-employment appears to have been largely caused by the overall increase in the number of women in the labour market as a whole (see Chapter 2). The rate of female self-employment has increased less, but is still a substantial growth, from approximately 3.12% of total females economically active in 1979 to 6.76% in 1997. During the same period, the rate of male self-employment increased from 9.27% of total males economically active in 1979 to 15.43% in 1997.

Table 10.1 UK male and female employment and self-employment, 1979–97 (thousands)

Year	Male employee	Male self-employed	% self-employed*	Female employee	Female self-employed	% self-employed*
1979	13,381	1,449	9.27	9,220	319	3.12
1981	12,427	1,753	11.12	9,147	438	4.16
1983	11,672	1,759	11.35	8,774	533	5.07
1984	11,643	1,988	12.65	9,030	619	5.65
1985	11,683	2,039	12.90	9,207	664	5.91
1986	11,583	2,057	13.07	9,399	661	5.79
1987	11,487	2,231	14.11	9,522	727	6.25
1988	11,836	2,375	14.86	9,872	761	6.43
1989	11,984	2,626	16.30	10,285	803	6.62
1990	12,082	2,647	16.39	10,406	824	6.75
1991	11,803	2,535	15.77	10,329	784	6.43
1992	11,363	2,374	14.96	10,214	773	6.36
1993	11,154	2,321	14.79	10,217	788	6.47
1994	11,209	2,414	15.40	10,265	806	6.61
1995	11,380	2,480	15.84	10,357	795	6.52
1996	11,551	2,403	15.34	10,534	810	6.58
1997	11,817	2,421	15.43	10,690	840	6.76

* Self-employed as percentage of total economically active.
Source: Labour Force Survey 1997, Spring Figures, Office for National Statistics © Crown Copyright 1999

Increases in the number of women starting in business have not only occurred in the UK, but have also been seen in many other countries. In Sweden, for example, women represent 23% of all business start-ups and account for around 25% of all private firms in the country (Nilsson 1997), a proportion common to many European states. In the USA, the total number of 'non-farm sole proprietorships' grew from 9.73 million in 1980 to 17.71 million in 1993, the last year for which figures are available – an increase of 82.06% (SBA 1996). In 1980 the number of female-owned businesses in the USA totalled 2.53 million, or 26.1% of the total. By 1993, the number of women-owned businesses had increased to 5.85 million, representing 33% of the total number of businesses (Table 10.2). The growth of female-owned businesses in the USA between 1980 and 1993 increased at a faster rate (130.81%) than for total businesses (82.06%). Carter and Allen (1997: 211) describe a slightly earlier period as demonstrating even faster growth in the proportion of female-owned businesses in the USA: 'Their share of all businesses in the USA grew over 550% between 1972 and 1987 ... and between 1987 and 1992 their number increased by another 125%.'

Table 10.2 The growth of women-owned businesses in the USA, 1980–93

USA total	1980	1993
All non-farm sole proprietorships	9,730,019	17,714,120
Women-owned businesses	2,535,240	5,851,514
Women's share of total	26.1%	33.0%
% change all non-farm businesses		82.06%
% change women's businesses		130.81%

Source: Small Business Administration (1996: 253)

10.4 The characteristics of female entrepreneurs

Until the mid 1980s very little was known about the female entrepreneur. Although a large number of studies had been undertaken investigating small-business owners, the bulk of the work concentrated upon the male-owned enterprise and there was an assumption that patterns of female behaviour conformed to those established using male samples. As Berg (1997: 259) states, theory-building in the area of entrepreneurship has been 'based on studies of men'. In the 1980s, however, there was the start of a new research interest in female-owned enterprise, reflecting both the rise in the number of women starting in business and also increasing academic interest in small business and the nature of entrepreneurship. Influenced by the existing small-business literature, early studies of female entrepreneurship concentrated mainly upon the motivations for business start-up (Schreier 1973; Schwartz 1976; Goffee and Scase 1985b; Hisrich and Brush 1986) and, to a lesser extent, the gender-related barriers experienced during this phase of business ownership (Watkins and Watkins 1984; Hisrich and Brush 1986; Carter and Cannon 1988). In Europe, researchers focused their attention on trying to establish linkages between motivations for female self-employment and the overall position of women in the labour market (Goffee and Scase 1985b; van der Wees and Romijn 1987; Cromie and Hayes 1988; Carter and Cannon 1988). As Berg's (1997: 259) critique highlighted, 'The aim of the majority of the studies [was] ... mainly to make comparisons with male entrepreneurs and to make women entrepreneurs visible.' Overall, these studies presented a *prima facie* picture of businesswomen with more similarities than differences to their male counterparts. Like men, the most frequently cited reason for starting in business was the search for independence and control over one's destiny. The greatest barriers to business formation and success were access to capital and mobilising start-up resources. Few of the early studies developed sophisticated taxonomies, preferring to identify female proprietors as a homogeneous group, and there was an implicit acceptance by researchers that, beyond the start-up phase, few significant differences existed between male- and female-owned and managed companies.

Many of the early studies from North America concentrated on describing the characteristics of female entrepreneurs and their motivations for self-employment. Schreier's (1973) pilot study of female business owners showed that the female entrepreneur had much in common with her male counterpart. One difference, however, which did emerge was in the business sectors in which female entrepreneurs tended to operate. Sectors in which women tended to own businesses reflected those with traditionally high levels of female employment, mainly services and retailing. A study by Schwartz (1976) also described a predominance of service-based businesses and also concluded that female motivations for starting businesses were similar to those of men. This study was, however, perhaps most notable for being the first to draw research attention to some specifically female barriers to business ownership. Schwartz (1976) found that the greatest barriers to female business success were financial discrimination, a lack of training and business knowledge, and generally underestimating the financial and emotional cost of sustaining a business.

Hisrich and Brush (1986) continued these broad, exploratory themes by attempting to draw a demographic profile of female entrepreneurs, and examining their motivations

169

for starting in business and their barriers to business success. Using a sample of 468 women entrepreneurs, the 'typical' female entrepreneur was described as being the 'first born child of middle-class parents ... After obtaining a liberal arts degree, she marries, has children, and works as a teacher, administrator or secretary. Her first business venture in a service area begins after she is thirty-five' (Hisrich and Brush 1986: 14). Motivations for start-up were described as being the search for job satisfaction, independence and achievement, while the major problems facing women were believed to be the initial undercapitalisation of new businesses, and a lack of knowledge and training in business skills. As Hisrich and Brush (1986: 17) described: 'For a woman entrepreneur who lacks experience in executive management, has had limited financial responsibilities, and proposes a nonproprietary product, the task of persuading a loan officer to lend start-up capital is not an easy one. As a result, a woman must often have her husband cosign a note, seek a co-owner, or use personal assets or savings. Many women entrepreneurs feel strongly that they have been discriminated against in this financial area.' Highlighting an issue of female credibility that would recur in several later studies, Hisrich and Brush (1986) also reported that half of their respondents reported difficulties in overcoming some of the social beliefs that women are not as serious as men about business. Their study also found evidence of contrasting experience of women operating in different types of industry sector: women in non-traditionally female sectors experienced greater financial problems, while in both non-traditional and newer sectors – such as computer services – women business owners were hampered by a lack of previous business training. The study concluded that many of the barriers which were experienced by female entrepreneurs related to the sectors in which they operated.

Early British studies also focused on describing the motivations and characteristics of women starting in business. Using a sample which compared the experiences of 58 female and 43 male business owners, Watkins and Watkins (1984) found that the backgrounds and experiences of women differed substantially from those of men. Men entering self-employment were more likely to have prior work experience which was related to their present venture. For them, self-employment provided an essentially similar occupation with the added attraction of independence and autonomy. Conversely, women were found often to have no relevant experience to enable them to enter self-employment, particularly in non-traditional business sectors. Watkins and Watkins (1984) concluded that their lack of prior work experience affected women's choice of establishing viable businesses, forcing them into traditionally female sectors. Within traditional sectors, however, other successful female entrepreneurs acted as role models, helping other women to confront and overcome problems. Watkins and Watkins (1984) found that most women were unprepared for business start-up and, as a consequence and often unwittingly, took greater risks. Choice of business sector for women's self-employment was largely determined by consideration of which areas posed the least obstacles to their success. These were perceived to be those where technical and financial barriers to business entry were low and where managerial experience was not essential to success. As Watkins and Watkins (1986: 230) emphasised in a later article, 'choice of business can be seen in terms of high motivation to immediate independence tempered by economic rationality, rather than by a conscious desire to operate "female-type" businesses'.

In a study undertaken in the same period, Goffee and Scase (1985b) analysed the experiences of 54 female proprietors in the UK. Central to this study was the development of a typology of female entrepreneurs based on two factors: firstly, their relative attachment to conventional entrepreneurial ideals in the form of individualism and self-reliance; and secondly, their willingness to accept conventional gender roles, often subordinate to men. Four types of female entrepreneur emerged in this taxonomy: 'conventional' entrepreneurs who were highly committed to both entrepreneurial ideals and conventional gender roles; 'innovative' entrepreneurs who held a strong belief in entrepreneurial ideals but had a relatively low attachment to conventional gender roles; 'domestic' entrepreneurs who organised their business life around the family situation and believed very strongly in conventional female roles and held low attachment to entrepreneurial ideals; and 'radicals' who held low attachment to both, often organising their businesses on a political, collectivist basis.

In the context of previous research, this study represented a significant advance, not least in highlighting the often-overlooked fact that female entrepreneurs are not a homogeneous group. This typology, however, was also subject to substantial criticism. Allen and Truman (1988) argued that the two factors underpinning the typology were fundamentally inappropriate for the analysis of female entrepreneurial behaviour and, moreover, that the socio-economic reality of women's lives implied that the majority have very little choice over their attachment to either entrepreneurial ideals or conventional gender roles. Carter and Cannon (1992) reiterated these concerns, but also suggested that the typology underestimated two key features of the entrepreneurial process. Firstly, it assumed that the process of business ownership was a static one. In reality, however, business ownership is a dynamic and often turbulent process: businesses expand, contract and diversify. Whilst small firms often remain small, diversity exists within these limits: cottage industries can become stable, thriving firms, self-employed designers can become manufacturers and manufacturers can diversify to produce specialised products. Secondly, the typology underestimated the effect business ownership has on the individual entrepreneurs, many of whom change with experience. Thus, women who may start as 'domestic' entrepreneurs may, by the very experience of business ownership, become dedicated business owners with a very strong attachment to entrepreneurial ideals.

While these early studies provided valuable descriptions of a group of entrepreneurs who had, hitherto, been overlooked by the mainstream small-business research effort, critics of the research drew attention to the exploratory nature of these early studies of female entrepreneurship. Criticism was levelled, in particular, at the small size of the samples used and their lack of representativeness and reliability (Curran 1986b; Carter 1993), the general lack of utility and rigour of the studies (Allen and Truman 1988; Solomon and Fernald 1988; Rosa and Hamilton 1994) and the limited extent of the cumulative knowledge (Stevenson 1983; Curran 1986b; Hamilton *et al.* 1992).

Studies using national data sets, notably Curran and Burrows' (1988b) analysis of the General Household Survey (see also Chapter 2), presented a more accurate demographic profile of female participation in self-employment. While this analysis lacked the depth of insight achieved in many of the smaller-scale, qualitative studies, the importance of the study lay in the challenges that it presented to what were becoming established orthodoxies. Perhaps most interestingly, it pointed out that some of the most notable and newsworthy findings of the smaller-scale studies – such as the claimed incidence of high divorce rates and marital breakdown among female entrepreneurs – were simply the result of sampling bias.

While the use of national data sets, such as the General Household Survey and the Labour Force Survey, would appear to be an appropriate way forward in investigating issues of gender and enterprise, their utility is restricted by the limited depth of the data collected. National data sets can provide no assistance in investigating some of the most interesting and the most controversial of the research themes, such as the existence and extent of female disadvantage in starting and running a business. Neither can they assist in developing an understanding of the processes and practices of gender relations, a prerequisite to the development of theories of gender and enterprise. By the late 1980s it was becoming clear that the research debates surrounding the issue of gender and business ownership were continuing largely because of the difficulties for researchers in providing clear and unequivocal evidence, either through empirical investigation or through more theoretical approaches. While several studies had suggested that it was considerably harder for women to both start and run their own enterprises, others had cited the gender literature to argue that start-up problems tended to be equally great for men, and that many women 'far from being discriminated against, thought that being a woman gave them a positive advantage over men' (Birley 1989: 36).

10.5 The management of female-owned businesses

In an attempt to refocus the research effort away from broad descriptions of the personal and business characteristics of female entrepreneurs, increasing attention was given to the attempt to understand the real nature of management differences in female-owned firms. In the UK, a study was commissioned by the Department of Employment and Shell (UK) Ltd in 1987 in order to develop a greater insight into the management of female-owned businesses (Carter and Cannon 1992). Based on case-study data drawn from seventy female-owned businesses in the UK, the study found that broadly the same operational problems were faced by all business owners, irrespective of sex. Certain specific areas of business ownership were, however, perceived by female business owners as being gender-related: late payment of bills; a tendency to undercharge; getting business and finding clients; and finally, the effect of proprietorship upon personal and domestic circumstances.

The effects of these operational problems and the strategies used to overcome them varied. Women running businesses with only a small capital base were less able to cope with late payments. Lack of assertiveness in collecting debts was perceived by some as a gender-related problem. Similarly, while price-cutting was used by many proprietors as a market entry strategy, for many women undercharging reflected a lack of confidence in both their products and their business skills. Difficulties in accessing start-up capital, coupled with delayed payments and undercharging, were assumed to have an inevitable impact on many companies. Drawing on interview data, the study suggested that the initial undercapitalisation of female-owned businesses had a long-term and deleterious effect on future survival and prospects for growth.

Despite the long-term effects of initial undercapitalisation, many female entrepreneurs stated that issues of employee relations posed the most difficult and intractable of all problems. Even women with previous management experience in larger companies felt a need to learn new skills. Older women were described as often successfully using an overtly matriarchal style, characterised by a unitaristic, family view of employment relations. Younger women, inexperienced in management and lacking the age to develop a credible management style, struggled most.

A substantial minority (40%) of proprietors interviewed for the study believed that aspects of business ownership were more difficult for women, often despite their inability to identify specific areas in which discrimination exists (Carter and Cannon 1992). As in the studies by Stevenson (1983) and Hisrich and Brush (1986), many respondents stated that they had to earn credibility, not just with their customers and suppliers, but also with their employees. Women who have been interviewed for various research studies have stated that problems of credibility are gender-related, and the lack of previous opportunities to develop business skills and knowledge is often given as the key difference between male and female business owners.

More recent studies have continued to explore the issue of management of female-owned businesses, but the field of study has developed to encompass more sophisticated methodologies, larger-scale samples and more robust sampling procedures, in particular the use of both male and female samples. Importantly, the focus of investigation has evolved to concentrate on the effect of gender on both the experience of self-employment and the relative performance of small businesses (Rosa and Hamilton 1994; Rosa et al. 1996; Berg 1997; Carter and Allen 1997; Marlow 1997). Two recurrent themes have emerged from this work. Following work by Buttner and Rosen (1989) and Riding and Swift (1990) in North America, and Fay and Williams (1993) in New Zealand, a major research theme has been the effect of gender differences on business financing (Read 1994; Carter and Rosa 1998). Developments have also been seen in the analysis of female entrepreneurs' use of business networks (Olm et al. 1988; Katz and Williams 1997). Overall, however, increasing theoretical sophistication – and engagement with sociological, geographical and feminist approaches in particular – has produced a more complete picture of female business ownership (Berg 1997). Work by Westwood and Bhachu (1988) and Allen and Truman (1993) has opened up the study of women's enterprise to include insights into race, class and family issues, providing a more nuanced view of women's participation in the small-firms sector. Research from other countries, such as Holmquist and Sundin's (1989) study on Sweden, and Padaki's (1994) and Premchander's (1994) work on India, has provided valuable information from different national and cultural contexts. Despite the relative sophistication of the current work it is, however, still an area notable for its broad neglect, a point strongly made by Baker, Aldrich and Liou (1997).

10.5.1 The financing of female-owned firms

Previous studies into gender and business ownership have resulted in conflicting evidence about whether finance poses problems for women starting and running businesses. Several studies have suggested both that it is more difficult for women to raise start-up and recurrent finance for business ownership and that women encounter credibility problems when dealing with bankers (Schwartz 1976; Hisrich and Brush 1986; Goffee and Scase 1985b; van der Wees and Romijn 1987; Carr 1990; Brush 1992; Carter and Cannon 1992). Other studies have not confirmed this (Buttner and Rosen 1989; Chrisman *et al.* 1990; Riding and Swift 1990). The debate has continued largely because of the difficulties for researchers in providing clear and unequivocal evidence. Four areas of the financing process have, however, been consistently noted as posing particular problems for women. Firstly, women may be disadvantaged in their ability to raise start-up finance (Schwartz 1976; Carter and Cannon 1992; Johnson and Storey 1993; Koper 1993; Van Auken *et al.* 1993). Secondly, guarantees required for external financing may be beyond the scope of most women's personal assets and credit track record (Hisrich and Brush 1986; Riding and Swift 1990). Thirdly, finance for the ongoing business may be less available for female-owned firms than it is for male enterprises, largely due to women's inability to penetrate informal financial networks (Olm *et al.* 1988; Aldrich 1989). Finally, female entrepreneurs' relationships with bankers may suffer because of sexual stereotyping and discrimination (Hisrich and Brush 1986; Buttner and Rosen 1989).

A recent study investigating the impact of gender on small-business management appears to have shed new light on how each of these four issues can be approached methodologically, even though definitive findings have yet to be achieved (Carter and Rosa 1998). Interviews with 600 business owners (300 women and 300 men) operating in three industry sectors (textile manufacturing, business services, and hotel and catering) in two different locations (Scotland and the West Midlands) revealed quantifiable gender differences in certain areas of business financing. Importantly, however, intra-sectoral similarities demonstrated that gender was only one of a number of variables that affect the financing process.

The results confirmed the findings of many previous studies which had suggested that female business owners use substantially less capital at start-up than do male business owners. In total, men used three times more start-up capital than women, and differences in start-up capital were apparent in all three sectors included in the investigation (Table 10.3). Importantly, start-up capital was related positively and significantly to current value of capital assets, sales turnover, total number of employees and number of core full-time employees. It would appear, therefore, that shortfalls in initial capitalisation can set women at a disadvantage in being able to attain growth in their business, and that the extent of this disadvantage may have been underestimated in previous studies. The sources of start-up capital were common to both men and women, however, with greatest use being made of personal and family savings, bank overdrafts and bank loans. Similarly, no significant gender differences were found in the use of guarantees for business financing. An analysis of financial arrangements for the ongoing business revealed both gender and sectoral differences in the sources used for ongoing finance. Men – particularly those in the hotel and catering sector – were more likely to make use of bank loans and overdrafts. Conversely, women were less likely to use institutional arrangements (such as bank loans and overdrafts) and were also less likely to take advantage of cheaper sources, such as extended supplier credit. Relationships with institutional lenders were generally reported as being good, although men operating in business services were more likely to describe their relationship as 'very good' (Carter and Rosa 1998: 237).

Table 10.3 Median starting capital by sex of respondent (nearest £500)

	Women (median) (£)	Men (median) (£)
Textile/clothing	1,000	3,000
Business services	1,000	2,000
Hotel/catering	15,000	25,000
Single owners	2,000	5,500
Multiple owners	3,000	6,000
Total sample	2,000	6,000

Source: Carter and Rosa (1998: 229)

Other research studies have extended the gender and finance debate further by considering the role of banks in providing finance to female business owners. In a development of an 'asymmetric information' approach (Fletcher 1994), gender researchers have attempted to determine whether banks have (unstated) differential lending policies to male and female business owners and, if so, whether these policies are a result of unwitting socialisation or outright discrimination (Fay and Williams 1993; Koper 1993). In a study undertaken in New Zealand, Fay and Williams (1993: 365) found some evidence that women encounter credit discrimination in seeking start-up funding, although the study concluded that this was not necessarily the fault of the banks. 'Commercial banks are risk averse institutions. Confronted by applications for finance from individuals with limited education and experience in the area they wish to operate and low proposed personal equity, as is commonly the case for would be female proprietors, loan officers not surprisingly refuse requests for finance. Bank staff are not guilty of discrimination in such situations. Rather, applicants' socialisation and work related experiences have disadvantaged them compared to male proprietors.'

Nevertheless, Fay and Williams emphasise (1993: 65) that 'the existence of discriminatory behaviour as a consequence of prejudice and stereotyping can be demonstrated only when all relevant factors up to the point of loan application have been equalised'. Researchers of female entrepreneurship are still a long way from being able to control factors so precisely. As Brush (1992: 15) points out, this area has been   studied insufficiently to enable firm conclusions to be reached.

10.5.2 Networks and female-owned firms

Research which has investigated the management of female-owned enterprises has often alluded to the important role of networks in the survival and success of individual firms (Carter and Cannon 1992; Rosa and Hamilton 1994) – see Chapter 21. Gender differences in the way networks are created and used have been cited as having an influence on certain aspects of the management process – for example, enabling improved access to finance and the development of strong relationships with financial backers (Carter and Rosa 1998). This view has been largely influenced by studies investigating entrepreneurial networks which have unequivocally demonstrated that the quantity and quality of external linkages between a firm and its environment are crucial to its success (see Chapter 21). Some have suggested that distinct gender differences might exist both in the establishment and management of social networks (i.e. the process of networking) and in the contents of social networks (i.e. what networks are used for) (Olm *et al.* 1988; Aldrich 1989). Such a view has been contested by others, however. In a review of research into entrepreneurial networks, Starr and Yudkin (1996: 40) concluded that 'the few studies that compare the networking activities of women and men business owners show differences in the sex composition of the networks of women, but not in how men and women use their networks'.

The influence of gender on the networking activities of business owners has been subject to very little dedicated investigation, and remains a highly contentious issue. Not only is there debate regarding the relative influence of networking activities on the performance of small firms generally and on female-owned firms in particular, researchers have yet to even conceptualise an appropriate starting hypothesis for research. This debate has occurred largely because of conflicting guidance in the research literature which has separately considered gender effects on business ownership and the influence of gender on networking activities. Researchers such as Rosa and Hamilton (1994) have argued that networking is both more critical and should be greater among female entrepreneurs than male entrepreneurs. This approach is, however, countered by research conducted by Aldrich (1989) which suggested that women's networking levels are lower than men's.

In a study specifically designed to investigate the influence of gender on networking, Katz and Williams (1997) analysed data from 361 respondents separated into four categories: self-employed females; self-employed males; salaried females; and salaried males. The study found that of all four groups, self-employed females showed demonstrably lower levels of 'weak-tie' networking than salaried males. Overall, however, salaried managers – regardless of gender – showed higher levels of networking than either of the self-employed groups. Katz and Williams (1997) concluded that the greatest differences in social networking activities were caused by employment status, rather than gender. Moreover, they asserted that 'Despite the centrality of social networking studies in entrepreneurship research, social networking ... is not a particularly powerful way of explaining gender differences' (1997: 195).

10.6 The performance of female-owned firms

The performance of small businesses – that is, their ability to contribute to job and wealth creation through business start-up, survival and growth – has become an important area of recent policy and academic debate (see Chapter 23). Comparatively little rigorous and in-depth research, however, has been undertaken on the issue of gender and business performance. Although many studies have made some mention of it, most shy away from direct examination of quantitative performance measures, preferring instead to engage in discursive debate concerning gender differences in qualitative assessments of success. These studies suggest that women perform less well on quantitative financial measures such as jobs created, sales turnover and profitability. This, it is argued, is usually because women do not enter business for financial gain but to pursue intrinsic goals (for example independence, and the flexibility to run business and domestic lives). Thus, it is argued that women assess their success in relation to their achievement in attaining these goals rather than on the more usual economic or financial measures.

An example of this approach was seen in a study which linked the self-reported motivations of women leaving organisations in order to start businesses and their subsequent success in achieving their goals (Buttner and Moore 1997). Four related issues were investigated in the study: firstly, the motivational influences which affect former managerial or professional women's entrepreneurial decisions; secondly, the role family concerns play in these former corporate women's entrepreneurial motivation; thirdly, how these female entrepreneurs measure success in their ventures; and finally, whether the women's entrepreneurial motivation is related to the ways they measure success in their own businesses. Using a sample of 129 American female entrepreneurs who were all formerly managers in large organisations, the data were collected by focus groups, interviews and structured questionnaires. In common with several previous studies of female entrepreneurship both in Europe and in the USA, the sample was both better educated and less likely to be married than the total population. Similarly, the profile of the businesses owned by respondents revealed a strong bias towards services (81%).

Reasons for exiting organisations were measured using 32 items on a rated scale. Of the five main reasons for leaving their former employment, the desire for 'challenge' (*to gain more respect; to be in charge; to regain excitement; to get recognition*) and 'self-determination' (*to make it on my own; self-esteem*) were the most influential. 'Family concerns' (*to balance family and work; to control my time*) and 'blocks to career advancement' (*discrimination; career barriers; didn't fit into corporate culture*) were the next most influential reasons for exiting organisations. Of least importance was the influence of 'organisational dynamics' (*little motivation to produce; no urgency to finish; lack of shared information; low quality standards*). Success was measured using six items on a rated scale. Of these items, 'self-fulfilment' was found to be the most important measure of success. This was followed, in order of importance, by 'achievement of their goals', 'profits', 'growth', 'balancing family and work' and, finally, making a 'social contribution'. Using correlation analysis, certain relationships emerged between reasons for leaving previous employment and how success was measured in their own enterprises. Women who had left employment for the 'challenge', for example, were found to measure entrepreneurial success in terms of 'self-fulfilment' and 'profitability', those who had left because of 'organisational dynamics' sought success in balancing work and family, while those who had left because of 'family concerns' measured success in balancing family and work and in making a 'social contribution'.

One methodological issue which emerged from this investigation was concerned with the attempt to isolate and rank measures of business success, particularly in studies which attempt to demonstrate differences between female and male respondents. Within the literature that deals with gender and performance, there is an implicit assumption that men measure business success using quantitative, 'external' criteria (i.e. profits, growth, etc.), while women use qualitative, 'internal' criteria (i.e. self-fulfilment, goal attainment, etc.). In this, there is a concern that researchers may be projecting particular value systems onto subjects and that the expectation of differences becomes a self-fulfilling prophecy. Assumptions such as these, which inadvertently result in trivialising women's entrepreneurial efforts, have generally been derived from studies using single-sex samples that lack the ability to pose identical questions to both genders.

The few studies that have used more sophisticated methodologies in pursuing issues of gender and performance have presented less clear-cut results. In a longitudinal study of 298 UK businesses, of which 67 were female-owned, Johnson and Storey (1993) found that women proprietors in their study had created more stable enterprises than had their male sample, although on average the sales turnover for women was lower than for males. Kalleberg and Leicht (1991) also found only slight and inconclusive differences in key performance measures in their sample of 400 businesses from three industrial sectors in Indiana. Rosa et al.'s (1996) study was one of the few large-scale studies specifically designed to investigate the impact of gender on small-business management. In analysing the comparative performance of businesses by gender, the study outlined four different measures: primary performance measures (number of employees, growth in employees, sales turnover, value of capital assets); proxy performance measures (geographical range of markets, VAT registration); subjective measures (including the ability of the business to meet business and domestic needs); and finally, entrepreneurial performance measures (the desire for growth, the ownership of multiple businesses).

The analysis of primary performance measures suggested that women's businesses employed fewer core staff, were less likely to have grown substantially in employment (more than twenty employees) after twelve months in business, had a lower sales turnover, and were valued at a lower level than male-owned businesses. The analysis of proxy performance measures also indicated that women-owned businesses were more likely to serve only local markets, although gender differences in export sales were not significant. Male-owned businesses were also more likely to be registered for VAT. The subjective measures of performance, however, were less clearly divided by gender. In considering how well their businesses had performed in the previous two years, men and women gave comparable responses. Women did, however, appear to be less optimistic than men in their expectation of future business success. Women were also less likely to believe that their business created sufficient income to meet domestic needs. This result appears to stem directly from the fact that women's businesses tended to be substantially smaller than male-owned businesses in the sample. Male respondents whose businesses had a similar-sized turnover were equally dissatisfied with their ability to meet domestic financial needs. The final measure (entrepreneurial performance) also demonstrated marked sex differences. Men were significantly more likely to own other businesses (19.6% compared with 8.6%) and also to have strong growth ambitions in so far as they wanted to expand their businesses 'as far as they could (43% versus 34%)' (Rosa et al. 1996: 469).

Although these results appear to demonstrate marked gender differences in business performance, they should be treated with caution. Not only are conclusions potentially premature given the scarcity of previous research, there are a number of complicating factors (such as industrial sector, business age and presence of co-owners) which, depending on how they are treated methodologically, appear to produce widely differing results in business performance (Rosa et al. 1996). Moreover, Rosa et al. (1996)

argue that, while the performance of women-owned businesses appears at first sight to be substantially lower than for their male counterparts, women have only recently emerged as an entrepreneurial group and their businesses are much younger and therefore less established. On this basis, they concluded that 'If female business owners have started from a much lower tradition of achievement in business, then this trend is encouraging and may provide support for Birley's (1989) view that the gender gap in the U.K. is narrowing' (1996: 475).

Collectively, the various studies which compare male and female performance differences offer mixed results. Overall, these studies suggest that the determinants of performance (i.e. the measures that are used by owners to assess their business performance) are similar by gender. Contrary to many of the earlier studies of gender and entrepreneurship, neither is there any evidence to suggest that men are more profit-orientated than women, or less likely to value intrinsic goals. Although the Rosa *et al.* (1996) study found some marked sex differences in performance indicators, the complexity of the overall pattern of results suggests that a more sophisticated interpretation is required than simply attributing differences to gender alone.

10.7 The neglect of female entrepreneurship

So far this chapter has concentrated on describing the growth in both the numbers of women entering business ownership and the volume of research studies that have been undertaken in an attempt to understand the true dynamics of this phenomenon. It has, however, been noted that, in comparison with the volume of academic research which has been undertaken on the small-firm sector, the female entrepreneur has been seriously 'neglected' by both the mass media and the academic community (Baker *et al.* 1997: 221). For some, the lack of attention paid to women's experience of entrepreneurship is evidence of a wider problem of gender effects being omitted from mainstream research studies into social phenomena. Carter (1993: 151), for example, notes that 'historically women have been left off the small business research agenda or made invisible by research practices or in other ways written out of the analysis of self-employment'. Hamilton (1990) cites an example of how this is done, using Rees and Shah's (1986) analysis of self-employment in the UK. As Hamilton (1990: 6–7) points out, their study 'excludes a number of categories of people and then a whole gender "in order to obtain sharper results". Among those excluded are "those who are not heads of household" (mainly women); "those who worked for less than thirty hours a week" (mainly women); "females" (on the basis that "self-employment is predominantly a male preserve").' The neglect of female entrepreneurship is, therefore, part of a much wider problem which has resulted in the social sciences being structured in a manner which favours the male experience. Concepts of entrepreneurship are traditionally assumed to be gender-neutral but, as Berg (1997: 261) points out, 'rely in fact on notions of humanity and rationality that are masculinist'. Dualities such as the rational–irrational distinction may appear to have no apparent gender bias, but in reality are 'thoroughly imbued with gender connotations, one side being socially characterized as masculine, the other as feminine, and the former being socially valorized' (Massey 1996: 113).

Although many of the early studies which examined the demographic characteristics and motivations of female entrepreneurs were subsequently criticised for their small scale and their lack of rigour, their importance cannot be underestimated in identifying and clearly delineating a (hitherto) 'invisible' group (Baker *et al.* 1997: 221). Although exploratory, these studies challenged for the first time the view that entrepreneurship is a gender-neutral activity. Their success can be judged in two main ways: firstly, by considering whether subsequent research has developed in a manner which addresses the methodological criticisms of the late 1980s; and secondly, by considering whether they have influenced the design and output of non-gender-specific studies.

As this chapter has demonstrated, research investigating female entrepreneurship has expanded and matured considerably over the past 15 years. This has been demonstrated by the re-focusing of attention away from early studies of women's business ownership which considered female experiences entirely in relation to male norms, and towards an increasing awareness of gender differences within entrepreneurship which are socially constructed and negotiated. As this chapter has attempted to present the research output in approximate chronological manner, developments in the methodological basis of many studies have been demonstrated. Where early studies were criticised for their use of small-scale samples and qualitative approaches, more recent research has moved towards large-scale, quantitative methods. Developments have not only occurred in the growing trend towards empiricism, however. Engagement with sociological approaches, in particular, has enabled a more insightful, qualitative analysis of the entrepreneurial principles and processes used by both men and women. On this basis, therefore, the field has matured to develop a cumulative knowledge.

Whether research investigating the effects of gender in entrepreneurship has been successful in influencing the remainder of the small-business research field is less certain. Although there appears to have been an increase in the number of studies which have included gender as a variable for analysis, there remains a pervasive assumption that female experience should be considered only in direct relation to male norms. Elsewhere, studies still assume a gender-neutral or androcentric position. As Shakeshaft and Nowell (1984: 187–8) point out in discussing the pervasive assumption of androcentrism in the social sciences, this results in the 'elevation of the masculine to the level of the universal and the ideal, it is the honoring of men and the male principle above women and the female. This perception creates a belief in male superiority and a value system in which female values, experiences and behaviours are viewed as inferior.'

10.8 Chapter summary

The past two decades have seen a rapid and dramatic growth in the number of women entering self-employment and business ownership. During the same period, the growing interest in the role and importance of small businesses within the overall economy has led to an increase in the volume of research studies which focus on the small-firms sector. Although the experiences of female entrepreneurs have been only a minority interest, research investigating the influence of gender on small-business ownership has developed considerably over the past fifteen years. While early research into female entrepreneurship focused on describing women's characteristics, motivations and experiences, the field has progressed beyond these exploratory and rudimentary studies. More recent research has not only developed a degree of methodological sophistication, it has also focused on increasingly specialised issues, such as the role of gender effects on the financing and the performance of firms.

This chapter has attempted to provide an overview of the growing literature on female entrepreneurship, highlighting some of the key debates within the field. It has also attempted to highlight more recent concerns that the female experiences of entrepreneurship and the effects of gender in small-business management are seriously neglected areas of study. Studies which have started to investigate key issues – such as the management and performance of female-owned firms – have revealed the extent of female disadvantage in business financing and the related and relative under-performance of women-owned firms. Although definitive results have yet to be attained, many recent studies unequivocally point to the same conclusion that, as women are a relatively new group of entrepreneurs, operating significantly younger businesses, women-owned firms may not yet have attained the same level of achievement as those owned by men, but as a group they are catching up fast.

Questions

1 What reasons account for the dramatic increase in the number of women starting in business?

2 In what specific ways do women experience disadvantage in business financing?

3 What factors should be taken into account when considering the performance of female-owned businesses?

CHAPTER 11

Ethnicity and enterprise

Monder Ram and Giles Barrett

11.1 Learning objectives

There are four learning objectives in this chapter:

1 To account for different levels of self-employment among Britain's ethnic minorities.
2 To understand the different explanations of the formation and development of ethnic-minority firms.
3 To describe the dynamics of financing ethnic-minority businesses.
4 To identify the challenges facing policy-makers in supporting ethnic-minority firms.

Key concepts

■ opportunity structure ■ culture ■ ethnicity ■ diversity ■ family

11.2 Introduction

Ethnic-minority-owned businesses are now an established and growing feature of many advanced industrial societies. In addition to fulfilling an important economic and social role for minority communities, ethnic-minority-owned firms have become particularly conspicuous within the general small-business population. This chapter reviews a number of the often-contentious themes that have characterised this emerging field of enquiry. These include: the myriad explanations of the formation of ethnic-minority businesses, which range from 'culturalist' accounts to more structurally orientated responses; factors behind different levels of self-employment activity; the material basis of 'family' labour; the nature of the market environment; financial experiences; and issues for business support agencies.

11.3 Ethnicity and enterprise

Throughout advanced industrial societies, the last decade has witnessed a significant increase in self-employment and small-business activity among ethnic minorities (Barrett *et al.* 1996; Light and Bonacich 1988; Waldinger *et al.* 1990a). Many of these businesses emerged from and are embedded in communities which grew out of post-war demand for low-skill and low-wage labour, particularly in labour-intensive manufacturing industry. De-industrialisation and the growing importance of the service sector have reduced traditional job opportunities for immigrant labour over the last 20 years (Phizacklea and Ram 1996).

In Britain, ethnic-minority businesses have been the subject of growing interest from a variety of sources. The media have not been slow to publicise the 'rags to riches' stories of conspicuously successful South Asian entrepreneurs, even though more careful accounts of this community in business convey a more complex picture. Researchers continue to offer competing explanations for the apparent entrepreneurial flair of some ethnic groups, noticeably South Asians, and the below-average propensity for self-employment among other communities, in particular African-Caribbeans. To varying degrees, business support agencies have attempted to respond, on the one hand, to high levels of unemployment in Black communities and, on the other, to the increasingly significant phenomenon of ethnic enterprise in particular localities and economic sectors. These developments need to be set against a political context which, during the 1980s, was punctuated by civil disturbances in a number of British inner-city areas. A consensus among policy-makers rapidly developed which exhorted the Black population to engage in 'productive pursuits' (Scarman 1981): encouraging self-employment among ethnic minorities therefore emerged as a means of maintaining social harmony in urban areas.

This interest is testimony to the growing importance of the ethnic presence in the small-firm population. In this chapter, key aspects of ethnic-minority business activity in Britain are assessed. These include explanations of the different patterns of self-employment among ethnic-minority groups, particularly African-Caribbeans and South Asians; the contentious question of entrepreneurial motivation and the apparent impact of 'cultural' resources on the business entry decision; the role of the often-lauded 'family' in the ethnic-minority firm; the constraining nature of the market environment; the relationship between ethnic enterprise and high-street banks; and the role of business support agencies in ethnic-minority business development. However, since ethnic-minority entrepreneurship is not a peculiarly British phenomenon, we begin with a brief assessment of ethnic-minority business activity from an international perspective.

11.4 Ethnic-minority enterprise: an international perspective

Across Europe as a whole, ethnic minorities have engaged in small-enterprise activities. Indicative of a tension that permeates the ethnic business literature, some observers have argued that particular groups are culturally predisposed to engage in these types of activities (see Werbner 1984, for example), whilst other contributors have stressed the importance of wider structures in governing the responses of ethnic minorities (Jones 1981; Ward 1991). In France, high levels of business activity among individuals of Moroccan, Tunisian and Chinese origin have been noted. These enterprises tend to offer the same product as indigenously owned firms but provide a different quality of service. Competitive advantage is achieved over their rivals through longer opening hours, easily available credit and the sale of produce in very small quantities (Ma Mung 1994; Ma Mung and Guillon 1986). The Tunisians are the smallest of the three groups but they have the greatest affinity towards self-employment. Research has shown the concentration of approximately 180 Tunisian catering establishments in only a few neighbourhoods of Paris. Within these outlets strong traditions are fostered and the firm provides much-needed work for family members and co-ethnics (Boubakri 1985).

Turkish-owned businesses have blossomed considerably in Germany and have also been the focus of research. A combination of factors – strong family tradition, market demand for culturally specific products, and self-employment as a vehicle of socio-economic progress against a backdrop of rising unemployment – has fuelled the rise of Turkish entrepreneurship. Many firms are intrinsically associated with the community and practise a high degree of ethnic communalism and networking. Business activity has not been restricted to serving a solely co-ethnic market, however. Blaschke and Ersoz (1986) identify the externalisation of Turkish enterprise towards providing such items as fast food and transport for consumption by the wider society. Turks in Belgium also appear to be following a similar pattern of self-employment activity, particularly in relation to restaurants (Kesteloot and Mistiaanen 1997).

The Netherlands too has witnessed growing ethnic-minority business activity. Ex-colonial subjects constitute the largest ethnic minorities in the country and the Surinamese are the largest single group (Blaschke et al. 1990). Low levels of entrepreneurial activity have been officially noted for Turks, Moroccans, Chinese, Javanese and Creoles among other groups. However, recent attention has turned to examining the informal economic activities of ethnic minorities in the Netherlands (Kloosterman et al. 1998; Rath 1998). Informal activities, defined as income-generating activities which do not meet the requirements of regulatory frameworks, are a feature of post-industrial urban economies throughout the world (Pugliese 1993). They not only provide income for the business owner but may also be instrumental in providing much-needed income for other members of ethnic minorities who may be, for example, between regular jobs or have no regular source of income whatsoever.

The immigration of Surinamese into the Netherlands has been characterised by a stop-start process. Immigration peaked in 1974–5 and then declined sharply following the independence of Surinam in 1975. The entrepreneurial behaviour of the Surinamese in Amsterdam reflects this pattern of migration. Hence businesses which were established in the 1960s were concerned with serving the dietary needs of the early migrants. As the numbers of co-ethnics rose in subsequent years, there occurred both proliferations in the number of these tropical food-stores and the diversification of entrepreneurial pursuits into other activities. Blaschke et al. (1990) record that in 1983 there were approximately 250 Surinamese ventures in Amsterdam. Most firms occupied the more inexpensive sites in the city in the older parts of the urban centre. This spatial pattern of business settlement also coincided with co-ethnic residential settlement patterns (Byrne 1998). These studies represent just a small sample of a recent rich seam of research undertaken on ethnic-minority sub-economies in Europe.

In North America, business ownership has been repeatedly promoted as a self-help strategy through which oppressed minorities can achieve economic advancement. Japanese-Americans, Chinese, Jews, Middle Easterners, French-Canadians and Cubans among others have all been the focus of research studies into the business activities of these diverse ethnic minorities (see Light 1972; Waldinger and Tseng 1992; Razin 1993; Light *et al.* 1993; Langlois and Razin 1995; Portes and Bach 1985 respectively). Much of this interest in ethnic business has tended to focus on the question posed by Waldinger (1995: 562) of 'why some visibly identifiable and stigmatized groups make it through business and others do not'. A recent manifestation of this is the comparison between Koreans and African-Americans in business (as we shall see, this has echoes of the juxtaposition of South Asian and African-Caribbean entrepreneurship in Britain).

'Business-minded' Koreans have been presented as the archetypal role model for all disadvantaged minorities to aspire to in their logical quest for socio-economic advancement. Both Kim (1981) and Min (1991) discuss the propensity of Korean-owned business to become established in low-income Black areas of central cities. The reason for their decision to service the population in these areas is twofold. Firstly, there is a desire to exploit the vacant niche which has not been filled by African-American entrepreneurs who lack the necessary cultural and class-based resources conducive to small-business formation. In New York City, the emergence of these niches has been precipitated by an ageing population of Jewish and Italian business owners whose fear of crime, age and the reluctance of whose heirs have prompted them to sell their businesses on.

Secondly, Korean entrepreneurs perceive that the Black ghettos represent a relatively less hostile environment than predominantly white areas. Whilst Korean entrepreneurs have brought much-needed services to central city ghettos, their strong ethnic ties and cultural attachment have served to exclude others (Light 1995). These exclusionary practices have prompted violent responses from inner-city Black communities angered by the failure of Korean-owned firms to employ African-American workers and to contribute finance to African-American community organisations. The organised boycotting of Korean-owned outlets has also been a feature. Hence the entrance of Korean businesses into African-American locales is often viewed as risky because of simmering inter-ethnic tensions (Jo 1992; McEvoy and Cook 1993; Ok Lee 1995).

Bates (1994) questions whether the educational merits of Korean entrepreneurs are sufficiently rewarded in their business activities. Min (1991; 1993) notes that the vast majority of Korean immigrants have received a high school or college education in South Korea; hence their employment in retail and service activities represents an underemployment of their human capital. Across the Atlantic a similar argument has been proposed for South Asians in Britain (Aldrich *et al.* 1981; 1982; Barrett 1997; Srinavasan 1992). Hence self-employment has afforded entrepreneurs the opportunity to make their own decisions about the operations of the enterprise but the wider structures of society regulate access to the different types of activities. Moreover, despite the ethnic and economic solidarity exhibited by Korean enterprises and their heavy investment in their ventures, actual returns on their human and physical capital are very small and inferior to the returns accruing to African-American-owned ventures (per dollar invested in capital) (Asante and Mattson 1992). This suggests that the appropriateness of the Korean entrepreneurship model as the benchmark for all marginalised minority groups to follow should be treated with caution.

As early as the 1880s some intellectual African-American leaders in the United States, such as Booker T. Washington, propagated the rise and development of a Black (African-American) bourgeoisie (Asante and Mattson 1992). This emerging strand of the middle classes would lead to the full emancipation of African-American people as business opportunities and property ownership became widespread and an accepted facet of African-American culture. These developments would be underpinned by the bond of shared values, racial co-operation and self-help.

However, Frazier (1957) points out that the capital mobilised within the African-American community was insignificant in relation to the American economy, and that African-American entrepreneurship provided very few jobs for co-ethnics. Hence, to promote African-American business activity as a panacea for the deep-seated and intractable problems of disadvantage and institutionalised racism is highly problematic. Frazier (1957: 153) labels the belief that entrepreneurship represented an overarching solution to the endemic problems of racism as a 'Social myth ... [and] ... one of the main elements in the world of "make-believe" which the Black bourgeoisie has created to compensate for its feeling of inferiority in a white world dominated by business enterprise'.

The comparatively low rates of African-American business ownership are generally attributed to the lack of socio-cultural and class resources which can be mobilised in the pursuit of entrepreneurship. Both Light and Bonacich (1988) and Waldinger et al. (1990b) affirm that the fragmented nature of African-American communities militates against the development of group social networks, and mechanisms of in-group attachment, which help to nurture business opportunities. The absence of petty bourgeois values is also a serious setback to encouraging new firms (Cashmore 1991). Low educational attainments among African-Americans, small amounts of financial capital and the absence of resource-generating mechanisms such as rotating credit schemes are among the class-related factors which severely hinder the processes of business formation (Bonacich and Modell 1980; Curran and Burrows 1986; Light and Rosenstein 1995).

However, a fundamental hindrance to Black progression is the persistence of racism. Unequal access to health, education, capital and labour market opportunities have stunted the growth of a Black entrepreneurial class (Guardian 1992; Marable and Mullings 1994). As Cashmore (1992) has observed, the promotion of an 'enterprise culture' during the 1980s under President Ronald Reagan actually involved considerable cuts in welfare and health expenditure and the proclaimed belief that poverty was a self-induced state of being. Hence socially, politically and economically marginalised groups such as the homeless, un/underemployed and visible minorities were held responsible for their own plight (Murray 1990). Neo-conservative thinking acted to create a pool of exploitable low-cost labour so that US industrial capital could begin to compete more readily with international competitors (Kasarda 1989; Sassen 1991). Whilst in the late 1990s some economic progress is detected for ethnic minorities in the United States, this is extremely uneven. The recent founding of initiatives such as inner-city enterprise zones and Specialised Small Business Investment Companies (SSBICs) have failed to galvanise a new generation of Black entrepreneurs in the USA (Bates 1997).

11.5 Ethnic-minority business activity: the British experience

One of the most conspicuous features of the ethnic-minority business population in Britain is the increasing disparity between the circumstances of different groups. This is clearly reflected in the patterns of self-employment among ethnic-minority communities. As Figure 11.1 indicates, South Asians are particularly well represented in self-employment. For example, 22% of those of Pakistani or Bangladeshi origins are self-employed; this compares with 7% for West Indians or Guyanese. Although not indicated in Figure 11.1, the equally high levels of self-employment among the Chinese and Mediterranean-origin populations (such as Greeks, Italians and Turks) indicate that the propensity for entrepreneurship is not confined to South Asians (Curran and Burrows 1988a).

Such is the extent of diversity among self-employed ethnic-minority groups that interest has now focused on the differences in the South Asian community itself (Basu 1995; Metcalfe *et al.* 1996). For example, Metcalfe *et al.* (1996) offer evidence of differences in cultural and economic factors affecting entry into self-employment, development of the businesses and satisfaction with self-employment. It appears that East African Asians and Indians are the real South Asian entrepreneurial 'success' stories; conversely, Pakistani and Bangladeshi enterprise still seems to arise out of a context of disadvantage. However, the most common point of contrast is still between South Asians and African-Caribbeans. Since the question posed by Kazuka (1980) – 'Why so few Black businessmen?' – has been the focus of interest, the next section reviews this recurring theme.

Figure 11.1 Total self-employed as a proportion of all employment by ethnicity (male and female)

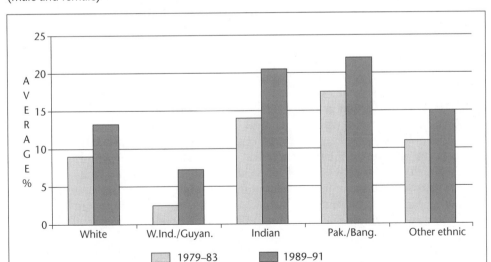

Source: Employment Gazette, June 1992, Office for National Statistics © Crown Copyright 1999

11.5.1 African-Caribbean experiences

Many of the explanations accounting for African-Caribbean 'under-representation' in self-employment appear to make reference to the apparent lack of cultural resources that are often documented in other ethnic-minority groups. They include the different value base of the African-Caribbean family unit, which apparently does not predispose them to running a family business (Reeves and Ward 1984); the legacy of slavery, which had a deleterious effect upon African-Caribbean culture (Fryer 1984; Gilroy 1987; Pajaczkowska and Young 1992; Rex 1982); and the absence of extended-family and community networks (Blaschke *et al.* 1990).

However, explanations that focus exclusively on the absence or otherwise of 'cultural' resources often fail to appreciate the impact that the opportunity structure can have on the facilitation of business opportunities. Basu (1991) in particular eschews culturalist interpretations and presents a cogent case for locating African-Caribbean under-representation in the socio-context of Black people in Britain. To this end, a number of factors need to be considered. First, many African-Caribbeans originally migrating to Britain were from a working-class background, as stated by Basu (1991: 102): 'Afro-Caribbeans [*sic*] were essentially a "replacement" workforce who came from working-class backgrounds to fill occupational and residential niches vacated by whites.'

'Class' resources (Light 1984) are important in developing attitudes, beliefs, educational qualifications and social networks conducive to entrepreneurship. South Asian migrants in Britain appeared to have a broader socio-economic profile and, therefore, greater access to class resources. The greater entrepreneurial success of the more affluent Blacks who migrated to the USA and Canada (Foner 1979; 1987) would seem to bear out the importance of class background. Ethnic identity is cross-cut by class background in this as in many other instances.

Secondly, comparatively high levels of unemployment among the Black community (Jones 1993) serve to induce self-employment in low-skill, highly competitive and poorly rewarded industrial sectors. Often such 'no-choice' businesses operate in the informal economy (and thus are not accounted for in official statistics); or remain marginal concerns with little prospect of real progress (Basu 1991).

Thirdly, negative stereotyping of African-Caribbeans in British society impinges upon their capacity to mobilise resources potentially useful in business. Less preferential treatment by the banks (Jones *et al.* 1994b) and racist customer behaviour (Jones *et al.* 1992) are important business processes where such stereotyping has been noted.

Fourthly, residential settlement patterns appear to influence business development among minority groups. For example, Reeves and Ward (1984) argue that the relative dispersal of African-Caribbean settlement (compared to the concentration of South Asians), their numerically smaller population and the apparent lack of culturally specific needs, combine to limit market potential for growth in small businesses.

Finally, African-Caribbeans are further constrained by their comparatively low levels of home ownership, which diminishes their capacity to offer collateral for business start-up funding (Basu 1991). It appears, then, that this group is faced with a powerful combination of structural handicaps to entrepreneurialism – handicaps which in themselves have little directly to do with ethnic cultural attributes. This needs to be borne in mind in comparative assessments of ethnic-minority entrepreneurship.

11.6 The business entry decision

One of the most keenly debated issues within the ethnic business literature concerns the decision to become self-employed. Various explanations have been advanced outlining the processes that give rise to ethnic-minority business ownership. Jenkins (1984: 231–4), for instance, has identified three basic explanatory models of ethnic involvement in business. The 'economic opportunity' model regards ethnic-minority business activity as essentially no different from routine capitalist activity, relying on the market for its fortunes. The 'culture' model asserts that some cultures predispose their members towards the successful pursuit of entrepreneurial goals. Finally, the 'reaction' model views self-employment by members of ethnic-minority groups as a reaction against racism and blocked avenues of social mobility, a means of surviving at the margins of white-dominated society. Waldinger *et al.* (1990b) have developed a more interactive approach for understanding ethnic business development. Essentially, it argues that ethnic enterprise is a product of the interplay of opportunity structures, group characteristics, and strategies for adapting to the environment.

A steady stream of studies since the 1980s has stressed the importance of external factors in their explanations of the proliferation of particularly South-Asian-owned small enterprises (Aldrich *et al.* 1981; 1982; 1984; Jones 1981; Jones *et al.* 1989; Mullins 1979; Nowikowski 1984; Robinson and Flintoff 1982). According to this perspective, self-employment is a survival strategy born out of the persistent discrimination that ethnic minorities face within the wider labour market. Compelling evidence for this view is presented by Jones *et al.* (1992) in their national study of 178 South Asian, 54 African-Caribbean and 171 white small-business owners. More than a quarter of South Asian owners turned to self-employment because of blocked opportunities or unemployment. Furthermore, Jones *et al.* (1992: 186) believed this to be an underestimate: 'Since there were also many other Asian respondents who had experienced periods of unemployment or unsuitable employment even while giving positive entry motives like money or independence, we take this as a sure sign that Asians in Britain are no more culturally predisposed or voluntaristically oriented towards enterprise than any other group.'

In contrast, there are strong proponents from a more 'culturalist' tradition who privilege what they regard as distinctively ethnic resources in their accounts of business formation (Basu 1995; Soni *et al.* 1987; Srinavasan 1992; Werbner 1980; 1984; 1990). For example, Werbner (1984) identifies a distinctive Pakistani ethos of self-sacrifice, self-denial and hard work that serves to fuel entrepreneurial activity. Basu (1995) also located a particularistic South Asian 'entrepreneurial spirit' in her survey of 78 South Asian retailers. Basu (1995: 16) maintained that 'It is difficult to support the hypothesis that the small businessmen in our sample were driven or pushed into self-employment as the only alternative to escaping unemployment'.

The controversy shows little sign of abating. But, nonetheless, it is clear that the simple concept of 'push' versus 'pull' (which has featured in some of the more quantitatively orientated studies of ethnic enterprise) is unlikely to grasp fully the complexity of entrepreneurial decision-making. As Granger *et al.* (1995: 513) note in their study of freelancers in the book-publishing sector, 'research designs which simply focus on the moment of transition from one labour market state to another, without exploring background career histories, are unlikely to grasp the real dynamics of self-employment career changes'.

This point is given added resonance by Ram and Deakins's (1996) study of African-Caribbean entrepreneurs. From a reading of employers' initial responses (using pre-set statements), the findings indicated that African-Caribbean entrepreneurs had in common with white small-business owners largely positive motivations for entrepreneurship (Curran 1986a). But more qualitative accounts from respondents were also elicited; these revealed that an unfavourable opportunity structure – in the guise of menial jobs or limited prospects at work – still had a bearing on the business entry decision.

From this review of the evidence, then, it would seem that pure culturalist explanations are not adequate in accounting for small-business formation in ethnic-minority communities. Of more significance is the nature of the opportunity structure and what Light (1984) has called *class resources*. This refers to tangible material resources like property and accumulated finance, which can be used to spin off new firms or branches; and less tangible properties such as contacts and information networks, and the self-confidence which goes with the possession of all these assets together with a track record. As noted above, such resources are not evenly spread across ethnic-minority groups.

11.7 Family and co-ethnic labour

A further prominent characteristic of ethnic-minority businesses is the use made of family and co-ethnic labour. Such labour is often portrayed as a critical source of 'competitive advantage' for ethnic businesses, since it is often cheap and the problem of supervision is made easier (Mitter 1986). It is widely held that their rapid expansion into such labour-intensive lines as clothing manufacture, catering and above all convenience retailing is enabled by their superior capacity to tap into a ready supply of labour power, thus equipping them to work long, unsocial hours at their customers' convenience (Ward 1991). South-Asian-owned firms are often seen as the exemplars of the 'family business'. Very similar tendencies have also been attributed to Greek Cypriots and the Chinese. For the former, Curran and Blackburn (1994) observe that because their entrepreneurs are intensely concentrated into the restaurant trade, they work very long hours boosted by ordering and collecting supplies. The Chinese are even more specialised in restaurants and take-aways and, consequently, exposed to extremely long hours of work in order to obtain a competitive cost advantage (Parker 1994: 622). Among many factors, it is above all this competitive undercutting which has enabled the Chinese take-away, in large part, to replace the traditional English 'chippie' in many areas (Liao 1992). The personal toll on the business families in question is often considerable, as Parker (1994: 622) notes: 'the whole of family life and the domestic economy [is] shaped by the takeaway'.

The facility of family labour does not appear to be as extensively utilised within African-Caribbean enterprise (Reeves and Ward 1984). Explanations accounting for this include the more 'egalitarian' nature of the African-Caribbean family unit (Basu 1991) and the lack of scope for enlisting unskilled family labour in the type of business sectors that the community tends to be involved in (Curran and Blackburn 1993).

Further corroboration is provided by Curran and Blackburn's (1993) study of Greek-Cypriot, Bangladeshi and African-Caribbean businesses: family labour was used least by African-Caribbeans. Curran and Blackburn explain this by reference not only to the nature of family culture, but also to the community's dispersed business activities. For instance, the type of unskilled or semi-skilled family labour which characterises many ethnic-minority firms may not be particularly appropriate in sectors like personal or professional services, where African-Caribbeans are involved.

However, two points that question the conventional wisdom on labour-intensiveness and family labour, particularly in relation to South Asian businesses, need to be made. Firstly, long working hours tend to be prevalent across the small-firm population (Curran and Burrows 1988a). When Jones *et al.* (1994a) examined this question with South Asian, African-Caribbean and white small-business owners, they found that ethnic-minority respondents did operate more labour-intensive practices than is customary; but these 'were as much a function of sectoral distribution and of external pressures as of specific ethnic cultural and behavioural traits' (Jones *et al.* 1994a: 201).

Secondly, the tendency to view the 'family' as an unqualified resource for the ethnic entrepreneur also needs to be more closely scrutinised. A growing body of evidence argues that 'culturalist' portrayals of the family at work are often one-dimensional; they fail to appreciate the extent to which primacy often accorded to the family can constrain business development (Barrett *et al.* 1996; Phizacklea and Ram 1996; Ram 1992; 1994a). In other words, over-reliance on the family can actually get in the way of economic rationality. Ram's (1994b) ethnographic study of South Asian employers in the West Midlands clothing sector documents many instances where family members were retained in the business despite a lack of competence; where regular breaches of discipline were ignored; and where family workers secured equal remuneration despite varying contributions to the business. Hence the role of the family in ethnic-minority enterprises is frequently 'double-edged', a point which is rarely given sufficient attention in the more celebratory accounts of minority business.

The 'family' label also tends to mask the unequal nature of gender relations in ethnic-minority firms (Dhaliwal 1998; Mitter 1986; Phizacklea 1990). This is evident in terms of ownership: Barrett *et al.* (1996) speculate that many male-owned businesses conceal the extent of women's centrality to the enterprise. It is also clear that women's contribution in the day-to-day activities of the business is often unacknowledged. Recent studies on the internal management processes in ethnic businesses (Phizacklea and Ram 1996; Ram 1992; 1994a) and, indeed, small firms *per se* (Fletcher 1997; Holliday 1995) illuminate the often critical contributions that women play in managing the business.

11.8 Restricted spatial markets

Most ethnic-minority businesses are located within Britain's inner cities, which is perhaps a reflection of ethnic settlement patterns (Basu 1991; Reeves and Ward 1984). Labour Force Survey data indicate that 70% of the economically active people in ethnic minorities live in metropolitan county areas. This compares with 30% of the white population (Employment Gazette 1994). An inner-city location can have important implications for the viability and growth prospects for small businesses. It was often 'white-flight' from decaying inner-city areas that provided the opportunity for ethnic minorities to take over businesses, particularly in the retail distributive sector (Jones *et al.* 1994a). But, despite providing this initial opportunity, the problems inherent in an inner-city location often temper the potential for the development of such businesses. For example, local environmental conditions like physical dilapidation, inadequate parking and vandalism are depressingly commonplace. They can often prove a major constraint in securing high-quality markets from outside the immediate locality (Basu 1991). Moreover, they accentuate the problem of raising appropriate finance (Deakins *et al.* 1994) and insurance cover (Patel 1988).

Although co-ethnic consumer tastes may provide an initial opportunity for business activities, continued reliance acts as a major constraint on business development. This is due to the comparatively small size of ethnic-minority communities. Furthermore, minority entrepreneurs tend to cater for mainly local residents within inner-city areas where customers have relatively low spending power (Basu 1991). Moreover, such 'community markets' are likely to be in long-term decline since successive British governments have made immigration progressively difficult; and there is the likelihood of later generations of ethnic minorities being more integrated with the dominant white culture and economy (Curran and Blackburn 1993). However, as Curran and Blackburn's own findings (1993: 60) show, break-out may be less of an issue for minority firms located in areas where there is still a large ethnic-minority population. They found that businesses in London, where there is a very significant ethnic-minority presence, were more dependent on co-ethnic markets for their sales than those in Sheffield and Leeds. Hence, demographic trends are likely to have a bearing on the urgency of break-out for ethnic-minority businesses.

In the light of such unpromising trading circumstances, encouraging break-out into majority markets has emerged as an issue of particular importance (Curran and Blackburn 1993; Ethnic Minority Business Initiative (EMBI) 1991; Ram and Jones 1998). But what actually constitutes break-out? Clearly, it is rather more than simply servicing white markets. For instance, a corner store in a white inner-city area may be in no better position than a similar business situated in an ethnic enclave; in both cases, highly competitive market conditions and geographic location militate against any real prospect of substantial growth. A recent study of African-Caribbean entrepreneurship in Britain (Ram and Deakins 1996) cautions against simplistic notions of ethnic business development. Contrary to many previous studies, Ram and Deakins found that firms in their investigation had an average of 50% sales to the majority population. Hence, at a basic level, many entrepreneurs may have heeded the advice of commentators advocating the servicing of 'white' markets as the way forward for ethnic enterprise. But it was not uncommon for these mixed-market-orientated firms to remain low-yielding marginal concerns with little prospect for significant development in the future.

Curran and Blackburn (1993: 12) provide a rather more sophisticated view of break-out. They argue for the assessment of plans for expansion with evidence of preparation for growth; examples of the latter would include investigating sources of finance, planning for the re-fitting of premises to enhance potential for growth, and the revamping of existing products or services offered by the business to appeal to a wider market or to achieve higher mark-ups. Precise measurement of these facets might be difficult but, none the less, a genuine attempt at break-out would need to address such issues. However, given the sectoral and spatial confines of many ethnic-minority firms, and their usually labour-intensive *modus operandi*, break-out in these terms is likely to be highly problematic.

11.9 Funding ethnic-minority enterprise

There can be little doubt that underfunding remains one of the most intractable problems facing ethnic-minority small-business owners. The difficult task of securing finance for business start-up is the most documented problem facing both existing and potential ethnic-minority business owners, whether in Europe or North America (Barrett 1997; Jones *et al.* 1992; Jones *et al.* 1994b; Woodward 1997). Problems of undercapitalisation perpetually thwart the growth and threaten the survival of many ethnic-minority businesses (Barrett 1997; Basu 1991). A major debate has been the extent to which the relationships between ethnic entrepreneurs and commercial banks serve to alleviate or exacerbate this problem. Recent research (Curran and Blackburn 1993; Deakins *et al.* 1994; Jones *et al.* 1994b) presents a mixed picture. For some groups, including Greek-Cypriots and Indians, the acquisition of bank finance does not appear to be problematic and, indeed, the positive entrepreneurial image often attached to such groups may even be an advantage. However, for Bangladeshis and African-Caribbeans in particular, negative experiences with mainstream financial institutions continue to be reported. This may be due to 'business-problems' (Curran and Blackburn 1993), which can be addressed by training and greater professionalism, or it may reflect the rather more insidious problem of institutionalised discrimination (Brooks 1983; Jones *et al.* 1992; Sawyer 1983). Whatever view is taken, it continues to be a major constraint upon the development of African-Caribbeans in business.

In addressing these problems, some progress has been made by Black-led enterprise support agencies, which appear to have been very active in assisting with business plans and even the provision of finance (Curran and Blackburn 1993). But Deakins *et al.* (1994) suggest a number of further steps that the banks could take. These include the training of staff to appreciate more fully the dynamics of ethnic-minority firms; employment of appropriately qualified ethnic-minority staff in more influential positions within the organisation; greater involvement in the social and cultural activities of minority groups; ethnic monitoring of customers; and more extensive networking with Black-led support agencies.

11.10 Ethnic-minority business and enterprise support

Encouraging ethnic-minority communities into self-employment has been a discernible feature of national and local policy-making since the early 1980s (see Chapter 4). There appear to be two particular reasons for this policy direction. Firstly, the civil disturbances in many inner-city areas that occurred in the early part of the decade focused attention on the often dire position of Black racialised minorities (Cross and Waldinger 1992). Following Lord Scarman's pronouncements in the wake of the disturbances in

Brixton, promulgating self-employment among the Black population was seen as an important means of tackling disadvantage and maintaining social harmony in urban areas. Secondly, some minority communities – notably South Asians, Chinese and Cypriots – have come to dominate particular sectors and local economies. Often this position of prominence has been achieved without the assistance of business support agencies (Marlow 1992).

There is a variety of agencies that ostensibly provide support to small businesses (see Storey 1994 for a critical discussion of the efficacy of such agencies). The emphasis here is on four layers of enterprise support, notably: Enterprise Agencies (EAs); Training and Enterprise Councils (TECs); Business Links; and local authorities. Of course, these institutions are not the only providers of business support for entrepreneurs. For example, accountants, solicitors and bank managers are important sources of advice which small-business owners probably use more often than the institutions that comprise the 'enterprise industry' (Curran and Blackburn 1994). Moreover, in the case of some ethnic-minority groups (notably South Asians) the family and co-ethnic community are thought to be significant to the process of business development (Ward 1991; Werbner 1990). But these other sources of enterprise support have been discussed in the course of this chapter and elsewhere (see Barrett *et al.* 1996 for review). In contrast, relatively little attention has been accorded to the issue of 'mainstream' providers of business services and ethnic-minority enterprise.

Perhaps the most significant of these layers for the purpose of ethnic-minority businesses is that of Enterprise Agencies (EAs). Although their remits and rationales may vary, EAs usually focus upon generating interest in business start-ups and meeting the perceived needs of smaller firms (that is, below ten employees). Many ethnic-minority businesses fall into the category of the smaller firm (Jones *et al.* 1994a). On the issue of start-ups, encouraging ethnic minorities into self-employment seems to have been an element of government policy since the inner-city unrests of the early 1980s (Storey 1994). Hence, some basic features of ethnic-minority businesses, notably their size and relative youth, would seem to suggest that they are a natural constituency for EAs.

Unfortunately, as Curran (1993) points out, such agencies have not proved popular with small-business owners in the past. EAs have been in existence since the late 1970s, but have never managed to reach more than a small proportion of the small-business population. Studies of small service-sector enterprises (Curran *et al.* 1991) and small manufacturing firms (Curran and Blackburn 1992) found that only a minority of firms had ever had contact with their local Enterprise Agency. A national study of ethnic-minority-owned and white-owned businesses showed that the use of public support services by small firms in a variety of urban locations throughout Britain was around one in twelve (Jones *et al.* 1992).

Ram's (1998) recent study of business support agencies (EAs in particular) highlighted further difficulties. For example, the actual delivery of services was rarely proactive and not always informed by an accurate profile of the extent, nature and dynamics of the local Black business community. Basic data on Black enterprises were not known. Service provision was largely reactive and often seen as 'top-down'. When it came to the issue of effectiveness, it was evident that satisfying fundholders' targets was a more pressing concern than endeavouring to address the complex issue of client needs.

TECs, in England and Wales, provide a further layer of support. Established since 1990, they have assumed control of major support schemes designed to encourage small-firm creation (the Business Start-Up Scheme, formerly the Enterprise Allowance Scheme) and enterprise growth (the Business Growth through Training scheme). Despite the potentially useful role that TECs can play in encouraging training and skills development, serious doubts have been raised about their capacity to deliver their enterprise remit in relation to small firms (Curran 1993; Peck 1991; 1993). Although TECs have generated considerable publicity and small-firm owners are increasingly aware of them, few entrepreneurs appear to have contact with their local TEC. For example, a survey by Curran and Blackburn (1992) showed that less than 10% of small-firm owners had used their TEC. Ram's (1992) study of South Asian employers in a West Midlands city found that only 4% had heard of their local TEC, and none had made use of its services.

The relatively recent creation of Business Links makes it difficult to draw firm conclusions on their effectiveness. There are, nonetheless, fundamental issues that impinge upon the operation of Business Links. Curran et al. (1995) identify two in particular. Firstly, a major assumption that appears to underpin Business Links is that SMEs are part of local networks and, therefore, the Links need to configure their services locally; yet many SME networks are shaped by other criteria, particularly economic sector. Secondly, in assuming a 'one-stop shop' role, there is a danger of Business Links becoming reactive service providers. Responding to client demands is important, but arguably of greater significance is the capacity of support agencies to be proactive and act as mentors for clients. How Business Links handle such issues will probably only become clear in time through the use of longitudinal evaluation studies (Curran et al. 1995: 54).

In many areas, local authorities have indicated a growing interest in supporting ethnic-minority enterprise (Brooks 1983; Mennon 1988). But Thomas and Krishnarayan (1993: 262, original emphasis) appear to question the sincerity of this interest. On the basis of a postal survey of 67 local authorities of England, Wales and Scotland, they conclude that 'The outstanding feature ... is the **absence** of policies and facilities targeted at the needs of ethnic-minority businesses'.

However, it does appear that many local authorities are now attempting to engage more directly with ethnic-minority enterprises. For example, many local authorities in the West Midlands region (where ethnic minorities constitute almost 20% of the population) have been instrumental in setting up discrete units to support ethnic-minority firms. Birmingham, Coventry, Sandwell, Walsall and Wolverhampton have gone down this path. Thomas and Krishnarayan (1993) report upon similar developments in Kirklees. Curran and Blackburn (1993) also point to the considerable efforts made by Enterprise Agencies to support ethnic enterprise in other inner-city areas.

11.11 Chapter summary

The increasing importance of self-employment among ethnic minorities has been one of the marked features of labour market change internationally over the past 20 years. As in many advanced industrial societies, ethnic-minority-owned businesses are now an established and growing feature of contemporary Britain. In addition to fulfilling an important economic and social role for the minority communities themselves, ethnic enterprise has also made a significant contribution to both the revival of the small-business population and the revitalisation of depressed urban retail landscapes. There is little doubt that particular areas of economic activity – such as retailing, clothes manufacture and catering – have been transformed by the dynamic presence of minority communities. Groups like the South Asians, Chinese and Greek-Cypriots have been notably conspicuous in effecting such transformations in often adverse competitive environments. Although African-Caribbean 'under-representation' in self-employment has precipitated much speculation, there is little doubt that African-Caribbeans are an emerging presence on the small-business scene. Recent evidence on African-Caribbean entrepreneurship (Curran and Blackburn 1993; Ram and Deakins 1996) points to the promising growth potential of this community in business.

In this chapter, we have attempted to scrutinise the growing literature on ethnic-minority enterprise with a view to assessing some of the key debates that have dominated this subject. The processes that underpin small-business formation have been shown to extend beyond pure culturalist arguments that, for instance, depict South Asians as natural entrepreneurs and African-Caribbeans as uninterested in entrepreneurial activities. The influence of the socio-economic context, or 'opportunity structure', continues to affect the life-chances of Britain's ethnic minorities; and its impact upon the decision to enter self-employment can rarely be detached.

Investigation of family and co-ethnic labour inside the ethnic small business further exposes the fragility of popular stereotypes. It is undoubtedly the case that in terms of hours worked, entrepreneurial rewards and commitment to the business, ethnic minorities (African-Caribbeans as well as the more commonly noted South Asians) are remarkably industrious. But it is equally evident that such practices are characteristic of the harshly competitive economic sectors that such minority groups trade in, rather than a culturally specific work ethic. Moreover, when the capacity of family labour to constrain business development and the often unequal nature of gender relations are highlighted, the image of the cosy, consensus-orientated ethnic-minority firm becomes even more illusory. This is not to deny the importance of particular ethnic resources, which can often serve as an important source of competitiveness. Rather, it serves to reinforce the importance of the context in which such firms operate. Hence, a comprehensive synthesis of the multi-faceted nature of ethnic-minority business enterprise is incomplete without an elaborate understanding of the intricacies of economic change and how and why the proclivity to entrepreneurship in advanced market economies varies between ethnic groups.

An important part of this context is the relationship with external agencies crucial to small-firm development, notably the high-street banks. Debate continues on whether the reported problems between ethnic-minority firms and the banks are business or 'race' related. However, there is little doubt that underfunding remains one of the most serious problems facing ethnic-minority small businesses. In attempting to assist with these and other problems, the 'mainstream' business support agencies appear to be constrained by major obstacles that seem endemic to the burgeoning 'enterprise industry'. These include a lack of clarity over objectives, inter-agency competition, scarce resources, inappropriate services and a lack of networking.

Questions

1 How adequate are 'culturalist' accounts in explaining ethnic-minority involvement in self-employment?

2 What factors account for the different levels of self-employment among ethnic minorities?

3 How feasible is 'break-out' for ethnic-minority firms?

CHAPTER 12

Franchising and enterprise

John Stanworth and David Purdy

12.1 Learning objectives

This chapter has four learning objectives:

1 To gain a basic understanding of the nature of a business format franchise.
2 To gain an understanding of the symbiotic nature of the franchisor–franchisee relationship.
3 To illustrate that franchising may be viewed as a growth strategy for small businesses or, alternatively, as a strategy for large businesses penetrating what have conventionally been recognised as small-firm markets.
4 To demonstrate the potentially contentious nature of statistics issued by commercial bodies with an interest in promoting their particular business sector.

Key concepts

■ franchising ■ enterprise ■ growth ■ symbiosis ■ survival rates
■ service economy

12.2 Introduction

At its best, franchising is an avenue into self-employment offered by franchisors (owners of a 'tried-and-tested' business format) to franchisees (typically aspiring small businessmen and women), in exchange for payment of a one-off front-end fee followed by an ongoing royalty. Based on the principle of 'cloning' success, a principal tenet of the franchise fraternity is that franchise failure rates are low. From the viewpoint of small-business researchers, franchising has been argued to be of particular importance, since most franchisors still are, or have recently been, small businesses themselves and most of their royalty-paying franchisees are also small businesses. Thus, in principle, franchising offers a route to growth for the would-be franchisor and small-business opportunities with limited risk for would-be franchisees. This chapter examines the advantages and disadvantages of franchising from the viewpoints of franchisor, franchisee and the wider society. It also examines growth rates, internationalisation, job creation, management challenges, future trends and, not least, risk levels. What emerges here is a striking similarity between the failure rates of young franchise systems and conventional small businesses at the same stage of development.

12.3 Franchising and enterprise

A franchise can be defined as comprising a contractual relationship between a franchisee (usually taking the form of a small business) and a franchisor (usually a larger business) in which the former agrees to produce or market a product or service in accordance with an overall 'blueprint' devised by the franchisor. The relationship is a continuing one, with the franchisor providing general advice and support, research and development, and help with marketing and advertising. In return, the franchisee usually pays an initial franchise fee and also an ongoing royalty or management service fee, normally based on the level of turnover and/or a mark-up on supplies purchased from the franchisor. The franchisee provides the capital for the outlet and is a legally separate entity from the franchisor.

Although the franchisor is usually a 'larger' business than the franchisee, in only a handful of cases does the franchisor truly meet the description of 'large'. Most franchisors remain very much SMEs (small and medium-sized enterprises), with no more than a small handful truly qualifying as large and these are almost invariably American in origin, e.g. McDonald's, ServiceMaster, Coke, Pepsi, Holiday Inn, Burger King, Kentucky Fried Chicken, Pizza Hut, Kwik-Kopy and Budget Rent-a-Car. Overall, in the UK, the average franchise involves around 30–40 outlets, according to British Franchise Association statistics, and could thus still certainly be considered an SME, if not a small business *per se*.

12.4 The nature of franchising: entrepreneurship or dependence?

At one extreme, it has been argued that the franchised enterprise is, in reality, a managed outlet featuring in the larger marketing pattern of another truly independent business – that of the franchisor (Rubin 1978: 223–33). This distribution strategy has certain advantages for the larger enterprise but just because the manager of the outlet has a capital stake in the business dressed up in the language of entrepreneurship, that is no reason to confuse a franchise outlet with a genuinely independent business. This is not to say that the arrangement cannot be highly beneficial to both parties but illusion should not be substituted for reality in a rigorous analysis of the status of the franchised outlet.

At the other extreme, the franchised small business may be viewed as an emerging form of independent small business in advanced industrial societies whose distinguishing characteristic is its overt and close relationship with another, usually larger, enterprise. This association might be seen as being little different – except in degree and the explicit form it takes – to that now found between many small businesses and other firms with whom they do business. In an increasingly interdependent economy, such a close association may simply be seen as a reflection of the fact that 'no firm is an island entire of itself'.

The independence of the small firm can never be absolute and is often difficult to assess accurately in practice. Any small enterprise, whatever its form, is part of a wider network of economic interaction summed up in the economist's notion of 'the market' and, arguably, it is from this source that the main limitations on independence are derived. Whilst economically, franchise relationships may appear to render franchisees highly dependent at a contractual level, at an operational level, higher levels of independence may manifest themselves than appear likely at first sight (Stanworth 1984).

The pioneering Bolton Committee researchers in the UK were attracted to the idea of classifying the roles of small firms according to the type of market they supply (Bolton Report, 1971: 31–2). Accordingly, they located small firms along a typology of reliance upon large firms:

- 'Marketeers' are those firms which actually compete in the same or similar markets as large firms (examples are computer software companies, fashion merchandise manufacturers and restaurants).

- 'Specialists' are those firms which carry out functions that large firms do not find it economic to perform at all, though they may include large firms amongst their customers (examples are repair and maintenance in the building industry, jobbing engineering and specialised retail outlets such as bookshops).

- 'Satellites', where the small firm is highly dependent upon a single larger business for the majority of its trade. The degree of dependence may be even greater if the large customer actually designs the product or service and merely subcontracts its manufacture or supply, as appears the case with a franchise. Franchisees would appear to fall under this third category.

'Product' franchises – embracing the fields of car and petroleum distribution, the soft-drink bottlers (Coke, Pepsi, Seven-Up, etc.) and, in the UK, tenanted public houses – are often categorised as 'first-generation' franchises and almost totally sidelined from most mainstream debates on modern franchising. The terms 'franchising' and 'business format franchising' are now used practically interchangeably in the franchise industry generally.

The relevance of business format franchising is perhaps best illustrated by US statistics which apportion just $200bn of a total of over $600bn franchise industry sales turnover to business format franchising. However, something in the region of 3,000 from a total of 3,500 franchisors and 400,000 from a total of 500,000 franchisees reside in the business format sector (Sen and Lee 1994).

In a nutshell, business format franchises are typically SMEs. However, given that the franchisor levies a royalty-based charge on the franchisee's level of turnover rather than profit, pressures to achieve market penetration and growth are institutionalised rather than optional. This can be achieved by expansion within a given franchise outlet or by expansion of the overall population of outlets – often involving multiple outlet ownership by more successful franchisees. For instance, this is particularly common in the field of fast-food franchising where, in the USA, it is not uncommon for 50% of a franchise company's outlets to be owned by less than 20% (and sometimes less than 10%) of its franchisees. A single large franchisee may own several hundred outlets (Bradach 1994). Multiple ownership in other sectors appears less common and, in the

UK, it is estimated that 82% of franchisees operate just a single unit (The NatWest Bank/British Franchise Association Franchise Survey 1993 – published March 1994).

Previous research has shown that approximately one in three of franchisees has prior experience of independent self-employment and that levels of prior educational attainment and previous earnings tend to correlate with the buy-in costs of particular franchises. Thus, individuals taking relatively high-cost franchises, in fields such as fast print, are more likely to be graduates and have professional backgrounds than, say, individuals taking up relatively low-cost carpet-cleaning franchises.

12.5 The advantages and disadvantages of franchising

The following section is assembled from three main sources – namely the published literature on franchising, previous research and discussions with key figures in the industry – and will be presented under four headings dealing with the franchisor, the franchisee, the consumer/local economy and, finally, the national economy.

12.5.1 Advantages and disadvantages to the franchisor

Advantages

- Franchising enables the franchisor to increase the number of distributive outlets for his/her organisation's product or service with limited capital investment. It is the franchisees who provide much of the capital with their stakes in the business.

- Since the franchisee owns his/her own business, he/she is assumed to be highly motivated to maximise growth and profitability. This situation may be compared to that of a manager of a retail outlet who is a direct employee of the parent company. Generally, such a manager earns a fixed salary (with possibly an element of bonus incentive incorporated) and lacks the extra incentive to succeed which may result from a personal financial investment in the business. A successful franchisee, with increasing profits, can be expected to contribute to the success of the franchisor.

- A franchise unit, being locally owned, is claimed to be readily accepted by the community as being a local business. It is not clear how far this is true, however, since very often local people may not be aware that a franchised unit is in fact owner-managed.

- The franchisor has limited payroll, rent and administrative overheads, because the very nature of the operation requires franchisees to be self-employed. Franchisees are themselves responsible for the staffing arrangements and operating costs of their particular outlets.

- As well as the franchisors achieving a wider distribution network for their product or service, the nature of most franchise contracts ensures that franchisees are in some measure 'tied' to the franchisor. They are often obliged to purchase equipment from or through the franchisor plus – as in the case of fast-food franchise restaurants – the necessary ingredients that go to make up the final product.

Disadvantages

- It may be difficult for the franchisor to exercise tight control over the franchisee simply because he/she is not a direct employee of the franchisor and cannot be closely supervised. In turn, the poor reputation of one outlet, in terms of product quality or service, can be damaging to the general trade name and reputation of the franchisor and, in turn, the whole franchise organisation.

- A franchisor cannot always be certain that a franchisee is declaring his/her true level of business activity. Many franchisors employ a central accounting system to combat this, although no system can be expected to be totally successful in this respect.

- If the franchisor believes that a franchisee has become demotivated and is not running his/her outlet efficiently, there is relatively little that can be done in the short term as long as the franchisee is operating within the terms of his/her contract.

- The management of a franchising company is limited in its flexibility. Conventional companies can move more quickly to exploit market potential when a modified selling strategy is required. However, to bring about changes can be a lengthy and cumbersome operation when dealing with individually owned franchised outlets. Any changes need to be carefully handled to avoid conflicts stemming from perceived threats to the franchisee's independence.

- There may be problems of information feedback from the franchisee to the franchisor. This can result from the franchisee's desire for independence or simply from channels of communication not being as well developed as they might be in company-owned and managed outlets.

- The franchisor is faced with a paradox. The franchise method of business tries to capitalise on the personal attention and service that characterise the owner-managed business. However, the franchisor's need for a standardised product or service, together with a uniform presentation – needed to give customers a sense of reliability and dependability – clashes with the former.

- The franchisor may have difficulty in recruiting suitable franchisees who (1) see franchising as an attractive method of doing business; (2) are motivated towards self-employment; and also (3) have the necessary capital available for investment.

12.5.2 Advantages and disadvantages to the franchisee

Advantages

- It is possible for an individual to run his/her own business yet gain the advantages and economies of scale of a larger company. Here the advantages range from initial and ongoing training, to centralised buying, ongoing product/service and market research.

- If the product or service has already achieved brand awareness, this relieves the franchisee of many of the normal demands of the sales and marketing function and allows him/her to concentrate on other aspects of the business. Most franchisors undertake both national and local advertising campaigns to keep franchisees' products or services firmly in the public mind.

- It is claimed that franchisees require less capital than would be the case to equip a business independently. The franchisor can help with raising bank loans, site selection, heading leases on properties, and getting the business open and running smoothly. However, franchise investment levels tend to be fairly high and it could be argued that one could start a business successfully for a similar investment (or less, perhaps) without the obligations imposed by a franchisor.

- Many franchisees operate within a defined territory, which involves the franchisor giving an undertaking not to set up another competing outlet within a given geographical radius. However, there is nothing to stop another franchisor, or other conventional competition, moving into the same area if it appears attractive and lucrative.

- There are other franchisees in the same network with the same challenges and problems and so any individual franchisee can use them as a source of non-threatening help and advice.

Disadvantages

- The tight control exercised by the franchisor in order to regulate the way in which the product or service is presented to the consumer may leave little opportunity for the franchisee to impose his/her personality on the business.

- Should the trade name of the franchise become tarnished – perhaps through mismanagement by the franchisor or the shortcomings of other franchisees – then there is the possibility that the franchisee may suffer simply because he/she is seen by the public as a representative of the franchise organisation in question.

- The service provided by the franchisor may constitute a heavy expense to the franchisee. The franchisee may be obliged to purchase equipment and ingredients from the franchisor which he/she could have bought more cheaply from other sources. Also, management service fees and charges may be high.

- There is the possibility that the franchise agreement may not fulfil the franchisee's expectations, both in terms of anticipated sales and profits and also possibly in terms of the franchisor not fulfilling his/her obligations.

12.5.3 Advantages and disadvantages to consumers and the local community

Advantages

- Consumers may have the convenience of an extended-hours service. Many franchises operate on the basis of long hours of service in order to maximise their markets, while many independent businesses, not bound by agreements to provide such service, may choose not to do so or may lack the resources.

- Franchisees, as owner-managers, should be able to offer a highly personal service.

- Although all franchised outlets are independent and separate, consumers can locate them under a single trade name and apply their knowledge of one outlet to all others because of uniform presentation and consistent standards of quality. Conversely, if a consumer is dissatisfied, he/she need not waste time with other outlets.

- If a conventional small business fails, dissatisfied customers may not get satisfaction. In the case of a franchise, failure rates may be lower and, in any case, customers can, in the final analysis, contact the franchisor.

- Franchisees receive training from their franchisors, usually ranging from 2 to 12 weeks. A portion of this will usually involve hands-on training in existing outlets run by other franchisees. Such training can be expected to add to the stock of business training and knowledge in the local economy.

Disadvantages

- Franchises may reduce levels of diversity in local economies due to their stress on standardisation.

- Franchising may 'export' money out of the local regional economy in terms of payments made to franchisors and may 'import' goods and services from the franchisor rather than from small suppliers locally.

12.5.4 Advantages and disadvantages of franchising to national economies

For individuals seeking self-employment opportunities but lacking the necessary experience and know-how, franchising can offer an avenue of opportunity. For others, already in business on a modest scale, a franchise as an addition, or alternative, to their existing business may offer the possibility of growth levels unlikely to be achieved by their existing business.

The role of the industry as a 'shop window' of business formats appears to have been recognised by leading franchisors who, over time, appear to have become generally less informative in response to early-stage enquiries. This has occurred in response to instances of individuals searching out information, under the guise of a potential franchisee, only subsequently to emerge in competition rather than in partnership.

The high level of publicity generated by the franchise industry, plus the steady flow of books and seminars, magazines and manuals on the topic, all act to reinforce this role. Overall, the franchise industry almost certainly plays a positive role in publicising and popularising the notion of self-employment.

12.6 Franchising in the United States of America: history and current trends

Franchising is more developed in America than in any other country. Also, research and data-gathering are far more advanced in the USA than elsewhere. Thus, much of what is known about franchising tends to be American in origin, and other countries look towards US experience as heralding the nature and scale of future developments in their own societies.

As a result of the large-scale development of franchising in the USA, the United States is the major exporter of franchising on a global scale, and American experience is invariably quoted (or misquoted) in justification of franchising in Britain and elsewhere. Three US statistics are quoted above all others:

- firstly, that franchising accounts for almost 35% of all retail sales in the USA;
- secondly, that franchising accounts for 10% of GDP in the USA;
- thirdly, that franchising expanded by around 300% between 1975 and 1990.

Allied to these claims is an assumption that franchising is both a low-risk business option and a largely recession-proof business strategy.

All of the above statistics appear essentially true. However, as Table 12.1 and Figure 12.1 illustrate, inflation-adjusted figures for the growth of franchising in the USA over recent years pull down the overall growth figure for 1975–90 dramatically from 284.6% to 58.5%, and the average annual growth rate from 9.4% to 3.1%. Moreover, in 6 years of this 16-year period, franchise growth in the USA was either zero or negative (Trutko, Trutko and Kostecka 1993). The franchise industry in the UK appears completely unaware of the existence of the latter adjusted statistics. (The data terminate in 1990 due to the abandonment of an annual survey of US franchisors and franchisees by the US Department of Commerce.)

Although academics, researchers and bodies such as the International Franchise Association (America's franchise association) use the terms 'franchising' and 'business format franchising' almost interchangeably, the fact remains that, for statistical purposes, 'product' and business format franchises are usually grouped together in the USA. In 1990, 48.4% of all franchising sales stemmed from the automobile and truck sector and a further 18.0% from franchised gasoline service stations.

Table 12.1 Trends in total USA franchising sales, 1975–90

Year	Actual franchise sales		Inflaton-adjusted franchise sales	
	Total ($bn)	% change from previous year	Total ($bn)	% change from previous year
1975	185.8	10.2	185.8	1.0
1976	217.9	17.3	205.9	10.8
1977	261.7	20.1	232.1	12.7
1978	282.2	7.8	232.6	0.2
1979	313.3	11.0	232.6	0.0
1980	334.4	6.7	218.5	–6.0
1981	364.8	9.1	215.4	–1.4
1982	376.0	3.1	209.3	–2.8
1983	422.8	12.5	228.1	9.0
1984	492.1	16.4	254.4	11.5
1985	543.0	10.3	271.0	6.6
1986	569.1	4.8	279.5	3.1
1987	599.4	5.3	283.8	1.5
1988	648.1	8.1	294.9	3.9
1989	677.9	4.6	294.3	–0.2
1990	714.5	5.4	294.4	0.0
Change 1975–90		284.6%		58.5%
Annual change 1975–90 (compound rate)		**9.4%**		**3.1%**

Source: Trutko, Trutko and Kostecka (1993)

Figure 12.1 Trends in total USA franchising sales, 1975–90

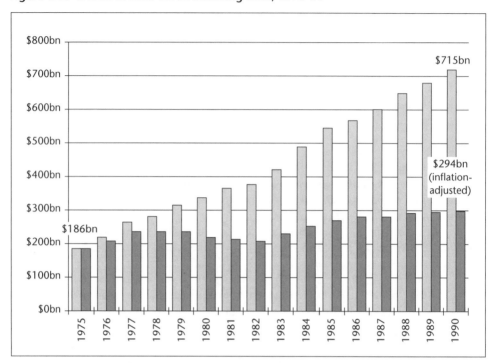

Source: Trutko, Trutko and Kostecka (1993)

Whereas product franchising grew by only 42.4% in inflation-adjusted (constant) dollars in the USA between 1975 and 1990, against an overall sector figure of 58.5%, business format franchising grew by 115.5%, or around 5.1% in real terms per annum.

The expansion and contraction of franchising in the USA seems to have closely followed general economic trends (Trutko, Trutko and Kostecka 1993: 3–19). Between 1975 and 1989, GNP in the USA grew by 52.7% in real terms against a comparable growth in franchise sales of 58.5%. The decline in franchise sales (in real terms) between 1979 and 1982 again closely reflected the wider economic situation. As the US economy recovered during the mid 1980s, franchise sales reflected the upturn, as they did the subsequent downturn towards the end of the 1980s.

Interestingly, however, whilst franchise sales performed relatively well between 1975 and 1990, the number of franchise establishments in the USA grew by only 13.3% compared to a 48.4% increase in the number of establishment units in the USA as a whole. It is predicted that this trend will continue, with franchisors concentrating on generating higher profits per establishment in the future rather than expansion via increased outlets (Trutko, Trutko and Kostecka 1993: 9–12). In this sense, franchising could be said to be limiting the number of small-business outlets.

The largest 88 US franchisors had more than 500 franchise units in 1986 and accounted for two-thirds (65.0%) of all franchise sales and establishments. By way of contrast, one-third (33.9%) of all franchising systems had 10 or fewer establishments and accounted for about 1% of sales and establishments.

Despite the overall dominance by large systems, there is some evidence that smaller systems have played an increasing role in recent years. Also, earlier thoughts that franchising might simply represent a temporary phase in a company's growth plans appear largely unfounded since the level of franchisee-owned stores appear to have remained virtually unchanged since 1975 at 81.5%.

Women and minorities appear to have increased their representation in franchising in recent years, though both groups are less visible than might be expected in terms of their general participation in the labour force at large. The evidence indicates that around 10% of franchise units are owned outright by women plus another 20% owned by women in alliance with men. Around 5% of franchise units were owned by minorities in 1986, compared with an 8.8% ownership level of US firms generally. This is despite government schemes targeted specifically at increasing the level of minority representation. Although there are no comparable figures collected for the UK, the position appears broadly similar, albeit with a heavy concentration of minority franchisees in the field of fast-food franchising.

It is felt by many that the help afforded by franchisors in setting up new franchisees, particularly those with no prior business experience, renders franchising user-friendly for women and minorities.

12.6.1 Franchise growth factors

A number of factors in particular are considered to have aided the general growth of franchising in the USA in recent decades. These include the growth of the US economy since World War II. They also include 'downsizing' policies exercised by large corporations which have released corporate executives with the necessary financial resources, experience in business management and a reduced faith in corporate security, often willing to consider self-employment.

Further, the post-war 'baby-boom' increased both consumer spending levels and the numbers of potential franchisees during the 1970s and 1980s. At the same time, the number of women in the US civilian workforce increased from 27.5 million in 1970 to 47.4 million in 1989 – a participation rate up from 42.6% to 57.2%. The growth in the numbers of working women and dual-income families led to increased needs for support services such as day-care services, educational products and services, home cleaning, fast food, home-delivery food and other services.

In addition, technological changes heralded a revolution in electronic data processing and materials handling. Technological benefits have often been made more available to small franchise outlets than conventional small firms due to the economies of scale delivered by the franchisor. Retailing in particular appears to have benefited from technological advances.

12.6.2 Franchising world-wide

A survey of franchise associations undertaken in 1995, by Arthur Andersen, revealed some marked differences between the number of franchise systems in the respondent countries, and also regarding the corresponding number of franchisees (see Table 12.2). The franchise data are shown in descending order, and the corresponding

Table 12.2 Franchising world-wide, 1995

Number of Franchisors		Number of Franchisees		Population (m)	GDP/head
United States	3,000	United States	250,000	266.5m	$27,500
Canada	1,000	Japan	139,788	125.4m	$21,300
Brazil	932	Canada	65,000	28.8m	$24,400
Japan	714	Brazil	60,000	162.7m	$6,100
Australia/NZ	600	France	30,000	58.3m	$20,200
France	520	**Britain**	**26,400**	**58.5m**	**$19,500 (UK)**
Germany	500	Australia/NZ	26,000	21.8m	$21,482
Britain	**414**	Mexico	18,724	95.8m	$7,700
Italy	400	Spain	18,500	39.2m	$14,300
Mexico	375	Italy	18,500	57.5m	$18,700
Netherlands	341	Germany	18,000	83.5m	$17,900
Spain	280	Netherlands	11,975	15.6m	$19,500
Austria	200	Hungary	10,000	10.0m	$7,000
Hungary	200	Sweden	9,000	8.9m	$20,100
Sweden	200	Norway	3,500	4.4m	$24,500
Norway	185	Argentina	3,500	34.7m	$8,100
South Africa	180	Belgium	3,083	10.2m	$19,500
Switzerland	170	Austria	3,000	8.0m	$19,000
Belgium	150	Singapore	1,600	3.4m	$22,900
Malaysia	125	Denmark	1,210	5.2m	$21,700
Indonesia	105	Finland	900	5.1m	$18,200
Argentina	100	Malaysia	800	20.0m	$9,800
Singapore	85	Yugoslavia	620	22.3m	$2,994 †
Hong Kong	84	Colombia	300	36.8m	$5,300
Portugal	70	Czech Republic	100	10.3m	$10,200
Finland	70	Philippines	61	74.5m	$2,530
Denmark	68	Chile	25	14.3m	$8,000
Philippines	56	Israel	15	5.4m	$15,500 ‡
Colombia	48	Bulgaria	7	8.6m	$4,920
Yugoslavia	45				
Chile	45				
Czech Republic	35				
Israel	18				
Bulgaria	0				

Note: The above franchise data were derived from a survey of the franchise associations in 40 countries, which achieved a 90% response rate. The population and GDP values are estimates (1996 and 1995 respectively).

† Bosnia and Herzegovina, Croatia, Macedonia, Serbia and Montenegro, Slovenia ‡ Excluding Gaza Strip and West Bank.

Source: Swartz (1995); Central Intelligence Agency (1996)

country population and Gross Domestic Product per head (as a measure of economic wealth) has been added to aid comparisons. At the forefront is the USA, but Canada and Australia – each also a 'land of opportunity' – have relatively large numbers of franchisees compared to their total population (Figure 12.2). All three of course had strong colonial ties to the UK. Some large-population countries were not included in

Figure 12.2 Country franchisee populations: number of franchisees vs total population

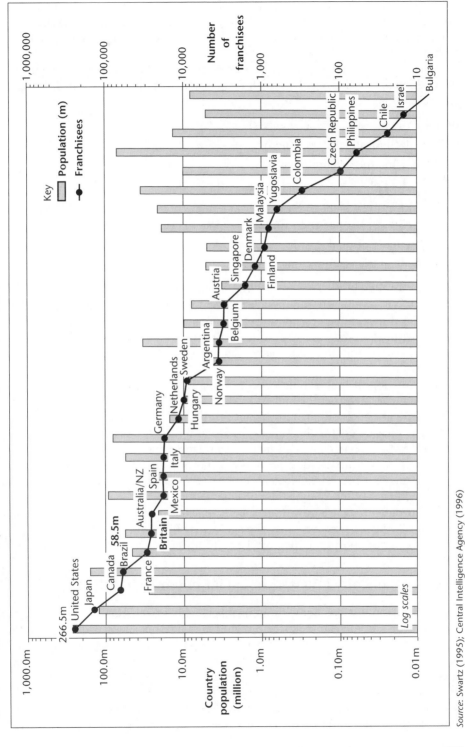

Source: Swartz (1995); Central Intelligence Agency (1996)

the survey data – such as China (1210m), India (952m), Indonesia (207m) and Russia (148m) – but data collection can be problematical in emerging markets, especially where there is no franchise association. Each of these missing countries is known to have a small number of franchise systems.

In the UK, the franchise industry has been strongly influenced by developments from the USA. In the mid 1970s, the British Franchise Association was formed by eight franchise companies:

- Budget Rent-a-Car (vehicle rentals)
- Dyno-Rod (drain cleaning and hygiene services)
- Holiday Inn (hotels and motels)
- Kentucky Fried Chicken (fast foods)
- Prontaprint (fast print services)
- ServiceMaster (carpet and furniture upholstery cleaners)
- Wimpy International (fast foods)
- Ziebart (vehicle rust-proofing services).

Only two of the above (Prontaprint and Wimpy) were distinctly British and even the latter was based upon an imported American idea, albeit developed by a British company. This dominant representation of American involvement in franchising has continued, with US companies exporting to Britain largely via the medium of granting 'master licenses' for an individual or company in Britain to develop their format nation-wide.

This situation of high-profile American involvement in international franchising is one which wins favour at the highest levels in the USA, as summarised in a recent analysis by Eroglu (1992: 19): 'from a balance-of-payments perspective, international franchising is considered [in the US] as a safe and speedy means of obtaining foreign currency with a relatively small financial investment abroad. It is notable in that it neither replaces [American] exports nor exports [American] jobs, all these reasons making this business arrangement one of the most preferred and government-supported forms of international involvement.'

The attitude of the US government here appears plain and one which recommends itself to other governments – the message is that home-produced franchises, particularly those with export potential, can be fruitfully considered for targeted support.

12.7 Ease of entry into franchising for potential franchisors

The franchise industry is not without members who are regarded by their peers as having staged an entry into franchising by other than 'textbook' methods. Usually, this has involved selling franchises to members of the public before the business in question had been properly tried-and-tested. In fact, on such occasions, it has been literally tried-and-tested on its early franchisees. When this happens, it is not necessarily the case that the franchisor in question has deliberately set out to defraud the public by selling franchises prematurely. Rather, the explanation may lie in ignorance or over-enthusiasm. In the author's own past career as a small-business trainer, there were occasions when an individual would attend a start-up course with the intention of selling franchises in his/her new business idea within weeks or months of starting in business for themselves.

The conventional wisdom in the industry is that any completely new small business will need at least two years in order to establish itself in terms of testing out sales, marketing, product/service, pricing and staffing strategies. After all, every small-business start-up plan inevitably requires considerable modification during the initial months of its implementation. High failure-rate figures, particularly during the first 30 months of operation, verify this fact.

Having established a basic business formula, the owner should then, ideally, establish an identical outlet in another location. The process of finding new premises, hiring personnel, organising a launch and all the other tasks accompanying a new outlet opening, is an essential test of the owner's ability to replicate the success achieved in the founding unit. Again, there will be a steep learning-curve here and the process could well take a further two years.

Finally, three key documents need to be drawn up prior to beginning franchising: firstly, an operating manual committing to paper detailed instructions for the guidance of franchisees when running an outlet for themselves, secondly, a franchise contract, stipulating the legal obligations of both parties – franchisor and franchisee – and, finally, a franchise prospectus as a marketing tool for use in recruiting franchisees. All three documents require a great deal of time, hard work and, usually, expensive external help from consultants, solicitors and accountants. Then begins the process of recruiting and training new franchisees and this, again, is liable to prove time-consuming and expensive, since the business involved has no previous experience or public awareness to draw upon.

Overall, adopting a 'textbook' approach, a business starting up from nothing may well find itself involved in five years of hard work before it recruits its first franchisee. The founder/s will find that they are not simply involved in testing out one business idea but two – a conventional business configuration plus an allied franchise format. Obviously, the final package has to be one capable of yielding notably better financial returns than the average small business since these must satisfy the franchisee's income needs, service bank loans and pay off loan capital, plus sustain the franchisor's need for management services fees, amounting to usually around 10% on sales turnover.

Once a franchise company is well established, it will find a range of specialist services and advice on offer from bodies such as the British Franchise Association and specialist units in the clearing banks. The weakest link in the chain of development is almost certainly at an earlier stage – between establishing a conventional small business with franchise potential and launching it as a fully-fledged franchise operation, without short-cuts being taken that could prove disastrous later.

Obviously, the above timetable can be safely reduced in the case of an already well-established SME wishing simply to convert to a franchise format by cloning their previous success, but the risks are still high. A recent report commissioned by the US Small Business Administration estimates that initial franchise development costs can exceed $500,000 (Trutko, Trutko and Kostecka 1993: 7): 'The development of a business from a proven concept through to the sale of its first franchise is typically a long, expensive, and risky process for the franchisor. Even excluding the costs of direct management involvement, the franchisor bears sizeable "upfront" costs for developing a programme before it can be marketed to franchisees.'

They also similarly identify the early stage of entry into franchising as a difficult time for the franchisee, since 'Prospective franchisees are often reluctant to use professional advisors to evaluate franchise offerings because of the cost and/or difficulty of identifying an attorney in the area of franchising'. Without doubt, most specialist franchise advisers see their principal area of vested interest as that of undertaking work for franchisors rather than franchisees.

12.7.1 Franchise contracts

The franchise relationship is governed, in the legal sense, by a written contract which commonly spans 30–40 pages in length and can be even longer. These contracts usually run for a specified period of time, though they are usually renewable. The most typical contract length is five years, followed by ten years.

The most detailed comparative work on franchise contracts is that undertaken by Dr Alan Felstead of the Centre for Labour Market Studies at the University of Leicester, England. He compared 83 different franchise contracts. His analysis compared contracts on six main component elements: guarantees granted to franchisees of territorial exclusivity; franchisors' rights to unilaterally impose changes to their operating manuals; post-termination restrictions on competition; franchisors' stakes in franchisees' businesses via ownership of sites, telephone lines or equipment; franchisors' rights to police the quality of the franchisees' output; and, finally, the franchisors' imposition of output targets.

Felstead (1993: 115) constructed an Index of Contractual Control (Figure 12.3). Each element of control is allotted a score of 0 if absent, 1 if present and, where appropriate, 2 if present in a stronger form. Although this scoring mechanism does not 'weigh' each of the components against one another, it does enable differentiation of 'hard' franchise systems (where the degree of contractual control is high) from 'softer' systems (where the degree of contractual control is low and franchisees enjoy greater degrees of autonomy).

Around two-thirds of the systems examined fell between the two extremes, with the overall distribution 'scores' skewed towards the 'hard' end. Felstead (1993: 116) feels that franchisees occupy an ambiguous position of being neither fully in control of 'their' business nor fully controlled:

> First, despite operating without close and direct supervision, franchisees are required to operate within procedures laid down and often subject to unilateral change. Moreover, franchisees are sometimes committed to adhere to franchisor-set performance targets, and, in any case, to give the aim of the franchisor (turnover maximisation) primacy in the running of the business. Secondly, while they appropriate the profits (and losses) of the business, they do so only after they have made turnover payments to the franchisor. Thirdly, although franchisees buy or lease much of the physical business apparatus, some parts remain in the hands of the franchisor, and some have franchisor-imposed restrictions on their use both during and after the currency of the agreement. Furthermore, franchisees have no ownership rights in the intangible business assets – they simply 'borrow' the business idea, trading name and/or format.

Figure 12.3 Index of Contractual Control

Component elements	Score	
a) Non-exclusivity:		
Exclusivity guaranteed in territory	0	49.4%
Qualified exclusivity	1	16.9%
Non-exclusive franchise	2	33.7%
b) Performance targets:		
None	0	62.7%
Turnover targets/expansion triggers	1	37.3%
c) 'Stake' in tangible business assets:		
No 'stake' evident in contract	0	33.7%
'Stake' in telephone lines/sites/equipment	1	66.3%
d) Operations manual:		
No rights to unilateral change	0	12.0%
Rights to unilateral change by franchisor	1	88.0%
e) Post-termination restrictions:		
None	0	13.3%
Non-compete or non-solicitation	1	25.3%
Both non-compete and non-solicitation	2	61.4%
f) Monitoring of output quality:		
No rights to police system	0	41.0%
Rights to inspect/communicate with clients on reasonable notice	1	10.8%
Rights to inspect/communicate without notice	2	48.2%
Index of Contractual Control		
'Soft' franchising (0–3)		13.3%
'Medium' franchising (4–6)		65.1%
'Hard' franchising (7–9)		21.7%

Source: Felstead (1993)

Felstead also traces a number of instances of franchisor–franchisee litigation. One particularly interesting case involved a Prontaprint franchisee in the UK who declined to renew his contract but continued to trade in the identical line of business and in the same premises, albeit under a different name. He lost a legal judgment on the grounds that:

■ he was still drawing benefit from the Prontaprint name via repeat business and, for some time at least, from being listed in local directories as 'Prontaprint'; and

■ the franchisee was deemed to have had little understanding of the print business prior to being trained by Prontaprint.

The latter fact may explain the frequently expressed franchisor preference for franchisees without prior experience in the operational line of the franchise.

12.8 Success and failure rates amongst franchisees

Research results identify quite clearly two principal appeals which franchising holds for 'potential franchisees'. One is 'independence/chance to be your own boss' and the other access to a 'proven business system'. Whilst both were chosen frequently and almost to the exclusion of other possible appeals of franchising, the precise ordering varied, depending upon whether or not respondents had prior experience of self-employment (see Figure 12.4).

Some causes of SME failure are seen as being due to 'generic' causes and should actually be remedied or reduced by franchising (Cross and Walker 1987). These are:

- undercapitalisation;
- absence of economies of scale;
- lack of business acumen;
- inability to survive intense competition in sectors (such as retailing) where barriers to entry are low.

Figure 12.4 Main appeal of franchising by current employment status

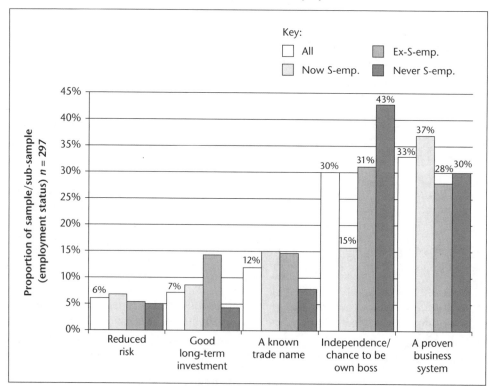

Source: Stanworth and Purdy (1993)

Franchising should reduce the probability of failure amongst franchisees due to such 'generic' causes, on condition, of course, that the franchisors' responsibilities are met and that the appropriate back-up services expand at a rate sufficient to cope with any growth of the franchise network. Thus, attempts by the franchisor to expand too quickly or, alternatively, to simply generate profits through the accumulation of once-and-for-all front-end fees, will act to the detriment of franchisees.

Failures due to 'franchising-related' factors, as opposed to 'generic' factors, are cited by Cross and Walker as falling essentially into five key categories:

- business fraud, such as the use of celebrities to attract franchisees to ill-founded franchise schemes in the USA during the 1960s and 1970s;

- intra-system competition, involving franchise outlets being located too close together and cannibalising each other's sales whilst maximising the franchisor's sales-based royalties; also, company-owned outlets may be sited close to franchisee-owned outlets;

- insufficient support of franchisees, encompassing advertising support, pre-opening programmes and management assistance;

- poor franchisee screening (possibly fuelled by a drive to maximise front-end fees), resulting in a mismatch between franchisee's attributes and criteria for success;

- persistent franchisor–franchisee conflict.

Mittlestaedt and Peterson (1980) have conducted work in this area which suggested franchise failure rates running at around 5% and turnover at around twice that level. Padmanabhan (1986) concluded that franchise operations fail generally less often than independents but that the opposite may be true of business services and automotive franchises. Ozanne and Hunt (1971) identified an annual failure rate of 6.7% amongst fast-food franchise systems but concluded that the actual failure rate could be two or even three times as high. The same went for franchisee failure rates, which were lower on a percentage basis, suggesting that franchisee failures tended to be concentrated in smaller franchise systems.

In summary, we still lack any harmonised methodology for assessing failure rates, and the difference between franchised business failures and independents is almost certainly much less than the impression given by promotional books and franchisee recruitment packages. However, the most honest and accurate statement that can be made on the issue of comparative failure rates probably remains that made by Housden (1984: 226): 'It has been claimed that as well as helping in the creation of new businesses, franchising substantially reduces the subsequent rate of failure in such businesses ... No firm evidence has yet been produced to support this contention, but it seems probable to assume that franchised outlets of a reputable system are less likely to fail than independently-owned outlets, because of the franchisor's vested interest.'

Statistics published in the USA appear to underline the possible effects of franchisor fees and market saturation in influencing franchisee failure rates and profit returns. Bates (1994: 4) drew up a sample of 7,270 small businesses started between 1984 and 1987, drawn from the US Census Bureau's Business Owners Database. Using 1987 as a baseline (year 1), he tracked these businesses through to 1991. Bates found that 34.9% of franchise businesses failed, compared to 28.0% of non-franchise businesses. Pre-tax income levels were also higher for independent businesses. Bates concluded that the difference in performance rates between franchised outlets and other small businesses was based in part on differences in industry distribution, with franchises over-represented in retailing and under-represented in services. Amongst other possible reasons for these findings, he includes:

- the recruitment by franchise companies of candidates poorly qualified to become franchisees;
- the saturation of key franchise markets;
- the high level of franchisor fees and royalties.

He hypothesises that what might once have been a prudent route to small-business success may now be undermined by excessive competition and/or fees relative to the value of franchisor services.

It should be remembered that, whilst a franchisee should – and hopefully will – receive the kind of professional managerial help and advice that is not normally available to SMEs, this is only delivered at a price, and often a substantial one at that – typically an ongoing rate of around 10% levied on sales turnover (in addition to front-end start-up fees and charges). Very many SMEs would almost certainly not make total profits of this magnitude and, by any measure, this kind of royalty regime is likely to take in the region of half the total profits of even a well-run franchised outlet. In short, the royalty regime is a heavy burden for outlets to bear, particularly where conditions of recession and market saturation also take their toll.

12.9 The quality of jobs created in franchising

Very little research has been undertaken concerning the quality of jobs provided by the franchise industry in terms of pay, training and job satisfaction levels. However, most franchised businesses tend to involve a limited range of products and services and appear to lend themselves to low-skill/low-pay human resource strategies. After all, franchise company outlets are essentially non-unionised small firms operating on the basis of human resource strategies devised by the franchisee. This is a fruitful area for future research and there are already movements on the part of researchers interested in becoming involved here.

Felstead (1993: 200) has presented some evidence which is, in all probability, fairly typical of the industry and thus generalisable. He makes the point that franchisees, in attempting to improve their profits, may be more motivated to save money on their payroll bills than by increasing turnover levels, since the latter attracts a 10% (or thereabouts) levy by the franchisor whereas the former does not. Felstead conducted a comparison of franchised and non-franchised high-street printers in the East Midlands (Felstead 1988). He found that those who worked for franchisees were more likely to be young, government-sponsored (i.e. on training schemes), women workers in receipt of payment levels and non-pay benefits (such as holiday pay) substantially below those paid by the industry's more traditional employers.

Felstead says that these findings are corroborated by a survey of American fast-food restaurants which indicate that, despite the common characteristics that employees of company-owned and franchise restaurants exhibit, wages and especially fringe benefits (paid holidays, sick leave, uniform allowance, free meals, etc.) are greater for workers employed in company-owned stores than those employed by franchisees (Krueger 1991; Katz and Krueger 1992).

12.10 Chapter summary

The world-wide growth of franchising appears set to continue on a long-term basis. The growth of franchising overall (in real terms) is strongly dependent on the performance of the economy as a whole. Against this, business format franchising – concentrated upon more service-oriented activities – is likely to experience growth rates notably faster than those which apply for franchising as a whole.

A number of factors appear likely to promote future growth. First is the general world-wide decline of traditional manufacturing industry and its replacement by service-sector activities. Franchising is especially well suited to service and people-intensive economic activities, particularly where these require a large number of geographically dispersed outlets serving local markets.

A second factor is the growth in the overall popularity of self-employment. Most governments throughout the world are looking towards self-employment and small business as an important source of future jobs. As franchising becomes increasingly well known and understood, it is likely to appeal to a growing number of people. Alongside this trend, we may expect to see an increase in the number of franchise opportunities. This process will be assisted, not least, by large companies following the current trend towards divestment from centralised control of an increasing proportion of their business activities. A notable example in the UK has been the franchising of domestic milk-delivery. Increasing female workforce participation will continue the current trend towards dual-career and dual-income families, resulting in both the need and the resources to purchase services. Home service franchises (cleaning, maiding, lawn-care, house-minding, etc.) are likely to feature here, as are child-care and child-development services.

The demands of an ageing population in many countries will also create opportunities, ranging from the need for special diets to special needs in the fields of leisure and care. In America the health-care industry is turning to franchised medicine, ranging from private-duty nursing agencies to the provision of alternative medicine. Greater awareness of health issues generally will also throw up opportunities in sectors ranging from food to exercise and counselling services. Entertainment and leisure activities will also offer additional franchise opportunities, ranging from travel agencies to ventures such as miniature golf courses, dance studios, specialist movie theatres, etc. American experience suggests that growth levels in the number of franchised outlets are unlikely to match growth levels in sales turnover figures, since franchise outlets tend to be larger than the average conventional small business in turnover terms.

On balance, it does not appear that franchise operations substantially displace conventional small businesses. Where they do challenge them, it is often because they act as a new force in the field with the flexibility to respond rapidly to changes in technology and market demand. They themselves may then subsequently be threatened by exposure to similar market forces, thus rendering their businesses and their profit margins more vulnerable than they and their franchisees would have expected or hoped. However, it is obviously untrue that those who eat at McDonald's do so without any measure of substitution concerning their former eating habits, or that customers of Kall-Kwik or Prontaprint still place their customary orders with traditional print firms. Encroachment and additionality appear to have developed hand in hand, usually aided by developments in technology, customer tastes and consumer spending power.

If we look at the quintessential icon of the industry – fast-food franchising – it is unlikely that it has not in some measure diverted trade away from more traditional providers in the field (many of them almost certainly small independents). However, the conditions fuelling a market restructuring here were almost certainly the development of technology capable of producing food quickly on a standardised basis, and a growth generally in trends towards convenience foods and eating out. Similarly, in the field of fast-print franchising, new technology reduced the training and skill levels required to produce print copy and final product from years to weeks. The result is that print products can now be produced in hours rather than days, using cheaper and less skilled labour, whilst relocating from manufacturing premises off the high street to 'business service' premises on the high street. An additional key factor assisting the growth of fast-print franchising was the trend of large firms in the 1980s to divest themselves of many internal services, and 'buy in' instead.

When a franchise first comes into being, it ideally requires some 'unique selling point', giving it an advantage over its competitors. Over time, however, competition arrives to challenge its market position. This may come in the shape of new franchise operations but may, equally, take the form of conventional small business operations.

Women and minorities appear to have increased their representation in franchising in recent years in the USA. Although both groups are less visible than might be expected in terms of their general participation in the labour force at large, the evidence indicates that around 10% of franchise units in the USA are owned outright by women, with another 20% owned by women in alliance with men. Around 5% of franchise units were owned by minorities in the USA in 1986 compared with an 8.8% ownership level of US firms generally. This is despite government schemes targeted specifically at increasing the level of minority representation.

The help afforded by franchisors in setting up new franchisees, particularly those with no prior business experience, renders franchising a potentially fruitful route for increasing female and ethnic participation in small business. Thus, any government assistance to franchising is best advised to be targeted on indigenous franchises – particularly those with export potential and the facility for spreading jobs and enterprise amongst ethnic groups where opportunities might otherwise be lacking.

Questions

1 Which is more logically consistent – to consider franchising as small businesses colonising territory which is usually the preserve of large firms, or vice versa?

2 In what ways can franchising combine the strengths of both small business and large business?

3 Why are American franchises such a success on the global platform and British franchises so relatively unsuccessful?

4 Consider why franchise trade associations routinely overstate industry achievements and the ethical implications of this stance.

CHAPTER 13

Technical entrepreneurship

Sarah Cooper

13.1 Learning objectives

There are five learning objectives in this chapter:

1 To examine the growth in interest in technical entrepreneurship over the last thirty years.

2 To identify characteristics of entrepreneurs in high-technology sectors.

3 To highlight possible differences between entrepreneurs in contrasting technology-based sectors.

4 To identify aspects of technology-based industries which pose specific challenges for technical entrepreneurs.

5 To examine the role of the technical entrepreneur in economic development.

Key concepts

- technical entrepreneurship
- typology of technical entrepreneurs
- agglomeration development
- management experience

13.2 Introduction

The rapid emergence of firms exploiting opportunities in new technology-based fields has been in stark contrast to the decline observed within traditional sectors. Small firms, particularly those within sunrise sectors, have been identified as important vehicles for achieving economic growth and have, thus, become targets for specific attention. New-firm formation and growth is dependent upon a supply of budding entrepreneurs, committed to transforming their new product and service ideas from dreams into realities. The relatively recent emergence of high-technology firm clusters, for example in Silicon Valley and around Cambridge, has brought the technical entrepreneur under close scrutiny and this chapter discusses some of the resulting research. Issues of policy relevance are highlighted since development agencies are keen to identify how more people can be encouraged to take a step towards independence and self employment.

13.3 Technical entrepreneurship

Over the last 20–30 years many economies have experienced marked structural shifts. Developed, Western economies have seen the decline of many traditional industrial sectors and a dramatic increase in the role played by services within the economy, with particular growth in the contribution of small firms to employment (see Chapter 2). While traditional manufacturing sectors have been changing fundamentally, expansion has occurred in technology-based fields which make an increasingly important economic contribution. The dramatic emergence and growth of high-technology-based areas in the United States of America, such as Silicon Valley and Route 128 in Massachusetts, brought technical entrepreneurship under the spotlight some time ago in the USA. However, it is only during the last 10–15 years that a burgeoning of technology-based entrepreneurial activity has occurred in Europe, exploiting existing and newly emerging technologies, bringing about a consequent growth in interest in the subject on the eastern side of the Atlantic. From an economic perspective local, regional and national governments and development agencies are focused on encouraging enterprise and are, understandably, eager to target their resources as effectively as possible into initiatives which will facilitate the emergence of new entrepreneurial business entities. Thus, they are keen to understand the entrepreneurial motives of founders and to identify the needs of fledgling and established technology-based businesses to maximise economic growth and regeneration.

This chapter explores some current issues in the field of technical entrepreneurship. Contrasting approaches adopted by researchers are discussed and a number of issues which impact upon the entrepreneurial process are examined, focusing specifically on the key or lead entrepreneur, including his/her motivations, education, employment background and expertise. In concluding, a number of areas are identified which may be of relevance to policy-makers wishing to encourage increased levels of entrepreneurship, to benefit local, regional and national economic development.

13.4 The environment for technical entrepreneurship

In their day James Watt and Alexander Graham Bell made significant technical breakthroughs which stimulated revolutionary economic and societal changes, altering the lives of millions. Wide-scale industrialisation was still in its infancy, and the pivotal role of technology in economic development had still to be recognised, but Britain was a breeding ground for such technical entrepreneurs who made major contributions to world development. More recently it has been in the USA that high-profile technical entrepreneurs have emerged: Bill Shockley with the transistor, Steve Wozniak and Steve Jobs developing the personal computer at Apple and – perhaps the most well-known – Bill Gates with his Microsoft empire. Against the background of such a 'Dream Team', Britain has continued to generate its share of entrepreneurs, notable recent examples being Clive Sinclair, revered for the Spectrum and notorious for the C5, Alan Sugar, renowned for his exploits at Amstrad and brushes with the City of London, and James Dyson, who succeeded in sweeping away the competition with his dual cyclone action technology.

Few business success stories escape the media spotlight, and modern communication technology and the investigative approach adopted by the media ensure that the life and times of those behind the business successes find their way into the newspapers and magazine bookstalls with increasing regularity. Such personalities form just the tip of a very large entrepreneurial iceberg, but perform a valuable task in raising the profile of technical entrepreneurship. The war-stories of their contrasting routes to success can stimulate latent entrepreneurs into taking the first step on the ladder to self-employment. Few who follow reach the heights achieved by their well-known counterparts; however, many do not seek their fortune but a rewarding career with challenges along the way. The massive growth in public interest in business personalities is a relatively recent phenomenon but it mirrors the increasing attention paid by academic researchers and policy-makers to the subject of entrepreneurship over the last 30–40 years. During that time the amount of effort invested into studies of technical entrepreneurship in particular has increased, partly as a result of significant structural economic changes.

13.4.1 The rise of the technology-based firm

Faced with marked declines in traditional sectors such as coal-mining, and job losses in other sectors due to downsizing and the application of new technology, many governments have been forced to look for new forms of enterprise on which to base their futures. Against a picture of falling employment in traditional areas of manufacturing, growth has occurred in sectors focusing on the exploitation of new technologies. Small firms in 'sunrise', high-technology sectors (including electronics, software and biotechnology) have been hailed as the future employment and wealth generators, 'largely based on the premise that such companies provide a powerful medium for the creation of new jobs, for regional economic regeneration, and for enhancing national rates of technological innovation and international competitiveness' (Berry 1998). They are more innovative than their large-firm counterparts, being less bound by convention (Pavitt *et al.* 1987), and are more flexible due to their organic and network-based structure, contrasting with the mechanistic and bureaucratic framework common in many large firms. Small firms also make an important contribution to economic growth and vitality 'by offering alternative career possibilities to those engineers and managers who do not function most effectively in larger organizations' (Cooper 1973).

Eisenhardt and Forbes (1984) point to the positive role of volatility inherent in many technology-based sectors, emphasising the way in which the peaks, troughs and fast-moving cycles reveal market niches suitable for occupation and exploitation by enterprising small firms. Although volatility presents opportunities, it also poses a threat as firms are forced to innovate and develop new products and services on a continuous basis, as competitors enter and overtake their market position; those working within such fields are forced to become acclimatised to a culture of instability and change. All this takes place in an environment supportive of risk-taking and dynamic action. In stressing the importance of maintaining and supporting such a system Eisenhardt and Forbes contend that 'technical entrepreneurship remains a key path to innovation and economic vitality throughout the world'.

13.4.2 Characteristics of new technology-based sectors

The search for a definition of 'high technology' has occupied many writers, and existing definitions are classified into those based on purely subjective criteria, those drawing a distinction between product and process innovation, and the final group using surrogate measures such as the proportion of employees in research and development (R&D). Discussions regarding 'high-technology' industry and of sectors falling within the classification often imply that firms are similar; however, research on small firms in specific sectors suggests that theoretical and practical differences exist between 'high-technology' industries and that technology strongly influences the ability of founders to establish and grow firms (Oakey and Cooper 1991; Oakey 1995; Cooper 1997a). The use of the term across a heterogeneous group of industries can lead to the mistaken assumption that all founders have similar entrepreneurial opportunities and experience similar problems.

Market entry by new technology-based firms depends upon barriers which may vary through time and between sectors. Technological progress creates business opportunities for new, small, research-intensive companies offering products, services or a combination of activities. Competition is generally less severe in 'new' sectors and more commercial opportunities exist for small firms; as sectors mature, larger firms tend to dominate and the small firms which remain are likely to occupy narrow niches, unattractive to larger firms. Collaboration between small and large firms often occurs as the activities of small, specialist product and service firms complement those of large organisations, allowing large companies to focus on their core business. An important factor in the growth and development of technology-based firms is the sectoral variation in the length of product life-cycle (Markusen 1985; Malecki 1981; 1991). In the electronics industry, for example, it is possible to take an idea from the drawing board to the marketplace in a matter of months; by contrast, product-based firms in sectors such as biotechnology experience long lead-times. The result is that some businesses are established on the basis of contract research, which is a low-cost method of start-up, on which future product development is built using revenue from service activities (Oakey *et al.* 1990).

Related to the question of time-scales and development and life-cycles is the issue of finance, as the requirement for long-term funding is generally greatest where development cycles are the longest. For example, the capital required for the translation of an electronics idea into a viable product is likely to be significantly less than that required by a biotechnology firm to finance six years of laboratory/development work, two years of testing and clinical trials before revenue is forthcoming. The dilemma for firms working in fields where the outcome of R&D is uncertain is that while potential long-term financial gains may be very high, so are the risks. The requirement for up-front finance often prevents a firm from being established or sinks the firm whose ability to spend exceeds its ability to generate income. Wider issues of finance and the firm are discussed in Chapter 19.

13.4.3 The emergence of technology-based start-ups

The culmination of entrepreneurial activity is the appearance of a new firm and there are two principal routes by which new enterprises are established within a region.

Spinning-off – resulting from the outward movement of personnel from a firm in which they have worked, either as the owner or as an employee – is a particularly important method of new-firm formation in areas of existing concentrations of high-technology industrial activity. The second method is the inward movement of individual and/or corporate capital into a region, often attracted by the quality of the local economic infrastructure or availability of incentives.

There is debate over whether entrepreneurs are born or made; whatever the case, some organisations appear to provide a greater stimulus to employees to be entrepreneurial and generate more spin-offs. Spin-off rates can vary dramatically between organisations: the spin-off rate from small firms is up to ten times greater than that of large organisations. Spin-off rates from business units within larger organisations tend to be greater than those where the activities of the organisation are not compartmentalised. Creating a culture supportive of enterprising behaviour within large organisations can bring performance improvements, which increase the feeling of achievement in staff and encourage individuals or groups to consider exploiting their capabilities through entrepreneurship. The decision to establish a business in the 'outside world' can, in turn, improve the prestige and social and professional standing of individuals. For this reason the culture both within the source organisation and in the local area is important in influencing the likelihood of entrepreneurial action.

Cooper (1973) identifies two types of organisation, generating above- and below-average numbers of new starts, which he categorises by their technical entrepreneur 'birth rates'. Low-birth-rate firms produce below-average numbers of entrepreneurs while high-birth-rate organisations contribute more than their 'fair share' to the economy. Low-birth-rate organisations employ large numbers of employees, are organised by function, recruit average technical people, are relatively well managed and are located in areas of little entrepreneurship. By contrast, high-birth-rate organisations have small numbers of employees, are product-decentralised, recruit very capable, ambitious people, are afflicted by periodic crisis and are located in areas of high entrepreneurship, where the presence of role models stimulates prospective entrepreneurs to found enterprises. This model implies that the structure and strategic orientation of existing organisations within a region strongly influence the likelihood of new enterprise creation by indigenous entrepreneurs. Locations such as Silicon Valley have seen significant levels of new technology-based firm formation through local spin-offs, while regions populated by low-birth-rate organisations do not exhibit high natural levels of spin-offs, nor are they likely to do so without proactive intervention.

13.4.4 The environment for technology-based firms

Planners and agencies wishing to attract firms to their areas or encourage indigenous entrepreneurship need to understand what influences the founders of technology-based firms to select a location in the first place. In the mid 1980s, Galbraith (1985) commented that high-tech firms operate on the basis of factors different from those for other types of manufacturing, the one common element being the importance of a complex local infrastructure (including universities, government research labs and mature companies), implying that the influence of materials and transport – so important in Weber's traditional location model – is less relevant in the context of new technology-based sectors.

The presence of institutions such as universities or research establishments plays a multidimensional role in encouraging and supporting new enterprise development. Institutions act as sources of entrepreneurs and of ideas on which firms are based and support innovation through the provision of specialist technical help to companies. While technical links may be maintained over long distances, links are most readily maintained within a local area; enthusiasm for the university science park is predicated on the belief that interaction will necessarily occur between firms on the park and academics in the university. There is debate between those who believe that universities and science parks play a role in stimulating industrial development (Monck *et al.* 1988) and those who question the precise nature of the relationship between universities, science parks and the growth of agglomerations of technology-based firms (Oakey 1985). While the level of interaction may vary, research-intensive organisations are viewed as an important part of the innovation infrastructure, improving the network to support and encourage new enterprise development and growth.

The tendency for firms to select similar locations results in the development of agglomerations or clusters of related firms and organisations, such as those in Silicon Valley and in the Silicon Glen of Scotland (Bell 1991; Cooper 1996). A location within an agglomeration frequently attracts higher costs, for example through high land, premises and wage rates, but yields benefits through ease of access to local customers, suppliers and financiers (Saxenian 1996). In spite of this, a minority of firms establish themselves in relatively remote locations where the entrepreneur enjoys the quality of life and a pleasant working and living environment. Roberts (1991) concludes that the supportive environment (including the presence of the Massachusetts Institute of Technology [MIT]) not only contributes to the high incidence of spin-off entrepreneurs in the Boston area but also influences the degree of success of those ventures.

The growth of industrial complexes leads to the development of specialist support infrastructure such as accountants, lawyers and financiers whose input can be vital, particularly in the pre-start and early days of the firm. A location providing ready access to those with the right skills/knowledge base should facilitate the establishment of the new business. Financial advisers with knowledge of technological sectors are not ubiquitous, and locations with a strong presence of high-technology firms establish a reputation for the quality of local specialist support (Cooper 1996).

13.5 The study of technical entrepreneurship

Among studies in small business the investigation of firms in new-technology fields has been growing in popularity; while many of the early studies were conducted in the USA, interest in the subject has risen in Europe over the last 15–20 years. A principal reason for the growth in interest is the increasing emphasis from government development and planning agencies on new forms of enterprise. Many of the early technical entrepreneurship studies were undertaken in the USA, partly as a result of the dramatic emergence and growth of technology clusters, such as those in Silicon Valley, California and alongside Route 128 near Boston. Researchers examined the influences on industrial development and at an early stage turned their spotlight onto the entrepreneurs themselves. The number of North American technical entrepreneurship investigators grew steadily; however, outside the USA research in the field was still in its infancy (Watkins 1973). The last 10–15 years have seen the burgeoning of technology-based entrepreneurial activity in Europe, exploiting existing and newly emerging technologies, accompanied by a consequent growth in interest in technical entrepreneurship.

The impetus for research comes from two contrasting directions. Academics interested in the development of new technology-based sectors have focused their attentions on the firm in general and, in particular, on the role of the entrepreneur in its establishment and growth. Meanwhile, local, regional and national agencies with an economic development remit are concerned to identify ways in which the environment can be improved to facilitate the emergence and growth of new firms. They wish to target resources at initiatives which will bear entrepreneurial fruit and, thus, draw on in-house and academic research to help them understand the influences on founders and identify the needs of fledgling and established technology-based businesses to maximise economic regeneration and growth.

13.5.1 Methodological approaches

Research in the field of technical entrepreneurship is still at a relatively early stage compared with its 'big brother' of general entrepreneurship. Even so a wide range of methodological approaches has been employed, from those based upon quantitative approaches to those founded upon qualitative principles. A number of early US studies adopted quantitative approaches, using questionnaires to sample hundreds of firms (Cooper 1973; Roberts 1991). They generated aggregate trends and profiles of entrepreneurial types, but provided little contextual and anecdotal information available via 'softer' methodologies. The approach was used due to the study of high-technology industry being relatively advanced; aggregate entrepreneurship data were interpreted in the context of a broad understanding of the sectors concerned. Perhaps the most comprehensive research database on technology-based firms and their founders is that developed by Ed Roberts. Through more than a quarter of a century of research, he has conducted numerous studies of spin-off activity, particularly around Boston and MIT (Roberts 1991). This approach contrasts with that of Bygrave (1988) who advocates that an understanding of the entrepreneurial process will be found in the descriptive background of the entrepreneur. The use of qualitative techniques, such as participant observation and in-depth personal interviews, allows the generation of a more multidimensional view of the start-up and subsequent development of the organisation, the role of the founder within the process and the influence of internal and external factors.

European researchers have employed approaches ranging from large-sample to case methodologies. Jones-Evans (1996a) suggests that research on the background of entrepreneurs should be largely exploratory but does not advocate the use of qualitative or quantitative approaches in isolation. Following quantitative survey work with in-depth exploratory interviews with a small number of survey participants can prove a powerful combination. Different approaches addressing similar themes sometimes yield contrasting results. Chandler (1996) used quantitative interviews to focus on the skills and degree of similarity between the founder's previous work and his new firm, while Jones-Evans (1996a) favoured the softer, in-depth case approach for his research. Using a particular approach may influence the result: for example, Cooper (1973) compares results of brief questionnaires and in-depth interviews. In the brief questionnaire a large number of respondents claimed socially acceptable 'pull' motives (such as 'desire for independence') as the reason for establishing their business; in interviews a large number cited 'push' factors such as redundancy or serious unhappiness in their previous employment. No approach is optimal; it is necessary to understand the research aims and to design an appropriate methodology.

The sharp increase in the number of studies of new technology-based firms poses problems for researchers. Firms are receiving increasing numbers of 'invitations' to contribute to studies through the completion of questionnaires and participation in interviews, and, while many managers wish to help, even the most tolerant find it increasingly difficult to respond positively to all requests. The firms most affected are those appearing in directories of organisations in specific sectors or in particular locations, such as science parks; they are 'sitting ducks' for researchers. In designing programmes and methodological approaches focusing on new technology-based sectors it is important to consider such wider issues and to be aware of potential 'research fatigue'.

The field of technical entrepreneurship research is highly dynamic; the rate of technological change is increasing, new sectors are emerging and, as the costs of R&D escalate, firms are adopting innovative strategies. Large firms are developing partnerships, often with small firms whose specialist input complements their capabilities and resources, and the skills required on the part of the technical entrepreneur and his firm to work in this more corporate mode are changing. Given that there is still much to find out about the technical entrepreneur and the entrepreneurial process, there is scope for purely quantitative and qualitative studies, and for those exhibiting a hybrid methodology, where trends identified using quantitative techniques are explored through softer qualitative approaches. Having briefly considered the background to current technical entrepreneurship research, the following discussion considers what studies have revealed about this key economic actor.

13.6 The technical entrepreneur

In considering the resources necessary to establish a technology-based firm, labour, capital and land are important but the key 'input' is the entrepreneur. Successful entrepreneurs of their day include Henry Ford, Alan Sugar and Bill Gates; however, while high-profile founders grab popular attention, the road to business ownership is less golden for most technical entrepreneurs. Individuals require a combination of skills and expertise to accept the entrepreneurship challenge. Some learn 'by doing' while others adopt a systematic approach, developing the skills and knowledge base 22 that culminates in the entrepreneurial step. Earlier contributions have considered aspects of the definition of what constitutes an entrepreneur. Definitions of the 'technical entrepreneur' range from that adopted by Jones-Evans (1995) – where a technical entrepreneur is 'the founder and current owner-manager of a technology-based business, i.e. primarily responsible for its planning and establishment, and currently having some management control within the organisation' – to that of Smith (1967), who suggests that an entrepreneur is an individual who is responsible for the setting-up of a new venture but is not necessarily involved in its subsequent management.

In his early research focusing on the technical entrepreneur Cooper (1973) identified a number of influences on the entrepreneurship process including the founder himself, the organisation for which he worked previously and external factors relating to the locality of the new firm. These elements interact to create a climate which is more or less favourable to entrepreneurial activity. In this highly dynamic environment the technical entrepreneur is the catalyst and leader (Collins and Lazier 1993). Given that high degrees of uncertainty surround technology development, especially sectors with a scientific base such as biotechnology, the technical entrepreneur has to tolerate risk. In leading-edge technology firms he has to generate support for a technology about which few people know, imparting his philosophy, spirit, vision and enthusiasm for his enterprise to all concerned with it. Surrounded by uncertainty, the financier is persuaded to place his money over a 'black hole' capable of swallowing thousands or millions of pounds with no guarantee of a return, and personnel are recruited, often from positions within other organisations. Thus, the technical entrepreneur is a risk-taker required to persuade others to put their faith, finance and careers in his hands. Risk may decrease as the sector matures, as the underlying knowledge base increases, improving the quality of decision-making.

13.6.1 Entrepreneurial motivations

Setting up a firm can be highly risky and it is logical to ask why entrepreneurs jeopardise the future stability of themselves and their family to risk everything. Roberts (1991) considers that a disproportionate number of technology-based firm founders had self-employed fathers, and have therefore grown up in an enterprising environment. Some founders start their firm as a part-time activity while still employed; this provides the opportunity to judge whether the business is viable. A number of technology areas are characterised by long lead-times, meaning that significant time and resources are invested in research before any saleable result is produced. The part-time method of market entry means business ideas are developed in parallel with other employment. The ideas and concepts on which the firm is based evolve until research advances to the stage of producing workable product or service ideas, and at this point the founder formally resigns and moves into business full-time.

A variety of 'pull' and 'push' factors stimulates technical entrepreneurs, whether acting on their own or in groups. The most commonly reported stimuli tend to fall into the 'pull' category, with the desire to be one's own boss rating highly, followed by the wish to exploit a market opportunity (Oakey *et al.* 1990; Roberts 1991; Oakey 1995; Cooper 1998). Market entry of a new firm implies that opportunities exist, either as a result of the technology-based sector being 'new' and, thus, competition less severe, or because the company is operating in a niche unattractive to larger firms. Start-up opportunities are dependent upon barriers to entry, including capital requirements and the extent of large-firm domination. Technological advances open up new business opportunities where small, research-intensive companies are able to flourish. Those reporting a negative, or push, stimulus have often become disgruntled and frustrated in their existing job which prompts them to 'go out on their own'; others have little choice and are forced (as a result of redundancy and difficulty finding alternative employment) into being entrepreneurial. Principal motives are frequently supported by secondary factors: founders harbour latent thoughts of self-employment but do not explore it until redundancy converts it from a good idea into a solution to unemployment. It may take such a precipitating event to trigger this action.

The life-cycle stage of the sector may influence the formation stimulus (Cooper 1998). A comparison of new firms in the electronics and software sector reveals greater numbers of founders in the relatively youthful software sector reporting (in in-depth interviews) the desire to work for themselves or exploitation of market/product opportunities as the primary motivator. The relatively mature electronics sector is affected by greater economic fluctuations, resulting in redundancy being a more common stimulus than in the software field. The pace and nature of change within a sector will influence the opportunities in the market suitable for exploitation by the new firm.

Self-employment offers entrepreneurs the opportunity to take control of their own destiny, and to control the direction and growth of their firm. Frequently, however, founders have little desire to grow their enterprises significantly, particularly when they have worked for large firms and in founding their own are trying to get away from that environment, with its hierarchies, impersonality and lack of meaningful involvement. Thus, many firms remain relatively small, limiting their contribution to employment generation. The optimal firm size will vary but a characteristic of the software sector is the strong representation of small firms. While there are high-profile firms such as Lotus and Microsoft, employing thousands, the majority of software firms are small, occupying small niches, founded by people who have left other enterprises to capitalise on their skills and expertise; there is often little need to employ large numbers of staff, each with a different skill – as will be explored in more detail later, software founders commonly possess a composite of required skills. In addition, small firms often collaborate with each other if contracts are larger than one can manage on its own.

13.6.2 Age and the technical entrepreneur

Bill Gates and Richard Branson both demonstrated entrepreneurial abilities at an early age, but there is no optimal age for 'going it alone' and some founders wait until they are in the twilight of their careers. In general, however, new-technology firms tend to be established by relatively young entrepreneurs, and a number of research studies have indicated that while technical entrepreneurs may range in age from their 20s to their 70s when founding their firm, the median tends to be in the mid-30s (Cooper 1973; Roberts 1991; Cooper 1997b). Roberts suggests that the pattern of young high-technology founders is a result of the 'youthful age structure of the technical organisations at which they previously worked', pointing towards a self-perpetuating pattern. The entrepreneur makes numerous sacrifices, sinking significant amounts of time and money into a venture; younger individuals tend to have fewer financial and family commitments than those in their mid-40s and have greater flexibility to focus on a business. Increased age brings with it a maturity of approach and a greater depth of experience, but a potential drawback is that older people may be more set in their ways – a major barrier in a dynamic and rapidly changing environment. Someone who has been with an employer for a long time thinks seriously before moving from a job offering pension and other benefits; for older entrepreneurs redundancy is a more common stimulus than the desire to be self-employed, as difficulties securing new employment result in them starting their own firm.

The sector or activity of the firm imposes certain constraints: for example, the experience and level of skills which the founder requires to set up within it, and the consequent length of time required to acquire that grounding. A long period of study and work experience can help establish credibility. An electronics founder may study to degree level, followed by a long period of work experience in order to develop a thorough understanding of electronics in an applied environment; this scenario contrasts with that of a computer science graduate who works in a product development role with much client contact and is able to set up after a relatively short period of paid employment. The age of the founder influences the length of time which he has had to develop skills and expertise on which to draw in his own venture. Some sectors require higher levels of funding and prospective founders wait until they have amassed sufficient resources of their own in order to minimise borrowing from external sources. In software, for example, people are becoming entrepreneurs at an earlier age; those with the right skills are identifying opportunities and the relatively modest levels of investment required mean that financial barriers to entry are low. In other sectors, such as electronics and biotechnology, funding proves a greater barrier for potential founders who need to gather experience and finance; thus, some sectors offer a swifter route to entrepreneurship.

13.6.3 Education and technical entrepreneurship

Bill Gates is perhaps one of the best-known Harvard 'drop-outs' but his is not the standard educational route. Many new technology-based sectors are highly competitive, and a firm's competitive advantage is usually based upon the knowledge and expertise of the founder. Contrasting patterns are evident among the results of a number of studies; however, when the qualifications of technical entrepreneurs are compared with those held by non-technical entrepreneurs the level of attainment in the latter group tends to be more modest. Fewer than 5% of founders of non-high-technology firms in Storey's (1982) study in Cleveland, UK, had a degree compared with high-technology science-park firms where 58% had a first degree and 38% a higher degree (Monck *et al.* 1988). This relative position may change with an increasing number of people going on to further and higher education prior to moving into employment of all types. The majority of high-technology entrepreneurs hold degrees in science or engineering disciplines and most founders hold Bachelor's and Master's degrees, with a lower proportion having a PhD. Roberts (1991) attributes the generally high 70–80% survival rate of new technology-based firms to the level of education of their founders.

While differences are apparent between high-technology and non-high-technology entrepreneurs, the pattern is not uniform between high-technology sectors. The proportion of degrees is higher in science-park-based than off-park firms (Monck *et al.* 1988), possibly as a result of the majority of science-park firms being at the R&D-intensive end of the spectrum. In addition, sectoral variations exist, with founders of science-based firms in biotechnology commonly having a Master's degree and frequently a PhD (Oakey *et al.* 1990). Vocationally orientated qualifications are more widespread in electronics, with founders undertaking practical, technically based training within firms, backed up by study at local colleges. Hisrich and Peters (1998) consider that an important aspect of education is that people develop the ability to deal with others and communicate clearly.

The education system plays a role in mobilising entrepreneurial capital. Taking a degree or further education qualification frequently means moving away from home to attend university or college; thus, institutions attract bright individuals into their locality, a minority of whom spin-off directly from university. Technology-based firms seeking able employees are drawn to university cities and towns to feed off the stream of graduates, as has happened in the Cambridge area. Ultimately, some employees spin-off and set up their own firms in the locality, aiding the development of agglomerations of related firms.

13.6.4 Background expertise and work experience

An entrepreneur needs to understand the environment within which his or her business operates, a process which is helped when s/he establishes his/her firm in a field with which s/he is familiar (Chandler 1996) – see Chapter 16. Most entrepreneurs in technology-based start-ups work for other organisations prior to establishing their own enterprise, and studies regularly report in excess of 80% of founders setting up within a similar market or using similar technology (Roberts 1991; Cooper 1998). There are two aspects of the previous work environment which are relevant to the technical entrepreneur: the task environment, related to the market in which the firm operates; and the skills and abilities developed by the founder (Timmons 1994).

A high degree of risk is associated with new-venture creation; however, knowledge of the target sector helps to reduce some of that risk. Sectoral familiarity makes it easier to recognise opportunities offered by a technology and also the limitations which it can impose on firm development. The technological complexity of many sectors makes this aspect very important if the technical entrepreneur is to avoid jeopardising the future of his/her business by making elementary mistakes. Timmons (1994) considers that being able to recognise an opportunity is an important advantage of having worked in a sector previously. Sector knowledge facilitates the identification of small, viable niches and competitor-free areas of the market, and results in the entrepreneur having a broad understanding of the customer and supplier environment. The technical entrepreneur is better placed to understand aspects of the competition and this allows him/her to place his/her firm in a stronger market position. Knowledge of the task environment, resulting from business similarity, enables the entrepreneur to make more informed decisions.

Roberts (1991) emphasises the role which the experience of the key founder plays in the business start-up, since there is a strong dependence on him/her to lead the organisation in a highly competitive marketplace. Lead entrepreneurs may surround themselves with capable managers and directors but there will be heavy reliance upon the entrepreneur to provide direction and motivation to those in the organisation. When persuading sceptical customers and financial backers of the viability of the business, technical and previous experience in the sector proves important in establishing credibility. In general, venture capitalists prefer technical entrepreneurs with experience in the field in which they intend to set up their own enterprise. Experience can be equated with the number of years spent in the sector; however, experience does not necessarily translate into success in the new venture (Chandler 1996).

Time spent working within a similar field enables individuals to enhance their technical and managerial skills, depending on the positions which they hold. Some entrepreneurs have held positions where they have developed specific skills which are similar to those required in their new business; useful skills include the ability to plan, organise and manage, all of which help an entrepreneur in the strategy implementation process. Oakey's (1984) entrepreneurial matrix represents the balance between business acumen and technical ability, in which different entrepreneurial types are identified depending on the degree of business and technical experience which they possess. Technical skills are important in the early stages of the business development process but a lack of supporting management skills frequently proves a drawback in the longer term, implying that evolution of the management team is required to progress the business beyond the start-up and early-growth stages.

The degree of sectoral similarity between the previous employer and the new enterprise may vary depending on the size and age of the sector. For example, most electronics spin-offs are generated from other electronics firms, while in a younger sector like software or biotechnology some new-starts originate from within the sector but a sizeable proportion come from organisations which share aspects of the underlying science/technology but are less closely related. At a practical level this implies that the number of related spin-offs generated within a particular sector is influenced by the profile of 'incubator' organisations.

The type of organisation for which the founder has worked may influence the breadth of knowledge which he develops. Common source organisations are other firms (both large and small) and public-sector institutions such as universities and government research establishments. Most provide a reasonable 'incubator' environment, allowing entrepreneurs to establish firms built upon their research and technical experience; what varies is the degree of exposure to commercial issues. Most entrepreneurs have experience primarily in technical areas since many have held mainly research and technical positions, providing limited management training; only a small minority have experience of functions such as finance and marketing. Cooper (1997b) revealed sectoral variations in expertise, with the majority of founders in the electronics sector having mainly technical expertise whereas software founders predominantly had a combination of technical and administrative/commercial skills. Many founders in the software sector had previously held technical/sales/commercial positions, involving product and service development, which resulted in them gaining a broad understanding of their sector and developing a wide range of skills. Electronics founders tended to have worked in relatively strict, usually technical, functional roles and so were less exposed to commercial issues. One area in which most technical entrepreneurs lack experience is marketing (Shanklin and Ryans 1988; Oakey *et al.* 1993). This is most extreme where academic entrepreneurs set up in business; while firm on the technical side, they usually lack a firm commercial base to grow a business beyond the start-up stage. Some faculty members do not sever links totally with their university but take on a part-time commitment to a new spin-off enterprise. Many 'academic' entrepreneurs have a strength in project management and, from co-ordinating research teams, have relevant people-management skills (Jones-Evans 1996a).

The commercialisation of public-sector technology from universities and other research laboratories is a valuable way of exploiting and obtaining a financial return on the resources invested in its development. It is likely that the number of university and research centre spin-offs will increase over time as universities place more emphasis on the commercialisation of their knowledge base. Staff are being encouraged to identify licensing opportunities for in-house developed technology and, thus, are working more closely with commercial firms, gaining greater insights into the commercial world. In the long term a minority may be tempted into heading up a spin-off team or into taking part-time directorships with spin-off companies. Given their relative lack of commercial expertise, the appropriate long-term role of academic entrepreneurs in the firm may be questioned.

13.6.5 Achieving 'balance' in the entrepreneurial team

Many high-profile figures are known for their individual entrepreneurial actions; however, while some like Alan Sugar start a firm on their own, many others establish a founding team. Even the lone entrepreneur usually draws on the support and expertise of others in respect of production, financial, commercial and marketing advice (Oakey *et al.* 1988; 1990). The founder who builds a firm with substantial levels of support from others compensates for any shortcomings in his own skill and knowledge base. Given that only a minority of technical entrepreneurs have both technical and commercial experience, the assistance of those with complementary skills is very important in many start-ups.

Entrepreneurial teams are important in helping to compensate for major weaknesses present in individuals, and many technology-based firms result from such collective actions (Cooper 1973; Roberts 1991; Cooper 1997b). Team members perform a valuable psychological function, providing mutual support and encouraging management to take the next step. Collins and Lazier (1993) stress that the development of a real team is essential to prevent the development of disparate agendas. Instances of institutional self-advancement are highly detrimental to the young firm as they smother the innovative spark which is vital in giving the organisation its competitive edge.

A variety of factors influences the composition of the start-up team. One is the need for particular sets of skills; the specialist knowledge on which products and services are based usually comes from the technical entrepreneur but the need for administrative, financial and marketing input causes the founder to seek collaborators. For this reason founding team members usually bring contrasting skills and expertise to the team. Cooper (1998) identifies sectoral variations in the size and composition of start-ups, with the number of single founders being much higher in the software sector than in electronics. Founders in the software sector typically possess a range of skills, including programming and technical knowledge and market awareness (developed through direct client contact), which provides them with a sound base on which to found their own business. In addition, the capital investment required in software is relatively modest and is more readily raised by one person. An electronics start-up often requires a range of skills which are less commonly possessed by an individual, and the greater level of capital investment frequently necessitates pooling financial resources. Oakey (1995) reveals that firms established by teams exhibit higher levels of growth; however, this does not imply a lack of business ability on the part of lone founders as some set up their own firm to escape from large organisations and have no major growth aspirations.

The previous workplace provides a fertile environment in which to identify possible business partners. It presents an opportunity to see how potential co-founders function within the business environment and means that team members bring appropriate skills and expertise, since the majority of technology-based start-ups are established within the field in which the lead entrepreneur has worked previously. Teams comprising former work colleagues tend to set up locally as, in all but the most extreme cases, it is uncommon for several households to relocate to establish a business. Lone founders have fewer constraints and are, thus, more footloose. The nature of the local, professional and social networks of potential entrepreneurs influences the composition of the start-up team; where networks are highly developed, aspiring entrepreneurs come into contact with potential entrepreneurial colleagues outside their workplace and immediate social circle. Highly developed networks in the Cambridge area are considered responsible for high numbers of non-work-related start-up teams (Cooper 1997b). A small minority of teams comprise family members: for example, a father with years of experience in a sector who teams up with a younger member of the family, who has completed a university education and brief period of work. Wider aspects of family enterprise are discussed in Chapter 9.

13.6.6 Location and the technical entrepreneur

The processes of spinning-off and the inward movement of entrepreneurial capital into an area govern the level of local new-firm formations, and in turn the size of the pool of firms from which future firms are generated. The *in situ* expansion of indigenous firms leads to industrial growth and increased sectoral employment in an area. These processes combine to result in the development of high-technology agglomerations like those which have emerged in the USA along Route 128 (near Boston) and in Silicon Valley, California, and in the UK along the M4 (Hall *et al.* 1987) and M11–Cambridge corridors (Segal Quince and Partners 1985) and in Scotland's Silicon Glen. Development agencies want to know where entrepreneurs come from, spatially, in order to ascertain the whereabouts of potentially enterprising types who can be targeted and encouraged into entrepreneurship.

Entrepreneurs setting up small firms are frequently influenced by the environmental quality of a region (Keeble 1987) and are attracted by the desire to live in a quiet and pleasant location, yielding not financial but psychic benefits (Tiebout 1957). The location of customers and suppliers exerts a degree of influence on firms, particularly those collaborating closely over development and contract-based work. Some need to be in close proximity to suppliers and locate as near as possible to their key service or materials provider; others with input needs which can be serviced by post or carrier can locate at a greater distance from their suppliers (Oakey and Cooper 1989). In a similar way some firms such as sub-contract electronics component manufacturers need to be located in close proximity to their main customers (Oakey 1984; Oakey *et al.* 1993). Other firms such as those producing sophisticated specialised equipment, where potential customers are located in any part of the world, are not subject to such strong external influences on their location, so a degree of footlooseness is possible.

The principal founder's previous workplace frequently influences the start-up location, with inertia resulting in entrepreneurs not moving from their current location. Research indicates that the majority of entrepreneurs (often in excess of 70%) set up firms in the locality where they previously worked (Oakey *et al.* 1988; Cooper 1997b). Setting up in a location with which the founder is familiar reduces some of the risk, and the benefit of moving has to outweigh significantly the disadvantages. Anecdotal evidence points to an emphasis on minimising disruption to domestic life – starting a business is stressful enough without uprooting the family unnecessarily. Much information is required when establishing a business, and setting up where the founder has been living and working means that numerous local contacts already exist and new ones are easily developed due to local knowledge. Some parts of the UK, especially agglomerations such as that around Cambridge, attract employees in to work for innovative organisations from which they spin-off to form indigenous firms.

Studies examining the childhood home and previous work location of technical entrepreneurs indicate that many people are not native to the region in which they set up their firm (Oakey *et al.* 1988; 1990; Cooper 1998). They are drawn in to work for local firms from which they spin-off, contributing to local economic development. The strong pattern of local spin-offs helps to increase the size of the agglomeration of related enterprises and intensifies the technology profile of a locality, as many new-starts are in the same technological sector. The emergence of new firms supplying goods and services improves the quality of the local supply infrastructure. The rich supplier pool acts not only as a stimulus to enhance local spin-off activity but also as a magnet to attract footloose entrepreneurs from elsewhere into the area.

Entrepreneurial mobility may be related to the sector of activity: for example, an electronics entrepreneur may be more likely to remain within the same locality than a software founder. Some electronics firms need to become highly integrated with local customers and/or supplier firms providing components and sub-contract services. As a consequence, the founder is reliant on his knowledge of the complex local inter-organisational network. The software founder trades information in its broadest sense and is less dependent upon the local environment. Knowledge of local suppliers and potential customers is, therefore, more important to new electronics than software firms, rendering the electronics start-up less mobile than the portable, software new-start.

To minimise costs many founders start up in their garage or spare room – firms such as Apple and Hewlett Packard grew from such humble beginnings. The home-based start is feasible where the process is 'clean', such as in software and some electronics firms. In sectors such as biotechnology the need for bespoke laboratory and factory space necessitates a rapid move into specialist facilities. These contrasting requirements pose differing barriers to start-up. In the longer term even clean businesses need physical and 'emotional' space, as entrepreneurs find that synonymous home and work locations become too stressful; the temptation not to 'leave' work or to keep going back risks ruling and ruining families' lives. These sharply differing premises need to be addressed by private or public-sector agencies attempting to encourage the development of technology-based entrepreneurship.

13.6.7 Continued entrepreneurial involvement and growth

For many founders of technology-based firms the organisation is their life. It develops from their idea, is based on their expertise, absorbs significant quantities of their personal and professional time, and allows them to pursue their interest and passion for a particular field of technology. Smith's and Jones-Evans' definitions of the technical entrepreneur differ in respect of this ongoing business involvement. For those involved with the firm from the start it is often difficult to consider, with a rational eye, what their long-term role and level of involvement should be; from their perspective they are crucial to the continued existence of the business. It is sometimes the case, however, that the long-term involvement of the technical founder in a controlling position within the enterprise is detrimental to the sustainability of the firm.

The extent to which some technical entrepreneurs lack an understanding of commercial issues at start-up has been discussed; few entrepreneurs attempt to gain a detailed knowledge of management concepts as their firm develops and consequently learn only 'by doing'. In some cases the continued involvement of a technical entrepreneur in a key decision-making role risks thwarting the development of the organisation and jeopardising its future. Some entrepreneurs recognise their shortcomings as 'managers' and adopt a central role in research and new product and service development, acknowledging their technical strengths. Many are happy to exchange the grey suit of management for the white coat of the laboratory, handing over to those more skilled and able to move the business onto a strong commercial footing. Reflecting this, Rubenson and Gupta (1990) conclude that technical entrepreneurs tend to stay in control of their businesses for shorter periods of time than entrepreneurs in other activities.

Some technical entrepreneurs possess all of the required skills but make a conscious decision not to pursue a strategy of rapid business growth. Many set up their own business expressly to distance themselves from large, bureaucratic, mechanistic and impersonal organisations. The prospects for employment growth in many technology-based businesses may, consequently, not be as great as they seem at first sight due to some entrepreneurs being economic satisficers rather than maximisers.

13.7 Technical entrepreneurs: an occupational typology

Earlier in this chapter brief definitions of technical entrepreneurs were presented, indicating their general nature. In the context of the above discussion it is clear that technical entrepreneurs take a variety of routes when progressing along the path to self-employment. Founders differ in their educational, employment and skill base, and yet all set up their firm alone or in consort with others. Each has a unique background which makes general classification difficult. It appears, however, that the occupational/work background is important for a number of reasons: the founder gains important sectoral and market knowledge and his/her occupation influences the extent of commercial and business expertise which s/he acquires. Authors have developed various entrepreneurial typologies. For example, Jones-Evans (1996b) divides technical entrepreneurs into four different types based on their occupational background: 'research entrepreneurs', 'producer entrepreneurs', 'user entrepreneurs' and 'opportunistic entrepreneurs'. Brief pen-portraits capture the essences of these entrepreneurial types, indicating the importance of occupational experience and educational background. Consideration of these types in the light of the earlier discussion of broad influences on the technical entrepreneur provides useful insights into the firms developed by these contrasting 'types'.

Research entrepreneurs

These have a knowledge-orientated, science and technology development background, having worked in higher education/academia or in a non-commercial laboratory. They have relatively little management experience but are experienced in the management of research programmes and possess good personnel management skills. Most have a high level of technical expertise and experience, coming from doctoral backgrounds, and only a few have experience in a production environment – and even then only in a research capacity. Due to their technical strength, research entrepreneurs provide the technical vision for the business; however, their lack of experience will often result in the formation of a firm with others possessing commercial management skills. Their levels of links to suppliers, customers and other external parties are extremely limited. Their long-term roles in the firm are likely to be in the technical development area.

Producer entrepreneurs

They come from an industrial background, having worked in production and development. They benefit from having direct commercial experience, combining both technical and management skills, often within the context of a large organisation. The majority of producer entrepreneurs have been educated to degree level, with a minority having served apprenticeships in technical subjects and moved into management later in their career, before themselves becoming entrepreneurs. Immediately prior to start-up some have worked in the technical environment while others have gained experience in management-intensive fields such as marketing. Producer entrepreneurs are perhaps the best placed of all four types to found a business on their own as they have the most highly developed all-round skills. Their company-based experience makes it likely that they have extensive business-related contacts, enabling them to build upon relationships with suppliers, customers and service providers when establishing their firms. Their all-round perspective makes them the most able of all four types to retain a central role in the management of the business.

User entrepreneurs

These entrepreneurs have been users of technology but have not been involved in its design or manufacture. Some have worked in technical sales or marketing, selling technology, but their direct experience of technical design aspects is peripheral. They are poorly placed to set up a firm on their own, due to their lack of technical design and development expertise. Their sales experience is highly valuable to the new enterprise and means that they are at ease working closely with customers.

237

Opportunist entrepreneurs

These have no technical background but have spotted a gap in the market; however, they have little or no previous experience in the field and are entering into relatively unknown territory. Opportunist entrepreneurs are in the minority. Their lack of sectoral experience makes it important for them to team up with others to develop a business. Their knowledge of the market, of customers and suppliers is either acquired from their business partners, or developed 'on the hoof'.

Technical entrepreneurs are acknowledged as playing an important role in economic development. It is apparent from this classification that entrepreneurs bring to the start-up situation a wide variety of skills. By considering these entrepreneurial types it is possible to see how an individual's background dictates the form and location of the enterprise which emerges. Such profiles also point to areas where entrepreneurs lack core skills and knowledge; many co-operate with others to compensate for their shortcomings but there are ways in which the development of technical entrepreneurship can be encouraged. Some implications for policy and practice arising from the above discussion are considered in the final section.

13.8 Chapter summary

Technology-based sectors have attracted the attention of policy-makers because they are seen as 'sunrise' industries, capable of compensating for declining traditional activities. The emergence and growth of new sectors is inextricably linked with issues of entrepreneurship since the business founder drives the enterprise development process; thus, the encouragement of entrepreneurship has become a major focus of attention from development organisations. A first step towards a greater understanding of ways to encourage entrepreneurship is to learn from those already in business. All have followed a slightly different path and had varying needs; while it is not possible to develop an individual support programme, there are some differences that agencies need to appreciate which may influence the rate and direction of enterprise development. Oakey and Cooper (1991) caution politicians and government planners eager to capitalise on 'opportunities offered by emergent key technologies' not to assume automatically that 'the encouragement of any new technology will result in rapid and sustained industrial growth'.

A high proportion of technology start-ups result from positive stimuli, but a sizeable number still occur due to the entrepreneur being pushed by redundancy or frustration. There are numerous niches suitable for small firms and setting up a business should be encouraged as a positive action rather than a response to a negative occurrence. Most people spin-off locally, suggesting that initiatives to increase levels of entrepreneurship need to be targeted at local people. The use of local role models will encourage those with ideas to appreciate that not all technical entrepreneurs are like Bill Gates.

A large proportion of firms are established in the same field in which the founder worked previously. Given the preponderance of local spin-off, the strong pattern of indigenous new-starts results in the intensification of a region's technology profile. The prevalence of local spin-offs assists the development of agglomerations of businesses, adding new firms, potential new suppliers, customers, contractors and service providers, increasing the visible presence of the agglomeration which in turn encourages the inward movement of entrepreneurs. For a location to remain attractive firms have to continue to innovate and adopt new techniques, otherwise the vitality of the agglomeration is reduced and competing clusters develop to become innovative centres, generating spin-offs and attracting inward investment.

Some organisations act as better entrepreneurial incubators than others, and agencies need to analyse the composition of their indigenous organisations in order to ascertain the likely level of local spin-offs and innovative potential of an area. Traditionally, large organisations have not acted as major generators of entrepreneurs but more firms are organising their activities into smaller product/service-based units, attempting to replicate the 'feel' of the small-firm environment; this is likely to encourage the creation of more spin-off teams as communication between employees increases and individuals from different functional areas identify opportunities and skill synergies. Areas lacking in local spin-offs need to attract more technical entrepreneurs from elsewhere in order to establish an innovative base on which to build. Stimulating entrepreneurship in areas which are under-represented is a challenge for development agencies. The creation of centres based around particular technologies, similar to the *technopôle* concept in France, might encourage entrepreneurship. The provision of appropriate support infrastructure and incentives or concessions might kick-start the process of encouraging predominantly local, latent, aspiring entrepreneurs into business ownership.

While a minority of entrepreneurs move some distance to set up firms, the majority spin-off in the local area, aiding the development of agglomerations of technology-based firms. Many entrepreneurs are embedded within professional and social networks which influence the decision on where to locate; once established, the firm becomes a node within a complex arrangement of organisational and personal relationships. Those who have worked in an area previously, in broadly the same field, possess local/market knowledge and are some way up the knowledge curve; remaining within the known environment reduces risk. Subsequent spin-offs increase the stock of firms and improve the attractiveness of an area to mobile entrepreneurs seeking a new location. A small minority of founders seek a location offering a high quality of life, and remote locations are viable if firms are able to operate at a significant distance from customers, suppliers and other service providers. The extent of local linkages in the short term might not be great so firms will use distant contacts, but in the long term peripheral areas have the potential to develop self-sustaining clusters of indigenous expertise. Improvements in information technology are making remote locations increasingly viable for certain firms. While many entrepreneurs still choose a non-peripheral location, anything which relieves pressure on existing industrial/commercial centres is beneficial.

Many founders in technology-based sectors have little business background and there is a danger that some potential entrepreneurs lack an appreciation of the opportunities offered by self-employment; others lack the management know-how and confidence to found a business. A two-pronged approach could raise business awareness and whet the appetite of bright scientists and engineers. Both aspects revolve around education: one addresses the student while the other focuses on the prospective entrepreneur who is at a later stage in his/her career.

Many schools offer students the opportunity to study management subjects, and greater integration of business into higher education programmes may prove fruitful. Gorman *et al.* (1997) advocate putting elements of entrepreneurship into formal education programmes, considering that entrepreneurs drive the economy. Courses socialise individuals into the idea of entrepreneurship as a viable and acceptable career path. Programmes incorporating entrepreneurship are relatively new in Europe, and until recently many 'would-be' technical entrepreneurs took a science/engineering degree which offered little exposure to management issues. Accreditation boards of professional institutes, such as those in civil and mechanical engineering, require that students on accredited degree programmes are exposed to management. Thus, management, accounting and legal concepts are becoming core elements in many college and university courses, ensuring that science and engineering graduates develop an understanding of the importance of management in organisations. In addition, increasing numbers of courses are incorporating industry placements. Hynes (1996) considers that 'non-business students have the talent of conceptualising new and original ideas'; thus, promoting ideas of entrepreneurship and business by putting them into the syllabuses of science and engineering courses may reap benefits.

In some technology-based fields a long 'apprenticeship' is not always required, and the route to entrepreneurship is relatively swift. For example, software graduates are well placed to establish firms straight out of university. In other sectors prospective founders need to gather financial, intellectual and human resources on which to base their business. The lead-time in some sectors is long and the provision of 'patient money' will enable founders to start firms at an earlier stage in areas where significant development funding is required. To support the increased level of management exposure in education and work, specialist courses targeted at more mature prospective technical entrepreneurs would enable them to gain a general understanding of business management. Once convinced of the merits of self-employment, those with specific business ideas would work up their concept into a formal business plan; those requiring external funding would receive help to develop proposals for investors. Such initiatives might encourage entrepreneurs to start their firm proactively rather than in response to a negative stimulus.

Technical people tend to remain in technical positions but, through education, may appreciate the pivotal role of business strategy and seek positions in which they can gain practical management experience. Ultimately, this may result in increased spin-off levels as founders develop a wider appreciation of the management function, making them better prepared for their role as founder. For those already running their own firms communication of the benefits of expanding the management team to maximise growth potential and share the burden may increase the number willing to grow their enterprises, maximising their contribution to wealth and employment generation.

The technical entrepreneur is an important economic actor, and the dynamic nature of most new technology-based fields means that there are numerous opportunities to further our understanding of what influences him/her into taking that 'one small step'.

Questions

1 Identify the key characteristics of technical entrepreneurs and contrast them with those of entrepreneurs in general. Do they differ and, if so, how?

2 Select a technology-based business and develop a short case-study profile of the firm and its founder (or principal founder in the case of a team-based start-up). How and in which areas is the influence of his or her personal and employment background most apparent with regard to the firm?

3 Which areas within your country have the greatest concentrations of technology-based firms? Why do you think that such firms are so common there and what resource or factor advantages exist?

4 How easy is it for technical entrepreneurs to set up firms in your local area – what forms of assistance are available to help them? What types of infrastructure, support and finance are provided by local and national government bodies and regional agencies to help potential founders, and how supportive is the local business environment in terms of potential customers, suppliers and information providers?

CHAPTER 14

Intrapreneurship

Dylan Jones-Evans

14.1 Learning objectives

There are five learning objectives in this chapter:

1 To identify the main differences between entrepreneurship and intrapreneurship.
2 To understand the key differences between a corporate and intrapreneurial culture within an organisation.
3 To understand the factors which can lead to intrapreneurship within the organisation.
4 To examine the barriers to intrapreneurship within a corporate setting.
5 To describe the personal and business characteristics of intrapreneurs.

Key concepts

▪ intrapreneurship ▪ corporate environment ▪ large organisations

14.2 Introduction

To compete effectively in dynamic and fast-changing world markets, many large organisations are adopting more innovative and enterprising approaches to management within their organisations. One of these approaches is the development of entrepreneurship within a corporate environment, generally known as intrapreneurship. This chapter will define the concept of intrapreneurship, especially the difference between developing entrepreneurial practices in a large firm and a new venture. It will examine the barriers that exist in creating an intrapreneurial culture within a corporate setting, and discuss some of the main factors that lead to the creation of a climate for intrapreneurship within an organisation. Finally, the specific characteristics of intrapreneurs will be discussed and contrasted with corporate managers and entrepreneurs.

14.3 Intrapreneurship

In many economies, large companies are a result of the favourable trading conditions enjoyed in the immediate years after World War II, with corporate bureaucracies set up to manage large-scale businesses operating in stable global conditions. As with the development of self-employment and the small firm (see Chapter 2), the growth in interest in entrepreneurship at a corporate level is due to a combination of various internal and external factors (Gibb 1990; Kanter 1989a), including:

- the blurring of boundaries between the formal and informal labour markets, with serious consequences for labour mobility and job security, especially for white-collar workers (see Chapter 2);
- a change in attitudes towards entrepreneurship, with a higher degree of individualism, particularly among the middle classes who make up the professional workers within many large organisations (see Chapter 3);
- increasing rates of product and market obsolescence – as life-cycles become shorter and the rate of process and technology change faster, there is demand for a higher degree of innovation within the organisation (see Chapter 13);
- the technological revolution, predominantly in computing and information science, which has had global consequences for industries as diverse as financial services and agriculture;
- economic uncertainties (such as the energy crises of the 1970s) leading to changing and unstable market conditions;
- pressures on the manufacturing sector to discard unnecessary overheads and externalise previously internalised services.

To cope with these changes, large firms have increasingly adopted more innovative and enterprising approaches to management within their organisations (Birkinshaw 1997; Stopford and Baden-Fuller 1994). One of these approaches is the development of entrepreneurship within a corporate environment, known as intrapreneurship, which is an attempt to integrate the strengths of small firms (such as creativity, flexibility, innovation and nearness to market) with the market power and financial resources of large companies – although there have been doubts whether this can be achieved successfully, and whether this may just be another management 'fad' adopted by large firms (Duncan 1988).

14.4 Defining intrapreneurship

As Chapter 8 in this book has demonstrated, there are a number of definitions of entrepreneurship. However, these tend to describe the activities of the owner-manager within a small organisation. With an increasing number of managers and professionals setting up new and small businesses within old and existing organisations during the 1970s, the term 'intrapreneur' was invented to describe those individuals who operated as entrepreneurs within existing organisations (Macrae 1976). During the 1980s, when entrepreneurs were again in favour, the concept was developed further to describe entrepreneurial behaviour within large organisations, rather than the establishment of small businesses within larger organisations. As Pinchot (1986) states, 'When I look at successful innovation in companies as diverse as Hewlett Packard, General Motors, Bank of California, 3M, General Mills, Du Pont or AT&T, I always find small independent groups of imaginative action takers working to circumvent or even sabotage the formal systems that supposedly manage innovation. These courageous souls form underground teams and networks that routinely bootleg company resources or "steal" company time to work on their own missions. They make new things happen while those trying to innovate by the official route are still waiting for permission to begin.' However, more recent work has also suggested that there is no reason why intrapreneurship cannot be initiated by employees working within established small firms (Carrier 1996).

So what makes intrapreneurs different to entrepreneurs? Like entrepreneurs, intrapreneurs take personal risks to make new ideas and innovation happen. However, unlike entrepreneurship, where the time and capital of the entrepreneur is placed at risk, intrapreneurship will often take the large organisation into new products and markets, away from their established core businesses. This may risk the company's capital, credibility and market share and, in so doing, the intrapreneur's position within the company. Therefore, an intrapreneur is an employee of a large organisation who has the entrepreneurial qualities of drive, creativity, vision and ambition, but who prefers, if possible, to remain within the security of an established company (Gibb 1988). A more detailed definition will be discussed later in this chapter.

As with entrepreneurship, the term 'intrapreneurship' has been used to describe a number of different organisational scenarios (Gibb 1990; Knight 1987; Pearson 1989), including:

- the development of an overall climate of entrepreneurship at a corporate level (Stopford and Baden-Fuller 1994);
- intra-corporate venturing – the creation of new ventures within an existing organisation to stimulate or develop new products or product improvements, including autonomous business units established within the corporation to develop a new product and/or market (David 1994; Gee 1994); venture groups or divisions set up for the cultivation of new ventures (Ginsberg and Hay 1994); and independent spin-offs (Jones-Evans and Klofsten 1997);
- initiatives by employees in the organisation to undertake something new, where an innovation is often created by subordinates without being asked, expected or even being given permission by higher management (Brazeal 1996);
- rationalisation of the business, including management personnel (Fulop 1991).

14.5 Entrepreneurial and intrapreneurial ventures

Therefore, intrapreneurship does not merely mean the development of a small business within a large organisation, and there are significant differences between creating a new independent venture and establishing a corporate venture through intrapreneurship (McKinney and McKinney 1989). These are most striking in the areas concerning the business environment, the decision to establish a new venture, sources and patterns of funding, and employment of staff.

14.5.1 Business environment

Whilst the entrepreneurial team within a new venture will gradually develop an understanding from which the right rules for running the business will evolve, staff within a corporate venture can be restricted by the parent corporation's existing 'rulebook', which has contributed to past corporate and managerial successes. As a result (and not always deliberately) the corporation can severely restrict the new venture by assuming that it must operate under the same old rules as other developments in the organisation. Therefore, for the intrapreneurial venture to succeed, its parent company must grant it the flexibility required to adapt to a previously unexplored and undefined market.

There can also be considerable differences in the degree of freedom each type of business has to develop its potential. Whilst a corporate venture – when it is part of a larger corporation – must subordinate itself to the parent firm's goals, new independent ventures are usually free to compete in any market, develop any product and utilise any technology (see Chapter 13). For example, when an intrapreneurial venture wishes to compete in a marketplace controlled by other parts of the firm, the intrapreneur – rather than being allowed to develop innovative advantages in any promising market – will, in the majority of cases, face severe resistance.

14.5.2 Establishing a new venture

One of the crucial resources for a new business is an adequate source of funding, both for start-up and for further development as the business grows. Many independent entrepreneurs will approach sources of funding such as venture capital firms or 'business angels' for this finance and, as Chapter 19 demonstrates, such funders will receive a large number of business plans from individual entrepreneurs each year, from which they will select only a few. On the other hand, the senior management of a large corporation will review only a few proposals for internal ventures every year. If the potential independent business is rejected by one source of funding, it can always apply to others who may better understand its potential. Within a corporate setting, rejected ideas have nowhere to go and thus a viable project may never realise its potential unless the intrapreneur takes the plunge, leaves the large organisation and starts a new independent business (see Chapter 13).

Funding sources such as venture capitalists will tailor their criteria to the proposal when making the decision to invest in the independent new venture. However, internal corporate ventures will be subject to the same traditional corporate decision-making criteria as other projects, such as minimum sales volume, minimum acceptable return on investment and special restrictions on use of capital and personnel. Innovation, as a criterion for choosing the project, will usually have little significance. Whilst the entrepreneur has control of the business, with responsibility for its management and, ultimately, its eventual success or failure, the intrapreneur must share control with top management. Consequently, the intrapreneur will have to operate under managerial constraints that would not be present in many independent businesses. Indeed, any problems with the venture can result in top management taking ultimate control over its future.

14.5.3 Sources and patterns of funding

The amount of funding allocated to each type of venture can differ considerably. Within large organisations, the pressure for short-term gains can lead to too much early-stage funding for intrapreneurial ventures. As a result, intrapreneurs may be tempted to commit resources before sufficiently understanding the new business area (new businesses can take over five years to become established in the marketplace). This can lead to the corporate venture being terminated early, when top management does not receive the expected short-term results it expects. On the other hand, early-stage funding within independent new ventures is usually limited to the entrepreneur's personal finances. This is because entrepreneurs are less willing to let in vast amounts of early equity funding, which can dilute their share of the company and thus their control of the management of the venture. In fact, new small ventures tend to be funded on a 'milestone' basis, rather than through traditional budgeting and resource allocation processes (as is found in established corporations), i.e. developing a new product or appointing a new director are 'milestones' that can attract additional capital.

The source of funds for business development also differs between independent and corporate ventures. The corporate venture is usually limited to one source of funds – the parent company. With no legal commitment, the funds may appear or disappear, and are mainly dependent on the parent's financial position. Within independent ventures, the entrepreneur negotiates a legal contract that guarantees initial funding with investors and sets guidelines for future funding. Should existing investors no longer wish to provide further funding, the entrepreneurial venture can seek additional funding from new investors.

14.5.4 Staff resources

A large organisation will recruit people to an internal venture on the basis of parent-company personnel in line for transfer or promotion, rather than on the basis of the needs of the venture. In contrast, an independent new venture is usually made up of eager, qualified individuals who share the founder's vision. Therefore, an important reward for leadership of an independent venture is control over the resources and strategic direction of the firm. Additional incentives can include financial gain, which is usually linked to the profitability of the business. In corporate ventures, long-term success can be linked to that of the parent corporation, rather than the venture, and developing an adequate reward system for intrapreneurs is one of the issues that will be discussed later in more detail.

Most independent ventures have a board of directors, made up of outside directors, experienced venture capitalists from investing firms, and other experts. These people provide valuable and wide-ranging experience in the technical or market areas related to the innovation. In most cases, the intrapreneurial venture does not have a board of directors and thus lacks a valuable source of advice. If the intrapreneurial venture reports to its management in the traditional hierarchical manner, its interests often lack adequate representation in the top management circles.

14.6 Climate for intrapreneurship within an organisation

As with independent entrepreneurs, many managers in a corporation are not capable of being successful intrapreneurs. Being an intrapreneur is not something that can be assigned to individuals within an organisation, like other job descriptions such as financial controller or marketing manager. In many cases, intrapreneurs are self-selected, i.e. they come up with an idea which they will develop further, often in their own time (see Chapter 8). Intrapreneurship can only be developed within an organisation by creating the right climate for such individuals to flourish (Kuratko *et al.* 1993), which includes the following factors.

14.6.1 Intrapreneurship sponsors

Within large companies where new innovations can often be lost in the bureaucracy and unresponsiveness of the organisation, intrapreneurs cannot sufficiently develop their ideas alone. A corporate environment favourable for intrapreneurship has sponsors and champions throughout the organisation who not only support the creative activity and resulting failures but have the planning flexibility to establish new objectives and directions as needed (Knight 1987). Such sponsors can be at all levels of the organisation, from chief executive to project manager to other intrapreneurs. The role of the sponsor should include:

- overcoming the financial concerns of other managers regarding risky ventures, in both initial review and follow-up evaluations;
- curing the need for resources by defending proposals in evaluation meetings, allocating initial exploration funding to new ideas and permitting flexibility in budgets in terms of money, people and equipment;
- ensuring that corporate venturing develops quickly within an organisation by putting the rewards and initiatives in place for intrapreneurs;
- fighting internal departmental issues, such as the hoarding of resources in one division, and 'empire-building'.

14.6.2 Continuous involvement of the original intrapreneur

In many large organisations, it is usually the case that an innovator of a new idea will be forced to hand that idea to another team of individuals for its development. This is particularly the case where a member of a division working in one industrial sector has come up with an idea that is applicable in another industrial sector in which the company operates. The intrapreneur may also be left behind if the idea reaches a stage of development where the intrapreneur has no direct experience (e.g. from development to manufacturing).

In many cases, the removal of the original intrapreneur from a project can often result in that project not reaching fruition. This is especially the case where an idea is new and innovative, and has been developed solely by the intrapreneur. In many cases, intrapreneurs are the motivational power behind new ideas within the company. When they are removed from projects, the very driving force behind the project is lost, as the new 'project leader' tends not to have the same degree of enthusiasm as the intrapreneur, as s/he will be working on someone else's idea. As Pinchot (1986) states, 'Intrapreneurs cannot exist if their passionate commitment is ignored and their visions given to people who don't understand them. Without intrapreneurs, innovation flounders.'

There have been criticisms of using a single intrapreneurial team to take an idea from development to commercialisation, mainly because of the reluctance of companies to have intrapreneurial teams led by inventors or researchers with very little commercial experience. In such scenarios, the inventor should become a member of the intrapreneurial team, perhaps in the role of technical leader, or alternatively act as a consultant to the intrapreneurial management team whilst still working on the development of the idea. In other cases, the inventor of the idea has sufficient skills to become the leader of the intrapreneurial team. One of the more important factors is that the intrapreneurial team stays together through the duration of the project, even after commercialisation. This is often because if the idea is new to the market, then imitations will soon follow, often with significant improvements. In order for the company to be able to counteract these 'follower' strategies, it is important that the original intrapreneurial team stays together for subsequent product generations.

14.6.3 The autonomy of the intrapreneurial team

As entrepreneurs have a desire to be 'their own boss', with responsibility for the destiny of their company, so intrapreneurs have a desire to have sole control over the destiny of their particular idea. In many cases, intrapreneurship is stifled within large organisations because the authority to develop innovation is often several management levels above that of the innovator, and with restricted access. If intrapreneurship is to work within large organisations, then intrapreneurs need the power to make decisions within their project remit (Garnsey and Wright 1990). This may include having the necessary authority to source people and resources from outside the parent organisation.

14.6.4 Crossing boundaries in the organisation

In developing an idea from first principles to final commercialisation, the intrapreneur will have to cross a number of boundaries within the organisation. These may include:

- inter-functional boundaries, such as between R&D and marketing;
- divisional boundaries between different business units within the company, e.g. an innovation may begin in the semiconductor division within a company, but may have more applicability in the instruments division;
- organisational boundaries between different levels of management in the hierarchy of the organisation (as mentioned earlier).

However, there is increasing evidence that managers within large organisations are recognising that vertically driven, financially oriented, authority-based processes, which for so long dominated company operations, are being overtaken by horizontal processes which cut across organisational boundaries (Goshal and Bartlett 1995). For intrapreneurship to be effective throughout the whole organisation, willing individuals in the intrapreneurial team, regardless of functional specialism, must modify the traditional boundaries between different parts of the organisation to encourage multi-disciplinary teamwork and participation.

14.6.5 Tolerance of risks, failures and mistakes *Recommedatn:*

Risk is a factor that is inextricably linked with entrepreneurship and innovation. However, large companies are risk-averse, as the concept of personal failure is anathema to the system of promotion and career development within traditional organisations, with managerial conservatism and performance measurement often inhibiting intrapreneurship (Schwab and Schwab 1997). In contrast, many entrepreneurs in small firms see failure as a learning experience, from which new products, services and ventures can be developed. To foster an intrapreneurial climate, this tolerance towards risk and failure through experimentation should be encouraged (Sathe 1989). If a large company wants to develop an entrepreneurial spirit, it has to establish an environment that allows mistakes and failures in developing new, innovative ideas. While this is in direct opposition to the established promotion and career system of the traditional organisation, without the opportunity to fail, few if any corporate intrapreneurial ventures will be undertaken.

14.6.6 Long-term philosophy towards success

There is a danger that the creation of internal corporate ventures, which are externalised from the main functions of the company, could lead to considerable problems. Whilst such decentralisation may lead to researchers and product developers becoming closer to the marketplace, it may lead to a focus on short-term market performance, in order to 'prove' the success of the new venture. Therefore, a company must be prepared to establish a long time horizon for evaluating the success of individual ventures as well as the overall intrapreneurship programme. An intrapreneurial climate should not be established within an organisation unless that company is willing to invest money with no expectation of return for five to ten years. It is also important that ideas are allowed to develop fully, and that the resources allocated to such an intrapreneurial project are not withdrawn before that idea has progressed to commercialisation (Pryor and Shays 1993).

14.6.7 Finding resources for ideas

Although intrapreneurs often will work on their new ideas in their own time, organisations need to make resources available to such individuals in order that these ideas reach the marketplace more quickly. This can be done by allocating either time or funds to the intrapreneur. Often, if intrapreneurs cannot find time to make their ideas marketable to the company, then those ideas will remain in the intrapreneur's head rather than becoming a marketable product, process or service. Once the idea has been

249

shown to be of some value to the organisation, then funds need to made available to develop this idea to the point where it can be adopted by the organisation. In many companies, available resources are often committed to solving problems that have immediate effects on the bottom line, rather than the development of new ideas. If discretionary funds are not available, the intrapreneur may become frustrated to the point of abandoning the commercialisation of the idea altogether. More worrying for the company, the idea may be taken elsewhere to be developed by the intrapreneur, either to a competing organisation or to a new small business.

14.6.8 An effective reward system

Although the attainment of commercialisation of their ideas is often sufficient, the energy and effort expended by the intrapreneurial team in the creation of the new venture needs to be appropriately rewarded (Brazeal 1996). However, as intrapreneurship is a relatively new phenomenon, many companies have yet to develop a reward system that is adequate in terms of pay and promotion.

In terms of pay, a study by Balkin and Logan (1988) has examined the different policies that organisations can develop to reward entrepreneurial staff. Their conclusions indicated that intrapreneurs should be paid below or at the market rate, with a significant portion of the individual's salary at risk in the form of pay incentives, which should be linked to individual and corporate venture performance. Therefore, the fixed-package portion of an intrapreneur's reward – salary and benefits – would be low. However, this should be compensated by a number of benefits including:

Short-term variable-pay benefits

These include profit-sharing, which can focus the intrapreneur's attention on the corporate venture's financial goals. This can also strengthen team spirit within the corporate venture, as all employees will receive a share of the profits proportional to their salaries. It is important within corporate entrepreneurship that a new internal venture does not imitate the reward policies of the corporation's other traditional business divisions, as these policies are usually designed for a complex bureaucracy and recognise the difference in pay scales according to an individual's status in the organisation.

Long-term variable-pay benefits

Equity ownership is a means for rewarding intrapreneurs. As well as being an excellent retention tool for the large organisation (with employees likely to remain within the venture as it develops), it also gives intrapreneurs a sense of ownership and responsibility for their venture, distinguishing it from other projects which the intrapreneur may have previously undertaken in a corporate capability for the large firm. In addition, stock ownership may also create a greater entrepreneurial spirit within a corporate venture, as employees look for more innovations and opportunities which will increase the profits (and stock value) of the venture.

Education and health benefits

These are to pay for travel, tuition and supplies for job-related education and training. Entrepreneurial employees frequently, in the development of new ideas, discover gaps in their education and training, and must develop new skills to continue to be productive and innovative. This is crucial in high-technology industries, where corporate entrepreneurship is prevalent. In addition, large firms initiating corporate venturing must be aware of the changes that will occur in the working lifestyles of intrapreneurs – as they assume 'ownership' for their ventures, their working hours will inevitably become longer (60–80 hours per week is not uncommon in these cases) and, as with entrepreneurs, the demands on their time will increase, as will the stress of the job. As a result, many companies are providing benefits in the form of health-club memberships so that intrapreneurs can develop positive coping behaviours.

Therefore, pay policies within corporate ventures should recognise that individuals assuming the role of intrapreneur should be treated differently to the rest of the organisation. However, this could cause potential problems in the development of the intrapreneurial venture, especially in the attraction of staff from other divisions of the large firm. Indeed, corporate entrepreneurship should pay more attention to internal pay equity than in independent small firms, because if it is to attract employees from other units of the large firm, it must be sensitive to the company's reward packages, and may have to match overall company pay and benefits levels, which may restrict its ability to design policies that reward innovation and creativity. However, this problem can be limited by:

- physically separating the corporate venture from the rest of the organisation;
- convincing possible transferees that the chance of greater long-term reward may be worth the cut in pay;
- not accepting transfers from other divisions in the large organisation.

The traditional reward within a corporate structure – promotion – is often not sufficient, as the motivation behind the development of the idea is often not career advancement. More importantly, intrapreneurs seldom make good corporate managers, as they rarely have the temperament for coping with the company's structure. This may cause problems in the organisation, especially with other corporate managers. 3M, for example, have developed a 'dual promotion system', where successful intrapreneurs can choose to be promoted on either the technical or the management hierarchy of the business. This recognises the needs of those intrapreneurs who do not wish to receive more administrative responsibilities. Those intrapreneurs who wish to remain in technical development – and indeed are more valuable in the laboratory than in the office – are given a higher rank but are not constrained to purely administrative positions. On the other hand, some companies prefer to reward their intrapreneurs through giving them a position of freedom within the organisation to develop new ideas, or even setting the intrapreneur up in a separate venture, with suitable equity as motivation for success. For example, within both 3M and Johnson and Johnson, the intrapreneur who successfully develops a new product, market or service, and then builds a business on it, will become the head of that business (Drucker 1985). This could be general manager or a division president, with the appropriate rank, bonuses and stock options.

Weaknesses

14.7 Barriers to intrapreneurship within a corporate culture

The success of entrepreneurial practices within companies such as Apple and Microsoft in the USA, and Virgin and Marks & Spencer in the UK, has resulted in attempts by many large companies to develop the positive side of small business and implement the spirit, culture and rewards of entrepreneurship within their organisations (Harris *et al.* 1995). However, large companies have a problem in being entrepreneurial for one simple reason – they are too big. The size of such organisations means that managers have to structure the corporation in order to control it and, as the company grows bigger, even more structures of management are added in order to manage the whole operation. Consequently, a number of barriers to intrapreneurship may be created as there are considerable differences between a traditional corporate culture and an intrapreneurial culture, with the former having an emphasis on a culture and reward system that tends to favour caution in decision-making.

For example, large businesses rarely operate on a 'gut feeling' for the marketplace, as many entrepreneurs do. Instead, large amounts of data are gathered before any major business decision is made, not only for use in rational business decisions, but also for use as justification if the decision does not produce optimum results. Risky decisions are often postponed until enough hard facts can be gathered or a consultant hired to provide extra advice and information. As a result of such a culture, large firms will often face difficulties in attracting suitably entrepreneurial staff. Entrepreneurs will not be attracted to large organisations, preferring the risk and adventure associated with ownership of a small business, although there are exceptions – such as John Harvey Jones of ICI – who develop an intrapreneurial style of management within a large organisation.

Moreover, large organisations may discourage the employment and advancement of entrepreneurial individuals. This is because the presence of entrepreneurs within a large company could possibly alienate other important managers within the organisation, especially if those individuals' career development is dependent upon conforming to the accepted structures and norms of the corporation. Other barriers to intrapreneurship within a corporate setting include the following.

14.7.1 Traditional corporate structures

The hierarchical nature of large corporations is not conducive to entrepreneurial behaviour, with considerable 'distance' between the top layers of management and the lowest level of the workforce, resulting in an impersonal relationship between management and staff. Multiple layers of management can also lead to many layers of approval between the potential intrapreneur and the person in charge of resources. For example, if a shop-floor worker in a manufacturing plant comes up with an idea to improve the production process, then the permission to develop the idea further usually comes from three or four levels of authority higher up, with each level having the potential to reject the proposal before it reaches someone with the responsibility and authority for funding.

14.7.2 Corporate culture

The nature of corporate culture itself – where job descriptions are rigidly enforced – may stifle innovation. The established procedures, reporting systems, lines of authority and control mechanisms of a traditional hierarchical organisation are there to support the existing management structure, and not to promote creativity and innovation (Krueger 1998). For example, the reporting procedures of large firms are usually centred on the short-term needs of budget officers and performance measurements. Managers are therefore taught to think in terms of short-term cycles.

14.7.3 Large-firm performance standards

The performance standards imposed by large businesses, especially in the short term, may adversely affect the development of intrapreneurial projects, many of which are long-term in nature. In many large organisations, short-term profits are generally used as the main measurement of a company's success. This is because increased short-term profits will support the company's share price and thus attract new investors. This will lead to pressure on managers to devise short-term strategies rather than look to long-term investment. Entrepreneurial activities, especially innovative new projects, will take time to develop sufficiently, and a short-term policy attitude will lead to problems with regard to financing such projects. Any mistakes may also be damaging to the personal reputation of the individual intrapreneur, who may be removed from the project prematurely and replaced with a less entrepreneurial corporate manager.

14.7.4 Planning procedures

The planning procedures within large organisations can stifle entrepreneurship. Generally, as companies get bigger, the corporate environment will require more control, and specific performance standards to exert this control. Thus paperwork and reporting standards on projects may take precedence over entrepreneurial and innovative behaviour. In some cases, this can lead to 'underground innovation', where intrapreneurs become involved in product innovations that are not authorised by the organisation (Abetti 1997). Instead, they are carried out in secret in the intrapreneur's own time until they are so near market readiness that they cannot be stopped.

14.7.5 Ownership

The total ownership, and the associated independence in decision-making, is one of the primary motivations in entrepreneurship. Within large companies, however, ownership of the assets of the intrapreneurial part of the business is rarely possible, except in the case of a management buy-out. Furthermore, the intrapreneur will have difficulty in retaining total ownership of the idea, from its development stage to its final marketing, due to the functional nature of management within a large organisation. As such, the influence of the intrapreneur on the innovative idea may be diluted by other individuals within the organisation.

14.7.6 Mobility of managers

Mobility of managers within large organisations may lead to a lack of commitment to specific projects, especially if those projects are of a long-term nature, as many intrapreneurial ones are. This may lead to a change in priorities by different managers for the project, thus losing the continuity associated with new product development within small companies. The flexibility to change the direction of projects may prove difficult if it impinges upon the activities of other departments within the company.

14.7.7 Inappropriate reward systems

In many large companies, there are often inappropriate methods to compensate creative employees. Rewards are normally based on improvements in strict performance measures laid down by management, with very little scope for a reward system based on creativity and innovation. Promotion to management – the normal route for talented individuals within a large corporation – is seldom an attractive reward to intrapreneurs. This is because it normally takes them out of the job in which they have displayed their innovative talents and places them into a managerial position with increased administrative responsibilities.

However, despite these problems, there are a number of initiatives a large organisation can take which can create an environment that is conducive to innovation and entrepreneurship.

14.8 Intrapreneurial characteristics – who is the intrapreneur?

As Vandermerwe and Birley (1997) suggest, intrapreneurial organisations often need a new type of person who can bridge the two worlds of the entrepreneurial and the corporate. Indeed, the set of skills that defines the intrapreneur is quite different to the skills needed by either the traditional corporate manager or the entrepreneur (Figure 14.1). For example, unlike entrepreneurs, intrapreneurs will need team-building skills and a firm understanding of both business and market realities, whilst also possessing the leadership and rapid decision-making qualities of successful owner-managers. Therefore, in developing intrapreneurs, the task for organisational managers is to identify those individuals who possess the managerial skills to manage a project within the boundaries of a large organisation *and* the entrepreneurial skills to be able to take the project forward (Jansen and van Wees 1994).

14.8.1 Managerial skills

The managerial skills required by an intrapreneur are as follows:

The ability to adopt a multidisciplinary role
At the beginning, only the intrapreneur will have a sufficient grasp of the concepts or ideas that they want to put forward within the organisation. Whilst intrapreneurs frequently have a background in one particular business discipline, such as development or marketing, they must be able to adopt a multidisciplinary approach when they become involved with the development of their own idea into a viable business. This may often mean crossing boundaries between functions in the organisation.

igure 14.1 Managers, entrepreneurs and intrapreneurs

	Traditional managers	Traditional entrepreneurs	Intrapreneurs
Organisationl attributes			
Attitude to organisation	Sees organisation as nurturing and protective, seeks position within it	May rapidly advance in a firm – when frustrated, rejects the system and forms his/her own	Dislikes the organisational system
Managerial satisfaction	Pleases others (higher in the organisational hierarchy)	Pleases self and customers	Pleases self, customers and sponsors
Primary motives	Wants promotion and other traditional corporate rewards	Wants freedom. Goal-oriented, self-reliant and self-motivated	Wants freedom and access to corporate resources
Relationship with others	Organisational hierarchy as basic relationship	Transactions and deal-making as basic relationship	Transactions within organisational hierarchy
Managerial attributes			
Decisions	Agrees with those in power/ delays decisions for superiors	Follows private vision. Decisive, action-oriented	More patient and willing to compromise than entrepreneur
Delegation of action	Delegates action – reporting and supervising takes most of time	Gets hands dirty and can upset employees by doing their work	Gets hands dirty – can do work but knows how to delegate
Management attention	Primarily on events inside the organisation	Primarily on technology and marketplace	Both inside – management on needs of venture – and outside of firm – focus on customers
Market research	Has market studies done to discover needs and guide product/service concepts	Creates needs. Talks to customers and forms own opinions	Does own market research and intuitive market evaluation like the entrepreneur
Problem-solving style	Works out problems within the system	Escapes problems in formal structures by leaving to start own business	Works out problems within the system, or bypasses it without leaving
Skills	Professional management. Abstract analytical tools, people management and political skills	Knows business intimately. More business acumen than managerial skill. Often technically trained	Very like the entrepreneur, but situation demands greater ability to prosper within the organisation
Personal attributes			
Personal attributes	Can be forceful and ambitious – fearful of others' ability to harm career development	Self-confident, optimistic, courageous	Self-confident; courageous – cynical about system but optimistic about ability to outwit it
Educational level	Highly educated	Less well-educated in earlier studies – some graduate work but rarely PhD	Often highly educated, especially in technical fields
Failure and mistakes	Strives to avoid mistakes and surprises. Postpones recognising failure	Deals with mistakes and failures as learning experiences	Attempts to hide risky projects from view so can learn from mistakes with-out public failure
Family history	Family members worked for large organisations	Entrepreneurial small business, professional or farm background	Entrepreneurial small business, professional or farm background
Risk	Careful	Likes moderate risk. Invests heavily but expects to succeed	Likes moderate risk – unafraid of dismissal so little personal risk
Status	Cares about status symbols	Happy sitting on an orange crate if job is getting done	Dismisses traditional status symbols – covets symbols of freedom

Source: adapted from Pinchot (1986)

Understanding the environment

The intrapreneur needs to understand the environment and its many aspects to establish a successful intrapreneurial venture. An individual must understand how his/her creativity can affect both the internal and external environments of the corporation.

Encouragement of open discussion

Open discussion must be encouraged to develop a good team for creating something new. A successful new intrapreneurial venture can only be formed when the team involved feels the freedom to disagree and critique an idea to reach the best solution. The degree of openness obtained depends on the degree of openness of the intrapreneur.

Creation of management options

The intrapreneur must challenge the beliefs and assumptions of the corporation and through this create something new in a largely bureaucratic organisation.

Building a coalition of supporters

Openness will lead to the establishment of a strong coalition of supporters and encouragers – the intrapreneur must encourage and affirm each team member, particularly during the problem times. This encouragement is very important, as the usual motivators of career paths and job security are not operational in establishing a new intrapreneurial venture.

14.8.2 Entrepreneurial skills

Some of the entrepreneurial skills required by the intrapreneur include:

Vision and flexibility

The intrapreneur must be a visionary leader, a person who 'dreams great dreams'. To establish a successful new venture, the intrapreneurial leader must have a dream and overcome all obstacles by selling this dream to others within the organisation, especially those in influential positions. However, whilst intrapreneurs are visionary, their dream is usually grounded in business experience, mainly because they realise that their dreams can only become reality if they themselves take action to turn an idea into a viable business proposition.

Action-orientation

Intrapreneurs tend to start doing immediately, rather than spending time planning the development of their idea in detail. Often, they do not wait for permission to begin work on their ideas. Instead, they will go ahead with the development of their idea, often in their own time. Unlike managers, who often delegate responsibilities to subordinates, intrapreneurs will often be involved in a number of tasks associated with the intrapreneurial project, predominantly because of their affinity towards turning their vision directly into reality through their own efforts.

Dedication

Traditional product development systems cannot compete with intrapreneurship for one simple reason – they are too bureaucratic to enable or encourage dedication. Traditional managers will divide marketing and technology, vision and action, and a host of other responsibilities into separate jobs, which will deny intrapreneurs the commitment, responsibility and excitement that inspire total dedication. In some cases, this dedication can be extreme, often to the extent of putting the priorities of the project before the people involved – they will prefer to get the job done on time rather than meeting people's needs.

Persistence in overcoming failure

The intrapreneur must persist through the frustration and obstacles that will inevitably occur during the creation of a new venture. Only through persistence will a new venture be created and successful commercialisation take place. More importantly, intrapreneurs (like entrepreneurs) tend to see failure as a learning experience – a temporary setback from which the idea can be improved.

Setting self-determined goals

The intrapreneur often sets personal goals for the project, rather than those corporate goals linked to short-term needs such as reporting procedures, etc. These goals are often related to high personal standards, as intrapreneurs gain little satisfaction from adhering to standards imposed by others.

14.9 Chapter summary

This chapter has briefly discussed much of the general knowledge regarding the concept of intrapreneurship, i.e. entrepreneurship within a corporate environment. It has demonstrated that under certain conditions in the large organisation, the enterprise, innovation and creativity of a small firm can be developed if specific barriers are overcome and certain policies and procedures put in place. It has also shown that the intrapreneur is quite different from the entrepreneur and the corporate manager, often possessing the competencies associated with both types of individual.

In examining this phenomenon, the chapter has drawn predominantly on literature from the USA to examine concepts such as the differences between an entrepreneurial and intrapreneurial venture; the barriers to intrapreneurship within a corporate environment; the climate for intrapreneurship; and finally, the characteristics of an intrapreneur. To date, very little work has been carried out in the European context on this area – this may be due to the fact that many modern and innovative management techniques could be described as falling within the sphere of 'intrapreneurship'; on the other hand, it could be that the general concepts of intrapreneurship have yet to penetrate the management of large European organisations in both the public and private sectors. However, it is clear that more work needs to be carried out to examine the entrepreneurial practices of organisations that are not classed as SMEs, and that a clear research agenda needs to be drawn up to test some of the concepts presented in this chapter, and to examine whether they exist in the UK and other European countries.

Questions

1 Discuss the main changes which need to take place within a large organisation to ensure that it changes its corporate style to one that is intrapreneurial.

2 What are the main differences in establishing a new venture independently and a new venture within an existing large organisation?

3 What are the main characteristics of intrapreneurs and how do these differ from those of the 'traditional' entrepreneur?

CHAPTER 15

Entrepreneurship in transitional economies

Milford Bateman and Lester Lloyd-Reason

15.1 Learning objectives

There are five learning objectives in this chapter:

1 To understand why small firms failed to emerge under central planning.

2 To appreciate the reasons for the early progress made by the transition economies after 1989.

3 To have some understanding of the early problems small enterprises faced after 1989.

4 To understand why policy intervention became important to promote the small-enterprise sector.

5 To appreciate the nature and extent of the problems with the main policy interventions.

Key concepts

■ 'Socialist black-hole'　■ spontaneous development　■ barriers to entry
■ policy intervention

15.2 Introduction

The unravelling and final collapse of Communism in Central and Eastern Europe at the beginning of the 1990s stands out as one of the most important events this century. It brought to an end an economic and political system based upon authoritarian bureaucratic rule, state ownership, one-party politics, and a lack of individual freedom. One of the most immediate effects of this enormous change – and the transition to democracy and the market economy which ensued – was the rebirth of entrepreneurship and small-scale private enterprise, features which had been largely suppressed under central planning. Millions of new private businesses began to spring up everywhere. As a result, many new and better-paying jobs were created. Taxation revenues were collected from the new private business sector, particularly by local governments, where before there was virtually nothing. New technologies, many of which were quite

259

commonplace in the Western economies, were rapidly brought into use in private business in order to lower costs and improve the quality of the goods and services produced. And the actual supply of consumer goods increased enormously in a very short space of time, in countries which had been characterised almost throughout the entire Communist period as 'shortage economies' (Kornai 1980). This chapter reviews the changes that have occurred over the past decade, concentrating in particular on the SME sector. Throughout the chapter a number of mini case studies are used to illustrate the differing issues experienced within the various countries of Central and Eastern Europe.

15.3 Entrepreneurship in transitional economies

The development of entrepreneurship and small businesses in Central and Eastern Europe has certainly not been easy. The overwhelming focus on importing and trade activities in the first wave of private businesses had a very immediate and damaging effect on domestic industry and the trade balance of nearly all of the post-Communist countries. There was also resentment at the fact that the previous Communist political élite was generally first in the queue to establish the most lucrative private businesses, especially those which required good connections and significant capital investment. Resentment of the old élite was particularly acute where it involved the Communist-appointed enterprise directors surreptitiously channelling state resources and assets into a so-called 'bypass' firm, which they discreetly owned or controlled. It is also the case that too many small businesses pay scant regard to health and safety standards, social contributions and holiday entitlements, and other traditional employee benefits, and otherwise exploit their employees in ways which are none too dissimilar from the early capitalism about which Karl Marx was so critical. At least partly because of this, historic antagonisms to private 'speculators' and 'profiteers' have taken some considerable time to recede, particularly in the former Soviet Union where the state had long propagandised against private business activities. But there was also the fact that in too many of the former Soviet countries, the new freedoms had led to a very disagreeable and dangerous 'mafia-isation' of the economy, reviled by many ordinary people and which, of course, gave licence to their previous suspicions of the private sector and entrepreneurs.

Broadly, however, the progress has been positive; or, at the very least, it has laid the foundations for a much more concerted attempt to develop and strengthen the SME sector from now on. The lack of progress has also thrown into sharp relief the importance of policy interventions – both those which have been implemented so far, and those which can be implemented in future. This chapter will consider the shape of the SME sector emerging in Central and Eastern Europe. We start with a look at the previous Communist system to see how and why SME development was handicapped, and then move on to the transition period to see how the SME sector has fared under the extremely difficult conditions of transition. The chapter finishes with a look at the policy interventions which have been undertaken with regard to the SME sector, particularly those designed and financed by the international assistance community.

15.4 Central planning

Central planning was the dominant economic model in Central and Eastern Europe from the mid 1940s until the beginning of the 1990s, but it had its origin in the former Soviet Union as far back as 1917. Building upon the experience of a prolonged period of Tsarist intervention and authoritarian control over the economy, central planning was retained as Communist economic policy in the newly established, but politically precarious, Soviet Union. But it was intended by the Communists to be a temporary measure – to be expediently used to efficiently mobilise the country's vast resources after the damage inflicted by World War I and the Russian Revolution which followed in late 1917 – but then set aside in favour of a broadly free-market economy. However, after just a short period of the market economy in the 1920s, the centrally planned economy was restored, as a way in which the Communist leadership under Stalin could effectively control the country and its people once more. It was to prove to be an enduring feature of Soviet life.

After World War II, pressure from the Soviet Union proved sufficient to forcibly introduce Communism and the centrally planned economy model into many of its neighbouring Central and Eastern European states to the west. These new Communist states enthusiastically set about constructing their own versions of the centrally planned economy, though they had to pay particular heed to what Moscow wished them to do. For example, the Soviet Union through the co-ordinating trade body for the Communist world, the Council for Mutual Economic Assistance (CMEA), was keen to ensure that the Communist bloc operated so as to prop up its own strength and activities, particularly with regard to its adversarial role in the Cold War with the USA and its propagandising role elsewhere in the world. Some Communist states resisted the exploitative nature of Soviet leadership of the Communist bloc, and this led them to attempt to reform their economic systems to give domestic enterprises and government policies more scope *vis-à-vis* their Soviet counterparts. But resistance was difficult. Prior to 1990, only the Yugoslavs were successful in standing up to Stalin and the Soviet Union and proved able to carry through their aim to abandon the Soviet economic model more or less completely, which they famously did in 1950.

Case study 15.1 Market socialism in the former Yugoslavia

The former Yugoslavia broke with the Soviet model in 1950 and established a system of 'worker self-management'. This was a pioneering experiment combining elements of the market mechanism, which led to a more efficient allocation of resources than under central planning, with common ownership of the means of production, which created a fairer and more equitable allocation of resources and wealth than under capitalism. The system also led to a more participative and dem-ocratic industrial management structure than in either Western or Eastern Europe, with an enterprise being responsive to the ideas and aspirations of its employees to a surprisingly large degree. However, after achieving much economic success in the 1950s and 1960s – the country was the 'tiger' economy of its day – the experiment went into decline in the mid 1970s when the Communist Party sought to re-impose its control over the enterprise sector once more. The worker self-managed economy was eventually legislated out of existence in the late 1980s as part of the Communists' 'shock therapy' stabilisation programme, which was carried out as a last-gasp effort to avoid further economic collapse and political turmoil.

In its most extreme form, central planning relied upon the complete control of industry through a central planning agency and relevant ministries, and permitted almost no strategic discretion at the enterprise level. In practice, enterprises were given orders regarding what to produce, when they would receive their inputs and raw materials, and when they were to be ready to distribute their final products and to whom. Because the procedure grew more cumbersome the more enterprises there were that had to be planned, the central authorities encouraged the development of giant and almost entirely self-sufficient enterprises. Enterprises themselves were only too happy to oblige the move towards so-called 'giantism', because a larger enterprise implied more political clout for the General Director. Also, the early experience with the central planning system was of poor-quality outputs, wrong specifications and continual delays in delivery, so it was far easier for an enterprise to ensure that its own plans would be realised if it produced as many of its required inputs and components as possible, rather than rely upon the planning system and the plan fulfilment of enterprises further up the supply chain.

It is often overlooked that the early experience of central planning in the former Soviet Union was generally positive, and indeed at one point its presumed efficiency seemed to be offering to the world an alternative to free-market capitalism. The central planning system allowed many of the Eastern European nations to proceed rapidly with the transition from an agricultural society towards an industrial one, and the system was also instrumental in rapidly repairing the enormous war-damage after 1917 and 1945. Living standards improved significantly in the 1950s for the bulk of the populations in Eastern Europe, particularly in the former Soviet Union (Nove 1986). However, the system's economic limitations began to become readily apparent from the 1960s onwards, and this led nearly all the Communist states to begin to experiment with a variety of reforms to the basic model of central planning. Some began to follow the lead set by the former Yugoslavia, and started to experiment with giving more power to employees and managers, and introducing elements of the market economy. Hungary and Poland were the main imitators, but all the other Central and Eastern European states were to follow suit and introduce their own home-grown variants of the basic reforms pioneered by the Yugoslavs.

However, it became clear in the 1980s that reforms to the system of central planning were no longer going to be enough to bring about the sort of transformation required to catch up with – never mind to overtake – the average living standards enjoyed in the West. Clearly, the Western market economies were able to allocate resources in a more efficient manner, and were far and away better at encouraging innovation and the utilisation of new product and process technologies, as well as the abandoning of outdated technologies and products. The desire for improved living standards and for greater political freedom – particularly the wish on the part of many of the Communist-bloc nations to become independent of the Soviet Union – became so strong that the ruling parties were forced to give way and abdicate power to the rule of the ballot box. Some ruling parties went voluntarily, for example in Central Europe, while others fought a desperate rearguard action to hold on to power, as in Romania and in the Soviet Union. In spite of these last-gasp measures, the reforms which began in 1989 very rapidly brought to an end the centrally planned economies in Central and Eastern Europe and ushered in a movement towards the market economy model.

15.5 SMEs under central planning

Notwithstanding the various reforms to the centrally planned economies in Central and Eastern Europe before 1989, the relative absence of self-employment, small-scale private ownership and SMEs remained throughout the Communist period one of its most distinctive features. For a number of reasons small enterprises were very much anathema to the planning authorities. For a start, they naturally further complicated the already highly complex planning process. After all, if it was difficult for the planning authorities to oversee the activities of just a few hundred giant firms, then it would have been virtually impossible for them to successfully incorporate many hundreds of thousands of small enterprises into their plans. The system would simply have ground to a halt. Secondly, small enterprises were ignored because they were seen as technically backward and unable to reap economies of scale. Finally, small private enterprises were feared by the political authorities because it was thought they could possibly be the harbingers of a return to capitalism. Many Communists sensed that once private ownership had gained a foothold in the economy – no matter how small initially – it would begin to generate pressure for further Western-style reforms to be made.

But in spite of the many restrictions to small enterprises, there was generally always some freedom to operate in the interstices of the planned economy and the large-enterprise sector, and so most of the Eastern European planned economies were not entirely without a small-enterprise sector during the period of Communism. Limited forms of officially sanctioned small-enterprise development were allowed as a way of ameliorating poor economic performance and lifting living standards, notably in the former East Germany, Poland and Hungary (see Aslund 1985). Also, there was a degree of official toleration for the 'second economy' in many Eastern European countries; while some countries, such as the former Yugoslavia, saw small businesses as a socially productive way of making use of their citizens' increasing wealth.

Case study 15.2 SMEs in the former Yugoslavia

The former Yugoslavia had probably the most liberal regime with regard to SMEs in Central and Eastern Europe, particularly in the northern Republics of Slovenia and Croatia. Part of the reason for this was related to the large number of Yugoslavs who worked in Western Europe as guest-workers, and the increasing

Case study 15.2 *continued*

personal wealth of much of the population as the country grew richer. The authorities were keen to see this increasing wealth invested in something other than holiday homes, a luxury car, and other luxury consumption items. They thus tried to encourage richer individuals to invest in small businesses in a variety of sectors, particularly tourism, transport, retailing and catering. In the 1960s and 1970s the authorities experimented with a variety of innovative profit-sharing enterprise structures. These allowed entrepreneurs to contemplate larger and riskier ventures, which would only be absorbed into the socially owned economy once the entrepreneur had extracted a suitable return on his/her initial investment and entrepreneurial expertise. These hybrid enterprises initially seemed to hold out much promise, but in reality the political élite would not allow them the freedom to develop as they were originally intended.

Pragmatism had its limits, however, and the freedom for entrepreneurs to operate remained closely circumscribed by the planners and the political authorities. Taxation of private enterprises was often punitive and arbitrary. Affordable business space was largely unavailable to private entrepreneurs. In addition, although governments were willing to allow some freedom for entrepreneurs to operate, they were manifestly unwilling to allocate resources to the sector to facilitate this growth. In Hungary, for example, the private sector remained largely outside of the financial flows available to state industry, which meant that small businesses found it difficult to raise capital in order to grow into production units of any meaningful size. In Poland, on the other hand, the extent of unofficial entrepreneurship was such that much capital was generated by the entrepreneurial sector. But, here, the problem was more the lack of meaningful opportunities for investment outside of the state sector, as well as the myriad of rules and regulations which effectively prohibited expansion and growth. In the former Soviet Union, Gorbachev promoted efforts to re-introduce private enterprise in the mid 1980s, but these failed to achieve as much as was hoped. Quite apart from having to cloak the new private sector in the ideologically acceptable rhetoric of co-operativism – the new initiatives were termed *ko-operativi* – the sector's emergence as a meaningful feature in the economy was greatly handicapped by charges of over-pricing, gangsterism and corruption involving local party officials. Very quickly these problems led to a furious back-pedalling by the Soviet leadership, and many restrictions were re-introduced which blocked the further growth of the sector in the period leading up to the collapse of Communism in 1991 (Jones and Moskoff 1991). Even in the former Yugoslavia, private enterprises faced a number of petty restrictions which hampered the development of a substantial sector. For example, aside from family members, for a long period private businesses could officially employ up to five persons only, rising to ten persons after 1983. There were very many instances of enterprises evading these employment regulations – for example, by employing large numbers of bogus family members – but such evasion was stressful and time-consuming, and ultimately prohibited the growth of the enterprise.

Case study 15.3 SMEs in Hungary

Hungary gave the green light to private enterprise in 1982. Capitalising on the general levels of inactivity during the normal working day, private enterprises were allowed to organise production outside normal working hours which could then be sold for private profit. The government did not think many individuals would be interested in such activity, but to their surprise – and alarm – by 1985 the number of private enterprises registered to take advantage of this opportunity had risen to 30,000.

Table 15.1 shows that the domination of the inefficient state sector was almost complete in the former Czechoslovakia, former East Germany and the former Soviet Union. The table also indicates that the former Yugoslavia, Hungary and Poland were already some way down the road as the transition process began in earnest. Notwithstanding such progress, the small-enterprise sector in all Central and Eastern European countries remained a minor component in the industrial structure in comparison to the Western European market economies and generally elsewhere. Essentially, for the sector to really grow, the overall political and economic system had to change fundamentally. This only came about in 1989, of course, when Communism finally collapsed.

Table 15.1 The state sector prior to privatisation

Country	% of total value added
Czech & Slovak Republics	97
Former East Germany	97
Former Soviet Union	96
Former Yugoslavia	87
Hungary	86
Poland	82

Source: adapted from Jones (1992)

15.6 SMEs in the early transition period

Once the decisive break with Communism was made in Central and Eastern Europe in 1989, and two years later in the then Soviet Union, small-enterprise development became one of the principal economic reform objectives to be adopted by the first post-Communist governments. The elimination of the main administrative and legal barriers to small private enterprise entry and development began right away. Also, the conversion process whereby state assets could be taken over by private owners was set in motion. As a result of these new freedoms and opportunities, almost everywhere in Eastern Europe there was a rush of new small-enterprise registrations. The small-scale privatisation programmes were extremely successful in transferring virtually all state-owned retail, catering and handicraft outfits into private hands just a few years into the transition. Then there was the large number of conversions from the informal sector. Here the new freedoms meant that many previously 'black economy' operations could now 'come out into the open' and become legitimate business operations, with the possibility to expand and develop, as well as tap into formal sources of finance. Other new registrations came from the first wave of genuine post-Communist entrepreneurs and innovators. Often in very well-paid and secure employment, these people were nevertheless keen to seek to benefit from the enormous opportunities which were being thrown up by the transition. Many of this group were part of the old Communist élite, many of whom had grown rich by privately abusing a system they so resolutely defended in public, but their efforts were at least able to inject dynamism into the post-Communist economies.

Some of the more enlightened governments, such as in Hungary, began to allocate direct financial support to small-enterprise development programmes. However, it was the Western governments and the bilateral and multilateral development agencies (e.g. World Bank, USAID, UNIDO/UNDP) which were most willing and able to underwrite the attempt to develop the SME sector. The European Union was perhaps the most important provider of assistance, through its 'Phare' programme of support for SME development in the early-reforming countries of Central and Eastern Europe, and later on in the former Soviet Union through its 'Tacis' programme. A new bank, the European Bank for Reconstruction and Development (EBRD), was also established to support private-sector development. The result of these new freedoms, and the establishment of a wide variety of SME support systems, was a major boom in the SME sector. Indeed, after nearly ten years of the transition, the SME sector is now widely pictured as one of the great success stories in the move to the market economy. Even though one could argue that the impressive early progress in the transition economies was really only filling the SME vacuum – or 'Socialist black-hole' as some termed it (Petrin *et al.* 1988) – which had been created by the Communist system, it was nevertheless the case that the SME sector very quickly came to account for a very sizeable share of employment, output, new-technology applications, tax revenue and wealth creation. Moreover, given the rapid decline of the social welfare systems in many post-Communist economies, SMEs began to play a vital role as a source of income for many who would otherwise be experiencing increasing poverty and deprivation.

15.6.1 Small-scale privatisation

Much early emphasis was put on small-scale privatisation. This process would allow the re-allocation of resources from inefficient state enterprises into the newly created, dynamic private sector. The start of the small-scale privatisation process instituted a scramble among would-be entrepreneurs eager to take advantage of the obvious opportunities on offer. The large state-owned enterprises were broken up and sold off in manageable units; retail outlets, restaurants and so on could now be registered and legally owned by their former managers; the myriad of 'unofficial' businesses was now legitimated and titles of ownership registered. Small-scale privatisation thus offered a quick, easy and relatively painless way to kick-start private-sector development.

Small-scale privatisation proceeded rapidly, with each country using different ways of defining those enterprises to be included within the small-scale privatisation programme. Poland and Hungary chose to include all those under local authority control. This comprised mostly retail outlets. The Czech and Slovak Republics decided to include all those that could be sold to a single buyer. Whilst some only included retail and consumer service business, others broadened the qualification to include industrial, transport and construction businesses.

Although small-scale privatisation appeared to be quick and easy, in practice this was not always the case. Not all the governments of the region have pursued small-scale privatisation with the same vigour. In Bulgaria, for example, small-scale privatisation was launched and aborted in March–June 1991. By March 1994 only 69 out of 5,000 enterprises had been sold by ministries and 93 had been sold by municipalities (Jeffries 1996). In those countries more committed to small-scale privatisation – notably Poland, Hungary and the Czech Republic – even where appropriate legislation was put in place, many problems emerged to hamper the development of the small-firms sector through the privatisation process. Such problems included intense political controversies, the state of the inherited organisational and administrative structure of the retail and service sectors, restrictive legislation and other policies which served to impede entry of new units and the restructuring of old ones (Frydman and Rapaczynski 1994). Once the state introduced the appropriate conditions favourable to the process, however, the anticipated increase in the stock of small firms usually followed.

Poland and Hungary concentrated on retail outlets in order to quickly generate a stock of small, owner-managed firms. Such firms were closer to the customer, best placed to deal with the re-allocation of the existing stock and able to respond to the changing business environment through their dynamism and flexibility. This process of the transfer of ownership was not without its problems, however. The existing employees within such units often claimed the right to take over the newly privatised firm, but exponents of the free market argued that the key criterion should be ability, and that only public auctions would allow a fair and efficient allocation through competition. There were also fears that the *nomenklatura* (the list of Communist Party members nominated to senior positions within government or industry) would use their influence to assume ownership, or that foreigners would move in to buy up the new stock of small firms. This was a particular concern in the Baltics where it was feared the neighbouring Russians would dominate the local economy.

In an attempt to deal with these issues, many countries of the region used voucher schemes and public auctions. Vouchers were used in the Baltics, for example, to exclude Russians from ownership of former state property. Although the voucher system made the process fairer and more open, it also slowed everything down and led to complications, such as arguments over property title or multiple ownership. Similarly, public auctions took much longer, and again slowed down the speed of the transfer in the ownership of power due to their complexity and the need to disseminate information widely. Residents were given priority, but the relatively high prices and the scarcity of capital made the purchase by foreign buyers much more likely.

Thus, there was a trade-off between speed and the degree of openness. Comparative results from two countries serve as an illustration. In Czechoslovakia (a country which adopted a much more regulated, formal approach to transition), of the planned 100,000 small firms earmarked for sale, only 25,584 had been sold by March 1992. By contrast, in Poland (where there was no such obsession with competitive procedures), in 1990 alone, 80,000 small stores were sold (Frydman and Rapaczynski 1994). In the early 1990s, Poland demonstrated a much more dynamic stock of small firms which operated in a much less regulated environment, whereas in Czechoslovakia corruption was less widespread and the processes much more regulated, but the stock of small firms grew at a much slower rate in the early stages of transition, and the firms were much less dynamic in their operations.

A highly problematic issue for all small firms registered through the small-scale privatisation process was the inability to purchase the premises on which the business activity took place. The only really desirable asset was the real estate within which the business operated. This, however, invariably remained in state hands, with the premises being leased to the owner-manager, short-term leases of two years being commonplace. To make matters worse, the property was often transferred to the previous managers or employees of the unit on preferential terms and they invariably imposed all sorts of restrictions on the owner-managers, such as business use, subletting and many others. In this way, although a stock of dynamic small firms was created at great speed, the ability of these units to compete effectively was often greatly hampered by the inefficiencies and corruption within the management of the property sector.

15.6.2 Growth of the small-firms sector

The small-scale privatisation programme, although responsible for the creation of many robust small firms, was not the main catalyst for the explosion in the number of small firms in the early years of the transition process: the main factors were elsewhere. Firstly, there was a 'push' factor in the shape of the threat of being made unemployed, thanks to the fact that the large state-owned enterprises were beginning to respond to the needs of a market economy and were starting to shed labour whenever possible. Many employees felt it would be far better to establish a new private business in their own time, rather than be pushed into it later on. The result was that, overwhelmingly, most new entrepreneurs came, not from the pool of the unemployed, but directly from large state enterprises in a process of 'job-to-job-transition' (Boeri 1994). Secondly, the steeply declining wage rates everywhere in the state sector significantly lowered the opportunity cost of embarking upon entrepreneurship – that is, the employed person had financially very little to lose by moving into a private business of his/her own. Thirdly, despite the fact that nearly all the transition economies were initially registering strongly negative growth and large declines in output, the huge mismatch between emerging demands and the inherited capacity to supply meant that there were many profitable business opportunities and niches which suitable 'first-comers' could exploit. Most of these 'first-comers' were keen to exploit new market opportunities through importing activities, with only a very small percentage seemingly willing or able to embark on manufacturing needed items themselves.

The overall result was that many people used the opportunities opening up within the rapidly changing economic environment to start up their own businesses. For example, long-distance lorry drivers bought the trucks they had been driving for many years and started operating as subcontractors to their former state-owned employer.

Others who could not afford such expenditure started using their private vehicles as taxis. Some with trades such as carpentry, plumbing or vehicle repair started trading on their own account from back-street premises. At the other end of the scale, many of the *nomenklatura* used their old network of contacts either to buy up privatised enterprises cheaply or to start up completely new ventures, often either supplying or buying from their former colleagues within the old state enterprises.

At first sight, the statistics appear impressive. By 1994, there were more than 1 million registered Hungarian enterprises, with more than 90% of those comprising micro-enterprises. Small-enterprise contribution to GDP represented 26% and 27% in 1992 and 1993 respectively (HFEP 1996). In Poland, by 1993 more than 1.5 million small-firm registrations were employing over 2.5 million people, more than 9% of the total population (Jeffries 1996). In Czechoslovakia, by the end of 1991, there were 900,000 small-firm registrations (Jeffries 1996). Even in Romania, where the conditions were much less favourable, there were over 400,000 registered small businesses by March 1993 (Nicolescu 1994).

Although this development of the small-firms sector can be celebrated, the statistics emanating from the countries of the region need to be looked at carefully, for all is not as it seems. The Czechoslovak Entrepreneurial Association estimated in 1991 that out of the 900,000 registered small firms, approximately 650,000 were not actually trading enterprises (EFER 1992). In Hungary in 1994, of 801,000 registered private entrepreneurs, just 481,000 presented tax statements. That is, 40% of all officially registered enterprises were in fact 'phantom' registrations (HFEP 1996). What is the explanation? The main reasons are as follows:

- Registration was simple, and therefore many people registered hoping to undertake some private business activity at some point in the future.
- Many of the registrations were undertaken by employees of the state who had a part-time business such as plumbing or car repair 'on the side'.
- Many state employees, particularly among the *nomenklatura*, registered businesses and then used these to trade with their employer for private gain, for example buying raw materials cheaply from the state enterprise and then selling them back at exorbitant rates. Of course, the state enterprise made a loss, but this was passed on to the government.
- As the regulations became tighter, many small companies required their employees to register as independent entrepreneurs to avoid having to make social security payments, wage taxes and so on. This also provided greater flexibility as wage levels were often restricted for normal employees.

These problems notwithstanding, Poland, Hungary and the Czech Republic have seen the most impressive development in their small-firm sectors. The developments in the Yugoslav successor states have been held back because of the disintegration of the country in 1991 and the civil war which followed, although Slovenia has emerged quite strongly since becoming an independent state. Bulgaria has suffered badly from its political environment and has witnessed what has become known as the 'mafia-isation' of its economy by the former *nomenklatura* which remains very powerful in that country.

Case study 15.4 The mafia-isation of the Bulgarian trading environment

By supplying raw materials at market prices to state-run firms managed by friends, and then buying back the finished products cheaply, companies can make money twice, first on the raw materials and then by selling the finished goods. Private companies with good connections to government were also able to take large credits and loans from the state banks with no intention of paying them back, giving rise to a small group of very rich people called the 'credit millionaires'.

In Russia too, a very hostile trading environment can be identified. Statistics on small firm registrations are very unreliable, and the majority of small traders prefer to operate outside of the mainstream business community in the 'grey' economy.

Case study 15.5 Small-firm trading in Russia

AK, a small businessman distributing batteries in St Petersburg, owns three ware-housing facilities and keeps three sets of accounts, each one relating to the level of stocks held in each warehouse. One warehouse is for when the inland revenue come calling. A second warehouse is for the 'mafia' who call to collect a percentage of the total stock value on the first Monday of each month. The third ware-house is to store any surplus to be hidden from one or the other. Each Sunday is dedicated to bookkeeping and stock control.

15.6.3 The later stages of transition

Following the initial flurry of activity, from 1994 onwards, the rate of new-firm formation in the region began to tail off significantly. Moreover, the number of small firms is starting to decrease relative to the number of micro-firms, which are beginning to represent a disproportionate percentage of the total stock of private enterprises. In other words, the private sector is 'hollowing out', with a general lack of strong small and medium-sized enterprises. To a large extent this is to be expected. In any young market environment, new entrants to that market are attracted by the prospects of easy start-up and future growth. As that market starts to mature, however, the trading environment becomes tougher, and many of the new entrants fail, not for lack of good ideas, but due to lack of expertise, of capital and so on. As the market continues to mature, the potential for fast growth diminishes and we find fewer small firms competing for fewer and fewer new customers. Finally, although there has also been a tremendous influx of foreign capital into many of the countries of the region, in practice the degree to which SMEs were able to take advantage of these business opportunities was quite limited. Thus the stimulation created by foreign investment has generally failed to reach the small and medium-sized enterprises.

One of the consequences of these trends has been the particular distribution of productive assets within the countries of the region. Whereas the traditional distribution could be represented by a pyramid structure, with, say, 10% of the productive assets owned by large firms, the position towards the end of the transition period could be represented by an hourglass shape (see Figure 15.1). That is, around 75% of all the productive assets are held by large-scale enterprises, with the majority of the remainder being held by small-scale enterprises. The difficulty of this situation therefore is the lack of an effective medium-sized sector. Small-scale operations provide the breeding-ground for many entrepreneurs, but in order for these enterprises to grow there must be effective interaction with the larger-scale firms. This interaction is effected through the interface provided by the medium-sized enterprises. The lack of such a sector results in a huge gap between the large-scale, hard-currency-orientated enterprises on the one hand and the small-scale, locally based organisations on the other.

Thus the majority of the productive assets remain with the small number of large-scale organisations. The majority of these enterprises will have foreign partners, and those who do not will derive most of their turnover from foreign trade. The remainder of the assets will rest with the myriad micro-businesses which derive their turnover from the local marketplace, dealing exclusively in the local currency. Such enterprises will prefer to operate outside the mainstream business community due to the lack of trust in the administration and to avoid taxes and social security payments.

The lack of an effective medium-sized sector ensures that there is little contact between these two forms of organisation, which could be said to operate in different worlds. This state of affairs is exacerbated by the inability or unwillingness of the banks to lend to small enterprises, together with the inability of the current governments to create a climate of confidence which may bring the small-scale entrepreneur into the mainstream business community.

Figure 15.1 Distribution of productive assets: firms by size

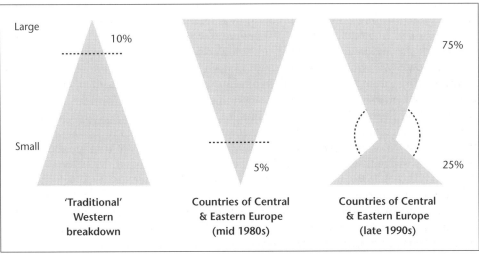

15.7 The need for policy intervention

Although the SME sector expanded considerably in the early years of the transition, it quickly became clear that policy support was desperately needed if the SME sector was to fulfil its early promise in terms of promoting rapid economic development. As was briefly touched upon above, most worrying was the fact that in the first few years of the transition the bulk of new SMEs were found to be engaged in petty services, simple retailing, catering and consumer goods importing activities, with the corollary to this being that very few were seriously engaged in manufacturing activity involving meaningful capital investment and the application of new technology. This was a negative development in Eastern Europe for a number of reasons. Firstly, such a structure clearly hinders the establishment of some very important economic development processes – industrial subcontracting and networking, increased R&D, innovation, technology and skills transfer, export activity, import substitution and so on. Almost without exception, the most successful models of small-enterprise development, such as in post-World War II Germany, Italy and Japan (Friedman 1988; Pyke and Sengenberger 1992), placed a very high premium on small enterprises as sophisticated manufacturers, industrial service providers and industrial subcontractors. Secondly, the petty importing activities which boomed after the instant liberalisation of trading relations, began to greatly undermine the local industrial structure in many regions. By facilitating very easy and very rapid access to imported goods (often without regard to customs duties and tariff restrictions) the rush of new importing businesses generated a real competitive threat to the vast majority of other local producers, most of which were desperately struggling to obtain the necessary capital and expertise which would enable them to quickly restructure, retool and retrain. Finally, one of the reasons for the shortage of affordable finance for manufacturing SMEs can be traced back to the high profits made by petty retailing, trading and importing concerns, particularly so in the early years. Given these 'abnormal' profits, the commercial banks were naturally keen to set a high price for capital (i.e. interest rates) in order to appropriate a share for themselves. Production- and technology-based SMEs, and other high-risk SMEs, thus found it difficult to service loan capital at these high interest rates, and so essentially desisted from attempting to obtain it. Effectively, they have been 'crowded out' of the financial market for both investment and working capital.

As with the macro-economic policies which the first post-Communist governments adopted, the SME policies put into practice from 1990 onwards were also very heavily influenced by the radical free-market or neo-liberal approach to managing an economy. Neo-liberalism was then held in very high regard in the Western democracies, thanks to the efforts of Mrs Thatcher in the UK and Ronald Reagan in the USA, who both pushed through a radical free-market economic policy agenda during their respective terms of office. Though it is now increasingly the case that these neo-liberal policies have actually failed in the West (see, for example, Amin and Tomaney 1995, Peck and Tickell 1994a), at the start of the transition Western governments and their advisers were encouraged to be decidedly outspoken about the need for Eastern Europe to adopt radical free-market policies to bring about a successful transition to the market economy. Pressure was exerted on Eastern European governments to go along with these radical ideas, sometimes with the implicit threat that if they did not toe the line they would not receive the financial support packages that they so desperately needed.

The SME policy interventions which emerged in Eastern Europe to support the SME sector thus tended to reflect the key elements of the radical free-market agenda, particularly its antipathy towards all forms of state intervention and support. However, the conditions prevailing in Eastern Europe were considered so severe as to require an initial helping hand from the state in order to establish the conditions for a market economy to emerge, and so three broad policy interventions were considered necessary to support SME development. These measures became the focus for much of the SME development policy in Eastern Europe.

15.7.1 Institution-building

Institution-building involved several aspects. Firstly, there was the provision of policy advice to government departments and ministries. Foreign advisers were brought in to address the whole range of government activities and propose new legislation, regulations and policies which would create an appropriately 'SME-friendly' environment. A second form related to the need to develop a national agency which would have the task of promoting and supporting the SME sector, and particularly the range of local institutions which would themselves support the local SME sector. With international support many countries thus established their own variant of a 'National Agency for SMEs'. The third form of institution-building – and by far the most important in terms of expenditure and commitment on the part of the international community – was the creation of local SME support institutions. These were the Business Support Centres (BSCs), which were established in most major towns and cities. The name of these centres varies between countries, but they are all meant to perform essentially the same service to the SME sector. Their role was to help develop SMEs in the locality through the provision of information, training, advice, access to capital, and hands-on assistance. Overwhelmingly, BSCs were established and initially financed by the international assistance community. By 1998, all of the post-Communist countries had created networks of BSCs of one form or another.

15.7.2 Financial support to SMEs

For a number of reasons, at the start of the transition most SMEs clearly found it extremely difficult to obtain access to affordable finance. Large enterprises were siphoning off most of the available credit, thanks to their access to the so-called 'soft money circuit', which left very little for the emerging SME sector to utilise. And what little cash there was potentially remaining for SMEs across the board tended to go to those which were well-established, well-connected and/or in high-profit/low-risk areas, such as retailing, trading and importing. Moreover, it was well known that in practice some commercial banks were 'red-lining' the SME sector – that is, refusing to deal with any SMEs as serious candidates for credit. Thus, special help of some sort was clearly desperately needed if a new generation of high-growth SMEs was to emerge.

Help came in the form of direct financial support through grants, credit lines, venture capital, and so on, again mainly thanks to the international assistance community.

This cash was meant to go to SMEs which had high growth and employment potential, and also if they were likely to be involved in exporting. At the same time, the local financial system itself was in need of reform in order to push it to provide affordable capital on its own. This objective was to be accomplished by channelling this financial support for the SME sector through private-sector institutions (e.g. commercial banks) who would then (it was hoped) be able to better see how to develop their own profitable SME loan portfolios. This was the so-called 'demonstration effect'. On a more modest scale, some local governments became active in financially supporting unemployed persons into entrepreneurship, utilising their own funds to encourage the unemployed to establish a new small business. Sometimes the unemployed person was allowed to capitalise on the funds earmarked for his/her future welfare payment support in order that they would have sufficient funds to become established, and thus also no longer require state financial support as an unemployed person. Many of these policies towards the existing and soon-to-be unemployed were part of the so-called 'Active Labour Market Policies' which were a feature of nearly all the transition economies (Godfrey and Richards 1997).

15.7.3 Regional development

A major feature of the SME policies which emerged as the transition began was the regional basis for much of this work. Many of the SME policies were structured to assist those regions which had been held back by the old system of central planning and/or which were suffering particularly adversely as a result of the transition to the market economy. SMEs were also central to many regional development programmes as a way to sponsor indigenous development and to link the regional economy to the other parts of the country, and to other countries through exports. Some SME programmes were also aimed at supporting regions with substantial minority communities, some of which were underdeveloped because of historical prejudice dating back to the pre-Communist period. Most importantly, the plans for integrating much of Central and Eastern Europe into the European Union shortly into the next millennium rely very much on comprehensive regional development programmes in which SME development has a pivotal role to play. These countries, particularly the five expected to be in the first wave (Poland, Hungary, Czech Republic, Slovenia and Estonia), are all busily strengthening their regional development networks to be able to absorb the variety of EU funds which are coming on-stream, with much of this investment earmarked for SME development. The hope is that SME development will spearhead the accelerated economic development of those regions which are at the bottom of the poverty and living standards indexes in each country, and thus facilitate the economic and social integration of the country.

15.8 SME policy interventions in practice

A number of years have now passed since the introduction of most of the main SME support policies, and it is now possible to look back and begin to assess the results of these various policy interventions. As we noted above, effectively the first policy intervention by governments in Central and Eastern Europe was to remove the many and varied barriers to SME entry which had prevailed for so long under Communism. This move directly led to the massive wave of 'spontaneous' entrepreneurship which was a feature of virtually all of the transition economies. Accordingly, there is a much larger population of SMEs virtually everywhere, in many cases reaching the same density (measured by number of SMEs per thousand head of population) as in parts of Western Europe. Moreover, removing the historical prejudice to SMEs and the many barriers to SME entry had the effect of creating a much more 'SME-friendly' environment, which in turn has encouraged other institutions to rapidly adapt to the new conditions. For example, universities quickly introduced the study of entrepreneurship into their curricula, and larger businesses absorbed many of the fundamental managerial concepts involved in entrepreneurship. Overall, the business culture in Central and Eastern Europe was pushed very much along from its bureaucratic-administrative inheritance, and towards the more entrepreneurial version found in most of the Western economies (Bateman 1997).

The results so far of the more proactive SME policy interventions are, however, somewhat more problematic. There was significant support for the establishment of BSCs in virtually all of the transition economies. Most now have a functioning network in place, in the main financed by the international assistance agencies (particularly the EU's Phare programme, USAID and UNIDO). The BSCs are intended to be driven by the immediate needs of the private sector, while being managed by a group of local 'stakeholders', such as local governments, banks, large firms, Chambers of Commerce, Chambers of Crafts, and so on. They are also supposed to be very commercially orientated in their manner of operations. By and large, most of these BSCs have fulfilled their mandate to offer to existing and potential entrepreneurs in most major towns and cities, if not a high-quality package of advice and support, then at least a 'first port of call' where the services of other agencies and individuals can be sought. Moreover, even though many studies indicate that only a very small proportion of new entrepreneurs actually use the BSCs' services, many nevertheless appear to have established a sufficiently high profile in the local business community.

But a number of interrelated problems have begun to emerge which are causing real concern, many of which can be attributed to the highly commercial orientation of the policy initiatives undertaken. First, many of the BSC networks are increasingly facing the prospect of collapse, on account of their international funding running out. In many cases it has so far proved impossible to illicit sufficient financial support from central or local government for the BSC networks to allow them to continue functioning in their present mode. After imbibing the neo-liberal approach to SME development promoted by the international community – and particularly its strong presumption that the free market with its 'invisible hand' was all that was really needed to promote entrepreneurship – many governments in Central and Eastern Europe were surprised by the need to cough up financial support for a variety of policy interventions. Many local governments resent the fact that they have been asked to assume the financial responsibility for an institution over which they were never meant to have any real control. Local governments also tend to be angry at the way that so much international funding has found its way into the private-sector-led BSC networks, while they themselves struggle to undertake an increasingly ambitious economic development agenda foisted onto them by the central government. One result is that the traditional economic departments within the local government structure have been allowed to atrophy. The second major problem with the BSC networks is the increasingly commercial nature of those BSCs which are determined to survive without government help. Most BSCs are now – or shortly will be – *de facto* private-sector consultancy bodies, competing with other private-sector consultancy companies in the SME sector for the best fee-paying clients. An increasing number of BSCs now almost exclusively survive on work provided by large companies (both state and privately owned) or incoming multinationals, and by doing consultancy and research work unrelated to SME development. The upshot of this trend is that many BSCs are clearly and increasingly losing touch with their original SME client base, many of which do not have the resources to pay them for their strictly commercial services. Finally, many BSCs have effectively withdrawn from the sort of strategic interventions in the SME sector which could have major positive longer-term effects, but which generate no revenue in the short term. Into this category of 'lost opportunities' would fall the promotion of industrial subcontracting, technology transfer and upgrading, sectoral upgrading, training initiatives, and so on.

Turning now to the special provision of financial support to SMEs, it was hoped that a major programme of financial support for SME development would be an extremely useful policy intervention by both governments and the international assistance agencies. Financial support was felt to be particularly important for new-starts and manufacturing-related SMEs. To date, however, the results from the many financial support programmes which have been established appear to be as problematic as in the case of the BSCs noted above. For sure, with a certain amount of targeting, or by simply ruling out any SME engaged in simple trading activities, most programmes have successfully managed to focus on some of those SMEs which have the capacity to make a real impact in the economy. Most surveys of the SME sector indicate that very many of the best-performing SMEs have become established thanks to support from these programmes. Programmes delivering micro-credits have been particularly successful in encouraging individual entrepreneurs to 'take the plunge' and try their hand at entrepreneurial activities. Some progress has also been made in terms of encouraging the commercial banks to develop their own SME lending capacity.

However, one obvious question which comes up here is: would the SMEs supported have been able to get into business without this special programme of financial support? The question arises because very many of the SMEs supported by the special financial programmes were quite easily capable of obtaining finance from local private-sector financial bodies, such as the commercial banks. They only went to the special financial support programmes because they offered better conditions than the local commercial banks, not because said banks had refused them access to a loan. Under these circumstances, the real contribution the financial programme makes to the local SME sector is minimal because the special programmes are simply substituting for money which would otherwise be available for the SME in the financial market. While this problem is not overwhelmingly pervasive, it has led to some modifications in lending practices by many financial programmes. For example, some special financial programmes now require potential clients to have first approached the local commercial bank for support, and only when unsuccessful in this would they be eligible for special support.

Another problem is that many of the financial programmes operated by governments and the international assistance agencies have tended to promote a relatively small number of new entrants with the funds at their disposal. High administrative costs can be avoided by working with a small number of projects, while the personnel directly involved in disbursing funds naturally desire to reduce their effort by concentrating on just a few of the very best projects. However, this limited entry strategy can very easily result in a small number of monopolistic/rent-seeking small enterprises becoming established, which is nice for those directly involved but overall will have a comparatively minor impact on local competition, the local industrial structure and production efficiency. Most financial programmes have not yet attempted to address this issue.

Finally, we turn to the regional programmes. With the moves to EU accession in a handful of the Central and Eastern European states now well under way, regional development programmes are increasingly coming to centre stage. Even countries as small geographically as Slovenia are experiencing significant regional economic development imbalances, particularly of a rural–urban nature, which are affecting the cohesion of the country. EU strategy for the accession process very much hinges on the successful reduction in regional differences, both within the country concerned and in relation to other member states. In addition, the EU places great store on the treatment of minority populations, and their economic inclusion into the emerging market economy. Some progress has been made here. In many regions, such as in Poland, the programmes have been successful in creating new SMEs and some SMEs out of failed or declining large state enterprises – and this was in spite of the reluctance of the central government to set out a regional development strategy and develop related policies. While this SME-driven regional development policy is not a magic cure, but at most a 'second-best solution', it has nevertheless managed to prevent an even larger decline in economic activity in regions which can ill afford it. Minority groups have also been able to secure greater access to resources in order to establish SMEs, and this has ameliorated their relative economic position and sense of injustice against the majority population. Other regional programmes unrelated to EU accession have also shown some success.

The main problem with regional development programmes involving SME development is that so much depends on the macro-economic framework: if it is not supportive, and large enterprises are going under, then very little can be done through SME development alone. In other words, SME development is a *complement* to a supportive macro-economic policy, and not a *replacement* for one. Moreover, the situation has not been helped in Eastern Europe by the substantial changes which have taken place in the structure of government since the collapse of Communism. Regional policies require strong and efficient regional governments, while most Eastern European countries inherited relatively weak regional governments.

15.9 Chapter summary

The SME sector has unquestionably progressed in the years since the collapse of Communism and central planning. The initial surge of new entrants in the period 1990–3 – overwhelmingly in the trading, importing and petty services sectors – has now subsided. The early and easy opportunities for high profits have now effectively all been found, exploited and competed away. Many prospective entrepreneurs are now setting up in more sophisticated ventures involving high levels of capital investment, technology and skills. This is a positive development for the future of Central and Eastern Europe. At the same time, new strategic policies are increasingly coming into view. Many governments are now keen to promote industrial subcontracting involving SMEs as suppliers to larger enterprises, a vital aspect of the industrial development process. Exporting SMEs are also being targeted for greater support, while import-substituting SMEs are getting more (though less publicised) help to wrest from importers a variety of traditionally local markets.

But in spite of this improved environment for SMEs, and the successes in SME development so far, there remains an enormous challenge for Eastern European governments to grasp. This is to use SME development not simply as a peripheral economic policy, but to base their development strategy far more around the potential offered up by SME development. There is much evidence that other countries, in similar circumstances to those which still prevail in Central and Eastern Europe, have been able to promote rapid economic development through a very strong focus upon SME development. For example, the overwhelming majority of what we can term 'post-conflict/post-chaos' reconstruction and development episodes, such as in post-World War II Germany, Italy and Japan, in the East Asian 'Tiger' economies from the 1960s onwards, and in China after the death of Mao in 1978, have involved SME development policies in a very big way (see Bateman 1999). The positive experiences and enormous development successes registered in these quite diverse examples of post-conflict/post-chaos reconstruction and development certainly seem to indicate that such a policy focus was entirely appropriate. This intervention took the form of establishing a well-financed network of local agencies providing advice and support directly to SMEs; encouraging the formation of a broader range of institutional structures; cajoling and negotiating with large enterprises to work with local SMEs as suppliers; and regional and local state planning to ensure scarce reconstruction and development resources (e.g. vacant land and buildings) were used efficiently and that local and regional comparative advantages were exploited fully.

The above type of intervention at the micro-economic level is somewhat akin to the 'transformative capacity' concept used by Weiss (1998) to explain the overall success of several of the most successful economies, such as Germany and Japan. A transformative local state seeks to ensure that the local economy and the small-business sector continually evolve, are upgraded, and take advantage of new technologies, markets, product and process innovations, and existing local comparative advantages, in order to respond to changes in the world outside of the locality. It recognises that the market mechanism will not do this alone. Nor will individual profit-seeking enterprises be able to bring about the extent of change required over the longer term. Instead, the local state must work alongside the small-business sector to ensure that a strategy is implemented which promotes the longer-term development and transformation of the local economy, and the local small-business sector as a whole. Thus, among other things, one could argue that local governments in Central and Eastern Europe rapidly need to develop a high level of 'transformative capacity' if they are now to go forward and build upon the obvious achievements made in the small-business sector since the collapse of Communism.

Questions

1 What role did small enterprises play under Communism?

2 What is meant by 'spontaneous entry'?

3 Why might small enterprises be important to the transition economies?

4 What have been the main problems in attempting to support small enterprises in Eastern Europe?

Management and the small firm

CHAPTER 16

Strategy and the small firm

Colm O'Gorman

16.1 Learning objectives

There are five learning objectives in this chapter:

1 To understand the strategies that are associated with success in small businesses.

2 To recognise the importance of focused and differentiated strategies for small businesses.

3 To appreciate the strategy-making process in small businesses.

4 To introduce the structural context that constrains the development of strategy in small businesses.

5 To note the strategic weaknesses of small businesses.

Key concepts

■ strategy ■ competitive advantage ■ focus strategy
■ the strategy-making process ■ the strategy-making context

16.2 Introduction

This chapter introduces students to the concepts of strategy and competitive advantage and their relationship to the management of the small firm. The owner-manager of a small business must choose 'where' to compete, and then, given a particular environment or industry context, the owner-manager must choose 'how' to compete. The first part of the chapter reviews research on the success strategies of small businesses. This review suggests that successful small businesses pursue 'focused' strategies and they emphasise competitive advantages such as flexibility, fast response times and closeness to the customer. Innovation can also provide the small business with an important competitive advantage. The second part of the chapter outlines the strategy-making process in small businesses, highlighting the fact that this is a highly informal and *ad hoc* process in most small businesses. The advantages of a formal strategy-making process are discussed. The chapter concludes by highlighting structural and strategic weaknesses that impact on the choice of strategy and the strategy-making processes of small businesses. These weaknesses make it difficult for the small-business manager to develop a clear competitive advantage. One of the most significant structural characteristics of small businesses that influences the strategy-making process is the centrality of the owner-manager. This prevents the delegation of authority and the sharing of responsibility for the strategic development of the small business. Strategic weaknesses include the lack of financial and managerial resource, reliance on a small customer base, and poor technological competence.

16.3 Strategy and the small firm

Strategy is about asking two questions: 'What business(es) should we be in?' and 'How do we compete in a given business?' (Hofer 1975). Drucker referred to these two challenges in terms of effectiveness and efficiency (1977). Efficiency means doing things right – ensuring that day-to-day operations are managed well. Effectiveness refers to ensuring that the business is doing the right things – that the focus of the business is correct in the context of customers, competitors and industry trends. Efficiency ensures short-term survival by producing a profit from existing activities, while effectiveness ensures long-term survival by focusing the business on activities that will continue to produce profits in the future. The essence of a good strategy is that it is feasible; that is, it is consistent with the resources and skills of the business; it provides a clear competitive advantage; and there is a 'fit' between the business and its external competitive environment (Rumelt 1991).

The concept of strategy has different meanings in different contexts. Mintzberg proposed that strategy can be defined in five different ways, i.e. as a plan, as a ploy, as a pattern, as a position and as a perspective (Mintzberg and Quinn 1991). Strategy as a plan refers to the intended actions that management have developed. When these plans refer to a specific decision they can be described as ploys. Mintzberg argues that not all strategies are planned but that in many situations strategy can be inferred from a pattern in a stream of decisions that management have made over time. Strategy can also refer to the position that the business has adopted in its external environment. This position can be defined in terms of the market that the business serves and in terms of the position that competitors have adopted. Finally, strategy can be conceptualised in terms of how a business perceives itself and its external environment, that is, in terms of the shared values and beliefs that guide the decisions made by the business.

The outcome of a strategy should be a clear competitive advantage. A competitive advantage is an advantage that is valued by customers and which distinguishes the business from its competitors. The source of a competitive advantage can be conceptualised in terms of the strategic positioning of the business or in terms of the resources and skills of the business. The positioning approach emphasises the need for the business to achieve 'fit' with the external environment. To develop a strategy the business must have a clear understanding of its market and of its competitors. The ongoing success of the business is dependent on the ability of the business to maintain the 'fit' between the business and the changing environment context.

The resource-based perspective argues that the source of a competitive advantage is the resources and capabilities of the business. By developing or acquiring resources the business can develop sustainable competitive advantages. Resources confer competitive advantage if they are hard to imitate, if they are heterogeneous – that is, different from the resources that other business have – and if there is uncertainty as to the value of the resource. However, the value of resources can only be understood in the context of the market that the business is operating in and in the context of a particular moment in time.

Strategy researchers traditionally focus on large organisations. However, differences in resource endowments and organisation structure between large businesses and small businesses mean that many strategy prescriptions appropriate to large businesses are inappropriate to small businesses. Therefore it is appropriate to ask: is it realistic for the small business to define its strategy and its strategic position? Should a small business have a formal strategy? And can a small business re-position itself strategically?

Small businesses differ from large businesses in their perception of opportunities and their commitment of resources to new opportunities (Stevenson and Gumpert 1985). Large organisations are typically characterised by an administrative management style. The growth and development of the business is driven by the resources that the business controls. Large businesses consider the pay-off of investments in the medium to long term. In making strategic moves the large business will typically analyse the opportunity and make a one-off commitment of resources. In contrast the small business is typically characterised by a lack of resources and management skills and by an entrepreneurial form of management. Small businesses can respond quickly to opportunities but may not be able to commit large amounts of resources to a new opportunity. Therefore, the small-business manager tends to commit small amounts of resources, in a number of different stages, as the opportunity emerges. These differences mean it is often inappropriate to compare large and small businesses in terms of the strategies associated with success and in terms of the strategy-making process.

In the context of developing strategic prescriptions for a business, 'small' can have several meanings. Small can refer to the actual size of the organisation, in terms of sales or staff numbers, but it can also refer to the size of a business relative to the total market and relative to competitors (Chen and Hambrick 1995). Small size need not be a competitive disadvantage. Small size can increase the flexibility of the business in responding to customer requests and to market changes. Small size can mean that the business can be more flexible in terms of production systems (Fiegenbaum and Karnini 1991) or in terms of price. Small size may mean that the business is faster to respond to changes in the market (Katz 1970). Small businesses may be less risk-averse and more inclined to initiate competitive actions (Chen and Hambrick 1995).

16.4 Success strategies in small firms

The owner-manager must choose where to compete, and then, given a particular environmental or industry context, the owner-manager must choose how to compete (McDougall and Robinson 1990). These choices have a significant and lasting effect on the organisation and its performance (Mintzberg and Waters 1982; Quinn and Cameron 1983). The choice of competitive strategy within a market determines the financial performance of the organisation: if the 'wrong' market is chosen, performance may be low. However, most owner-managers of small businesses adopt a 'me-too' or 'copy-cat' strategy – replicating what has been done before. Typically, owner-managers of small businesses claim that they compete on quality but that, in contrast, most of their competitors compete on cost.

Industry structure impacts on the success of new ventures and has a critical impact on the choice of strategy (Sandberg and Hofer 1987). Periods of high-demand conditions, such as industry growth and industry maturity, offer better opportunities for the small business than do periods of low demand such as the emergent stage of the product life-cycle (Carroll and Delacroix 1982; Romanelli 1989). However, while market choice is a critical managerial decision, it is not a choice that is, or can be, subject to frequent change. The choice of environment is constrained by the owner-manager's past experience, by previous choices made by the owner-manager, and is therefore not an active decision variable (Eisenhardt and Schoonhoven 1990).

Many researchers have focused on the strategic attributes of successful small businesses. Success is typically measured in terms of existing competitive position and the change in this position over time. Measuring success in a small-business context is inherently difficult as success should be related to the owner-manager's objectives rather than measured in terms of competitive, financial or market success. Studies on the strategies pursued by small businesses typically focus on some measure of success in terms of these latter criteria rather than in terms of the owner-manager's personal definition of success.

16.4.1 Choosing 'where' to compete: a broad or narrow focus?

The prescriptive advice from the strategy literature is that small businesses should focus on market niches. The focus strategy involves the owner-manager targeting the product/service at a narrow market niche. The advantages of such a strategy are that the owner-manager can conserve limited resources and ensure that all attention is given to the chosen target market.

The early strategy content literature attempted to identify strategies associated with different sizes of business. Katz (1970) suggested strategy prescriptions for both large and small businesses, the thrust of his suggestions being that the small business must focus and conserve its resources while the larger competitor must play to the advantages of its size by planning activities carefully to ensure resources are allocated to activities in relation to their contribution to the business. Abbanat (1967) concluded with reference to his comparison of the strategies of small companies with the strategies of large companies that 'If there was a pattern to the results, it was a pattern of difference and in this sense the impression that small manufacturing companies compete directly with large corporations is erroneous. Rather these companies probed for soft spots and gaps in the market.'

This theme was repeated by Porter who suggested that a focus strategy is most appropriate for smaller businesses (1985). According to Porter the business pursuing a focus strategy competes by selecting a segment or group of segments in its industry and by tailoring its strategy to serving these segments to the exclusion of others. By optimising its strategy in the target segments the business with a focus strategy achieves a competitive advantage even though it does not possess a competitive advantage for the whole market.

Research on small businesses has suggested that there is evidence supporting a market niche strategy in high-growth small businesses. The essence of a market niche strategy in the context of many small businesses appears to be the avoidance of direct competition with both larger and smaller competitors. The evidence from the studies of fast-growth businesses in Ireland and the UK suggests that, despite attempts in the research to control for sector influences on growth by choosing 'matched pairs', high-growth companies rarely competed directly with low-growth companies (Kinsella and Mulvenna 1993; Storey 1994).

Research on low-market-share competitors has suggested a number of strategies that the smaller-share business can successfully employ. The most common conclusion of these studies is that the smaller business should avoid head-to-head competition by seeking out protected market niches (Buzzell and Wiersema 1981; Cooper, Willard and Woo 1986). Combined with this strategy of segmentation, smaller-share competitors should seek to differentiate their product offering and should offer a high-quality product.

Studies of successful medium-sized companies have suggested that a market niche strategy is an important characteristic of these companies. Cavanagh and Clifford (1983: 10) concluded that 'most winning companies are leaders in market niches, often in markets they have created through innovation'. Research evidence from the UK suggests that market position is an important characteristic of fast-growth businesses (Macrae 1991; Solemn and Stiener 1989). This research suggests that while the choice of overall sector may influence profitability and growth, the choice of specific market position is more important to the performance of an individual enterprise.

The empirical identification of a market niche strategy in small businesses is fraught with operational and definitional difficulties. It is difficult for researchers to precisely define the product market a business is competing in. How does a small food manufacturer producing speciality frozen desserts for supermarkets define their product market arena? Such a business could define its business very narrowly: 'a producer of premium frozen desserts for supermarkets'; or broadly: 'a dessert producer'. The classification of its competitive strategy will be a function of the choice of business definition and more importantly this definition may broaden as the business seeks to grow and expand. Neither Kalleberg and Leicht (1991) nor Westhead and Birley (1993) were able to provide conclusive evidence of market niche strategies among fast-growth small businesses in the UK. Biggadike (1976) compared the relative attractiveness of a niche strategy and an aggressive market-share-seeking entry strategy and suggested that the latter is more appropriate for new ventures seeking to establish themselves. He suggested that the poor performance of many new ventures is the direct consequence of limiting market focus at the time of entry.

The dangers of pursuing a focus strategy are that the business may incorrectly identify a market niche. Unless the business gets a competitive advantage by focusing on the niche then it should pursue a more broadly based strategy. For example, a soft-drinks manufacturer could not identify the market for carbonated orange drinks as a market niche. Customers do not identify this product as any different and competitors supplying a wider range of products, such as carbonated water, cola, lime, etc., will have an advantage due to lower production, distribution and promotion costs. An additional problem of pursuing a focused strategy is that the chosen market niche may be too small for the business to survive or may require that the small business become involved in export markets at a stage when they lack the resources to support these markets.

Rather than focusing on a market niche the entrepreneur might try to gain a large share of the market. Some new businesses must pursue a broad entry strategy because of the large capital investment required at start-up. These businesses are only viable if they achieve high utilisation of their large capital investment. The advantage of a broad market strategy is that if the business is successful it will be on a large scale. Additionally, a broad strategy might be more attractive to distributors, retailers or consumers. It suggests that there will be continuity in the business and it might include a more comprehensive service for the customer. Most new businesses do not have the resources to pursue such a strategy and therefore start on a small scale. Despite inconclusive empirical evidence, the prevailing wisdom in the strategy literature is that small businesses should optimise the use of their limited resources by competing in a limited market niche. In the literature on small businesses the prescriptive advice is that the best way to avoid direct competition with larger competitors is to pursue a niche strategy (Vesper 1990).

16.4.2 Choosing 'how' to compete: cost or differentiation?

Having chosen which market to compete in, the SME must then choose how it is going to compete within this market. Porter (1985) identified two types of competitive advantage, which he termed cost leadership and differentiation. Based on these two advantages and on the competitive scope of the business, which he classified as either industry-wide or focused, he developed three generic competitive strategies, namely 'cost leadership', 'differentiation', and 'focus'. According to Porter businesses must choose one of these generic strategies – failure to do so results in below-average profitability.

Research suggests that a differentiation strategy is the most appropriate strategy for small businesses. The limited resources of small businesses suggests that the owner-manager should focus resources and pursue a differentiation strategy. A large number of firms pursuing different differentiation strategies may be successful in the same environment (Eisenhardt and Schoonhoven 1990; McDougall and Robinson 1990; Porter 1980).

Product quality was the most important competitive advantage identified by SMEs across a number of European countries (Bamberger 1989). In addition, factors such as reliability of delivery, reputation of firm and the competence of the workforce were ranked as important competitive advantages. Interestingly, pricing factors were only rated 16th out of the 26 factors important to the development of competitive advantage. New ventures pursuing undifferentiated strategies performed less well than new ventures pursuing differentiated strategies (Sandberg and Hofer 1987).

Successful mid-sized companies compete by being unique (Kuhn 1982). Kuhn defined uniqueness as aspects of the business's interaction with the external environment which set it apart from competitors. Uniqueness was achieved by differentiating both the company and its products from those of competitors. Kuhn included market segmentation by product uniqueness, market segmentation by geographic specificity, market segmentation by customer/industry specificity, evidence of corporate uniqueness, and dependence on brand names as measures of uniqueness. A finding which surprised Kuhn was that successful mid-sized companies were product-orientated. The companies in his study emphasised product quality, product brand name and product value to customers as essential elements of their strategy. According to Kuhn the corporate claims of product leadership were 'vigorous, persistent and widespread among our sample' (1982: 170).

There are many ways in which a business may have a better product/service. These include superior product/service performance, faster delivery service, better location, wider product range, personal advice and after-sales service, longer credit terms, more flexible service, personalised attention, etc. It is important that the entrepreneur tries to maximise the number and the extent of advantages that the product/service has. This strategy is often not successful because the 'better' service/product that the business is offering is not of value to customers. Another reason why this strategy is unsuccessful is because small businesses fail to communicate their better service/product to their customers. This may be because of the financial investment and time required for promotion, advertising and sales support – activities and areas of expenditure that most small businesses consider to be a luxury.

Porter (1985) proposes that a business differentiates itself from competitors by being unique at something which is of value to buyers. To be sustainable a business's differentiation must perform unique activities that impact on the customers' purchasing criteria. Porter (1985: 152) identifies several methods that a business can employ to enhance its differentiation. These are:

- to enhance its sources of uniqueness;
- to make the cost of differentiation an advantage;
- to change the rules of competition to create uniqueness; and
- to reconfigure the value chain to be unique in entirely new ways.

Intuitively most owner-managers believe that a low-cost strategy will be successful – customers should be willing to pay less for the same product/service. However, this strategy is not that easy to pursue and many owner-managers fail to pursue it successfully, with the result that their business performs poorly. To pursue a low-price strategy the new business should have a lower cost base than competitors. Many small businesses pursue this strategy of lower costs by ensuring that they have lower overheads, by operating outside the tax system, or by using low-cost labour and not costing their own time at the market rate. The danger with this approach is that the entrepreneur may not have identified all the overheads that the business will incur and that, as the business develops, overheads will increase. The advantage of a low-price strategy is that the new business should be able to attract customers. Lower prices should encourage customers to try the new business and may encourage new customers into the business.

However, this strategy does not always work for small businesses. Often the net effect of lower prices is lower profits for the entrepreneur rather than increased sales. There are a number of reasons why this strategy may not work for the small business. The first is that for many products the price charged is assumed by customers to be a reflection of the quality of the product. Low prices may be interpreted by customers as a lower-quality service rather than as a more efficient supplier. To overcome this problem it might be necessary for the entrepreneur to inform customers why they are cheaper, e.g. 'cheaper because we buy direct from the factory'.

The second reason why this strategy may not work is that the owner-manager fails to invest in promotion and advertising. The owner-manager may incorrectly assume that a low-cost strategy means not investing in marketing and selling costs. The net effect of this is that the customer is unaware of the lower-cost alternative and the new business remains small. Many small businesses fail to generate revenues to invest in advertising and promotion because of their low prices and low turnover.

16.4.3 Innovation as a source of advantage

Within the literature on innovation researchers have sought to establish a relationship between business size and the level of innovation. An alternative perspective is to compare the level of innovation with business profitability, growth and survival. To the extent that this has been done (mostly indirectly by studies examining the characteristics of better-performing companies in a particular size/industry sector), it appears that there is a relationship between better performance and higher levels of innovation (Cavanagh and Clifford 1983; Kuhn 1982; Peters and Waterman 1982). Scherer (1980: 422) concluded that 'what we find ... is a kind of threshold effect. A little bit of bigness – up to sales levels of $250 million to $400 million at 1978 price levels – is good for invention and innovation. But beyond the threshold further bigness adds little or nothing, and it carries with it the danger of diminishing the effectiveness of inventive and innovative performance.'

Innovation may manifest itself in terms of the introduction of new products. Research suggests that the ability to introduce new products is positively related to performance in small businesses (Cambridge Small Business Research Centre 1992; Kinsella *et al.* 1993; Murray and O'Gorman 1994; Woo *et al.* 1989; Wynarczyk *et al.* 1993). Other evidence suggests that those businesses that are technically more sophisticated or technologically more innovative are likely to grow faster (Boeker 1989; Phillips and Kirchhoff 1989). However, it may be that these technically more sophisticated sectors are experiencing faster growth.

Buzzell and Wiersema (1981) used the PIMS database to test what strategies were characteristic of businesses that were increasing their market-share position. They found that the strategic factors generally involved in market-share gains included increases in new product activity, increases in relative product quality and increases in sales promotion, relative to the growth rate of the served market. Cohn and Lindberg (1972) concluded that the key advantage of small businesses is their flexibility in relation to customer service and making product changes.

Cavanagh and Clifford (1983), in a study of the strategies of successful mid-sized companies, concluded that innovation was 'a way of life' among the top-performing mid-sized growth companies. Most of their survey respondents achieved their first major success with either a unique product or a distinctive way of doing business. On average 25% of sales in their successful companies came from products which were not offered in the previous five years.

Small businesses face a number of disadvantages in trying to be innovative. Most small businesses lack the financial, technical and human resources needed to innovate. The lack of time for long-term thinking by the owner-manager prevents the development of both technical and market-led innovations. The absence of a marketing function and marketing expertise restricts the development of customer-driven innovations. Even those small businesses that are technologically competent, for example small engineering or software firms, face problems in the management of technology. The competitive strength of these small businesses – their specialist technical knowledge – exposes them to the possibility of being exposed to technical developments outside their area of expertise. This problem is particularly apparent in sectors where developments have been driven by the fusion of two or more existing technologies. The small business typically does not have the expertise or the financial resources to cope with external developments. The solution to this problem often necessitates co-operation with other businesses or with universities or technical institutes. However, small businesses are reluctant to co-operate with other businesses. While universities may provide technical assistance, they seldom provide access to investment and therefore can only partially solve the problems facing the small business.

16.4.4 Exporting and internationalisation strategies

Exporting or internationalisation can provide the small business with access to larger markets and to more attractive markets (see Chapter 24). However, most small businesses do not engage in any exporting or international activities. In particular, small businesses in the services sector have very low levels of direct international activity. Small firms face significant barriers in trying to internationalise their activities. Of particular significance are a lack of knowledge and a lack of resources (Johanson and Vahlne 1984). However, it is important to note that many small businesses are involved indirectly in international markets through their sub-supply activities with larger indigenous and multinational companies. The globalisation of some new high-technology sectors facilitates small companies internationalising at an earlier stage of development than is typical among small businesses (see Chapters 13 and 24).

16.5 Strategy-making in the small business

The small-business owner typically relies on previous industry experience to develop a strategy for the business. In many cases there may be no need for this strategy to be clearly articulated or for any formal plan to be developed to justify the choice of strategy or to set out how the strategy will be implemented. However, over-reliance on industry experience can result in a 'me-too' or 'copy-cat' strategy and no clear competitive advantage. In many industries with low barriers to entry, the cycle of 'me-too' new start-ups results in low profitability and high failure rates for all small businesses.

One approach to developing a successful strategy is to engage in a formal planning process. The models of planning suggested for small businesses have been adopted from the strategic management literature. However, small businesses differ from large businesses with regard to their planning needs and processes (Curtis 1983). Small businesses generally do not have the resources to plan and to purchase external advice and support; they are very susceptible to small environmental changes; owner-managers may not have the necessary experience for managing all aspects of a small business and owner-managers cannot devote a lot of time to consciously working through plans because of day-to-day pressures of work. A consequence of this is that owner-managers tend to take a shorter and more functional approach to planning.

Formal and comprehensive planning systems are rare in small businesses. The planning processes observed in most small businesses have been described as 'informal, unstructured, and sporadic' (Cohn and Lindberg 1972) and as 'a passive search for alternatives' (Bracker 1982). The structure of the small business and the centrality of the entrepreneur mean that all 'strategic planning' is typically concentrated in the owner-manager. Owner-managers may see no advantage in formalising the planning process that they use to develop the strategy of the business. Often the owner-manager will see disadvantages such as the potential loss of control, the loss of secrecy and the loss of flexibility. The reality of planning in the new-venture context is that it is opportunistic and informal rather than formal. Founders analyse ideas parsimoniously and they integrate analysis and implementation (Bhide 1994). However, the lack of formal planning does not imply the absence of strategic thinking. Planning can be thought of as any reflective activity which precedes the making of decisions (Foster 1993).

The essential components of a successful planning process in a small business are that the owner-manager is central to the planning process; the owner-manager and, where relevant, managers must have sufficient time to devote to the planning process; and effective planning will only be possible if sufficient internal information is available. This means that an adequate financial record-keeping and financial control system should be in place in the business. Financial information must be timely and accurate.

16.5.1 Planning and financial performance in small business

Within the literature on small business, research on planning has concentrated on establishing a link between planning and performance. Many researchers make the inference that the ultimate survival of a small business is dependent on the presence of formal planning activity (Bracker and Pearson 1986). There is evidence that small-business failure is linked to a lack of planning activity (Bracker and Pearson 1986). However, this research on the significance and the impact of planning in small businesses has proved to be inconclusive (Cragg and King 1988; Schwenk and Shrader 1993; Stone and Brush 1996).

Schwenk and Shrader (1993) reviewed studies on the relationship between planning and financial performance and found conflicting results. In a comparative study between planners and non-planners, Cragg and King (1988) found no correlation between planning activities and financial performance. They also found a negative correlation between planning and size of sales and marketing team. Within this sample, however, younger firms performed better than older ones. Bracker and Pearson (1986) compared small mature firms in terms of age, size and planning history. They concluded that level of sophistication of planning had a positive impact on financial performance; younger firms performed better than older firms; and firms with a longer planning history performed better.

In many cases, the act of planning cannot necessarily be correlated with the success of a business venture (Robinson and Pearce 1984). It is possible that the contribution of planning to new and small businesses cannot be measured quantitatively. Rather than compare planning and financial performance, a more useful measure of planning might be the amount of vicarious experience that the owner-manager acquires by undertaking the planning process. Planning helps focus owner-managers on their resources, their market and their product. In this way, it could be argued that the main contribution of planning to a business is an increased level of environmental awareness. Similarly, the absence of planning cannot be used as the sole explanation of business failure. In fact, it has been argued that a higher proportion of unsuccessful firms co-ordinate written plans and performance; set goals; and monitor goal achievement (Frank, Plaschka and Roessl 1989).

16.5.2 The benefits of a formal planning system for a small firm

Planning is generally perceived as a crucial element in the survival of new and small businesses (Hisrich and Peters 1992; Kinsella *et al.* 1993). Business plans are essential if entrepreneurs are to acquire external financial support. By planning you increase your chances of success by choosing the right battlefield to suit your skills (Hay *et al.* 1993). Timmons (1994) argues that plans give the new business a results orientation which it would not otherwise have; that they force the new business to work 'smarter' so that goals can be attained in the most effective and efficient manner possible; and that planning results in the consideration of alternatives which may not otherwise have been thought of and this allows planners to choose the optimum way of approaching a problem and, at the same time, it also makes them think ahead.

There are two main roles and uses of plans. Plans are used as communication devices and as aids to controlling the business's factors of production (Baker *et al.* 1993; Mintzberg 1994). The preparation of a business plan by an owner-manager is often seen exclusively as an external communications device. For some owner-managers a plan is written merely to improve legitimacy and satisfy demands from external agencies in order to acquire funding (Frank, Plaschka and Roessl 1989). A clear description of how the entrepreneur will exploit the business opportunity allows investors to decide whether the project is a worthwhile investment and what is the risk attached to it. The second role of a plan is as a control device. Plans provide benchmarks against which subsequent performance can be evaluated. This is particularly important in small businesses as the owner-manager's time tends to be consumed by day-to-day management issues. The benefits of formal planning for small businesses are as follows.

Statement of goals and objectives

A formal planning system will require key managers and promoters to state the goals and objectives of the business. Essential to planning is the choice of a future direction, for 'if you do not know where you are going, any road will take you there' (The Koran). By clearly specifying objectives, promoters and staff should be more focused in their daily work activities.

Efficient use of time

By engaging in a planning process the owner-manager and, where appropriate, the directors of the business should make better use of their own management time.

Planning should result in the identification and monitoring of a small number of key success factors.

Consideration of alternatives

A formal planning system allows the small business to explicitly consider alternatives for the development of the business. This may include addressing issues such as succession planning in family businesses.

Better internal management and staff development

By focusing on the future development of the business, a planning system should highlight the need for internal systems and processes and the future staff and managerial requirements of the business. The owner-manager should be able to develop these processes and systems in advance of the actual need. In many cases the development of these internal systems and structures will facilitate the strategic development of the business.

Better financial management

Planning systems are closely tied to financial systems. In order to plan, the small business will need a basic financial system which provides timely information on current performance. This should improve the financial control of the business and result in better decisions.

16.5.3 Reasons for the absence of formal strategic planning in small businesses

Research suggests that most new and small businesses do not plan (Bhide 1994; Curtis 1983; Robinson and Pearce 1984; Stratos Group 1990). In many cases the structure of the small business is such that the owner-manager is intimately linked to all day-to-day activities. This allows the entrepreneur to control the direction of the business on a day-to-day basis. Where there is a planning process, it is often seen as a separate activity to the day-to-day management of the business rather than as a tool for improving day-to-day management. There are several barriers which inhibit the practice of planning in new and small businesses, as follows.

Clear sense of strategic direction/position

Most owner-managers have a clear sense of the strategic position and direction of their business. Management activity is typically focused on striving to implement more effectively the strategy chosen at start-up.

Centrality of the owner-manager

The close proximity of the entrepreneur to environmental issues often makes objective judgement difficult (West 1988).

Environment context

Many small businesses operate in highly turbulent environments. Formal planning may be counter-productive in such environments as it reduces the strategic flexibility of the business (Chaffee 1985; Fredrickson and Mitchell 1984).

Rigidity of formal systems

Formal planning systems may be too rigid for a small business (Mintzberg 1994). The small business often relies on its flexibility and speed of response as a competitive strength, and a formal planning system with tight financial controls may restrict the responsiveness of the small business. Once a plan is developed, there are so many links between issues and areas, one change can upset the whole plan. In addition, some goals are planned in 'lock step immutable order', which means that the entire plan can be ruined by one unexpected difficulty (Timmons 1994).

Lack of time

The owner-manager is typically involved in the day-to-day management of the business and may not have the time to invest in formal planning. Many owner-managers have to complete administrative and record-keeping activities outside of work hours.

Lack of experience

Owner-managers typically have little formal management training and little exposure to budgeting, controlling or planning systems.

Lack of openness

Owner-managers typically are sensitive about their business plans and their business performance. They are slow to share this information and key decisions with staff or external advisers.

Fear of failure

The explicit statement of goals and objectives, an essential element to a planning process, may result in a failure to achieve these goals and a sense of overall failure by the entrepreneur. By avoiding stating the goals and objectives of the business the entrepreneur can avoid commitment to any one direction or goal.

16.6 The strategy-making context for small businesses

Most small businesses are characterised by a 'simple' structure (Mintzberg 1979). This structure reflects the personality traits of the owner-manager (Miller and Droge 1986). Typically the owner-manager is actively involved in the day-to-day management of the business and is often involved in the direct production of the product or the provision of the service. The customer base of the business is typically limited and is known directly to the entrepreneur. The entrepreneur relies on informal communication channels to communicate internally and externally. Due to a lack of time the entrepreneur tends to keep incomplete and outdated financial records and/or spends 'out of work' hours updating financial accounts.

The benefits of this entrepreneurial structure are that the entrepreneur is in close contact with the key issues of the business and is 'on the spot' to deal with problems; quality standards are maintained through direct supervision by the entrepreneur; staff are involved in the business and engage in frequent informal communication with the entrepreneur. These advantages allow the business to respond to the needs of customers in a quick, innovative and flexible manner. It is these latter qualities that many larger bureaucratic organisations are now trying to emulate through delayering, down-sizing and teamwork (Kanter 1983).

However, in many cases it appears that the management style of the owner-manager is the antithesis of good management practices. The skills, competencies and behaviours necessary for successful new-venture creation become barriers to the growth and development of a business (Churchill and Lewis 1983; Kazanjian 1988). Traits such as a strong need for control and a high sense of distrust can result in owner-managers engaging in behaviours that prevent the organisation growing (Baumback and Mancuso 1993; Churchill and Lewis 1983; Kets de Vries 1985). Such behaviours might include the centralisation of control and 'scape-goating' when activities are not successful (Kets de Vries 1985). The pervasive involvement of the entrepreneur in the business means that it is difficult for the entrepreneur to attend to important, though non-urgent, issues. The high need for achievement that drives the entrepreneur may result in the centralisation of decision-making (Miller and Droge 1986).

The nature of the managerial problem facing the entrepreneur shifts as the organisation grows and develops. Stages of growth models suggest that the owner-manager must implement increasingly formal systems and procedures in the 'entrepreneurial' organisation if it is to grow and develop (Churchill and Lewis 1983; Kazanjian 1988). Kazanjian (1988) emphasises how the managerial problem shifts from one of acquiring resources and organising production during start-up to the generation and management of sales and organisational issues as the organisation grows. Churchill and Lewis (1983) highlight how many businesses stagnate at a small size. These businesses are characterised by simple systems and planning systems that are no more than extended cash-flow forecasting. The model of 'evolution and revolution' described by Greiner (1972) highlights how skills needed for success at one stage become barriers to the future growth of the business. This model assumes that movement from the 'growth through creativity' phase to the 'growth through direction' phase requires the introduction of formal systems and procedures and the introduction of professional management. Many of the changes and the increasing professionalism of management necessary for growth are beyond the scope of most small businesses; for example, most small businesses do not have the resources to hire professional management. For the small business to grow and develop the entrepreneur may have to relearn some of the skills and competencies that were effective during start-up.

16.7 The strategic problems of small businesses

The strategy pursued by a small business is influenced by the structure of the business and the environmental context in which the business is operating. The strategic weaknesses that characterise most small businesses are the consequence of the managerial deficiencies of the owner-manager and the resource deficiencies of the small business.

16.7.1 Lack of financial resources

Most small businesses are undercapitalised and are inappropriately capitalised, in terms of both a high debt–equity ratio and an over-reliance on short-term debt

(Davidson and Dutia 1991). Inadequate and inappropriate capitalisation is a significant contributory factor to the high levels of failure among new businesses. Poor capitalisation may be the result of the difficulties that new businesses face in raising capital (Hall 1989) and the low levels of profitability in small businesses (Davidson and Dutia 1991). When capital is available entrepreneurs may choose debt capital in preference to equity capital due to its perceived lower cost (Brigham and Smith 1967).

However, the capital structure decision is not purely a financial decision. Strategic factors also determine debt–equity ratios (Changanti, DeCarolis and Deeds 1995). The desire to maintain control of the business may increase the use of personal equity investment. The level of personal equity investment by the entrepreneur may reflect the entrepreneur's 'insider' knowledge of the business and his evaluation of the likelihood of success, with low levels of investment resulting in non-value-maximising behaviours such as higher CEO salaries. Entrepreneurs may substitute financial capital with cheaper 'sweat equity'.

16.7.2 Marketing problems and customer concentration

Small businesses engage in little marketing activity. Most small businesses have few resources to devote to marketing and many owner-managers have no experience of marketing and prefer to devote their time to activities that are more familiar, for example production, with the result that little time is spent on either marketing or selling activities. Some of the marketing problems of small businesses relate to their lack of product differentiation. This makes it difficult for the owner-manager to position the product or service as a distinctive offering. A distinguishing characteristic of small businesses is their high dependency on a small number of customers. Research evidence suggests that as many as one-third of all small businesses are dependent on one customer for 25% or greater of their sales (Cambridge Small Business Research Centre 1992). This is a high-risk strategy for the small business as the loss of one customer may result in business failure. Finally owner-managers tend to have very little knowledge of export markets.

16.7.3 Management resources and human resources

By their nature most small businesses are owner-managed. The owner-manager is required to manage all functions of the business, including operations, finance, staff and marketing. However, the narrow expertise of the owner-manager and the lack of management skills mean that the small business is deficient in a number of these functional areas. Most small businesses do not have the resources to hire outside managers to strengthen functional areas of the business. Where resources are available the pervasive involvement of the entrepreneur in the business may make it difficult for outside managers to function in the business.

Small firms have difficulty in attracting good staff. For many potential employees, a small business will not offer the scope for training and development. Additionally, potential employees perceive working in a small business as a risky career move as the small business may subsequently fail. Due to a lack of resources and low levels of profitability, small businesses often pay lower salaries than competing larger businesses.

16.7.4 Lack of systems and controls

Small businesses are characterised by informality and poor information systems. Specifically, small businesses are characterised by poor formal control systems (Huff and Reger 1987). During the start-up period informality dominates in many aspects of the new business, including its control system (Quinn and Cameron 1983; Walsh and Dewar 1987). The lack of information results in poor decision-making.

16.7.5 Technological skills

The majority of small businesses can be classified as technologically contingent – having no influence on the technological trends and innovations that impact on the business. Most small businesses lack the capacity to investigate and assess new technical developments that might impact on their competitive position. In many cases small businesses operate in sectors which have a stable technological trajectory, allowing the small business to pursue a reactive strategy, that is, to respond to external changes as they happen. However, with technological developments the technical demands on many small businesses have increased significantly and technological competence has become a prerequisite to survival in many sectors.

16.8 Chapter summary

This chapter outlined the research that explores which strategies are associated with success in small business. It is evident that some strategies, such as a focused market position and a differentiated competitive advantage, are positively associated with success in small businesses. In addition, the importance and significance of innovation as a means of developing competitive advantage was discussed. However, most small businesses face significant strategic and structural weaknesses. In particular, small businesses lack the managerial skills necessary to develop and implement a strategy. The strategy-making process is typically *ad hoc* and informal, and frequently the entrepreneur's personality prevents the sharing of information about the business's strategic position. Strategic weaknesses also prevent the implementation of a strategy. Small businesses are typically characterised by insufficient financial and managerial resources. The lack of financial resources prevents investment in activities such as product development and marketing. The owner-manager's lack of financial skills means that the information necessary for managerial decisions is not available.

The implications of the research presented in this chapter for the owner-manager are that the development of a clear competitive advantage is essential to both short-term and long-term survival. Owner-managers must understand that choices in relation to 'where' they compete, and 'how' they compete, impact on the viability and performance of their business. In addition, owner-managers need to understand that the structural characteristics of the business and their own managerial style may restrict the development of both an effective strategy-making process and an effective strategy.

The implication for the policy-maker is that most small businesses are characterised by significant strategic and structural weaknesses. For individual small businesses to develop and prosper these deficiencies must be reduced. Clearly, the role of the policy-maker is to facilitate the owner-manager in the development of a strategy and competitive advantage. It is important that policy-makers appreciate that the problem is not with the strategy-formulation process but rather with the development of a clear competitive advantage. Pressurising owner-managers to produce formal plans does not assist the owner-manager in addressing the strategic and structural deficiencies of the small business. Policy-makers need to systematically address the strategic and structural deficiencies of small businesses by providing the owner-manager with the opportunity to develop the skills and acquire the resources that are needed for the development and implementation of an effective strategy.

Questions

1 What strategies are associated with success in small businesses?

2 How appropriate is it for policy-makers to require owner-managers of small businesses to prepare formal business plans prior to receiving any financial assistance?

3 What strategic and structural weaknesses impact on the development and implementation of effective strategies in small businesses?

4 Given the strategic and structural weaknesses of small businesses, do the concepts of 'strategy' and 'competitive advantage' have any relevance to small businesses?

CHAPTER 17

People and the small firm

Susan Marlow

17.1 Learning objectives

There are four learning objectives in this chapter:

1 To understand the role of small firms as employers within the wider context of industrial relations in the UK.

2 To be able to critically evaluate contemporary accounts of labour management in small firms.

3 To appreciate the internal and external influences upon small firms which generate specific approaches to labour management.

4 To be able to comment upon and critically assess the extent to which the management of people in the small firm accords with the industrial relations policies of the current government.

Key concepts

- employee relations ■ managing people in small firms
- terms and conditions of employment

17.2 Introduction

Evidence indicates that the majority of people currently employed in the private sector work in small firms (Department of Trade and Industry 1998). Yet, we still know comparatively little about the terms and conditions under which these people work and how such terms are agreed upon by managers, owners and employees. When the Bolton Report (1971) referred to the harmonious nature of the employment relationship in the small firm, this pronouncement was based on the assumption that proximity of owner and employee within the workplace would overcome the tensions evident between the interests of capital and labour, which so often lead to industrial relations problems in larger firms. It was taken as read that such an axiomatic association required little further investigation. It has only been relatively recently that this assumption has been questioned, with a small number of empirical studies emerging to challenge the harmony thesis. From the relatively little we do know about managing people in small firms, existing empirical studies suggest that it is inappropriate to presume that size will denote harmony between employers and employees or that there is a homogeneity of terms, conditions and experience regarding employment in smaller firms. Whilst there are some qualified generalisations which can be applied, it is essential to recognise the variety of policies and practices which firm owners utilise to manage their employees; moreover, it is essential to place these practices in the context of national trends and policies. Consequently, this chapter will explore issues surrounding employee relations in smaller firms whilst also placing them in the larger context of the national framework.

17.3 People and the small firm

Given the challenges of establishing a consensual definition of a 'small business' (Storey 1994) and the evident heterogeneity of the sector, it is with caution that comment will be made upon the management of labour in small firms. Added to the general difficulty of definition and variety is the relative paucity of empirical evidence or theoretical debate pertaining to employee relations in the small enterprise. Scase (1995) comments at some length upon this issue, highlighting a number of reasons for such a lacuna. Primarily, there is a tendency for academics and policy-makers to focus on industrial relations in larger firms. Whilst there is some interchanging of the terms 'industrial relations' and 'employee relations' in contemporary texts, for the purpose of this discussion the consensus is that 'industrial relations' refers to the collective management of labour at work. This encompasses the study of trade unions, management and state policy to constrain, control and reform the employment relationship. As such, the term is *more likely*, but not exclusively, to be applicable to the labour process of large, unionised organisations but this does not exclude medium-sized or large non-union organisations. The term 'employee relations' has developed to reflect the greater individualisation of the labour process in all firms in recent years, particularly within the non-union sector where many smaller firms are located. However, this is not to say that the terms are not used interchangeably in many texts but, for our purpose, employee relations will be used to relate to smaller firms, with industrial relations referring to larger organisations and national trends.

To date in the study of industrial relations, large organisations are deemed to be indicators of national trends in policy and practice and are used as the basis of theoretical constructs and critiques, with many robust workplace studies emerging over the years to examine such (see, for example, the time-series data of the Workplace Industrial Relations Series – Daniel and Milward 1983; Milward and Stevens 1986; Milward *et al.* 1992). Moreover, until recently, larger firms have dominated modern economies and so constituted the foundation for the development of industrial relations theory and research with a concentration on collective forces and influences. Consequently, there is a certain rationality and tradition for some continued focus upon the larger firm; however, this should be reviewed given recent evidence indicating that 46% of those in employment work in establishments with fewer than 50 employees (Small Business Action Update 1998: 2). Indeed, for some time there has been a lively debate surrounding the small firm 'job generation thesis' (Birch 1979; Armington and Odle 1982; Daly 1991b), with the overall conclusion that smaller firms make an important contribution to net employment creation. So, small firms are significant as job creators and employers, making the paucity of research puzzling.

Some of the explanation for this lack of interest in smaller firms lies in the notion of 'academic élitism', by which it is suggested that there has been a certain dismissal of the importance and credibility of investigating and commenting upon the employment relationship in smaller firms. Such a dismissal is premised on reasons other than a failure to recognise the contribution of small business to contemporary labour management policies and practices. As Curran and Burrows (1986: 274) commented, 'the small firm has been taken up as the articulating principle of *right wing* reaction to economic crisis' (italics inserted). As such, there is a sense that industrial relations research and theory formulation will be diminished by association with smaller firms, whose development and ethos reflect an academically unpopular political and economic philosophy articulated in an era which saw savage attacks upon the traditional elements of established industrial relations practices in larger firms. Closer examination of existing research does, however, suggest that such views are blinkered and are, in fact, ensuring continued ignorance of a critical area of employment. Indeed, if we consider the foremost textbooks on contemporary industrial relations we find a minority have a dedicated chapter on the employment relationship in small firms (Towers 1992; Edwards 1995). The majority of texts instead regard non-unionism and smaller firms as synonymous areas of debate – even though successive Conservative governments since 1979 have explicitly articulated the growth of employment in smaller firms as a key element of their employment relations policy (Blyton and Turnbull 1998).

A further problem for this particular research agenda is the prevailing presumption that employee relations in smaller firms are relatively unproblematic, and still reflect the Bolton Report's (1971) superficial analysis of homogeneous harmony and unitarism across the sector – a presumption supported once again in 1983 by the Conservative government whose 'Moving Forward' pamphlet declared that a major advantage that small businesses enjoy is the generally good state of relations between owners, managers and employees. The notion is that absence of overt conflict is positively correlated with harmonious employee relations and a sense of partnership, made possible because of small-group interaction. However, whilst research evidence (Rainnie 1989; Scott *et al.* 1989; Goss 1991; Earnshaw *et al.* 1998) may be limited, findings and ensuing debate indicate that a blanket presumption of equanimity in employment relations in smaller firms is both simplistic and inaccurate. Therefore, there is considerable scope for investigation regarding the varied experiences of employment in smaller firms and any implication this has for national trends and policy development.

In terms of research credibility, sample identification, contact and access (if existence and durability are highly volatile, identifying appropriate firms which will exist at the culmination of research is a challenge; equally, given the informality of management techniques, analysing styles and strategies is often not welcome as well as difficult), it is apparent that undertaking research into the employment relationship in smaller firms is problematic. Although somewhat limited in number, the existing studies do indicate that, whilst it is hard to generalise, there will be some common features regarding labour management in small firms. Such firms are unlikely to be unionised, or to have formal personnel management, or to have formal policies and procedures in place when compared to larger organisations, and the owner will take a critical role in determining labour management practices and styles (Scott *et al.* 1989; Marlow and Patton 1993; Earnshaw *et al.* 1998). Thus, there are differences in the employment environments generally attributable to larger and smaller firms, with the latter now acting as substantial employers in the UK; consequently there is an urgent need for further investigation into employment issues in smaller firms. In order to comment on contemporary approaches to labour management in UK small firms, this chapter will review existing evidence relating to employee relations. To undertake this task, it is necessary to place employment management practices in small firms within the context of the national management of industrial relations in the UK rather than isolate them as separate from national trends and policies. Thus, a brief overview of contemporary industrial relations in the UK will outline the influence of the post-war consensus in establishing the large firm as the focus of study; and will consider how the initiatives of successive Conservative governments since 1979 encouraged the growth of smaller firms, and if employment initiatives taken by the Blair government will affect the sector. Existing studies pertaining to employee relations in smaller firms will then be outlined and discussed. Building upon such evidence, we will conclude and comment upon how the evidence from the small-firm sector relates to the wider assessment of national trends and current government ambitions for industrial relations.

17.4 The changing context of post-war British industrial relations

To comprehend the development of the contemporary form and context of employee relations in smaller firms, it is imperative to perceive the relationship as part of the wider set of issues surrounding the management of labour. This will be facilitated through a short review of major influences upon industrial relations in the post-war period, which can be cautiously divided into three periods, each associated with identifiable trends and policies: 1945–79 (the post-war consensus); 1979–97 (contemporary Conservatism); 1997 – present (New Labour). Whilst making such divisions for purposes of clarity, it should be noted that industrial relations practice and theory identify great areas of continuity so, for example, within the market economy labour must always sell itself for a price such that negotiation around the wage/effort bargain is a permanent feature of such economies. For a greater discussion of such continuities see Edwards (1995); Kelly (1998); and Blyton and Turnbull (1998).

17.4.1 The post-war consensus

Successive Labour and Conservative governments adhered to a number of economic and social policies which generated a particular approach to managing labour at work, as follows:

■ *Keynesianism:* a state commitment to support full employment to create a cycle of strong demand for goods and services; theoretically, such demand would then underpin full employment. Support for full employment was a priority over public debt containment.

■ *Voluntarism*: where terms and conditions of employment were agreed through collective negotiation by management and trade unions on a voluntary basis with minimal state regulation or interference – a collective laissez-faire approach.

■ *Corporatism*: joint discussion between employers' federations/organisations, trade union leaders and government to agree policy outlines for national terms and conditions of labour and economic management.

■ *Pluralism*: dominance of an analysis which argues that, within a market economy, there are conflicting aims between the interests of capital and labour, but consensus is desirable and possible. This is best achieved by joint regulation through collective bargaining between personnel/IR management and trade union representatives. When consensus eventually breaks down (almost inevitably), collective bargaining practices effectively manage and institutionalise conflict whilst generating new forms of consensus. The role of the state is to encourage and facilitate collective bargaining whilst providing minimal protection for a minority of labour excluded from such practice.

■ *Public sector*: utilised as an example of 'good industrial relations' which during this era focused upon offering secure employment, encouraged union membership and promoted collective bargaining.

Until the 1970s, post-war industrial relations were characterised by a focus upon voluntary collective bargaining in large organisations with a pluralist ethos. This structure was supported by the state which largely refrained from overt employment regulation. However, growing pressures from ensuing economic difficulties generated by crises of accumulation and production in the late 1960s, and throughout the 1970s, prompted successive governments to focus on reforming industrial relations as an important part of the solution to such problems. Edward Heath attempted to do this through an extensive piece of legislation (the Industrial Relations Act 1971) which was firmly rejected by both management and trade unions, jealous of their voluntary regulation (see Deakin and Morris 1995). The ensuing Labour government repealed the Act, appealing instead for voluntary restraint on incomes and a renewed focus on productivity. When this proved ineffective, the government imposed incomes policies in the public sector, exhorting the private sector to follow suit. The resentment of the public sector at such restraint was articulated as extensive industrial action – the so-called 'winter of discontent' of 1978/9.

Despite the claim from the Thatcher administration of a new approach to government after election in 1979, in their last few years of power the Callaghan government had already tacitly adopted monetarist policies of constraining public spending to control inflation. These had failed, however, in the face of high inflation, strong union protest and the ability of the private sector to circumnavigate restraint. Consequently, the failure of the Labour government to cope with growing economic crises facilitated the election of a Conservative administration committed to radical reform.

17.4.2 Contemporary Conservatism 1979–97

The mandate of the 1979 Thatcher administration firmly rejected the post-war consensus. In its stead, a combination of free markets, monetarism, entrepreneurialism and individualism would address the economic, social and industrial challenges of the late 20th century. Each individual was deemed responsible for his/her own needs, encapsulated in Margaret Thatcher's claim that there is 'no such thing as society', whilst, in 1983, Norman Tebbit (Secretary of State for Employment) advised the unemployed to 'get on their bikes' to seek jobs rather than wait for the state to provide them. Thus, inequality was considered the motor of enterprise whilst unemployment was seen as an individual failing and as a necessary evil to control inflation.

A key element in the realisation of Conservative policies and philosophies was the reform of industrial relations in large firms, along with the creation of a buoyant small-firm sector where the employment relationship would constitute the exemplar of harmony (see the Conservative pamphlet 'Small Firm, Big Future', 1983). However, certain changes were essential to industrial relations policies and practices if the management of labour in large firms was to be reformed and employment in small firms facilitated, namely the following.

Monetarism

A fiscal policy focused upon the control of the money supply and lowering inflation. This was articulated through a contraction of public spending, the reduction of public-owned enterprises and, during serious recession (1983, 1987), a refusal to support a struggling manufacturing industry and toleration of resulting high unemployment.

Market forces

In keeping with the Austrian school of economic thought (Hayek 1979), it was argued that a free market was critical to encourage individuals to act independently and entrepreneurially whilst enabling them to fully benefit from their actions. So, it was necessary to deregulate markets for goods and services in society. Regarding the labour market, this entailed removing protective legislation, extending periods of employment before claims for unfair dismissal could be registered, disbanding wages councils and making it altogether easier to 'hire and fire' labour. As state regulation, influence and protection declined, public spending savings would be transformed into tax concessions, further enhancing disposable income for individuals who had greater freedom and choice in the free market for goods and services.

Trade union decline

A basic tenet of contemporary Conservatism is individualism. Thus, it was argued that the collective power of trade unions undermined individual enterprise, constrained productivity, acted as a false lever in the market and indeed was cited as the major cause of the economic problems of the 1970s. Union organisation and influence were consequently subject to a number of formal and informal forces to constrain and reduce power, namely:

■ Unemployment: this denies unions new members because of reduced job opportunities whilst redundancies of existing members deplete ranks. Consequently, membership declined significantly in the 1980s as high and growing levels of unemployment during recession were tolerated by the state as a necessary consequence of monetarism and free-market policies.

- Legislation was focused on the constraint of official union action and the reform of their democratic processes (Edwards 1995). The failure of Heath's wholesale attempt at legislative reform in 1971 had been noted so, consequently, a *series* of employment Acts was placed on the statute books over the 1980s and 1990s. However, evidence would indicate that legislation 'registered the decline in union power . . . rather than precipitated it' (Blyton and Turnbull 1998: 166). Rather, a combination of environmental pressures (such as unemployment), political initiatives (for example encouragement of small firms, non-unionism) plus a lack of strategic recruitment activity by unions themselves (Kelly 1998) have proved to be more damaging than legislation.

- Small-firm growth characterised by non-unionism (Scase 1995) has presented a further challenge to established trade unions. With their focus on large firms, unions have in the past found recruiting small-firm employees costly, time-consuming and more likely to meet with owner/management resistance. As such, with government facilitation of small-firm growth and criticism of union collectivity, the decline of large firms and little tradition of union achievements for those employed in small business, unions have been challenged in attracting new members in the sector.

- Privatisation/contracting-out/internal markets: such policies represented government efforts to reduce the level of public-owned stock and introduce competition into that which remained. The public sector had been a bastion of union strength, but the contraction of the sector and the absorption of much redundant labour into private-sector services further depleted union ranks. Furthermore, in public-sector services subject to internal markets, the efforts to make service cheaper coupled with greater management prerogative and political encouragement led to the narrowing of the collective bargaining agenda and challenges to union strength, further undermining union credibility (Edwards 1995).

Flexibility was envisaged as fundamental to new forms of working which would transform the labour market (Atkinson 1984; Piore and Sabel 1984) but in the UK, there has been little evidence for the emergence of a retrained, multiskilled, polyvalent worker commanding high status and high rewards. Instead, the deregulated labour market combined with weak unions and high unemployment encouraged flexible working practices characterised by low pay, low skill and insecurity (Noon and Blyton 1997). The greatest growth area of employment in the 1980s and 1990s has been in part-time work, defined largely as a feminised sector with all the accompanying disadvantages (see Cockburn 1993 for greater discussion). Thus, dominant forms of flexibility in the UK – numerical and temporal working – act to further reduce the cost of labour and have contributed to the ease with which labour can be 'hired and fired'.

Human resource management – HRM – has been the subject of substantial debate regarding its form, content, existence and influence upon the management of labour (Storey 1989; Legge 1995; Storey 1995; Sparrow and Marchington 1998). HRM practices engage with the individual to gain compliance and commitment to the labour process. Simplistically explained, this may involve 'developing' employees to new levels of skill and competence to gain autonomous commitment to the organisation (soft HRM) or through subjecting individuals to arduous and repressive forms of labour discipline (hard HRM). More realistically, evidence indicates a selective adoption of differing 'bundles' of HRM within an organisation in response to product, labour, finance and other market pressures (Storey 1995). Consequently, with government encouragement of individualism and the growth of managerial power, the introduction of HRM initiatives should have been facilitated. Indeed, there is some evidence for the growth of hard HRM in non-union, smaller firms (Sisson 1993) but, paradoxically, HRM initiatives to gain individual compliance to firm objectives are most evident in unionised environments (see Legge 1995 for an overview). Hence, HRM might be more appropriately viewed as a new managerial strategy to gain labour compliance which has evolved to reflect changes in markets for goods, services and labour over recent years.

Overall, the employment relationship has been deregulated and subject to market discipline. For many employees this has resulted in greater job insecurity, loss of union protection, greater flexibility, a move from larger to smaller employers or venturing into self-employment or small-firm ownership. There can be little doubt that the adoption of monetarism, then supply-side economics articulated through individualised laissez-faire policies, has facilitated the growth of a low-paid, low-skilled, insecure workforce whose productivity gains have been obtained through redundancy, fear, managerial prerogative and change to the labour process (Noon and Blyton 1997). This has been at the expense of investment in fixed and human capital epitomised by the fact that, by the early 1990s, almost half of the working population in the UK lived below the European decency threshold (based on an income of at least 68% of all full-time mean earnings [Pearson and Quincy 1992: 1]). Consequently, it is difficult to defend the fiscal and industrial policies adopted by successive Conservative governments as the instigators of a wealthier society with secure, long-term employment prospects for its members – although the wealthiest members of society have undoubtedly benefited (Hutton 1996). But, regardless of whatever other effects contemporary Conservatism may have had on inequality and opportunity, it cannot be disputed that the focus on the individual in a deregulated labour market, within the rhetoric of an enterprise society, facilitated self-employment and the start-up of many new small firms. Added to this, the complexities of recruiting, managing and firing labour were simplified to encourage employment by small firms – whilst the growing debate around individualised HRM practices drew the non-union firm into the discussion surrounding the contemporary employment relationship. Thus, by the end of the 20th century the small-firm sector has been established as a significant employer in the UK economy. With the election of the Blair government, it remains to be seen whether New Labour wishes to challenge such trends or offer coherent policies to create a viable alternative to short-termism and insecurity.

17.4.3 New Labour

The current UK administration has no intention of repealing repressive labour legislation enacted to constrain the power of trade unions or to return to the corporatism of the post-war consensus. Instead, the government wishes to establish voluntary social partnerships between employers, trade unions and employees to agree appropriate workplace terms and conditions – although, as one critic comments, 'it is difficult, if not impossible, to achieve a partnership with a party who would prefer that you didn't exist' (Kelly 1998: 88). However, the Labour government believes such partnerships to be possible but will also enact legislation for a base-line of employment regulation, and is pledged to recognise European social policy directives. Thus, a national minimum wage will be established although indications are for a very low rate (£3.60 per hour, 1998) with some employees excluded. A major legislative act will establish new rights for individuals (parental leave, shorter qualifying period for unfair dismissal, removal of ceiling for Employment Tribunal payments) and make provision for trade union recognition where a majority of all the relevant workforce vote in favour. The government has also signed up to the Maastricht social chapter so the UK will observe the Working Time Directive, the Works Council initiative and future policies relating to the employment relationship. These proposals, however, will not apply to firms with less than 20 employees. Regarding small firms, the government has been anxious to allay fears of burdensome regulation – hence the persistence of exclusion policies and a voluntarist approach. It is unlikely that small-firm employee relations policies and practices will be challenged by the current Labour government. Indeed, it is more likely that small-firm owners will perceive their organisations to be good examples of 'social partnerships' on the basis of existing indications regarding owner and management perceptions of the firm's internal social relations (Goss 1991). One potential area of challenge might come from trade unions pursuing recognition agreements in smaller firms but evidence regarding trade union recruitment strategies and employee demand make such a scenario unlikely (Abbot 1993; Kelly 1998).

In summary, the post-war consensus, constructed upon collective laissez-faire, Keynesianism, voluntarism and collective bargaining articulated through a pluralist analysis, was challenged in the 1970s by crises of capital, accumulation and labour resistance to government policies. Since 1979, Conservative governments have promoted individualism and free-market policies aiming to create wealth, choice and competition; however, there is little evidence for such – rather, a growth in insecurity, poverty and poor-quality employment (Hutton 1996; Noon and Blyton 1997), but there is some indication of an unsustainable short-term productivity improvement (Nolan 1989). However, there can be little doubt that one identifiable outcome of contemporary Conservatism has been the expansion of smaller firms and self-employment (see Chapter 3). Unemployment, redundancies, a positive image of the entrepreneur, some financial inducement and an expansion of opportunity in the service sector where entry costs are low, have all combined to 'push' and 'pull' people into firm ownership. Such pressures have combined with changes to the labour market and the employment relationship to ensure that small firms now make a significant contribution to employment in the UK. Whilst the *quantitative* expansion of employment opportunities is a positive factor, it is also important to consider the *quality and durability* of the jobs that are being created. It is this aspect we now consider.

17.5 Managing people in small firms

As stated, many more people now find themselves employed by smaller firms than was the case 15 years ago but relatively few studies exist which explore the experience of employing and being employed in the small-firm sector. From studies which have been undertaken we will identify some tentative trends pertaining to labour management in smaller firms. In keeping with many other contemporary commentators on employee relations in small firms (Rainnie 1989; Goss 1991; Stanworth and Gray 1991) the discussion will commence with a famous quote from the Bolton Report (1971).

> In many aspects, the small firm provides a better environment for the employee than is possible in most large firms. Although physical working conditions may sometimes be inferior in small firms, most people prefer to work in small groups where communication presents few problems: the employee in a small firm can more easily see the relation between what he [*sic*] is doing and the objectives and performance of the firm as a whole. Where management is more direct and flexible, working rules can be varied to suit the individual. Each employee is also likely to have a more varied role with a chance to participate in several kinds of work. . . . turnover of staff in small firms is very low and strikes and other kinds of industrial dispute are relatively infrequent. The fact that small firms offer lower earnings than larger firms suggests that the convenience of location and generally the non-material satisfactions of working in them more than outweigh any financial sacrifice involved. (Bolton Report 1971: 21)

Thus, a unitarist image of harmonious employee relations in small firms was suggested where the antagonism between labour and capital was successfully overcome through partnership and shared ambition, and the scale of operations enabled individuals to identify their contribution to the organisation, thus overcoming the anomie associated with working for the larger bureaucracy. This was an image which was presented during a period when focus was renewed upon small-scale activity, with the 'small is beautiful' thesis generated by Schumacher (1974) becoming increasingly influential. Further support for individual job satisfaction was offered by Ingham (1970) who argued that small-firm employees 'self-select' themselves to such enterprises precisely because the identification with the firm, its owner and other employees is sufficient compensation for lower wages and a restricted career path. Emphases on small-scale enterprise also emerged in the early 1980s with theoretical debates surrounding the emergence and existence of post-modernism.

In post-modernist society, Piore and Sabel (1984) argued that a second industrial divide would emerge with skills as a defining feature. Production would be focused on small and medium-sized enterprises with a core group of multiskilled employees working with advanced technologies. The emphasis was upon *flexibility* in that the size of the firm would facilitate a rapid, flexible response to changing market demand; the polyvalent nature of the employee would enable a quick response to such changes whilst advanced technology would make such flexible production possible. Core employees in smaller enterprises would be highly valued and rewarded – thus collective protection such as that offered by unions would be needless, whilst 'secondary labour' utilised casually, where and when necessary, would be too weak to resist either individually or collectively. When such theoretical considerations were aligned with an ideology of harmonious labour relations, an image of the entrepreneur as pioneer of risk and uncertainty with rewards shared by all, and the individualistic free-market philosophy of the newly elected Conservative government in the early 1980s, the advantages of supporting small-firm development were strong and convincing.

However, into this 'brave new world' image emerged a number of studies which questioned the harmony of small-firm employment or the possibility that the sector would herald the advent of a new epoch of production. As early as 1979, Curran and Stanworth questioned Ingham's (1970) view of 'self-selection', pointing out that it was in fact employers who had greater prerogative in terms of recruitment and selection. Moreover, it was argued that a blanket presumption of harmonious employee relations could not be applied to such a heterogeneous sector as that of the small firm, an issue which formed the basis of many subsequent studies (Scott *et al.* 1989; Goss 1991; Storey 1994).

In the 1980s a number of papers and texts emerged which developed a theoretical critique of the harmony thesis. Rainnie and Scott (1986) argued that as part of the market economy small firms still have to address the tension inherent within capitalism. From a Marxist perspective, the researchers argued that it is necessary for small-firm owners to purchase labour and extract surplus value (profit) through exploitation, so the challenge is to identify how exploitation is experienced, and how it is made effective. Rainnie and Scott reject the notion that the absence of trade unions in small firms facilitates harmony but argue that, whilst there may be a positive correlation between non-unionism and absence of overt dispute, this does not denote a causal relationship (given that a wide range of variables will impinge upon union presence such as sector, age, locality and labour characteristics such that any inference must recognise and adjust for complexity). Rather, there is a need to consider other channels for articulating discontent such as turnover, absence and industrial tribunal referrals. Hence, attention is drawn to the importance of class relations, the limited opportunities small-firm employees have for expressing overt discontent and the necessity of analysing the complexity of intervening variables underpinning any such assertions.

In a more comprehensive study of labour management in small manufacturing firms, Rainnie (1989) also critically assesses the notion of independence of small-firm owners and managers. When considering their position in the wider labour market, Rainnie argues that labour management styles of small-firm owners are constrained by the demands and competitive position of their larger counterparts (as customers or suppliers) and by the market for goods itself. To demonstrate this, Rainnie offers a typology of relations between small firms and the market:

- *dependent* – where survival is totally dependent on a relationship with a larger firm (for example as a subcontractor);
- *competitive dependent* – competition is directly with larger firms, therefore survival depends on ability to cut costs and is likely to result in extreme exploitation of labour;
- *old independent* – niche-market firms where growth is constrained due to market demand;
- *new independent* – where larger firms may invade new or developing markets if the opportunities for profit and expansion are attractive.

To fully comprehend the manner in which labour is managed, the market conditions under which the firm operates must be analysed, so awareness of heterogeneity and labour markets is critical. These studies were useful in identifying the heterogeneity of small firms and locating them in the wider economy – in particular, Rainnie draws attention to the falseness of the 'dual' approach where small and large firms are deemed as being separate spheres without overlapping confluence. There are some problems with this analysis which depends on a deterministic presumption that external pressures will fully dictate labour management strategies; it must be questioned whether typologies can realistically be applied to markets or whether they can only exist as 'ideal types' or conceptual examples. Finally, the empirical work which Rainnie utilises to illustrate his theory is based largely upon manufacturing firms whereas the majority of small firms are located in the service sector (Curran 1991), so a question of representation remains.

In his study of social harmony in smaller firms, Goss (1988) criticises the reliance on employer perception of the quality of employee relations which leads to positive reporting. To evaluate such perceptions, Goss argues that conflict is submerged beneath 'intergroup credibility' (p. 116) which emerges from the pragmatic response to powerlessness by small-firm employees. It is argued that the proximity of owner, managers and labour when at work ensures that 'trouble-makers' can be identified or removed and conflict is masked. Goss (1988: 116) states that 'small firms provide an environment in which contradictions implicit in the labour/capital relation can be relatively effectively contained or neutralised by employers'. In his critique of the social harmony thesis, Goss focuses upon the ability of employers, combined with market pressures, to limit opportunities for employee resistance to labour management tactics. Using evidence from a small study of printing firms, Goss found that owners identified 'good' and 'bad' employees according to their willingness to tolerate labour process changes, demands for overtime and flexible working. Those deemed 'bad' were denied pay bonuses and had their jobs threatened – thus compliance with the owner was based on powerlessness, not identification. Even though there was a union presence, the members felt that the union lacked interest in smaller firms and were reluctant to get 'involved'. So, Goss reiterates the view of Rainnie (1989) that harmony and conflict are complex issues which cannot be presumed from the presence or lack of overt conflict. In a later work, Goss (1991) develops this debate further by developing a typology to demonstrate the manner in which employers exert control over both employees and the labour process itself, but also how employees might resist such control. A number of categories are identified, as follows.

Fraternalism

Where there is a shared sense of skill and effort, owners tend to work alongside employees, for example in construction. There is a reliance on negotiation between employer and employee with a realisation that all are needed for the firm to survive; thus, the circumstance of mutual reliance and close working generates a form of partnership.

Paternalism

There is a differentiated power relationship between employer and employee but an effort is made to generate an identification from labour with the ethos of the enterprise, for example in agricultural communities. Other forms of employment may be scarce but employers still need commitment from labour to undertake unsupervised work, unscheduled overtime and other forms of flexibility. Identification with the workplace extends into the community with some evidence of mutual obligation (for more discussion, note the concept of the 'deferential worker': Newby 1977).

Benevolent autocracy

There is a clear identification of the role of the employer and the power this commands but this is solely based within the workplace; there is a tendency towards informality with a pragmatic acceptance of labour/capital inequality but some evidence of joint identification of organisation needs.

Sweating

Again there is a clear imbalance of power but the employer makes no effort to cultivate employee identification and there is a critical focus on cost containment.

Goss notes the complexity of managing employee relations in smaller firms and, importantly, notes that there is potential for some employees to influence social relations at work. This analysis again underpins the complexity of the employee relationship and the need to consider carefully definitions of harmony, but the dependence of typologies is not always useful (see above) and the study is, again, overly dependent upon manufacturing firms for conclusions.

17.5.1 General labour management practices in the small firm

Research which attempted to address some of the problems noted with the work above was completed by Scott *et al.* (1989). This study was undertaken with the objectives of recognising the heterogeneity of the small-firm sector and analysing daily labour management practices. The authors identified a sample of 400 firms (larger than had previously been utilised) and adopted a two-stage approach with the use of a survey and case studies. The firms were geographically dispersed to control for local labour markets and drawn from different sub-sectors to control for heterogeneity. The authors wished to establish the particularistic processes evident in small-firm employee relations which would then question previous attempts to impose large-firm industrial relations norms upon the sector. As a result, a number of major components of daily labour management were discovered.

It was found that the major problems were with cash flow, but in terms of personnel the greatest task was finding skilled staff who 'fitted in'. Employment expansion depended on rising demand and the owner's perception of the firm's position in the market; employment contraction occurred with a fall in demand or improved productivity. Male manual workers were most likely to be fired. Throughout the sample there was a high level of procedural informality, with unionised, manufacturing firms displaying most formality. Traditional services with a high percentage of female labour had fewest formal procedures.

Recruitment processes were influenced by sector, with traditional services and manufacturing relying heavily on informality. On the other hand, high-technology firms (where skill requirements were critical) depended far more on formal processes. Owners reiterated the need to find the right skills in people who fit, and appeared to be seeking 'clones' of themselves. The service sector had a greater dependence on women and casual labour whilst there was a notable growth in the dependence on part-time labour for both traditional manufacturing and services.

In all sectors, labour turnover was high but for different reasons. As a result of skill shortages, high-technology employees were able to move between jobs to seek improved conditions, but for other sectors bad management, poor firm performance and autocratic attitudes led to high levels of churning. As a result, employment stability within firms was the exception rather than the rule. This finding lends some support to the hypothesis that 'management get the employee relations they deserve!'

A unitary view of employee relations dominated the study but there appeared to be no strategic policies to achieve this. Rather, there was a positive perception of employer 'reasonableness' and the opinion that if people continued to work, there were no problems – this was compounded by the view that, at least for traditional manufacturing and services, people were free to leave whenever they wished. In high-technology firms, employees had a positive view of work, welcomed change and engaged in career planning. In other sectors, it was found that employees felt relatively powerless to command their own futures and resented change to the labour process which they perceived as threatening.

If problems arose, these were individualised through attribution of blame to 'trouble-makers' which transposed the difficulty into an individual failing, thus averting challenge to the owner/management control of the labour process. So, there was no channel for such issues to become 'industrial relations problems'. For owners and managers, this was reinforced by the lack of complaints. When questioned, employees felt there was no point in complaining as nothing could be achieved. It is clear that significant differences existed in perceptions of 'social harmony'.

Where discipline issues were concerned, service-sector firms had least formality and manufacturing the most, with high-tech firms also having formalised procedures but experiencing few disputes (such formality was largely related to intellectual property rights). Discipline proved to be a difficult issue to manage for most firms. If the true nature of the employment relationship is relatively obscured by informality, fraternalism and proximity between employer and labour, the sudden exposure of the power imbalance within employment – when discipline is overtly applied – is very challenging. Thus, even where formal discipline codes existed, owners and managers were most inclined to have a 'quiet word' with a friend of the person concerned, who was expected to pass the message on. Alternatively, there was some tendency to tolerate the perceived deviant behaviour by turning a 'blind eye'. As a result, the problem was often left until tempers erupted, leading to snap decisions to dismiss under traumatic circumstances. The lack of formal warning or procedure laid the basis for tribunal claims.

Wages were found to be dependent on sectoral and skill issues, with high-technology employees perceiving themselves to be appropriately paid and undertaking individual negotiation. In service firms, both employer and employees agreed pay was low but reflected going rates; these were not subject to negotiation but to management prerogative. In manufacturing firms, there was some guidance from union minimums which employers considered good, while employees felt rates were relatively poor. With regard to payment, skills, sector and location were particularly influential. Informal perks or fringe benefits were rare, except for the most skilled.

Union recognition was concentrated in larger manufacturing firms, and there was surprisingly little hostility from employers towards unions, which were believed to be largely irrelevant to their firms, due to the existing strength of the employment relationship. However, the owners did express some antagonism regarding union activity, with such opinions largely formed as a result of negative media reporting. Overall, there was indifference rather than hostility and employees generally felt unions were a 'good' thing but believed there would be difficulties in joining or gaining union recognition; moreover, it was considered that unions would have limited influence even if present. Unions themselves had little inclination to recruit in small firms because of the access barriers and problems of organising small-firm labour whose characteristics and working patterns present specific challenges.

Employers in all sectors made limited and pragmatic use of employers' federations or other support agents, calling upon them for advice when problems arose. However, interference from external bodies such as industrial tribunals, the Health and Safety Executive or the Inland Revenue was perceived in highly personal terms by the small number of employers who had been subject to attention. Apart from this group, other owners felt indifferent to them and took little interest in their advice or literature.

Although legislation was deemed a 'burden' on small firms by the government in the 1980s, this was not raised as an issue by most firm owners, who displayed considerable ignorance concerning regulation. Only 70% of the sample offered a statutory employment contract; 33% in traditional services offered no statutory sick pay, with sickness leading to dismissal; maternity benefit was not relevant to most firms but where women had become pregnant this was deemed as resignation; there was little compliance with health and safety regulations and almost total ignorance of the discrimination Acts.

Therefore, it was found that a unitary view predominates in all but the largest firms. There was no evidence for strategic employee relations throughout the sample, and informal labour management was endemic. Such systems undermined the development of collectivity but were not synonymous with harmony – rather, they were evidence of 'submissive agreement'. The interaction of family employment and personal styles upon labour management obscured the true nature of the employment relationship. However, such informality created problems when the owner needed to take back control such as when imposing workplace change or disciplining employees. The study identified a growth in feminised part-time work in services but a decline in the number of male full-time workers. Furthermore, the high level of churning in all but high-tech firms indicated an undercurrent of insecurity.

This study by Scott *et al.* (1989) effectively drew attention to the specifics of employee relations in small firms. The reliance on owner perceptions of appropriate management tactics, the dependence on informality, the ignorance of legislation and regulation, the individualisation of problems and attribution of such indicate a highly personalised approach to employee relations. However, as Rainnie (1989) argued, the external market was also influential such that high-tech firms had to adopt greater formality to recruit and retain skilled employees within tight labour markets. So there was an unstable relationship between sectors, markets, localities and owner perceptions of the employment relationship which generated certain forms of small-firm employee relations. From the evidence of this study, the researchers argue that greater regulation of employment which would promote greater formality upon labour management could only be beneficial in creating fairer and more secure jobs in small firms. However, the study again over-emphasised manufacturing firms, given the predominance of service-sector firms in the small-firm sector – and whilst some employee comment was obtained, this is limited in comparison to owner perceptions.

Other studies (Rainnie 1989; Goss 1988; 1991) also indicated that the harmonised small-firm employee relations hypothesis was founded on false premises. Whilst the heterogeneity of the sector makes robust conclusions difficult, it is possible to tentatively suggest that evidence indicates that labour relations in smaller firms are largely based on informality, and there are poorer terms and conditions of employment than in larger firms, with employers and employees having differing perceptions regarding the reality of the work experience. To some extent more recent studies have supported these tentative findings. Using survey data from 3,289 firms in the UK, Thompson and Wilson (1991) found that wages for all groups in all sectors increase with firm size as businesses move away from dependency on 'parochial labour markets', i.e. casual and family labour, and seek better-quality staff. In summary it was found that smaller firms paid up to 30% less than larger firms, but it is essential to recognise sectoral and geographical variation and that wage rates are a very crude measure which alone cannot determine job quality or satisfaction.

In terms of hours worked, there already exists strong anecdotal evidence regarding the long hours worked by small-firm owners, with Jones *et al.* (1993) finding an average working week of 53 hours. This is also reflected in the working week of employees (Storey 1994) but this does require some qualification. The trend for lower wages will lead to greater dependency upon overtime payments through longer hours, but it is also important to note that this trend is focused on male manufacturing workers. However, there is also a noticeable trend for more female part-time labour to be utilised in smaller firms so working hours are skewed to either end of a continuum.

17.5.2 Training and the small firm

With the growing realisation that a considerable challenge to UK competitiveness has been the dearth of skilled labour, there has been government encouragement for firms to invest in more training. However, as this remains at the level of voluntary activity, there is little evidence that uniform training provision is being made throughout the economy (Marlow 1998). Existing evidence, however, suggests that smaller firms are even less inclined to develop their employees and any training offered is more likely to be informal and short-term (Keep and Mayhew 1997). A Labour Market Quarterly Report survey (1998) found that older, larger and innovative firms which had problems recruiting skilled staff were more likely to invest in training. Whilst there was some evidence that firms which trained enjoyed greater durability, this was linked with several other variables such that a positive correlation between training, survival and profitability cannot be made. It should also be noted that as the majority of small firms are found in the service sector (Curran 1991) where there is a higher incidence of part-time, lower-skilled labour, training could be of little relevance to employees or make little contribution to firm performance.

It is, however, slightly paradoxical that whilst employers in small firms offer fewer training opportunities to their employees, they complained of experiencing considerable skill shortages. A British Chamber of Commerce (1998) survey found that a third of firms felt competitiveness suffered through a lack of labour skills but few firms were

training ✓ , seek from labor market ✗

involved in education. The survey concluded that to meet this challenge small firms need to identify and provide the skills they need rather than depend on the labour market to provide them. On this point, Atkinson and Meager's (1994) study of over 3,000 small firms focused on how appropriately the labour market serves the needs of small firms, rather than how small firms develop their labour. To fully understand how employee relations and labour market issues interact, Atkinson and Meager focused on five firm variables, namely age, sector, owner characteristics, size and managerial approach and professionalism. The first three are deemed to be fixed, the latter two will vary, but all interact internally and externally with the market. Such firm variables will affect 'thresholds' which, Atkinson and Meager argue, will be key influences upon employment practices:

- entry threshold – first employee;
- delegation threshold – first manager;
- formalisation threshold – formal recruitment;
- function threshold – professional personnel employed.

As each threshold is attained, different levels of formality develop which require differing responses from the labour market. Firms with between 10 and 14 employees experienced problems with recruitment and these persisted until the firm exceeded 50 employees.

So, it would appear that small firms in the 1990s are still experiencing difficulties in recruitment, but this can be linked to informal approaches and a failure by the labour market to provide appropriate employees. This latter issue is complex as it relies upon informal perceptions of 'suitability' from firm owners and managers which, evidence would suggest, are based on 'fit' as well as skills. Further to problems finding labour, it appears that small firms still experience difficulties when disciplining and dismissing staff.

17.5.3 Discipline and dismissal in small firms

A recent study of Industrial Tribunal (IT) cases (Earnshaw *et al.* 1998) found that many decisions against small firms occurred because of the lack of formal procedures and policies. Indeed, it was often the experience of a tribunal hearing which prompted the adoption of formal policies. It was also noted that even where firms did have formal policies, some had failed to utilise them, preferring the 'quiet word' approach as owners found resorting to formality in a personalised employment situation too difficult. Thus, there was some evidence for what Gouldner (1964) termed 'mock bureaucracy' whereby formality exists but is largely ignored as it is deemed inappropriate. The consequences of this often meant that if the 'quiet word' failed, the next step was dismissal with little intervening activity. Even rarer than discipline procedures were grievance policies, so channels for employees to draw attention to their complaints – which may have prevented some discipline problems – were limited. Earnshaw *et al.* (1998) did find more formality and use of procedures in unionised firms (note problems of correlation) and accompanying such formality was an increased chance for employee success in the case.

Employers felt the IT system was not appropriate for small firms and difficulties arose because of individual trouble-makers rather than a failure of labour management processes. Consequently, the problem lay in recruitment decisions rather than poor employee relations or inadequate policies and procedures. However, employers felt extending the employment qualification period to two years for IT claims was not helpful as they generally identified and excluded most unsuitable employees after a few weeks. There was no evidence for strategic dismissal just prior to two years' service. Overall, it was concluded that small sites and employers were and remain the principal source of claims for unfair dismissal. Some surprise is expressed that more cases are not brought forward from the sector as a whole.

17.5.4 The advantages of employer–employee relationships in the small firm

Whilst most studies of employee relations in smaller firms highlight problem areas, some recent research has found more positive aspects regarding employment in the sector. Curran *et al.* (1993b) found a high degree of mutual satisfaction regarding terms and conditions of employment in their study of service-sector firms. Even where disputes and dismissals had occurred, both employers and employees felt the actions taken had been justifiable. Whilst there was little evidence for training and development, it was found that the employees did not wish to participate in development schemes, considering them of little relevance to their work. So, it may be unfair to castigate employers for not providing training opportunities – it may be that characteristics of the product and of labour make such provision inappropriate, so a more complex analysis of national labour markets, skill deficiency and product competition is necessary.

Further evidence for greater levels of job satisfaction in smaller enterprises is offered by Abbot (1993). In a study of union recognition and membership issues, Abbot found substantial levels of indifference from owners and managers regarding trade union presence (reflecting initial survey findings from Scott *et al.* 1989), with a minority (40%) who would resist a recognition request. This may be perceived as encouragement for union recruitment strategists, but somewhat more discouraging was the indication that less than a quarter of the sample (24.4%) wished to join a union. It was felt that a union would form a communications barrier between individuals and their employers and, overall, the study revealed that most employees reported good relations with their employer.

It may be wise to view such findings with a little caution. When reporting similar findings from survey evidence, Scott *et al.* (1989) found that closer questioning during case-study analysis revealed contradictory opinions. Many owners felt that union recognition was not an issue because it would never occur. It would be enlightening to review this situation if such firms were faced with a recognition bid. Goss (1991) may also suggest that employees may not seek union membership as they have 'submitted' to owner prerogative and, therefore, believe changes to their situation to be impossible. Moreover, given the lack of traditional activity and representation in smaller firms, particularly in the service sector, there will be few positive examples of union achievement to encourage worker affiliation.

17.6 Human resource management and the small firm

The growth of literature and empirical study pertaining to human resource management (HRM) as a new managerial strategy has, to some extent, been reflected in recent studies of smaller firms. Much of this work has been focused on North America (Ng and Maki 1993; Deshpande and Golhar 1994; Rowden 1995) and indicates a growing awareness of the importance of appropriate labour management to maintain competitiveness in tight markets. Arguing that trends in HRM in the UK reflect those of the USA, Bacon et al. (1996) undertook a survey of 229 small and medium-sized firms to test this assertion. It was found that many firms claimed to be practising new managerial strategies, were sustaining such initiatives and reporting positive outcomes. Whilst the study revealed some 'over-claiming' by survey firms, follow-up case studies indicate that 'the take up of new initiatives remains surprisingly high' (Bacon et al. 1996: 88), with activities such as devolved management, flexibility, team briefing, work and culture change programmes dominating. Overall, small-firm management competencies were greater than the researchers expected given previous empirical findings. Bacon et al. suggested that this may reflect the growing influx into smaller firms of managers who had previously worked for 'down-sized' larger firms, and had assimilated beliefs in employee professionalism and development from their previous employers. It was noted, however, that smaller firms faced specific challenges when pursuing new managerial strategies as they lack resources and management expertise and are less likely to be aware of developments in other companies.

In larger firms, shifts towards HRM have been prompted by changes in the competitive environment (Storey 1989). For smaller firms more specific triggers were evident, namely:

- a change in ownership followed by introduction of new forms of labour management;
- introduction of professional management with new ideas and standards;
- increase in size and formality;
- customer pressure for new standards of service.

Whilst many respondents had awareness of HRM issues, the most frequent source of new policies and practices came from management experience. Where such experience remained limited, this was reflected in stagnation regarding labour process management. Firms most resistant to change were found to be family-owned, not growth-orientated, and managed by those with limited career experience and who regarded professional management with suspicion.

This study is useful in drawing attention to dynamic elements in small-firm ownership and management willing to employ new initiatives to improve competitiveness. More studies of HRM in small firms in the UK are emerging (Duberley and Walley 1995) and these are useful as a reminder of heterogeneity of labour management in the sector as a whole. However, it should be noted that the study sample in the Bacon et al. survey included a number of firms which might be deemed medium or even large (up to 199 employees). With just under half the sample drawn from the manufacturing sector it might be argued that the survey is not representative of small business as a sector. It would also be useful to assess employee perceptions of such HRM initiatives.

17.7 Chapter summary

This chapter has shown that there can be little doubt that the Bolton Committee's (1971) assessment of employee relations in small firms was both simplistic and ill founded. However, it was a major contributor towards successive Conservative governments' (1979–97) policies to encourage the growth of self-employment and a buoyant small-firm sector. There was a strong belief that the style of employee relations associated with small business could overcome the industrial relations problems believed to be endemic in large firms. Moreover, the individualised nature of labour management in small firms would contribute to the Conservative aim of constraining and controlling the power of trade unions. To accommodate their free-market philosophies and monetarist policies and also to facilitate the growth of smaller firms, Conservative policies focused upon deregulation of markets for labour, goods and services, privatisation and calling for greater individual enterprise. Such policies did indeed lead to a growth in self-employment and small-firm ownership such that whilst debate has been fierce, there can be little doubt that smaller firms have been responsible for the generation of most new jobs in recent years. However, some concern has been expressed regarding the quality and durability of such employment.

Primarily, commentators on employee relations in small firms stress the heterogeneity of the small-firm sector which makes blanket statements of harmony or dissent a nonsense. To accommodate such difference, researchers now recognise the need to address issues of sector, size, age, locality, funding, labour characteristics and ownership context (i.e. family-owned, owner-managed, professionally managed, etc.) and in recognising such complexities are able to draw some tentative conclusions regarding identifiable trends or traits within labour management.

During the 1980s, a number of studies of small-firm employee relations did identify some trends pertaining to employee relations in small firms, whilst still recognising the influence of differing variables. Such studies also disputed that smaller firms enjoyed specific and separate forms of operation, compared to larger organisations, which exempted them from similar market pressures. Rainnie and Scott (1986) and Rainnie (1989) argue that ideological divisions between labour and capital are equally pertinent in small as well as large firms, all being part of a market economy. Thus, we must reject false notions of duality when analysing the determinants of labour management. Rather, the market position of large and small firms and their consequent dependency relationships are critical in determining systems of employee relations. Goss (1988; 1991) rejected the prevalence of the 'social harmony' in smaller firms. Rather, he argued that the informal, individual nature of the employment relationship masked the tension inherent in labour management and generated 'submission' to employer prerogative, rather than identification. The complexity of 'submission processes' was recognised with the identification of a number of typologies which noted differing pressures on employment associated with the range of variables which affect the structure of small firms.

Scott et al. (1989) also disputed the social harmony thesis. Evidence from a survey and case studies based on a range of firms, reflecting differing variables such as sector and size, indicated that specific forms of employee relations were identifiable in small businesses. This does not contradict Rainnie's (1989) assertion that smaller and larger firms share the same need to generate surplus value, but suggests that within smaller firms, influential variables will interact to create a 'particular approach' to managing people in small firms. Such trends as Scott *et al.* identified were individuality, informality and insecurity, but external pressures such as skill shortages were important in determining whether these developed. Overall, it was established that owners had positive perceptions of terms and conditions of employment, resented external interference and were largely ignorant of legal regulation. Most employees, however, did not share such positive perceptions, were more resigned to employment conditions but could affect employee relations when in command of scarce skills or other attributes which afforded leverage.

By the end of the 1980s, evidence grew indicating that the image of social harmony in small firms was false but heterogeneity in the sector still ensured that whilst trends can be identified, firm conclusions cannot be drawn. More recent studies of labour management (Atkinson and Meager 1994; Earnshaw *et al.* 1998) have largely supported the overall view that there is a problem with the durability and quality of work in the small-firm sector. Such jobs appear to command lower pay and offer fewer opportunities for training and development; small internal labour markets constrain career progression; hours worked are either longer to enhance wages or are more likely to be part-time. However, it is interesting to note that there is some indication that employees are not necessarily discontented in such work and that employers do not fear external regulation which would improve conditions, such as that from trade unions (Abbot 1993; Curran 1993). Equally, there is evidence for the emergence of new managerial strategies which recognise the importance of gaining employee commitment and compliance to enhance competitiveness, with indication that these will grow (Bacon *et al.* 1996).

Notwithstanding, the overall findings from a range of studies which have acknowledged the complex variables which determine how labour is managed in small firms show that standards are likely to be lower and terms and conditions of employment tend to be poorer. Such aspects are critically affected by the competitive position of the firm in the marketplace and the level of professionalism applied to labour management. So, it becomes apparent that if most small firms are located in the service sector – which is characterised by competition based on cost containment, low skill, low pay and dependency on more vulnerable labour (women, older/younger workers) – they are unlikely to be able to offer, or indeed need to offer, preferable employment terms. Equally, given that responsibility for labour management is deemed the prerogative of the owner (who will rarely have previous experience or qualification in personnel issues) and that a personnel specialist is likely to be one of the last management professionals to be employed in smaller firms (Wynarczyk 1993), it is again unlikely that professional standards will prevail. Consequently, in any assessment of employee relations in smaller firms it is imperative to consider not only the internal dynamics of the firm, but external market pressures and competitive environments in which they operate. If all of these are assessed it is then possible to suggest that terms and conditions of employment in many smaller firms appear, *overall*, to be poorer than those in many larger firms whilst acknowledging that there will always be important exceptions to this trend.

Having established that there has been a growth of low-paid, low-skill work concentrated in a growing service sector in the UK whose output ensures poor competitive national performance (Noon and Blyton 1997), it would appear that the growth of employment in small firms has contributed to this trend. Consequently, if this situation is to be addressed, the contribution of small firms to this deterioration must be recognised. Scott *et al.* (1989) called for greater regulation of employment as the only channel to introduce greater formality and hence security to such work. This is reflected by Rainnie (1989: 151) who argues that 'much *greater* control should be exercised over the wages and conditions provided by small firms . . . there exists a crying need for a far more extensive and detailed regulatory framework for small firms'. Blyton and Turnbull (1998) reiterate the call for statutory protection and suggest unions may be the best enforcers of regulation.

Currently, it would be inappropriate to elect trade unions as regulatory enforcers for a number of reasons. It is difficult to force employers to grant union recognition and even more challenging to ensure bargaining occurs in good faith. Employers cannot be forced to welcome trade unions – it is questionable if they could be forced to even tolerate them where they were unwanted. It is debatable to what extent private service-sector employees, in particular, would support union regulation, having little experience of union benefits and no tradition of union affiliation. So, unions would require some official status and funding to 'police' workplaces where they were not recognised – this is unlikely. Also, it must be questioned whether unions would be up to such a task in the short, or even medium, term as regulation would require coherent strategies and significant numbers of well-trained organisers. This is clearly not beyond the scope of unions given time, resources and official encouragement. However, given the somewhat distant relationship which currently exists between trade unions and the Blair government, this is not a very likely scenario. Alternatively, existing bodies such as the Health and Safety Executive could be further empowered, or new regulatory organisations pertaining to wages and conditions could be formed. These bodies would require substantial funding, professional advisers and powerful sanctions to be effective, all of which is perfectly possible and would ensure greater professional management and uptake of advice.

So, it is clear that, on the balance of existing evidence, the argument for greater regulation to improve employment conditions in small firms is persuasive. Yet, it is difficult to imagine how focusing on one particular sector of the economy, which is noted for its heterogeneity, could be adequately justified – given the criticisms this would elicit. Also the effect on production costs and consequent implications for firm survival must be recognised. Moreover, whilst the Labour government has made a pledge to promote fair employment through a floor of regulation, in keeping with traditional UK approaches the emphasis is on voluntary regulation through social partnerships. So, whilst formal regulation might be the most effective manner to address inequality and exploitation in employment, it is unlikely to occur.

For voluntary regulation to be effective, it must offer sustainable benefits for all interested stakeholders. This might be obtained through extending and developing the system which in the past pertained to local government contracting whereby tenders were considered on not just cost, but also issues such as employment standards. Given the dependency of many smaller firms upon such contracts in the private and public sector, this would encourage a review of standards whilst offering the benefit of contracts. Whilst this would necessitate larger firms extending their remit for tenders, given the formality/bureaucracy of such organisations this would not be excessively demanding. Of course many firms, as non-contract enterprises, would be excluded but without formal regulation this is inevitable.

A point of further contention in current government policies is the exclusion of the smallest firms (less than 20 employees) from much employment legislation. This is problematical as it infers that those working in such firms do not deserve the same degree of protection as those in larger firms and also creates a barrier to growth as employers are reluctant to expand beyond this threshold. This is a false barrier and should be removed, as all employees deserve a uniform standard of protection.

Finally, whilst it may be desirable to promote fairer employment conditions for waged labour in modern economies, it is also vital to recognise the reality of the weak competitive position of the UK. As Rainnie (1989) argued, some time ago, small firms are part of the whole market economy so whilst it is feasible and appropriate to call for improvements in segments of that market, it requires a coherent national policy regarding strategic development of the whole economy to drag the weakest elements forward. Examples from relatively robust economies would indicate that regulation, rather than voluntarism, is the way forward. It would therefore appear that, in the case of the UK, poor employers – whether in smaller or larger firms – will continue in their current role for the foreseeable future.

Questions

1 Discuss how and why the management of labour in small firms differs from approaches in larger organisations.

2 Evaluate whether the size of an enterprise can critically affect the tension inherent in the labour–capital relationship in modern market economies.

3 Examine the reasons why the majority of small-firm owners and their management teams adopt an informal *ad hoc* approach to the management of employees.

4 Outline the approach of your current government to the management of people at work and discuss how contemporary attitudes towards managing people in small firms will accord with such an approach.

CHAPTER 18

Training and the small firm

Harry Matlay

18.1 Learning objectives

There are four learning objectives in this chapter:

1 To develop an understanding of the specific training needs of small-business owner-managers and their workforce.

2 To understand the role of owner-managers within small-business management in general and the training function in particular.

3 To evaluate a number of contemporary training initiatives aimed at the small-business sector of the British economy.

4 To gain an understanding of directly and indirectly relevant factors that affect the provision of training in smaller firms.

Key concepts

- training initiatives ▪ vocational and educational training
- Industry Training Organisations ▪ Investors in People ▪ Business Links
- Training and Local Enterprise Councils

18.2 Introduction

Small-business owner-managers make most, if not all, of the important decisions in relation to the day-to-day operation of their firms. The success or failure of government-inspired training initiatives aimed specifically at the small-business sector must be evaluated in terms of actual impact upon owner-managers and their workforce. This chapter evaluates the impact that a number of important support programmes and initiatives have had upon small businesses in terms of owner-manager awareness of, interest in, intention to provide and actual take-up rates of training. These issues are discussed in the light of a national research study involving 2,000 small-business owner-managers which evaluated owner-manager usage of training provision and support in individual firms. Even though, in recent years, the position of the small-business sector in relation to contemporary national training policies has improved dramatically, it appears that the actual provision of vocational education and training (VET) in small firms fails significantly to keep pace with the perceived skills needs of owner-managers and their workforce. The disappointingly low impact that most contemporary training initiatives appear to have upon small businesses in Britain ultimately betrays the wide credibility gap that still exists between politically inspired VET rhetoric and owner-managers facing rapidly changing economic realities.

18.3 Training and the small firm

During the 1980s and 1990s the business scene in most industrially developed countries was characterised by a growing interest in support measures and policies aimed specifically at small enterprises. Increasingly, the business community, governments, investors, bankers and other stakeholders came to view the small-business sector as the 'driving force' behind the quest for economic growth and renewal. Within the European Union, in particular, small businesses were viewed as crucial for the generation of employment opportunities and GDP growth. It is not difficult to see why, on average, small firms represent 99.8% of all businesses active in the European Union. Typically they account for 68% of total employment and 63% of the overall business turnover (Tacis 1997). Furthermore, over the same period, the average employment growth rate in small businesses was greater than that recorded in larger enterprises. In particular, the small-business-dominated services sector has been a major source of jobs in the Member States, where alarmingly high rates of youth and adult unemployment have dominated political and economic agendas since the early 1970s (ENSR 1997).

The general trend towards downsizing of large-firm operations and contracting-out of marginal activities continued to provide small businesses with both challenges and new opportunities. The rapidly changing global business environment and the increased internationalisation of markets (see Chapter 24) impacted considerably upon national economies by providing new opportunities and threats which translated into an unprecedented growth in domestic small-business sectors (Matlay 1999). In Britain, following the virtual full employment of the post-war period, the oil crises of the early 1970s heralded the onset of long-term (youth and adult) unemployment and the collapse of both the manufacturing sector and the related apprenticeship system of training. The overall downsizing trend, characteristic of this period, was particularly noticeable in the manufacturing sector of the British economy. Here, a large proportion of operations that were traditionally carried out 'in-house' were either contracted out or exported to areas of the world that offered substantially lower labour costs (see Chapter 3). Most of the resulting domestic subcontract activity was mopped up by newly created small businesses often equipped with obsolete machinery and using workers made redundant by larger firms.

The increase in the overall incidence of general, as well as specific, support targeted at the SME sector of the British economy could be attributed to a number of interrelated factors. During the 1979–97 period, general and specific support aimed at start-ups as well as established small firms appears to have been boosted by the 'free-market' economic policies pursued by the Conservative governments led by Margaret Thatcher and John Major (Matlay 1996). Furthermore, the appropriation of post-Fordist rhetoric by the New Right since the late 1970s appears to have promoted the small-business sector to a key position in the quest for the regeneration of the British economy. The explicit emphasis placed by the Conservative government upon small firms was based mainly upon the belief that a healthy small-business sector was a fundamental prerequisite for an expanding and globally competitive economy. Most importantly, and for similar reasons, the subsequent Labour government appears to be fully committed to the continuing improvement and expansion of the small-business sector (Hyland and Matlay 1997; McGoldrick 1997). Future policy measures, designed both to encourage new start-ups and to assist the development and growth of existing firms, are likely to continue to support this crucially important sector of the British economy well into the next millennium (Corney 1997).

In the past two decades, a number of costly training programmes and initiatives have been implemented in Britain, in the knowledge that limited resources were to be targeted at a massive and diverse domestic small-business sector (Curran 1990; DTI 1996b). A segmented approach to the delivery of support to this sector was suggested and justified by a number of academics, commentators and policy-makers (Storey and Johnson 1987; Storey 1993; DTI 1995a). In the event, most of the strategic approaches to small-business support appear to have involved some type of screening which, in accordance with specific characteristics and/or needs, was deemed either to ensure positive outcomes or to guarantee overall success (Matlay 1997a). Similarly, discriminant means of resource allocation were used in an attempt to maximise – in terms of employment and/or sustainable competitiveness – the benefits arising from the distribution of public funds (Baldock *et al.* 1997). Interestingly, most of the support programmes and initiatives implemented since the late 1970s were deemed, by the government of the time, to have been successful, even though few independent or methodologically consistent evaluation studies were commissioned or undertaken. Furthermore, a small number of such programmes were either unceremoniously dropped or simply disappeared from government-inspired or dominated economic agendas (Matlay 1997b).

This chapter aims to evaluate the impact that training has had upon small businesses in terms of owner-manager awareness of, interest in, intention to provide and actual take-up rates of a number of important support programmes and initiatives. It is suggested that the success (or otherwise) of support programmes or training initiatives aimed specifically at the small-business sector should be evaluated in terms of their actual impact upon owner-managers and their workforce. Government-inspired training statistics as well as related and often inflated expenditure statements must be carefully scrutinised in order to detect, as far as possible, cases of double accounting or similar irregularities. It appears that, so far, much of the openness and accountability advocated by representatives of all the major political parties in Britain has failed to significantly influence the 'quangos' that largely administer the considerable sums allocated exclusively for the support and improvement of the small-business sector. It is further suggested that the apparent paucity of independent research on VET and related issues is perhaps symptomatic of an increased government involvement in, and a strict control of, a large proportion of academic and research funding.

18.4 Training and HRD strategies in the small-business sector

There exists an extensive body of academic and practitioner literature that emphasises the factors most likely to influence the overall performance of small firms. The body of knowledge focusing upon small-business performance covers most, if not all, of the important areas of management: finance, marketing, production, research and development (Hughes 1992). Until recently, however, there was a noticeable paucity of research focusing upon the training and human resource development (HRD) needs of small-business owner-managers and their workforce (see Chapter 17). It appears that these issues have been largely neglected by academic researchers and human resource development specialists who were content to offer solutions which were more relevant to the business strategies of larger firms rather than their smaller counterparts. In practice, downscaled human development strategies and large-scale training solutions were of little use to owner-managers of small businesses (Holme 1992: 16). Furthermore, the academic and professional neglect of this aspect of small-business strategy appears to have been compounded by the discriminant economic policies of successive governments that were perceived by owner-managers and their representatives to be mostly biased towards larger firms and their needs. As a result, the majority of small-business owner-managers tend to be sceptical towards government involvement in their affairs and would prefer to be left to their own devices (Hyland and Matlay 1997; Matlay 1997a).

Conventional wisdom relating to training in the small-business sector (and indeed in medium-sized or large firms) appears to promise considerable benefits to all those involved in the process. Furthermore, it is widely believed that undergoing training and gaining certain vocational qualifications will confer a range of benefits to employers, individual employees and society as a whole (Osowska 1996). In the short term, employers could expect to recover their investment in training and, in the medium and long term, to benefit significantly from the increased productivity of their employees. Similarly, to the trained employees there would accrue benefits in terms of pay increments, job satisfaction and/or increased employment security (Matlay 1995). *Prima facie*, small-business owner-managers would be well advised to invest in the future of their workforce. In practice, however, the small-business sector has a longstanding reputation for lower educational and training achievements (Matlay 1996). Similarly, training and skill levels in Britain have been repeatedly criticised for falling significantly behind the achievements of both its major and minor competitors (Hyland and Matlay 1997).

The lack of interest in the human aspect of small businesses became patently obvious following the publication of the largest study on training funding, activity and attitudes undertaken in Britain (Training Agency 1989). The four reports arising from this study revealed a number of shortcomings, including an overly narrow definition of 'training', a partiality towards quantitative methods of data collection/analysis and a size-related preference towards investigating larger enterprises. This prompted Pettigrew *et al.* (1990) to comment that the training literature in Britain was distinguished by a lack of specialised research to ascertain the importance (or otherwise) of human resource strategies to small-business development and growth. Hendry *et al.* (1991) further argued that in the growing field of small-business research the human resource dimension has been largely neglected by academics and practitioners alike.

More recently, as it became increasingly obvious that more training should be provided in British organisations of all sizes – if they were to compete successfully in globalised markets – the human resource strategies of small firms have come under close scrutiny (Matlay 1997b). In this context, it appears that the importance of the skill levels and training needs of individuals working in small enterprises has belatedly been recognised. However, in common with the wider training debate in this country, there appears to be little agreement as to how much training should be or has been provided in small firms. For example, Matlay and Hyland (1997) argue that, in general, small-business owner-managers and their workforce are poorly trained and exhibit lower skill levels. In contrast, Curran *et al.* (1996: 2) have shown that although in some sectors of economic activity this might be true, in others over three-quarters of owner-managers reported providing training over a period of 12 months prior to the interviews.

Important insights can be gained from Westhead and Storey's (1997) study of training provision in the small-business sector of the British economy. They found that training in small businesses differed considerably from that provided in larger firms. The authors argue that training in small firms was more likely to convey informal work skills and/or knowledge, mostly from one employee to another. In contrast, training in larger firms usually led to formal qualifications and was mostly externally provided and validated. It appears that 'quality of training' is the key measure of its provision and that individuals working in small firms are less likely to receive training than those employed by larger organisations. Furthermore, the authors claim that they could find no evidence of well-conducted research which clearly and consistently linked training provision to enhanced business performance.

18.4.1 Investigating training in the small-firms sector

Important implications for research are also drawn by Westhead and Storey (1997: 30). Firstly, there is an obvious need for longitudinal and qualitative studies to evaluate the long-term benefits of training provision in small firms. Secondly, control groups should be used in order to compare and contrast outcomes in firms that provide training and in those that choose to ignore this route to sustainable competitiveness. Thirdly, it is suggested that multivariate statistical techniques should be utilised in order to establish the direction and strength of causal links between training provision and subsequent business performance. To a great extent, the research study upon which this chapter is based conforms with their recommendations, even though in view of dominant replies to the survey questionnaire it was decided that multivariate statistical techniques were not applicable in this case.

A number of commentators have noted the lack of well-documented and methodologically sound research on the topic of training and human resource development in the small-business sector. For example, Storey and Westhead (1994: 17) point out that, following an extensive literature review on training in the small-business sector, they were unable to 'consistently document methodologically well conducted research'. Furthermore, much of the literature that they reviewed, originating in both Europe and the USA, exhibited substantial flaws and omissions as well as some blatant methodological shortcomings. Other authors have reached similar conclusions in their own reviews of the state of research on this topic (see, for example, Hendry *et al.* 1991). Typically, most of the research in this area appears to be quantitative and, in view of recurrent low response rates, empirical results of such 'snapshot' studies should not be generalised across a wider population. Thus, it appears that well-conducted qualitative or longitudinal research appears to be notably absent from the body of knowledge relating to training and human resource development in the small-business sector of the British economy.

A recent study of training in the small-business sector attempted to overcome many of these problems by combining three different investigative and analytical approaches. Firstly, it involved a cross-sectional, exploratory telephone survey carried out in 1993. This survey collected a set of attitudinal, sectoral and compositional data from 2,000 firms, randomly selected from the Yellow Pages business database (Yellow Pages 1993). The response rate for this survey was 89%. Secondly, the research included a longitudinal analysis of a subset of 200 owner-managers over a five-year period (1993–7). This allowed annual analysis of changes in the adoption of specific training programmes. Finally, over the same period, 74 matched cases of small-firm owner-managers were conducted in order to compare and contrast the main strategies and approaches adopted by small-business owner-managers in relation to their training and human resource needs.

18.5 Who makes training-related decisions in small firms?

It is increasingly acknowledged that owner-managers play a pivotal role in the day-to-day running of small businesses (e.g. Goss 1991; Storey 1994). It appears that, in most cases, owner-managers are directly involved in all the important aspects of the decision-making processes appertaining to management and training strategies (Curran *et al.* 1996: 11).

As Table 18.1 shows, in micro-firms (size band A and B), the locus of training-related decision-making processes rested solely with the owner-manager. In the majority of very small businesses (size band C and D), training control remained the prerogative of owner-managers but, in a small proportion of this type of firm, personnel managers were given responsibility for this function. Interestingly, in small businesses (size band E), just over 80% of owner-managers retained the prerogative of making training-related decisions. In a further 2.6% of cases, personnel managers were involved in the decision-making process and in 17.3% of firms key personnel (mainly line managers or operational supervisors) were responsible for the training function.

Table 18.1 The locus of training decision-making in small firms

Band code	Number of employees	All firms (N = 2,000) (%)	Who Makes Training Decisions?			
			Owner/ manager (%)	Personnel manager (%)	Key personnel (%)	Other employees (%)
A	1–5	63.60	100.00	0.00	0.00	0.00
B	6–10	15.70	100.00	0.00	0.00	0.00
C	11–19	12.40	96.60	3.40	0.00	0.00
D	20–49	5.70	82.70	17.30	0.00	0.00
E	50–99	2.60	80.10	2.60	17.30	0.00

As argued elsewhere (Matlay 1997b), it becomes crucial that any attempts to improve the quality of the workforce in the small-business sector should focus upon the expressed needs of owner-managers. Support programmes and initiatives directed at the small-business sector must take into consideration the extent of owner-managers' involvement in the decision-making process related to training as well as their tendency to retain control of most, if not all, of the functions relevant to the management of their firms.

18.6 Training initiatives and their impact upon small firms

In theory, small firms can draw upon training support from a wide range of sources, including trade associations, government-sponsored organisations, private training consultancies, clients and suppliers, as well as some of the individuals connected with the business. Potentially, government-sponsored initiatives represent the most important and consistent source of training support for small-business owner-managers. These are usually well resourced and can benefit from a wide base of specialist expertise and an extensive administrative and marketing base. According to the prevalent wisdom, government-inspired and/or sponsored training initiatives – and in particular those that include specific small-business remits – should have been widely used by owner-managers in their quest for competitiveness and organic growth. The apparently low take-up rates of such initiatives, as demonstrated by the owner-managers in the research sample, could be attributed to a number of interrelated factors, the most important of which are identified and analysed in this chapter.

18.6.1 Industry Training Organisations (ITOs)

ITOs date back to the beginning of the 1980s, from the time of the Industrial Training Boards' dissolution. Although these are voluntary-sector organisations, ITOs have close links with government, including support and guidelines on their role, focus and performance. The development of ITOs has been uneven and a large proportion of them only became operational in the late 1980s or early 1990s (Curran *et al.* 1993b: 33). Similarly, ITO performance in relation to the small-business sector has also been uneven, due mainly to budgetary constraints and short-term strategies targeted to maximising returns (HOST 1994).

Only a relatively small proportion of owner-managers appears to have been aware of the existence and purpose of ITOs (Table 18.2). In micro-firms (band code A and B), just over 17% of owner-managers interviewed knew about ITOs and claimed to understand their function in relation to training and support. About 12% of these showed an interest in them but just over 8% admitted to having used the training-related services that were on offer. In the case of very small businesses (band code C and D), just over 21% of owner-managers were aware and understood the activities of ITOs. Only about 14% showed an interest in their training potential and just over 9% of these actually used them. Over one-third (34.72%) of owner-managers in small firms (band code E) were aware and understood the training policies of ITOs, yet less than half (14.87%) of these were interested in or actually used the training schemes on offer.

Table 18.2 Owner-manager awareness, understanding, interest in and actual usage of ITOs

Band code	Number of employees	Industry Training Organisations (ITOs)			
		Awareness (%)	Understanding (%)	Interest in (%)	Actual usage (%)
A	1–5	16.38	16.38	11.84	8.32
B	6–10	17.27	17.27	12.62	8.64
C	11–19	21.19	21.19	12.89	9.17
D	20–49	21.84	21.84	14.51	9.26
E	50–99	34.72	34.72	14.87	14.87

18.6.2 Investors in People (IiP)

Since its launch in November 1990, Investors in People (IiP) actively encouraged owner-managers to make a public commitment to training in their firms. Under the auspices of this scheme, an investment in training would be rewarded not only in financial terms but also in other, less tangible but nevertheless important ways. For example, the IiP Badge of Achievement can be, and often is, exhibited by achieving firms, as a guarantee of the quality of their products and services. Furthermore, these firms are periodically targeted, by the awarding TECs, for regular training briefs and updates.

Most of the firms that have achieved IiP recognition continue to train their workforce and can benefit from discounted training packages available from their local TECs. Generally, TECs are the main drivers of this training scheme, both as providers and as assessors (Rix *et al.* 1994). In practice, local TECs are called upon by owner-managers to assist and supervise the development of a flexible and updatable business plan. With the active help of an advisory team, aspiring firms set out to achieve, within a relatively short time-span, a national standard of training. Significantly, IiP was aimed at organisations of all sizes and economic activity, including micro-, small and medium-sized businesses as well as large corporations (DTI 1995b).

However, despite concerted efforts and regular advertising campaigns, the uptake of IiP amongst firms operating in the small-business sector has been relatively low (Table 18.3). For example, amongst micro- and very small firms in the research sample (band code A, B, C and D) owner-manager awareness of IiP has yet to reach the 10% mark. Even amongst those owner-managers who claim to be aware of it, understanding of IiP was typically very low (less than 5%). Furthermore, none of the owner-managers of micro-firms (band code A and B) appeared to be interested in, or have achieved, IiP accreditation. Amongst very small businesses in the research sample (band code C and D), owner-manager interest in IiP stood at less than 2% and just under 1% claimed to have completed the accreditation process. Much better overall rates were reported by owner-managers of small businesses (band code E): 26.12% of them reported an awareness, understanding and interest. Better still, 12.17% of these owner-managers have successfully completed the IiP accreditation process.

Table 18.3 Owner-manager awareness, understanding, interest in and actual usage of Investors in People

Band code	Number of employees	Investors in people (IiP)			
		Awareness (%)	Understanding (%)	Interest in (%)	Actual usage (%)
A	1–5	6.82	3.13	0.00	0.00
B	6–10	7.38	3.83	0.00	0.00
C	11–19	9.55	4.27	1.58	0.82
D	20–49	9.83	4.93	1.93	0.87
E	50–99	26.12	26.12	26.12	12.17

18.6.3 Business Links (BLs)

Business Links (BLs) were established in 1992 and since then an increasing number of local and regional outlets have been set up to provide a single point of access for all the support needs of businesses across Britain. The principal, stated objective of BLs was defined as 'outlets for the full range of DTI business services' (DTI 1995b: 31). Initially, it was hoped that smaller businesses would benefit significantly from a focal point of reference and a local outlet where owner-managers could access all the information and support that they might need during the normal course of their chosen economic activity. Interestingly, however, the target market that later emerged from the specific remit given to BLs seemed to explicitly exclude micro-businesses (i.e. those firms employing fewer than 10 individuals). As a result, a comparatively large proportion of firms operating in the small-business sector of the British economy were left to seek support for their specific needs elsewhere or fend for themselves as best they could (Curran *et al.* 1996: 39). To date, an explanation is yet to emerge for the exclusive targeting of Business Link services towards the more sizeable firms operating in both the small-business sector and the wider economy.

The exclusion of micro-business owner-managers from the target market appears to have succeeded in barring the majority of them from using the services provided by Business Links (Table 18.4). Interestingly, however, just under 4% of the micro-business owner-managers interviewed (band code A and B) were both aware of and claimed to understand the services available from such 'one-stop shops'. Furthermore, just under 3% of them were interested in benefiting from their services, but just over 1% reported to have used them. Just over 7% of owner-managers in very small businesses (band code C and D) claimed to be aware, understand or have an interest in the services provided by Business Links. However, less than half of these admitted to having used these services. Almost one-third of the small-business owner-managers interviewed (band code E) were aware, understood and claimed to be interested in Business Links. More than half of these also claimed to have used the services made available to them. In view of their relatively short existence, Business Links appear to have made a good impression upon the owner-managers of the more sizeable small businesses in the sample. It is suggested, therefore, that a refocusing of the BLs' target market towards the specific needs of micro- and very small firms could significantly increase their relevance to the training effort in this important sector of the British economy.

Table 18.4 Owner-manager awareness, understanding, interest in and actual usage of Business Links

Band code	Number of employees	Business Links (BLs)			
		Awareness (%)	Understanding (%)	Interest in (%)	Actual usage (%)
A	1–5	1.38	1.38	1.27	0.52
B	6–10	1.52	1.52	1.62	0.67
C	11–19	7.18	7.18	7.18	2.38
D	20–49	7.68	7.68	7.68	2.59
E	50–99	31.55	31.55	31.55	23.6

18.6.4 Training and Local Enterprise Councils (TECs/LECs)

The 1988 White Paper *Employment for the 1990s* set out, in broad terms, the reasoning behind the creation of Training and Enterprise Councils (TECs) in England and Wales and Local Enterprise Councils (LECs) in Scotland. Fundamental to this document was the concept of employer involvement in, and responsibility for, the management and delivery of training (Department of Employment 1988). Furthermore, TECs and LECs were conceived not only to promote training arrangements linked to the particular skill needs of a local workforce, but also to increasingly generate private investment in training. Most importantly, for the small-business sector, this training initiative was aimed to meet (quantitatively and qualitatively) the needs of both new and established firms, through a combination of local enterprise support networks and specific national training programmes (Johnson and Gubbins 1991). The launch in 1989 of TECs/LECs has been seen by many as the latest and most ambitious scheme to promote an enterprise culture movement (Storey 1994). Although since inception a wide range of initiatives, styles and approaches has been used, the actual impact of these councils on national training standards remained difficult to ascertain.

As Table 18.5 shows, the owner-managers of micro- (band code A and B) and very small businesses (band code C and D) exhibited very low rates of awareness and understanding of the training provisions available from TECs/LECs: about 4% and 8% respectively. Just over half of these owner-managers (respectively, 2% and 4%) showed an interest in using the training services available through TECs and LECs. Interestingly, however, less than 1% of micro-business owner-managers have actually taken advantage of the training support available from these councils. In the case of very small businesses, training take-up rates stood at just under 3%. Significantly better rates of TECs/LECs usage were exhibited by the owner-managers of small businesses (band code E): 38.58% of them asserted that they were aware, understood and were interested in the services available from these organisations. Furthermore, just over 30% of these owner-managers claimed to have used the training services on offer from TECs/LECs.

Table 18.5 Owner-manager awareness, understanding, interest in and actual usage of TECs/LECs

Band code	Number of employees	TECs/LECs			
		Awareness (%)	Understanding (%)	Interest in (%)	Actual usage (%)
A	1–5	3.47	3.47	2.12	0.85
B	6–10	3.93	3.93	2.27	0.88
C	11–19	8.12	8.12	4.67	2.92
D	20–49	8.23	8.23	4.89	2.93
E	50–99	38.58	38.58	38.58	30.12

18.6.5 National and Scottish Vocational Qualifications (NVQs/SVQs)

The National Council for Vocational Qualifications (NCVQ) framework and the related Scottish Vocational Qualifications (SVQs) were introduced in 1986, as a 'quiet revolution' in the British vocational education and training system (Burke 1989). NVQs, and their Scottish equivalent SVQs, are both underpinned by a system of competence-based education and training (CBET) that extends throughout all educational levels, from school to university (Hyland 1994). Although very similar, there are some significant differences between NVQs and SVQs. In contrast to NCVQ, the Scottish Vocational Education Council (Scotvec) is both an awarding and an accrediting body. While NVQs are perceived to be 'industry-led', SVQs are mainly thought of as 'education-led' (Wojtas 1993). Policy-makers, politicians, educators, trainers, employers, academics, trade unions and many other parties claim to have an interest in, or a contribution to make to, the S/NVQ system of competence-based education and training in Britain. As another ostensibly 'employer-led' initiative, the introduction of S/NVQs has proved to be central to the concerted effort to upskill small-business owner-managers and their workforce (Matlay and Hyland 1997).

As Table 18.6 shows, owner-managers exhibited significantly higher rates of awareness, understanding and interest in S/NVQs than in any of the other support programmes reviewed in this chapter. Since its inception in 1986 this type of vocational qualification has benefited from a sustained and continuously improved marketing campaign. About half the owner-managers of micro- and very small businesses (band code A to D) claimed to be aware of S/NVQs. Just under 14% of micro-business owner-managers (band code A and B) claimed to understand them, about 6% were interested in them yet less than 1% actually managed to implement these qualifications within their firms. Similarly, although just over 20% of very small business owner-managers claimed to understand S/NVQs and about half of them were interested in these vocational qualifications, just over 1% admitted to have implemented them. Even the relatively high rates of awareness (84.73%), understanding and interest (54.42%) exhibited by small-business owner-managers (band code E) only materialised as a 4.16% rate of implementation. Most of the owner-managers interviewed for this research blamed their low rates of S/NVQ implementation upon the complexity, time-scale and expense involved in adopting the NCVQ framework of vocational qualifications.

Table 18.6 Owner-manager awareness, understanding, interest in and actual implementation of NVQs/SVQs

Band code	Number of employees	NVQs/SVQs			
		Awareness (%)	Understanding (%)	Interest in (%)	Actual imple-mentation (%)
A	1–5	49.46	13.62	6.11	0.71
B	6–10	49.52	13.98	6.24	0.78
C	11–19	50.54	20.28	10.56	1.36
D	20–49	50.61	20.61	10.13	1.09
E	50–99	84.73	54.42	54.42	4.16

18.7 Factors affecting the provision of training in small firms

The owner-managers participating in this study identified a number of directly and indirectly relevant factors that affected the provision of training in their firms (Table 18.7). 'Directly relevant' factors, such as market positioning, prevailing economic conditions and the availability of relevant training, were considered of primary importance to their training strategies. 'Indirectly relevant' factors were of secondary importance but nevertheless exerted some influence upon both the quantity and quality of the provision in these firms. Secondary factors included the cost of training, time constraints, lack of in-house trainers and determinants relating to trainee cover, motivation and interest.

Across the two main sectors of economic activity, 91% of respondents in the manufacturing sector and 93% in services identified the market positioning of their firms as the most important factor affecting training provision in their firms. The specific market orientation of a small organisation (with a relatively narrow portfolio of products or services) and its perceived positioning in relation to known competitors appeared to

Table 18.7 Factors affecting the provision of training in small firms

Factors affecting actual provision of training	No. of respondents nominating factor (manufacturing) (%)	No. of respondents nominating factor (services) (%)
1. Directly relevant:		
Market positioning of firm	91	93
Prevailing economic conditions	89	87
Availability of relevant training	83	80
2. Indirectly relevant:		
Cost of training	46	45
Time constraints	40	37
Lack of trainee cover	34	32
Lack of in-house trainers	28	29
Lack of trainee motivation	26	25
Lack of trainee interest	13	12

determine the choice, quantity and quality of training provision. Thus, small firms that focus on low-quality products and services rely mostly on reactive strategies and appear to have little need to train their workforce on a regular basis. Conversely, a focus on better-quality products and services appears to involve a proactive human resource development approach. Prevailing economic conditions as a directly relevant determinant of training provision was nominated by 89% of respondents in manufacturing and 87% in the service sector. Interestingly, favourable economic circumstances resulted in higher staff turnover rates and also increased growth-related training needs. Conversely, unfavourable economic circumstances tended to stabilise staff turnover and increase the external pool of trained personnel. Importantly, however, 83% of respondents in the manufacturing sector and 80% in the services claimed to have experienced acute shortages of relevant training. Shortages of relevant training appear to have significantly handicapped these owner-managers in their drive to fulfil their business objectives. Typically, they claim that most of the training on offer was geared for, or better suited to, the strategies of larger organisations, to a great extent ignoring their specific, small-firm needs.

'Indirectly relevant' factors included six interrelated constraints that, in the experience of these respondents, had a curtailing effect upon the actual provision of training in their firms. Due to a shortage of specific training, owner-managers were forced to purchase either exorbitantly priced customised training or expensive, large-firm solutions that invariably turned out to be of limited use. Some respondents claimed to have encountered considerable difficulties in identifying and costing training schemes pertinent to their specific needs. As a result, few respondents were able to compute the full extent of actual, marginal or incidental costs relating to their training strategies. At various stages, time constraints frustrated the training activities of these respondents, including needs evaluation, the search for relevant training, and cost-effectiveness feedback exercises; in some cases, they even precluded them from checking the overall impact of related strategies. Many owner-managers had to rely on superficial assessment or unreliable and biased trainee feedback. The lack of in-house trainers mainly reflected either the small size of the respondent organisation or the owner-manager's preference for external training programmes. Other trainee-related constraints, including lack of cover, motivation and interest, appear to have hampered some of the respondents' training efforts. Solutions to this type of problem varied widely across the sample, ranging from 'drastic measures', such as disciplinary action, to financial incentives for training-related increases in productivity. Significantly, however, those respondents who adopted a 'proactive' approach to training appeared to be better prepared for dealing with strategic problems than their more 'reactive' counterparts.

18.8 Chapter summary

The main training initiatives reviewed in this chapter exhibit a number of important common trends. Typically, these initiatives are government inspired and supported, in terms of both sourcing and orientation. As part of the economic strategies of consecutive governments, these training initiatives included in their remit a focus on the specific needs of firms operating in the small-business sector of the British economy.

Owner-manager awareness, understanding and interest in the training services on offer were generally low. The take-up incidence of the training solutions incorporated in these initiatives was even more disappointing. The owner-managers of micro- and very small businesses exhibited very low rates of awareness, understanding, interest and take-up of training services on offer. This would suggest that, in the main, the specific needs of such firms are yet to be properly assessed, supported or fulfilled. Much higher rates of success could be claimed in relation to small-business owner-managers who appear to increasingly benefit from government-inspired and supported training initiatives. It appears, however, that the specific training needs of the vast majority of owner-managers operating in the small-business sector of the British economy remain unfulfilled despite the concerted efforts and sizeable funding that have been invested, over the last two decades, in this type of support initiative. There is an obvious need for a wide-ranging independent review which could establish the specific training needs of small-business owner-managers and the best and most effective way to fulfil them. Perhaps a long-overdue small-business White Paper could achieve this important objective, with the impact that could significantly improve the competitiveness of British firms forced to operate in increasingly globalised markets.

Questions

1 What are the perceived benefits accruable to all those involved in the training process in small firms?

2 Which of the contemporary training initiatives aimed at small businesses appears to be more successful and why?

3 What are the directly and indirectly relevant factors that appear to affect the provision of training in small firms?

4 How could the relatively low take-up of training provision in smaller firms be improved?

CHAPTER 19

Finance and the small firm

Robin Jarvis

19.1 Learning objectives

There are five learning objectives in this chapter:

1 To understand the arguments as to whether or not a finance gap exists for small firms.
2 To appreciate the types of finance used by small firms.
3 To recognise that capital structure theory is not influential when small firms make capital structure decisions.
4 To appreciate the importance of small firms' annual reports and accounts to the providers of finance.
5 To understand the reasons why small firms and large firms are financed differently.

Key concepts

- finance gap ■ capital structure decision
- the separation of ownership and management
- the importance of annual reports to finance providers

19.2 Introduction

The information available on how small firms are financed is limited because little is in the public domain. However, through a careful search of the literature a picture emerges which indicates that small firms use different types of finance compared to large firms. Large firms benefit from established markets where they can raise funds. There are no similar markets for the vast majority of small firms. Therefore, the proportion of equity invested in small firms is much less than that of large companies. In general, small firms tend to rely on bank lending and other types of financial products.

The question of whether a finance gap exists for small firms has been examined and debated over many years. Through government initiatives and the introduction of new products by the financial institutions much has been done to bridge this gap. However, many argue that the gap still exists, particularly for firms starting up or wishing to grow. The influential variables in the capital structure decision of large firms are not so critical in small-firm decisions. The markets in which the small firm operates, the firm's life-cycle and the preferences and desires of the owner(s) are influential. The research also shows that there is an important link between small firms' annual reports and accounts and the providers of finance. A number of studies have identified that this information is used by the providers in their decisions to grant credit and to monitor the firm's progress.

19.3 Finance and the small firm

The main purpose of this chapter is to examine the range of finance available to small firms and their source. It is important to recognise that the financing of small enterprises differs considerably from that of large entities. From a financial-economic perspective, the main difference lies in the lack of availability of capital markets where small firms can raise funds compared with their larger counterparts for whom established markets exist such as the London Stock Exchange. The differences from a socio-economic perspective are primarily associated with the relationship between the finance provider and the enterprise. In the case of small firms the owners normally represent the enterprise in the capacity of both the owner and manager. In large firms which are often companies, the relationship is between the providers of finance (the shareholders who are the owners of the company) and the directors (the managers) who are invariably separate from the owners (shareholders). The significance of these differences will be a main theme running throughout this chapter.

Although much has been written about the different types of finance employed by small businesses, only limited information is available on the extent to which each type is actually used. This is because not all the information relating to the financing of small businesses is in the public domain. By contrast, information relating to the different types of finance used by large companies is publicly available from a variety of sources including these companies' own annual reports and accounts. One of the main sources of information on finance and the small firm is survey data (for example, surveys by the ESRC Centre for Business Research, Cambridge). These surveys, although limited in scope, give useful insights into the types of finance used by small firms. However, the results of such studies should be interpreted with caution for two reasons: firstly, there is no standard definition of a 'small' business and, secondly, there is the problem of aggregation of the data. This is particularly important when examining how small businesses are financed because it is likely that the extent and source of funds will depend upon the size of business. For example, small firms with a turnover of £50,000 are likely to have very different capital structures from small firms with a turnover of £1 million. Another important factor that tends to affect the type of finance employed by a small enterprise is the industrial sector in which it operates. For example, a firm which has tangible assets such as land and buildings that can be offered as security – such as a firm in the property sector – is likely to find it easier to obtain funds than a firm in a sector whose assets are intangible in nature – such as a firm in the advertising industry whose main assets tend to be creative, reflecting the skills of the personnel employed.

This chapter begins by examining what is referred to as the 'finance gap' or, more specifically, the 'equity gap'. The importance of this gap is reflected in the significant proportion of small-business literature devoted to the subject, as well as the number of government committees that have been set up to investigate it. This is followed by a review of the main sources of finance employed by small enterprises and an examination of the relative risk, from the perspective of the providers of the finance and the owner-managers of the firms receiving the funds. Next, the capital structure of small enterprises is examined and this focuses on the critical issue of the choice of financing the firm with equity only or with both equity and debt. This section looks at some theoretical models, followed by some evidence of practice. Finally, the role of financial information is considered, with specific reference to financial reporting, and comparisons are made with the users and uses of large-company financial reports.

19.4 The finance gap

The finance gap refers to a situation where a firm has profitable opportunities but there are no (or insufficient) funds (either from internal or external sources) to exploit the opportunity. In finance theory this situation is known as 'hard capital rationing', as opposed to 'soft capital rationing' which, to a great extent, is a self-imposed restriction. Hard capital rationing occurs when there is a mismatch between the supply and demand for finance from equity and debt sources. The term 'equity gap' is also commonly used and specifically refers to the gap between funds that can be profitably employed by the firm and their inability to raise equity as opposed to debt. Clearly, if a gap in the funding of small businesses exists, it may seriously curtail the growth of such enterprises, which could adversely affect the economy. Not surprisingly, therefore, the subject has attracted much attention from government, policy-makers and academia.

Historically, the existence of a 'finance gap' was formally recognised nearly 70 years ago. In 1931 the government-sponsored Macmillan Committee reported that the financing needs of small business were not well served by the then existing financial services institutions. The committee, consisting of such eminent academics as John Maynard Keynes and politicians such as Ernest Bevin, illustrates the importance given to the subject of financing small firms by government in the 1930s. Since then this criticism of financial institutions has been echoed by other important inquiries (Bolton Report 1971; Wilson Committee 1979). In response to these criticisms successive governments have introduced a number of initiatives with varying success. For example, the Small Firms Loan Guarantee Scheme is a lending scheme for firms which have limited security to act as collateral for bank loans, and this scheme is examined in more detail later in the chapter. In recent years financial services institutions have broadened their scope and for commercial reasons have introduced new products that have made access to funds easier for smaller firms. It has been argued that if a finance gap still exists, it has been substantially narrowed because of these initiatives and subsequent responses by the market since the 1930s (Deakins 1996). However, others dispute this claim on both empirical and theoretical grounds (for example Harrison and Mason 1995). The following examines the nature of the gap and some of the evidence of whether it exists and whether it is a constraint on the financing of small enterprises.

In terms of equity capital most small firms depend on the capital the owner(s) put into the business when they started the enterprise, together with a proportion of retained profits generated from operating the business. There is a very limited opportunity for small firms to raise funds in the equity markets. The main market for small businesses to raise funds is the Alternative Investment Market (AIM), but only a very tiny proportion of small businesses in the UK are eligible for listing. In addition, there is some evidence to suggest that a large proportion of owner-managers of small firms are reluctant to seek equity finance from external sources (e.g. Binks, Ennew and Reed 1990b; Cowling, Samuels and Sugden 1991). This reluctance is primarily due to the owner-manager's desire to maintain his or her independence and control of the business. AIM will be discussed later in this chapter.

In terms of debt finance (for example, bank loans) financial institutions should assess the application for funds from small firms applying the principle of risk–return trade-off. Figure 19.1 illustrates the relationship between risk and return. Simply, the economic rationale of the principle dictates that the higher the risk, the higher the return that can be expected. With reference to Figure 19.1, point a on the graph is the base rate and the gradient from points a to b represents the increase in interest rates as the risk increases. The point X on the horizontal risk axis represents the risk associated with Firm X, X1 indicates the interest rate (the return) relating to that level of risk. In contrast, point Y on the horizontal axis indicates the risk associated with the much riskier Firm Y and point Y1 on the vertical axis the interest rate related to this higher level of risk. Risk is conventionally measured by the variability in returns of a firm; the higher the variability of returns, the higher the risk and vice versa. The variability in a firm's returns and thus risk is a function of the type of business, the structure of the industry and other similar business characteristics.

Whilst this explanation of the relationship between risk and return is blessed with sound economic logic and is widely used for assessing large firms, it suffers from one major problem when applied to small firms, since it is impossible to measure risk with any reasonable accuracy. At first sight, this is not necessarily apparent because the word 'risk' in this context is very much a part of institutional financiers' rhetoric, whether referring to large or small firms; for example, the phrase 'well, it all depends upon the risk' is commonly heard from clearing bankers when considering business loans. The inability of financial institutions to measure risk and make some assessment of the debt interest that should be charged has resulted in the use of secured lending and crude credit-scoring systems to control exposure to risk. Security is normally based on the assets of the borrower or a personal guarantee. The amount of security available is clearly a constraint on borrowing by small-business owners. Credit-scoring is a system of analysing information for making lending decisions. Points are allocated based on the characteristics of the applicant. The sum of the points is the credit score, which indicates the degree of risk (Berry, Faulkner, Hughes and Jarvis 1993a: 202). Security and credit scoring both limit the extent to which small firms can borrow and therefore contribute to the finance gap.

It would appear that a subset of small businesses who wish to grow have more acute financing problems because of their need for development finance (Buckland and Davis 1995). The Wilson Committee some 28 years ago, for example, recognised that the finance gap was a particular problem for such firms. Research shows that only around

Figure 19.1 The relationship between risk and return

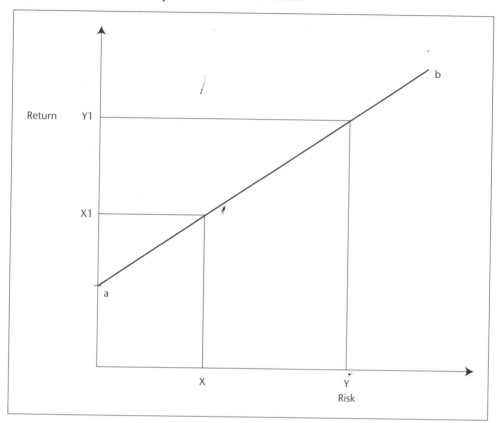

10% of firms want to grow (Hakim 1989a) and of these only approximately 10% will actually do so. However, this subset of small firms has attracted much attention (e.g. Buckland and Davis 1995) because of their significant actual or perceived contribution to the economy. A particular problem for growth firms is their lack of access to equity capital. The problem is that businesses can only increase loan capital in proportion to assets held and the equity interest prevailing. Therefore, the only way the firm can increase capital is through injections of equity capital. In recognition of the difficulties faced by small enterprises the capital markets have introduced AIM and financial institutions have developed products known as venture capital. Venture capital normally takes the form of equity in high-risk small firms. These firms are characterised by high growth and are often in the high-tech industries.

The shortage of start-up and early-stage equity capital in general, not necessarily for growth firms only, has also been cited as a particular problem for small enterprises (e.g. Robson Rhodes 1984; ACOST 1990). The problem often relates to insufficient start-up capital (the amount the owner-manager(s) initially invest(s) in the enterprise) and subsequently this affects the ability to raise loan capital.

It has been strongly argued by academics, policy-makers and owner-managers that a finance gap exists for small companies, particularly in high-growth firms, yet there is a lack of clear evidence to support this view. Although research indicates that many small enterprises which wish to grow experience difficulties in raising finance, at the same time owner-managers are often very reluctant to seek external finance and do not attempt to obtain external funding from sources other than the bank for fear of losing their independence (Keasey and Watson 1993).

Much attention in recent times has been given to informal risk capital provided by investors, known as 'business angels', as a means of providing small amounts of equity capital to close the gap. A number of initiatives have been developed to make this form of finance more accessible. However, the main problem is one of matching potential investors with the firms that need the funds. Business angels are considered in more detail in the next section.

Research into the finance gap has also highlighted an 'information gap'. It is claimed that the reason why small enterprises have problems raising finance is because owner-managers are insufficiently informed of funding opportunities with regard to both equity and loan capital, the quality and cost of information which can drive and sustain bank lending decisions (Bovaird *et al.* 1995; Binks and Ennew 1995). In recent years, however, the information flows and the advice available have improved substantially with the setting up of government agencies, such as Business Links, and the growing amount of literature on the range of sources of finance available to small firms.

It would appear that the evidence from past research on whether or not there is a finance gap is inconclusive. However, the attention of successive governments to the problems faced by small businesses with regard to raising finance has resulted in a number of initiatives which have improved matters for some owner-managers. At the same time financial institutions have developed a number of products which have increased the range of options for financing small enterprises.

19.5 Sources of finance

In this section empirical evidence is drawn upon in order to provide an overview of the nature and usage of varying types of finance employed by small businesses. Usage, it is assumed, is a reasonable surrogate for importance. As already mentioned, the results of the surveys reviewed must be interpreted with care due to the problems associated with the lack of a standard definition for what constitutes a 'small' business and other limitations of survey methods. The main sources of finance are reviewed.

19.5.1 Banks

There is considerable evidence that banks are the main source of finance for many different sizes and types of small firms. For example, the results of one survey (ESRC Centre for Business Research 1996) indicates that over 50% of small and medium-sized companies are financed by banks. Although small firms are constrained in the amount they can obtain from banks because of the security required as collateral for the loan, the survey shows a greater dependency by small firms on loan capital compared with equity capital. Latest figures from CSO (Financial Statistics – Sources of new finance for UK industrial and commercial companies) show that bank borrowing by large companies in contrast was negative. This means that large companies are depositing more with the bank than they borrow which contrasts vividly with the picture for small enterprises.

The pattern of bank lending to small firms has changed dramatically in recent years. Two-thirds of lending by the UK clearing banks is on a fixed-term basis, only a third is in the form of overdrafts. This can be contrasted with the situation in 1994 when there was an even split between overdrafts and fixed-term loans (65% of these fixed-term loans were for a period of five years or more: British Bankers Association 1997). An overdraft is a short-term loan that banks grant customers giving them the right to overdraw their bank account by an agreed amount and is normally repayable on demand.

The term of any loan should ideally be matched with the life of the investment for which the loan is required. For example, if finance is required to purchase a printing machine, the term of the loan ideally should match the commercial life of the printing machine. This ensures that monies generated from the use of the machine are available to repay the loan. The life of the assets used by business to generate funds should be for periods commensurate with long or medium-term loans which are for a fixed term. On the other hand, if finance is required to fund working capital, a short-term loan, perhaps in the form of an overdraft, is likely to be more appropriate.

Although matching the term of the loan with the life of the investment makes commercial sense, this does not always take place in practice because time is associated with uncertainty and therefore risk. The longer the time period, the greater the uncertainty and the risk associated with predicting outcomes. This notion of uncertainty due to the passing of time is therefore extremely relevant in the lending decision. The length of the loan, in terms of the period of repayment, will be strongly influenced by the other perceived risks associated with the applicant for the loan and the purpose of the loan. Therefore, in the case of the more risky (but still acceptable) applications the lending banker is likely to lend only for a short period ignoring the matching principles relating to the life of the investment and the repayment of the loan.

Smaller businesses are generally perceived as being more risky than their larger counterparts and this has tended traditionally to lead to short-term rather than long-term lending by banks. A survey of small firms by Binks, Ennew and Reed (1988) found that 25% of the fixed assets (i.e. long-term investments) were funded by overdraft rather than by fixed, longer-term forms of funding. This strategy, it is argued, was one of the major causes of the liquidity crisis when banks called in overdrafts during the credit squeeze in the early 1990s. The banks suffered considerable criticism for this policy. More recent moves towards increased fixed-term lending may be a reflection of the banks' sensitivity to these criticisms, since such a policy means that they are more exposed to risk.

The provision of finance and other services offered by the clearing banks to small firms has been subject to much criticism since the early 1970s. In 1979 the Wilson Committee concluded that bank managers tend to be overly cautious in their lending decisions, finding evidence of banks demanding a high level of security as collateral for loans which constrained the financing of small firms in the economy. More recent research (Binks *et al.* 1988; 1990a; 1993) provides evidence that banks have continued to demand high levels of security. However, some relief has come from the introduction of the Small Firms Loan Guarantee Scheme which is examined in the next section.

19.5.2 Loan Guarantee Scheme

The Loan Guarantee Scheme was introduced by the government for small firms which have a viable business proposal, but have tried and failed to obtain a conventional loan from a bank, either because of the lack of security or business track record, or both. The provision by government to guarantee against the potential default by borrowers enables banks to reduce their exposure to risk. Currently the government guarantees 85% of the loan, the other 15% being taken on by the banks. The maximum amount of the loan is currently £250,000 for a maximum term of ten years.

The scheme is intended to be in addition to normal commercial finance and is not available if a conventional loan can be obtained. Under the scheme the applicant applies initially to a bank. Once the loan officer has decided that the applicant has a viable business proposal and is eligible for a loan under the scheme, the bank applies to the Department of Trade and Industry (DTI) for a guarantee. The scheme is self-financing and a premium is charged on top of the normal interest rate to recover bad debts. The premium currently stands at 1.5% variable rate and 0.5% fixed rate lending.

The scheme was originally introduced in 1981 from a recommendation of the Wilson Committee 1979 to counter the criticism of the high levels of security required by small enterprises as collateral for a loan. Initially, there was a lower-than-expected take-up and there have been many critics of the scheme. The main criticism is that it is costly (because of the premium). In addition, banks are reluctant to use the scheme because it is excessively bureaucratic and expensive to administer (Robson Rhodes 1984). For these reasons it has been described as a scheme of last resort lending for small-business owners who have limited security. However, the scheme has been amended and has become more popular over time.

19.5.3 Leasing and hire purchase

Leasing and hire purchase (HP) are often considered together in surveys and, excluding equity, studies show that after bank loans and overdrafts, leasing and HP represents the second most important source of finance to small firms. In this section further evidence is considered with regard to the use of leasing and HP by small firms, the nature of leasing and HP and the main reasons why it is an attractive source of finance to small firms.

Leasing can be described as a form of renting. The ownership of the asset rests with the lessor who allows the lessee to rent the asset. There are two types of lease. An operating lease is a lease under which an asset is leased in the short term, for a period that is substantially shorter than the asset's useful economic life. The responsibility, in this case, for servicing and maintenance normally rests with the lessor. Typically, equipment such as photocopiers, computers and cars are acquired by firms under operating leases. Such leases are very attractive to small businesses not only because they are convenient, but because by leasing instead of buying, small firms can insure against the risk of future uncertainty as to the asset's value (for example, changes in technology) as the risk is transferred to the lessor.

A finance lease is a lease that transfers substantially all the risks and rewards of ownership to the lessee (Hussey 1995). It is a contractual commitment to make a series of payments for the use of an asset over the majority of the asset's life which normally cannot be cancelled. The lessee therefore acquires most of the economic value of the ownership although the lessor retains the title. Finance leases are long-term and are very similar, apart from the question of ownership, to purchasing an asset with a bank loan.

HP is a method of buying goods in which the purchaser takes possession of them as soon as an initial instalment of the price (known as the deposit) has been paid. Ownership of the goods passes to the purchaser when all the agreed number of subsequent instalments, which include an interest charge, have been made. The purchaser has the use of the goods over the period that he or she is making the payments and, as with leasing, benefits from being able to use the asset without incurring a large capital outlay. It is because of this similarity that HP and leasing are often grouped together when considering the sources of finance of firms, as in the studies discussed next.

A survey of 90 small businesses (Berry, Jarvis, Lipman and Macallan 1990) found that 70% had some assets financed by leasing or HP with 12% of the total value of assets leased and 65% acquired via HP. Of 238 different assets acquired by the sample businesses, 45% were financed by leasing or HP. The sample comprised firms in printing, computer services and professional services and some significant variation was found in the relative importance of leasing compared with HP. In the printing industry only 9% of the total value of the assets were leased, whilst 77% were acquired using HP. The main reason for this difference was because the assets acquired (in this case printing machines) tend to appreciate in value and there was a very active second-hand market for them. Therefore, printers preferred to use HP as a source of finance since the ownership of the asset eventually transferred to them. If firms in the printing industry are excluded from the analysis because of this particular preference for HP, the percentage of the value of the assets leased by the remaining sample would be just above 20%.

The study demonstrated that the use made of leasing and HP was related to certain characteristics of both the business and the asset. The larger the size of the firm, the more likely it was to use both leasing and HP. The firm's past experience of various sources of finance in negative or positive terms was also found to affect the firm's future preference for a particular source of finance. Of the sample firms, 21% expressed negative attitudes towards leasing whilst only 4% of the sample responded negatively to HP. The type of asset was found to influence the type of finance used; for example, assets such as photocopiers and cars have traditionally been marketed via leasing. Finally, the study found that the number of firms using leasing appears to increase with the upward growth rate of the firm, although the number using HP does not.

Previous research, which was mainly focused on large firms, indicates that the influence of tax is the most significant factor influencing the decision to lease. This relates to tax benefits via capital allowances which are obtainable when using finance leases as opposed to operating leases (for example, Drury and Braund 1990). A study by Jarvis, Lipman, Macallan and Berry (1994) gathered the views of owner-managers of small firms on the perceived advantages of leasing. The findings showed that tax was not important in the leasing decision and suggested that few owner-managers could undertake the complex tax computations necessary to establish the cost of leasing compared to other forms of finance. The main advantages to owner-managers of leasing were that it avoids a large capital outlay; it is cheaper; it helps cash flow; and it is easier to arrange.

19.5.4 Equity

The term 'equity' is used here to mean the finance contributed by the owner(s) of the enterprise. This definition ignores whether the enterprise is a company, a partnership or a sole trader. Although funds from business angels and venture capital could be included within this definition, these forms of finance are considered in detail separately. Individuals starting a business normally need to invest a certain amount of their own money in the business, whether they are a sole trader, partnership or a company. After the start-up owners can choose whether to withdraw profits from the business or to re-invest these funds. Funds retained in the business are another form of equity finance, which together with start-up funds are often referred to as 'internal equity'. Finally, during the life of the business, owners may make further investments from their own personal funds to finance the business.

The amount of equity invested by the owners in the business depends on a number of factors, the most influential of which are the owners' wealth and the profitability of the business's activities. From a survey of small firms, Keasey and Watson (1992) estimated that internal equity contributed approximately 30% of the capital structure. This suggests that the amount of equity contributed to the business after start-up from owners, and funds derived from the retention of profits, is relatively low compared to other sources of finance. A more recent survey (ESRC Centre for Business Research 1996) estimated that only 6% comes from this source. The Keasey and Watson study also found that approximately 70% of operating income is withdrawn by the owners of small firms, leaving a relatively small residue to re-invest. This evidence has attracted the attention of policy-makers to the need to develop strategies to encourage owner-managers, through tax incentives, to retain a greater proportion of profits in the business.

Access to sources of equity other than that contributed by the original owners (external equity) is limited to formal venture capital and informal venture capital (business angels), and raising finance from the Alternative Investment Market (AIM). All of these sources will be discussed separately. However, it should be borne in mind that, as already mentioned, the overriding evidence is that many owner-managers resist any form of external involvement and therefore do not seek external equity sources.

The extent of a small firm's overall funding generally depends on the owner-manager's wealth and the equity in the business. Other forms of finance, such as bank lending, normally depend on the security provided by the business. Such collateral usually takes the form of a charge on the firm's assets or on the personal assets of the owner-manager, or a combination of the two. The limitations of equity sources of small firms therefore constrain the assets acquired by the business and the wealth of the owner-manager further limits his or her ability to raise finance elsewhere. Binks *et al.* (1990b) argue that this reliance on collateral effectively creates a 'debt gap'.

19.5.5 The Alternative Investment Market (AIM)

When AIM was established in 1995, Michael Heseltine (then President of the Board of Trade in the UK) said: 'smaller and growing firms are critical to Britain's long-term economic prosperity and a market which will enable them to raise capital for investment and have their shares more widely traded can only help to strengthen this sector of the economy'. The support of the government was an important factor in the initial success of the market, but perhaps more important was the timing of its launch in the middle of a bull market when investors had been lured by easy profits to be made from the sensational share price gains. For example, the shares of ViewInn were placed at 100p and in June 1996 were traded at 650p.

In the first 12 months of its existence, 162 companies obtained a listing on AIM and by 1998 the number had grown to more than 260. This high volume of companies joining AIM in its short life-time provides strong evidence of the need for an alternative market for small companies. However, during 1998 a series of companies crashed shortly after they were listed on AIM and this has made companies wishing to join the market a little cautious. Generally, prospective companies considering joining, in particular computer and high-tech companies, are looking for a higher profile and a wider source of funds. A survey by a firm of accountants (Kidson Impey 1998) found that potential users of AIM felt that the market is less accessible than a year ago and argue that this is attributable to the increase in due diligence required by nominated advisers as a result of well-publicised failures.

Conditions for listing on AIM are that companies must have a nominated adviser, broker and reporting accountant in order to give investors some degree of reassurance about the quality of the company. Once listed, the company must appoint, and retain at all times, a nominated adviser and nominated broker. The nominated adviser is selected by the corporation from a register of firms approved by the Stock Exchange. The adviser and broker are required to ensure that the company has complied with the listing rules for AIM. The reporting accountant is required to ensure that the company complies with the rules regarding the publication of price-sensitive information and the quality of the interim and annual reports. A prospectus must be produced, but not necessarily a trading record.

A listing currently costs between £200,000 and £400,000, plus around 3% funds raised. The annual cost of listing is at least £25,000. It is generally claimed that AIM is suitable for companies wishing to raise between £1m and £50m. Therefore, only the larger small companies tend to be listed. At this stage in its life, it would appear that AIM makes very little contribution to the overall funding of small enterprises in the UK since the 260 companies currently listed represent a mere 0.025% of the total number of companies filing accounts.

19.5.6 Venture capital

Venture capital is finance provided to unlisted companies by specialist financial institutions. Venture capitalists tend to be very selective, concentrating on fairly risky investments typically in the form of backing for entrepreneurs, financing a start-up, or developing business, or assisting management buy-outs (MBO) and management buy-ins (MBI). Usually the venture capital is represented by a mixture of equity, loans and 'mezzanine finance'. Mezzanine finance is finance that is usually provided by specialist institutions and is neither pure equity nor pure debt. It can take many different forms and can be secured or unsecured. It usually earns a higher rate of return than pure debt but less than equity, yet carries higher risk than debt although less than equity. It is often used in the financing of MBOs (Hussey 1995). It is used for medium-term to long-term investments where the venture capitalist is looking eventually for an exit route.

Although much has been written about venture capital as a major source of funds for small enterprises, the evidence is that the majority of firms that receive funds from this source are relatively large enterprises. The average investment of a venture capitalist is £1 million to £2 million and the smallest investment £100,000. A large and an increasing proportion of capital has been invested in MBOs. Although Murray (1995) contends that venture capital 'represents a small but important part of the finance for new firm formation and industrial restructuring in both the UK and continental Europe', earlier in the same paper Murray graphically shows start-ups and other early-stage finance as representing 6% in terms of percentage allocation of UK venture capital investments as opposed to MBO/MBI investments of over 50% in 1991. Arnold (1998) claims that 75% of venture capital in 1995 went into MBO/MBI investments, with only 4% being placed in early-stage companies. The ESRC (1996) survey shows that between 1% and 2% of small firms used venture capital to finance their business. There has, however, been a slow recognition in the more popular texts and journals that venture capital plays very little part in the financing of small enterprises!

19.5.7 Informal venture capital (business angels)

Business angels are a source of informal venture capital and are wealthy individuals, rather than financial institutions, who tend to have considerable business experience and are willing to invest in start-ups, early-stage or expanding enterprises. Another description of business angels, or more precisely informal venture capitalists, that focuses on the nature of the capital, is: equity or near-equity risk finance invested by private individuals directly into businesses which are not listed on a stock exchange (Gaston 1989). The term 'informal' venture capital derives from the fact that it is individuals rather than financial institutions who invest venture capital in a more controlled environment. Although informal venture capital is well developed in the USA, and has also been a significant form of finance in the UK, it has only been in the last ten years that this source of finance has attracted that much attention from academics and policy-makers (Mason and Harrison 1992).

It has been argued (Harrison and Mason 1995) that the use of informal venture capital provides an appropriate resolution for the new small-business equity gap because it lowers the information and monitoring costs that are incurred in borrowing from external sources and there is less likelihood of owner-equity value dilution. Loans and other forms of finance from external sources normally involve the preparation of detailed credit reviews and the collection of information for formal reviews and monitoring of the progress of the enterprise. However, informal venture capitalists normally have prior knowledge of the industry – which is a crucial factor in their investment decision – and of the business and its owner(s). Information is also disclosed to private informal investors on a more informal and informative basis.

Harrison and Mason claim informal venture capitalists are more patient than venture capitalists and are willing to invest smaller amounts of capital in line with the needs of the owner-managers of small firms. Business angels tend not to look for quick exit routes and typically invest sums up to £10,000. Only a small proportion invest more than £50,000. Very few business angels have high incomes or are millionaires. They tend to have average income of less than £50,000 p.a. and their worth, excluding their own residence, rarely exceeds £100,000. Business angels sometimes join together to become investment syndicates and, in such cases, the sums invested can be relatively large.

The major problem associated with informal venture capital is that of matching investors with smaller firms seeking finance. The main way in which firms and business angels find one another is through friends, family and business connections. In recognition of the importance of this source of income, formal networks have been set up to aid this matching; for example, most Business Links and TECs maintain databases of interested parties. However, it would appear that only a small proportion of proposals are attractive to business angels since between 90% and 97% of proposals are rejected.

The extent to which business angels contribute to the pool of finance available to small enterprises is extremely difficult to determine. There does appear to be an acknowledgement, however, that informal venture capital contributes considerably more funds to financing small enterprises than venture capital does. A recent survey estimated that in 1996 4% of funds for a sample of small firms was derived from business angels (ESRC 1996). Therefore, business angels play an important role in the financing of small enterprises, but not significantly enough to claim that this source of funds will resolve the finance gap.

19.5.8 Factoring

Factoring is the purchase by a factor of the trade debts of a business, usually for immediate cash. The sales accounting functions are then provided by the factor who will manage the sales ledger and collection accounts, under terms agreed by the seller. The factor may agree to take the credit risk within limits or this risk may be retained by the seller. This source of finance is to a certain extent dependent upon the nature of the business (i.e. where the business has reasonably high debtor's balance). In the right circumstances factoring can provide a significant source of finance on a continuing basis to firms.

An interesting paper published by the Policy Unit of the Institute of Directors in 1993, that examined the late payment of debt, convincingly argued that the 'majority of overdue debts could be reduced by better credit management'. Good credit management itself is, of course, a source of finance. Research shows that small firms in particular suffer from late payment and tend to have weak credit management (Wilson *et al.* 1995). Factors employ specialist credit controllers and tend to use state-of-the-art computer software which enables them to manage efficiently the credit given to the customers of small firms. The effectiveness of factors in credit management is demonstrated by figures published by the Factoring and Discounters Association (FDA) in 1995: the average waiting period for payment was 75 days as compared with the factoring industry's own average of 58 days. Over the last several years factoring has increased in popularity. Turnover in the factoring industry rose from £4.4 million in 1984 to £47.2 million in 1997. Ignoring currency fluctuations this still represents a significant increase. However, it would appear that only 8% of small and medium-sized firms in the UK currently use factoring (Grant Thornton 1998: 31). A survey of the perceptions of accountants (Berry and Simpson 1993) identified three main reasons why small and medium-sized enterprises do not use factoring: the high cost, reduced customer relations and the issue of confidentiality. There is, however, very little independent evidence on the perceptions of owner-managers of small enterprises since much of the literature in this area tends to be anecdotal and speculative.

19.6 The capital structure decision

Finance theory assumes that the firm is a vehicle for shareholders to maximise their wealth and ignores other stakeholders. Much of the finance literature also assumes there is a separation of ownership and control by directors/managers. Therefore, it is not surprising that the main question when deciding how the firm should be financed is whether there is an optimal capital structure that will maximise the value of the firm and hence shareholders' wealth.

Traditionally, the starting-point for examining the capital structure decision is the seminal paper by Modigliani and Miller (1958). Modigliani and Miller demonstrated that, assuming a perfect capital market with no information costs, the value of the firm is independent of its capital structure. Thus there is no optimal capital structure, the financing decision is irrelevant and the value of the firm is solely dependent upon the firm's ability to generate profits (cash flows) from operations. Their assumptions importantly include a world with no taxes. Since this paper a number of researchers have examined the effect on the capital structure decision of the relaxing of one or more of the market imperfections which Modigliani and Miller in their 1958 paper assumed did not exist (e.g. Ross 1977; Myers 1984). Perhaps the most influential research which allowed for one of these market imperfections was in a paper by Modigliani and Miller themselves in 1963 which considered the effect of corporate and personal taxes on the capital structure decision. Modigliani and Miller in this later paper demonstrate that when other things are held constant, firms with high tax rates should use more debt than firms with low rates, because the value of debt financing is tax deductibility *vis-à-vis* equity, and the value of this benefit increases with the tax rate. Therefore, financing the firm using debt rather than equity implies that firms should obtain as much debt finance as possible. Clearly this does not happen in practice, primarily because of the countering effects of other market imperfections such as bankruptcy. However, this is not to say that this tax effect is not influential to some extent in the overall capital structure decision.

Despite these developments in finance theory it does not yet fully explain the different capital structures that firms adopt in practice nor do we know how firms choose the debt, equity or hybrid securities they issue (Myers 1984). Nevertheless, from a careful inspection of real-world market imperfections we get a good idea of the factors that will affect the capital structure decision (Higson 1993). However, large firms have also been the main focus of the research on capital structure decision (Michaelas *et al.* 1996) and thus the literature is less well developed and restricted to a few papers (Keasey and Watson 1993).

Small firms, of course, are subject to very different financial economic and socio-economic structures as compared to large firms. For example, as previously mentioned, there tends not to be a separation between ownership and control of firms, and large firms are listed and quoted on markets. These are two significant characteristics of small firms that are likely to influence the capital structure decision. Therefore, capital structure decision theory related to large firms has very limited applicability to small firms.

Norton (1990; 1991a and 1991b) is one of a few researchers to have examined the capital structure decision from the perspective of small firms. In examining a number of market imperfections which it is claimed are influential in the capital structure decision of large firms, Norton argues that bankruptcy costs, agency costs and information asymmetries seem to have very little effect on small firms' capital structure decisions. He also highlights the importance of certain factors relating to the market the firm operates in, and the preferences and desires of the owner(s). Small firms, Norton concludes, are less likely to have target debt ratios and there is a preference for using internal finance rather than external finance.

Michaelas, Chittenden and Poutziouris (1996) conducted a study of the financial and non-financial factors that determine the capital structure of small privately owned firms. Their findings show that the life-cycles of small firms are influential in determining their capital structure. When firms start up, and as they grow, they use debt finance. However, as they mature the reliance on debt declines. A positive relationship was found between gearing and the collateral value of the assets and this emphasises the importance of security in the bank lending decision. The research also found that tax and bankruptcy costs were not influential in the decision and no relationship was found between gearing levels and profitability, growth, risk and the level of debtors. Firms in different industrial sectors seem to differ in their capital structure preferences and it was found that economic conditions also had a bearing on the capital structure decision.

There are clearly a number of missing pieces to Myers' puzzle but research to date from a small-firm perspective does highlight that financial theory related to large firms, and particularly that related to the theory of the capital structure decision, is not necessarily appropriate to smaller enterprises.

19.7 Financial reporting considerations

An important link between the sources of finance for a business, particularly for small firms, is the financial reports produced periodically by firms which primarily give an account of the performance for a stated period – normally a year (the profit and loss account) – and the financial position of the business on a stated date (the balance sheet). The evidence is that this information is required by the providers (creditors) of finance in their assessing of the applicant firm requesting the finance (A. Berry *et al.* 1993a). Also there is evidence that some creditors such as banks require financial reports to monitor the progress of the business to which they have provided finance (A. Berry *et al.* 1993b).

Sole traders and partnerships are not required by statute to disclose such information, but may do so in order to satisfy the needs of creditors. In contrast, companies are required by statute to file annual accounts (whether or not they are seeking external finance) with the Registrar of Companies and give copies to their shareholders. However, it is the legal requirements and accounting regulations that influence and drive the form and nature of the annual accounts produced by small enterprises that are outside the scope of these requirements. In the main the legal and regulatory requirements have been designed for large quoted companies where there is a separation of ownership and management. The primary concern of the regulations is one of stewardship; that is, the annual financial report forms an integral information liaison between the managers (directors) of the company, who run the operations of the business, and the owners (shareholders) of the business. There are currently just over 2,000 of these large quoted companies out of a total of over 1 million companies who file annual accounts. Of these companies 995 are small. Therefore, the way in which these small companies report, as with other small businesses that follow similar reporting regimes, has very little to do with their needs. Consequently, it may be the case that the financial reports for small businesses would look very different if they considered what they are used for and who uses them.

Generally, there is very limited knowledge of the use of these small-business annual reports and their users. The main published work that does exist relates to small and medium-sized companies. In a recent review of the literature (Jarvis 1996) on the use of financial reports and their users, banks were identified as a major user (for example, A. Berry *et al.* 1987; 1993b; Deakins and Hussain 1994b). Within the bank lending process, it is recognised that financial reports play a significant role (A. Berry *et al.* 1993b). In fact, the 'excessive' use of financial reports and other financial information in this process has been heavily criticised by some; for example, Deakins and Hussain (1994b) argue: 'we find that there is an excessive reliance on financial information such as forecast balance sheets and profit and loss accounts and standard financial ratios'.

The findings of research into bankers' use of financial reports recognise that the use of financial information is dependent upon a number of contingent variables (R. Berry *et al.* 1993). An influential factor in the use of financial information is whether or not the applicant is currently a customer with the bank and whether the business in question is new or existing (A. Berry *et al.* 1993b). For example, if the application is from an owner-manager of a new business no financial reports would be available. There is also evidence that this user group can obtain additional information in support of figures in financial statements – for example, management accounting information and valuation reports commissioned by the business. Banks are able to successfully demand this information because they are in a relatively powerful position within the relationship.

In the literature review identified earlier (Jarvis 1996) a study by Mitchell *et al.* (1995) was identified that examined venture capitalists' use of financial reports in investment decisions. The financial statement was seen as an important source of information in the process of making decisions.

Recent research (Dugdale *et al.* 1998) provides evidence of owner-managers' use of financial reports. It is clear that managers recognise the importance of financial statements to creditors of the enterprise. In that context it is likely that they, the owner-managers, will monitor the reports to ensure that everything looks all right in respect of creditors, otherwise this may cause concern (Jarvis 1996).

Although there is no further evidence of other creditors' (for example, business angels') use of financial reports it is generally assumed that these investors into small companies are significant users of financial reports of small and medium-sized companies, although they may not necessarily reflect the needs, as previously mentioned, of users of the reports.

19.8 Chapter summary

This chapter examined the types and sources of finance used by small firms and three important related issues: the finance gap, the capital structure decision and financial reporting. Small firms use different types of finance as compared with large firms. Large firms have established markets where they can publicly raise funds. There are no similar markets for the majority of small firms. The proportion of equity invested in small firms tends to be less and there is more reliance on bank lending. Over the years the question as to whether a finance gap exists has been debated. Although the finance gap is never likely to completely disappear, through the introduction of government initiatives and new products by financial institutions it has become much less of a constraint for the majority of firms.

Finance theory relating to the capital structure decision was found not to be wholly applicable to small firms. A significant influential variable is the life-cycle of small firms. When firms start up and as they grow they tend to rely on debt, but when the firm matures this reliance on debt declines. The amount of security available, however, restricts the extent to which the firm can obtain debt financing. The concept of stewardship (reporting to the owners of the business on the performance of the firm's management) is irrelevant in the reporting of the financial affairs of small businesses. However, financial reports are an important source of information for financial institutions in making credit decisions and monitoring the client's progress. Therefore, it is clear that from a number of perspectives, the financing of small businesses differs significantly from the way in which large firms are financed.

Questions

1 Are small enterprises constrained in their operations by lack of finance?

2 Why do large companies use different types of finance as compared to small firms?

3 From a financial perspective compare businesses where there is a separation between the owners and the managers, and where the owner is also the manager.

4 What are the influential variables in the capital structure decision of businesses? Do they differ if the business is small or large?

CHAPTER 20

Marketing and the small firm

David Stokes

20.1 Learning objectives

There are four learning objectives in this chapter:

1 To understand the importance of marketing to small firms and their owners.
2 To appreciate the typical marketing problems which small firms face.
3 To gain insight into how entrepreneurs and owner-managers interpret the marketing function.
4 To understand the characteristics of entrepreneurial marketing and the processes and methods which are typical of its implementation.

Key concepts

■ entrepreneurial marketing   ■ marketing competencies   ■ networking

20.2 Introduction

This chapter considers the role that marketing plays in the fortunes of small businesses and their owners. Although marketing is a key factor in their survival and development, small firms share a number of characteristics, which cause marketing problems. These include a restricted customer base, limited marketing expertise and impact, variable, unplanned effort and over-reliance on the owner-manager's marketing competency. However, entrepreneurs and small-business owners interpret marketing in ways that do not conform to standard textbook theory and practice. They tend to be 'innovation-orientated' rather than customer-orientated. They target markets through 'bottom-up' self-selection and recommendations of customers. They shy away from formalised research, relying more on informal networking. They prefer interactive marketing methods to the mass communications strategies of larger companies. It is more useful to summarise 'entrepreneurial marketing' using 'Is' rather than the 'Ps' of existing marketing models. As a strategic process it involves innovation, identification of target markets, informal information-gathering and interactive marketing methods – methods which can be summarised as a marketing mix of influence (word-of-mouth communications), image-building, incentives and involvement ('four + four Is' rather than 'four Ps').

20.3 Marketing and the small firm

There has been a tendency amongst both marketing theorists and small-business owners to associate marketing with large, rather than small organisations. Marketing theory was developed from studies of large corporations, and most textbooks (e.g. Kotler 1997) still reflect these origins in the concepts and case studies which they present. Even owner-managers of small firms seem to give marketing a low priority compared to the other functions of their business, often regarding marketing as 'something that larger firms do' (Stokes *et al.* 1997).

Yet there is considerable evidence that marketing is crucial to the survival and development of small firms. Research findings are summarised below which indicate that marketing is particularly important to smaller organisations because it represents (i) a vital interface between a small firm and an uncertain, fast-changing external environment, and (ii) a key internal management skill which differentiates between surviving and failing firms.

20.3.1 Marketing as the interface between a small firm and the external environment

A key feature that distinguishes small from large firms is the much higher closure rates of small firms (Storey 1994). Businesses are at their most vulnerable when they are very young and very small. Only a small percentage stay in business in the long term; over two-thirds close in the decade in which they opened. Businesses exist in fast-changing environments, and the youngest and smallest are particularly exposed in this unpredictable world (Hall 1995). Their lack of market power and dependency on a relatively small customer base make their environments more uncontrollable and more uncertain than those of larger organisations (Wynarczyk *et al.* 1993).

How can small firms best cope in this hostile business environment? Marketing is certainly important in the early, vulnerable years, because it provides a vital interface between the organisation and its external environment. Research involving case studies of surviving and non-surviving small manufacturing firms by Smallbone, North and Leigh (1992) indicated that *adjustment* is the key. The most important adjustment for both survival and growth was active market development – a continuous search for new market opportunities and a broadening of the customer base of the business. Those firms that are most active in making adjustments in what they do, and how they do it, particularly in relation to the marketplace, seem to have a greater chance of survival than those who carry on as before. As the function that supplies the necessary information and direction to guide such adjustments, marketing provides a key interface between a small business and its external environment.

20.3.2 Marketing management and small-firm survival

It is not surprising therefore that research has identified marketing management as a key internal function which influences survival. The judgement of individual investors in small business, or so-called 'business angels', is interesting in that it indicates what they have discovered to be critical factors which make a venture more likely to succeed or fail (see Chapter 19). According to Harris (1993) the principal reasons given by business angels for not investing are:

- lack of relevant experience of entrepreneur and any associates;
- deficiencies in marketing;
- flawed, incomplete or unrealistic financial projections.

Cromie (1990) interviewed 35 manufacturing and 33 service firms which had been trading for four to five years, asking each of them open-ended questions on the major problems they had encountered and the mistakes they had made. His overall conclusion was that 'Small, young organisations experience problems particularly in the areas of accounting and finance, marketing, and the management of people' (Cromie 1990: 58–9).

There is some consensus in this literature on why firms close which indicates the centrality of what has been referred to as the 'three Ms' of 'Marketing, Money and Management of people' (Stokes 1998). Marketing represents a key management discipline, which differentiates between survival and failure of small firms.

20.4 Characteristics of small firms and marketing problems

However, small organisations tend to suffer from a number of distinctive marketing problems. Certain characteristics which differentiate small from large organisations lead to marketing issues, which are especially challenging for small-business owner-managers.

20.4.1 Limited customer base

A number of studies have shown a relationship between size of firm and number of customers, with a high percentage of small businesses dependent on less than 10 customers, and some on only one buyer (Storey 1982; Hall 1995). As well as depending on a small number of customers, small businesses tend to trade only in a limited geographical area (Curran and Blackburn 1990). This ties their fortunes closely to the cycles of the local economy, with limited opportunities to compensate for any downturn.

20.4.2 Limited activity

Lack of access to financial and human resources restricts marketing in small firms. A small enterprise has less to spend on marketing as a percentage of income because of the impact of fixed costs which take up a higher proportion of revenues; financial constraints also restrict their ability to employ marketing specialists (Weinrauch *et al.* 1991). Carson (1985) concluded that the marketing constraints on small firms took the form of restricted resources, lack of specialist expertise and limited impact.

20.4.3 Lack of formalised planning and evolutionary marketing

As we have already discussed, small firms have to cope with an ever-changing environment, meaning they have to continually adapt and adjust as a business to survive (see Chapter 16). It would seem that those firms which do survive adjust to the new conditions in a continual process of evolution (Smallbone *et al.* 1992). The marketing implication is that short-term considerations take priority over longer-term planning. Research has confirmed that planning is a problem for small-firm management, which tends to be reactive in style (Fuller 1994). Cromie (1990) characterised this as an operational as opposed to a strategic orientation. However, just as the firm must evolve to survive, so marketing evolves to reflect the owner-manager experience and the needs of the firm. Carson (1985) has suggested four stages in the evolution of marketing in small firms:

- initial marketing activity in the set-up stages;
- reactive selling as demand grows;
- a DIY marketing approach under the direction of the owner-manager as the firm realises the need for a more positive marketing stance; and finally
- integrated, proactive marketing as the firm adopts longer-term marketing strategies usually involving the recruitment of specialist marketing management.

20.4.4 Innovation, niches and gaps

Small firms today are often seen as playing a key role in the innovation of new products and processes because of their flexibility and willingness to try new approaches. However, innovation is neither a unique nor a universal characteristic of small firms: large organisations are also important innovators and not all small firms can be considered innovative. Nevertheless, innovation is an important characteristic of small firms in certain industry sectors (Rothwell 1986). Niches or market focus can help small firms overcome their inherently lower profitability compared to larger firms. But the marketing problem which arises for smaller firms is not only how to develop innovative products and services, but also how to defend their competitive advantage and exploit innovations to the full with limited resources. Cannon (1992) saw this as an important weakness of small firms because of their lack of access to the resources to realise fully the potential of the gaps in the market they identify. He warned of what he called 'poisoned apple marketing' in which it is not unusual for large firms to wait for smaller enterprises to open up markets and make the mistakes before they use their resource base to capitalise on the opportunity (Cannon 1992: 473). Exploiting niche markets to the full can be as big an issue as developing them in the first place.

20.4.5 The owner-manager's marketing competency

Scholhammer and Kuriloff (1979) recognised a personalised management style as a distinguishing feature of small enterprises. This is typified as personal knowledge of all employees, involvement in all aspects of management and lack of sharing of key decisions. The dominant influence of the owner-manager has led to a large literature which seeks to establish relationships between the psychology, type and background of owners and the performance of their firms (Chell *et al.* 1991). If the personal characteristics of the owner-manager are the dominant internal management influence, then the marketing management of a small enterprise will be much affected by the marketing

Figure 20.1 Small organisations: characteristics and marketing issues

Small-organisation characteristics	Marketing issues
■ Relatively small in given sector	■ Limited customer base
■ Resource constraints	■ Limited activity, expertise and impact
■ Uncertainty	■ Little formalised planning; intuitive, reactive marketing
■ Evolutionary	■ Variable marketing effort
■ Innovation	■ Developing and defending niches
■ Personalised management style	■ Dependent on owners' marketing competency

competency of the owner. Carson *et al.* (1995) describe entrepreneurial marketing in terms of the experience, knowledge, communication abilities and judgement of the owner-manager – key competencies on which marketing effectiveness depends. As the competency of SME owners varies widely in these areas, so does the marketing performance of their firms (Carson *et al.* 1995: 12–13). These characteristics of small organisations, and the marketing issues and problems which typically arise, are summarised in Figure 20.1.

20.5 Is marketing different in small organisations?

Advisers, educators and policy-makers attempting to overcome these marketing problems have met with little success. Curran and Blackburn (1990) concluded that small-business owners are not 'joiners', with only a minority having contact with Training and Enterprise Councils and Business Links, and they often reject approaches from advisers and consultants because of a 'fortress enterprise' mentality. But there is also a danger that notions of best practice amongst larger firms are automatically assumed to be appropriate for small businesses, providing they can be given the resources to adopt them. For example, there is evidence that SMEs implement the concept of market orientation less fully than larger companies (Brooksbank *et al.* 1992; Liu 1995). However, there is little to suggest that traditional marketing concepts such as this are relevant to smaller firms.

20.5.1 Marketing defined

One of the problems in investigating small-business marketing is the lack of clarity over what 'marketing' actually means in any context. Even marketing in larger firms is not clearly defined; for example, Crosier (1975) compiled a list of fifty different definitions of marketing in the literature, an indication of the difficulties marketers have had in defining their own discipline. In order to investigate and describe marketing in smaller organisations we will adopt Webster's (1992) classification of marketing into three distinct elements: as an organisational philosophy or culture, as a strategic process, and as a series of tactical functions or methods.

Marketing as an organisational philosophy

This relates to a set of values and beliefs concerning the central importance of the customer to the success of the organisation. This has been refined as the concept of market or customer orientation, which requires that an understanding of customer needs should precede and inform the development and marketing of products and services (Kotler 1997). Most definitions of marketing relate mainly to this level of meaning; for example, the definition of the (UK) Institute of Marketing states that marketing is 'the management process responsible for identifying, anticipating and satisfying customer requirements profitably'.

Marketing as a strategy

This defines how an organisation is to compete and survive in the marketplace. Most marketing textbooks (e.g. Kotler 1997) review marketing strategy through the stages of market segmentation, targeting and positioning. This involves, firstly, research and analysis of the marketplace in order to divide it into meaningful groups or segments of buyer-types. Secondly, one or more segments are chosen as the most appropriate targets for marketing activities. Thirdly, an appeal is made to this target group through an appropriately positioned product or service.

Marketing tactics

These use specific activities and techniques, such as market research, product development and advertising, to implement the strategy. These are referred to as elements in the 'marketing mix', commonly summarised as the four 'Ps' of product, pricing, promotion and place.

20.5.2 Marketing defined by small-business owners

Entrepreneurs and owner-managers of small businesses tend not to see marketing this way. They define marketing in terms of tactics to attract new business – in other words, at the third level of meaning in the definitions above. They are less aware of the other, philosophical and strategic meanings of the term. Research by Kingston University's Small Business Research Centre (Stokes *et al.* 1997) indicated that most small-business owners equated marketing with selling and promoting only. Unprompted definitions of marketing focused on customer acquisition and promotions whilst identifying customer needs, and other non-promotional aspects of marketing, such as product development, pricing and distribution, were largely ignored. Many owners suggested that their business was reliant on word-of-mouth recommendations and therefore 'they did not have to do any marketing'.

This does not necessarily mean that they overlooked other aspects of marketing, only that they were unaware of the terminology. The business owners' narrow view of marketing was not borne out by what they actually did. Their activities indicated a strategic marketing awareness, particularly in areas such as monitoring the marketplace, targeting individual market segments and emphasising customer service and relationships. When asked to rank their most important marketing activities, recommendations from customers came first in all sectors and sizes of small firms. However, this reliance on recommendations was not necessarily an indication of minimal marketing effort, as such recommendations were often hard won. To an outside observer, it is all too easy to accept the owner-manager's comment that they 'do not have the time or resources for marketing', when those same owners do indeed devote much of their time to building relationships with satisfied customers who then recommend the business to others. In other words, they spend considerable time and resources on marketing, but they call it by another name.

20.6 Entrepreneurial interpretations of marketing

Marketing in small firms is not the simplistic, promotional activity that it appears at first sight. Nor is it marketing according to the textbook. If we examine each of the three elements in the definitions of marketing as described earlier, we discover distinct variations between what successful small-business owners actually do and what marketing theory would have them do.

20.6.1 Customer orientation versus 'innovation orientation'

Marketing as an organisational philosophy indicates that an assessment of market needs comes before new product development. Entrepreneurial business owners frequently do it the other way round. They start with an idea, and then try to find a market for it. Creativity and innovation in product or service development are the hallmarks of successful entrepreneurship (Drucker 1985), not careful research into customer needs. Well-known entrepreneurs such as Roddick and Branson did not found their early businesses on market analysis, but on an intuitive feel for what was required. Innovation is a key entrepreneurial activity, which takes new ideas and turns them into useful products or services which customers need (Adair 1990). But often this is achieved through a zeal for the development of new concepts and ideas – an 'innovation orientation' – rather than through a dedication to the principles of customer orientation.

20.6.2 'Top-down' versus 'bottom-up' strategies

Marketing as a strategy involves the processes of segmentation, targeting and positioning, so that products and services are focused on appropriate buyer groups. Entrepreneurial owner-managers identify closely with a specific group of customers whose needs are well known to them, in accordance with these theories of strategic marketing. However, most marketing textbooks advocate a 'top-down' approach to the market in which the strategy process develops in the following order:

- the profiles of market segments are developed first using demographic, psychological and other buyer-behaviour variables;
- an evaluation of the attractiveness of each segment concludes with the selection of the target segment;
- finally, the selection and communication of a market position differentiates the product or service from competitive offerings.

This process implies that an organisation is able to take an objective overview of the markets it serves before selecting those on which it wishes to concentrate. This usually involves both secondary and primary market research with evaluation by specialists in each of the three stages.

Although successful entrepreneurs do seem adept at carefully targeting certain customers, the processes they use in order to achieve this do not seem to conform to the three stages described above. Evidence suggests that successful, smaller firms practise a 'bottom-up' targeting process in which the organisation begins by serving the needs of a few customers and then expands the base gradually as experience and resources allow. Research into 'niche marketing' approaches indicates that targeting is achieved by attracting an initial customer base and then looking for more of the same (Dalgic and Leeuw 1994). The stages of entrepreneurial targeting are:

- **Identification of market opportunities.** Matching innovative ideas to the resources of a small enterprise identifies possible opportunities. These opportunities are tested through trial and error in the marketplace, based on the entrepreneur's intuitive expectations which are sometimes, but not often, backed up by more formal research.

- **Attraction of an initial customer base.** Certain customers, who may or may not conform to the profile anticipated by the entrepreneur, are attracted to the service or product. However, as the entrepreneur is in regular contact with these customers, he or she gets to know their preferences and needs.

- **Expansion through more of the same.** The entrepreneur expands the initial customer base by looking for more customers of the same profile. In many cases, this is not a deliberate process as it is left to the initial customers who recommend the business to others with similar needs to their own. A target customer group emerges and grows, but more through a process of self-selection and some encouragement from the entrepreneur, rather than through formal research and proactive marketing.

This bottom-up process has advantages over the top-down approach. It requires fewer resources and is more flexible and adaptable to implement – attributes which play to small-business strengths. It has corresponding disadvantages. It is less certain of success and takes longer to penetrate the market to full potential – weaknesses which characterise many small firms.

20.6.3 Four Ps versus one-to-one marketing tactics

Marketing strategies are implemented through marketing activities of various types, which have been summarised as the marketing mix, the set of tools at the marketer's disposal. As these tools are numerous, various attempts have been made to categorise them into a manageable form, including the 'four Ps', as discussed earlier. Entrepreneurial marketing activities do not fit easily into these existing models of the marketing mix. Owner-managers do not define their own marketing mix in terms of product, pricing and place decisions, although they usually include promotions.

Instead, a different theme seems to run through the marketing methods preferred by entrepreneurs: they involve direct interchanges and the building of personal relationships. Entrepreneurs prefer interactive marketing. They specialise in interactions with their target markets because they have strong preferences for personal contact with customers rather than impersonal marketing through mass promotions. They seek conversational relationships in which they can listen to, and respond to, the voice of the customer, rather than undertake formal market research to understand the marketplace. Interactive marketing methods imply one-to-one contact through personal or telephone selling and perhaps direct or electronic mail. In smaller firms, the ability of the owner-manager to have meaningful dialogues with customers is often the unique selling point of the business.

20.6.4 Market research versus networking

In each stage of the traditional marketing process, whether strategic or tactical, formal market research plays an important part. Market orientation relies on research to determine customer needs. Strategic segmentation and targeting is determined by market research. The success of adjustments to the marketing mix is tracked by consumer research. Successful entrepreneurs shy away from such formal research methods. They prefer more informal methods of gathering market information, usually through networks of contacts involved in the industry or trade (Carson *et al.* 1995).

20.7 Entrepreneurial marketing

So what does entrepreneurial marketing consist of? We have described a marketing process common amongst entrepreneurs and successful small-business owners which encompasses innovation, identification of a target market, interactive marketing methods and information-gathering. We will examine each of these further to uncover more about how a typical entrepreneur carries out this marketing process.

20.7.1 Innovation

We have already echoed the views of several commentators who have stressed the importance of innovation to entrepreneurship (Drucker 1985; Adair 1990). However, we should not assume that entrepreneurial innovation consists of major breakthroughs and inventions. It is more likely to consist of incremental adjustments to existing products and services or market approaches, rather than larger-scale developments (Henry and Walker 1991). Whilst a few small firms may make the big innovative breakthrough and grow rapidly as a result, the majority which survive do so by growing more slowly through making small but regular improvements to the way in which they do business. This may mean stocking new lines, approaching a new market segment with a particular service, or improving services to existing customers – in other words incremental, innovative adjustments which together create a competitive edge.

20.7.2 Identification of target markets

We have described how the identification of a market for new products often comes after the development of the idea, when customers are found through a bottom-up process of self-selection and recommendation. In this way, many successful small firms occupy 'niche' markets in which they supply specialised products or services to a clearly identified group of customers. Others find a gap in a particular marketplace for the provision of more general services. Either way, success is dependent on identifying a particular group of customers who need the product or service on offer.

However, target markets need not be solely concerned with customers in the conventional sense of the term. Small businesses survive in their changeable environment not only by successfully marketing to those who buy their products or services, but also by developing important relationships with other individuals and organisations. Suppliers, bank managers, investors, advisers, trade associations, local government and public authorities may be as vital as customers to a small business's success. Entrepreneurs may target marketing strategies at these other markets which go beyond conventional definitions of the term 'customer'. In this sense, entrepreneurial marketing resembles relationship marketing which defines the need to develop a supportive framework around the organisation: 'Marketing can be seen as relationship management: creating, developing and maintaining a network in which the firm thrives' (Gummesson 1987). In other words, entrepreneurial marketing can target any organisation or individual, which can have a positive or negative effect on the small firm.

20.7.3 Interactive marketing methods

A selling point for a small business often lies in its ability to stay in touch with customers. Owner-managers themselves usually spend a considerable part of their working day in contact with customers (Orr 1995) – see Chapter 21. This allows them to interact with their customer base in a way which large firms, even with the latest technological advances, struggle to match.

Interactive marketing for small firms implies responsiveness – the ability to communicate and respond rapidly to individual customers. Entrepreneurs interact with individual customers through personal selling and relationship-building approaches, which secure not only orders but recommendations to potential customers as well. These interactive marketing methods have some common themes too. They rely on the influence of word-of-mouth marketing, which can be stimulated by image-building, involvement and incentives, as discussed below.

The influence of word-of-mouth marketing

Entrepreneurial marketing relies heavily on word-of-mouth marketing to develop the customer base through recommendations. Research studies inevitably cite recommendations as the number one source of new customers for small firms. Such recommendations may come from customers, suppliers or other referral groups. Word-of-mouth marketing has been defined as 'Oral, person-to-person communication between a perceived non-commercial communicator and a receiver concerning a brand, a product or a service offered for sale' (Arndt 1967). This definition makes two crucial distinctions between word-of-mouth and other forms of marketing activity:

- it involves face-to-face, direct contact between a communicator and a receiver; and
- the communicator is perceived to be independent of the product or service under discussion.

The importance of such communications is well documented in the marketing literature which suggests that word of mouth is often crucial to purchase decisions in many consumer and business-to-business markets. For many small firms, reliance on recommendations is no bad thing as it is more suited to the resources of their business. Referrals incur few, if any, additional direct costs; most owner-managers prefer the slow build-up of new business which word-of-mouth marketing implies because they would be unable to cope with large increases in demand for their services. Word-of-mouth marketing has two major disadvantages:

- *It is self-limiting*: reliance on networks of informal communications restricts organisational growth to the limits of those networks. If a small business is dependent on recommendations for new customers, its growth is limited to those market areas in which its sources of recommendations operate.

- *It is non-controllable*: owners cannot control word-of-mouth communications about their firms. As a result, some perceive there to be few opportunities to influence recommendations other than providing the best possible service.

In practice, however, successful entrepreneurs find ways of encouraging referrals and recommendations by more proactive methods.

Image-building

Successful owner-managers recognise the importance of building favourable images of their business in the marketplace in order to encourage the influence of positive word-of-mouth marketing. Image-building is particularly important for the great majority of small businesses, which are involved in selling services, rather than tangible products. Prospective buyers cannot easily test or sample services, so their perceptions of the selling organisation become even more important in the purchase decision. A number of factors influence such perceptions including the ethos or atmosphere of the place of work, the physical appearance of anything associated with the business from letterheads to lorries, and the attitudes of people who have customer contact – which is usually everyone in a small firm.

Incentives

Like most organisations, owner-managers promote their business by offering a variety of incentives including reduced prices and promotional offers. However, some incentives can be used not only to generate immediate business, but also to encourage the development of supportive networks in which the business owner can operate. For example, Shaw (1997) demonstrated that small graphic designers used bartering, hospitality, flexible pricing and differential handling of work to help in the development of their networks. Entrepreneurs use such incentives not only to encourage existing customers but also to develop new markets by expanding their networks.

Involvement

A feeling of involvement or participation with a small business can also encourage customer loyalty and recommendations. From a study of lawyers' practices in the USA, File *et al.* (1992) suggested that the intensity and variety of client participation during the service delivery process was predictive of positive word-of-mouth and referrals. Stokes (1997) found that the more parents became involved with their children's school, through helping in class or fund-raising activities, the more they were likely to become strong advocates of the school. (This reinforces the need for owners who wish to improve word-of-mouth communications to adopt interactive marketing practices which encourage involvement of some sort with the business, so that customers feel an added sense of commitment to it.)

20.7.4 Informal information-gathering

Successful entrepreneurs maintain an external focus to their activities which alerts them to opportunities and threats in their environment. Their informal information-gathering techniques allow them to monitor their own performance in relation to competitors and react to competitive threats. They are also open to new ideas and opportunities through a network of personal and inter-organisational contacts. This process restarts the marketing cycle by forming the basis for further innovative adjustments to the activities of the enterprise.

The four main elements of entrepreneurial marketing, together with the four types of interactive marketing methods, can be conceptualised as the 'four + four Is' of entrepreneurial marketing as shown in Figure 20.2.

Figure 20.2 The entrepreneurial marketing process: four + four Is

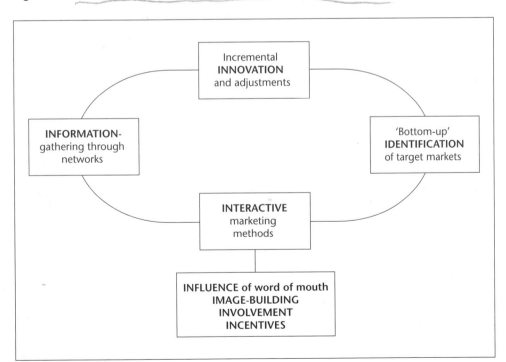

20.8 Chapter summary

This chapter has shown that marketing is particularly important to very small, young firms as it represents the interface between a small firm and its external environment. In particular, the marketing competency of owner-managers is a key discriminator between the survival and failure of small firms. It has also been demonstrated that the inherent characteristics of small firms lead to distinctive marketing problems, although this can be due to the owner-manager's conceptualisation of marketing being narrow and concentrating largely on promotions. Successful owner-managers and entrepreneurs are active in marketing, although they may not call it that. Indeed, entrepreneurial marketing is innovation-orientated, rather than customer-orientated, and entrepreneurs target customers through bottom-up, rather than top-down approaches. They also gather information informally through networks of contacts and prefer interactive marketing methods, relying on the influence of word-of-mouth communications, supported by image-building, incentives and the involvement of customers. Entrepreneurial marketing can thus be simplified as four process stages – innovation, identification of markets, information-gathering and interactive methods – and four elements of the marketing mix – influence, image-building, incentives and involvement (four + four Is rather than four Ps).

In summary, entrepreneurial marketing can be conceptualised as a process and as specific activities typical of entrepreneurial business owners. Innovative developments and adjustments to products and services are targeted at identified customer and other influential groups. Interactive marketing methods work through the influence of word-of-mouth communications, stimulated by image-building, incentives and involvement. Information-gathering through informal networks monitors the marketplace and evaluates new opportunities, which may, in turn, lead to further innovations, to begin the entrepreneurial marketing process all over again. In this way successful owner-managers have overcome the inherent marketing problems in running a small business.

Questions

1 Why do many owners of small firms seem to be wary of marketing?

2 How can entrepreneurs market their business effectively with the limited resources at their disposal?

3 As entrepreneurs rely on word-of-mouth marketing to promote their business, how can they stimulate recommendations and referrals?

4 Is it possible for a business to be both innovation-orientated and customer-orientated?

CHAPTER 21

Networking and the small firm

Eleanor Shaw and Stephen Conway

21.1 Learning objectives

There are eight learning objectives in this chapter:

1 To explain why networking is an important entrepreneurial activity.

2 To define what is meant by the entrepreneur's 'personal contact network'.

3 To compare and contrast alternative perspectives on small-firm networks.

4 To identify and describe the interactional and morphological dimensions of social networks.

5 To identify trends in recent small-firm networking research.

6 To discuss the contents of small-firm networks and consider the impact which these have across their life-cycle.

7 To discuss the implications that small-firm research has for the small-firm policy.

8 To provide recommendations for future research in the area of small-firm networks.

Key concepts

■ social networks ■ personal contact network ■ industrial district
■ network morphology ■ network contents ■ network brokers ■ multiplexity

21.2 Introduction

This chapter identifies and discusses the contribution which networks make to the entrepreneurial process. It starts by considering how networks can be defined and by discussing the different perspectives from which the study of small-firm networks can be approached. Research has typically drawn distinctions between 'industrial', 'support' and 'personal' networks. However, such perspectives offer a relatively narrow view of small-firm networks, concentrating more on the individual sets of dyadic relationships of which such networks are comprised. Consequently, it is argued, little is understood about the wider social context within which small firms are created and developed. Social network theory is then introduced as a framework within which the impact that this wider environment has upon small firms' actions and behaviours can be researched. The chapter then moves to a discussion of what research to date has revealed about small firms' networks. This section reviews the membership, transactions, linkages and morphology of small-firm networks as well as the contribution which networks have been found to make to, for example, problem-solving and innovation. The chapter concludes by identifying emerging issues in small-firm network research and considering the implications that these have for future small-firm research and policy.

21.3 Networking and the small firm

Traditionally, entrepreneurs have been viewed as individuals with a high drive for individualism and independence (Scase and Goffee 1980; 1982). Recently, however, the relevance that network research has for understanding entrepreneurs and small firms has been recognised. The reason for this is that while entrepreneurs may be characterised by their autonomy, paradoxically they are 'very dependent on ties of trust and cooperation' (Johannisson and Peterson 1984: 1). Research has now established that 'networks' and 'networking' are important entrepreneurial tools that contribute to the establishment, development and growth of small firms. For example, networks have been found to assist small firms in their acquisition of information and advice (Birley 1985; Carson et al. 1995; Shaw 1997). It has also been established that networks make important contributions to the smaller firms' innovation processes (Birley et al. 1991; Johannisson and Peterson 1984; Leonard-Barton 1984; Rothwell 1991; Rothwell and Dodgson 1991). Consequently, it is now accepted that 'comprehensive explanations of entrepreneurship must include the social context of [such] behaviour, especially the social relationships through which people obtain information, resources and social support' (Aldrich and Zimmer 1986: 9). For this reason, this chapter will identify the networks of relationships in which small firms are embedded (Granovetter 1985; 1992) and discuss the impact which these have on the behaviour, activities and outcomes of small, entrepreneurial firms.

While 'networks' and 'networking' have attracted the recent attention of small-firm researchers and policy-makers, it is recognised that there is much confusion over the meaning of these terms (Easton 1992; Grandori and Soda 1995; Harland 1995; 1996; Kanter and Eccles 1992). The variety of subject areas from which the study of small-firm networks has been approached, together with a failure to distinguish between small-firm 'networks' and small-firm 'networking' activities, has led to a number of competing definitions and perspectives of networks. Because of this, a second purpose of this chapter is to provide a comprehensive review of the literature on small-firm networks which makes clear the different types of network in which small firms have been found to exist and identifies the types of networking activities in which small firms have been found to engage.

21.4 Defining 'networks'

Network studies of the organisation have received attention from a diverse range of subjects including: transaction economics (Bradach and Eccles 1989; Powell 1990;

Williamson 1985; 1991; 1996); industrial marketing (Axelsson and Easton 1992; Ford 1990; Hakansson and Snehota 1995; Metcalf *et al.* 1991); organisational behaviour (Kanter 1989c); small business (Aldrich and Zimmer 1986; Birley *et al.* 1989; 1991; Conway 1997; Curran *et al.* 1993a; Filion 1990; Johannisson 1986; 1988; Shaw 1997; Szarka 1990) and entrepreneurial marketing (Carson *et al.* 1995). However, a review of this literature establishes that while networks are currently 'in vogue' (Nohria 1992) in the organisational and management research literature, there is a scarcity of literature available which defines and/or explains what is meant by the term 'network'.

Recent interest in network studies of the organisation can be traced to Aldrich's (1979) proposition that as organisations are essentially open systems which exist within and interact with a wider social environment, their behaviour is best understood by studying the network of relationships in which they are involved. Accepting this view, organisational networks can be defined as constructs which conceive of the environment in which small firms exist as forming a network structure of overlapping relationships. More specifically, small-firm networks can be defined as the composite of the relationships in which small firms are embedded which serve to link or connect small firms to the environments in which they exist and conduct their business.

21.5 Alternative perspectives on small-firm networks

Within the small-firm literature, the term 'networks' has been used very loosely to describe a variety of small-firm activities. In particular, small-firm networks have been used with reference to industrial districts (Piore and Sabel 1984; Pyke 1992; Saxenian 1985; 1990); support structures (Chaston and Mangles 1997) and the personal contacts of small-business owner-managers and entrepreneurs (Aldrich and Zimmer 1986). The first of these areas has explored networks of small firms in such industrial districts as Emilia-Romagna in Northern Italy (Piore and Sabel 1984; Pyke 1992) and Silicon Valley, California (Saxenian 1985; 1990). Research in this area has sought to use an understanding of the collaborative arrangements present within these networks to inform policy of the impact that these can have upon the competitiveness of the small firms of which they are comprised. Similar interests have motivated research into networks of support organisations, such as Business Links in England and Local Enterprise Companies in Scotland, which now exist to support the creation and growth of small firms. Encouraged by government enthusiasm for collaborative relationships between small firms, this branch of research has sought to inform policy of the ways and extent to which umbrella organisations, such as local chambers of commerce and business clubs, serve as a catalyst for small-firm networking activities and, by doing so, indirectly assist in the establishment and subsequent development and growth of small firms (Chaston 1995; 1996; Chaston and Mangles 1997).

By contrast, research which has considered the personal contact networks of the entrepreneur and small-firm owner-manager is encouraged by an interest in understanding the impact which these networks have upon their ability to create, develop and grow small firms (Aldrich and Zimmer 1986; Aldrich *et al.* 1986; Aldrich 1987; Aldrich *et al.* 1989; Aldrich and Reese 1993; Birley 1985; Birley *et al.* 1989; 1991; Carsrud *et al.* 1987; Dubini and Aldrich 1991; Zimmer and Aldrich 1987). While industrial district and support network research are interested in exploring the organising mechanisms by which small, entrepreneurial firms effectively arrange their activities for the purposes of maximising their creation, development and competitiveness, this branch of small-firm and entrepreneurial research has different motivations. Specifically, while each of the preceding research areas focuses on the sets of dyadic 'business' relationships in which small firms are involved, this branch of small-firm network research is interested in exploring *all* of the relationships in which entrepreneurs and their firms are embedded (Granovetter 1985; 1992). In contrast then to each of the former research areas, this third branch of small-firm network literature does not abstract the relationships which small firms share with others in their environment out of the ongoing, concrete social relationships within which small-firm activities occur (Granovetter 1973; 1982; 1985; 1992; Mitchell 1969; 1973). Instead, by introducing to the analysis of the behaviour of owner-managers and small firms the possibility that other, 'non-business' relationships in which they are involved may influence their economic or business behaviour, this third area of small-firm network literature distinguishes itself.

The small-firm owner-manager's personal contact network has been defined as 'the relationships or alliances which individuals develop, or may seek to develop, between themselves and others' (Carson *et al.* 1995: 200). Also termed the owner-manager's 'focal' network of contacts and the small firm's 'social network', such networks have been found to play a number of important roles. The personal contact networks of small-firm owner-managers have been found to generate social support; to extend the strategic competencies of the entrepreneur in relation to their identification of opportunities and threats; and to supplement internal resources to resolve acute operating problems (Johannisson and Peterson 1984). In short, the small-firm owner-manager's personal network can be regarded as an important, if not critical, business resource. Support for this suggestion is offered by Leonard-Barton (1984: 113) who argued that 'entrepreneurs who, for geographic, cultural or social reasons, lack access to *free* information through personal networks, operate with less *capital* than do their well-connected peers'. Similarly, Shaw's (1997) research identified social networks as playing a critical role in the development of small service firms. Her study of the impact which social networks have on the development of such firms established that the time and money saved when entrepreneurs access information, advice and resources through their social networks is influential in increasing the resource base of their small firms. Consequently, social networks contribute to the growth and development of small firms in a time- and money-efficient manner.

21.6 Conceiving of small-firm networks

The social network concept has been identified as useful in developing a comprehensive understanding of the impact which personal contact networks have on the creation, development and growth of small, entrepreneurial firms (Aldrich and Zimmer 1986; Conway 1997; Granovetter 1985; 1992; Shaw 1997; 1998; Szarka 1990). Developed by social anthropologists as a construct for exploring and understanding social action and behaviour in terms of the social relationships shared between social actors, the concept of a 'social' network offers a useful way of conceiving of the environment in which small, entrepreneurial firms exist. As such, it is a useful construct from which to approach network studies of the small firm and develop a detailed understanding of the relational factors which impact upon their behaviours and outcomes.

By viewing society as a 'network' structure of overlapping social relationships which bind individuals, groups and organisations together, social anthropologists believe that social action and behaviour can be understood both in terms of the positions which individuals hold within these social networks and also as a consequence of the interactions which they share (Bott 1971; Mitchell 1969). For the purposes of analysing the structural and interactional dimensions of social action and behaviour, social networks are conceived as possessing both *morphological* and *interactional* dimensions. These two dimensions are discussed in more depth below.

21.6.1 Morphological characteristics

Morphological characteristics consider the pattern and structure of social networks and the impact that these have upon the behaviour of social actors (Mitchell 1973; Tichy *et al.* 1979; Tichy 1981). The dimensions that Mitchell (1973) described as 'germane' to the structural analysis of social behaviour in network terms are:

- anchorage;
- reachability;
- density;
- range.

Anchorage

'*Anchorage*' is the term used to identify the focus of social network enquiries. As social network theorists argue that relationships lie along a continuum from personal to inter-organisational, the anchorage of social networks of small, entrepreneurial firms can range from the owner-manager, to the quasi-small organisation, to the established small, entrepreneurial firm. Despite this, network studies of the small firm have typically selected the entrepreneur or the small-firm owner-manager as the anchorage point of their research and sought to identify the impact which their social network has on the establishment of small firms (Aldrich and Zimmer 1986; Birley 1985). Aside of the work of a handful of researchers, including Shaw (1997; 1998), most network studies of the small firm have selected the entrepreneur or owner-manager rather than the small firm as the anchorage of their research.

Reachability

Once the focal point of a social network study has been identified, the '*reachability*' of this anchorage point is useful in identifying all of the relationships that should be examined if the behaviour of the anchorage is to be fully understood in relational terms. '*Reachability*' is a measure of how far and easily an anchorage is able to contact other social actors within the same conceptually distinct social network. The reachability of anchorage is measured by the number of interactions, represented by the number of lines drawn on a network map, which they have to make in order to reach other social actors (see Figure 21.1). The fewer the number of interactions, the greater their reachability. By giving an indication of the effort required to make contact via direct relationships with those to whom they are not directly connected, reachability assesses the extent to which relationships far removed from anchorage have the potential to influence the behaviour of anchorage. Consequently, measures of reachability can help decide where the boundary of a social network study should be drawn. The distinguishing feature of social network theory is that it includes, in the analysis of small-firm behaviour and action, both the direct and indirect relationships in which small firms are involved. By providing an indication of the extent to which indirect relational influences can, via direct relationships, impact upon the behaviour of small firms, the reachability dimension of social networks stresses the importance placed by social network theory on 'brokers'. Tichy et al. (1979) define brokers as 'special nodes within the network' who link together social actors who do not share a direct relationship. While Business Links, for example, provide a formal brokering service to introduce small firms to relevant third parties which can offer advice on marketing and finance etc., social network studies have established that informal brokers exist within small-firm networks which serve to link small firms, for example, to sources of information, finance, advice and product ideas (Conway 1997; 1998; Shaw 1997; 1998).

Density

The third morphological dimension is 'density'. Also referred to as the 'connectedness', 'complexity' or 'social cohesiveness' of a social network, density is a measure of the extent to which social actors are connected to one another by social relationships. The density of a social network is calculated by the percentage of lines that actually exist in relation to the number that potentially would be created if every person in a social network were directly connected to every other person. Measures of density can be used

Figure 21.1 Example of a social network map

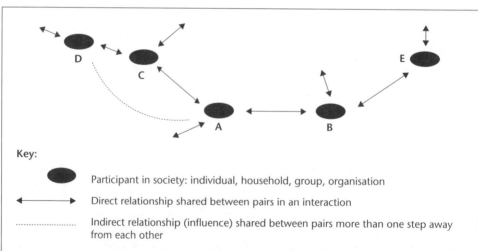

Key:

⬤   Participant in society: individual, household, group, organisation

←——→   Direct relationship shared between pairs in an interaction

····················   Indirect relationship (influence) shared between pairs more than one step away from each other

to distinguish between social networks which are 'tight' and 'loose-knit'. Such measures have been used to assess, for example, the ease with which information travels through social networks (Bott 1971). Consequently, density is an important indicator of the impact that the structure of a social network can have upon the activities and behaviours of its social actors. Applied to small firms, Granovetter (1973; 1982) argued that the more dense an entrepreneur's social network, the less opportunity they have of accessing a wide range of information and advice from their social networks.

Range

The final morphological dimension of social networks is '*range*'. This refers to 'the number of actors in direct contact with anchorage and the social heterogeneity of these actors' (Wheeldon 1969). An entrepreneur's social network can be described as being either 'narrow' or 'diverse' in its range. Again, Granovetter argued that the narrower the range of an entrepreneur's social network, the less opportunity they have of acquiring, from their social networks, a variety of information and advice. Similarly, Gibson (1991: 117–18) contends that 'the more extensive, complex and diverse the web of relationships, the more the entrepreneur is likely to have access to opportunities, the greater the chance of solving problems expeditiously, and ultimately, the greater the chance of success for a new venture'.

21.6.2 Interactional characteristics

While it is revealing to examine the morphological dimensions of social networks, it has been argued that a concentration on analysing these dimensions restricts our understanding of small firms' actions and behaviours to the ways in which these are influenced by the structure of relationships in which they are involved (Mitchell 1973). As the social network concept was developed for the purposes of also understanding social action as a consequence of the interactions shared between social actors, it possesses a number of interactional or relational dimensions. In contrast to the morphological dimensions detailed above, the interactional dimensions of social networks are particular to individual relationships. Consequently, they can only be understood by interpreting the perceptions which individuals have about the relationships in which they interact. Five interactional dimensions can be identified, as follows:

- content;
- intensity;
- frequency;
- durability;
- direction.

Content

The '*content*' of social networks refers to the meanings which people attach to relationships and the understandings they have about the implications which their involvement in particular relationships have for their actions and behaviours in respect to those relationships. This suggests, for example, that if an entrepreneur defines a relationship as a 'friendship', they will engage in activities and behaviours that they perceive to be appropriate to those of a 'friend'. As the contents of relationships are not directly observable, Mitchell (1969) suggested that the meanings which social actors attach to relationships can be interpreted in terms of their information, communication or normative contents.

Similarly, Tichy *et al.* (1979) distinguish between four types of transaction content. They argue that the contents of social networks can be described as:

- *'expressive'*: the exchange of friendship;
- *'instrumental'*: the exchange of power and influence;
- *'cognitive'*: the exchange of data, ideas, information or know-how;
- *'objective'*: the exchange of goods, money, technology or services.

Identification of these contents is, however, complicated by the 'multiplexity' of social relationships. As social actors typically engage in a variety of interactions within the relationships which they share, a number of contents typically exist within each of these relationships.

While recent discussion of the content of social networks has sparked debate over whether, for example, economic small-firm networks can be distinguished separately from those comprised of information and normative contents (cf. Blackburn *et al.* 1990; Szarka 1990), social network theory asserts that while social networks are conceived to comprise of each of the contents mentioned, this does not imply that each content is representative of a conceptually distinct social network. Rather, within multiplex relationships, the interactions between social actors are comprised of a variety of contents. For example, the same two people may share an employer–employee relationship comprised of an economic content and also a friend–friend relationship containing normative expressions. Consequently, the behaviour of social actors *vis-à-vis* multiplex relationships cannot be understood unless all of their contents are identified. Writing about the individual relationships existing within the owner-manager's social network, Johannisson and Peterson (1984: 3) agree that such relationships are 'multi-stranded involving unique syntheses of instrumental, affective and moral' contents.

Intensity

The second interactional dimension of social networks is *'intensity'*. This refers to the 'degree to which individuals are prepared to honour obligations, or feel free to exercise the rights implied in their link to some other person' (Mitchell 1973). Consequently, the intensity of a relationship provides an important indication of the influence which relationships have upon social action and behaviour. Considered alongside the dimension of multiplexity, intensity provides some indication of how complicated relationships between small firms and the environment can be. For example, where a relationship is comprised of economic and normative contents, the interactions involved in its economic content will be influenced by the obligations which actors feel towards one another as a consequence of the friendship relationship which they share. As the intensity of a relationship cannot be observed, the frequency and durability which social networks are also conceived to possess are suggested as suitable indicators.

Frequency

'*Frequency*' refers to the amount of time entrepreneurs spend interacting in relationships. Social network theory asserts that a high frequency of interaction is indicative of intensity. Considered, however, alongside the content of relationships, Mitchell (1973) cautions that frequency is not always an appropriate indicator of the intensity of relationships comprised of normative contents. This, he explained, was because such relationships often have a low level of frequency yet share a very strong relationship. For example, while sisters, one living in Glasgow and the other in San Francisco, may not communicate on a regular basis, this does not imply that the feelings of friendship and affection which they feel towards one another are diminished.

Durability

As the membership of social networks is voluntary and participation in them changes over time, the '*durability*' which they are conceived to possess is an indication of the length of time over which a relationship continues. As such *durability* is often used as an indication of the intensity of relationships. The durability of a relationship is affected not only by its contents, but also by the extent to which both parties to the relationship perceive it to be mutually satisfying. The logic behind this assertion is that if parties to a relationship perceive that they are providing and receiving the type of behaviour which they expect from the relationship, they are more likely to continue to interact than if they perceive that their investment in the relationship is not being reciprocated by the other party.

Direction

Mutuality and reciprocity are, in turn, dependent upon the final interactional dimension of '*direction*'. This refers to the person from whom a relationship is orientated and provides an indication of the direction of the power of a relationship. As with frequency, the extent to which relationships can be described as being orientated in one particular direction is influenced by their content. For example, where relationships are comprised of normative expressions and are defined by their participants as 'friendship' relationships, their direction is less of an issue than where relationships are defined by their parties as 'economic'.

21.7 What has research told us about the nature of small-firm networks?

As a consequence of the informality of the relationships in which small firms engage and the relatively few staff they employ, the social networks in which they are embedded are more readily identifiable than those of their larger counterparts. Despite this, social network studies of small and entrepreneurial firms have tended to be restricted to analysing the relationships between the entrepreneur's personal contact network and their ability to create a new venture (cf. Aldrich and Zimmer 1986). Further, while the concept of a social network has been used for the analysis of entrepreneurial behaviour, this analysis has concentrated on understanding the structural influences on such behaviour to the neglect of understanding interactional influences. Specifically, it has been noted that little is known about the variety of contents of the relationships in

375

Figure 21.2 Classification of SME network research findings

▨ Network membership	e.g. profession networks or user networks
▨ Nature of linkages	e.g. formal versus informal networks
▧ Type of exchanges or transactions	e.g. information, goods, friendship or power
▧ Network function or role of network	e.g. problem-solving or idea-generation
▧ Network morphology	e.g. size, diversity, density and stability of links in network
▧ Geographical distribution of network	*i.e.* balance between local, national or international members

which small and entrepreneurial firms engage (Blackburn *et al.* 1990; Brown and But-ler 1995; Curran *et al.* 1993; Curran and Blackburn 1994). Moreover, little is under-stood about the motives which such firms have for engaging in some relationships rather than others, or the impact which relationships comprised of particular contents have upon their actions and behaviours across their life-cycle (Joyce *et al.* 1995).

Nevertheless, research has provided insight into the networks and networking patterns of entrepreneurs and small and medium-sized firms. These findings may be usefully distinguished as shown in Figure 21.2 (Conway 1998).

21.7.1 Membership

A number of studies have sought to reveal the membership of the networks of small firms and entrepreneurs. Some of these focus on specific activities, such as innovation (Conway 1994; 1997); others are more general in nature and look at the overall com-position of the network (Birley *et al.* 1991; Donckels and Lambrecht 1997). What is common amongst the findings of such studies is the importance of the diversity of actors within the network of the entrepreneur or small firm (Beesley and Rothwell 1987; Conway 1994; 1997; Dodgson 1989; Shaw 1997; 1998). This network diversity allows small firms to draw upon a range of external resources, such as technical knowledge, market information and finance, to supplement the internal resources of the organisation. Donckels and Lambrecht (1997: 13) go further, arguing that 'the fragility which accompanies small size can be offset by the supportive environment provided by resilient networks'.

In more general studies of entrepreneurial and small-firm networks, the importance of family and friends is highlighted, particularly at the earlier stages of the firm's life-cycle (Birley and Cromie 1988; Birley *et al.* 1991; Donckels and Lambrecht 1997). In their study of the impact of entrepreneurial characteristics and network structure, Donckels and Lambrecht (1997) found that highly educated entrepreneurs were more likely to have a wider network, which allowed them to rely less on the advice and judgements of friends and family. However, research has also indicated that as the business survives start-up and begins to grow, so does the diversity of network mem-bership to include professional bankers, suppliers, lawyers and accountants, for ex-ample (Birley and Cromie 1988). Interestingly, studies have shown that entrepreneurs tend not to include other small-firm owner-managers in their personal network (Birley *et al.* 1991).

The diversity of the small-firm network is highlighted by Conway (1997) in a study of the set of relationships mobilised in the development of a sample of successful technological innovations. The networks revealed were often found to be large, predominantly informal, localised and diverse, stretching *upstream* along the supply chain to suppliers, *downstream* to various users and distributors, and incorporating other individuals such as university academics. Of particular importance to the innovation process were linkages with users and suppliers. The research also revealed that the 'ego-centred' network of entrepreneurs frequently plugged into a series of other networks, allowing them to tap knowledge and information from a wider set of relationships within which they were embedded. Five broad categories of network were identified:

- scientific and technical networks organised around scientific or technological domains;
- profession networks, comprising of individuals within a given profession, such as medicine or education, and bound by 'professional ethics of co-operation';
- user networks, that evolve with the end-users of a firm's products;
- friendship networks, referring to the personal networks of individuals based predominantly on friendship;
- recreation networks, a particular type of friendship network whose cohesion arises from the mutual sense of attachment to some recreational activity, such as sailing, mountaineering or rugby, where the feelings of challenge, achievement and comradeship, through participation, create and maintain personal bonds.

21.7.2 The nature of network linkages

Research has also focused on the nature of the linkages between actors within small-firm networks. A key distinction is made between informal or personal relationships and formal relationships, such as joint ventures, licensing agreements, and supply-chain linkages with either suppliers or users. The importance of informal or personal relationships and the role of trust are frequently cited. Furthermore, the network of external relationships built, nurtured and mobilised by small firms is frequently found to be centred largely around one individual: the founder or entrepreneur.

A comparative study of successful small- and large-firm technological innovations found that external inputs into the development process were more frequently sourced informally by small firms (Conway 1994). In particular, relationships with users tended to be informal, with the principal mechanisms for interaction being customer-site visits, chance meetings at exhibitions, and contact over the phone. In contrast, supplier input into the innovation process of small firms was found to be largely formal. However, friendship and informality were seen to be important elements of successful formal relationships with suppliers, highlighting the value of multiplex relationships. Informal boundary-spanning relationships therefore represent a valuable intangible organisational resource, both in their own right and in 'breathing life' into formal relationships.

Informality would appear to play an important role in allowing entrepreneurs to resolve the apparent paradox raised earlier in this chapter: that while on the one hand 'the entrepreneur personifies individualism and independence', on the other s/he 'is ... very dependent on ties of trust and cooperation'.

21.7.3 The nature of transactions within the network

Small-firm networks may also be described and researched according to the nature of what flows through the network, and is exchanged between actors. These flows are termed 'transaction content' (Fombrun 1982). As noted earlier, transaction content may be, for example, affect, power, information and goods (Tichy *et al.* 1979). Networks constructed using this approach are generally expressed in terms of the category of social exchange selected, hence friendship networks, influence networks, communication networks and economic or exchange networks, respectively. Similarly, Krackhardt and Hanson (1993: 111) identify three types of network according to their contents and argue that because of what is exchanged between network members, social networks provide an illustration of how the 'informal organisation gets work done'. The three networks which they identify are:

- *the advice network:* to reveal the prominent players in an organisation on whom others depend to solve problems and provide technical information;
- *the trust network:* to reveal the pattern of sharing with regard to delicate political information, and support in a crisis;
- *the communication network:* to reveal the employees who talk to each other on a regular basis.

Although Krackhardt and Hanson (1993) are referring to internal networks within larger organisations, this typology is clearly of relevance to the study of small-firm networks. Indeed, Shaw (1998) utilises a similar typology in her study of the impact of social networks on the innovative behaviour of small service firms in the UK. In this research she highlights the variety of transaction content flowing through small-firm networks, such as information, advice, friendship, economic and bartering exchanges, each of which was found to impact on the innovation processes of the sample of small service firms.

21.7.4 The function or role of the network

Studies have also revealed a variety of functions or roles that small-firm networks play. Once again these range from the more general (e.g. firm development or competence building), to the more specific (e.g. development of discrete innovations). Shaw (1997; 1998), for example, highlights the role social networks play in the development of small firms. Her research reveals that social networks may play both positive and negative roles, depending on network membership and the nature of what flows through the network. Specifically, it was found that the more heterogeneous or diverse the social network in which the small firm was embedded, and the greater the variety of information and advice flowing through the network, the more positive the impact the social network was found to have on the firm's development. Research has also highlighted the role that networks play in the building of technological competence within small firms. In their study of the influence of networks on new biotechnology firms in the UK and France, Estades and Ramani (1997) develop a typology of three technological competence trajectories:

- *competence 'widening'*: a diversification of the technological competence of the firm;
- *competence 'deepening'*: an improvement of existing technological competencies of the firm;
- *competence 'narrowing'*: an abandoning of a set of existing projects, processes or products, without the development of new technological competencies.

Estades and Ramani then consider which of the various actor attribute-defined networks revealed in the study (e.g. scientific networks, inter-firm networks) lead to the emergence of the three different technological competence trajectories in the new biotechnology firms. They found, for example, that the decisive networks associated with the deepening or widening of technological competence in these small firms were scientific or inter-firm networks (i.e. those linking them to large firms).

The importance of external inputs and of external or boundary-spanning networks to the innovation process has already been noted. This holds true for both small and large firms, although small firms are more reliant on such boundary-spanning networks to overcome internal resource constraints (Conway 1994). However, the importance of the small-firm network, and of particular actors within it, will vary depending on the task at hand. In his study of small-firm technological innovation, introduced earlier, Conway (1997) distinguished between the nature and importance of the contribution of the network towards different stages or activities in the innovation process, that is:

- project stimuli;
- concept definition;
- idea-generation regarding features and functionality of innovation;
- technical problem-solving;
- field-testing prior to commercialisation.

Users were found to be a major source of inputs into idea generation, and this was particularly evident during *re-innovation*, that is, the modification of earlier models (Rothwell and Gardiner 1985). For example, one developer of a software package noted that: 'The substantial number of changes have come from the users ... We try and be really careful about putting our own ideas in unless a user agrees with it.' In addition, users were also seen to represent a major source for the pre-commercialisation field-testing of the innovations in the sample. This adds support to Habermeier's (1990) hypothesis that product characteristics and user requirements can often only be discovered if the innovation is actually used, sometimes for long periods of time. It is also worth noting that in most of these cases field-testing was undertaken by what Hippel (1986) has termed *lead-users*. Field-tests were seen as an important test-bed not only for the technical performance of the innovations, but also for the suitability of the embodied features and functionality. However, it is also true to say that a fair amount of what may be considered as post-commercialisation field-testing was highlighted by the research. That is, a number of the innovating companies either consciously or unwittingly commercialised rather 'rough and ready' versions of their innovations, which were subsequently tested by users in a commercial situation. This led directly to new product versions that incorporated debugging and/or much improved functionality. This point was expressed quite openly in relation to the development of an electronic gadget: 'I suppose at the back of your mind you're realising that you're doing development, to a certain extent, maybe, on your customers.' A lack of financial resources was cited as the main reason for this occurring. The analysis also highlighted the key role played by suppliers in providing inputs into the technical solutions embodied in the commercialised innovations, sometimes developing critical components in response to specific requests from the small-firm innovators. The cases in the study provide clear illustrations of both the 'complementary' and the 'substitutive' nature of external sources of knowledge and technology in relation to indigenous innovative activity in small firms.

21.7.5 Network morphology

Research on the heterogeneity of entrepreneurs suggests that differences in experience and career background may have a significant consequence for an individual's 'know-how' and 'know-who'. This may be expressed by the different patterns and types of social relationships found within entrepreneurial networks. In exploring this link between entrepreneur type and network morphology, Conway and Steward (1998) mapped the innovation networks mobilised by innovative small firms in the development of a sample of successful products. The cases were distinguished by employing the typology developed by Jones-Evans and Steward (1995). This identifies three types of entrepreneur: the 'research' entrepreneur, previously involved in scientific work, usually with an academic institution; the 'producer' entrepreneur, originating from an industrial organisation, with involvement in product development; and the 'user' entrepreneur, previously an end-user of a technological product or process.

The networks revealed clearly highlight two features which are common to all the cases: within each of the small firms there is a strong formal link between two individual key actors, with a division of responsibility between the technical and business dimensions of the innovation process; each small firm also exhibits a wide range of external links with other organisations, which are predominantly informal in nature and which are mobilised as part of an individual's set of personal network relationships. In the cases where the entrepreneur has a business background, whether in a producer or user organisation, it is evident that the individual concerned is responsible for the majority of external network links. The other internal actor, who has a primary role in the technical aspects of the innovation, appears to play a minor role in external boundary-spanning activity. In the cases where the entrepreneur has an academic research background, there is a different pattern. In these instances both of the internal actors play an active role in the utilisation of external network links and thus share this boundary-spanning role between them. Here the academic mobilises a research-orientated network, while the business entrepreneur boundary-spans to the marketplace.

A recent explorative study by Baaijens (1998) sets out to test the hypothesis that the social structure in which entrepreneurial actors operate has important effects on the success of the SME. He looks at a number of Innovation Groups or innovation clusters instigated by a number of Dutch Innovation Centres to stimulate innovation and industrial renewal. His conceptual framework is derived from the ideas of Burt (1992), particularly those in relation to 'structural holes'. He concludes that certain positions in the social structure (i.e. 'structural holes') provide actors with novel opportunities, and have the potential to better equip entrepreneurs and SMEs who are able to occupy these broker positions.

21.7.6 Geographical distribution of the network

Research has also highlighted a number of factors that influence the geographical distribution of the network of an entrepreneur or small firm: the amount of experience of the entrepreneur; the level of education of the entrepreneur; the size of the firm; and the growth-orientation of the firm. Birley *et al.* (1991: 59) note that 'entrepreneurs, at an early stage of enterprise development, rely heavily on an informal network of friends, family members and social contacts from the local neighbourhood to gather relevant data. At a later stage, entrepreneurs rely increasingly on professional bankers, accountants, lawyers, suppliers, government agencies, etc. to gain access to requisite business information.' In addition, a study by Donckels and Lambrecht (1997) revealed that highly educated entrepreneurs were significantly more likely to have networks that spanned national boundaries into the international arena, and that the bias towards local contacts in the network was lower for small businesses of more than ten employees and for growth-orientated small firms.

21.8 Emerging research issues in small-firm networks

To date, where social network theory has been applied to small-firm research, the predominant method of investigation has been quantitative in nature. Specifically, methods such as mailed questionnaires have been used to collect cross-sectional data about the structural dimensions of small-firm networks, in particular their size and membership composition. Consequently, while much has been written about the membership of small-firm networks and the transactions which they contain, less is known about the reasons why small firms choose to engage in particular networks or about the outcomes which result from their involvement in different relationships and the impact which these have upon their creation, development and growth.

Emerging within the small-firm research literature is a call for network studies of the small firm to collect more detailed data about the interactional dimensions of small-firm networks (cf. Blackburn *et al.* 1990; Curran *et al.* 1993a) and for researchers interested in small-firm networks to 'look for indicators of their impact' on small firms (Joyce *et al.* 1995: 12). Shaw (1997), in particular, has argued that the failure to collect data about the interactional dimensions of the social networks of small firms has led to a lack of understanding of the impact of networks on small firms. Moreover, she argues, current research in this area has produced an incomplete understanding of the structural dimensions of small-firm networks. As a consequence of these gaps in the small-firm network literature, the emerging issues detailed in Figure 21.3 have been identified as suitable areas of future investigation.

Figure 21.3 Gaps in the small-firm network research literature

Focus of previous small-firm network research	Research gaps
▪ Owner-manager as unit of analysis	▪ Small firm as unit of analysis
▪ Networks at start-up	▪ Networks during development
▪ Cross-sectional studies, snapshot data, hypothesis testing	▪ Sector-specific, in-depth studies which collect rich data and generate understanding
▪ Structural dimensions and quantitative data, e.g. size and shape of network	▪ Interactional dimensions and qualitative data, e.g. contents and impact of network
▪ Concentration on conceptualisation	▪ Empirical data

Small-firm networking research has tended towards selecting the owner-manager as the unit of analysis. As such, it can be argued that, to date, a restricted view of those relationships with the potential to impact upon small firms has prevailed. Additionally, a concentration on small-firm creation and growth, together with a concentration on testing relationships between the structural dimensions of the entrepreneur's network of relationships and their successful creation of small firms, has characterised small-firm network research. Apart from the work of a small number of researchers (cf. Brown and Butler 1995; Butler and Hansen 1991; Ramachadran et al. 1993), few published studies exist about the processes of interactions involved between small firms and the social networks in which they are embedded as they survive start-up and develop. Related to this, while studies involving the collection of quantitative data from large, cross-sectional samples of small firms have contributed significantly to current understanding about the structural dimensions of the social networks in which small firms are embedded, there is a scarcity of data about the interactional dimensions of these networks or about the impact which they have upon small firms as they develop. One reason for this may be that the collection of data about the interactional dimensions of social networks requires that a qualitative approach is adopted. In contrast to quantitative methods which have dominated research on the topic of small-firm networks, such an approach allows the researcher to understand and interpret the perceptions which small-firm network members have about the contents and the outcomes of network relationships. While such studies are able to generate a rich and detailed understanding of the interactions between small firms and their environments, the time investment which they require, together with the restrictions which they place on the generalisability of their findings, may have encouraged researchers to focus on the structural dimensions of such networks.

21.9 Chapter summary

This chapter has sought to demonstrate the important role played by networks in the process of small-firm creation, development and growth. However, it is important to highlight that networks do not emerge without considerable endeavour and that their maintenance and development are a major investment for entrepreneurs and small firms. This point is stressed by Birley *et al.* (1991: 58–67) who note that 'entrepreneurs have to work hard to develop relationships: they have to persuade, socialise, bargain, reciprocate with others to create a relationship and maintain it ... networks are inclined to become more useful with age as relationships develop and individuals learn how to get the best out of them'.

The chapter has also provided a review of alternative perspectives on small-firm networks and has detailed the advantages of adopting the concept of a social network when seeking to understand the behaviour of the small firm in relational terms. A comprehensive review of the small-firm network literature has been provided, identifying key aspects of their membership, linkages, transactions, function, morphology and geographical distribution. From this review a number of emerging issues are highlighted together with gaps in this literature. The chapter concludes by identifying a number of recommendations for both small-firm researchers and policy-makers.

Questions

1 What are the advantages of conceiving of the small firm's environment as a social network?

2 Compare and contrast each of the following types of small-firm network: industrial districts; support networks; personal contact networks.

3 In what way is the concept of a social network distinct from each of the following networks: industrial; support; personal?

4 What relevance does an understanding of each of the following network dimensions have for our understanding of small firms: density; content; range; anchorage; and direction?

5 In what ways can networks contribute to the development of small, innovative firms?

CHAPTER 22

Information and communication technology in the small firm

Jürgen Kai-Uwe Brock

22.1 Learning objectives

There are six learning objectives in this chapter:

1 To argue the importance of information and communication technology (ICT) for small firms.

2 To explain what is meant by the key terms 'ICT', 'digital convergence', 'Internet' and related terms.

3 To describe the key technological developments in ICT.

4 To identify key differences in the adoption, implementation and use of ICT among small firms compared to larger firms.

5 To list key influential internal and external factors in the adoption, implementation and use of ICT among small firms.

6 To discuss implications for researchers, practitioners and policy-makers.

Key concepts
- information and communication technology
- organisational adoption, implementation and use of technology - the Internet

22.2 Introduction

Computer-based information and communication technology (ICT) plays an important role for any organisation. Still, little empirical research has addressed the specifics of ICT adoption, implementation and use in the context of the small firm. This chapter reviews the current state of art in ICT adoption, implementation and use in small firms. After defining and delineating key terms, as well as giving a short historical overview of key technological developments, a general overview of the research field is presented. A review of empirical studies relating to the adoption, implementation and use of ICT in small firms follows, focusing on key influential organisational and environmental factors. This review is extended by a section that focuses specifically on the Internet. The Internet's theoretical impact, focusing on the marketing function and the internationalisation process of the firm, is discussed and a review of empirical studies relating to the Internet among small firms follows and concludes the review. An overall summary of the review's key findings and its implications for researchers, practitioners and policy-makers ends the chapter.

22.3 Information and communication technology (ICT) in the small firm

Organisations are consumers, managers and distributors of information, its use being an essential element of organisational operations (Feldman and March 1981; Evans and Wurster 1997) in order to reduce uncertainty and equivocality about its external environment and its internal operations (Daft and Lengel 1986). The consumption, management and distribution of information necessitates an organisation and its members to communicate, both internally and externally, turning communication into a central phenomenon in organisations (Guetzkow 1965; Euske and Roberts 1987). Since a large share of modern communication is mediated and since today's information unit of widest use is the digital bit (Morrison and Morrison 1998), computer-based information and communication technology (ICT) plays an important role for organisations, being the key mediating technology to facilitate the above-outlined core processes of collecting, managing and distributing information.

The importance of information technology (IT) for organisations has been known for quite some time, with articles first theorising about its organisational impact in the late 1950s (Leavitt and Whisler 1958), when computer technology started to become commercially available. Since their early observations, the importance of IT for organisations to support information processing has increased, particularly due to its technological 'convergence' with communication technology (CT). Nowadays, ICT impacts the entire organisational value chain and its linkages, changes industry structures, creates new competitive advantage and spawns new businesses (Porter and Millar 1985). ICT can play a crucial role in almost any business process (Hammer and Champy 1993) and, most importantly for the context of this book, it is nowadays economically and strategically feasible to even the smallest organisations (McFarlan 1984; Raymond 1989; Thong and Yap 1995).

ICT's value potential for organisations is reflected in its increasing adoption and implementation among firms. Currently, it is estimated that the share of employees using ICT has increased from less than a quarter in the mid 1980s to between 40% and 56% by the mid 1990s in several OECD member states (OECD 1998).

Most research has, however, focused on large organisations. Historically, this large-firms bias reflected the economic imperative of strong financial resources and expert know-how. Computer power in its early years was very expensive and difficult to operate. Small firms simply did not have the financial resources and expertise needed to operate such technology. As computer power expanded and prices dropped, as computers became widely available and as computer usability and ease of use increased, so did the adoption and diffusion of computer technology in small firms. A recent study estimated computer ownership in SMEs (10–250 employees) in five of the world's main economies (France, Germany, Japan, UK and USA) to be above 90% and in micro-firms (1–9 employees) to be above 70% (Department of Trade and Industry 1998). Nevertheless, over 20 years after the first commercially successful personal computer (PC) was introduced by Apple Computer in the USA, little empirical research has addressed the specifics of ICT adoption, implementation and use in the context of the small firm (Thong and Yap 1995; Igbaria *et al.* 1998).

The following sections are intended to give the reader an overview of current research related to the organisational use of ICT. Since comparatively little research has focused on small firms, the next section will start with a general overview of the field, followed by a review of empirical studies of ICT use in small firms. This review will specifically focus on the key organisational and environmental factors of small-firm ICT use and highlight its difference to ICT use in large organisations. In order to reflect IT's technical 'convergence' with communication technology (CT), a section on the Internet – the most popular and important manifestation of this convergence – and the small firm follows. This section will focus on the Internet's potentially most important impact – its impact on the internationalisation process of the firm – as well as the few existing empirical studies of Internet use in small firms. A summary and evaluation of the reviewed studies and their implication for researchers, policy-makers and practitioners will conclude this chapter. Before proceeding to give an overview of research on ICT in organisational settings, the next section will provide a brief historical background of IT's evolution and a working definition of the key terms used in this chapter, as well as related terms.

22.4 Definition and historical background

It is commonly assumed that the term 'information technology' was first introduced by Leavitt and Whisler in 1958 in their seminal article 'Management in the 1980s' (Markus and Robey 1988). In this article, the authors highlighted the increasingly important value of the technical power of computer technology to support and enhance organisations in their information processing and decision-making. Ever since, computer technology was regarded as a salient data and information providing and processing tool for organisations. The term 'information technology' was widely adopted to express this. A lot has changed since Leavitt and Whisler (1958) introduced the term: change mainly driven by technological advances in the field of computer technology, as well as in the field of communication technology.

Various similar 'paradigms' or 'eras' have been suggested to describe the technological development of IT and its main implications over time (see, for example: Tesler 1995; Chandler 1997; Strassman 1997). Tesler (1995) divided the history of computing into four paradigms (see Figure 22.1), a classification which will be used here to illustrate some of the key changes that have been taking place.

Following the classification in Figure 22.1, computer technology has changed mainly in two key ways. Firstly, computers have become mainstream. The days when experts and specialists 'controlled' central computers (mainframes) are gone and computer power is now in the hands of the end-user, the individual. This trend is mainly a reflection of the increase in computer power, paired with a decrease in computer cost, an increase in usability and ease of use and an increase in average user expertise. Secondly, the technological base of computers has expanded and merged with the technological base of communication technology, a phenomenon typically refered to as

Figure 22.1 The four paradigms of computing

	Batch	Time-sharing	Desktop	Network
Decade	1960s	1970s	1980s	1990s
Location	Computer room	Terminal room	Desktop	Mobile
Users	Experts	Specialists	Individuals	Groups
User status	Subservience	Dependence	Independence	Freedom
Data	Alpha-numeric	Text, vector	Fonts, graphs	Script, voice
Objective	Calculate	Access	Present	Communicate
User activity	Punch & try (submit)	Remember & type (interact)	See & point (drive)	Ask & tell (delegate)
Operation	Process	Edit	Layout	Orchestrate
Interconnect	Peripherals	Terminals	Desktops	Palmtops

Source: abbreviated from Tesler (1995)

'digital convergence'. Communication technology and computer technology can no longer be strictly separated, as they share the same underlying digital technology, which led to a convergence on the product and industry level (for a more in-depth discussion see, for example: Baldwin *et al.* 1996; Duysters 1996; Messerschmidt 1996; Collis *et al.* 1997; Greenstein and Khanna 1997; Yoffie 1997). This technological trajectory has expanded the traditional domain of IT, to include nowadays not only computer hard- and software but also communication technology as its key components (O'Connor and Galvin 1997). To reflect this change, the term ICT will be used rather than the term IT.

Various other terms like information systems (IS), management information systems (MIS), information management (IM) and communications-intensive information systems (CIIS) have been used in the literature with regards to IT and its usage (for a more in-depth discussion see, for example, Boaden and Lockett 1991). Although authors have often used the terms interchangeably, Boaden and Lockett (1991) have synthesised the various terminologies. They suggest that the term IT should be used to refer to the general technical developments in the field (IT as technology). The term information system (IS), which the authors consider to be congruent with the term MIS,

Figure 22.2 The relationship between IM, IT, CT, IS and CS

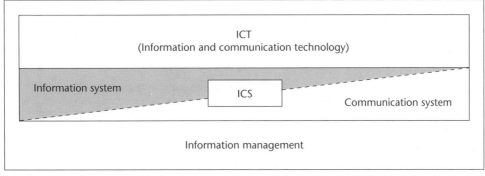

Source: adapted and expanded from Boaden and Lockett (1991)

should be used to refer to a specific system used within an organisation (IT as applied technology). The term information management (IM) should be used as an overall reference to the field of research (IT as computer-supported management of information). In order to reflect the above-mentioned digital convergence of IT and CT, their framework will be expanded here to include CT (see Figure 22.2). In summary, information management refers to a function within an organisation using information and communication systems (ICS) based on information and communication technology in order to enhance data and information processing supporting business processes and organisational decision-making.

22.5 Overview of research streams and the problem of the dependent variable

As an interdisciplinary research field, there are various research streams influencing research in ICS ranging from computer science, behavioural science, decision science, organisation science, social science and management science to economics and political science (for a broader overview see, for example: Davis 1980; Culnan and Swanson 1986; Lyytinen 1987). The key research areas that have developed over time can be classified according to their main focus into the following groups:

- *adoption research* (see, for example: Thong and Yap 1995; Fink 1998);
- *implementation research* (see, for example: Lucas 1981; Cooper and Zmud 1990; Saga and Zmud 1994);
- *strategic management research* (see, for example: McFarlan *et al.* 1983; Ives and Learmonth 1984; Hammer and Mangurian 1987; Cecil and Goldstein 1990; Sethi and King 1994; Elliot and Melhuish 1995);
- *impact research* (see, for example: Lucas 1975; DeLone and McLean 1992; Hitt and Brynjolfsson 1996).

Adoption research is interested in the determinants of organisational adoption of ICT. One of its key questions is to determine organisational differences between adopters and non-adopters.

Implementation research is interested in the various post-adoption processes, mainly the implementation process. Following organisational innovation and diffusion theory (Zaltman *et al.* 1973; Rogers 1995), one can distinguish between initiation, adoption, implementation, routinisation and infusion phases (Zmud and Apple 1992; Saga and Zmud 1994). A major substream in this field focuses on the effects of user involvement, user participation, user acceptance and the interaction between ICS users and ICS designers on the success of ICS implementation (see, for example: Swanson 1974; DeBrabander and Thiers 1984; Ives and Olson 1984; Davis 1989; Hartwick and Barki 1994; McKeen *et al.* 1994; Kappelmann 1995; Szajna 1996).

The strategic management research stream is interested in the potential strategic value of ICS for organisations. Various normative planning and strategic analysis models have been suggested (see, for example: Ives and Learmonth 1984; McFarlan 1984; Rockart and Scott-Morton 1984; Hammer and Mangurian 1987; for an overview:

Earl 1989). These models are usually grounded in generic strategic management frameworks such as the ones developed by Porter (1980; 1985). In contrast to the above research streams, most studies are not based on empirical investigations and, although Sethi and King (1994) have proposed a measure to assess the strategic impact of ICS, ICS impact on the strategic performance of firms still remains one of the key ambiguities in ICS research (Blili and Raymond 1993).

Impact research is interested in the various effects of an ICS on the operations of individuals, work groups or the whole organisation and is thus an implicit part of most of the above research streams. Yet, it was listed as a separate group, because assessing the performance of an ICS is difficult, as several dependent variables and categories of dependent variables can be investigated (DeLone and McLean 1992; see Figure 22.3 for an overview of categories and measures).

Performance research on the organisational level is particularly controversial, because it is very difficult to calculate the overall value of an ICS to an organisation. Besides the problem of measuring productivity in a world that depends more and more on intangible goods, there usually exists a time-lag between an investment in an ICS and its economic impact (Brynjolfsson and Hitt 1998), a time-lag that is difficult to capture in cross-sectional investigations – the most popular form of empirical enquiry in this field. Furthermore, as ICT becomes more and more integrated into business processes, it becomes more and more difficult to isolate its impact from other influential variables (Dempsey et al. 1998).

In addition, recent empirical investigations have shown that around 50% of ICS value is due to unique characteristics of the firm and not due to the ICT in itself (Brynjolfsson and Hitt 1998), supported by a recent international investigation by McKinsey and Co. into the corporate use of ICT and its impact on corporate effectiveness and efficiency of manufacturers (Kempis et al. 1998; Kempis and Ringbeck 1998). One of the studies' key findings is that a key moderator between an ICS and organisational performance is the design and redesign of key business processes to fully exploit ICT's potential; a moderating variable that distinguished high from low performers. These findings suggest that it is increasingly becoming necessary and important to structure an organisation and its processes in ways that can leverage the value-potential of ICT (Rai et al. 1997; Brynjolfsson and Hitt 1998) – an observation which will be important with regards to ICT in small firms.

It follows that a key problem with many of the research findings of the above research streams is that they are very difficult to compare, due to the problem of the variety in dependent variables that can be investigated. Besides the speedy change of the underlying technology (decade-old research findings about mainframe use are not necessarily congruent with more recent studies investigating PC use) and the above-mentioned measurement problems, the difficulty also arises because ICT can manifest itself in a broad variety of services and products. It can have a value of a few pounds (e.g. a piece of software) or millions of pounds (e.g. mainframes), and its use can vary as well. An off-the-shelf database, for example, can be used for a simple customer database or it can be used as an integrated part of an inventory control system. Furthermore, an ICT application can be used in different functional areas within a firm and can thus cause different organisational impacts. Therefore, as noted above, a broad variety of dependent variables can be investigated, leading to different and

Figure 22.3 Categories of ICS measures

Quality of external support	System quality	Information quality	Information use	User satisfaction	Individual impact	Organisation impact
Support level	Technical level	Semantic level	Effectiveness of ICS and impact			
■ informal sources	data accuracy	importance	■ amount/duration of use:	Satisfaction with specifics	information understanding	■ application portfolio:
– reliability of support	data currency	relevance	– enquiries	overall satisfaction	learning	– range and scope of applications
– technical competence	database content	usefulness	– connect time	single-item measure	accurate interpretation	– number of critical applications
– small-firm competence	ease of use	informativeness	– functions used	multi-item measure	information awareness	operating cost reduction
– availability	ease of learning	usableness	– records assessed	information satisfaction (difference between information needed and received)	information recall	staff reduction
■ formal sources (vendor)	convenience of access	understandability	– access frequency	enjoyment software satisfaction	problem identification	overall productivity gains
– reliability of support	human factors	readability	– frequency of report requests	decision-making satisfaction	■ decision effectiveness:	increased revenues
– technical competence	realisation of user requirements	clarity	– reports generated		– decision quality	increased sales
– small-firm competence	usefulness of system features and functions	format	– charges for system use		– improved decision analysis	increased market share
– availability	system accuracy	appearence	– regularity of use		– correctness of decision	increased profits
■ formal sources (consultant)	system flexibility	content	■ use by whom?		– time to make decision	return on investment

Quality of external support	System quality	Information quality	Information use	User satisfaction	Individual impact	Organisation impact
– reliability of support	system reliability	accuracy	– direct vs chauffeured use		– confidence in decision	return on assets
– technical competence	system sophistication	precision	▪ binary use:		– decision-making participation	ratio of net income to operating expenses
– small-firm competence	integrations of systems	conciseness	– use vs non-use		improved individual productivity	cost/benefit ratio
– availability	systems efficiency	sufficiency	– actual vs reported use		change in decision	stock price
	resource utilisation	completeness	▪ nature of use:		causes management action	increased work volume
	response time	reliability	– use for intended purpose		task performance	product quality
	turnaround time	currency	– appropriate use		quality of plans	contribution to achieving goals
		timeliness	– type of information used		individual power or influence	service effectiveness
		uniqueness	– purpose of use		personal valuation of ICS	
		comparability	▪ levels of use:		willingness to pay for information	
		quantitativeness	– general vs specific			
		freedom from bias	– recurring use			
			– institutionalisation of use			
			– report acceptance			
			– percentage used vs opportunity for use			
			– voluntariness of use			
			– motivation to use			

Source: adapted and expanded from DeLone and McLean (1992)

non-comparable empirical results. An additional problem in the case of small firms lies in the owner-manager's typical reluctance to report exact financial results. Hence, several measures, particularly on the organisational level, are not applicable and more subjective rather than objective criteria have to be applied.

The difficulties of comparing studies are further pronounced if investigations are undertaken at an aggregated level, that is, if the adoption and implementation of different ICS is compared across firms, as in some of the above-stated adoption and implementation studies. The adoption, implementation and use of ICT in an organisation is contingent upon the nature of the specific ICS, the nature of the organisation and the nature of the ICS's intended use. Innovation research has shown that different organisational structures and strategies are needed to facilitate the implementation for different innovations (see, for example: Ettlie *et al.* 1984; Zmud 1984). These limitations should be kept in mind with regards to the review of empirical studies of ICT use in small firms that follows below.

22.6 ICT in the small firm

While empirical research on the impact of ICT on large and medium-sized organisations started early (see, for example: Whisler 1970a; 1970b; Pfeffer and Leblebici 1977), research with a focus on small firms started later due to factors that were outlined above. Early contributions and several contributions that followed were mainly normative or descriptive in nature (see, for example: West 1975; Heintz 1981; Senn and Gibson 1981; Garris and Burch 1983; Malone 1985; Geisler 1992). Today, still little empirical research has addressed the specifics of computer use in small firms (Thong and Yap 1995; Igbaria *et al.* 1998) and findings derived from large organisations, particularly those with internal ICS departments, are not or only to a limited degree applicable to small firms. Besides the general structural differences between large and small firms, in the case of ICT use in small firms, the following differences can be observed:

- Large organisations often use ICT to co-ordinate and communicate across different organisational levels, divisions and, in the case of MNEs (multinational enterprises), across different subsidiaries; while small firms seldom use ICT for formal, internal communication, due to their informal and less specialised organisational structures.

- Small firms use ICT more as tools to support specific organisational tasks like administration and accounting. Due to a lack of financial resources and ICT in-house expertise, small firms usually do not develop ICS on their own. They rely more on standard, off-the-shelf ICT. Due to a lower level of internal ICT expertise compared to larger firms with internal IS departments, small firms usually rely more on external support from friends, vendors and/or consultants.

While the use and implementation of ICT among small firms, particularly in the early phases of computing (see Figure 22.1, paradigms one and two) was low or non-existent, empirical studies have found comparatively high levels of ICT diffusion among their samples of small firms (see for example Nickell and Seado 1986; DeLone 1988; Chen 1993). It is currently estimated that around 90% of SMEs and slightly over 70% of micro-firms use ICT (Department of Trade and Industry 1998).

However, differences exist with regards to the following organisational and environmental aspects of small firms that will be discussed below:

- the size of the firm;
- the age of the firm;
- the industry sector of the firm;
- the firm's experience with ICT, including the role of the top manager and the end-user;
- the role of external support;
- the usage pattern of ICT.

22.6.1 Firm size

Firm size often correlates with ICT use (Niedleman 1979; Nickell and Seado 1986; Raymond 1987; 1990; Thong and Yap 1995; OECD 1997b; DTI 1998b). It is argued that firm size is an indicator of the firm's accrued internal financial and human resources. Ceteris paribus, the lower its resource base, the lower the economic and strategic feasibiliy of ICT. However, firm size is only a crude indicator and nowadays even micro-firms can utilise ICT. Recent empirical investigations support this view (Fink 1998; see also the review of empirical studies in the Internet section giving further support). Thus, it is less the overall size of the firm than its internal resource base, than particularly its ICT experience and skills, that explain actual ICT use. This is an important aspect which will be discussed further below.

22.6.2 Firm age

Although a strong relationship between firm age and firm size is usually assumed (Aldrich and Auster 1986), which would suggest that young firms do use less ICT than older firms, it was found that younger firms are more likely to use ICT (Chen 1993), with more mature firms exhibiting higher levels of ICT use (Raymond 1990). While it could be argued that this is a reflection of an overall increase of ICT experience in the population (see for example an investigation by Doukidis *et al.* 1994) and a reflection of more mature firms' accumulation of internal ICT experience, it could also be argued that the firm's age is a less important indicator and the average employee age within a firm is a more informative dimension. Studies have shown that employee age in small firms seems to be negatively related to ICT use (Nickell and Seado 1986; OECD 1998; Igbaria *et al.* 1998). Nickell and Seado (1986) found that older respondents were on average less ICT experienced and attended less training courses. Montazemi (1987) found additional support for the notion of a negative relationship between user age and user ICT literacy. A recent compilation of various studies by the OECD (1998) also found strong evidence that computer use among elder employees is lower compared to employees in their thirties. In a different context, such behaviour was explained by reference to an individual's life-cycle, consisting of four phases: 'schooling', 'career path', 'end-of-life easing' and 'retirement' (Swanson *et al.* 1997). The authors found evidence that older workers, entering stage three, choose not to adopt new technology. Taking the average age of employees within a firm into consideration might shed a new light on the findings regarding the age of the firm. However, it should be remembered that overall, use of computers is rising for all age groups, as time series data from France and the USA have revealed (OECD 1998).

22.6.3 Firm sector

Some empirical evidence for industry sector differences exists. Kagan *et al.* (1990) found that particularly small firms in transaction-intensive industries like wholesaling and retailing showed a high degree of ICT use and sophistication. They regarded their findings as an evidence that small firms' ICT use can be highly sector-specific, an observation that a later study further supports (Julien 1995). However, although theorists have noted before that ICT will play a more important role in transaction- and information-intensive industry sectors (Porter and Millar 1985), a study by Thong and Yap (1995) could not empirically validate this assumption. Neither information intensity nor more competitive environments showed an effect on small firms' likelihood to adopt ICT. However, it seems logically appealing that a link between transaction and information intensity and ICT use among small firms should exist. Future research will clarify whether such a link can be empirically demonstrated.

22.6.4 Firm and user experience

It was noted above that some empirical evidence exists suggesting that older employees are less likely to use ICT than younger employees. As Nickell and Seado's (1986) study showed, older respondents were on average less ICT experienced. Hence, all things being equal, ICT experience seems to be an important factor in ICT use in small firms. The importance of ICT experience within a small firm, and the problems with a lack of it, are among the most commonly found research findings, and the latter is still one of the biggest impediments to proper ICT use in small firms (Financial Times 1997; Department of Trade and Industry 1998), despite an overall increase in ICT sophistication (Doukidis *et al.* 1994). ICT experience has a positive effect on users' attitudes towards computers (Nickell and Seado 1986), subsequently increasing adoption and usage levels. Lees (1987) showed that long experience with computers was positively related to the use of ICT. Raymond (1990) and Yap *et al.* (1992) could also demonstrate that ICS sophistication had a positive influence on the level of system success. Montazemi (1988) further supported the importance of user ICS experience. In his study of service and manufacturing firms, end-user satisfaction with ICS correlated with the level of end-user ICT literacy. More recently, studies by Igbaria *et al.* (1998) and Fink (1998) gave additional evidence for the positive effect of ICT experience within a small firm. However, as noted and empirically supported by DeLone (1988), experience as measured by length of computer use is not necessarily associated with successful use of ICS. He argues that it is less the existence of ICT within the firm *per se*, but the resources and energies devoted to its use and development over time. In particular providing user training is an important factor (Igbaria *et al.* 1997). Furthermore, it can be assumed that small firms differ in their ability to convert experience with ICT into ICT expertise, enabling them to make more effective future uses of their ICS.

22.6.5 Top management support

Due to small firms' typical high degree of centralisation, the owner-manager or top manager within a small firm plays an important role. This influential role is also mirrored in the adoption and implementation process of ICT, especially since ICT projects in small firm are usually initiated at the top (Montazemi 1987; Igbaria *et al.* 1998). Several investigations have shown that support from the small firm's top manager – in the form of commitment and involvement – is conducive to successful ICS use (DeLone 1988;   Martin 1989; Yap *et al.* 1992), as well as his level of ICT literacy (DeLone 1988; Martin 1989; Thong and Yap 1995; Igbaria *et al.* 1997; Fink 1998). On the other hand, a lack of managerial support can lead to implementation problems (Chenney 1983).

22.6.6 User participation

In addition to top management support, user participation is another important factor in the implementation process. Besides the studies noted above in the context of larger organisations, studies investigating smaller organisations have also shown that user participation in the implementation process is associated with successful use or user satisfaction (Montazemi 1988; Yap *et al.* 1992; Doukidis *et al.* 1994). User participation is not only likely to reduce the key barrier, user resistance (Chenney 1983), by involving employees in the implementation process and listening to their needs, but it can also increase usage levels since the ICS might be more tailored to the specific needs of the user. However, while user participation is important, in the context of the small firm, particularly micro-firms with less than 10 employees, it can be assumed that user participation is naturally relatively high, since initiators and users of ICT are more likely to be the same persons.

Users in small firms are on average less likely to exhibit high levels of ICT expertise (Raymond 1987; Mønsted 1993). Hence, small firms often need to rely on external provision of expertise. A study by Naylor and Williams (1994) for example showed that 60% of their sample utilised externals in the ICT acquisition process. Raymond (1985) reports a level of 70%, Chen (1993) noted nearly 75% and DeLone (1988) reports an even higher percentage of 83%. Additionally, the use of external expertise is often not confined to inexperienced firms: experienced small firms also use externals to help implement new ICS (Soh *et al.* 1992).

22.6.7 The importance of external support

There are basically two external sources of support (Mønsted 1993): informal sources like ICT-knowledgeable friends and collegues, or formal sources of ICT expertise like ICT vendors, consultants or governmental support programmes. However, although informal networks were found to be of importance (Mønsted 1993; Zinatelli *et al.* 1996), most of the few studies investigating external ICT support in small firms focus on the formal sources of external support.

While government programmes (see, for example, Yap and Thong 1997) are usually helpful to lower knowledge-based barriers of adoption (e.g. by supplying information and/or training classes) and can aid in overcoming some of the resource-based problems of small firms (e.g. by offering financial support schemes or specific tax allowances), vendors and consultants are usually key sources of formal expertise in the actual planning and implementation stages.

Intuitively one would assume that external support potentially increases the likelihood of ICS success by overcoming the internal lack of ICT expertise. This assumption found support in a study by Lees (1987). Extensive vendor support increased user satisfaction and ICS usage in his sample. Likewise, Yap *et al.* (1992) report that consultant effectiveness and the level of vendor support showed a positive relationship with ICS success. Thong *et al.* (1996) even found that top management support is not as important as effective external ICS expertise. Findings by other researchers paint a slightly different picture. Soh *et al.* (1992) found no differences between small firms that did use consultants and those that did not. Furthermore, they observed no difference between use of consultants and the overall success of ICS. Another striking finding in their study is that small firms with consultant support were less likely to complete implementation in time and within budget. The authors argue that this might be an indication of a more fomalised planning and needs evaluation approach compared to small firms implementing without consultant support. Their subsequent finding of a higher system use for small firms with consultant support can be interpreted as an indication of a higher organisational congruence with the potential of the newly implemented ICS, potentially based on the more thorough planning process. Still, the non-existence of overall differences between firms using consultants and those that did not is surprising.

Thong *et al.* (1994) compared the effectiveness of small firms using both, consultant and vendor support, with small firms using only vendor support. Their findings indicate that the vendor-only approach led to higher user satisfaction levels. Besides the potentially higher co-ordination costs in the consultant-vendor approach, the authors argue that consultants are usually more trained in dealing with large firms. Their lack of understanding of the peculiarities of small firms might be a source of lower effectiveness. This observation might also explain the above-stated findings by Soh *et al.* (1992).

It thus seems that it is not so much the technical expertise of the external sources *per se*, but their capability and experience in dealing with small firms (Soh *et al.* 1992). ICT consultants, as well as ICT vendors, tend to speak a different language, which can cause communication problems; some authors even refer to a potential cultural clash between external ICT 'techies' and small-firm management (Mønsted 1993). In addition, DeLone (1988) argues that external support is no substitute for a knowledgeable and involved top management. This notion is supported by a recent study, showing that internal factors are more important than external factors in the adoption process (Fink 1998). Thus, it is more the combination of internal skills and management support with external support that is likely to contribute to effective ICT implementation in small firms (Igbaria *et al.* 1997). Examples of small firms adopting sub-optimal ICT solutions due to a passive engagement in external networks (Robertson *et al.* 1996) further stress the importance of the development of internal skills.

Furthermore, it is also important to distinguish between the role of externals at the various stages of ICT initiation, adoption, implementation and post-implementation.

A first study by Cragg and King (1993) addressed the post-adoption stages in small firms. Although they did not focus on the role of externals, they found a considerable variability in ICT growth over time and attributed it to various factors. It would be intersting to see how the role of externals evolves over the various stages and how they influence ICT use in the small firm.

Taking into consideration what type of ICT adoption decision the firm undertakes is also crucial. One could for example differentiate between ICT innovation, ICT update and ICT expansion decisions. ICT innovation refers to a firm's decision to invest in a new ICS, including its first-time investment decision. ICT update decisions refer to updating an existing ICS and ICT expansion decisions refer to expanding the use of existing ICS within the firm. Mahmoud and Malhotra (1986), for example, report that small firms' perceptions of the usefulness of consultants versus vendors differ. Small firms planning to use ICT emphasised the importance of greater consultant involvement, while for current users of ICT, vendor support was stated as a key criterion. Therefore, a small firm's needs for external support relating to ICT innnovation decisions and ICT update and expansion decisions are different. Additionally, ongoing maintenance and service support is important, which often requires a different skill set from the external party (Mønsted 1993).

It is important to bear in mind that the above-mentioned stages will differ depending on what type of ICS will be implemented. All the above studies are related to a mix of different ICT applications. It can be assumed that, depending on the type of ICS and depending on the existing internal ICS skills, effectiveness of externals will differ and different skills will be asked for. Therefore, no final straightforward conclusion can be drawn from the empirical investigations, but that externals in general play an important role in ICT implementation in small firms.

22.6.8 ICT usage pattern

The importance of internal ICT experience, top management support and user participation and the importance of the efficient and effective use of external expertise discussed so far were found to be salient for the successful implementation and use of ICS in small firms. But one important question was not yet discussed. What do small firms actually use ICT for?

Despite the comparatively high level of computerisation among small firms and their view of ICT use being a competitive necessity (Cragg and King 1993), small firms do not yet utilise ICT's full potential. In reviewing the empirical studies analysing the use pattern of ICT in small firms, it becomes apparent that small firms use ICT mainly for operational and administrative support functions rather than for strategic decision-making (Raymond and Magenat-Thalmann 1982; Malone 1985; Mahmoud and Malhotra 1986; Nickell and Seado 1986; Martin 1989; Chen 1993; Mønsted 1993; Department of Trade and Industry 1998), mainly relying on standard off-the-shelf applications (Montazemi 1987; 1988; Martin 1989; Heikkilä et al. 1991). However, a more recent study paints a more positive picture, with over 70% of top management starting to use ICS for decision-making (Igbaria et al. 1998). While this high percentage might be due to the nature of the population of the firms investigated (manufacturing and engineering firms) being on average more prone to use ICT and exhibit higher levels of ICT expertise compared to small firms in other sectors (cf. industry sector variability as noted above), additional evidence suggests that the overall percentage of small firms using ICT for strategic planning is rising (Department of Trade and Industry 1998). Furthermore, using ICT for competitive advantage is currently a top issue among small firms (Pollard and Hayne 1998), also indicating that small firms are moving beyond simply using ICT to support their administrative functions.

In addition to the lack of resources and expertise as an explanation of the low strategic level of ICT use in small firms, another important factor relates to the structural characteristics of small firms. As noted earlier and elsewhere in this book, on average, small firms' degree of specialisation and formalisation is low and their degree of centralisation is usually high. Such an 'unstructured structure' is less congruent with the 'structured structure' of ICT. Therefore, findings by, for example, Raymond (1990), stating that mature and more formalised small firms exhibited higher level of ICS sophistication, are not surprising and are in line with the above-mentioned findings of an increased benefit derived from ICT if business processes are redesigned to leverage ICT's value potential. Furthermore, evidence mounts that ICT can not only lead to decentralisation (Pfeffer and Leblebici 1977), but that particularly combining ICT with decentralised work practices can increase productivity (Brynjolfsson and Hitt 1998). Raymond (1987) also noted that end-user computing was associated with a higher level of decentralisation. Therefore, in order to achieve higher levels of benefits provided by ICS in small firms, structural and work process changes need to be considered, too. But particularly decentralisation might turn out to be a key barrier, as it means that owner-managers have to give up some degree of their control and delegate more power to their employees. A potential loss in power and control is something owner-managers are often unwilling to accept (Kets de Vries 1977).

The above section showed that small firms' adoption, implementation and use of ICT differs from the adoption, implementation and use of ICT in large organisations. Various environmental and organisational specifics were observed. Salient factors in the implementation process could be derived from the reviewed empirical investigations, with creating internal ICT expertise, top management support, user participation and making efficient and effective use of external expertise as key factors for the successful implementation and use of ICS in small firms.

The section that follows moves beyond internal ICS to first theoretically discuss the impact of the Internet, an ICS that crosses the boundaries of the firm. The theoretical discussion will focus on the Internet's role in the internationalisation process of the firm. Secondly, the following section will review empirical studies related to the use of the Internet in small firms.

22.7 The Internet and the small-firm sector

The section above reviewed studies of internal or intra-organisational ICS in small firms. Whereas intra-organisational ICT-based applications are used inside a firm (e.g. an inventory system, a PC), inter-organisational ICS are used by two or more organisations in order to support the sharing of data and/or applications among end-users in different organisations (Barrett and Kosynski 1982; Johnston and Vitale 1988), in essence they constitute electronic computer links between different organisations, crossing their organisational boundaries (e.g. electronic order systems). Inter-organisational ICS offer a variety of advantages for participating firms like lower transaction costs and a speedier flow of data and information (Cash and Konsynski 1985). But until recently, most inter-organisational ICS were either proprietary, developed by large firms for their international communication with geographically dispersed subsidaries (e.g. Apple's AppleLink), or specific to the participating parties (e.g. electronic data interchange), that is, not open for third parties to participate without the consent of the other parties or the network owner. Particularly for new firms, due to their 'liabilities of newness' (Stinchcombe 1965), this meant that tapping into electronic networks was difficult, since they needed not only to identify a potential trading partner, but also to establish themselves as a trustworthy business partner, *before* an electronic link could be established.

The non-proprietary, universally accessible Internet, which can thus be regarded as a supra-organisational ICS, has radically changed this and thereby increased the importance and viability of inter-organisational ICT for small firms. The Internet can be viewed as the largest connected set of computer networks in the world, based on the open TCP/IP (Transmission Control Protocol/Internet Protocol) standard which regulates and directs the flow of data from the sender to the receiver (for more details and a more elaborated definition focusing on the technological features and the communication abilities of the Internet, see December 1996). The two core characteristics that set the Internet apart from other technological innovations are that it is global, i.e. it is universally accessible and globally interconnected, and that it is a digital, multimedia environment. Due to its digital, multimedia nature, the Internet can be simultaneously regarded as a global data and information source, a global communication infrastructure, a global marketplace and a distribution channel of digitisable products.

Although its most important service, the World Wide Web, is still comparatively young, Internet diffusion among organisations is already at a comparatively high level. It is currently estimated that between 73% and 24% of all firms have Internet access and between 14% and 45% of firms have a web site (see Figure 22.4). However, in line with the studies discussed above, the diffusion level among small firms is lower and estimated to be around 40% for SMEs (10–250 employees) with Internet access and to be around 21% for micro-firms (up to 9 employees) with Internet access (Department of Trade and Industry 1998). The technological features of the Internet have several important implications for firms, regardless of their size and age. The main implications, focusing on the marketing function of the firm, are the blurring of:

- national and international marketing boundaries;
- the traditional marketing mix;
- traditional marketing domains.

National and international marketing boundaries

Being present on the Internet in the form of a corporate web site means being globally accessible by everyone having access to the Internet's World Wide Web (www). A corporate web site crosses all existing national borders and whatever the communicated

Figure 22.4 Percentage of firms with Internet access and a web site

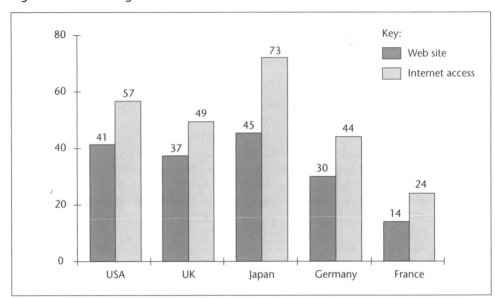

Source: Department of Trade and Industry (1998)

corporate message actually is, it is a global message. Particularly small firms can appear like large firms, operating internationally in ways that were previously not possible. Thus, national and international communication distinctions become irrelevant on the Internet (for an in-depth discussion on the implications of the Internet on international marketing please refer to Quelch and Klein 1996; Hamill 1997).

The traditional marketing mix

The traditional *market mix* distinguishes between product, price, place and promotion (originally introduced by Borden [1958; 1964] and popularised by Kotler's four Ps). On a digital and interactive medium like the Internet, these categories are no longer meaningful and the traditional marketing mix no longer applies (Rayport and Sviokla 1994). For example, a web site can be place and promotion simultaneously; their boundaries blur.

Traditional marketing domains

If the traditional marketing mix does not apply on the Internet, it logically follows that some of the traditional marketing domains blur as well, in addition to the merge of international and national marketing as noted above. Marketing departments in large firms usually have different departments for above-the-line marketing communication, below-the-line marketing communication and direct marketing activities. Since traditional communication models merge on the Internet as well (for a more detailed discussion please refer to December 1996; Morris and Ogan 1996), branding, the traditional domain of above-the-line marketing communication, and direct marketing overlap on the Internet, to give but one example. Thus, marketing on the Internet means crossing marketing domains that were traditionally separated (at least in most large firms).

As a result, it is postulated that, for small firms in particular, Internet-related services like the World Wide Web can be of strategic significance. Besides potential savings in interaction costs (Benjamin and Wigand 1995; Rayport and Sviokla 1995; Booz-Allan and Hamilton 1997; Butler *et al.* 1997) with suppliers, partners, distributors and customers, Internet-related services can help small firms to address international markets, access international market and customer information and compete globally (Quelch and Klein 1996; Hamill 1997).

Although there has been a huge increase in the literature dealing with the Internet, most contributions are rather anecdotal and serious scientific research, particularly empirical research, is still in its infancy (Hamill 1997). However, due to its wide-ranging impact, various research streams, besides technology-based studies, are currently emerging, ranging from advertising (see, for example, *Journal of Advertising Research*, 1997, 37/2, special issue on the World Wide Web) to international marketing (Quelch and Klein 1996; Bennett 1997a; 1998; Hamill 1997; Hamill and Gregory 1997).

22.7.1 The Internet and the internationalisation of the firm

Arguably the Internet's most important value for small firms lies in its potential to enable and facilitate small firms' internationalisation, a growth option for small firms (see Chapter 24) that has become more and more relevant as the globalisation of the world economy increases. Besides various barriers in the internationalisation process (see Chapter 24) that can be overcome or lowered with the technological potential of the Internet (Bennett 1997a; 1998; Hamill 1997), some authors have argued that the traditional incremental school of internationalisation, as postulated by the Uppsala model of internationalisation (see Chapter 24), is called into question when the Internet provides firms of any size with a low-cost and instant access to global markets (Bennett 1997a; Hamill 1997).

This view needs to be differentiated by incorporating an important distinction: the distinction between what has been termed 'marketplace' and 'marketspace' (Rayport and Sviokla 1995). The marketplace represents the physical world of resources or what Negroponte (1995) has termed the world of atoms. The marketspace represents the virtual world of digitised information (Rayport and Sviokla 1995), the world of 'bits' according to Negroponte (1995). This distinction is important as both worlds represent unique characteristics (Rayport and Sviokla 1994; 1995), albeit being interconnected, which means that companies have to operate in both 'worlds'.

With regard to the internationalisation process and the traditional or contingent internationalisation stages in marketspace, there are no internationalisation stages and there exists no internationalisation process (see Figure 22.5). Every firm that presents itself in marketspace via, for example, a corporate web site, is a 'virtual global' the day its web site is accessible. Whereas in the marketplace a firm has to be physically present everywhere to be truly global, so that customers can go to a shop or any other form of physical distribution system to see and buy a firm's wares, in marketspace a firm's offerings are instantly globally accessible, though not physically, by everybody with an Internet access.

Figure 22.5 Internationalisation – marketplace vs marketspace

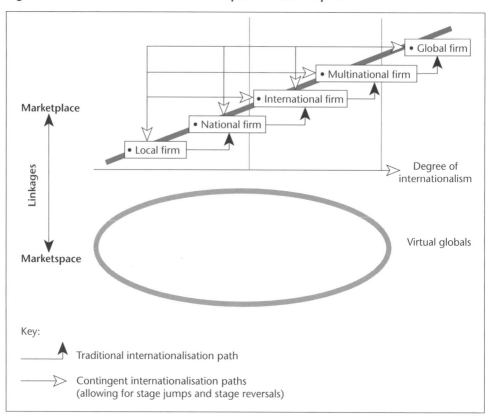

Since there are no internationalisation stages and no internationalisation processes, one of the classical internationalisation barriers, psychic distance, becomes obsolete in marketspace. The Internet's marketspace superimposes a global virtual market with its own rules and characteristics on the geographically-bound markets in the marketplace. These rules and characteristics are, as opposed to foreign markets in the marketplace, independent of spatial aspects; geographic location, nationality and culture matter less. A technical distance (for example, access to hard- and software that enables Internet access, as well as technical expertise to use the access devices) and a language distance, where the role of English as a global language will strengthen further in marketspace (Quelch and Klein 1996; Cairncross 1997), are likely to supersede the classical concept of psychic distance, at least in marketspace. Taking the Internet's current speed of technological, software-based innovations into consideration underlines the important effect of technical distance.

The Internet's marketspace thus opens up a new mode of international operations for firms. Besides the three traditional generic modes of international operation, exporting, licensing and foreign direct investment (see Chapter 24), a 'virtual' mode of international operations can be added (see Figure 22.6).

Figure 22.6 The virtual mode of international operations

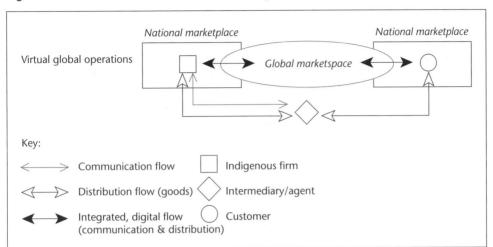

In most cases, the virtual mode of international operations will still rely on operations in the marketplace, as only very few products like software and information services can be digitised and distributed over the Internet, thereby blurring the traditional marketing mix distinction between place and promotion. The distribution of non-digitisable products will therefore follow the traditional physical route – in the case of a small firm, most probably via an intermediary due to their resource poverty. Amazon Books (www.amazon.com) for example markets all its books in marketspace and uses agents like Federal Express in the marketplace to distribute its wares to the customer (for a detailed case study on amazon.com, see Kotha 1998).

Additionally, as customer power in marketspace is likely to increase due to reduced search costs for information (Bakos 1991; 1997; Butler *et al.* 1997), the amount of unsolicited enquiries and unsolicited orders from foreign customers is likely to increase, a notion that a recent case-study-based investigation supports (Honeycutt *et al.* 1998). Hence, marketspace activities are likely to have an impact on the marketplace activities and vice versa. Though these potential linkages have not yet been thoroughly empirically assessed, one can theorise that extensive marketspace activities will have a positive effect on the degree of internationalisation activities in the marketplace. Bennett (1997a) reports for example that the Internet encouraged nearly 20% of firms in his sample a lot to expand their foreign operations. Furthermore he noted that Internet users felt less of a need to establish foreign branches. These are first indications of a linkage between marketspace and marketplace activities.

22.7.2 The Internet and the small firm – empirical studies

Little empirical evidence currently exists with regard to the Internet's role in small firms. However, the few empirical findings that do exist are often in line with the findings of intra-organisational ICT as discussed above. Still some differences are observable.

While external help in implementing and operating Internet-based technologies (Auger and Gallagher 1997; Bennett 1997a; 1998) and the lack of skills and resources being a major reason for non-adoption (Coyne *et al.* 1996; Auger and Gallagher 1997; Bennett 1997a; Hamill and Gregory 1997; Nath *et al.* 1998) are in line with the findings in the intra-organisational ICT research domain, firm size seems to be less relevant in Internet use. Several studies have found no significant difference between large and small firms regarding use and most small firms using the Internet are rather very small (micro-firms with between 1 and 10 employees and small firms with less than 50 employees) than medium-sized (Abell and Lim 1996; Abell and Black 1997; Bennett 1997a; Fink *et al.* 1997; Poon and Strom 1997; Poon and Swatman 1997). Furthermore these firms are relatively young and more likely to use the Internet than more established firms (Bennett 1997a; Fink *et al.* 1997). A major reason for these findings is probably the little financial investment that is needed to use Internet-related services.

Industry specifics are also observable. Small firms operating in the ICT sector are more likely to use the Internet (Abell and Lim 1996; Abell and Black 1997; Fink *et al.* 1997; Poon and Swatman 1997; Soh *et al.* 1997; Poon and Swatman 1998), possibly because the technical entrepreneurs in those firms are more familiar with the technology and its value compared to the 'average' owner-manager in small firms (see Chapter 13). Furthermore, since technology-intensive small firms often exhibit a strong international orientation early on, the Internet's potential to support international operations might be another influential factor.

Due to the Internet's reciprocal nature (Markus 1987), an important influential factor in Internet use among small firms is the 'wiredness' of its trading partners and its network of business contacts. Since communication in the form of e-mail is currently the main use of the Internet among firms (Abell and Lim 1996; Abell and Black 1997; Feher and Towell 1997; Poon and Strom 1997; Poon and Swatman 1997; Department of Trade and Industry 1998), firms whose trading partners do not use e-mail have little incentive to adopt e-mail as a communication tool, unless they are willing to expand their existing network of business contacts or are able to convince its existing partners to get 'wired'. Empirical investigations by Abell and Lim (1996) and Sillince *et al.* (1998) support this notion, reporting that the number one reason for non-adoption of firms is the non-wiredness of suppliers and customers.

However, besides the benefits of easily accessing information, the Internet's promise as a virtual market is not yet fulfilled for most participating firms. Most studies indicate a comparatively low level of on-line ordering via the Internet (Abell and Lim 1996; Abell and Black 1997; Feher and Towell 1997; Fink *et al.* 1997; Soh *et al.* 1997), with the above-mentioned success story of amazon.com being rather an exception than the rule. A major reason for this is that the Internet is not yet considered to be a secure medium by most firms (Abell and Lim 1996; Coyne *et al.* 1996; Auger and Gallagher 1997; Feher and Towell 1997; Soh *et al.* 1997; Nath *et al.* 1998) and that some firms question the reliability and credibility of the information obtained from the Internet (Soh *et al.* 1997).

Despite this, a key advantage of the Internet for small firms, its information richness as a global data and information pool, is becoming more and more of a disadvantage as the Internet's content continues to grow. Internet search engines have serious limitations, covering only a fraction of the Internet (Jenkins *et al.* 1998) and the most valuable information for firms can often only be found in what has been termed 'the hidden Internet', a part of the Internet that is not covered by most search engines (Notess 1997). It thus comes as no surprise that firms report difficulties in locating relevant information on the Internet (Abell and Lim 1996; Soh *et al.* 1997). Hence, small firms adopting Internet services early on might gain first-mover advantages by accruing expertise from using the Internet (learning by using) that will be difficult to match for later entrants. A longitudinal investigation by Poon and Swatman (1997) indirectly demonstrated the existence of organisational learning effects. The authors found that the stated extent of saved time to find resources on the Internet increased over time, indicating that firms' expertise in using the Internet effectively has increased.

This section showed that the Internet as a global, supra-organisational ICS differs from the intra-organisational ICS discussed in the previous section. While similarities regarding its adoption and implementation in small firms were observed, four differences stand out. Firstly, due to its low-cost access, the Internet is financially feasible to even the smallest firms. Secondly, due to its reciprocal nature, effective use of the Internet as a communication medium necessitates 'wired' business partners. Its value depends on the amount and quality of a firm's present and future business partners. Thirdly, effective use the Internet as an information medium is not easy. Its exponential growth in contents makes it more and more difficult to retrieve relevant information, which in turn prompts a firm to devote time and resources to using the Internet as an effective information source. Fourthly, despite all the hype in the media, the Internet as a virtual market is still in its infancy. Security and credibility concerns among firms still slow down the process of turning the Internet into a viable way to do business for most firms.

22.8 Chapter summary

This chapter intended to give the reader an overview of research into the organisational use of ICT, particularly the current empirical state of ICT research in small firms. It is apparent that the adoption, implementation and use of ICT in small firms differs from that in larger organisations. The chapter showed that internal ICT skills, top management support, user participation and the role of externals are among the most salient characteristics of successful ICT use in small firms.

Although an increase in ICT use among small firms was reported, most small firms still under-utilise ICT's value potential by restricting its use to administrative tasks. The chapter highlighted that in order to derive a higher level of ICT sophistication, small firms need to align their processes to leverage ICT's value potential. Such processes, including higher degrees of formalisation and decentralisation, are however unlikely to be implemented in a large proportion of small firms, since their 'unstructured structure' and high degree of centralisation are usually organisational characteristics that small firms' owner-managers may be unwilling to give up (Kets de Vries 1977), which is often reflected in their 'stay small attitude' (Davidsson 1989b).

Besides intra-organisational ICS, inter-organisational ICS, particularly the supra-organisational Internet, are of increasing importance. In the future, as more and more large firms connect via electronic links, it is likely that the role of inter-organisational ICS will become essential for most small firms in order to tap into these networks, especially if they want to participate in the international business arena. Previous limitations, due to proprietary systems leading to ex-post dependencies, are about to be overcome with the Internet's open standards. But inter-organisational ICS are not only important for small firms relying on links to large organisations (like suppliers). Small firms can also use this new medium to market their services to consumers. Especially due to its global nature, small firms are now in a position to market their products and services on a global basis, an exposure that was previously not possible for small firms. Still it was also observed that most of the theoretical postulations are not yet observable in the day-to-day business of most small firms. While Internet start-ups and success stories like amazon.com might suggest otherwise, the average small firm still has a lot of concerns about the Internet and would rather wait before they jump on the bandwagon. However, it was also shown that small firms actively participating early on might gain learning-based first-mover advantages. Hence it might depend on the specific industry sector a small firm operates in, as well as its products, to decide on its organisational approach to the Internet as a new medium.

These conclusions have several implications. The need for more empirical research is the main implication for researchers. Still too little is known about ICT use in small firms, especially in the case of Internet use in small firms. Besides more detailed investigations into the use of specific ICT like CAD/CAM, MRP or the Internet and investigations into specific small firms like start-ups or family firms, a fruitful research approach would be to conduct more longitudinal and inductive research, as opposed to the traditional cross-sectional, postal questionnaire-based investigations. In addition, researchers should address the issue of comparability by employing similar categorisations and levels of analysis, or at least reporting the characteristics of the sample along these dimensions. Such a categorisation should include the following:

- size of the firm;
- age of the firm;
- stage of adoption;
- dependent variable.

The main implications for owner-managers lie in the crucial need to develop internal ICT skills (those of the owners and of their employees) and to personally support ICT implementations. Although external support is often essential, it cannot substitute for a complete lack of internal skills. Internal managerial ICT skills are the only source that can provide sustainable competitive advantage from ICT (Mata *et al.* 1995). The technology *per se* is available to every firm. It is the internal skill of a firm to put it to effective use that makes the difference. In addition, ongoing user training and user participation in the implementation process are crucial in order to maximise ICS usage. Furthermore, due to the importance of external support, it is crucial for the owner-manager 'to listen to the right people' and select the right sources of support; and these might be less the most technically sophisticated, but more the small-firm experienced vendors and consultants. The owner-manager should also make sure that an ICT-supporting infrastructure is in place. Particularly in the case of the Internet as a virtual market, providing a small firm with global exposure, the risk of overexposure is high. Customers on the Internet not only expect short response times, but they can also access a corporate web site 24 hours a day. If the small firm has not the needed resources in place to respond in time, customer dissatisfaction is likely to follow. Besides the risk of overexposure, the owner-manager should also make sure that international in-house expertise is present, including foreign language skills (particularly in the case of non-English-speaking firms) and expertise to ship products internationally, since being on the Internet automatically means participating in international business, at least in the marketspace.

Although the need for other structural alignments like business process redesign and decentralisation were mentioned, it is unlikely that most small firms' managers will pursue such restructuring unless their organisational growth, transforming their small firm into a medium-sized firm, necessitates such realignments.

Since the small-firms sector can be considered as a relatively untapped market with a higher growth potential compared to the more saturated markets in the medium- and large-firm sector, ICT producers, consultants and vendors should take the above-stated small-firm specifics into account when devising their marketing programmes. Marketing programmes tailored to large firms' internal IS departments with their ICT experts are not applicable in the case of most small firms, due to their lower level of ICT expertise. It is more valuable for small firms if vendors focus more on ICT competence transfer than on merely selling hardware, software and after-sales maintenance services.

Policy-makers should focus their support on providing the needed national technical infrastructure, particularly in the case of supra-organisational ICT, in order to reduce technical distance. In addition, they should help address the concerns raised about Internet security by internationally co-ordinating policies to increase its viability as a virtual market. In particular, policy-makers need to address the three related security issues of authentication, integrity and confidentiality. Authentication refers to the reliable identification of the originator or sender of a message, integrity refers to a mechanism that ensures that data were not altered during transmission and confidentiality refers to a mechanism that prevents the unwanted disclosure of the sent information (Feit 1996). Most importantly policy-makers should also ensure that they offer support programmes that enhance ICT skill development among small firms and provide financial support schemes to help small firms invest in ICT. Due to the heterogeneity of small firms, generic support schemes will only reach a limited number of small firms. Policy-makers are therefore advised to develop specific support programmes tailored to specific classes of small firms (for a detailed discussion see, for example, LaRovere 1998). But while the national technology infrastructure and the related security issues are high on the political agenda of most industrialised countries, support programmes to enhance internal ICT skills of small firms are usually less widely diffused.

Questions

1 Is ICT important for small firms? Why?

2 What is meant by the term 'coverage' and how does it relate to IT and IM?

3 What is meant by 'the problem of the dependent variable'? And what are its implications?

4 What factors constitute key success factors in the implementation of ICT in small firms? And how do these differ compared to larger firms?

5 Why is the Internet a very special ICT?

CHAPTER 23

Growth and development in the small firm

David Smallbone and Peter Wyer

23.1 Learning objectives

There are four learning objectives in this chapter:

1 To consider what is meant by growth in small firms.

2 To consider how growth in small firms can be explained.

3 To assess the main barriers and constraints to growth in small firms.

4 To identify some of the main issues facing managers in growing small firms and to discuss ways in which these may be successfully dealt with.

Key concepts

■ business growth ■ development ■ management constraints
■ external environment

23.2 Introduction

There has probably been more written about small-business growth in recent years than any other aspect of the development or management of small firms. One of the reasons for this is the contribution of growing firms to economic development and employment generation, which has attracted the attention of policy-makers in many countries. In the UK in the 1990s, growing SMEs have been the prime target for business support services by Business Links, as part of a national strategy for increasing the contribution of the SME sector to the competitiveness of the national economy (HMSO 1994; 1995; DTI 1995c). For private-sector business service providers such as banks, growing businesses are potentially attractive customers because business growth is likely to be associated with a demand for finance and other services. For some individual business owners, the high casualty rates among new firms in particular focus attention on the elusive 'success factors', the identification of which have been the subject of a large number of studies. Whilst growth may be judged by some as an indicator of business success, it can also present managers with problems which often focus on the need to relate expansion to the resources available, or those which can be realistically mobilised.

In this context, this chapter considers some of the main issues relating to growth that confront small-business owners/managers, as well as those individuals and organisations concerned with assisting or doing business with them. After a brief discussion of what is meant by 'growth' in small firms, the question of how growth can be explained is considered, drawing on a number of major research studies. The second half of the chapter focuses on some of the management issues associated with growth in small firms, including the main barriers to growth and how these can be managed.

23.3 Growth and development in the small firm

Much of the literature that has been written about small-business growth defines growth in terms of employment (Keeble 1993; Storey 1994). Part of the reason for this is the interest of public policy-makers in facilitating a growth in employment opportunities. In this context, various studies have demonstrated the disproportionate contribution of a minority of fast-growth firms to employment generation (see Chapter 3). For example, among new firms, it has been suggested that 'out of every 100 created, the fastest growing four firms will create half the jobs in the group over a decade' (Storey *et al.* 1987). Another study, which was concerned with the development of a group of 306 mature manufacturing SMEs over an 11-year period, showed that 23% of the firms (i.e. those achieving high growth) contributed 71% of all new jobs created in the panel (Smallbone *et al.* 1995).

Although employment generation may be an appropriate growth criterion for public policy, for most SME owners/managers it is a consequence rather than a prime objective of business development. Where owners seek to expand their business, this is more likely to be in terms of profitability, sales turnover or net assets than employment *per se*, since few have set up their businesses primarily to create employment for others. At the same time, a number of studies has demonstrated the close correlation that exists between employment growth and sales growth in small firms over a long period of time (Storey *et al.* 1987; Smallbone *et al.* 1995), although increased employment is less clearly related to a growth in profitability.

Although the policy context is one of the reasons why many academic studies define small-business growth in terms of increased employment, another concerns data availability and reliability. Financial data (such as sales turnover or profits) are notoriously less reliable in small firms than in large firms and less commonly available because of exemption of the smallest firms from annual financial reporting requirements. This means that researchers typically have to rely on self-reported financial data which presents both confidentiality and reliability issues, with respect to sales and profitability in particular.

One of the issues that need to be recognised in any discussion of small-business growth is that not all owners see growth as an important business objective. One of the reasons is that there is a variety of factors that contribute to individuals starting and running a business, which means that lifestyle and non-business objectives may result in a lack of growth orientation (Curran 1986b). Moreover, the importance of business growth in relation to an individual entrepreneur's other goals can change as s/he gets older.

The growth orientation of an individual small firm can also vary at different stages of business development, as well as in response to changes in external factors. For example, in a newly established business, some growth is likely to be a necessity for survival, although a period of rapid growth may need to be followed by a period of consolidation if expansion is not to outstrip the ability of the firm's resource base to support it. For these reasons, the extent to which the owner of a small firm is seeking to grow (i.e. its growth orientation) can vary over time as well as between firms.

23.4 Explaining growth in small firms

Although a great deal has been written about the growth of small enterprises, there is no single theory which can adequately explain it nor, as Gibb and Davies (1990; 1991) have suggested, is there much likelihood of such a theory being developed in the future. The main reason for the absence of such a model is the variety of different factors which can affect the growth of small firms and, in particular, the way in which these factors interact with one another. For this reason, the approach used here is based on a modified version of a framework presented by David Storey (1994) to consider the factors influencing small-firm growth. This will incorporate aspects of the four main theoretical approaches to small-business growth identified by Gibb and Davies (1990; 1991) as well as selected empirical evidence where appropriate. The aim is to highlight those aspects which appear to be characteristic of high-growth enterprises.

Our framework includes the three influences on growth identified by Storey: characteristics of the entrepreneur; characteristics of the firm; and management strategies. It also incorporates the additional influence of the external environment, since it is our intention to make explicit that a prime determinant of growth is the way in which the small business addresses the enabling and constraining nature of its operating context (Figure 23.1). Each of these components will be discussed in turn.

23.4.1 Characteristics of the entrepreneur

Since one of the distinguishing characteristics of small firms compared with large firms is the close correspondence between ownership and management, the characteristics of individuals who start and run small firms can have a major impact on their growth orientation and performance, as well as on their organisational culture (see Chapter 8 for a more detailed discussion).

In this context, one of the approaches to understanding small-business growth identified by Gibb and Davies (1990; 1991) was the so-called 'personality-dominated approach', in which the entrepreneur is seen as the key to the development of the business. For example, the entrepreneur's personal goals are likely to influence why a business was started in the first place, as well as the strength of the firm's growth orientation once it was established. *A priori*, one might expect that a business which was set up to exploit a clearly defined market opportunity for a product or service (and/or because the entrepreneur is strongly motivated to make money) would show a higher propensity to grow than a start-up where the main drivers are 'push' factors such as unemployment (or the threat of it), dissatisfaction with present employment or personal lifestyle reasons.

Figure 23.1 Growth in small firms

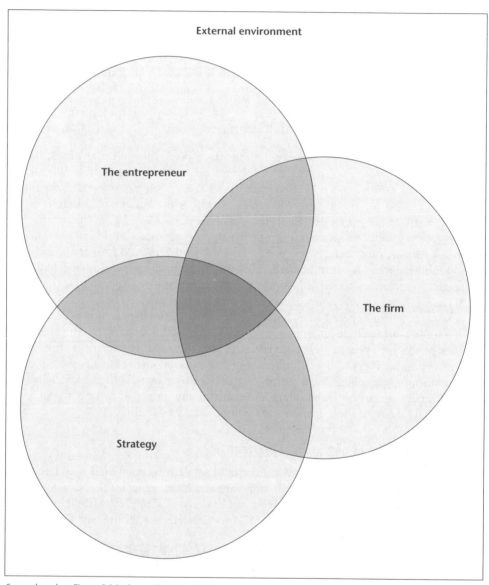

Source: based on Figure 5.1 in Storey (1994), p. 124

In their seminal work on small-business growth, Stanworth and Curran (1976) distinguished between three different identities of small-business owners, thus emphasising the variety of goals that is apparent in relation to why individuals start and run small firms (see Chapter 8). The identities were defined as:

■ an artisan identity, where the owner's role centres on the intrinsic satisfaction associated with the personal autonomy that running one's own business can entail;

- the 'classical entrepreneurial' identity, where the owner's role emphasises earnings and the generation of profits; and

- the 'managerial' identity, where it is suggested that the owner's priorities are focused on looking for the recognition of others.

Empirical evidence suggests that whilst growth orientation does not necessarily lead to actual growth performance, one of the characteristics which distinguishes high-growth firms from other firms is the commitment of the owner(s) to expand the business. For example, in a survey of 306 established manufacturing SMEs (up to 100 employees), it was found that the propensity to achieve high growth between 1979 and 1990 was significantly associated with the strength of their commitment to grow: 70% of high-growth firms referred to strong commitment to grow during this period compared with 32% of other firms (Smallbone *et al.* 1995).

Researchers who have focused on the role of the entrepreneur's personality on the firm's growth performance (e.g. Kets de Vries 1977; Chell *et al.* 1991) have highlighted its influence on attitudes to risk (which can affect the willingness to use external finance), the emphasis placed on personal autonomy (which can affect the willingness of the entrepreneur to collaborate with other firms, or even to use consultants) and managerial competencies, particularly in relation to strategic management skills.

Whilst such factors can undoubtedly affect the performance of the firm in a number of respects, some types of research in this paradigm are more controversial. These include attempts to use typologies based on a profiling of entrepreneur personality traits to predict business success, which tend to ignore the capacity of people to learn and change over time, or indeed their motivation. For example, an owner's motivation for expanding a business may decline once they have achieved what they consider to be a satisfactory level of income from their enterprise and/or their personal/family circumstances change as they grow older. In this respect, Chell and Haworth (1992) have pointed to an association between the age and experience of the leader of the firm and the stage of development of the business reached.

Some of the manufacturing SMEs that achieved high growth in the longitudinal study referred to above (Smallbone *et al.* 1995) were started by what Stanworth and Curran characterised as 'artisans' but who changed to a more entrepreneurial stance over time. An example includes a business started by a founder from a craft printing background but who 10 years later was beginning to think like an entrepreneur, seeking to manage the assets of the business to increase his returns, rather than simply to run a production plant. This had involved firms setting up a property management arm to the business which the owner ran himself, recruiting a production manager to run the core printing activity with which the owner had become increasingly bored.

Storey's emphasis on the role of the characteristics of entrepreneurs in business performance places less emphasis on personality *per se* and more on those personal characteristics which influence access to resources. These include educational background and qualifications, which can affect both the management resource base of the business as well as the entrepreneur's motivation for running it, because of the higher earnings expectations of more educated business owners. Whilst recognising that educational qualifications are no guarantee of business success, Storey suggests that their role is likely to vary between sectors and will be higher in technology and knowledge-based activities and lower in the more traditional and craft-based sectors (see Chapter 13). Other personal characteristics of entrepreneurs considered by Storey include:

- previous management and/or entrepreneurial experience (if any) prior to establishing the current enterprise;
- family history;
- functional skills and previous training;
- previous knowledge and/or experience of the sector in which the business has been established.

However, whilst most of these factors can be shown to contribute to small-business growth in one or more major empirical studies, none appears to make a dominant contribution. Indeed, the search for the identikit picture of the successful entrepreneur has not proved fruitful and, whilst undoubtedly relevant, the characteristics and previous experience of the founder appear to have only a modest effect on the success of the business in terms of its growth performance. Moreover, for many of us, it is the unpredictability and variety of conditions associated with small-business success that help to make the topic so fascinating.

One characteristic that has been attracting increasing attention in recent years has been portfolio ownership (Scott and Rosa 1997) which refers to the fact that some entrepreneurs may be involved in a number of enterprises. Some studies have suggested that portfolio entrepreneurs are more likely to be associated with growth-orientated firms, since multiple ownership is itself a sign of a degree of entrepreneurial flair. It has also been pointed out that, whilst early studies of portfolio entrepreneurship tended to emphasise its role in reducing business risk, it has been increasingly recognised as an important growth strategy, particularly in sectors where economies of scale can be achieved at a low level (Carter 1998).

23.4.2 Characteristics of the firm

Although organisational characteristics may reflect those of the entrepreneur, they are different in the sense that they are based on decisions made by the owner either at the time that the business was started, or at some time after. Storey's review of the relationship between organisational profile characteristics and the propensity of small firms to grow includes age and size, as well as other variables. With respect to age, Storey reports that most UK and US research shows that younger firms grow more rapidly than older firms, reflected in the statement that 'most small firms grow only in the first few years and stabilise' (Burns 1989). Whilst this may be statistically accurate, it partly reflects the need for newly established firms to increase the scale of their operations if they are to accumulate sufficient resources to be able to withstand unforeseen external shocks (see Chapter 7). Other research has demonstrated that even some very mature firms can grow strongly, sometimes following a long period of stagnation (Smallbone and North 1996). Indeed, growth in small firms (where it occurs) is rarely a continuous and sustained process, so that a firm's age will never be a completely reliable predictor of its growth prospects.

One of the approaches used to explain small-business growth identified by Gibb and Davies (1990) was the so-called 'organisational' approach, which emphasises the development sequence of a firm as it passes through a series of stages at different points in its so-called life-cycle – the original idea being that if every product or service faces a life-cycle, then so does any business. There are a number of variants of these 'life-cycle' or 'stages of growth' models, of which that described in Figure 23.2 is an example.

Churchill and Lewis (1983) propounded a five-stage developmental model. This model considers each developmental stage in terms of five management factors:

- managerial style;
- organisational structure;
- formality of systems;
- organisational objectives;
- level of involvement of the owner.

The framework depicts changing development objectives over the *introduction* and *take-off stages* with two phases in each stage. The objectives relate to survival and consolidation/control phases in the introduction stage and control/planning and

Figure 23.2 An indicative 'stages of growth'/life-cycle model

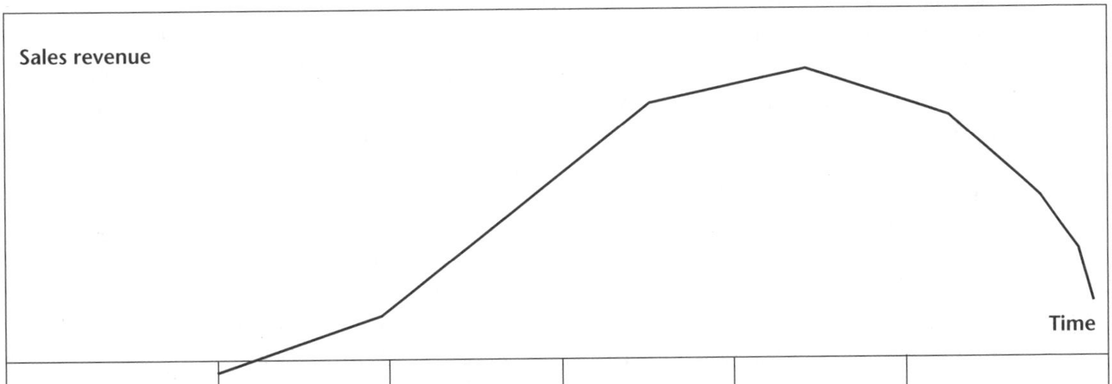

Business life-cycle	Initiation	Development	Growth	Maturity	Decline
Example					
Changing nature of impacting problems:	Need to identify market	Need to consolidate and develop	Need to counter competition	Need to seek alternative markets	Need to develop extension strategies
The need to progressively develop management ability:	Informal marketing ability	Formulation of marketing approach	Competition analysis	Broadening of market analysis	Adjustment to existing products and market focus

expansion phases within the take-off stage. Each of these phases is epitomised by particular management styles and organisation forms, together with particular problems, all of which change as the developmental phases of the business unfold. Application of such a model could, for instance, portray that, at the initial survival phase, the owner *is* the business: (s)he performs all major tasks and undertakes direct supervision of staff. By the time the business reaches the control/planning phase, recruitment of staff is a priority and simple organisation has given way to the delegation of responsibilities to staff that is underpinned by tight controls. A typical marketing problem at the initial survival phase is building an adequate customer base. By the time the small business has developed to the control/planning phase the marketing problems have begun to centre on achieving market penetration by combating the activities of competing firms (Burns 1989).

Whilst critical thresholds separating distinctive phases of the development of a small firm often exist, the formalised 'stages' models, such as those of Churchill and Lewis or Steinmetz (1969), have little application as tools to explain the growth of small firms for a number of reasons. In practice, boundaries between phases may be fuzzy rather than distinct and some small businesses commonly develop more rapidly in relation to certain functions or dimensions than others. As a result, it is often difficult to position firms empirically and thus apply the model in practice.

More fundamentally, such an approach implies that a firm's development path is determined, whereas in practice the number of stages that can be identified is variable. Moreover, in practice, the order of stages is not fixed which means that some firms that may ultimately grow further may move back then forward, rather than continuously forward in the sequence of stages. Overall, the value of such models is more to help to diagnose organisational problems and bottlenecks that need to be addressed by the owner-manager if the firm is to grow further, rather than as an explanation of what actually occurs. At the same time, such models are only concerned with internal constraints and thresholds, divorcing the firm's development path from any interrelationship with the firm's external environment (for an excellent critique of stage models of growth, see O'Farrell and Hitchens 1988).

Empirical studies have shown that one of the most critical thresholds with respect to growth as far as organisational development is concerned, relates to the willingness of the owner to delegate decisions (Storey 1994). This can be illustrated with reference to an analysis of the distinctive characteristics and strategies of a group of high-growth SMEs over an 11-year period (Smallbone *et al.* 1995). One of the most significant differences between high-growth firms and their low-growth or non-growth counterparts was their propensity to have made changes that were designed to create more time for the leaders to manage the firm strategically. Previous writers had suggested that 'creating time to manage is one of the key internal factors influencing the process of change in small firms' (Gibb and Dyson 1982). The results from the long-term longitudinal research showed it to be a key discriminating feature between firms which were able to achieve high growth over 11 years and those that were simply able to survive. Whether this is a cause or effect of growth is less important in practical terms than recognising that the issue needs to be prioritised by entrepreneurs if sustained growth over a long period of time is to be achieved.

23.4.3 Management strategy

In considering the role of strategy as a factor influencing small-firm growth, we refer to management actions taken by the owner once the business has started to trade, that affect the development path of the firms – which may be planned and explicit but more typically is not in smaller companies (see Chapter 16). David Storey's review of areas where management strategy may influence the growth of a small firm includes product development and innovation, market strategy, business planning, production technology, the financial base and external equity, management training and recruitment, workforce training and the use of external advice and assistance (Storey 1994). As a result, strategies for mobilising resources are included, and, by implication, management competence, since this is central to the way in which finance, labour and other resources are mobilised.

Several key strategy factors which underpin growing firms were identified by Storey. Firstly, a willingness to share equity with external individuals or organisations was felt to be an issue central to small firms achieving growth. A second factor relates to the ability of rapidly growing firms to identify market segments or niches where they can build customer bases founded on their distinct quality advantages (see Chapter 20). Moreover, exploitation of this quality advantage will often relate to the utilisation of relevant technologies and a willingness to introduce new products. Finally, an owner-manager's willingness to delegate and devolve decision-making was felt to be a crucial facilitator of growth, which would also require an ability to attract, retain and enthuse quality managerial personnel who are capable of accepting this delegated authority.

One of the main approaches to understanding the growth process identified within the literature is characterised by Gibb and Davies (1990; 1991) as the 'business management' approach, which focuses on the importance of business skills and the role of functional management, planning, control and formal strategic orientations. This body of literature provides valuable guiding insights into how the growing business might achieve sustainable development through making internal adjustments commensurate with identified opportunities in its external change environment. Thus, informative works such as that of Johnson and Scholes (1993) emphasise the growing need for managers to sensitise themselves to what is an increasingly turbulent operating environment, offering management approaches and techniques to aid the manager in this respect. Certainly, their work would offer support to Storey's propositions on key strategy factors. However, much work within the 'business and management' field continues to be based upon assumptions that organisations should or could undertake rational decision-making approaches to identifying and acting upon development opportunities within their external change environment. This rationality manifests itself in recommendations and prescriptions with regard to the essential roles of long-term planning and financial control for the underpinning of organisational growth. However, such prescription seems to overlook the ability of management tools of this nature to accommodate the nature and form of contemporary change situations which impact on today's businesses (Stacey 1990), particularly smaller firms which have limited ability to shape or control external environmental influences (see Chapter 16).

For Gibb and Davies 'business management approaches can be useful in providing frameworks for understanding the way in which firms might grow through product/

market combinations'. Whilst management activities such as 'strategic planning' and 'control' may have a part to play in sustaining the growth of some small firms, the use of formal strategic planning is rare in small firms, being more characteristic of larger businesses. This is partly because of the higher propensity of large firms to employ managers who are professionally trained, although it also reflects a greater ability to reduce some of the uncertainties in the external environment that are typical in the case of small firms. It appears, therefore, that whilst propounded management approaches within the business literature may have great potential in aiding the understanding of organisational growth, there is a need to be highly selective in the use of this insight in the small-business development context.

23.4.4 External environmental influences

Arguably, it is the impact of external influences and the unpredictable manner in which they emerge or change that provide the major impact on the nature and pace of small-business growth (Wyer 1997). Small businesses can face severe problems with environmental change because of a lack of understanding, expertise and time. In this context, Cohn and Lindberg (1974: 14) emphasise that 'because small firms generally engage in a narrower range of activities, use a narrower range of materials, employ fewer skills and serve single markets, it is probably even more important for them to anticipate changes in the factors impinging on their welfare than it is for large firms. A great change in one factor is likely to have more effect on a small company.' For example, within a financial context, Welsh and White (1984) underline how 'external forces tend to have more impact on small businesses than on large businesses. Changes in government regulations, tax laws and labour and interest rates usually affect a greater percentage of expenses than they do for large organisations' (see Chapter 4).

Certainly, two of the broad categories of approaches to growth identified by Gibb and Davies (1990; 1991) address the importance of the impact of the external environment upon organisations: the so-called 'business management' approaches discussed above and the 'sectoral and broader market-led approaches'. For Gibb and Davies (1991), these sectoral studies concentrate predominantly on the identification of external constraints and opportunities underpinning the small-firm growth process. For example, within the context of small high-tech businesses, the need to keep abreast of technological change and 'the importance of building marketing into quality, design and development from the early stages' are key sectoral conditions affecting business success (see Chapter 13). The position and role of the large company within the external operating environment can be a further crucial issue, with small-business growth being closely related to the attitudes and strategies of the large firm. For example, large-company strategies with regard to subcontracting, 'make or buy' and strategic partnerships are viewed as key determinants of small-firm growth potential. Integral to the concept of partnership is the potential for the small firm to access large-company R&D, technology and management and resource support.

Whilst Gibb and Davies emphasise that the existing literature does not provide clear guidelines in the form of predictive theory, the existing knowledge base does provide a partial guiding framework of insight regarding the small-firm growth process.

In relation to external environmental influences, sectoral variations on the growth rates of small firms are to be expected because of differences in market trends and competitive conditions between different activities (see Chapter 16). However, since market conditions vary between individual product markets, the amount of sectoral variation in growth performance which is identified in practice tends to vary according to the level of sectoral disaggregation that is used. This is because the narrower the sectoral definition that is used, the less variety that exists within sectoral categories, which means there is less of a tendency for buoyant conditions in one product market to be offset by weak trends in another, or vice versa.

A firm's location is another characteristic that can affect its growth prospects, since it reflects spatial variations in local environmental conditions. On the demand side, variations in the size, scope and buoyancy in local markets might be expected to affect a firm's opportunities to grow. On the supply side, variations in the cost and availability of some factors of production (such as labour and premises) and resources (such as access to information and business services) may also be an influence. At the same time, the adaptability of SMEs to local external conditions should not be underestimated. Whilst the employment growth of small firms may vary considerably between different types of location (Keeble *et al.* 1992) because of differences in labour market conditions, the growth performance of small firms measured in terms of sales growth tends to show much less variation (Smallbone *et al.* 1993). This is because of differences in the types of strategy used by SME owners/managers to develop their businesses in different locations, which is an indication of the adaptability of successful SMEs to local conditions (North and Smallbone 1996).

23.5 Barriers and growth constraints – the external operating context

In this section we build on the foundation of insight offered in the previous section to consider the major external barriers which may constrain small-business development and which have to be circumvented or managed if effective growth is to be sustained.

23.5.1 The differing nature of change situations impacting on contemporary businesses

Contemporary business organisations, if they are to survive and prosper, must cope with unprecedented levels of change. The origins of such change are multi-sourced, deriving from sources such as the liberalising activities of countries forming co-operative economic blocs, unfolding patterns of globalisation (Goman 1994) which have in turn been built out of factors such as ease of communication and transportation, the arrival of the better-educated and discerning consumer and advances in technology which substantially enhance the competitive nature of the change environment.

For the small business, its weakness in being able to control and relate to the environment is a key distinguishing characteristic (Gibb 1983a). Moreover, when one conceptualises 'change' at a more specific level, the complexity of the management task in small firms becomes highly apparent. For Stacey (1990) it is necessary to consider change situations in terms of closed, contained and open-ended change. With closed change a firm can predict events and actions with regard to timing and consequences, such as if a major customer increases his or her order. In such circumstances, the form and timing of its consequences are knowable and allow for prediction in terms of the required resources and cash flows. Contained change relates to events occurring whereby repetitions of the past, the laws of large numbers and concepts of probability apply. Change events such as the seasonal patterns of sales allow predictability within limits. With both closed and contained change situations the small-business manager can undertake rational short-interval planning activity in order to underpin organisational control.

However, as Stacey emphasises, much of the change that faces contemporary business organisations is unknowable and unpredictable in terms of its timing and its consequences. In other words, such change is open-ended, with it often being unclear what is changing or why it is changing. For example, Britain's exit from the European Exchange Rate Mechanism was unexpected, and its consequences for individual businesses could not be clearly determined. The unanticipated emergence of cost reductions and quality-improving technology from an overseas competitor can have an indeterminate impact on the small business.

Under such operating conditions, sustainable business development can therefore only be effected by small-business management processes that can facilitate identification and understanding of open-ended change situations as a basis for determining appropriate internal adjustment activity within the small firm.

23.5.2 Industry structure, competition and market limitations

Porter (1980) emphasises that the key aspect of a firm's environment is the industry or industries in which it competes. For Porter, the competitive rules of the game and strategies potentially available to the firm are substantially influenced by industry structure (see Chapter 16). He sees the intensity of competition in an industry transcending well beyond the behaviour of current competitors with its roots firmly implanted in the industry's underlying economic structure. It is, for him, the collective strength of five basic competitive forces which determine the profit potential in an industry. These forces which drive industry competition are: the threat of new entrants; bargaining power of suppliers; bargaining power of buyers; the threat of substitute products or services; and the intensity of rivalry among existing firms.

In order to effect sustainable development within a given industry, a small firm would need to build up an understanding of the underlying structural features which underpin the above basic competitive forces, for it is knowledge of the underlying sources of these competitive forces which allows a firm to determine its critical strengths and areas of weakness. For example, the threat of new entrants to an industry (or put another way, the difficulty of gaining access to an industry) can be understood by reference to the major underlying sources of barriers to entry. These might include: existence of economies of scale within the industry; established firms having achieved product differentiation; high-level capital requirements; the presence of switching costs; the need for new entrants to secure access to distribution channels; and the possession by established firms of cost advantages independent of scale (such as product know-how or design characteristics retained through patents or secrecy; access to raw materials; or favourable locations).

For the smaller business one keystone to growth may be a recognition that 'markets tend to become more heterogeneous over time, evolving into progressively finer segments as buyer tastes and technological opportunities change'. Such 'heterogeneity of the market permits market segmentation and the use of product differentiation to create "specialist" or "niche" strategies by firms' (McGee 1989). Inherent here, however, are significant potential barriers which may prevent the small firm from effecting such development. These barriers include firstly the need to identify and respond to such market segments or niches. This will require both the determination of the form of the 'distinctiveness' which will provide the differentiation of product which matches the customers' needs; and the ability to produce and sustain that distinctiveness. For example, O'Farrell and Hitchens (1988) suggest that those firms which achieve growth are those which can identify the key criteria upon which to compete in certain segments (including design, price, quality, delivery) and are then able to develop a competitive advantage around these criteria. The barriers also include the difficulty of coping with direct competitors who may ultimately be attracted by the returns associated with the emerging segment or niche, and the broader forces of competition, as discussed above.

Moreover, even where a small business has appropriately identified underlying industry and market structure characteristics in a manner which continues to facilitate ongoing sustainable development, the unfolding of unknowable open-ended change situations can confound that development without warning. For example, the recent sudden emergence of political and financial turmoil across South-East Asia, Russia and Brazil has affected the development of many businesses which heretofore had successfully effected growth through building up trade with these countries.

23.6 Barriers and growth constraints – the internal operating context

This section reviews some of the major internal constraints which affect growth in the small firm. These relate to the influence of the owner-manager and the relative small scale of the enterprise.

23.6.1 Owner-manager- and size-related constraints

Smallbone and Wyer (1997) have demonstrated how, for many small to medium-sized enterprises, 'size-related factors affect their ability to identify and respond to developmental opportunities in their external environment'. They emphasise how owner-manager- and size-related characteristics help to shape the enabling and constraining forces which affect the ability of small firms to identify, cope with and positively respond to environmental changes. Size-related characteristics thus contribute substantially to the shaping of strategic activity and underlying management actions. Such owner-manager- and size-related characteristics include the following.

Organisational culture
In an owner-managed business, the 'organisational culture' typically reflects the personality traits and aspirations of the owner-manager that, in turn, help to shape the

enabling and constraining forces affecting the firm. The pervading sets of norms and values, the ways of doing things and the freedoms afforded to different individuals, are often reflected in informal and idiosyncratic structures, systems and processes which themselves often reflect the personality traits of the main owner (see Chapter 6). Whilst over time a firm's historical development path and its markets and its technologies will all affect this small-firm culture, the owner-manager is likely to predominate particularly in the early stages. In this context, a key potential constraint on future development can be the extent to which the small-business culture/structure remains embedded in the owner-manager. This is a key management issue which we address later.

Finance

A well-documented constraint on small-business growth is that of an inadequate financial resource base (see Chapter 19). On the one hand, this can result from a lack of the required levels of collateral and of a proven track record that can affect the firm's ability to raise external development finance, whilst it also reflects the firm's outlook of financial management skills which can affect its ability to generate investment funds internally. Whilst David Storey (1994) has identified a willingness to share equity as a factor influencing the growth potential of a small firm, the operation of the formal venture capital markets makes it difficult for firms to raise sums of less than £250,000 from this source. Whilst informal risk capitalists (or 'business angels') are a possible source of such finance, entrepreneurs must have the knowledge and ability to identify a feasible development project and produce a supporting business plan to realise it. As it is, an ignorance of this financing concept may itself be a constraint on the growth of many potentially successful small businesses.

Attracting and retaining quality people

Many small businesses face a marginal labour market whereby they cannot offer the same wage and salary levels or career-path opportunities as large companies. A frequent corollary of this is that they attract less able, less committed and/or less experienced workers which can result in lateness, absenteeism or leaving without notice (Curran 1988). This can impact severe constraints on development when, for example, consistency in quality, reliability and delivery are essential prerequisites for the build-up of image and customer base, but cannot be realised because of staffing problems (see Chapter 17). The solution must be to encourage more owners to adopt a more staff-focused approach to human resource management, recognising that potentially the workforce can be one of the firm's most important assets.

Marketing problems

Developing effective marketing and distribution systems can be a particularly exacting challenge for the small business, especially for those firms attempting to grow through market development activities into overseas markets (see Chapter 24). For example, Smallbone et al. (1998) find that, within a recent seven-country study of internationalisation and SME development, in all countries SMEs faced difficulties in obtaining information about foreign markets, which was, in part at least, due to their tendency to rely on informal marketing methods. It was felt that whilst reliance upon informal methods is typically appropriate in some domestic markets, such methods may be inadequate abroad.

Carson (1991) suggests that the understanding and enhancing of small-business marketing will derive from greater consideration of factors such as the character and personality of the owner-manager and the inherent flexibilities and informalities of small-business management (see Chapter 20). Implicit in this is the possibility that any small-business attempt to draw upon the essentially large-company-oriented formal marketing management literature for guidance could in some instances act as a constraint on the firm's development rather than a facilitator.

We conclude this subsection by emphasising that 'potential unique problem-types implicit' (Wyer 1990) may threaten the flexibility and fast-responsiveness advantages (Wyer and Mason 1998a) which small firms can potentially exploit (Chisnall 1987) in competing with larger firms. Thus, if such problems are not circumvented or effectively managed they can prove a major constraint on growth.

23.6.2 Inadequacy of existing assets for underpinning growth

Many of the above size-related constraints can exert pressure upon management to attempt to 'squeeze more' out of existing assets to facilitate the growth path to which they are committing themselves. For example, 'rapidly growing companies are especially vulnerable to cash difficulties. This is because working capital increases in a more or less constant ratio to turnover. So there will be an ever increasing demand for finding working capital as turnover increases' (Winckles 1986: 61). Over-trading can result from failure to carefully plan the underlying financial requirements of a significant development project or from an attempt to expand too rapidly. For instance, taking on increased customer orders on the assumption that existing resources can cope can lead to cash-flow problems and the souring of relations with the firm's workforce and suppliers as the firm finds itself unable to pay staff wages or suppliers.

Growth can also lead to pressure on the firm's human resource base, which is exacerbated if the firm is either unwilling or unable to recruit externally. Such firms must focus on existing human resources within the firm and the emphasis must be upon getting the best out of those workers. Within this context, small businesses have been found to be constrained in several areas. For example, in order to motivate and enthuse management and supervisory-level staff and to fully utilise their expertise and capabilities, it may be necessary to give them more responsibility and involve them more substantially in the decision-making processes. However, the management style of many owner-managers has tended to be autocratic and underpinned by a reluctance to delegate decision-making (Kets de Vries 1977). A further issue concerns confidence and capability levels of staff (including the owner-manager) to undertake new tasks which they will inevitably be asked to complete as the firm proceeds along its growth path. This in turn raises the issue of the need for training and the fact that a number of constraining forces has been found to restrict the uptake of management training within the small firm. These include: an owner-manager reluctance to utilise outside advice; time constraints; unwillingness to pay the market price; and the relevance and digestibility of training materials (Gibb 1983a).

The pace of growth can also exert pressure on physical resources. For example, a reluctance to invest in additional or new machinery may be the result of a lack of confidence or ability to assess new available technologies, or of concern with regard to the integrating of new systems and processes into existing activities. Bosworth and Jacob (1989) emphasise how 'small business owners lack the evaluation skills necessary for costing technological change'. They stress that 'hidden' costs can be overlooked, leaving management with the later difficulty of having to absorb those costs. A further developmental difficulty revolves around premises. The pace of growth may find the small business outgrowing its existing facilities. Both availability and cost of alternative premises can result in the firm attempting to utilise existing premises to the limit which has severe repercussions in terms of efficiency of operation and ability to meet customer quality and delivery demands. Moreover, a fear that increased overheads associated with any expansion may not be adequately covered because of the firm's inability to achieve requisite rates of growth in sales can also result in a reluctance to take up new premises (Smallbone and Wyer 1994).

23.6.3 Difficulties associated with team-building and team management

In order to establish a newly developing firm as an effective organisation capable of sustaining itself in the marketplace, the owner-manager has to ensure that all tasks are allocated as appropriate on an individual and/or small-group basis. At this early stage of the firm's development those 'sub-units' of individuals organised to work together may be working as a 'team' but often may be no more than a 'group', lacking a collective rationale, in which it is clearly understood that individual performance contributes directly to the overall good (Godfrey 1990).

Arguably, however, for a small organisation to sustain ongoing development, there is a need for the management to recognise that the concept of the 'team' is preferable to that of the 'group', and that this is the working unit they should strive to create (Godfrey 1990). Recognition of such a working unit addresses the possibility that workplace 'groups' may be made up of individuals working together but not necessarily for the good of the whole; rather, they may be underpinned by rivalries and individual differences. For Godfrey, 'ensuring the transition from group to team is the fundamental starting point of good management'. However, whilst ensuring transition from 'group' to 'team' working is arguably a pre-condition for effecting sustainable small-business development, bringing with it crucial benefits such as synergising the talents and abilities of team members to team and small-business objectives, the problems associated with team-building and team management can prove a major constraint on organisational development (see Chapters 17 and 18).

23.7 Managing growth

Since one of the major challenges facing the contemporary small business is that of coping with unknowable, unpredictable open-ended change, a key issue relates to how small firms attempt to strategically control their operations. This section first considers the potential and limitations of formal, rational long-term planning modes of management to underpin small-firm development. Empirical insight is then utilised to suggest the potential utility of an organisational learning perspective to effecting small-business growth.

23.7.1 The uses and limitations of rational long-term planning modes of management

Considerable support continues to be afforded to the view that a rational, systematic step approach to managing the dynamic, volatile and fast-changing operating environment in which the modern-day small business finds itself is the most effective way to underpin sustainable long-term development. Brown and McDonald (1994: 4) emphasise how it is critical 'to recognise that a series of systematic steps can be useful in formulating strategies when the stakes are high and the resource commitment is significant to the firm. It reduces the risk of leaving out key issues, and it highlights the assumptions on which strategies are based and resources are committed.' McDonald (1980) underlines that business problems are in fact less amenable to highly structured analytical methods to be found in the sciences, but that it is the very complexity of business problems which lends itself to some kind of structured procedure to help identify problems.

A structured approach to problem-solving underpins the rational analytical planning models of management, which typically involve the following:

- awareness of the problem;
- exploration of the problem;
- deciding what to do;
- taking action to implement the decision;
- examination and feedback of results (Luffman *et al*. 1991).

Within a strategic planning context, the approach assumes that a small business can approach the strategic control of its fast-changing operating environment through undertaking a series of rational, systematic steps. This process is depicted in Figure 23.3.

Figure 23.3 Indicative steps in strategic control

- External analysis (reveal opportunities and threats in the operating environment)
- Internal analysis (identify the organisation's strengths and weaknesses)
- SWOT analysis
- Formulate long-term development objectives
- Choice of strategies for achieving objectives
- Development of action plans
- Implementation of strategies (through action plans)
- Control and review (monitor progress and feedback)

The propounded strength of this model lies in its processual form. Strategic planning encourages a careful and systematic reading of shifts in technology, competitor position and customer tastes, leading to the formulation of actions in response. Moreover, it has been suggested that strategic planning helps the small business concentrate on its competitive nature by encouraging an external focus on key environmental factors to determine where the firm fits, as well as internally focusing on the firm's strengths and weaknesses. The overall analytical and evaluatory process should then lead to the setting of a formal direction for the business, helping to determine where the business is going (Fry and Stoner 1995).

However, the real utility of rational planning models in small organisations is debatable (Wyer 1997). Firstly, the utility of rational analytical planning should be considered within the context of the assumptions upon which the concept is based, which include the quality of information and an ability to extrapolate future events from past experiences. Its value is also affected by the fact that resource constraints limit the ability of most small firms to formally scan their external environment. Much change with which contemporary small business must cope is, then, open-ended change which is unknowable and unpredictable rather than closed or contained change, to be coped with in the context of more limited internal resources than are available to most larger firms. As a consequence, it is questionable whether formal, rational long-term planning methods of management are compatible with the idiosyncrasies and informalities of small-firm management processes or whether such modes of management are adequate for dealing with open-ended change situations (Stacey 1990).

23.7.2 An organisational learning perspective

Drawing upon personal construct theory (Kelly 1955) and contemporary learning theory (Hawkins 1994), Wyer and Boocock (1996) have offered insight into the ways in which small-business owner-managers learn and have provided foundations for considering how the small firm copes with open-ended change. The thrust of their work is founded on Kelly's proposition that all individuals utilise a personal construct system (derived from inherent personal characteristics and accumulated experience) which is used as a frame of reference to interpret the world. In brief, we all have personal constructs that act as frames of reference to help us view the world which confronts us and deal with new situations which arise.

If change situations impact on a small-firm owner-manager s/he will use his/her existing personal constructs to cope with the change. On many occasions minor adjustments to the construct may allow the owner-manager to deal with the change, simply because a *similar situation* has been dealt with in the past. This can be characterised as *simple* learning (Stacey 1996), whereby the owner-manager has confirmed the validity of his/her current constructs by using them to make sense of a new situation. However, sometimes change situations arise for which existing constructs are inadequate. This requires them to be extended through a process that entails the questioning of the underlying assumptions upon which the existing constructs are based. It is a more *complex* learning process, which is why simple learning is more common (Stacey 1996).

Such a conceptualisation of how individuals cope with change has far-reaching implications for the growth-oriented small business. If the owner is confronted by unknowable, unfolding change forces, success in coping with such a challenge in a manner which can lead to sustainable business development will depend to a considerable extent on an ability and willingness to 'extend' personal construct systems; that is, to change his or her mindset or frames of reference and to engage in complex learning. This may include an ability and willingness to anchor the understanding and learning of other key members of the organisation to enhance collective organisational understanding (Wyer and Mason 1998b), which means that the role of dialogue – both between internal organisational members and with key external informants on the boundaries of the small firm's operating environment – is a crucial learning activity.

Foundation studies which have drawn on an organisational learning perspective to investigate strategic development processes in small firms based on in-depth case studies have revealed a number of insights (Wyer 1997; Wyer and Mason 1998b). They confirm that whilst few small firms have written short- or long-term plans, many owner-managers demonstrate strategic awareness (Gibb and Scott 1985) in the sense of having a mentally held target of the preferred development path for the business. The study also demonstrated the role of informal networking with key external actors and informants in contributing to emergent strategy, which was typically developed in a trial-and-error way (see Chapter 21). Significantly, however, some of the most successful firms in the study were able to loop back the results of what they had learned to make adjustments to their strategic or operational activities. In other words, successful SMEs in the study were led by owner-managers who appeared to have learned how to learn!

23.7.3 Managing finance to facilitate expansion

In order to facilitate sustainable growth it is necessary for the small firm's management to progressively enhance its financial management capabilities (see Chapter 19). In the early stages of development when activity and sales levels are relatively low, control can be maintained through the use of relatively informal systems. However, as the business grows not only is it necessary to enhance finance skills and formalise the approach to financial management, it is also necessary to recognise the interdependencies between finance and other areas of functional activity within the firm. For example, the projection of financial requirements to underpin a period of expansion must derive to a considerable extent from the forecasting of future sales and the determination of income and costs associated with that sales expansion. This requires a marketing capability to provide an understanding of the target customer base and of change forces to which that customer base is, or may become, sensitive, in order to provide such estimates. In other words, effective financial management depends to some extent on other functional management capabilities.

With regard to the financing of growth, two crucial areas are the management of fixed and working capital. Expansion will require close attention to fixed capital needs in terms of ability to acquire requisite premises, plant and/or equipment. The firm needs to acquaint itself with the various methods of raising long-, medium- and short-term finance and to develop understanding of what would be an appropriate mix of these categories of finance to effectively underpin development. Integral to this is consideration of the wider variety of sources of such finance, including the ability to recognise innovative sources of finance (such as 'business angels', already discussed above) and how innovative 'finance packages' can be used to leverage further funds from elsewhere (Krantz 1999). A crucial underpinning ability relates to the need to consider the appropriate balance of external and internal funds. For example, the balance of debt (long- and medium-term external funding) to equity (the owner's own internal funding) is a crucial issue. The ratio of this funding (known as the gearing ratio) can be critical in terms of facilitating or constraining small-firm growth. With a high gearing ratio (where the firm is relying on external interest-bearing borrowings), in times of slow sales and high interest rates, a firm may find its potential for future growth severely constrained because of the financial drain imposed upon it by having to meet high interest costs on borrowings.

The small business will also have to make sufficient provision for working capital in order to facilitate growth. Working capital relates to the ongoing provision of stocks of appropriate levels of raw materials and component parts, the financing of debtors and the access to cash to meet day-to-day expenditures and running costs. It thus incorporates the firm's current assets and current liabilities. The complexity of the management tasks underpinning the determination of working capital forms and levels to facilitate growth include the need to forecast sales from which estimates of the costs likely to be incurred and anticipated income can be made; plans for future growth, including time-scales for each step and estimation of all inherent costs; consideration of possible developmental problems which may result in delay (hold-ups and inefficiencies); and examination of the current and likely costs of borrowing and consideration of repayment periods (Bennett 1989).

Inevitably, over time, growth will require additional fixed and working capital, and the ability to ensure that adequate and appropriate funding underpins that growth clearly points to the need for an ongoing enhancement of financial capabilities. For example, the management of working capital will require close control of debtors to ensure a balance between, for example, credit being used as a 'promotional' and competitive tool, whilst controlling debtor periods to avoid undue financial pressures on the business. Stock levels must be managed to ensure a free-flowing production activity and an ability to serve customers in a timely manner, whilst not at a level which results in stocks of raw materials or component parts idling on the shelves and thus tying up cash. With regard to creditors, there is a need to negotiate credit periods which contribute effectively to a positive cash flow, whilst at the same time recognising that creditors should not be exploited in a manner which can sour the relationship and lead to a deterioration in quality or timing of supplies, or which precludes the uptake of discounts for early settlement.

However, a crucial issue is that the nature of financial management skills developed by the growing small business must reflect and accommodate the nature and form of the growth and change patterns of the business. For example, Bennett's proposition, that decisions on working capital needs should be based on consideration of anticipated activity levels and require the forecasting of sales and costs, will be a more straightforward task if the small business is operating in a relatively stable external environment, in which it has been able to track a pre-determined development path.

However, if a small firm is facing open-ended unknowable change, in which it may have to seek development opportunities through trial and error, the relationships between financial management skills, marketing capabilities and strategic awareness are closely interrelated.

23.7.4 Developing the marketing function

Analysis of the small business in its early stages of development is unlikely to reveal a marketing approach or activity which even vaguely reflects formal marketing management as represented by the mainstream marketing literature (see Chapter 20). Instead, it is an understanding and application of the concept of marketing that is important, namely 'a matching between a company's capabilities and the wants of customers in order to achieve the goals of the firm' (McDonald 1984). Whilst this may appear to be an obvious and fundamental concept which must underpin any sustained development of any successful small business, there is much evidence of small firms going out of business because of a failure to fully understand the needs of their targeted customers and of firms founded on the mistaken premise that they have the 'company capability' to serve the needs of an identified group of customers (Smallbone 1990).

At the early stages of small-business development the nature and form of marketing are often embedded in the owner-manager him/herself. In many instances it is the owner-manager's close interface and relationship with his or her customers which allows for the 'matching process' between the small-firm capability and the wants of customers to be effectively achieved.

Whilst an informal 'market orientation' may be a keystone for sustainable growth and development of the small firm, the effective facilitation of sustainable growth may require an increasing formulation of the firm's marketing activity. For McDonald, it is not essential for a firm 'to have a formalised marketing department for the analysis, planning and control of the matching process'. However, with growth in a firm's product range and customer types, the management of marketing may need to be brought under one central control function. Growth brings with it the need to co-ordinate all of those functional activities within the firm which participate in the matching process. The crucial issue is not that of whether a department, or an individual or a group of individuals, is responsible for a firm's marketing, but the extent to which all those individuals in the firm have clear understanding that the profit which the company strives to earn is a return founded on depth of understanding of the needs of its target customer groups and ability to organise the firm's resources in their totality so as to satisfy those needs. Within the context of the growing small business, a key management art appears to relate to the ability to extend the marketing concept in the business as it develops.

23.7.5 Broadening the customer base whilst coping with existing customers

A major challenge facing the growth-oriented small business is to sustain the level of service provision to an existing clientele, which may itself be exerting increasing quantitative and qualitative demands on the firm, whilst seeking to broaden its customer base. However, as we have already seen, the actual process of identifying opportunities which can facilitate a widening of the customer base is itself a difficult one, which is likely to exert considerable strain upon the small firm's ability to continue to serve the increasing demands of its existing customer base. The process of effecting internal adjustments to exploit new opportunities can place such stress on the operations of the small firm that the service to existing customers is adversely affected. The broadening of the firm's product-market definition will require an expansion of physical, financial and human resources at a time when the existing customer base may be demanding ongoing management attention and additional resource allocations. Within a highly competitive environment, the small firm will find itself having to continuously seek efficiency improvements within the business and in interface with service providers such as suppliers and distributors in order to maintain a competitive edge in its existing markets. This, together with the need to improve existing products, will be a prerequisite to protect existing customer bases and market shares so as to cement current foundations, both to maintain current levels of activity and to facilitate any future expansion. Clearly, any move to broaden the existing product-market definition within the small business must be accompanied by a careful evaluation of the adequacy of existing resources and abilities as a basis for sustainable development of the firm in its totality (that is, an ability to expand into new areas of activity whilst effectively maintaining and enhancing those existing areas with ongoing developmental potential). Such evaluation should also incorporate the potential for complementing existing resources and abilities in a manner which can facilitate the identified expansion opportunities.

23.7.6 Deciding when to introduce new managers and modify organisational structure

A key developmental issue is to what extent a small business which is striving for growth can continue to rely upon an organisational framework in which the owner-manager is the pivotal centre of all activity and depends on an informal loose structure for the direction and fulfilment of operational activities. The answer is that it is likely to be contingent upon the individual business and its personnel, the nature of its development path and of its impacting operating environment and focal industry/markets.

Handy (1976) explains how 'each organisation, each part of an organisation has a culture, and a structure and systems appropriate to that culture'. Thus, in a large company we may find several subcultures and different forms of structure throughout the organisation. For the small business it is common to find culture in a form which Handy terms a *power* culture; its structure is depicted by a *web*: 'the culture depends on a central power source, with rays of power and influence spreading from that central figure. They are connected by functional or specialist strings but the power rings are the centre of activity.' The organisation with its few rules and procedures tends to work on precedent, with staff often anticipating the wishes and decisions of the owner-manager, the central power source. The owner-manager often exercises control by selection of key individuals for particular activities, or through 'occasional summonses to the centre'.

As the small business grows, this culture/structure is likely to prove inadequate to facilitate pace of development. Indeed, as reported earlier in the chapter, firms that are successful in achieving high growth over an extended period are characterised by an ability to modify the structure to accommodate an evolving role for the leader of the firm. A typical evolving response by the owner-manager might be to gradually formal-ise structure in terms of the allocation of formal responsibilities and the development of linking mechanisms between the newly emerging roles with a resultant formal *hierarchy*-type structure and an underpinning *role*-type culture (see the pioneering work in this area by Taylor [1947] and Fayol [1949]). But for a small business to evolve into a formal hierarchical structure in its pure form would be to overlook the inherent weaknesses of such a structure: the classical model views a business in terms of a network of interlinking job descriptions rather than a network of human relation-ships and it treats the organisation as a closed system (the inputs of the business are viewed as easily controlled), when in reality any business is faced with the complexities of a dynamic external environment, that is, it is an open system (Lawrence and Lee 1989). Thus, the timing and form of adjustment to small-firm structure is a complex issue and one which is underpinned by the danger that adjustment takes a naturally evolving route toward a pure formal hierarchy which, with its rigidity and inward-focusing tendency, will reduce the ability of the small firm to relate to its fast-changing environment.

Greater depth of understanding of the development of small-firm organisational structure may well derive from the work of Handy (1976) who suggests that busi-nesses should differentiate structure and culture according to the dominant activities of the organisation. For Handy there is a general way of looking at the activities of all organisations – large and small, manufacturing or service. In every organisation there are four sets of activities:

- *Steady state* refers to all activities which are routine, which can be programmed. These may include up to 80% of an organisation's workforce, embracing the infra-structure of the organisation in terms of the accounting and secretarial systems, office services and most of the production function, and sales but not marketing.

- *Innovative/developmental* includes all activities directed to effecting change in what the organisation does or the way that it does it. It incorporates parts of marketing, R&D, production development and corporate planning-type activities.

- *Breakdown/crises* refers to the organisational need to deal with the unexpected and will thus include top management and parts of production and marketing.

- *Policy/direction* refers to the overall guidance and direction of activities and includes the direction and allocation of resources, the setting of priorities, the initia-tion of action and the establishing of standards.

The underlying rationale is that organisational effectiveness will be increased if an appropriate culture/structure prevails where a specific set of activities prevails. Thus, applying this rationale to the growing small business, growth will certainly require an increased formalisation, but it should encourage different cultures/structures for differ-ent situations.

Such a conceptualisation underlines, as a facilitator of growth, the predominant need to identify the sets of pragmatic activities which will have to be undertaken in the growing business and the need to accommodate those activities by the

431

owner-manager's encouragement of different cultures/structures appropriate to those activities. It also provides a parallel guiding frame for consideration of the adequacy of existing management capability and the need for complementing that capability through external recruitment, including increased supervisory capability and the need for the introduction of a more 'professional' approach to management.

23.8 Chapter summary

Growth-oriented small businesses make a major contribution to economic development and employment generation within local communities and are a crucial underpinning engine of development of national economies. For this reason they attract a great deal of attention, not least from those support providers hoping to encourage and influence their ongoing growth. Little is known, however, about how successful growth businesses effectively sustain development. Commencing from the premise that there is no single theory which can adequately explain small-firm growth, this chapter firstly sought to draw upon major research studies to highlight aspects which appear to be characteristic of high-growth enterprises. Crucial in many small firms is the central and pivotal role of the owner-manager, though many research studies have had limited success in their attempts to identify key personality traits and characteristics which can be said to typify owner-managers of growth-oriented firms. However, the juxtaposition of ownership and management is a major feature which distinguishes small firms from large companies, and the characteristics and capabilities of individuals operating small firms impact substantially on the form of organisation culture of particular small firms and their orientation toward, and success in achieving, sustained growth.

Many studies have also focused on the characteristics and development issues of the small firm itself. One such approach is the life-cycle or stages model approach which – whilst a useful vehicle for aiding in the diagnosis of organisational problems and difficulties which an owner-manager may have to circumvent if growth is to be achieved – again falls short of effectively explaining growth. Similarly, the body of 'business management' literature provides guiding insight to enhance understanding of ways in which organisations may sustain growth through adoption of development choices regarding potential adjustment to their market, product and/or process activities. But much of such insight appears over-rational and systematic and thus incompatible with the idiosyncrasies and informalities of small-business management processes, and inappropriate for coping with the unpredictable contemporary change environment with which the modern-day small business must struggle. Indeed, an emphasis throughout this chapter has been that a prime determinant of growth is the way in which the growth-oriented small business must successfully address the enabling and constraining nature of its external operating context.

It appears, therefore, that the literature provides a foundation insight and guiding frameworks for enhancing understanding of key issues underpinning small-firm growth and for aiding the small business in effecting sustainable development, without providing an integrated theory of growth. Moreover, much of those areas of literature which are 'business management' based seem to be substantially large-company-oriented and fail to fully address the idiosyncrasies and impacting problems of the smaller firm. It is, then, a selective utilisation of relevant literature which has facilitated within this chapter a consideration of major barriers which may constrain small-business development and which must be circumvented or managed if effective growth is to be sustained. Commencing with the external operating context, emphasis is on the predominance of totally unpredictable open-ended change and how this must be identified and understood if the small firm is to effectively grow. With regard to the competitive environment, the small business needs to be sensitive to underlying industry and market structure characteristics if it is to understand the broad sources of competition.

In terms of the internal operating context of the small firm, it was suggested that the small business can be viewed as a 'potential unique problem-type' facing problems and barriers to growth which are owner-manager- or size-related – thus distinguishing it from the large firm. Particular attention was afforded to internal barriers impacting on growth in the form of the potential inadequacy of existing assets and to management ability to team-build and team-manage to effectively facilitate the nature and pace of development.

Having focused on key barriers which can potentially impede on growth, the final section of the chapter considered the limited utility of rational long-term planning and an alternative organisational learning perspective to the effecting of sustainable strategic development of the small business. The totality of the chapter to this point then provided the context for consideration of key management issues which are significant in the growing business.

Questions

1 To what extent do life-cycle and stages models of business development help in enhancing understanding of the small-firm growth process?

2 In what ways may rational long-term planning modes of management be inadequate for aiding the small business to effect sustained growth?

3 What are likely to be the key constraints impacting upon a small business in its attempts to effect growth through the broadening of its customer base?

Internationalisation and the small firm

Kevin Ibeh

24.1 Learning objectives

This chapter has five learning objectives:

1 To understand the meaning of internationalisation, and the various ways in which it is attained.

2 To appreciate the changing face of SME internationalisation, including its underlying dynamics.

3 To understand the major theories advanced to explain SME internationalisation, as well as the critical decision-maker, firm and environmental influences.

4 To explain the major barriers and problems which impinge upon SME internationalisation.

5 To understand the policy measures and institutional mechanisms which currently assist SME internationalisation, as well as possible policy initiatives that may yield improved results.

Key concepts

- SME internationalisation process
- 'stages' models
- networks
- barriers
- effective policy support

24.2 Introduction

This chapter is concerned with internationalisation and the small firm. It starts with some reflections on the growing status of SMEs as international market actors, and the economic and technological imperatives that have driven SME internationalisation policy-making and research since the 1970s. It next considers theories of small-firm internationalisation, covering such relevant approaches as the stage of development models, the network theories, and the strategy/resource-based perspectives. Further discussions centre on the factors which stimulate SME internationalisation; the range and variety of barriers which impede them from so doing; the decision-maker and firm-specific characteristics which enhance the likelihood of successful international market entry among SMEs; and the policy measures assisting SME internationalisation across OECD countries.

24.3 Internationalisation and the small firm

One of the major landmarks of the 20th-century business scene is the phenomenal growth of firm internationalisation. Impelled by significant and continuing advancements in production, transportation, information technologies, financial systems, regulatory environments, and business networks, firms – large and small – have increasingly initiated international operations in order to exploit technological and organisational advantages, as well as reduce business costs and risks. That SMEs are not insignificant actors in this changing landscape is evident in the OECD's (1997a) report that internationalised SMEs account for about 25–35% of the world's manufactured exports, with their export contribution to GDP representing 4–6% for OECD countries and 12% for Asian economies.

This seems very different from the period, not too long ago, when internationalisation was regarded as the domain of large corporations. Based on their presumed lack of internationalisation potential, small firms were largely ignored by most governments, policy-makers and researchers seeking to promote national economic position through foreign operations. This explains why the dominant theories and models of internationalisation – product life-cycle, market imperfection, internalisation (transaction cost), and the eclectic paradigm – have an essentially multinational enterprise (MNE) focus, explaining the conditions under which MNEs extend and establish their activities (particularly production) overseas.

The serious difficulties experienced by Western MNEs during the 1970s and early 1980s, and the knock-on effect on their national economies, however, served to expose the weakness of this exclusive reliance on the large firm. Assailed by such developments as the oil crisis of 1973/4, depressed global demand, intense international competition from Japan and newly industrialising countries, and revolutionary new technologies, Western MNEs lost their grip on world trade and were forced into plant closures, downsizing and process re-engineering. Their governments soon reacted with massive programmes of deregulation and privatisation – see Chapter 3. From the ashes of resulting redundancies, however, emerged many new small firms – their formation fuelled by rising trends in outsourcing, greater demand for services, and micro-electronics (Bell 1994). Subsequent evidence of the small-firm sector's economic contribution was reported in a number of studies, notably the Bolton Commission's (1971) in the UK; Birch's (1979, 1981) in the USA; and Storey and Johnson's (1987) in the European Community.

Concerns were, however, expressed about the disproportionate under-representation of small firms in the international market. Cannon and Willis (1981), for example, observed that while small firms accounted for nearly 25% of the UK's Gross National Product, they contributed less than 10% of all manufactured exports. Even more insightful was the indication that a significant proportion of SMEs with exporting potential had restricted themselves to domestic operations, in the erroneous 'belief that size is an insuperable disadvantage' in internationalisation (Bolton Report 1971). It was hardly surprising, therefore, that policy-makers, faced with burgeoning trade deficits and an inert large-firm sector, would begin to focus on developing the little-tapped export potential of smaller firms (Bell 1994). This favourable policy climate transformed SME internationalisation into an important area of enquiry – a situation which has continued to date.

24.4 SMEs and internationalisation: concepts, context and extent

The term 'internationalisation' commonly refers to 'the process of increasing involvement in international operations' (Welch and Luostarinen 1988). It describes the continuum which stretches from the firm's first import activity or extra-regional expansion or 'domestic internationalisation' to full globalisation (Wiedersheim-Paul et al. 1978; Luostarinen 1994). Full globalisation is characterised by the establishment of manufacturing plants and marketing affiliates across major international regions; extensive outsourcing of inputs and marketing of outputs across borders; and worldwide integration and co-ordination of resources and operations in pursuit of global competitiveness. Sometimes used interchangeably with globalisation (its most evolved form), internationalisation is attained through a variety of international market entry and development modes (Young 1990). These include: exporting; licensing; franchising; management contract; turnkey contract; contract manufacturing/ international subcontracting; industrial co-operation agreements; contractual joint venture; equity; wholly owned subsidiaries; mergers and acquisitions; and strategic alliances.

A number of authors have tried to classify internationalisation modes. This chapter employs Luostarinen's (1980) approach, whose distinctions between home and overseas production, and direct and non-direct investments (see Figure 24.1), offer useful insights into understanding SME versus large-firm internationalisation. In general terms, the progression from home-based internationalisation modes to overseas production modes, and from non-direct investment modes to direct investment modes, is marked by increased resource commitments/transfer and risks. Given their obvious resource (financial and managerial) and attitudinal (to risk/control) differences, small and large firms have tended to adopt divergent internationalisation modes. Indeed, SMEs are most likely to supply their international markets from domestic production bases (through indirect and direct exporting, and sales/service subsidiaries). This explains why the bulk of the literature on SME internationalisation originates from exporting research.

According to a recent OECD (1997a) report, SMEs' share of export in each of the surveyed OECD and Asian economies ranges between 15% and 50%, with 20% and 80% respectively being active exporters (Table 24.1). In general, SME internationalisation is greater in small, open economies and less in larger, more self-contained economies. This, however, is not always the case. France and Italy still have 30% and 70% of exports respectively contributed by SMEs, while internationalisation in small, open economies like Australia, Malaysia and Greece is less than might be expected (OECD 1997a).

Figure 24.1 Forms of international market entry and development

Production in home market		Production overseas	
Non-direct investment marketing operations	Direct investment marketing operations	Non-direct investment production operations	Direct investment production operations
Indirect goods exports	Sales promotion subsidiaries	Licensing	Assembly
Direct goods exports	Warehousing units	Franchising	Wholly owned / Joint ventures / Minority holdings / Fade-out agreements
Service exports	Service units	Contract manufacturing/ international subcontracting	Manufacture
Know-how exports	Sales subsidiaries	Turnkey operations	
Partial project exports			

Source: Luostarinen (1980)

That SMEs are not restricting their internationalisation forays to exporting, how-ever, is evident in the rising trend towards small firms' adoption of more direct forms of international marketing, including low-level foreign direct investments (FDI), strate-gic alliances, licensing, joint ventures and similar co-operation-based modes (Oman 1984; Young 1987). An OECD (1997a) study indicates the extent of SME internation-alisation thus: 'about 10% of SMEs are engaged in FDI and about 10% or more for-eign investment appear to be attributable to SMEs. Around 10 to 15% of SMEs have licences, franchises or other arrangements with firms outside their home country ... It is estimated that about 1% or less of SMEs (30,000 to 40,000) can be said to be glo-bal, in the sense of being active in multiple countries and/or across several continents, or having the ability to operate wherever they see fit ... another 5 to 10% of SMEs in manufacturing ... can be said to be extensively internationalised ... [with] a further 10 to 20% ... active in up to three foreign countries.'

These internationally active SMEs are growing faster than their domestic counter-parts. Those in niche markets and new (including high-tech) industries constitute the fastest-growing segment (20%), while those in traditional industries (around 50%) internationalise incrementally via exporting. It would, indeed, appear that most SMEs now see internationalisation as not only fashionable, but imperative. This is based on the realisation that pressures from inward internationalisation are likely to be most unkind to firms which stand still, and are not internationally active. As the OECD (1997a) reports, probably less than 40% of SMEs are insulated from any effects of globalisation, and the proportion of such firms (mainly small service providers) is expected to contract further to 20%. This does not imply that service firms are not active internationally. Many play an increasingly important international role (Erramilli and Rao 1990; Sharma 1993; Hellman 1996), although measurement diffi-culties prevent an overall picture of the extent of service SMEs' internationalisation. It should be noted, nevertheless, that the easily measured physical manufactured exports are often accompanied by significant international SME service activity, including customer service, design, distribution, marketing, etc. (OECD 1997a).

Table 24.1 Estimates of the extent of SME internationalisation

	[Percentages]		
	Exports from SMEs	Percentage of SMEs exporting	Notes
Australia	n.a.	5–10*	0–100 employees
Belgium		20*	0–500 employees
Canada		14*	5–200 employees
Denmark	46*		< 500 employees
Finland	23*		
France	M 26		
Greece	n.a.	n.a.	SME exports as % of industry turnover = 15–20%
Ireland		25	
Italy	52.7		< 500 employees
		68	51–100 employees
		80	101–300 employees
		83	301–500 employees
Japan	13.5		< 300 direct
	30–35		< 300 indirect
Netherlands	26		< 100 indirect + direct
		17	0–9 employees
		43	10–99 employees
		67	100+ employees
Portugal	–	–	No figures available
Spain		18	< 20 employees
		50	51–100 employees
		70	101–200 employees
Sweden	36		< 200 employees
Switzerland	40		
United Kingdom		16–20	
United States	11*	12*	
China	40–60		
Republic of Korea	40		
Indonesia	10.6		
Chinese Taipei	56		
Thailand	10		
Malaysia	15		
Singapore	16		
Vietnam	20		

*Manufacturing.
Source : OECD (1997a), *Globalisation and Small and Medium Enterprises (SMEs)*, vol. 1., Copyright © OECD 1997

24.5 Explaining SME internationalisation

Firm internationalisation has been studied from the perspective of both export development (involving mostly SMEs) and the emergence of the MNEs (Bell and Young

1998). Focusing on SME internationalisation, three theoretical perspectives can be identified:

- stage of development (or internationalisation process) approaches;
- network theory;
- resource-based, business-strategy-based and contingency perspectives.

24.5.1 Stage of development approaches

A number of 'stage' models have emerged to explain the process of a firm's development along the internationalisation route. Common to all these models is the view of export development as a sequential, 'staged' process. All have their roots in the behavioural theory of the firm (Cyert and March 1963) and Penrose's (1959) theory of the growth of the firm. According to 'stage' theorists, firms adopt an incremental, evolutionary approach to foreign markets; gradually deepening their commitment and investment with increasing international market knowledge and experience, more positive perception of risks, and so on (Johanson and Vahlne 1977; 1978; 1990). Firms are believed to target neighbouring, 'psychically close' countries initially, and subsequently enter foreign markets with successively larger psychic distance. 'Psychic distance' refers to extent of proximity in geography, language, culture, political systems and business factors like industry structure and competitive environment (Zafarullah *et al.* 1998).

Pioneering this approach was Johanson and Vahlne's (1977) model of knowledge development and increasing foreign market commitment, which built on Johanson and Wiedersheim-Paul's (1975) study of the internationalisation behaviour of four Swedish firms from their early beginnings. They found that the internationalisation process was the consequence of a series of incremental decisions, rather than large, spectacular foreign investments. Four different stages were identified in relation to a firm's international involvement:

1 no regular export;

2 export via independent representation (agent);

3 sales subsidiaries;

4 production/manufacturing.

As Johanson and Vahlne (1990) stated: 'the firm's engagement in a specific foreign market develops according to an establishment chain, i.e. at the start no export activities are performed in the market, then export takes place via independent representatives, later through a sales subsidiary, and, eventually manufacturing may follow'.

A further dimension was added to the internationalisation model by Wiedersheim-Paul *et al.*'s (1978) model of pre-export behaviour, which extended the establishment chain backwards to include a pre-export stage. Export start was found to be influenced by the interplay between 'attention-evoking factors' and the individual decision-maker, the environment and history of the firm, including experience in extra-regional expansion (domestic internationalisation). Thus, the establishment chain model attempts to explain the whole process of a firm's internationalisation, from the pre-export stage to the post-export stage, including FDI.

Cognisance should be taken of the differences in perspectives adopted by these 'stage theorists'. Anderson (1993), for example, distinguished between the 'Uppsala Internationalisation (U) Models' and innovation-related (I) models. While the former clearly refers to the models that emerged from a Swedish school of that description, the composition of the latter is not so clear. It seems appropriate, however, to include as innovation-related models those works that present export development as an innovation-adoption cycle (Lee and Brasch 1978; Reid 1981), and those that see it as a 'learning curve', influenced by external attention-evoking stimuli (e.g. unsolicited orders or enquiries) and internal factors, such as managerial ambitions and excess capacity (Bilkey and Tesar 1977; Cavusgil 1980; Czinkota and Johnston 1982; Crick 1995). The actual number of 'stages' undergone by internationalising firms also differs according to models, but this, as observed by Anderson (1993), 'reflects semantic differences rather than real differences concerning the nature of the internationalisation process'. Anderson's (1993) major criticisms, however, are 'the lack of proper design to explain the development process', the absence of clear-cut boundaries between stages, and the lack of 'tests of validity and reliability'.

Recent findings on a new genre of firms variously referred to as 'born globals', 'global start-ups', 'International New Ventures', 'high-technology start-ups' and 'committed internationalists' have reinforced earlier evidence which questioned the relevance of stage theories, particularly in respect of entrepreneurial, high-tech firms (Bell 1995); service firms (Sharma and Johanson 1987; Lindqvist 1988; Engwall and Wellenstal 1988); and subcontractors (Anderson et al. 1995). As Bell (1995) explains, stage theories use linear models to explain dynamic, interactive, non-linear behaviour. Clark et al. (1997) observed that the establishment model was one of several paths to FDI, noting that 'firms often bypass the intermediate stages to FDI'. Cavusgil (1984) was even more forthright: 'the overwhelming export success of smaller, high value-added exporters ("born globals") discredits the conventional wisdom that firms ought to pursue export opportunities cautiously, in a series of incremental steps'. Suffice to say that 'the stages theory has merit in its use as a framework for classification purposes rather than for an understanding of the internationalisation process' (Turnbull 1987). They are also of limited relevance 'insofar as they merely identify the internationalisation patterns of certain firms – but not of others – and as they fail to adequately explain the processes involved' (Bell and Young 1998). Madsen and Servais (1997) sought to clarify the situation by categorising internationalising firms into three groups: firstly, the traditional exporters whose internationalisation patterns largely reflect the traditional stages model; secondly, firms that leapfrog some stages, e.g. 'late starters' that have only domestic sales for many years, but then suddenly invest in a distant foreign market; and thirdly, the 'born global' firms.

Findings supportive of the 'psychic distance' concept have been reported in a variety of studies. The more a firm can recognise and adapt its way of doing business to the cultural environment (i.e. reduce the psychic distance), the better the chances of success. Styles and Ambler's (1994) findings were broadly similar, hence their conclusion that 'firms should focus on those countries which are closest in "psychic distance" for early export endeavours'. There have, however, been refutations of the psychic distance concept, most notably by Czinkota and Ursic (1987), and to a lesser degree by the 'network school' (Johanson and Mattsson 1988). The latter ascribes limited relevance to the concept in the face of vastly improving global communications and transportation infrastructures, as well as increasing market convergence. Evidence of 'client follower-ship' has also been reported (Bell 1994), which is inconsistent with the 'intuitive logic' (Sullivan and Bauerschmidt 1990) of the psychic distance concept. A recent Canadian study identified a 'psychic distance paradox': operations in psychically close countries are not necessarily easy to manage, because assumptions of similarity can prevent exec-utives from learning about critical differences (O'Grady and Lane 1996).

Despite valid criticisms, the stage of development perspective remains a significant contribution to the understanding of SME internationalisation. Prior to its emergence, internationalisation was essentially theorised and discussed in terms of the MNE. It is also the case that its focus on initial internationalisation attracted considerable research attention and illumination to SME internationalisation, extending even to the pre-export stage. The postulations on psychic distance may now appear dated, given recent advancements in IT (see Chapter 22), but few would disagree that they resonate with the market selection pattern intuitively associated with exporters (Madsen and Servais 1997). Criticisms of the model, based on its failure to reflect the internationali-sation behaviour of entrepreneurial, high-technology and service firms, are acknowl-edged. Nevertheless, most studies involving firms in mature industries have been consistent in supporting the model's basic propositions.

24.5.2 Network theory

Another significant strand of internationalisation research was the development, from international industrial marketing, of the network or interaction and relationship con-cepts (see Chapter 21 for a further analysis of this concept). The basic tenet is that internationalisation proceeds through an interplay between increasing commitment to, and evolving knowledge about, foreign markets, gained mainly from interactions in the foreign markets. These interactions – dynamic, evolving, less structured – yield increased mutual knowledge and trust between international market actors and, subse-quently, greater internationalisation commitment. In summary, 'a firm begins the export process by forming relationships that will deliver experiential knowledge about a market, and then commits resources in accordance with the degree of experiential knowledge it progressively gains from these relationships' (Styles and Ambler 1994).

In network theory, markets are seen as a system of relationships among a number of players including customers, suppliers, competitors, family, friends and private and public support agencies. Strategic action, therefore, is rarely limited to a single firm, and the nature of relationships established with others in the market influences and often dictates future strategic options. For example, firms can expand from domestic to international markets through existing relationships which offer contacts and help to develop new partners and positions in new markets. At the same time, network relationships may restrict the nature of a firm's growth initiatives.

Internationalisation driven by customer/client followership, or what Hellman (1996) referred to as 'customer driven internationalisation', has been seen in service sectors and in the computer software sector. As observed by Johanson and Mattsson (1988), a firm's success in entering new international markets is more dependent on its relationships with current markets, both domestic and international, than it is on the chosen market and its cultural characteristics. This subtle shift from the core Uppsala internationalisation model (the psychic distance concept) was further endorsed by Johanson and Vahlne's (1992) remarks that many firms enter new foreign markets almost blindly, propelled not by strategic decisions or market research, but by social exchange processes, interactions and networks.

A growing body of evidence exists on the role of network relationships in SME internationalisation. Coviello and Munro (1995; 1997), for example, found that successful New Zealand-based software firms are actively involved in international networks, and that they outsource many market development activities to network partners. As they observed, 'the network perspective goes beyond the models of incremental internationalisation by suggesting that firm's strategy emerges as a pattern of behaviour influenced by a variety of network relationships'. Coviello and Munro's evidence, while supportive of network theory, recognised the occurrence of internationalisation stages, albeit in a much condensed and accelerated form. This attempt to reconcile the network perspective with the work of the stage theorists and the 'international new venture' scholars also formed the substance of Madsen and Servais' (1997) theory-building effort.

There is no doubt that the network perspective has brought immense value to the understanding of the internationalisation process, particularly among SMEs. It presents a view of SME internationalisation which should be seen more as a complement than an alternative to the incremental internationalisation model. More importantly, it moves discussion away from the largely sterile debate which, until recently, raged for and against the Uppsala model. It can, arguably, be credited with stimulating recent efforts being made toward a more holistic view of small-firm internationalisation (Bell and Young 1998; Madsen and Servais 1997). It is this emerging perspective that is considered below.

24.5.3 Resource-based, business-strategy-based and contingency perspectives

An integrative perspective on SME internationalisation appears to have emerged in the form of the resource-based theory (Bell *et al.* 1998a; 1998b). According to these authors, 'the resource-based perspective presents a holistic view of the firm', such that decisions like country market choice, mode of entry, product strategies and so on are made not on a stand-alone basis, but within a co-ordinated framework of resources and capabilities (whether internal or externally leveraged), as well as environmental (including competitive) realities. They elaborated that 'firms will have a different mix of resources/competencies and resource/competence gaps, and their strategic responses to these allow for the possibility of different paths to growth and internationalisation'. It could be argued that the resource-based theory of internationalisation is actually a more grounded restatement of the business-strategy and contingency frameworks. It would appear to have met the need 'to root contingency frameworks within an underlying theory'. As its proponents observe, there is a close relationship with contingency approaches which are designed to show the influence of a range of internal and external variables. This perspective is equally implicit in the business-strategy frameworks.

The business-strategy perspective proposes a strategically planned, rational approach to internationalisation, such that decisions on foreign market entry, servicing strategies (entry mode), and so on are made in the context of the firm's overall strategic development, and guided by rigorous analysis of relevant internal and external environmental factors (Young 1987; Young *et al.* 1989). This is consistent with Chandler's (1962) view that 'structure follows strategy'. It also reflects Turnbull's (1987) conclusion that a company's stage of internationalisation is largely determined by the operating environment, industry structure and its own marketing strategy. The business-strategy perspective is implicit in much of the mainstream export literature, notably Aaby and Slater's (1989) model (widely referred to as the 'strategic export model'); Namiki's (1994) taxonomic analysis of export marketing strategy; Cavusgil and Zou's (1994) path analysis of export marketing strategy and performance; as well as Reid's contingency framework (Reid 1983a).

The contingency approach to internationalisation views foreign expansion and export mode choice as severally influenced and situation-dependent. Reid (1983a) argued that 'since exporting results from a choice among competing strategies that are guided by the nature of the market opportunity, firm resources, and managerial philosophy, it represents a selective and dynamic adaptation to the changing character of the foreign market. ... Market factors and requirements are therefore closely intertwined with deciding whether to go international and what form this expansion should take.' Reid (1983b; 1985) further employed the economics-orientated transaction cost theory to explain firms' export mode decisions, as dependent on the costs involved in initiating, negotiating and co-ordinating export transactions – reflecting Williamson's (1975) observation that transactional considerations are 'typically decisive in determining which mode of organisation will obtain in what circumstances, and why'.

A common denominator of these three frameworks is the recognition that internationalisation is affected by multiple influences, and that a range of the firms' internationalisation decisions, incorporating products, markets and entry modes, is made in a holistic way. There appears to be an increasing realisation of this extended base of internationalisation parameters. This is apparent in the emerging trend towards a more inclusive and holistic explanation of firm (particularly small-firm) internationalisation. Having identified partial and situational relevance for each of the existing internationalisation models, Bell and Young (1998) invited more attention to their 'potential complementarities'. Researchers seem to have accepted this challenge. For example, Coviello and Munro's (1997) study of New Zealand software SMEs reported evidence of incremental internationalisation, network-driven internationalisation, as well as accelerated internationalisation (International New Ventures) which is similar to the range of propositions offered by Madsen and Servais (1997) in their conceptualisations on 'born globals'. It will be interesting to see what explanatory frameworks will emerge in the growing area of small-firm internationalisation. Of more immediate relevance, however, is the role of internal (firm/decision-maker) and external (environmental) factors which stage theorists, network scholars, and business-strategy-/resource-based theorists have identified as significant to SMEs' initial internationalisation decisions.

24.6 Stimulating internationalisation

To initiate and subsequently develop international (export) activity, a firm must first be influenced by stimulating or 'attention-evoking' factors. The nature of these stimuli may offer invaluable insights into why some SMEs successfully internationalise while others do not. Building on previous typologies of internationalisation stimuli, Albaum *et al.* (1994) identified the following four categories:

- *internal-proactive* (factors associated with the SME's own initiative to exploit its unique internal competencies, e.g. potential for export-led growth);

- *internal-reactive* (responding to pressures from the internal environment, e.g. accumulation of unsold goods);

- *external-proactive* (active exploitation by management of market possibilities, e.g. identification of better opportunities abroad);

- *external-reactive* (reaction to factors from the external environment, e.g. receipt of unsolicited foreign orders).

Nevertheless, research on initial internationalisation suggests that stimuli are not sufficient on their own. They need to be supported by facilitating factors associated with the decision-maker, the organisation and the environment. These factors constitute the real impetus behind the firm's decision to go international.

24.6.1 Decision-maker characteristics

Decision-maker characteristics are generally considered to have, in Brooks and Rosson's (1982) words, 'a decided impact on export decision'. All the major review articles on empirical exporting research have similarly concluded on the decisive importance of decision-makers' characteristics. As Reid (1981) noted, 'empirical evidence points exclusively to the decision makers' attitude, experience, motivation and expectations as primary determinants in firms engaging in foreign marketing activity'. This is particularly so 'in small firms, where power, particularly decision-making power, is generally concentrated in the hands of one or very few persons'. According to Miesenbock (1988), 'the key variable in small business internationalisation is the decision maker of the firm. He or she is the one to decide starting, ending and increasing international activities.' Empirical findings on the specific decision-maker characteristics which increase the likelihood of SME internationalisation have, however, been inconsistent. This is particularly true of findings on decision-makers' age and level of educational attainment. Garnier's (1982) remarks that it was not possible to ascertain whether there were statistically significant differences between managers of internationalised and non-internationalised firms with respect to age and level of education would appear to reflect the available evidence.

With regard to international orientation, variously defined as foreign education or work experience, travel, foreign birth, world-mindedness (Boatler 1994), the balance of empirical evidence is that decision-makers of internationalised SMEs are likely to have spent part of their lives abroad, and are generally less affected by foreign-business-related uncertainties. Miesenbock (1988) concluded from an extensive review of the literature that 'the external contacts of the decision maker seem to be the most important objective characteristic'. Closely related to international orientation is another characteristic which may be referred to as international ethnic ties or contact networks. There is growing evidence that decision-makers whose contact networks (see Chapter 21) are internationally spread are more likely to exploit international market opportunities than those who lack such ties. Jackson (1981), indeed, found the Zionist links of British Jews to be significant in explaining the flow of Israeli exports into Britain. Further supportive evidence has been reported by Crick and Chaudhry (1995) and Zafarullah *et al.* (1998) in their respective studies of British-Asian and Pakistani SMEs (see Chapter 11).

Decision-makers' psychological traits are a further set of variables which have been widely studied. A large number of empirical findings have associated decision-makers of internationalised SMEs with such characteristics as: favourable perception of exporting risks, costs, profits and growth; more positive attitudes toward exporting; aggressiveness and dynamism; flexibility; and self-confidence. As observed by Ford and Leonidou (1991), 'firms with a decision maker perceiving risk in the export market as being lower versus risk in the domestic market, profits in the export market as being higher versus profits in the domestic market, and costs in the export market as being lower versus costs in the domestic market are more likely to become exporters'. Nevertheless, as Miesenbock (1988) stated, 'the explanatory power of psychologically-oriented research in internationalisation ... [is] controversial'.

24.6.2 Firm characteristics and competencies

Very few issues in SME internationalisation research have as much empirical support as the positive link between management support, commitment, perceptions and attitude, and internationalisation behaviour. As Aaby and Slater (1989) remarked, 'management commitment and management perceptions and attitudes towards export problems and incentives are good predictors of export [behaviour]'. Studies have also found a much higher propensity to internationalise (export) among firms with market (or organisational) planning, or exploration. As Aaby and Slater (1989) concluded, 'the implementation of a process for systematically exploring, analysing, and planning for export seems to be a very powerful discriminator between ... exporters and non-exporters'.

Findings on the impact of firm size (whether measured by employee number, sales, ownership of capital equipment, financial capability or a combination of criteria) on internationalisation behaviour have been mixed, if not outright controversial. The balance of evidence, however, suggests the importance of size, particularly in initiating international activity. As a general rule, larger firms are more likely to internationalise than small firms. Beyond some point, however, exporting would appear not to be correlated with size, a view corroborated by Withey's (1980) critical mass of 20 employees for crossing the internationalisation threshold. Reid (1982) explained it thus: 'absolute size using traditional indicators (assets, employees, functional specialisation, and sales) predominantly affect ... [small firms'] export entry'. The above standard does not, however, apply to SMEs in high-technology and service sectors (Bell 1994). Indeed, the use of e-commerce and on-line marketing via the World Wide Web and Internet is increasingly removing whatever deterrence size brings to internationalisation of SMEs, even in traditional industries (see Chapter 22).

The SME's industry or product type has also been found to influence international market entry. As Tybejee (1994) remarked, industry membership, or the structural characteristics of the industry, determine the conditions in which a firm competes and consequently its internationalisation. Garnier (1982), for example, in a study of Canadian printing and electrical industries, reported that 'the most immediate cause of export[ing] ... is the nature of the product or service offered by the exporting firm'. While SMEs in industries characterised by low skill level, low intrinsic value, bulkiness and high transportation costs are less likely to internationalise, those in sectors marked by short life-cycles are 'motivated to accelerate their entry into the international markets' (McGuinness and Little 1981; Tybejee 1994). Another firm characteristic which appears to influence an SME's internationalisation is its history, including previous experience of extra-regional expansion, importing experience or 'inward internationalisation'. Such experiences and attendant (network) relationships have been found to be significant precursors of internationalisation.

Empirical studies on SME internationalisation have also underscored the importance of firm competencies. It has, indeed, been suggested that 'firm competencies are probably more important than firm characteristics' (Aaby and Slater 1989). The specific dimensions of firm competency which, on balance, have been empirically supported include: technology intensity; R&D; systematic market research; product development; unique product attributes and quality; distribution, delivery and service quality; and advertising and sales promotion.

24.6.3 Characteristics of the firm's environment

Relative to larger firms, SMEs tend to lack the necessary resources and political clout to control their operating environment. Empirical findings can broadly be categorised into two: those related to the firm's domestic environment and those concerned with foreign (target) market attractiveness.

As observed by Miesenbock (1988), 'the home country of the firm also determines the performed export behaviour'. The legal system 'may facilitate (e.g. tax advantages in exporting) or complicate (e.g. foreign exchange regulations) international business. The same holds for infrastructure (e.g. distribution facilities or impediments).' Wiedersheim-Paul et al.'s (1978) model of pre-export behaviour and Garnier's (1982) theoretical model of the export process in a small firm both reflect the impact of the domestic environment. The former suggests that firms' location within an 'enterprise environment' facilitates an efficient exchange of information as well as creates 'possibilities for "contagion transmission" of ideas from other firms, in different stages of expansion'. Garnier (1982) also sees general characteristics of the environment as well as industry in which small firms operate as affecting their decision 'to export or refrain so doing'. Bilkey (1978) and Pavord and Bogart (1975) identified 'adverse home market conditions' as a push factor in export initiation, one example being 'home market saturation'.

With respect to foreign (target) market environment, studies have reported foreign government-imposed barriers and poor infrastructure – road and telephone systems – to be significant impediments to export market choice. Ford and Leonidou (1991) concluded that 'firms producing products which have to be modified in order to conform with the rules and regulations of foreign governments ... are less likely to become exporters'. Further discussions on these and related issues are undertaken in the next section on internationalisation barriers and problems.

24.7 Barriers in SME internationalisation

This section reviews empirical evidence on the obstacles that confront SMEs at different stages in the internationalisation process, including the export initiation stage. Leonidou (1995) defined export barriers as 'all those attitudinal, structural, operational, and other constraints that hinder the firm's ability to initiate, develop, or sustain international operations'. Different classificatory schemes have been used in the literature with respect to these problems. In an extensive review of export barrier research, Leonidou (1995) combined his earlier framework with Cavusgil's (1984), into a 'two-dimensional export barrier schema' (Kaleka and Katsikeas 1995). This identified four categories of problem:

- internal-domestic;
- internal-foreign;
- external-domestic;
- external-foreign.

Internal-domestic

These problems encompass obstacles emanating from within the firm, and relating to its home-country environment. They include: (i) the lack of personnel with requisite information and knowledge about export marketing, including expertise in handling such problems as foreign government regulations; (ii) negative perceptions of risks involved in selling abroad; and (iii) management emphasis on developing domestic market activities, particularly in large-sized domestic markets.

Internal-foreign

These problems arise mainly from the SMEs' limited marketing ability, and are experienced in the foreign (target) market environment. For some SMEs, international market entry is inhibited if product modifications are required to meet foreign safety or health standards or customers' specifications. As Moini (1997) remarked, 'adapting a product to foreign standards may require a large initial investment which many non-exporters lack'. Similar difficulties have also been reported with regard to providing repair and technical services, pricing and communicating with overseas customers. Other typical obstacles here include both high transportation cost and transportation, service and delivery-related difficulties.

External-domestic

These problems emanate from the SMEs' domestic environment, but are typically beyond its control. Among the most cited obstacles in this category is the vast amount of time and complex documentation involved in international marketing. Also often reported are the absence of adequate government support – incentives and infrastructural – to overcome internationalisation barriers and the lack of reasonable access to (or prohibitive cost of) capital needed to finance internationalisation.

External-foreign

These problems originate from outside the SME and are typically experienced in the international markets. Several studies have reported on the inhibiting impact of foreign government-imposed restrictions, including exchange rate, import and tariff regulations. Equally problematic for the SME is the development of reliable overseas contacts/distributors/representatives, including the overcoming of language and cultural differences. Other often-cited internationalisation barriers in this category are the intensity of competition in international markets or SMEs' lack of price competitiveness and the difficulties of getting payments.

The nature of a firm's response to these obstacles depends broadly on the background, decision-maker and firm characteristics, specifically organisational size; international business experience; international market research orientation; and export involvement. Inexperienced exporters, relative to regular exporters, perceived strict import quotas and confusing import regulations as much more important in hindering their entry into the Japanese market (Namiki 1988). Marginal exporters, compared to their more active counterparts, have significantly different perceptions of shipping complexity, uncertainty of shipping cost, and complexity of trade documentation. Similar conclusions were reached by Tesar and Tarleton (1982) in respect of passive and aggressive exporters among their Wisconsin and Virginia sample; and Bell (1997) with regard to occasional, frequent and aggressive exporters.

It appears, also, that firms at different stages of internationalisation face problems of differing types and severity (Bilkey and Tesar 1977; Bilkey 1978; Dichtl *et al.* 1984; Bell 1997). A recent three-nation study by Bell (1997), for example, reported that while 'finance-related problems often intensify with increased international exposure, ... marketing-related factors tend to decline as firms become more active in export markets'.

24.8 Policy and institutional support for SME internationalisation

This section highlights the existing policy frameworks and support programmes which underpin SME internationalisation in most OECD countries. Currently used measures can be classified into direct and indirect, in terms of whether they are specifically designed for export development, or with a general aim of enhancing SME overall competitiveness – internationalisation benefits being only implied (Bell 1994). As observed by Seringhaus and Rosson (1991), direct assistance encapsulates 'an array of programmes that range from awareness-creating, interest-stimulating, research support, export preparation, export market entry, to export market development and expansion-focused activities'. These have broadly been categorised by Crick and Czinkota (1995) into export service programmes (e.g. seminars for potential exporters, export consultancy, and export financing) and market development programmes (e.g. dissemination of sales leads to local firms, participation in trade shows, and preparation of market analyses). Indirect assistance extends to those aspects described as economic infrastructure (Owualah 1987), whether hardware (financial, fiscal, and plant and machinery-leasing) or software (training, advice, information). They are generally aimed at effecting structural and process change within companies (Seringhaus and Rosson 1991), and are often integrated into the industrial policy implemented by various governments at central and/or regional levels (Bell 1994). Such programmes also, increasingly, seek to facilitate the adoption of innovative new technologies and best practices (including networking) among firms. Programmes of direct and indirect support include:

- providing access to foreign market information;
- providing some form of financial assistance (export credit or foreign investment guarantees, venture capital, grants and subsidies);
- improving SMEs' capability through management advisory services and help with R&D and technology;
- providing SMEs with a better business environment, by facilitating networking and subcontracting arrangements and offering simplified, one-stop assistance units, industrial parks and arbitration assistance.

Importantly, the extent of involvement of the government and the private sector in actual support provision varies between countries. While government involvement appears to be dominant in countries such as the UK, Ireland and Canada, others like Finland, Denmark and Germany tend to emphasise private-sector leadership in support provision. Yet, a few others (notably France, the Netherlands and Austria) seem to provide highly rated support at both public- and private-sector levels. Granted that no firm conclusions have been reached regarding the relative merits of public versus quasi-public-sector support mechanisms (Bell 1997), it is safe to suggest that 'delivery systems that make use of existing and potential private sector activities are more likely to be cost-effective' (OECD 1997a).

Despite the sophistication and comprehensiveness of policy measures available in advanced (as well as developing) economies, empirical findings on SMEs' level of awareness, usage and satisfaction with these programmes have been generally negative. This highlights the challenging nature of the task of seeking to improve SME internationalisation policy – a task which the concluding section attempts to address.

24.9 Chapter summary

It would appear from the unremitting pressures of globalisation drivers that the trend towards SME internationalisation can only intensify. The OECD's (1997a) prognosis of a continuing shrinkage in the percentage of SMEs insulated from (inward) globalisation effects implies also that SMEs which ignore internationalisation realities risk losing their competitiveness. These make it even more imperative that as many SMEs as possible are given whatever support is necessary to encourage their internationalisation.

A consensus appears to have emerged among academic researchers and policy-makers that SMEs negotiate varying paths to internationalisation. Having been extensively and successfully challenged, the 'stage' approach would seem to have lost its traditional hegemony to a more inclusive, integrative view of SME internationalisation. This perspective, recently articulated by Bell and Young (1998), presents extant frameworks – incremental models; network-driven models, including the accelerated 'born internationals' perspective; and the rationalistic strategy-/resource-based models – as complementary rather than competing explanations. It is now clear that while some SMEs internationalise in an incremental manner, others accelerate through the process, driven possibly by their existing network relationships or entrepreneurial factors, and yet others adopt a rational, strategy-based process involving some consideration of relevant internal and external factors. Thus, it behoves policy-makers to seek greater understanding of SMEs as the objects of their policy measures (see Chapter 4). Such an understanding should inform the segmentation of these SMEs for policy-making purposes, and subsequently lead to needs-based targeting of appropriate assistance and support.

The idea of segmenting assistance targets is not new in the literature, and is integral to the much-criticised stage models. What should, perhaps, be new is the rethinking of the segmentation framework, such that the 'stage-by-stage' approach is seen, not as *The Way*, but as one of the ways to internationalise; across a spectrum that includes network-driven, including accelerated, internationalisation as well as strategy-/resource-based internationalisation. Hopefully, this perspective would translate to a broadening of the focus of programmes supporting SME internationalisation beyond their traditional exporting emphasis (Bell 1994). Whatever the approach taken, policy-makers should recognise the existence of different internationalisation pathways. For incrementally inclined firms, usual methods of assistance targeting based on stages of internationalisation may be appropriate. SMEs at lower stages may need intensive information support, one-to-one counselling and so on to nudge them along their learning curve, while those at more advanced stages may require more experiential-type knowledge, and perhaps assistance aimed at easing the financial obstacles facing foreign target customers (Crick and Czinkota 1995). Proper acknowledgement of the reality of accelerated internationalisation should imply, for example, programmes of support for network building and activation among SMEs. Existing efforts in this direction, at industry, national and regional levels (such as BC-NET in Europe, Unisphere in America and Global Entrepreneur Forum in Asia), should be strengthened. It seems appropriate, also, to widen the assistance programmes on offer to reflect a more diversified mix of internationalisation possibilities than is currently the case, such that SMEs which wish to establish joint-venture operations overseas or engage in strategic alliances or even acquire a production plant abroad would find requisite support and encouragement. In these immensely exciting days of e-commerce and on-line marketing, SMEs should be sensitised and supported with appropriate training and consultancy to optimise the benefits of Internet-based internationalisation.

To effectively target SMEs and their decision-makers with the appropriate kind of competence-enhancing support, it may be useful to employ a classification scheme built around their current characteristics and competencies, thus: internationalised entrepreneurial firms; internationalised less entrepreneurial firms; non-internationalised entrepreneurial firms; and non-internationalised less-entrepreneurial firms (see Figure 24.2).

For the non-internationalised, less entrepreneurial SMEs, the focus should be on improving the entrepreneurial and international orientation of their key decision-maker(s) through seminars and workshops, export information provision, and sponsorship to trade fairs. This should also involve introducing an external agent (Wiedersheim-Paul *et al.* 1978) on a part-time or consultancy basis. Ideally, non-internationalised SMEs, lacking in entrepreneurial orientation, should be assisted in the search for, and employment of, managers with requisite profiles: experienced, internationally orientated and connected decision-makers. Other measures which may

Figure 24.2 Recommendations to assist SME internationalision by SME categories

	Entrepreneurial	Less entrepreneurial
Internationalised	**[IV]** Encourage best practices – R&D, IT, innovation Facilitate participation in network structures Mitigate operational problems: assist foreign customers, ease market access, etc.	**[III]** Seek positive reinforcement Deploy liaison officer/problem-solver Encourage networking; export clubs Establish mentoring scheme
Non-internationalised	**[II]** Assist to redress competency gap Provide consultancy support and training Ease access to available support Introduce mentoring scheme Encourage best practices – R&D, IT, innovation, networking	**[I]** Introduce change agents Provide training/information support Help with foreign market contacts Encourage networking Establish and utilise international market brokers

Source : adapted from Ibeh (1998)

be useful here include encouraging networking and linking them with foreign customers. The latter could be particularly crucial given the strength of empirical evidence on the impact of unsolicited orders from abroad in stimulating initial internationalisation.

As the name indicates, non-internationalised entrepreneurial SMEs have not yet internationalised but appear to have the right entrepreneurial disposition to do so. This category of firms, by definition, are likely to have top management or key decision-makers with the requisite characteristics. Their resource gap may arise from any of such areas of firm competencies as product quality and technology, market intelligence, or intermediaries' network. These areas of resource lack (Bell and Young 1998) would have to be addressed in order to enable these firms to internationalise, as they apparently wish to do. Potentially useful support measures may comprise providing access to market survey reports, assisting with consultancy, foreign market contacts and networks, including mentoring relationships.

Internationalised, but less entrepreneurial SMEs are those which have found themselves in the international market, but appear to lack a strong motivation for so doing. Such firms may have started exporting accidentally, through the receipt of unsolicited foreign orders or allied external-reactive stimulus (Albaum *et al.* 1994). The policy focus here should be on ensuring that such SMEs receive positive reinforcement from

451

their international market experience. Suggested measures include providing requisite assistance – information, training, counselling; easing operational problems; seconding 'change agents' or helping them to employ more decision-makers with requisite qualities; encouraging private-sector organisations to draw them into their networks, hence availing them of opportunities for sharing of experiences and learning.

Finally, the policy focus in respect of internationalised entrepreneurial SMEs should be on shoring up their key competencies and renewing their international and entrepreneurial vision. Such firms should be equipped to continually respond to the inevitable competitive challenges of an increasingly globalised market through appropriate adjustments and innovations in products, processes, organisations, markets and technology (OECD 1997a; Hyvarinen 1990). Increased attention needs to be given to relationships with key market actors (regular market visits and so on), particularly given the strength of empirical support on the potential benefits of so doing (Styles and Ambler 1994; 1997; Bell 1994). SMEs in this category, relatively speaking, need less assistance from the government and its relevant agencies. The direction in which government assistance would, none the less, be most appreciated is the minimisation of operational or access problems in foreign markets (Katsikeas 1994; Katsikeas and Morgan 1994). This is the standard service provided by government to its businesses, the most notable example, arguably, being the US government's deployment of their might in favour of their international companies. Policy-makers can also make a real difference by facilitating sectoral and/or industry-level export co-operative arrangements among SMEs to assist them in meeting the increasingly stiff competition from other regions (Arnould and Gennaro 1985). The potential benefits of this initiative may be quite immense, extending to cost-sharing in R&D and technology sourcing, more innovative and quality products, better reputation of country's products in export markets, better leverage in relationships with distributors, agents, government officials (domestic and foreign), and, indeed, a whole lot of other network-related spin-offs (Ibeh 1998).

Questions

1 An SME can be exposed to relevant stimuli, but constrained from internationalising owing to some barriers or lack of requisite managerial, organisational and environmental back-up. What implications has this statement for government policy-making and support provision?

2 A fuller understanding of SME internationalisation can be gained by focusing on the potential complementarities of existing explanatory frameworks as opposed to the current practice of viewing them as competing alternatives (Bell and Young 1998). Discuss.

3 Internationalised SMEs have progressed from being a rarity, to a significant exporting presence and are now serious contributors to direct foreign investments, especially the co-operation-based modes. Please explain this statement, focusing on the internal (within the firm) and external developments that have furthered SME internationalisation.

4 Speculate on the future of SME internationalisation over the next five years.

References

Aaby, N. and Slater, S. F. (1989) 'Management influences on export performance: a review of the empirical literature 1978–1988', *International Marketing Review*, 6(4), 7–23.

Abbanat, R. (1967) *Strategies for size*, PhD dissertation, Harvard University.

Abbot, B. (1993) 'Patterns of privatisation and market trends in local government', Kingston Business School Working Paper.

Abell, P., Khalif, H. and Smeaton, D. (1995) 'An exploration of entry to and exit from self-employment', Centre for Economic Performance, LSE Discussion Paper No. 224.

Abell, W. and Black, S. (1997) *Business Use of the Internet in New Zealand: A Follow-Up Study.* http://www.lincoln.ac.nz/ccb/staff/abell/webnet.htm.

Abell, W. and Lim, L. (1996) *Business Use of the Internet in New Zealand: An Exploratory Study.* http://elmo.scu.edu.au/sponsored/ausweb/ausweb96/business/abell/paper.html.

Abetti, P. A. (1997) 'Underground innovation in Japan: the development of Toshiba's word processor and laptop computer', *Creativity and Innovation Management*, 6(3), 127–39.

Ackerman, P. L. and Humphreys, L. G. (1990) 'Individual differences theory in industrial and organizational psychology', in Dunnette, M. D. and Hough. L. M. (eds) *Handbook of Industrial and Organizational Psychology*, 2nd edition, vol. 1, 223–82. Palo Alto, CA: Consulting Psychologists Press, Inc.

ACOST (1990) *The Enterprise Challenge: Overcoming Barriers to Growth in Small Firms*, Advisory Council on Science and Technology, Cabinet Office. London: HMSO.

Adair, J. (1990) *The Challenge of Innovation.* Guildford: Talbot Adair Press.

Agar, J. (1994) *Walking on Water: Some Recommendations on the Role of the Personal Business Adviser.* Durham: Durham University Business School.

Ajzen, I. (1991) 'The theory of planned behavior', *Organizational Behavior and Human Decision Processes*, 50, 179–211.

Ajzen, I. (1995) 'Attitudes and behavior', in Manstead, A. S. R. and Hewstone, M. (eds) *The Blackwell Encyclopedia of Social Psychology*, 52–7. Oxford: Blackwell Publishing Ltd.

Albaum, G., Strandstov, J., Duerr, E. and Dowd, L. (1994) *International Marketing and Export Management*, 2nd edition. Wokingham: Addison-Wesley.

Aldrich, H. E. (1979) *Organisations and Environments.* Englewood Cliffs, NJ: Prentice Hall.

Aldrich, H. E. (1987) 'The impact of social networks on business founding and profit: a longitudinal study', in *Frontiers of Entrepreneurship Research.* Wellesley, MA: Babson College.

Aldrich, H. (1989) 'Networking among women entrepreneurs', in Hagen, O., Rivchum, C. and Sexton, D. (eds) *Women Owned Businesses*, 103–32. New York: Praeger.

Aldrich, H. E. and Auster, E. (1986) 'Even dwarfs started small: liabilities of age and size and their strategic implications', in Staw, B.M. and Cummings, L.L. (eds) *Research in Organizational Behavior* 8, 165–98. Greenwich: JAI Press.

Aldrich, H. and Reese, P. R. (1993) 'Does networking pay off? A panel study of entrepreneurs in the Research Triangle', unpublished paper.

Aldrich, H. and Zimmer, C. (1986) 'Entrepreneurship through social networks', in Sexton, D. L. and Wilson, R. W. (eds) *The Art and Science of Entrepreneurship*, 154–67. Massachusetts: Ballinger.

Aldrich, H., Cater, J., Jones, T. and McEvoy, D. (1981) 'Business development and self-segregation: Asian enterprise in three British cities', in Peach, C., Robinson, V. and Smith, S. (eds) *Ethnic Segregation in Cities*, 170–90. London: Croom Helm.

Aldrich, H., Cater, J., Jones, T. and McEvoy, D. (1982) 'From periphery to peripheral: the South Asian petite bourgeoisie in England', in Simpson, I. and Simpson, R. (eds) *Research in the Sociology of Work*, vol. 2, 1–32.

Aldrich, H., Jones, T. and McEvoy, D. (1984) 'Ethnic advantage and minority business development', in Ward, R. and Jenkins, R. (eds) *Ethnic Communities in Business*, 189–210. Cambridge: Cambridge University Press.

Aldrich, H., Rose, B. and Woodward, W. (1986) 'Social behaviour and entrepreneurial networks', in *Frontiers of Entrepreneurship Research*, 239-240. Wellesley, MA: Babson College.

Aldrich, H., Reese, P. R. and Dubini, P. (1989) 'Women on the verge of a breakthrough: networking among entrepreneurs in the United States and Italy', *Entrepreneurship and Regional Development*, 1, 339–56.

Aldrich, H. E., Renzulli, L. and Laughton, N. (1997) *Passing on privilege: resources provided by self-employed parents to their self-employed children*. Paper presented at the American Sociological Association.

Allen, J. (1992) 'Fordism and modern industry', in *Political and Economic Forms of Modernity*, Cambridge: Polity Press.

Allen, S. and Truman, C. (1988) *Women's work and success in women's businesses*. Paper presented to 11th UK National Small Firms Policy and Research Conference, Cardiff Business School.

Allen, S. and Truman, C. (1993) *Women in Business: Perspectives on Women Entrepreneurs*. London: Routledge.

Allen, T. (1977) *Managing the Flow of Technology: Technology Transfer and the Dissemination of Technological Information within the R&D Organization*. Boston, MA: MIT Press.

Amabile, T. M., Hill, K. G., Hennesey, B. A. and Tighe, E. M. (1994) 'The work preference inventory: assessing intrinsic and extrinsic motivational orientations', *Journal of Personality and Social Psychology*, 66 (5), 950–67.

Amin, A. and Tomaney, J (eds) (1995) *Behind the Myth of European Union: Prospects for Cohesion*. London: Routledge.

Amsden, A., Kochanowicz, J. and Taylor, L. (1994) *The Market Meets its Match: Restructuring the Economies of Eastern Europe*. Cambridge, MA: Harvard University Press.

Anderson, J. (1995) *Local Heroes*. Glasgow: Scottish Enterprise.

Anderson, O. (1993) 'On the internationalisation process of firms: a critical analysis', *Journal of International Business Studies*, Second Quarter, 209–31.

Anderson, O. and Strigel, W. H. (1981) 'Business surveys and economic research – a review of significant developments', in Laumer, H. and Ziegler, M. (eds) *International Research on Business Cycle Surveys*, 25–54. Munich: Springer-Verlach.

Anderson, P. H., Blenker, P. and Christensen, P. R. (1995) *Generic routes to subcontractors'*

internationalisation. Paper presented at the RENT IX Conference on Entrepreneurship and SMEs in Milano, Italy, November.

Argyle, M. (1969) *Social Interaction*. Atherton: Methuen.

Armington, J. and Odle, C. (1982) 'Small business, how many jobs?', *Barclays Review*, Winter, 14–17.

Arndt, J. (1967) 'Word-of-mouth advertising and informal communication', in Cox, D. (ed.) *Risk Taking and Information Handling in Consumer Behaviour*. Boston: Harvard University.

Arnold, G. (1998) *Corporate Financial Management*. London: Financial Times Pitman Publishing.

Arnould, O. and Gennaro, E. (1985) 'Enhancing the market for new products and services by export co-operation between innovative SMEs', in *Developing Markets for New Products and Services through Joint Exporting by Innovative SMEs*, Commission of the European Committee Report EUR 9927, 27–32.

Arthur Andersen/Singapore Trade Development Board (1997) *Franchising in Asia-Pacific*.

Asante, M. K. and Mattson, M. (1992) *Historical and Cultural Atlas of African Americans*. New York: Macmillan.

Aslund, A. (1985) *Private Enterprise in Eastern Europe*. New York: St Martin's Press.

Atherton, A. and Sear, L. (1996) *Finance and the SME: mapping current configurations of provision in the North-East of England*. Paper presented to the 26th efmd European Small Business Seminar, Vaasa, Finland, 24–6 September.

Atherton, A. and Sear, L. (1997) *Support for the exporting SME: current configurations of provision in the North-East of England*. Paper presented to the 20th National Small Firms Policy and Research Conference, Belfast, November.

Atherton, A., Gibb, A. and Sear, L. (1996) *Reviewing the Case for Business Start-ups*. Report by Small Business Centre, Durham University Business School, University of Durham.

Atkinson, J. (1984) 'Manpower strategies for flexible organisation', *Personnel Management*, August, 28–31.

Atkinson, J. and Meager, N. (1994) 'Running to stand still: the small business in the labour market', in Atkinson, J. and Storey, D. (eds) *Employment, the Small Firm and the Labour Market*. London: Routledge.

Audit Commission (1988) *Urban Regeneration and Economic Development: The Local Government Dimension*. London: HMSO.

Auger, P. and Gallagher, J. M. (1997) 'Factors affecting the adoption of an Internet-based sales presence for small businesses', *The Information Society*, 13 (1), 55–74.

Autio, E. (1995) 'Four types of innovators: a conceptual and empirical study of new, technology-based companies as innovators', *Entrepreneurship & Regional Development*, 7 (3), 233–48.

Axelrod, R. (1981) 'The emergence of cooperation among egoists', *American Review of Political Science*, 75, 306–18.

Axelsson, B. and Easton, G. (eds) (1992) *Industrial Network: A New View of Reality*. London: Routledge.

Baaijens, J. (1998) *The social structure of innovation and entrepreneurship*. Paper presented at the 10th International SASE Conference.

Bacon, N., Ackers, P., Storey, J. and Coates, D. (1996) 'It's a small world: managing human resources in small business', *International Journal of Human Resource Management*, 7 (1), 82–100.

Badaracco, J. (1991) *The Knowledge Link: How Firms Compete through Strategic Alliances*. Harvard Business School Press.

Badenoch, D., Reid, C., Burton, P., Gibb, F. and Oppenheim, C. (1994) 'The value of information', in Feeney, M. and Grieves, M. (eds) *The Value and Impact of Information*, 9–77. London: Bowker-Saur.

Bagby, R. (1988) 'Editorial: the winds of change', *Entrepreneurship, Theory and Practice*, Fall, 5–6.

Bagozzi, R. P. and Kimmel, S. K. (1995) 'A comparison of leading theories for prediction of goal-directed behaviours' *British Journal of Social Psychology*, 34, 437–61.

Bagozzi, R. P. and Warshaw, P. R. (1992) 'An examination of the etiology of the attitude–behavior relation for goal-directed behaviors', *Multivariate Behavioral Research*, 27 (4), 601–34.

Baker, T., Aldrich, H. E. and Liou, N. (1997) 'Invisible entrepreneurs: the neglect of women business owners by mass media and scholarly journals in the USA', *Entrepreneurship and Regional Development*, 9 (3), 221–38.

Baker, W. H., Adams, L. and Davis, B. (1993) 'Business planning in successful small firms', *Long Range Planning*, 26 (6), 82–8.

Bakos, J. Y. (1991) 'A strategic analysis of electronic marketplaces', *MIS Quarterly*, 15 (3), 295–310.

Bakos, J. Y. (1997) 'Reducing buyer search costs: implications for electronic marketplaces', *Management Science*, 43 (12), 1676–92.

Baldock, R., Smallbone, D. and Bridge, M. (1997) *Targeted support for new and young businesses: the case of North Yorkshire TEC's 'Backing Winners' programme*. Paper presented at the Small Business & Development Conference, University of Sheffield, 19–20 March.

Baldwin, T. F., McVoy, D. S. and Steinfield, C. (1996) *Convergence – Integrating Media, Information and Communication*. Thousand Oaks: Sage.

Balkin, D. B. and Logan, J. W. (1988) 'Reward policies that support entrepreneurship', *Compensation and Benefits Review*, 20 (1), 18–25.

Bamberger, I. (1989) 'Developing competitive advantage in small and medium-sized firms', *Long Range Planning*, 22 (5), 80–8.

Bandura, A. (1982) 'The psychology of chance encounters and life paths', *American Psychologist*, 37 (7), 747–55.

Bandura, A. (1986) *Social Foundations of Thought and Action: A Social Cognitive Theory*. Englewood Cliffs, NJ: Prentice Hall.

Bandura, A. (1991) 'Social cognitive theory of self-regulation', *Organizational Behavior and Human Decision Processes*, 50, 248–87.

Bandura, A. (1995) 'Perceived self-efficacy', in Manstead, A. S. R. and Hewstone, M. (eds) *The Blackwell Encyclopedia of Social Psychology*, 434–6. Oxford: Blackwell Publishers Ltd.

Barberis, P. and May, T. (1993) *Government, Industry and the Political Economy*. Buckingham: Open University Press.

Baron, R. A. (1998) 'Cognitive mechanisms in entrepreneurship: why and when entrepreneurs think differently than other people', *Journal of Business Venturing*, 13, 275–94.

Barrett, G. A. (1997) *Multiple disadvantage and black enterprise: aspects of African-Caribbean and South Asian small business*, unpublished PhD thesis, Liverpool John Moores University.

Barrett, G. A., Jones, T. P. and McEvoy, D. (1996) 'Ethnic minority business: theoretical discourse in Britain and North America', *Urban Studies*, 33 (4/5), 783–809.

Barrett, S. and Konsynski, B. R. (1982) 'Inter-organisational information sharing systems', *MIS Quarterly*, Fall, 93–105.

Barry, B. (1989) 'Development of organization structure', *Family Business Review*, 2 (3), Autumn, 293–315.

Bartlett, W. (1991) *Privatisation and quasi-markets*. Paper presented at EACES First Trento Workshop, University of Trento.

Basu, A. (1995) *Asian small businesses in Britain: an exploration of entrepreneurial activity*. Paper to the Second International Journal of Entrepreneurial Behaviour and Research Conference, Malvern, 18–20 July.

Basu, D. (1991) *Afro-Caribbean Businesses in Great Britain: Factors Affecting Business Success and Marginality*, unpublished PhD thesis, Manchester Business School.

Bateman, M. (ed.) (1997) *Business Cultures in Central and Eastern Europe*. Oxford: Butterworth-Heinemann.

Bateman, M. (1999) 'Small enterprise development policy in the transition economies of Central and Eastern Europe: progress with the wrong model?', *Zagreb International Review of Economics and Business*, 2 (2).

Bates, T. (1994), reported in *The Franchise Update Report*, Issue 94–1.

Bates, T. (1997) 'The minority enterprise small business investment company program: institutionalizing a nonviable minority business assistance infrastructure', *Urban Affairs Review* 32(5), 683–703.

Baumback, C. and Mancuso, P. (1993) *Entrepreneurship and Venture Management*. London: Prentice Hall.

Becker, G.S. (1962) 'Investment in human capital', *Journal of Political Economy*, 70, 9–49.

Beckhard, R. and Dyer, W. G. (1983) 'Managing change in the family firm – issues and strategies', *Sloan Management Review*, 24, 59–65.

Beesley, M. and Rothwell, R. (1987) 'Small firm linkages in the UK', in Rothwell, R. and Bessant, J. (eds) *Innovation, Adaptation and Growth*. Amsterdam: Elsevier.

Beesley, W. and Wilson, P. E. B. (1984) 'Public policy and small firms', in Levicki, C. (ed.) *Small Business Theory and Policy*. London: Croom Helm.

Begley, T. M. and Boyd, D. P. (1987) 'Psychological characteristics associated with performance in entrepreneurial firms and smaller businesses', *Journal of Business Venturing*, 2, 79–93.

Bell, C. G. (1991) *High-Tech Ventures: The Guide for Entrepreneurial Success*. Reading, MA: Addison Wesley.

Bell, J. D. (1994) *The role of government in small-firm internationalisation: a comparative study of export promotion in Finland, Ireland, and Norway, with specific reference to the computer software industry*, unpublished PhD thesis, Department of Marketing, University of Strathclyde, Glasgow.

Bell, J. (1995) 'The internationalisation of small computer software firms – a further challenge to "stage" theories', *European Journal of Marketing*, 29 (8), 60–75.

Bell, J. (1997) 'A comparative study of the export problems of small software exporters in Finland, Ireland and Norway', *International Business Review*, 6 (6), 585–604.

Bell, J. and Young, S. (1998) 'Towards an integrative framework of the internationalisation of the firm', in Hooley, G., Loveridge, R. and Wilson, D. (eds) *Internationalisation: Process, Context and Markets*. London: Macmillan.

Bell, J., Crick, D. and Young, S. (1998) 'Holistic perspective on small firm internationalisation', *Proceedings of the AIB (U.K. Chapter) Conference*, April.

Bellu, R. R. (1988) 'Entrepreneurs and managers: are they different?', in Kirchhoff, B. A., Long, W. A., McMullan, W. E., Vesper, K. H. and Wetzel, W. E. J. (eds) *Frontiers of Entrepreneurship Research*, 16–30. Wellesley, MA: Babson College.

Bellu, R. R. (1993) 'Task role motivation and attributional style as predictors of entrepreneurial performance: female sample findings', *Entrepreneurship and Regional Development*, 5, 331–44.

Bellu, R. R. and Sherman, H. (1995) 'Predicting firm success from task motivation and attributional style. A longitudinal study', *Entrepreneurship and Regional Development*, 7, 349–63.

Benjamin, R. and Wigand, R. (1995) 'Electronic markets and virtual chains on the information superhighway', *Sloan Management Review*, Winter, 62–72.

Bennett, M. (1989) *Managing Growth*, NatWest Small Business Shelf. London: Pitman.

Bennett, R. (1997a) 'Export marketing and the Internet – experiences of web site use and perceptions of export barriers among UK businesses', *International Marketing Review*, 14 (5), 324–44.

Bennett, R. (1998) 'Using the World Wide Web for international marketing: Internet use and perceptions of export barriers among German and British businesses', *Journal of Marketing Communications*, 4, 27–43.

Bennett, R. and Errington, A. (1995) 'Training and the rural small business', *Planning, Practice and Research*, 10 (1), 45–54.

Bennett, R. J. (1995) *Meeting Business Needs in Britain*. London: British Chambers of Commerce.

Bennett, R. J. (1997) *SMEs, Business Associations and their contribution to business competitiveness*. Paper presented to the 20th National Small Firms Policy and Research Conference, Belfast, November.

Bennett, R. J. and Krebs, G. (1991) *Local Economic Development: Public–Private Partnership Initiatives in Britain and Germany*. London: Belhaven.

Bennett, R. J. and McCoshan, A. (1993) *Enterprise and Human Resource Development: Local Capacity Building*. London: Paul Chapman Publishing.

Bennett, R. J., Wicks, P. and McCoshan, A. (1994) *Local Empowerment and Business Services: Britain's Experiment with Training and Enterprise Councils*. London: UCL Press.

Berg, N. G. (1997) 'Gender, place and entrepreneurship', *Entrepreneurship and Regional Development*, 9 (3), 259–68.

Berry, A. and Simpson, J. (1993) *Financing Small and Medium Sized Businesses and the Role of Factoring – The View of Accountants and User Companies*, Brighton Business School Research Papers. Brighton University.

Berry, A., Citron, D. and Jarvis, R. (1987) *The Information Needs of Bankers Dealing with Large and Small Companies*, The Chartered Association of Certified Accountants Research Report No. 7. London.

Berry, A., Jarvis, R., Lipman, H. and Macallan, H. (1990) *Leasing and the Smaller Firm*, ACCA Occasional Paper No. 3. London: The Chartered Association of Certified Accountants.

Berry, A., Faulkner, S., Hughes, M. and Jarvis, R. (1993a) *Bank Lending: Beyond the Theory*. London: Chapman and Hall.

Berry, A., Faulkner, S., Hughes, M. and Jarvis, R. (1993b) 'Financial information: the banker and the small business', *British Accounting Review*, 25 (2).

Berry, M. (1998) 'Strategic planning in small high tech companies', *Technovation*, 31 (3), 455–66.

Berry, R. H., Crum, R. E. and Waring, A. (1993) *Corporate Performance Appraisal in Bank Lending Decisions*. London: CIMA.

Bessant, J. (1995) 'Networking as a mechanism for enabling organisational innovations: the case of continuous improvement', in Andreasen, L. E. Coriat, B. and Friso, D. H.

(eds) in *Europe's Next Step: Organisational Innovation, Competition and Employment*, London: Frank Cass & Co, 253–70.

Bhaskar, R. (1986) *Scientific Realism and Human Emancipation*. London: Verso.

Bhide, A. (1994) 'How entrepreneurs craft strategies that work', *Harvard Business Review*, 72 (2), 150–62.

Biggadike, R. (1976) *Corporate Diversification: Entry, Strategy and Performance*. Boston, MA: Division of Research, Graduate School of Business Administration, Harvard University.

Bilkey, W. J. (1978) 'An attempted integration of the literature on the export behaviour of firms', *Journal of International Business Studies*, 9, Spring/Summer, 33–46.

Bilkey, W. J. and Tesar, G. (1977) 'The export behaviour of smaller-sized Wisconsin manufacturing firms', *Journal of International Business Studies*, 8 (1), 93–8.

Binks, M. and Ennew, C. (1991) 'Banks and the provision of finance to small businesses', in Stanworth, J. and Gray, C. (eds) *Bolton 20 Years On: The Small Firm in the 1990s*, 50–75. London: Paul Chapman Publishing.

Binks, M. R. and Ennew, C. T. (1995) 'Bank finance and the growing firm', in Buckland, R. and Davis, E. W. (eds) *Finance for growing enterprise*. Routledge.

Binks, M. R., Ennew, C. T. and Reed, G. V. (1988) 'The survey by the Forum of Private Business on banks and small firms', in Bannock, G. and Morgan, E.V. (eds) *Banks and Small Businesses: A Two Nation Perspective*. London: Forum of Private Business/ National Federation of Small Business.

Binks, M. R., Ennew, C. T. and Reed, G. V. (1990a) *Small Business and Their Banks 1990*. Knutsford: Forum of Private Business.

Binks, M. R., Ennew, C. T. and Reed, G. V. (1990b) *Finance gaps and small firms*. Paper presented to the Royal Economics Society Annual Conference, Nottingham.

Binks, M. R., Ennew, C. T. and Reed, G. V. (1993) *Small Business and Their Banks, 1992*. Knutsford: Forum of Private Business.

Birch, D. (1979) *The Job Generation Process*. Massachusetts: MIT Program on Neighborhood and Regional Change.

Birch, D. (1981) 'Who creates jobs?', *The Public Interest*, 65, 3–14.

Birkinshaw, J. (1997) 'Entrepreneurship in multinational corporations: the characteristics of subsidiary initiatives', *Strategic Management Journal*, 18 (3), 207–29.

Birley, S. (1985) 'The role of networks in the entrepreneurial process', *Journal of Business Venturing*, 1, 107–17.

Birley, S. (1989) 'Female entrepreneurs: are they really any different?', *Journal of Small Business Management*, January, 32–6.

Birley, S. and Cromie, S. (1988) *Social networks and entrepreneurship in Northern Ireland*. Paper presented at the Enterprise in Action Conference, Belfast.

Birley, S. and Macmillan, I. (eds) (1995) *International Entrepreneurship*. London: Routledge.

Birley, S., Myers, A. and Cromie, S. (1989) *Entrepreneurial networks: some concepts and empirical evidence*. Paper presented at the 12th National Small Firms Policy and Research Conference, The Barbican, London.

Birley, S., Cromie, S. and Myers, A. (1991) 'Entrepreneurial networks: their emergence in Ireland and overseas', *International Small Business Journal*, 9 (4), 56–74.

Black, J., De Meza, D. and Jeffreys. D. (1996) 'House prices, the supply of collateral and the enterprise economy', *Economic Journal*, 106 (434), pp. 60–75.

Blackburn, R. A., Curran, J. and Jarvis, R. (1990) *Small firms and local networks: some theoretical and conceptual explorations*. Paper presented at the 13th National Small Firms Policy and Research Conference, Harrogate, November.

Blanchflower, D. G. and Oswald, A. (1991) 'Self-employment and Mrs. Thatcher's enterprise culture', Centre for Economic Performance, LSE Discussion Paper No. 30.

Blaschke, J. and Ersoz, A. (1986) 'The Turkish economy in West Berlin', *International Small Business Journal*, 4 (3), 38–47.

Blaschke, J., Boissevain, J., Grotenberg, H. *et al.* (1990) 'European trends in ethnic business', in Waldinger, R., Aldrich, H. and Ward, R. (eds) *Ethnic Entrepreneurs*, 79–105. London: Sage.

Blili, S. and Raymond, L. (1993) 'Information technology: threats and opportunities for small and medium-sized enterprises', *International Journal of Information Management*, 13 (6), 439–48.

Blyton, P. and Turnbull, P. (1998) *The Dynamics of Employee Relations*. London: Macmillan.

Boaden, R. and Lockett, G. (1991) 'Information technology, information systems and information management: definition and development', *European Journal of Information Systems*, 1 (1), 23–32.

Boatler, R. (1994) 'Manager worldmindedness and trade propensity', *Journal of Global Marketing*, 8 (1), 111–27.

Boeker, W. (1989) 'Strategic change: the effects of founding and history', *Academy of Management Journal*, 32, 489–515.

Boeri, T. (1994) '"Transitional" unemployment', *Economics of Transition*, 2 (1).

Boissevain, J. (1974) *Friends of Friends: Networks, Manipulations and Coalitions*. Oxford: Basil Blackwell.

Bolton Report (1971) *Report of the Committee of Enquiry on Small Firms*, Chaired by J. E. Bolton, Cmnd. 4811. London: HMSO.

Bonacich, E. and Modell, J. (1980) *The Economic Basis of Ethnic Solidarity in the Japanese American Community*. Berkeley: University of California Press.

Booz-Allen and Hamilton (1997) *Zukunft Multimedia – Grundlagen, Märkte und Perspektiven in Deutschland*, 4. Auflage [Future Multimedia – Basics, Markets and Perspectives in Germany, 4th edition]. Frankfurt: IMK.

Borden, N. H. (1958) 'Note on concept of the marketing mix', in Lazer, W. and Kelley, E.J. (eds) *Managerial Marketing – Perspectives and Viewpoints*, 272–5. Illinois: Homewood.

Borden, N. H. (1964) 'The concept of the marketing mix', *Journal of Advertising Research*, 2–7.

Boswell, J. (1973) *The Rise and Decline of Small Firms*. London: Allen and Unwin.

Bosworth, D. and Jacob, S. C. (1989) 'Management attitudes, behaviour and abilities as barriers to growth', in Barber, J., Metcalfe, J. S. and Porteous, M. (eds) *Barriers to Growth in Small Firms*, 20–38. London: Routledge.

Bott, E. (1971) *Family and Social Networks*, 2nd edition. London: Tavistock.

Boubakri, H. (1985) 'Mode de gestion et reinvestissement chez les comercants Tunisiens à Paris', *Revue Européene des Migrations Internationales*, 1 (1), 49–66.

Bourdieu, P. (1984) *Distinction: A Social Critique of the Judgement of Taste*, translated by R. Nice. London: Routledge.

Bourdieu, P. (1990) *The Logic of Practice*. Cambridge: Polity Press.

Bourdieu, P. (1996) 'On the family as a realised category', *Theory, Culture and Society*, 13 (3), 19–26.

Bovaird, T., Hems, L. and Tricker, M. (1995) 'Market failures in the provision of finance and business services for small and medium size enterprises', in Buckland, R. and Davis, E. W. (eds) *Finance for the Growing Enterprise*. London: Routledge.

Boyd, N. G. and Vozikis, G. S. (1994) 'The influence of self-efficacy on the development of entrepreneurial intentions and actions', *Entrepreneurship Theory and Practice*, 18 (4), 63–77.

Boyer, R. (1990) *The Regulation School: A Critical Introduction*. New York: Columbia University Press.

Boyle, E. (1984) 'The rise of the reluctant entrepreneurs', *International Small Business Journal*, 12 (2).

Bracker, J. (1982) *Planning and financial performance among small entrepreneurial firms: an industry study*, unpublished doctoral dissertation, Georgia State University.

Bracker, J. and Pearson, J. (1986) 'Planning and financial performance of small mature firms', *Strategic Management Journal*, 7, 503–22.

Bradach, J. (1994) 'Chains within chains: the role of multi-unity franchisees', *Proceedings of the 8th Conference of the Society of Franchising*, Nevada, 13–14 February.

Bradach, J. and Eccles, R. G. (1989) 'Price, authority and trust: from ideal types to plural forms', *Annual Review of Sociology*, 15, 97–118.

Branson, R. (1998) *Losing My Virginity: The Autobiography*. London: Virgin Publishing.

Brazeal, D. V. (1996) 'Managing an entrepreneurial organizational environment', *Journal of Business Research*, 35 (1), 55–68.

Brigham, E. and Smith, K. (1967) 'Cost of capital to the small firm', *The Engineering Economist*, 13 (3), 1–26.

British Bankers Association (1997), quoted in *Finance for small Firms*, Fifth report, Bank of England, January 1998.

British Chamber of Commerce (1998) 'Small firms survey – skills'. London.

Brockhaus, R. H. S. (1980) 'Risk taking propensity of entrepreneurs', *Academy of Management Journal*, 23 (3), 509–20.

Brockhaus, R. H. S. (1982) 'The psychology of the entrepreneur', in Kent, C. A., Sexton, D. L. and Vesper, K. L. (eds) *Encyclopedia of Entrepreneurship*, 39–71. Englewood Cliffs, NJ: Prentice Hall.

Brogger, J. and Gilmore, D. D. (1997) 'The matrifocal family in Iberia: Spain and Portugal compared', *Ethnology*, XXXVI (1), 13-30.

Brooks, A. (1983) 'Black businesses in Lambeth: obstacles to expansion', *New Community*, 11, 42–54.

Brooks, M. R. and Rosson, P. J. (1982) 'A study of behaviour of small and medium-sized manufacturing firms in three Canadian provinces', in Czinkota, M. R. and Tesar, G. (eds) *Export Management: An International Context*, 39–54. New York: Praeger Publishers.

Brooksbank, R., Kirby, D. and Wright, G. (1992) 'Marketing and company performance: an examination of medium sized manufacturing firms in Britain', *Small Business Economics*, 4, 221–36.

Brown, B. and Butler, J. E. (1995) 'Competitors as allies: a study of the entrepreneurial networks in the US wine industry', *Journal of Small Business Management*, 33 (3), 57–66.

Brown, L. and McDonald, M. H. B. (1994) *Competitive Marketing Strategy for Europe*. London: Macmillan.

Brown, P. and Scase, R. (1994) *Higher Education and Corporate Realities*. London: UCL Press.

Brush, C. G. (1992) 'Research of women business owners: past trends, a new perspective, future directions', *Entrepreneurship Theory and Practice*, Summer, 5–30.

Brynjolfsson, E. and Hitt, L. M. (1998) 'Beyond the productivity paradox: computers are the catalyst for bigger changes', *Communications of the ACM*, 41 (8), 49–55.

Buchanan, J. M. and Di Pierro, A. (1980) 'Cognition, choice, and entrepreneurship', *Southern Economic Journal*, 46, 693–701.

Buckland, R. and Davis, E. W. (1995) *Financing for Growing Enterprises*. London: Routledge.

Burchell, B. and Wilkinson, F. (1997) 'Trust, business relationships and the contract environment', *Cambridge Journal of Economics*, 21 (2), 217–37.

Burke, J. (1989) *Competency Based Education and Training*. Lewes: Falmer Press.

Burns, P. (1989) 'Strategies for success and routes to failure', in Burns, P. and Dewhurst, J. (eds) *Small Business and Entrepreneurship*, 32–67. London: Macmillan.

Burns, P. (1996) 'Introduction: the significance of small firms', in Burns, P. and Dewhurst, J. (eds) *Small Business and Entrepreneurship*, 2nd edition. London: Macmillan.

Burrows, R. (1990) 'A socio-economic anatomy of the British petty bourgeoisie: a multivariate analysis', in Burrows, R. (ed.), *Enterprise Cultures, Entrepreneurship, Petty Capitalism and the Restructuring of Britain*. London: Routledge.

Burrows, R. (1991a) 'The discourse of the enterprise culture and the restructuring of Britain', in Curran, J. and Blackburn, R. (eds) *Paths of Enterprise: The Future of Small Business*. London: Routledge.

Burrows, R. (1991b) 'Introduction: entrepreneurship, petty capitalism and the restructuring of Britain', in Burrows, R. (ed.) *Deciphering the Enterprise Culture – Entrepreneurship, Petty Capitalism and the Restructuring of Britain*. London: Routledge.

Burt, R. S. (1992) *Structural Holes. The Social Structure of Competition*. Harvard University Press.

Butler, J. E. and Hansen, G. S. (1991) 'Network evolution, entrepreneurial success and regional development', *Entrepreneurship and Regional Development*, 3, 1–16.

Butler, P., Hall, T. W., Hanna, A. M., Mendonca, L., Auguste, B., Manyika, J. and Sahay, A. (1997) 'A revolution in interaction', *McKinsey Quarterly*, 1, 4–23.

Buttner, E. H. and Moore, D. P. (1997) 'Women's organizational exodus to entrepreneurship: self-reported motivations and correlates with success', *Journal of Small Business Management*, January, 34–47.

Buttner, E. H. and Rosen, B. (1989) 'Funding new business ventures: are decision makers biased against women entrepreneurs?', *Journal of Business Venturing*, 4 (4), 249–61.

Buzzell, R. D. and Wiersema, F. D. (1981) 'Successful share-building strategies', *Harvard Business Review*, 53 (1), 135–44.

Bygrave, W. D. (1988) *The entrepreneurship paradigm (I): a philosophical look at its research methodologies*. Paper presented at the Entrepreneurship Doctoral Consortium, Babson Research Conference, University of Calgary.

Byrne, D. (1998) 'Class and ethnicity in complex cities – the cases of Leicester and Bradford', *Environment and Planning A*, 30, 703–20.

Cairncross, F. (1997) *The Death of Distance*. Boston: Harvard Business School Press.

Calder, G. H. (1961) 'The peculiar problems of a family business', *Business Horizons*, 4 (3), 93–102.

Cambridge Small Business Research Centre (1992) *The State of British Enterprise*. Cambridge: Department of Applied Economics, University of Cambridge.

Campbell, D. J. (1988) 'Task complexity: A review and analysis', *Academy of Management Review*, 13 (1), 40–52.

Campbell, M. and Daly, M. (1992) 'Self-employment in the 1990s', *Employment Gazette*, June, 269–92.

Cannon, T. (1992) 'Marketing for small business', in Baker, M. J. (ed.) *The Marketing Book*. Oxford: Butterworth-Heinemann.

Cannon, T. and Willis, M. (1981) 'The smaller firm in overseas trade', *European Small Business Journal*, 1 (3), 45–55.

Carr, M. (1990) 'Women in small-scale industries – some lessons from Africa', *Small Enterprise Development*, 1 (1), 47–51.

Carrier, C. (1996) 'Intrapreneurship in small businesses: an exploratory study', *Entrepreneurship Theory and Practice*, 21 (1), 5–20.

Carroll, G. and Delacroix, J. (1982) 'Organisational mortality in the newspaper industries of Argentina and Ireland: an ecological approach', *Administrative Science Quarterly*, 27, 169–98.

Carson, D. (1985) 'The evolution of marketing in small firms', *European Journal of Marketing*, 19 (5), 7–16.

Carson, D. (1991) 'Research into small business marketing', *European Journal of Marketing*, 9, 75–91.

Carson, D., Cromie, S., McGowan, P. and Hill, J. (1995) *Marketing and Entrepreneurship in SMEs: An Innovative Approach*. Prentice Hall International.

Carsrud, A. L. and Johnson, R. W. (1989) 'Entrepreneurship: a social psychological perspective', *Entrepreneurship and Regional Development*, 1, 21–31.

Carsrud, A. L., Gaglio, C. M. and Olm, K. W. (1987) 'Entrepreneurs, mentors, networks and successful new venture development: an exploratory study', *American Journal of Small Business*, Fall, 13–18.

Carter, N. M. and Allen, K. R. (1997) 'Size determinants of women-owned businesses: choice or barriers to resources?', *Entrepreneurship and Regional Development*, 9 (3), 211–20.

Carter, S. (1993) 'Female business ownership: current research and possibilities for the future', in Allen, S. and Truman, C. (eds) *Women in Business: Perspectives on Women Entrepreneurs*, 148-60. London: Routledge.

Carter, S. (1998) 'The economic potential of portfolio entrepreneurship: enterprise and employment contributions of multiple business ownership', *Journal of Small Business and Enterprise Development*, 5 (4), 297–306.

Carter, S. and Cannon, T. (1988) *Female Entrepreneurs: A Study of Female Business Owners; Their Motivations, Experiences and Strategies for Success*, Department of Employment Research Paper No. 65, pp. 1–57.

Carter, S. and Cannon, T. (1992) *Women as Entrepreneurs*. London: Academic Press.

Carter, S. and Rosa, P. (1998) 'The financing of male- and female-owned businesses', *Entrepreneurship and Regional Development*, 10 (3), 225–41.

Cash, J. I. and Konsynski, B. R. (1985) 'IS redraws competitive boundaries', *Harvard Business Review*, Mar–Apr, 134–42.

Cashmore, E. (1991) 'Flying Business class: Britain's new ethnic elite', *New Community*, 17 (3), 347–58.

Cashmore, E. (1992) 'The new Black bourgeoisie', *Human Relations*, 45 (12), 1241–58.

Castrogiovanni, G., Justis, R. and Julian, S. (1993) 'Franchisee failure rates: an assessment of magnitude and influencing factors', *Journal of Small Business Management*, April, 105–14.

Cavanagh, R. E. and Clifford, D. K. (1983) 'Lessons from America's mid-sized growth companies', *The McKensey Quarterly*, Autumn.

Cavusgil, S. T. (1980) 'On the internationalisation process of firms', *European Research*, 8, November, 273–81.

Cavusgil, S. T. (1984) 'Differences among exporting firms based on their degree of internationalisation', *Journal of Business Research*, 12 (2), 195–208.

Cavusgil, S. T. and Zou, S. (1994) 'Marketing strategy–performance relationship: an investigation of the empirical link in export market ventures', *Journal of Marketing*, 58, January.

Cecil, J. and Goldstein, M. (1990) 'Sustaining competitive advantage from IT', *McKinsey Quarterly*, 4, 74–89.

Central Intelligence Agency (1996) *World Factbook*.

Chaffee, E. (1985) 'Three models of strategy', *Academy of Management Review*, 10, 89–98.

Chandler, A. (1962) *Strategy and Structure*. Cambridge, MA: MIT Press.

Chandler, A. D., Jr (1997) 'The computer industry – the first half-century', in Yoffie, D. B. (ed.) *Competing in the Age of Digital Convergence*, 37-122. Boston: Harvard Business School Press.

Chandler, G. (1996) 'Business similarity as a moderator of the relationship between pre-ownership experience and venture performance', *Entrepreneurship: Theory and Practice*, 20 (3), 51–65.

Chandra, S. (1997) *Indonesia – Franchise – IMI970603*, US Department of Commerce (International Market Insight), June.

Chaney, D. (1996) *Lifestyles*, London: Routledge.

Changanti, R., DeCarolis, R. and Deeds, D. (1995) 'Predictors of capital structure in small ventures', *Entrepreneurship Theory & Practice*, 20 (2), Winter, 7–18.

Chapman, S. (1996) 'The Fielden fortune. The finances of Lancashire's most successful antebellum manufacturing family', *Financial History Review*, 3 (1), 7–28.

Chaston, I. (1995) 'Small firm growth through the creation of value-added networks', *Proceedings of the 18th ISBA National Small Firms Policy and Research Conference*, Paisley, 45–57.

Chaston, I. (1996) *Small business networking: evolving an appropriate UK national process model*. Paper presented at the 19th ISBA National Small Firms Policy and Research Conference, Birmingham, November.

Chaston, I. and Mangles, T. (1997) *Small business structures and networking: identification and marketing collaboration opportunities*. Paper presented at the MEG Special Interest Group in Entrepreneurial Marketing Meeting, Dublin, January.

Chau, P. Y. K. and Tam, K. Y. (1997) 'Factors affecting the adoption of open systems: an exploratory study', *MIS Quarterly*, March, 1–21.

Chell, E. and Haworth, J. (1992) 'A typology of business owners and their orientation towards growth', in Calay, K., Chell, E., Chittenden, F. and Mason, C. (eds) *Small Enterprise Development: Policy and Practice in Action*. London: Paul Chapman.

Chell, E., Haworth, J. and Brearley, S. (1991) *The Entrepreneurial Personality: Concepts, Cases and Categories*. London: Routledge.

Chen, C. C., Gene Greene, P. and Crick, A. (1998) 'Does entrepreneurial self-efficacy distinguish entrepreneurs from managers?', *Journal of Business Venturing*, 13 (4), 295–316.

Chen, J. C. (1993) 'The impact of microcomputer systems on small businesses: England, 10 years later', *Journal of Small Business Management*, 31 (3), 96–102.

Chen, M. and Hambrick, D. (1995) 'Speed, stealth and selective attack: how small firms differ from large firms in competitive behaviour', *Academy of Management Journal*, 38 (2), 118–27.

Chenney, P. H. (1983) 'Getting the most out of your first computer system', *American Journal of Small Business*, 7 (3), 50–60.

Chisnall, P. M. (1987) *Small Firms in Action: Case Histories in Entrepreneurship*, 1–10. London: McGraw-Hill.

Chrisman, J., Carsrud, A. L., DeCastro, J. and Herron, L. (1990) 'A comparison of assistance needs of male and female pre-venture entrepreneurs', *Journal of Business Venturing*, 5 (4), 235–48.

Churchill, N. C. and Lewis, V. C. (1983) 'The five stages of small business growth', *Harvard Business Review*, 61 (3), 30–9.

Clark, K. and Drinkwater, S. (1998) 'Ethnicity and self-employment in Britain', *Oxford Bulletin of Economics and Statistics*, 60 (3), 383–401.

Clark, T., Pugh, D. S. and Mallory, G. (1997) 'The process of internationalisation in the operating firm', *International Business Review*, 6 (6), 605–23.

Cloke, P. (ed.) (1996) *The Rise of the Rustbelt*. London: UCL Press.

Clutterbuck, D. (1991) *Everyone Needs a Mentor: Fostering Talent at Work*, 2nd edition. London: Institute of Personnel Management.

Cochrane, A. (1993) *Whatever Happened to Local Government*. Buckingham: Open University Press.

Cockburn, C. (1993) *In the Way of Women*, London: Methuen.

Cohn, T. and Lindberg, R. (1972) *How Management is Different in Small Companies*. New York: Harper & Row.

Cohn, T. and Lindberg, R. A. (1974) *Survival and Growth: Management Strategies for the Small Firm*. New York: Amacom.

Collins, J. C. and Lazier, W. C. (1993) 'Vision', *ERM*, Spring, 61–75.

Collis, D. J., Bane, P. W. and Bradley, S. P. (1997) 'Winners and losers – industry structure in the converging world of telecommunications, computing, and entertainment', in Yoffie, D.B. (ed.) *Competing in the Age of Digital Convergence*, 159–200. Boston: Harvard Business School Press.

Conway, S. (1994) 'Informal boundary-spanning links and networks in successful technological innovation', PhD Thesis, Aston Business School.

Conway, S. (1997) 'Informal networks of relationships in successful small firm innovation', in Jones-Evans, D. and Klofsten, M. (eds) *Technology, Innovation and Enterprise: The European Experience*, 236–73. Macmillan.

Conway, S. (1998) *Developing a classification of network typologies*. Paper presented at the 14th EGOS Colloquium – Subtheme 4: Inter-organisational relations and networks, July.

Conway, S. and Steward, F. (1998) 'Mapping innovation networks', *International Journal of Innovation Management*, 2 (2), 165–96.

Cookson, G. (1997) 'Family firms and business networks: textile engineering in Yorkshire', *Business History*, 39 (1), 1–20.

Cooper, A. C. (1970) 'The Palo Alto experience', *Industrial Research*, May, 58–84.

Cooper, A. C. (1973) 'Technical entrepreneurship: what do we know?', *R&D Management*, 3 (2), 59–64.

Cooper, A., Willard, G. and Woo, C. (1986a) 'Strategies of high-performing new and small firms: a re-examination of the niche concept', *Journal of Business Venturing*, 1, 247–60.

Cooper, A. C., Dunkelberg, W. C. and Woo, C. Y. (1986b) 'Optimists and pessimists: 2994 entrepreneurs and their perceived chances for success', in Ronstadt, R., Hornaday, J. A., Peterson, R. and Vesper, K. H. (eds) *Frontiers of Entrepreneurship Research*, 563–77. Babson Park, MA: Center for Entrepreneurial Studies, Babson College.

Cooper, R. B. and Zmud, R. W. (1990) 'Information technology implementation research: a technological diffusion approach', *Management Science*, 36 (2), 123–39.

Cooper, S. Y. (1996) *Small high technology firms: a theoretical and empirical study of location issues*, unpublished PhD thesis, Edinburgh, Heriot-Watt University, Department of Business Organisation.

Cooper, S. Y. (1997a) 'Technological and behavioural influences in the location of high technology small firms', in *Generating Growth: Proceedings of 20th National Small Firms Policy & Research Conference, Belfast*, 585–604. Leeds: Institute of Small Business Affairs.

Cooper, S. Y. (1997b) *You take the high road and I'll take the low road: contrasting routes to entrepreneurship in high technology small firms*. Paper presented to IntEnt97, the 7th International Entrepreneurship Conference, Monterey, California, 25–7 June.

Cooper, S. Y. (1998) 'Entrepreneurship and the location of high technology small firms: implications for regional development', in Oakey, R. P. (ed.) *New Technology Based Firms in the 1990s*, 245–67. London: Paul Chapman.

Corner, J. and Harvey, S. (1991) *Enterprise and Heritage*. London: Routledge.

Corney, M. (1997) 'Beauty contest to woo the favour of small businesses', *Times Educational Supplement*, 28 February.

Coviello, N. and Munro, H. (1995) 'Growing the entrepreneurial firm: networking for international marketing development', *European Journal of Marketing*, 29 (7), 49–61.

Coviello, N. and Munro, H. (1997) 'Network relationships and the internationalisation process of small software firms', *International Business Review*, 6 (4), 361–86.

Cowling, M., Samuels, J. and Sugden, R. (1991) *Small Firms and Clearing Banks*, Report prepared for the Association of British Chambers of Commerce.

Cox, C. and Jennings R. (1995) 'The foundations of success: the development and characteristics of British entrepreneurs and intrapreneurs', *Leadership and Organisational Development Journal*, 16 (7), 4–9.

Coyne, R. D., Sudweeks, F. and Haynes, D. (1996) 'Who needs the Internet? Computer-mediated communication in design firms', *Environment and Planning B*, 23 (6), 749–70.

Cragg, P. and King, M. (1988) 'Organisational characteristics and small firms' performance revisited', *Entrepreneurship Theory & Practice*, Winter, 49–64.

Cragg, P. B. and King, M. K. (1993) 'Small firm computing: motivators and inhibitors', *MIS Quarterly*, 17 (1), 47–60.

Creigh, S., Roberts, C., Gorman, A. and Sawyer, P. (1986) 'Self-employment in Britain: results from the Labour Force Surveys 1981–1984', *Employment Gazette*, June, pp. 183–94.

Cressy, R. (1996) *Small Business Failure: Failure to Fund or Failure to Learn?* Coventry: Centre for SMEs, University of Warwick.

Cressy, R. and Storey, D. J. (1996) *New Firms and Their Bank*, NatWest/Warwick SME Centre, University of Warwick.

Crick, D. (1995) 'An investigation into the targeting of UK export assistance', *European Journal of Marketing*, 29 (8), 76–94.

Crick, D. and Chaudhry, S. (1995) 'Export practices of Asian SMEs: some preliminary findings', *Marketing Intelligence and Planning*, 13 (11), 13–21.

Crick, D. and Czinkota, M. R. (1995) 'Export assistance: another look at whether we are supporting the best programmes', *International Marketing Review*, 12 (3), 61–72.

Cromie, S. (1990) 'The problems experienced by young firms', *International Small Business Journal*, 9 (3), 43–61.

Cromie, S. and Hayes, J. (1988) 'Towards a typology of female entrepreneurs', *Sociological Review*, 36 (1), 87–113.

Crosier, K. (1975) 'What exactly is marketing?', *Quarterly Review of Marketing*, 1, (2).

Cross, J. (1994) 'Franchising failures: definitional and measurement issues', *Proceedings of the 8th Conference of the Society of Franchising*, Nevada, 13/14 February.

Cross, J. and Walker, B. (1987) 'Services marketing and franchising: a practical business marriage', *Business Horizons*, 30, 10–20.

Cross, J. and Walker, B. (1988) 'Franchise failures: more questions than answers', *Proceedings of the 2nd Conference of the Society of Franchising*, California, 31 January/1 February.

Cross, M. and Waldinger, R. (1992) 'Migrants, minorities and the ethnic division of labour', in Feinstein, S., Gordon, I. and Harloe, M. (eds) *Divided Cities: New York and London in the Contemporary World*. Cambridge, MA: Blackwell.

Crossick, G., Haupt, H. G. and Merriman, J. (1996) 'The petite bourgeoisie in Europe, 1780–1914: enterprise, family and independence', *Economic History Review*, XLIX (3), 619–20.

Csikszentmihalyi, M. (1992) *Flow – The Psychology of Happiness*. London: Rider.

Culnan, M. J. and Swanson, E. B. (1986) 'Research in management information systems, 1980–1984: points of work and reference', *MIS Quarterly*, 10, 289–302.

Curran, J. (1986a) 'The survival of the petit bourgeoisie: production and reproduction', in Curran, J., Stanworth, J. and Watkins, D. (eds) *The Survival of the Small Firm*, 204–27. Aldershot: Gower.

Curran, J. (1986b) *Bolton Fifteen Years On: A Review and Analysis of Small Business Research in Britain 1971–1986*. London: Small Business Research Trust.

Curran, J. (1988) 'Training and research strategies for small firms', *Journal of General Management*, 13 (3), Spring.

Curran, J. (1990) 'Rethinking economic structure: exploring the role of the small firm and self employment in the British economy', *Work, Employment and Society*, May, 125–46.

Curran, J. (1991) 'Employment and employee relations', in Stanworth, J. and Gray, C. (eds) *Bolton, 20 Years On: The Small Firm in the 1990s*. London: PCP.

Curran, J. (1993) *TECs and small firms: can TECs reach the small firms other strategies have failed to reach?* Paper presented to the All Party Social Science and Policy Group, House of Commons, London, 17 April.

Curran, J. and Blackburn, R. (1990) *Small Firms and Local Economic Networks: A Report to Midland Bank*. Kingston-upon-Thames: Small

Business Research Centre, Kingston Business School.

Curran, J. and Blackburn, R. A. (1991) 'Small firms and networks: methodological strategies: some findings', *International Small Business Journal*, 11 (2), 13–25.

Curran, J. and Blackburn, R. (1992) *Small Business Survey*, February, Small Business Research Centre, Kingston University.

Curran, J. and Blackburn, R. (1993) *Ethnic Enterprise and the High Street Bank*. Kingston upon Thames: Kingston Business School, Kingston University.

Curran, J. and Blackburn, R. A. (1994) *Small Firms and Local Economic Networks: The Death of the Local Economy?* London: Paul Chapman Publishing Ltd.

Curran, J. and Burrows, R. (1986) 'The sociology of petit capitalism: a trend report', *Sociology*, 20 (2), 265–79.

Curran, J. and Burrows, R. (1988a) *Ethnicity and enterprise: a national profile*. Paper presented to the 11th Small Firms Policy and Research Conference, Cardiff.

Curran, J. and Burrows, R. (1988b) *Enterprise in Britain: A National Profile of Small Business Owners and the Self-Employed*. London: Small Business Research Trust.

Curran, J. and Burrows, R. (1989) 'National profiles of the self-employed', *Employment Gazette*, July, pp. 376–85.

Curran, J. and Stanworth, J. (1979a) 'Self selection and the small firm worker – a critique and an alternative view', *Sociology*, 13 (3), 427–44.

Curran, J. and Stanworth, J. (1979b) 'Work involvement and social relations in the small firm', *Sociological Review*, 27 (2), 317–42.

Curran, J. and Stanworth, J. (1981a) 'Size of workplace and attitudes to industrial relations in the printing and electronics industries', *British Journal of Industrial Relations*, 19 (1), 14–25.

Curran, J. and Stanworth, J. (1981b) 'A new look at job satisfaction in the small firms', *Human Relations*, 34 (5), 343–65.

Curran, J., Stanworth, J. and Watkins, D. (1986) *The Survival of the Small Firm*, vols I and II. Aldershot: Gower.

Curran, J., Blackburn, R. A. and Woods, A. (1991) *Profiles of the Small Enterprise in the Service Sector*. Kingston-upon-Thames: ESRC Centre for Research on Small Service Sector Enterprises, Kingston Business School, Kingston University.

Curran, J., Jarvis, R., Blackburn, R. A. and Black, S. (1993a) 'Networks and small firms: constructs, methodological strategies and some findings', *International Small Business Journal*, 11 (2), 13–25.

Curran, J., Kitching, J., Abbot, V. and Mills, V. (1993b) 'Employment and employment relations in the small service sector enterprise – a report'. ESRC Centre for research on small service sector enterprises, Kingston Business School.

Curran, J., Blackburn, R. and Kitching, J. (1995) *Small Business, Networking and Networks: A Literature Review, Policy Survey and Research Agenda*. Small Business Research Centre, Kingston University.

Curran, J., Blackburn, R., Kitching, J. and North, J. (1996) *Establishing Small Firms' Training Practices, Needs, Difficulties and Use of Industry Training Organisations*. DfEE Research Studies RS17. London: HMSO.

Curtis, D. A. (1983) *Strategic Planning for Smaller Businesses*. Toronto: Lexington Books.

Cyert, R. M. and March, I. G. (1963) *A Behavioural Theory of the Firm*. Englewood Cliffs, NJ: Prentice Hall.

Czinkota, M. and Johnston, W. J. (1982) 'Exporting: does sales volume make a difference? – A reply', *Journal of International Business Studies*, Summer, 157–61.

Czinkota, M. R. and Ursic, M. L. (1987) 'A refutation of the psychic distance effect on export development', *Developments in Marketing Science*, X, 157–60.

Dabinett, G. and Lawless, P. (1992) 'Public subsidy, property development and economic activity: an evaluation of Britain's RDC's Redundant Building Grant', *Environment and Planning C: Government and Policy*, 10 (2), 211–28.

Daft, R. L. and Lengel, R. H. (1986) 'Organizational information requirement, media richness and structural design', *Management Science*, 32 (5), 554–71.

Daily, C. M. and Dollinger, M. J. (1993) 'Alternative methodologies for identifying family versus nonfamily managed businesses', *Journal of Small Business Management*, April, 79–90.

Dalgic, T. and Leeuw, M. (1994) 'Niche marketing revisited: concept, applications and some European cases', *European Journal of Marketing*, 20 (1), 39–55.

Daly, M. (1991a) 'The 1980s: a decade of growth in enterprise', *Employment Gazette*, March, 109–34.

Daly, M. (1991b), 'VAT registrations and de-registrations in 1990', *Employment Gazette*, November, 579–88.

Daly, M., Campbell, M., Robson, G. and Gallagher, C. (1991) 'Job creation 1987–1989: the contribution of small and large firms', *Employment Gazette* 99 (11), 589–94.

Daniel, W. and Milward, N. (1983) *Workplace Industrial Relations in Britain, The DE/PSI/SSRC Survey*. London: Heinemann.

Das, T. K. and Teng, B.-S. (1997) 'Time and entrepreneurial risk behavior', *Entrepreneurship Theory and Practice*, 22 (2), 69–88.

David, B. L. (1994) 'How internal venture groups innovate', *Research Technology Management*, 37 (2), 38–45.

Davidson, W. and Dutia, D. (1991) 'Debt, liquidity, and profitability problems in small firms', *Entrepreneurship Theory & Practice*, Fall, 53–64.

Davidsson, P. (1989a) *Continued Entrepreneurship and Small Firm Growth*. Stockholm: Stockholm School of Economics, The Economic Research Institute.

Davidsson, P. (1989b) 'Entrepreneurship – and after? A study of growth willingness in small firms', *Journal of Business Venturing*, 4 (3), 211–26.

Davidsson, P. (1995) *Determinants of entrepreneurial intentions*. Paper presented at the Rent IX Conference, Piacenza, Italy, November.

Davies, S. (1995) 'Training policy and practice in Wales and North-Rhine-Westphalia', in Cloke, P. (ed.) *The Rise of the Rustbelt*. London: UCL Press.

Davis, F. D. (1989) 'Perceived usefulness, ease of use, and user acceptance of information technology', *MIS Quarterly*, 13 (3), 319–39.

Davis, G. B. (1980) 'The knowledge and skill requirements for the Doctorate in MIS', *1st Annual International Conference on Information Systems*. Proceedings, Philadelphia, December, 174–86.

Davis, P. (1983) 'Realising the potential of the family business', *Organizational Dynamics*, Summer, 47–56.

Davis, P. and Stern, D. (1988) 'Adaptation, survival and growth of the family business: an integrated systems perspective', *Family Business Review*, 1 (1), Spring, 69–85.

Deacon, B. (1992) *The New Eastern Europe*. London: Sage.

Deakin, N. and Edwards, J. (1993) *The Enterprise Culture and the Inner City*. London: Routledge.

Deakin, S. and Morris, G. (1995) *Labour Law*. London: Butterworth.

Deakins, D. (1996) *Entrepreneurs and Small Firms*. London: McGraw-Hill.

Deakins, D. and Freel, M. (1997) *Entrepreneurial learning and the growth process in SMEs*. Paper presented to the 4th ECLO International Conference, Sophia Antipolis, France, May.

Deakins, D. and Hussain, G. (1994a) 'Risk assessment with asymmetric information', *International Journal of Bank Marketing*, 12 (1), 24–31.

Deakins, D. and Hussain, G. (1994b) 'Financial information, the banker, and the small business: a comment', *British Accounting Review*, 26 (4).

Deakins, D., Hussain, G. and Ram, M. (1994) *Ethnic Entrepreneurs and Commercial Banks: Untapped Potential*. Birmingham: University of Central England Business School.

Deakins, D., Graham, L., Sullivan, R. and Whittam, G. (1997a) *New venture support: an analysis of mentoring support for new and early stage entrepreneurs*. Paper presented to the 20th ISBA National Small Firms Policy and Research Conference, Belfast, November.

Deakins, D., Majmudar, M. and Paddison, A. (1997b) 'Developing success strategies for ethnic minorities in business: evidence from Scotland', *New Community*, 23 (3), 325–42.

Deakins, D., Mileham, P. and O'Neill, E. (1998) *The role and influence of non-executive directors in growing small firms*. Paper presented to Babson Entrepreneurship Research Conference, Ghent, Belgium.

Deakins, D., Mileham, P. and O'Neill, E. (1999) *The Role and Influence of Non-Executive Directors in Growing Small Firms*, ACCA research report. London: ACCA.

DeBrabander, B. and Thiers, G. (1984) 'Successful information system development in relation to situational factors which affect effective communication between MIS-users and EDP-specialists', *Management Science*, 30 (2), 137–55.

December, J. (1996) 'Units of analysis for Internet communication', *Journal of Communication*, 46 (1), 14–38.

Deci, E. L. (1992a) 'On the nature and functions of motivation theories', *Psychological Science*, 3 (3), 167–71.

Deci, E. L. (1992b) 'The relation of interest to the motivation of behavior: a self-determination theory perspective', in Renninger, K. A., Hidi, S. and Krapp, A. (eds) *The Role of*

Interest in Learning and Development, 43–70. Hillsdale, NJ: Erlbaum.

Delmar, F. (1996) *Entrepreneurial Behavior and Business Performance*. Stockholm: Stockholm School of Economics, Economic Research Institute.

Delmar, F. (1997) 'Measuring growth: methodological considerations and empirical results', in Donckels, R. and Miettinen, A. (eds), *Entrepreneurship and SME Research: On Its Way to the Next Millennium*, 199–216. Aldershot: Ashgate.

DeLone, W. H. (1988) 'Determinants of success for computer usage in small business', *MIS Quarterly*, 12 (1), 51–61.

DeLone, W. H. and McLean, E. R. (1992) 'Information systems success: the quest for the dependent variable', *Information Systems Research*, 3, 60–95.

Dempsey, J., Dvorak, R. E., Holen, E., Mark, D. and Meehan, W.F. (1998) 'A hard and soft look at IT investment', *McKinsey Quarterly*, 1, 126–37.

Department of Employment (1988) *Employment for the 1990s*, Cmnd 540. London: HMSO.

Department of Trade and Industry (1992) *A Prospectus for One Stop Shops for Businesses*. London: DTI.

Department of Trade and Industry (1995a) *Small and Medium-sized Enterprise Statistics for the United Kingdom – 1993*. Sheffield: Department of Trade and Industry Small Firms Statistics Unit.

Department of Trade and Industry (1995b) *Small Firms in Britain Report 1995*. London: HMSO.

Department of Trade and Industry (1995c) *Competitiveness: Helping Smaller Firms*. London: DTI.

Department of Trade and Industry (1996a) *Personal Business Advisers: Policy Guidelines*. London: DTI.

Department of Trade and Industry (1996b) *Small Firms in Britain Report 1996*. London: DTI .

Department of Trade and Industry (1998) *Our Competitive Future: Building the Knowledge Driven Economy*, Cm. 4176. London: HMSO.

Department of Trade and Industry/Information Society Initiative (1998) *Moving into the Information Age – An International Benchmarking Study*. London: DTI.

Deshpande, S. and Golhar, D. (1994) 'HRM practices in large and small manufacturing firms: a comparative study', *Journal of Small Business Management*, 32 (1), 49–56.

Dess, G. G. and Robinson, R. B., Jr (1984) 'Measuring organizational performance in the absence of objective measures: the case of the privately-held firm and conglomerate business unit', *Strategic Management Journal*, 5 (3), 265–74.

Dhaliwal, S. (1998) *Silent Contributors – Asian Female Entrepreneurs and Women in Business*. London: Roehampton Institute.

Dichtl, E., Leibold, M., Koglmayr, H. G. and Muller, S. (1984) 'The export decision of small and medium-sized firms: a review', *Management International Review*, 24 (2), 47–60.

Dickson, P. R. and Giglierano, J. J. (1986) 'Missing the boat and sinking the boat: a conceptual model of entrepreneurial risk', *Journal of Marketing*, 50 (July), 58–70.

Dodgson, M. (1989) *Technology Strategy and the Firm, Management and Public Policy*. Harlow: Longman.

Doll, J. and Ajzen, I. (1992) 'Accessibility and stability of predictors in theory of planned behavior', *Journal of Personality and Social Psychology*, 63 (5), 754–6.

Donckels, R. and Lambrecht, J. (1997) 'The network position of small businesses: an explanatory model', *Journal of Small Business Management*, April, 13–25.

Donnelley, R. G. (1964) 'The family business', *Harvard Business Review*, March–April, 42, 93–105.

Doukidis, G. L., Smithson, S. and Lybereas, T. (1994) 'Trends in information technology in small business', *Journal of End User Computing*, 6 (4), 15–25.

Down, S. and Bresnen (1997) 'The impact of Training and Enterprise Councils on the provision of small business support: case studies in London and the Midlands', *Local Economy*, 11 (4), 317–32.

Drucker, P. (1977) *Management: Tasks, Responsibilities, Practices*. London: Pan Books.

Drucker, P. (1985) *Innovation and Entrepreneurship*. London: Pan Books.

Drury, J.C. and Braund, S. (1990) 'The leasing decision: a comparison of theory and practice', *Accounting and Business Research*, Summer.

Duberley, J. and Walley, P. (1995) 'Assessing the adoption of HRM by small and medium sized manufacturing organisations', *The International Journal of Human Resource Management*, 6 (4), 891–909.

Dubini, P. and Aldrich, H. (1991) 'Personal and extended networks are central to the entrepreneurial process', *Journal of Business Venturing*, 6, 305–13.

Dugdale, D., Hussey, J. and Jarvis, R. (1998) *Financial Reporting by Small and Medium-Sized Companies*, Small Business Research Centre, Kingston University.

Duncan, W. J. (1988) 'Intrapreneurship and the reinvention of the corporation', *Business Horizons*, 31 (3), 16–21.

Duncan, W. J., Ginter, P. M., Rucks, A. C. and Jacobs, T. D. (1988) 'Intrapreneurship and the reinvention of the corporation', *Business Horizons*, 31 (3), 16–21.

Duysters, G. (1996) *The Dynamics of Technical Innovation – The Evolution and Development of Information Technology.* Cheltenham: Edward Elgar.

Dyer, W. G. (1989) 'Integrating professional management into a family owned business', *Family Business Review*, 2 (3), 221–35.

Eagly, A. H. and Chaiken, S. (1993) *The Psychology of Attitudes*, 1st edition. Fort Worth, TX: Harcourt Brace Jovanovich, Inc.

Earl, M. J. (1989) *Management Strategies for Information Technology.* New York: Prentice-Hall.

Earnshaw, J., Goodman, J., Harrison, R. and Marchington, M. (1998) 'Industrial tribunals, workplace disciplinary procedures and employment practice', *Employment Relations Research Series 2.* London: DTI.

Easton, G. (1992) 'Industrial network: a review', in Axelsson, B. and Easton, G. (eds) *Industrial Network: A New View of Reality.* London: Routledge.

Edwards, P. (1995) *Industrial Relations, Theory and Practice in Britain.* Oxford: Blackwell.

EFER (1992) *The Conditions for Entrepreneurship in the C.S.F.R.* Brussels: European Foundation for Entrepreneurship Research.

Egge, K. A. (1987) 'Expectations vs. reality among founders of recent start-ups', in Churchill, N. C., Hornaday, J. A., Kirchhoff, B. A., Krassner, O. J. and Vesper, K. H. (eds) *Frontiers of Entrepreneurship Research*, 322–36. Wellesley, MA: Babson College.

Eisenhardt, K. M. and Forbes, N. (1984) 'Technical entrepreneurship: an international perspective', *The Columbia Journal of World Business*, 19 (4), Winter, 31–8.

Eisenhardt, K. and Schoonhoven, C. (1990) 'Organisational growth: linking founding team, strategy, environment, and growth among US semiconductor ventures, 1978–1988', *Administrative Science Quarterly*, 35, 504–29.

Elliot, A. J. and Harackiewicz, J. M. (1994) 'Goal setting, achievement orientation, and intrinsic motivation: a mediational analysis', *Journal of Applied Psychology*, 66 (5), 968–80.

Elliot, S. and Melhuish, P. (1995) 'A methodology for the evalation of IT for strategic implementation', *Journal of Information Technology*, 10 (2), 87–100.

EMBI (1991) *Assisting Ethnic Minority Businesses: Good Practice Guidelines for Local Enterprise Agencies.* London: Home Office.

Employment Gazette (1994) 'Ethnic minorities and the labour market', 2, 147–59.

English, W. and Willems, J. (1994) 'Franchise vs. non-franchise restaurant attrition: year-four of a Yellow Pages longitudinal analysis', *Proceedings of the 8th Conference of the Society of Franchising*, Nevada, 13/14 February.

Engwall, L. and Wellenstal, M. (1988) 'Tit for tat in small steps. The internationalisation of Swedish banks', *Scandinavian Journal of Management*, 4 (3/4), 147–55.

ENSR (1997) *The European Observatory for SMEs – Fifth Annual Report.* European Network for SME Research, Zoetermeer: EIM Small Business Research and Consultancy.

Enterprise Dynamics (n/d) *Small Firms: Survival and Job Creation: The Contribution of Enterprise Agencies.* London: Business in the Community.

Epstein, J. A. and Harackiewicz, J. M. (1992) 'Winning is not enough: the effect of competition and achievement orientation on intrinsic interest', *Personality and Social Psychology Bulletin*, 18 (2), 128–38.

Ernst and Young (1996) *Evaluation of Business Links.* London: DTI.

Eroglu, S. (1992) 'The internationalisation process of franchise systems: a conceptual model', *International Marketing Review*, 6 (5), 19–30.

Erramilli, M. K. and Rao, P. (1990) 'Choice of foreign market entry modes by service firms: the role of market knowledge', *Management International Review*, 30 (2), 135–51.

ESRC Centre for Business Research (1996) *The Changing State of British Enterprise*, Cosh, A. and Hughes, A. (eds). University of Cambridge.

Estades, J. and Ramani, S. (1997) *Technological Competence and the Influence of Networks: A Comparative Analysis of NBFs in the Biotechnology Sectors in France and Britain*, conference paper.

Ettlie, J. E., Bridges, W. P. and O'Keefe, R. D. (1984) 'Organization strategy and structural differences for radical vs incremental innovation', *Management Science*, 30, 682–95.

Euske, N. A. and Roberts, K. H. (1987) 'Evolving perspectives in organization theory: communication implications', Jablin, F. M., Putnam, L. L., Roberts, K. H. and Porter, L. W. (eds) *Handbook of Organizational Communication*, 41–69. Newbury Park: Sage.

Evans, P. B. and Wurster, T. S. (1997) 'Strategy and the new economics of information', *Harvard Business Review*, Sept–Oct, 70–83.

Eyton, R. (1996) 'Making innovation fly', *Business Quarterly*, 61 (1), 59–65.

Factoring and Discounters Association (1995), quoted in Bickers, M. (1998) *Factoring in the UK*. London: HMSO.

Fagenson, E. A. (1993) 'Personal value systems of men and women entrepreneurs versus managers', *Journal of Business Venturing*, 8, 409–30.

Fass, M. and Scothorne, R. (1990) *The Vital Economy*. Edinburgh: Abbeystrand Publishing.

Fay, M. and Williams, L. (1993) 'Sex of applicant and the availability of business "start-up" finance', *Australian Journal of Management*, 16 (1), 65–72.

Fayol, H. (1949) *General and Industrial Management*. London: Pitman.

Feher, A. and Towell, E. (1997) 'Business use of the Internet', *Internet Research: Electronic Networking Applications and Policy*, 7 (3), 195–200.

Feit, S. C. (1996) *TCP/IP – Architecture, Protocols, and Implementation with IPv6 and IP Security*, 2nd edition. New York: McGraw-Hill.

Feldman, M. S. and March, J. G. (1981) 'Information in organizations as signal and symbol', *Administrative Science Quarterly*, 26, 171–86.

Felstead, A. (1988) *Technological change, industrial relations and the small firm: a study of small printing firms*, unpublished PhD thesis, University of London.

Felstead, A. (1993) *The Corporate Paradox – Power and Control in the Business Franchise*. London and New York: Routledge.

Fiegenbaum, A. and Karnini, A. (1991) 'Output flexibility – a competitive advantage for small firms', *Strategic Management Journal*, 12, 101–14.

File, K. M., Judd, B. B. and Prince, R. A. (1992) 'Interactive marketing: the influence of participation on positive word-of-mouth and referrals', *Journal of Services Marketing*, 6 (4), Fall, 5–14.

Filion, L. J. (1990) 'Entrepreneurial performance, networking, vision and relations', *Journal of Small Business and Entrepreneurship*, 7 (3), 3–12.

Financial Times (1997) 'Small companies lack IT support', *Financial Times*, 2.12.1997, 14.

Fink, D. (1998) 'Guidelines for the successful adoption of information technology in small and medium enterprises', *International Journal of Information Management*, 18 (4), 243–53.

Fink, K., Griese, J., Roithmayr, F. and Sieber, P. (1997) 'Business on the Internet – some (r)evolutionary perspectives', in Vogel, D. R., Gricar, J. and Novak, J. (eds) 10th *International BLED Electronic Commerce Conference: 'Global Business in Practice'*, vol. 2: Research. Bled, Slovenia, 9–11 June.

Fletcher, D. E. (1997) *Organisational networking, strategic change and the family firm*. PhD thesis, Nottingham Business School.

Fletcher, D. E. (1998) 'Swimming around in their own ponds: the weakness of strong ties in developing innovative practices', *International Journal of Innovation Management*, 2 (2), Special Issue, June, 137–59.

Fletcher, M. (1994) *How bank managers make lending decisions to small firms*. Paper presented to the 17th ISBA UK National Small Firms Policy and Research Conference, Sheffield Hallam University.

Foner, N. (1979) 'West Indians in New York and London: a comparative analysis', *International Migration Review*, 13, 284–95.

Foner, N. (1987) 'The Jamaicans: race and ethnicity among migrants in New York City', in Foner, N. (ed.) *New Immigrants in New York*, 195–217. New York: Columbia University Press.

Ford, D. (ed.) (1990) *Understanding Business Markets: Interaction, Relationships and Networks*. Academic Press.

Ford, D. and Leonidou, L. (1991) 'Research developments in international marketing', in Paliwoda, S. J. (ed.) *New Perspectives on International Marketing*. London: Routledge.

Foster, M. J. (1993) 'Scenario planning for the small business', *Long Range Planning*, 26 (1), 123–9.

Fox, M., Nilikant, V. and Hamilton, R. T. (1996) 'Managing succession in family-owned businesses', *International Small Business Journal*, 15 (1) (57), 15–25.

Frank, H., Plaschka, G. and Roessl, D. (1989) 'Planning behaviour of successful and non-successful founders of new ventures', *Entrepreneurship & Regional Development*, 1, 191–206.

Frazier, E. F. (1957) *Black Bourgeoisie: The Rise of a New Middle Class*. New York: The Free Press.

Fredrickson, J. and Mitchell, T. (1984) 'Strategic decisions processes: comprehensiveness and performance in an industry with an unstable environment', *Academy of Management Journal*, 27 (2), 399–423.

Freeman, C. (1991) 'Networks of innovators: a synthesis of research issues', *Research Policy*, 20 (5), 499–514.

Friedman, A. (1977) *Industry and Labour*. London: Macmillan.

Friedman, D. (1988) *The Misunderstood Miracle: Industrial Development and Political Change in Japan*. Ithaca, NY: Cornell University Press.

Fry, F. L. and Stoner, C. R. (1995) *Strategic Planning for the New and Small Business*. Chicago: Upstart.

Frydman, R. and Rapaczynski, A. (1994) *Privatisation in Eastern Europe: Is the State Withering Away?*, Central European University Press, Budapest.

Fryer, P. (1984) *The History of Black People in Britain*. London: Pluto Press.

Fuller, P. B. (1994) 'Assessing marketing in small and medium-sized enterprises', *European Journal of Marketing*, 28 (12), 34–49.

Fulop, L. (1991) 'Middle managers: victims or vanguards of the entrepreneurial movement?', *Journal of Management Studies*, 28 (1), 25–44.

Furnham, A. and Steele, H. (1993) 'Measuring locus of control: a critique of general, children's, health- and work-related locus of control questionnaires', *British Journal of Psychology*, 84, 443–79.

Galbraith, C. S. (1985) 'High technology location and development – the case of Orange County', *California Management Review*, 28 (1), 98–109.

Garnier, G. (1982) 'Comparative export behaviour of small Canadian firms in the printing and electrical industries', in Czinkota, M. R. and Tesar, G. (eds) *Export Management: An International Context*, 113–31. New York: Praeger Publishers.

Garnsey, E. and Wright, S. M. (1990) 'Technical innovation and organizational opportunity', *International Journal of Technology Management*, 5 (3), 267–91.

Garris, J. M. and Burch, E. E. (1983) 'Small businesses and computer panic', *Journal of Small Business Management*, 21 (3), 19–24.

Garrison, T. (1996) *International Business Culture*. Huntingdon: ELM Publications.

Gartner, W. B. (1988) '"Who is an entrepreneur?" is the wrong question', *American Journal of Small Business*, 12 (4), 11–32.

Gartner, W. B. (1990) 'What are we talking about when we talk about entrepreneurship?', *Journal of Business Venturing*, 5 (1), 15–28.

Gaston, R. J. (1989) *Finding Private Venture Capital for Your Firm: A Complete Guide*. New York: Wiley.

Gavron, R., Cowling, M., Holtham, G. and Westall, A. (1998) *The Entrepreneurial Society*. London: IPPR.

Gee, R. E. (1994) 'Finding and commercializing new businesses', *Research Technology Management*, 37 (1), 49–56.

Geisler, E. (1992) 'Managing IT in small business: some practical lessons and guidelines', *Journal of General Management*, 18 (1), 74–81.

Gersick, K. E., Davis, J. A., McCollom Hampton, M. E. and Lansberg, I. (1997) *Generation to Generation: Lifecycles of Family Business*. Boston, MA: Harvard Business School Press.

Gibb, A. (1983a) 'The small business challenge to management education', *Journal of European Industrial Training*, 7 (5), 6–8.

Gibb, A. A. (1983b) *Enterprise Agencies: Exploring Their Future Potential*. Durham: Durham University Business School.

Gibb, A. A. (1988) 'The enterprise culture: threat or opportunity?', *Management Decision*, 26 (4), 5–12.

Gibb, A. A. (1990) 'Entrepreneurship and intrapreneurship – exploring the differences', in Donckels, R. and Miettinen, A. (eds) *New Findings and Perspectives in Entrepreneurship*. Aldershot: Avebury.

Gibb, A. A. (1993) 'Key factors in the design of policy support for SME development process: an overview', *Entrepreneurship and Regional Development*, 5, 1–24.

Gibb, A. (1996) 'Entrepreneurship and small business management: can we afford to neglect them in the twenty-first century business school?', *British Journal of Management*, 7, 309–21.

Gibb, A. A. (1997) 'Small firms' training and industrial competitiveness: building on the small firm as a learning organisation',

International Small Business Journal, 15 (3), 13–29.

Gibb, A. and Davies, L. (1990) 'In pursuit of frameworks for the development of growth models of the small business', *International Small Business Journal*, 9 (1), 15–31.

Gibb, A. A. and Davies, L. G. (1991) 'Methodological problems in the development and testing of a growth model of business enterprise development', in *Recent Research in Entrepreneurship*, 286–323. Aldershot: Avebury.

Gibb, A. and Dyson, J. (1982) *Stimulating the growth of the owner-managed firms*, UK National Small Business Policy and Research Conference, Glasgow.

Gibb, A. A. and Haas, Z. (1995) *Strategic issues in the development of Local Enterprise Agency support for small business in Central and Eastern Europe and the CIS*. Paper presented to the 25th efmd European Small Business Seminar, Industrial Training Authority, Cyprus, 20–2 September.

Gibb, A. and Scott, M. (1985) 'Strategic awareness, personal commitment and the process of planning in small business', *Journal of Management Studies*, 22 (6), 597–632.

Gibb, A., Dyer, W. and Handler, W. (1994) 'Entrepreneurship and family business: exploring the connections', *Entrepreneurship Theory and Practice*, Autumn, 71–83.

Gibson, D. (1991) *Technology Companies and Global Markets: Programs, Policies and Strategies to Accelerate Innovation and Entrepreneurship*. Rowan and Littlefield.

Gilder, G. (1971) *The Spirit of Enterprise*. New York: Simon & Schuster.

Gilroy, P. (1987) *There Ain't No Black in the Union Jack: The Cultural Politics of Race and Nation*. London: Macmillan.

Ginsberg, A. and Hay, M. (1994) 'Confronting the challenges of corporate entrepreneurship: guidelines for venture managers', *European Management Journal*, 12 (4), 382–90.

Godfrey, M. and Richards, P. (eds) (1997) *Employment Policies and Programmes in Central and Eastern Europe*. Geneva: ILO.

Godfrey, P. (1990) 'Management – theories and practice', in Armstrong, M. (ed.) *The New Manager's Handbook*, 37-49. London: Kogan Page.

Goffee, R. and Scase, R. (eds) (1985a) *Entrepreneurship in Europe*. London: Croom Helm.

Goffee, R. and Scase, R. (1985b) *Women in Charge: The Experience of Female Entrepreneurs*. London: Allen and Unwin.

Goffee, R. and Scase, R. (1995) *Corporate Realities: The Dynamics of Large and Small Organisations*. London: Routledge.

Goldberg, L. R. (1993) 'The structure of phenotypic personality traits', *American Psychologist*, 48 (1), 26–34.

Goman, C. K. (1994) *Managing in a Global Economy: Keys to Success in a Changing World*. California: Crisp Publications.

Gordon, C. (1996) *The Business Culture in France*. Oxford: Butterworth-Heinemann.

Gorman, G., Hanlon, D. and King, W. (1997) 'Some research perspectives on entrepreneurship education, enterprise education and education for small business management: a ten-year literature review', *International Small Business Journal*, 15 (3), 56–77.

Goshal, S. and Bartlett, C. A. (1995) 'Changing the role of top management: beyond structure to processes', *Harvard Business Review*, 73 (1), 86–96.

Goss, D. (1988) 'Social harmony and the small firm: a reappraisal', *Sociological Review*, 36 (1), 114–32.

Goss, D. (1991) *Small Business and Society*. London: Routledge.

Gouldner, A. (1964) *Patterns of Industrial Bureaucracy*. London: RKP.

Grabher, G. (ed.) (1993) *The Embedded Firm Or the SocioEconomics of Industrial Networks*. London: Routledge.

Grandori, A. and Soda, G. (1995) 'Interfirm networks: antecedents, mechanisms and forms', *Organisational Studies*, 16 (2), 183–214.

Granger, B., Stanworth, J. and Stanworth, C. (1995) 'Self-employment career dynamics: the case of "Unemployment Push"', *Work, Employment and Society*, 9 (3), 499–516.

Granovetter, M. S. (1973) 'The strength of weak ties', *American Journal of Sociology*, 78 (6), 1361–81.

Granovetter, M. S. (1982) 'The strength of weak ties: a network theory revisited', in Marsden, P. V. and Lin, V. (eds) *Social Structure and Network Analysis*, 105–30. London: Sage.

Granovetter, M. (1985) 'Economic action and social structure: the problem of embeddedness', *American Journal of Sociology*, 91, 481–510.

Granovetter, M. S. (1992) 'Networks and organisations: problems of explanation in economic sociology', in Nohria, N. and Eccles, R. G. (eds) *Networks and Organisations: Structure, Form and Action*. Boston, MA: Harvard Business School Press.

Grant, W. and Sargeant, J. (1987) *Business and Politics in Britain.* Basingstoke: Macmillan Education Ltd.

Grant Thornton International and Business Strategies Ltd (1998) *European Business Survey.*

Green, H. and Cruttenden, M. (1990) *Enterprise Support Agencies in Leeds: An Analysis of Current Patterns – A Report for Leeds TEC.* Leeds: CUDEM, Leeds Polytechnic.

Green, H. and Johnson, S. (1992) *Localisation and quasi-markets and enterprise support: implications for TECs.* Paper presented to the 15th National Small Firms Policy and Research Conference, Southampton, November.

Greene, F. and Kirby, D. (1998) *Overcoming asymmetries in the relationship between accountants and their small business clients.* Paper presented to the 21st National Small Firms Policy and Research Conference, Durham, 18–20 November.

Greenstein, S. and Khanna, T. (1997) 'What does industry convergence mean?', in Yoffie, D.B. (ed.) *Competing in the Age of Digital Convergence,* 201–26. Boston: Harvard Business School Press.

Greiner, L. E. (1972) 'Evolution and revolution as organisations grow', *Harvard Business Review,* July–August, 37–46.

Grell, O. P. and Woolf, S. (ed.) (1996) 'Domestic strategies: work and the family in France and Italy 1600–1800', *Historical Journal,* 39 (1), 257–63.

Guardian (1992) 'Poverty and prejudice trap America's black businesses in small-time ghetto', *Guardian,* 6 June.

Gubrium, J. F. and Holstein, J. A. (1990) *What is Family?* Mayfield Publishing.

Guetzkow, H. (1965) 'Communications in organizations', in March, J. G. (ed.) *Handbook of Organizations,* 534–73. Chicago: Rand McNally.

Gummesson, E. (1987) 'The new marketing – developing long term interactive relationships', *Long Range Planning,* 20 (4), 10–20.

Haahti, A. (1987) *A Word on Theories of Entrepreneurship and Theories of Small Business Interface. A Few Comments.* Helsinki School of Economics, Working Papers F-170.

Haggett, P. (1983) *Geography, A Modern Synthesis.* New York: HarperCollins.

Hakansson, H. and Snehota, I. (1995) *Developing Relationships in Business Networks.* London: Routledge.

Hakim, C. (1988a) 'Women at work: recent research on women's employment', *Work, Employment & Society,* 2 (1), 103–13.

Hakim, C. (1988b) 'Self-employment in Britain: recent trends and current issues', *Work, Employment & Society,* 2(4), 421–50.

Hakim, C. (1989a) 'Identifying fast growth small firms', *Employment Gazette,* January, pp. 29–41.

Hakim, C. (1989b) 'New recruits to self-employment in the 1980s', *Employment Gazette,* June, 286–97.

Halkier, H., Danson, M. and Damborg, C. (eds) (1998) *Regional Development Agencies in Europe.* London: Jessica Kingsley Publishers and Regional Studies Association.

Hall, E. (1959) *The Silent Language.* New York: Doubleday.

Hall, G. (1989) 'Lack of finance as a constraint on the expansion of innovative small firms', in Barber, J., Metcalfe, J. and Porteous, M. (eds) *Barriers to Growth in Small Firms.* London: Routledge.

Hall, G. (1995) *Surviving and Prospering in the Small Firm Sector.* London: Routledge.

Hall, P., Breheny, M., McQuaid, R. and Hart, D. (1987) *Western Sunrise: The Genesis and Growth of Britain's Major High Tech Corridor.* London: Allen & Unwin.

Hall, S., Held, D. and McGrew, T. (1992) *Modernity and Its Futures.* Cambridge: Polity Press.

Hamill, J. (1997) 'The Internet and international marketing', *International Marketing Review,* 14 (5), 300–23.

Hamill, J. and Gregory, K. (1997) 'Internet marketing in the internationalisation of UK SMEs', *Journal of Marketing Management,* 13 (1–3), 9–28.

Hamilton, D. (1990) *An 'ecological' basis for the analysis of gender differences in the predisposition to self-employment.* Paper presented to the Research in Entrepreneurship (RENT) Conference, Cologne.

Hamilton, D., Rosa, P. and Carter, S. (1992) 'The impact of gender on the management of small business: some fundamental problems', in Wetford, R. (ed.) *Small Business and Small Business Development – A Practical Approach,* 33–40. Bradford: European Research Press.

Hammer, M. and Champy, D. (1993) *Re-Engineering the Corporation.* London: Nicholas Breasley.

Hammer, M. and Mangurian, G. (1987) 'The changing value of communication technology', *Sloan Management Review,* 28 (2), 65–71.

471

Hampden-Turner, C. and Trompenaars, F. (1994) *The Seven Cultures of Capitalism*. New York: Doubleday.

Handy, C. B. (1976) *Understanding Organisations*. Middlesex: Penguin.

Hansen, J. V. and Hill, N. C. (1989) 'Control and audit of electronic data interchange', *MIS Quarterly*, 13 (4), 402–13.

Harackiewicz, J. M. and Elliot, A. J. (1993) 'Achievement goals and intrinsic motivation', *Journal of Personality and Social Psychology*, 65 (5), 904–15.

Hareven, T. (1975) 'Family time and industrial time: family and work 1912–22: the role of family and ethnicity in the adjustment to urban life', *Labor History*, 16, 249–65.

Harland, C. M. (1995) 'Networks and globalisation: a review of research', Warwick University Business School Research Paper, ESRC Grant No. GRK 53178.

Harland, C. M. (1996) 'Supply chain management: relationships, chains and networks', *British Journal of Management*, 7, 63–80.

Harris, B., Holt, C. P., Hatsopoulos, G. N., De-Simone, L. D. and O'Brien, W. F. (1995) 'How can big companies keep the entrepreneurial spirit alive?', *Harvard Business Review*, 73 (6), 183–90.

Harris, D. (1993) 'Where those business angels fear to tread', *The Times*, 13 March.

Harrison, R. T. and Mason, C. M. (1987) 'The regional impact of the small firms loan guarantee scheme', in O'Neil, K., Bhambri, R., Faulkner, T. and Cannon, T. (eds) *Small Business Development: Some Current Issues*, 121–44. Aldershot: Avebury.

Harrison, R. and Mason, C. (1995) 'The role of informal venture capital in financing the growing firm', in Buckland, R. and Davis, E. W. (eds) *Finance for Growing Enterprises*. London: Routledge.

Hartwick, J. and Barki, H. (1994) 'Explaining the role of user participation in information systems use', *Management Science*, 40 (4), 440–65.

Harvey-Jones, J. (1994). in Leach, P. *The Stoy Hayward Guide to the Family Business*. London: Kogan Page.

Haughton, G. (1993) 'The local provision of small and medium enterprise advice services', *Regional Studies*, 27 (8), 835–42.

Hawkins, P. (1994) 'The changing view of learning', in Burgoyne, J., Pedlar, M. and Boydell, T. (eds.) *Towards the Learning Company: Concepts and Practices*, 9–27. McGraw-Hill Europe.

Hay, M., Verdin, P. and Williamson, P. (1993) 'Successful new ventures: lessons for entrepreneurs and innovators', *Long Range Planning*, 26 (5), 31–44.

Hayek, F. (1979) *Law, Legislation and Liberty*. London: RKP.

Hayton, K. (1991) 'The coming of age of local economic development?' *Local Government Policy Making*, 18, 53–6.

Heath, C. and Tversky, A. (1991) 'Preference and belief: ambiguity and competence in choice under uncertainty', *Journal of Risk and Uncertainty*, 4, 5–28.

Heelas, P. and Morris, P. (1992) *The Values of the Enterprise Culture*. London: Routledge.

Heikkilä, J., Saarinen, T. and Sääksjärvi, M. (1991) 'Success of software packages in small businesses: an exploratory study', *European Journal of Information Systems*, 1 (3), 159–69.

Heintz, T. J. (1981) 'On acquiring computer services for a small business', *Journal of Small Business Management*, 19 (3), 1–7.

Hellman, P. (1996) 'The internationalisation of Finnish financial service companies', *International Business Review*, 3 (2), 191–207.

Hendry, C., Jones, A., Arthur, M. and Pettigrew, A. (1991) *Human Resource Development in Small to Medium Sized Enterprises*, Research Paper No. 88. Sheffield: Employment Department.

Henry, J. and Walker, D. (1991) *Managing Innovation*. London: Sage.

Herron, L. and Robinson, R. B. J. (1993) 'A structural model of the effects of entrepreneurial characteristics on venture performance', *Journal of Business Venturing*, 8, 281–94.

Heuberger, G. (ed.) and Gutwein, D. (1997) 'The Rothschilds: essays on the history of a European family (review)', *Journal of Economic History*, 57 (1), 214–16.

HFEP (1996) *Annual Report: State of Small and Medium Sized Businesses in Hungary*, Budapest.

Higson, C. (1993) *Business Finance*, 2nd edition. London: Butterworths.

Hinden, R. M. (1996) 'IP next generation overview', *Communications of the ACM*, 39 (6), 61–71.

Hisrich, R. and Brush, C. G. (1986) *The Woman Entrepreneur: Starting, Financing and Managing a Successful New Business*. Lexington, MA: Lexington Books.

Hisrich, R. D. and Peters, M. P. (1992) *Entrepreneurship: Starting, Developing, and Managing a New Enterprise*. Chicago: Irwin.

Hitt, L. and Brynjolfsson, E. (1996) 'Productivity, profit and consumer welfare: three different measures of information technology's value', *MIS Quarterly*, 20 (2), 121–42.

HMSO (1985) *Lifting the Burden*. London: HMSO.

HMSO (1994) *Competitiveness: Helping Business to Win*. London: HMSO.

HMSO (1995) *Competitiveness: Forging Ahead*. London: HMSO.

HMSO (1996) *Competitiveness: Creating the Enterprise Centre of Europe*. London: HMSO.

Hofer, C. (1975) 'Toward a contingency theory of business strategy', *Academy of Management Journal*, 18, 784–810.

Hofstede, G. (1991) *Cultures and Organisations: Software of the Mind*. London: McGraw-Hill.

Hofstede, G. (1994). 'Defining culture and its four dimensions', *European Forum for Management Development: Focus: Cross-Cultural Management*, Forum 94/1, 4.

Hofstede, G. (1996) *Cultures and Organisations*. London: HarperCollins.

Hogan, R., Hogan, J. and Roberts, B. W. (1996) 'Personality measurement and employment decisions: questions and answers', *American Psychologist*, 51 (5), 469–77.

Hogan, R. T. (1991) 'Personality and personality measurement', in Dunnette, M. D. and Hough, L. M. (eds) *Handbook of Industrial and Organizational Psychology*, 2nd edition, vol. 2, 873–919. Palo Alto, CA: Consulting Psychologists Press, Inc.

Hogarth, R. (1987) *Judgment and Choice*, 2nd edition. Chichester: John Wiley and Sons.

Holland, P. G. and Boulton, W. B. (1984) 'Balancing the "family" and the "business" in family business', *Business Horizons*, March–April, 16–21.

Hollander, B. (1984) *Towards a model for family-owned business*. Paper presented at the meeting of the Academy of Management, Boston.

Hollander, B. S. and Elman, N. S. (1988), 'Family-owned businesses: an emerging field of inquiry', *Family Business Review*, 1 (2), 145–64.

Holliday, R. (1995) *Nice Work?: Investigating Small Firms*. London: Routledge.

Holliday, R. and Letherby, G. (1993) 'Happy families or poor relations – an exploration of familial analogies in the small firm', *International Small Business Journal*, 11 (2), 54–63.

Holme, C. (1992) 'Self development and the small organisation', *Training and Development UK*, August, 16–19.

Holmquist, C. and Sundin, E. (1989) *The growth of women's entrepreneurship – push or pull factors?* Paper presented to the EIASM Conference on Small Business, University of Durham Business School.

Honeycutt, E. D. Jr, Flaherty, T. B. and Benassi, K. (1998) 'Marketing industrial products on the Internet', *Industrial Marketing Management*, 27, 63–72.

Hornaday, J. A. (1982) 'Research about living entrepreneurs', in Kent, C. A., Sexton, D. L. and Vesper, K. L. (eds), *Encyclopedia of Entrepreneurship*, 281–90. Englewood Cliffs, NJ: Prentice Hall.

Hornaday, R. (1992) 'Thinking about entrepreneurship: a fuzzy set approach', *Journal of Small Business Management*, 30 (4), 12–23.

Hoselitz, B. (1951) 'The early history of entrepreneurial theory', *Explorations in Entrepreneurial Theory*, 3, 193–220.

HOST (1994) *ITO Non-Members Survey – Summary Report*. Sheffield: Employment Department.

Housden, J. (1984) *Franchising and Other Business Relationships in Hotel and Catering Services*. London: Heinemann.

Hoy, F. and Verser, T. G. (1994) 'Emerging business, emerging field: entrepreneurship and the family firm', *Entrepreneurship Theory and Practice*, Autumn, 9–23.

Huff, A. and Reger, R. (1987) 'A review of strategic process research', *Journal of Management*, 13 (2), 211–36.

Hughes, A. (1992) *The Problems of Finance for Smaller Businesses*, Working Paper No. 15, University of Cambridge: Small Business Research Centre.

Hussey, R. (ed.) (1995) *A Dictionary of Accounting*. Oxford University Press.

Hutton, W. (1996) *The State We're In*. London: Vintage.

Hyland, T. (1994) *Competence, Education and NVQs – Dissenting Perspectives*. London: Cassell.

Hyland, T. and Matlay, H. (1997) 'Small businesses, training needs and VET provision', *Journal of Education and Work*, 10 (2), 129–39.

Hynes, B. (1996) 'Entrepreneurship education and training – introducing entrepreneurship into non-business disciplines', *Journal of European Industrial Training*, 20 (8), 10–17.

Hyvarinen, L. (1990) 'Innovativeness and its indicators in small and medium-sized industrial enterprises', *International Small Business Journal*, 9 (1), 65–79.

Ibarra, H. (1993) 'Personal networks and minorities in management: a conceptual framework', *Academy of Management Review*, 18 (1), 56–87.

Ibeh, K. (1998) *Analysing the critical influences on export entrepreneurship in a developing country environment*, unpublished PhD thesis, Department of Marketing, University of Strathclyde, Glasgow.

Igbaria, M., Zinatelli, N., Cragg, P. and Cavaye, A. L. M. (1997) 'Personal computing acceptance factors in small firms: a structural equation model', *MIS Quarterly*, 21 (3), 279–305.

Igbaria, M., Zinatelli, N. and Cavaye, L. M. (1998) 'Analysis of information technology success in small firms in New Zealand', *International Journal of Information Management*, 18 (2), 103–19.

Ingham, G. K. (1970) *Size of Industrial Organisation and Worker Behaviour*. London: Cambridge University Press.

Institute of Directors (1993) *Late Payment of Debt – A Position Paper*. London: IOD.

Institute of Directors (1996) *Business Link IoD Research Paper*. London: Institute of Directors.

Ives, B. and Learmonth, G. (1984) 'The information system as a competitive weapon', *Communications of the ACM*, 27 (12), 1193–1201.

Ives, B. and Olson, M. H. (1984) 'User involvement and MIS success: a review of research', *Management Science*, 30 (5), 586–603.

Izard, C. E. (1984) 'Emotion–cognition relationships and human development', in Izard, C. E., Kagan, J. and Zajonc, R. B. (eds) *Emotions, Cognition, and Behavior*, 17–37. Cambridge: Cambridge University Press.

Jackson, G. I. (1981) 'Export from the importer's viewpoint', *European Journal of Marketing*, 15, 3–15.

Jansen, P. G. W. and van Wees, L. L. G. M. (1994) 'Conditions for internal entrepreneurship', *Journal of Management Development*, 13 (9), 34–51.

Jarvis, R. (1996) *Users and Uses of Unlisted Companies' Financial Statements: A Literature Review*. The Institute of Chartered Accountants in England and Wales.

Jarvis, R., Lipman, H., Macallan, H. and Berry, A. (1994) *Small Business Finance: The Benefits and Constraints of Leasing*, Occasional Paper No. 28, Kingston University.

Jarvis, R., Kitching, J., Curran, J. and Lightfoot, G. (1996) *The Financial Management of Small Firms: An Alternative Perspective*, Research Report No. 49. London: The Association of Chartered Certified Accountants.

Jeffries, I. (1996) *A Guide to the Economies in Transition*, London: Routledge.

Jenkins, A. (1998) *Trends in Business Support*. Durham: Small Business Foresight.

Jenkins, C., Jackson, M., Burden, P. and Wallis, J. (1998) 'Searching the World Wide Web: an evaluation of available tools and methodologies', *Information & Software Technology*, 39 (14/15), 985–94.

Jenkins, R. (1984) 'Ethnic minorities in business: a research agenda', in Ward, R. and Jenkins, R. (eds) *Ethnic Communities in Business*, 231–8. Cambridge: Cambridge University Press.

Jenkins, S. P. (1994) 'Winners and losers: a portrait of the UK income distribution during the 1980s', University College of Swansea, Department of Economics, Discussion Paper No. 94–07.

Jo, M. H. (1992) 'Korean merchants in the black community: prejudice among the victims of prejudice', *Ethnic and Racial Studies*, 15 (3), 395–411.

Johannisson, B. (1986) 'New venture creation: a network approach', in *Frontiers of Entrepreneurship Research*, 236–40. Wellesley, MA: Babson College.

Johannisson, B. (1987a) 'Anarchists and organisers: entrepreneurs in a network perspective', *International Studies of Management and Organisations*, XVII (1), 49–63.

Johannisson, B. (1987b) 'Toward a theory of local entrepreneurship', in Wyckham, R., Meredith, L. and Bushe, G. (eds), *The Spirit of Entrepreneurship*, Proceedings of the 32nd International Congress of Small Business, Vancouver.

Johannisson, B. (1987c) 'Beyond process and structure: social exchange networks', *International Studies of Management and Organisation*, XVII(i), 3–23.

Johannisson, B. (1988) 'Business formation: a network approach', *Scandinavian Journal of Management*, 4, 83–99.

Johannisson, B. and Peterson, R. (1984) *The personal networks of entrepreneurs*. Paper presented at the Third Canadian Conference of the International Council for Small Business, Toronto, 23–5 May.

Johanson, J. and Mattsson, L. G. (1988) 'Internationalisation in industrial systems – a network approach', in Hood, N. and Vahlne, J. E.

(eds) *Strategies in Global Competition*. Kent: Croom Helm.

Johanson, J. and Vahlne, J. (1977) 'The internationalisation process of the firm – a model of knowledge development and increasing foreign market commitments', *Journal of International Business Studies*, 8 (1), 23–32.

Johanson, J. and Vahlne, J. E. (1978) 'A model for the decision making affecting the pattern and pace of internationalisation of the firm', in Ghertman, M. and Leontiades, J. (eds) *European Research in International Business*, 283–305. New York: Croom Helm.

Johanson, J. and Vahlne, J. E. (1984) 'The mechanism of internationalisation', *International Marketing Review*, 7 (4), 11–23.

Johanson, J. and Vahlne, J. E. (1990) 'The mechanism of internationalisation', *International Marketing Review*, 7 (4), 11–24.

Johanson, J. and Vahlne, J. E. (1992) 'Management of foreign market entry', *Scandinavian International Business Review*, 1 (3), 9–27.

Johanson, J. and Wiedersheim-Paul, F. (1975) 'The internationalisation of the firm – four Swedish cases', *The Journal of Management Studies*, 12, 305–22.

Johnson, B. R. (1990) 'Toward a multidimensional model of entrepreneurship: the case of achievement motivation and the entrepreneur', *Entrepreneurship Theory and Practice*, 14 (3), 39–54.

Johnson, G. and Scholes, J. (1993) *Exploring Corporate Strategy: Text and Cases*. London: Prentice Hall International.

Johnson, S. (1990) *Small firms policy – an agenda for the 1990s*. Paper presented to the 13th National Small Firms Policy and Research Conference, Harrogate.

Johnson, S. (1993) *TEC's and enterprise support: developing a strategic role*. Paper presented to the Skills and Enterprise Network Conference, University of Nottingham, 29 March.

Johnson, S. and Gubbins, A. (1991) *Training in small and medium sized enterprises: lessons from North Yorkshire*. Paper presented at the 14th National Small Firms Policy and Research Conference, Blackpool, 20–2 November.

Johnson, S. and Storey, D. (1993) 'Male and female entrepreneurs and their businesses', in Allen, S. and Truman, C. (eds) *Women in Business: Perspectives on Women Entrepreneurs*, 70–85. London: Routledge.

Johnston, H. R. and Vitale, M. R. (1988) 'Creating competitive advantage with interorganisational information systems', *MIS Quarterly*, June, 153–65.

Jones, A. and Moskoff, W. (1991) *Ko-ops: The Rebirth of Entrepreneurship in the Soviet Union*. Bloomington and Indianapolis: Indiana University Press.

Jones, C. (1992) *Privatisation in East Europe and the Former Soviet Union*. Financial Times Management Reports.

Jones, G. (1991) *Starting Up*, 2nd edition, NatWest Business Handbooks. London: Pitmal Publishing.

Jones, M. (1995) *Business Link: One stop (or Enterprise Monster) shop?* Paper presented to the ESRC seminar programme on the North in the 1990s, University of Durham, 4–5 July.

Jones, M. (1996) 'Business Link: a critical commentary', *Local Economy*, 11 (1), 71–8.

Jones, T. (1981) 'Small business development and the Asian community in Britain', *New Community*, 9, 467–77.

Jones, T. (1989) *Ethnic minority business and the post-Fordist entrepreneurial renaissance*. Paper presented to the conference on Industrial Restructuring and Social Change in Western Europe, University of Durham, 26–8 September.

Jones, T. (1993) *Britain's Ethnic Minorities*. London: Policy Studies Institute.

Jones, T. and McEvoy, D. (1986) 'Ethnic enterprise: the popular image', in Curran, J., Stanworth, J. and Watkins, D. (eds) *The Survival of The Small Firm*, 197–219. Aldershot: Gower.

Jones, T., Cater, J., De Silva, P. and McEvoy, D. (1989) *Ethnic Business and Community Needs*. Report to the Commission for Racial Equality. Liverpool: Liverpool Polytechnic.

Jones, T., McEvoy, D. and Barrett, G. (1992) *Small Business Initiative: Ethnic Minority Business Component*. Swindon: ESRC.

Jones, T., McEvoy, D. and Barrett, G. (1993) 'Labour intensive practices in the ethnic minority firm', in Atkinson, J. and Storey, D. (eds) *Employment, the Small Firm and the Labour Market*. London: Routledge.

Jones, T., McEvoy, D. and Barrett, G. (1994a) 'Labour intensive practices in the ethnic minority firm', in Atkinson, J. and Storey, D. (eds) *Employment, the Small Firm and the Labour Market*, 172–205. London: Routledge.

Jones, T., McEvoy, D. and Barrett, G. (1994b) 'Raising capital for the ethnic minority small firm' in Hughes, A. and Storey, D. (eds) *Finance and the Small Firm*, 145–81. London: Routledge.

Jones-Evans, D. (1995) 'A typology of technology-based entrepreneurs – a model based on previous occupational background', *International Journal of Entrepreneurial Behaviour and Research*, 1 (1), 26–47.

Jones-Evans, D. (1996a) 'Technical entrepreneurship, strategy and experience', *International Small Business Journal*, 14 (3), 15–39.

Jones-Evans, D. (1996b) 'Experience and entrepreneurship: technology-based owner-managers in the UK', *New Technology, Work and Employment*, 11 (1), 39–54.

Jones-Evans, D. and Klofsten, M. (1997) *Technology, Innovation and Enterprise: The European Experience*. London: Macmillan.

Jones-Evans, D. and Steward, F. (1995) 'Technology, entrepreneurship and the small firm', in Bennett, D. and Steward, F. (eds) *Technological Innovation and Global Challenges: Proceedings of the First IAMOT European Conference on Management of Technology*, 272–79.

Joyce, P., Woods, A. and Black, S. (1995) 'Networks and partnerships: managing change and competition', *Small Business and Enterprise Development*, 2, 11–18.

Joynt, P. and Warner, M. (1996) *Managing Across Cultures*. London: International Thomson Business Press.

Julien, P. A. (1995) 'New technologies and technological information in small businesses', *Journal of Business Venturing*, 10 (6), 459–75.

Kagan, A., Lau, K. and Nusgart, K. R. (1990) 'Information system usage within small business firms', *Entrepreneurship Theory and Practice*, 14 (3), 25–37.

Kahneman, D. and Tversky, A. (1979) 'Prospect theory: an analysis of decision under risk', *Econometrica*, 47 (2), 263–91.

Kaleka, A. and Katsikeas, C. S. (1995) 'Exporting problems: the relevance of export development', *Journal of Marketing Management*, 11, 499–515.

Kalleberg, A. and Leicht, K. T. (1991) 'Gender and organisational performance: determinants of small business survival and success', *Academy of Management Journal*, 34 (1), 136–61.

Kanfer, R. (1991) 'Motivation theory and industrial and organizational psychology', in Dunnette, M. D. and Hough, L. M. (eds) *Handbook of Industrial and Organizational Psychology*, 2nd edition, vol. 1, 75–170. Palo Alto: Consulting Psychologists Press, Inc.

Kanter, R. (1983) *The Change Masters*. London: Allen and Unwin.

Kanter, R. M. (1989a) *When Giants Learn to Dance – Mastering the Challenges of Strategy, Management and Careers in the 1990s*. London: Unwin.

Kanter, R. M. (1989b) 'Work and family in the United States: a critical review and agenda for research and policy', *Family Business Review*, 2 (1), Spring, 77–114.

Kanter, R. M. (1989c) 'Becoming PALS: pooling, allying and networking across companies', *Academy of Management Executive*, III (3), 183–93.

Kanter, R. M. and Eccles, R. G. (1992) 'Making network research relevant to practice', in Nohria, N. and Eccles, R. G. (eds) *Networks and Organisations: Structure, Form and Action*. Boston, MA: Harvard Business School Press.

Kappelmann, L. A. (1995) 'Measuring user involvement – a diffusion of innovation perspective', *Data Base for Advances in Information Systems*, 26 (2–3), 65–86.

Kasarda, J. (1989) 'Urban industrial transition and the underclass', *Annals of the American Academy of Political and Social Science*, 501, 26–47.

Katsikeas, C. S. (1994) 'Perceived export problems and export involvement: the case of Greek exporting manufacturers', *Journal of Global Marketing*, 7 (4), 29–57.

Katsikeas, C. S. and Morgan, C. E. (1994) 'Differences in perceptions of export problems based on firm size and export market experience', *European Journal of Marketing*, 28 (5).

Katz, J. A. (1992) 'A psychosocial cognitive model of employment status choice', *Entrepreneurship Theory and Practice*, 17 (1), 29–37.

Katz, J. A. and Williams, P. M. (1997) 'Gender, self-employment and weak-tie networking through formal organizations', *Entrepreneurship and Regional Development*, 9 (3), 183–98.

Katz, L. and Krueger, A. (1992) 'The effect of the minimum wage on the fast food industry'. *Working Paper No. 3997*. Cambridge, MA: National Bureau of Economic Research.

Katz, R. L. (1970) *Cases and Concepts in Corporate Strategy*. Englewood Cliffs, NJ: Prentice-Hall.

Kazanjian, R. K. (1988) 'Relation of dominant problems to stages of growth in technology-based new ventures', *Academy of Management Journal*, 31 (2), 257–79.

Kazuka, M. (1980) *Why So Few Black Businessmen?* Report on the Findings of the Hackney Ethnic Minority Business Project, London.

Keasey, K. and Watson, R. (1992) *Investment and Financing Decisions and the Performance of Small Firms*, study commissioned by the National Westminster Bank, September.

Keasey, K. and Watson, R. (1993) *Small Firm Management: Ownership, Finance and Performance*. Blackwell.

Keat, R. and Abercrombie, N. (eds) (1991) *Enterprise Culture*. London: Routledge.

Keeble, D. (1987) *Entrepreneurship, high-technology industry and regional development in the United Kingdom: the case of the Cambridge Phenomenon*. Paper presented to the seminar on 'Technology and Territory: Innovation Diffusion in the Regional Experience of Europe and the USA', Instituto Universitario Orientale, University of Naples, 20–1 February.

Keeble, D. (1993) 'Small firm creation, innovation and growth and the urban–rural shift', in Curran, J. and Storey, D. (eds) *Small Firms in Urban and Rural Locations*, 54–78. London: Routledge.

Keeble, D. and Lawson, C. (1997) *Networks, links and large firm impacts on the evolution of regional clusters of high-technology SMEs in Europe*, Report on the Presentations and Discussions, Barcelona Meeting of the TSER European Network on 'Networks, Collective Learning and RTD in Regionally-Clustered High-Technology Small and Medium Sized Enterprises', 17–18 October, ESRC Centre for Business Research, Department of Applied Economics, University of Cambridge.

Keeble, D., Tyler, P., Broom, G. and Lewis, J. (1992) *Business Success in the Countryside: The Performance of Rural Enterprise*. London: HMSO.

Keen, L. and Scase, R. (1998) *Local Government Management: The Rhetoric and Reality of Change*. Milton Keynes: Open University Press.

Keep, E. and Mayhew, K. (1997) *Vocational education and training and economic performance*. Paper presented to the ESRC Seminar Presentation, Cranfield University.

Kelly, G. A. (1955) *The Psychology of Personal Constructs*, vols 1 and 2. Norton.

Kelly, J. (1998) *Rethinking Industrial Relations*. London: Routledge.

Kempis, R.-D. and Ringbeck, J. (1998) 'Manufacturing's use and abuse of IT', *McKinsey Quarterly*, 1, 138–50.

Kempis, R.-D., Ringbeck, J., Augustin, R., Bulk, G., Höfener, C. and Trenkel-Bögle, B. (1998) *Do IT Smart – Chefsache Informations Technology; Auf der Suche nach Effektivität* [Do IT Smart – Top Management Affair Information Technology; In Search of Effectiveness]. Wien (Vienna): Ueberreuter.

Kepner, E. (1983) 'The family and the firm: a coevolutionary perspective', *Organizational Dynamics*, 12 (1), 57–70.

Kesteloot, C. and Mistiaanen, P. (1997) 'From ethnic minority niche to assimilation: Turkish restaurants in Brussels', *Area*, 29 (4), 325–34.

Kets de Vries, M. F. R. (1977) 'The entrepreneurial personality: a person at the crossroads', *Journal of Management Studies*, 14, 34–57.

Kets de Vries, M. (1985) 'The dark side of the entrepreneur', *Harvard Business Review*, 63 (6)m 160–7.

Kidson Impey (1998), quoted in *Accountancy Age*, 30 April 1998.

Kilby, P. (1971) 'Hunting the Heffalump', in Kilby, P. (ed.) *Entrepreneurship and Economic Development*. New York: The Free Press.

Kim, I. (1981) *New Urban Immigrants: The Korean Community in New York*. Princeton, NJ: Princeton University Press.

Kim, M.-S., and Hunter, J. E. (1993) 'Attidude–behavior relations: a meta-analysis of attitutional relevance and topic', *Journal of Communication*, 43 (1), 101–42.

Kimhi, A. (1997) 'Intergenerational succession in small family businesses: borrowing constraints and optimal timing of succession', *Small Business Economics*, 9 (4), August, 309–18.

Kinsella, R. and Mulvenna, D. (1993) 'Fast growth businesses: their role in the post-Culliton industrial strategy', *Administration*, 41 (1), 3–15.

Kinsella, R., Clarke, W., Coyne, D., Mulvenna, D. and Storey, D. J. (1993) *Fast Growth Firms and Selectivity*. Dublin: Irish Management Institute.

Kirchhoff, B. (1991) 'Entrepreneurship's contribution to economics', *Entrepreneurship, Theory and Practice*, 16 (2), 93–112.

Kirzner, I. (1979) *Perception, Opportunity and Profit Studies in the Theory of Entrepreneurship*. Chicago/London: University of Chicago Press.

Kloosterman, R. C., van Der Leun, J. and Rath, J. (1998) 'Across the border: economic opportunities, social capital and informal business activities of immigrants', *Journal of Ethnic and Migration Studies*, 19 (1), 40–54.

Knight, F. H. (1921) *Risk, Uncertainty and Profit*. Boston, MA: Houghton Mifflin Company.

Knight, R. M. (1987) 'Corporate innovation and entrepreneurship: a Canadian study', *Journal of Product Innovation Management*, 4, 284–97.

Kolvereid, L. (1992) 'Growth aspirations among Norwegian entrepreneurs', *Journal of Business Venturing*, 7, 209–22.

Kolvereid, L. (1996a) 'Organizational employment versus self-employment: reasons for career choice intentions', *Entrepreneurship Theory and Practice*, 20 (3), 23–31.

Kolvereid, L. (1996b) 'Prediction of employment status choice intentions', *Entrepreneurship Theory and Practice*, 21 (1), 47–57.

Kolvereid, L. and Bullvag, E. (1996) 'Growth intentions and actual growth: the impact of entrepreneurial choice', *Journal of Enterprising Culture*, 4 (1), 1–17.

Koper, G. (1993) 'Women entrepreneurs and the granting of business credit', in Allen, S. and Truman, C. (eds) *Women in Business: Perspectives on Women Entrepreneurs*, 57–69. London: Routledge.

Kornai, J. (1980) *Economics of Shortage* (2 vols). Amsterdam: North Holland.

Kotha, S. (1998) 'Competing on the Internet: the case of amazon.com', *European Management Journal*, 16 (2), 212–22.

Kotler, P. (1997) *Marketing Management*, 9th edition. Englewood Cliffs, NJ: Prentice Hall.

Krackhardt, D. and Hanson, J. (1993) 'Informal networks: the companies behind the chart', *Harvard Business Review*, July–August, 104–11.

Kram, K. E. (1986) 'Mentoring in the workplace', in Hall, D. T. *et al.* (eds) *Career Development in Organisations*. San Francisco, CA: Jossey-Bass.

Krantz, S. (1999) 'Small business', in *Sunday Business* Essex, W, 11 April.

Krueger, A. (1991) 'Ownership, agency and wages: an examination of franchising in the fast food industry', *Quarterly Journal of Economics*, 56 (1), 75–101.

Krueger, N. (1998) 'Encouraging the identification of environmental opportunities', *Journal of Organizational Change Management*, 11 (2), 174–83.

Krueger, N. F. (1993) 'The impact of prior entrepreneurial exposure on perceptions of new venture feasibility and desirability', *Entrepreneurship Theory and Practice*, 18 (1), 5–21.

Krueger, N. F. and Brazeal, D. V. (1994) 'Entrepreneurial potential and potential entrepreneur', *Entrepreneurship Theory and Practice*, 18 (3), 91–104.

Krueger, N. F. J. and Carsrud, A. L. (1993) 'Entrepreneurial intentions: applying the theory of planned behavior', *Entrepreneurship and Regional Development*, 5 (4), 315–30.

Krueger, N. F. J. and Dickson, P. R. (1993) 'Perceived self-efficacy and perceptions of opportunity and threats', *Psychological Reports*, 72, 1235–40.

Krueger, N. J. and Dickson, P. R. (1994) 'How believing in ourselves increases risk taking: perceived self-efficacy and opportunity recognition', *Decision Sciences*, 25 (3), 385–400.

Kuhn, R. (1982) *Mid-Sized Businesses: Success Strategies and Methodology*. New York: Praeger Press.

Kuratko, D. F., Hornsby, J. S., Naffziger, D. W. and Montagno, R. V. (1993) 'Implement entrepreneurial thinking in established organisations', *SAM Advanced Management Journal*, 58 (1), 28–34.

Kuzmina, E. (1997) *Russia – Franchising – ISA970701*, US Department of Commerce (Industry Sector Analysis), July.

Labour Market Quarterly Report (1998). Department for Education and Employment, May.

Langlois, A. and Razin, E. (1995) 'Self-employment among French-Canadians: the role of the regional milieu', *Ethnic and Racial Studies*, 18 (3), 581–604.

LaRovere, R. L. (1998) 'Small and medium-sized enterprises and IT diffusion policies in Europe', *Small Business Economics*, 11 (1), 1–9.

Larson, A. (1992) 'Network dyads in entrepreneurial settings: a study of the governance of exchange relationships', *Administrative Science Quarterly*, 37, 76–104.

Lawrence, P. A. and Lee, R. A. (1989) *Insight into Management*. Oxford: Oxford University Press.

Leach, P. (1994) *The Stoy Hayward Guide to the Family Business*, London: Kogan Page.

Leavitt, H. J. and Whisler, T. L. (1958) 'Management in the 1980s', *Harvard Business Review*, Nov–Dec, 41–8.

Lee, T. Y. and Low, L. (1990) *Local Entrepreneurship in Singapore: Private and State*.

Singapore: Singapore Institute of Policy Studies and Times Academic Press.

Lee, W.-Y. and Brasch, J. J. (1978) 'The adoption of export as an innovation', *Journal of International Business Studies*, 9 (1), 85–93.

Lees, J. D. (1987) 'Successful development of small business information systems', *Journal of Systems Management*, 25 (3), 32–9.

Legge, K. (1995) *Human Resource Management, Rhetorics and Realities*, Basingstoke: Macmillan.

Leiner, B. M., Cerf, V. G., Clark, D. D., Kahn, R. E., Kleinrock, L., Lynch, D. C., Postel, J., Roberts, L. G. and Wolff, S.S. (1997) 'The past and future history of the Internet', *Communications of the ACM*, 40 (2), 102–8.

Leonard-Barton, D. (1984) 'Interpersonal communication patterns among Swedish and Boston-area entrepreneurs', *Research Policy*, 13 (2), 101–14.

Leonidou, L. C. (1995) 'Empirical research on export barriers: review, assessment, and synthesis', *Journal of International Marketing*, 3 (1), 29–43.

Lessem, R. and Neubauer, F. (1994) *European Management Systems*. Maidenhead: McGraw-Hill.

Levin, I. (1993) 'Family as mapped realities', *Journal of Family Issues*, 14 (1), 82–91.

Liao, Y. (1992) 'The geography of the Chinese catering trade in Greater Manchester', *Manchester Geographer*, 14, 54–82.

Light, I. (1972) *Ethnic Enterprise in America: Business and Welfare among Chinese, Japanese and Blacks*. Berkeley, CA: University of California Press.

Light, I. (1984) 'Immigrant and ethnic enterprise in North America', *Ethnic and Racial Studies*, 7, 195–216.

Light, I. (1995) 'The "other side" of embeddedness: a case-study of the interplay of economy and ethnicity', *Ethnic and Racial Studies*, 18 (3), 555–80.

Light, I. and Bonacich, E. (1988) *Immigrant Entrepreneurs*. Berkeley, CA: University of California Press.

Light, I. and Rosenstein, C. (1995) *Race, Ethnicity and Entrepreneurship in Urban America*. Hawthorne, NY: Aldine de Gruyter.

Light, I., Sabagh, G., Bozorgmehr, M. and Der-Martirosian, C. (1993) 'Internal ethnicity in the ethnic economy', *Ethnic and Racial Studies*, 16 (4), 581–97.

Lindqvist, M. (1988) 'Internationalisation of small technology-based firms: three illustrative

case studies on Swedish firms', Stockholm School of Economics Research Paper 88/15.

Litz, R. A. (1995) 'The family business: toward definitional clarity', *Family Business Review*, 8 (2), Summer, 71–81.

Liu, H. (1995) 'Market orientation and firm size: an empirical examination in UK firms', *European Journal of Marketing*, 29 (1), 57–71.

Locke, E. A. (1991) 'The motivation sequence, the motivation hub, and the motivation core', *Organizational Behavior and Human Decision Processes*, 50, 288–99.

Lombardini, S. (1996) 'Family, kin and the quest for community: a study of three social networks in early modern Italy', *History of the Family*, 1 (3), 227–58.

Losee, R. M. (1997) 'A discipline independent definition of information', *Journal of the American Society for Information Science*, 48 (3), 254–69.

Low, M. B. and MacMillan, I. C. (1988) 'Entrepreneurship: past research and future challenges', *Journal of Management*, 14 (2), 139–61.

Lucas, H. C., Jr (1975) 'Performance and the use of an information system', *Management Science*, 21 (8), 908–19.

Lucas, H. C., Jr (1981) *Implementation: The Key to Successful Information Systems*. New York: Columbia University Press.

Luffman, G., Sanderson, S., Lea, E. and Kenny, B. (1991) *Business Policy: An Analytical Introduction*. Oxford: Blackwell.

Luostarinen, R. (1980) *The Internationalisation of the Firm*. Helsinki School of Economics.

Luostarinen, R. (1994) *Internationalisation of Finnish Firms and Their Response to Global Challenges*, 3rd edition, Helsinki: UNU/WIDER.

Lyytinen, K. (1987) 'Different perspectives on information systems: problems and solutions', *ACM Computing Surveys*, 19, 7–46.

Ma Mung, E. (1994) 'L'entreprenariat ethnique en France', *Sociologie du Travail*, 2, 195–209.

Ma Mung, E. and Guillon, M. (1986) 'Les commercants étrangers dans l'agglomération Parisienne', *Revue Européene des Migrations Internationales*, 2 (3), 105–34.

Ma Mung, E. and Simon, G. (1990) *Commercants Maghrebins et Asiatiques en France: Agglomération Parisienne et villes de l'est*. Paris: Masson.

Macaulay, S. (1963) 'Non-contractual relations in business: a preliminary study', *American Sociological Review*, 45, 55–69.

Macmillan Committee (1931) *Report of the Committee on Finance and Industry,* Cmnd 3897. London: HMSO.

Macrae, D. (1991) *Characteristics of high and low growth small and medium sized businesses.* Paper presented at 21st European Small Business Seminar, Barcelona, Spain.

Macrae, N. (1976) 'The coming entrepreneurial revolution', *The Economist,* Christmas edition, London.

Madsen, T. K. and Servais, P. (1997) 'The internationalisation of born globals: an evolutionary process?', *International Business Review,* 6 (6), 561–83.

Mahmoud, E. and Malhotra, N. (1986) 'The decision-making process of small business for microcomputer and software selection and usage', *INFOR – Information Systems and Operational Research,* 24 (2), 116–33.

Malecki, E. J. (1981) 'Product cycles, innovation cycles, and regional economic change', *Technological Forecasting and Social Change,* 19, 291–306.

Malecki, E. J. (1991) *Technology and Economic Development.* Harlow: Longman Scientific and Technical.

Malone, S. C. (1985) 'Computerising small business information systems', *Journal of Small Business Management,* 23 (2), 10–16.

Marable, M. and Mullings, L. (1994) 'The divided mind of Black America: race, ideology and politics in the post Civil Rights era', *Race and Class,* 36 (1), 61–72.

Markus, M. L. (1987) 'Toward a critical mass theory of interactive media – universal access, interdependence and diffusion', *Communication Research,* 14, 491–511.

Markus, M. L. and Robey, D. (1988) 'Information technology and organizational change: causal structure in theory and research', *Management Science,* 34 (5), 583–98.

Markusen, A. (1985) *Profit Cycles, Oligopoly, and Regional Development.* Cambridge, MA: MIT Press.

Marlow, S. (1992) 'Take-up of business growth training schemes by ethnic minority-owned small firms', *International Small Business Journal,* 10, 34–46.

Marlow, S. (1997) 'Self-employed women – new opportunities, old challenges?', *Entrepreneurship and Regional Development,* 9 (3), 199–210.

Marlow, S. (1998) 'So much opportunity, so little take up – training in small firms', *Journal of Small Business and Enterprise Development,* 5 (1), 38–49.

Marlow, S. and Patton, D. (1993) 'Managing the employment relationship in the small firm: possibilities for HRM', *International Small Business Journal,* 11 (4), 57–64.

Martello, W. E. (1994) 'Developing creative business insights: serendipity and its potential', *Entrepreneurship and Regional Development,* 6 (2), 239–58.

Martin, C. J. (1989) 'Information management in the smaller business: the role of the top manager', *International Journal of Information Management,* 9 (3), 187–97.

Martin, S. and Oztel, H. (1996) 'The business of partnership: collaborative-competitive partnerships in the development of Business Links', *Local Economy,* 11 (2), 131–42.

Mason, C. M. and Harrison, R. T. (1991) 'The small firm equity gap since Bolton', in Stanworth, J. and Gray, C. (eds) *Bolton 20 Years On: The Small Firm in the 1990s,* 112–50. London: Paul Chapman Publishing.

Mason, C. M. and Harrison, R. T. (1992) *Promoting Informal Venture Capital: Some Operational Considerations for Business Introduction Services,* Venture Finance Research Project, Paper No. 5. University of Southampton.

Mason, C. M. and Harrison, R. T. (1995) 'Informal venture capital and the financing of small and medium sized enterprises', *Small Enterprise Research,* 3 (1), 33–56.

Massey, D. (1996) 'Masculinity, dualisms and high technology', in Duncan, N. (ed.) *Bodyspace – Destabilizing Geographies of Gender and Sexuality,* 109–26. London: Routledge.

Masters, R. and Meier, R. (1988) 'Sex differences and risk-taking propensity of entrepreneurs', *Journal of Small Business Management,* 26 (1), 31–5.

Mata, F. J., Fuerst, W. L. and Barney, J. B. (1995) 'Information Technology and Sustained Competitive Advantage: A Resource-Based Analysis', *Management Information Systems Quarterly,* (United States) 19 (4), 487–506.

Matlay, H. (1995) *The Training Needs of Small Business Owner-Managers.* Warwick University: Department of Continuing Education.

Matlay, H. (1996) *Paradox resolved? Owner-manager attitudes to, and actual provision of, training in the small business sector of the British economy.* Paper presented at the 19th ISBA Conference, Birmingham, 20–2 November.

Matlay, H. (1997a) *Evaluating the effectiveness of training initiatives: factors influencing the provision of training in the small business sector*. Paper presented at the Small Business & Development Conference, University of Sheffield, 19–20 March.

Matlay, H. (1997b) 'The paradox of training in the small business sector of the British economy', *Journal of Vocational Education and Training*, 49 (4), 573–89.

Matlay, H. (1999) 'Vocational education and training in Britain: a small business perspective', *Education and Training*, forthcoming.

Matlay, H. and Hyland, T. (1997) 'NVQs in the small business sector: a critical overview', *Education and Training*, 39 (9), 325–32.

Matthews, C. H. and Moser, S. B. (1995) 'Family background and gender: implications for interest in small firm ownership', *Entrepreneurship and Regional Development*, 7, 365–77.

May, T. C. and McHugh, J. (1991) *Government and small business in the UK: the experience of the 1980s*. Paper presented at the Annual Conference of the Political Studies Association of the United Kingdom.

McCarthy, E. J. and Perreault, W. D. (1987) *Basic Marketing*. Illinois: Irwin.

McClelland, D. C. (1961) *The Achieving Society*. Princeton, NJ: Van Nostrand.

McClelland, D. C. and Winter, D. G. (1969) *Motivating Economic Achievement*. New York: Free Press.

McCloy, R. A., Campbell, J. P. and Cudeck, R. (1994) 'A confirmatory test of a model of performance determinants', *Journal of Applied Psychology*, 79 (4), 493–505.

McCollom, M. E. (1988) 'Integration in the family firm: when the family system replaces controls and culture', *Family Business Review*, 1 (4), Winter, 399–417.

McCollom, M. E. (1992) 'Organizational stories in a family owned business', *Family Business Review*, V (1), Spring, 3–23.

McDonald, M. H. B. (1980) *Handbook of Marketing Planning*. Bradford: MCB Publications.

McDonald, M. H. B. (1984) *Marketing Plans: How to Prepare Them and Use Them*. London: Heinemann.

McDougall, P. and Robinson, R. (1990) 'New venture strategies: an empirical identification of eight "archetypes" of competitive strategies for entry', *Strategic Management Journal*, 11, 447–67.

McEvoy, D. and Cook, I. G. (1993) *Transpacific Migration: Asians in North America*. Paper presented at the 2nd British Pacific Rim Seminar, Liverpool John Moores University.

McFarlan, F. W. (1984) 'Information technology changes the way you compete', *Harvard Business Review*, May–June, 98–103.

McFarlan, F. W., McKenney, J. L. and Pyburn, P. (1983) 'The information archipelago – plotting a course', *Harvard Business Review*, 61, 145–56.

McGee, J. (1989) 'Barriers to growth: the effects of market structure', in Barber, J., Metcalfe, J. S. and Porteous, M. (eds) *Barriers to Growth in Small Firms*, 173–95. London: Routledge.

McGoldrick, J. (1997) 'Just the job?', *People Management*, 3 (17), 32–5.

McGrath, R. G., MacMillan, I. C. and Scheinberg, S. (1992) 'Elitists, risk-takers, and rugged individualists? An exploratory analysis of cultural differences between entrepreneurs and non-entrepreneurs', *Journal of Business Venturing*, 7, 115–35.

McGuinness, N. W. and Little, B. (1981) 'The influence of product characteristics on the export performance of new industrial products', *Journal of Marketing*, 45, Spring, 110–22.

McKeen, J. D., Guimaraes, T. and Wetherbe, J. C. (1994) 'The relationship between user participation and user satisfaction: an investigation of four contingency factors', *MIS Quarterly*, 18, 427–51.

McKinney, G. and McKinney, M. (1989) 'Forget the corporate umbrella – entrepreneurs shine in the rain', *Sloan Management Review*, 30 (4), 77–82.

Meadow, C. T. and Yuan, W. (1997) 'Measuring the impact of information: defining the concepts', *Information Processing and Management*, 33 (6), 697–714.

Meager, N. (1991), 'Self-employment in the United Kingdom', *IMS Report* No. 205, Institute of Manpower Studies.

Meager, N. (1992) 'Does unemployment lead to self-employment?', *Small Business Economics*, Vol. 4 , pp.87–103.

Meager, N., Court, G. and Moralee, J. (1996) 'Self-employment and the distribution of income', in Hills, J. (ed.), *New Inequalities*. Cambridge: Cambridge University Press.

Mellers, B. A., Schwartz, A. and Cooke, A. D. J. (1998) 'Judgment and decision making', *Annual Review of Psychology*, 49, 447–77.

Mendelsohn, M. (1993) *The Guide to Franchising*. Cassell.

Mennon, S. (1988) 'Greater London Council ethnic minority business development initiatives: a policy review', *Policy and Politics*, 16, 55–62.

Messerschmidt, D. G. (1996) 'The convergence of telecommunications and computing – what are the implications today?', *Proceedings of the IEEE*, 84 (8), 1167–86.

Metcalf, L. E., Frear, C. R. and Krishman, R. (1991) 'Buyer-seller relations: an application of the IMP interaction model', *Journal of Marketing*, 26 (2), 27–46.

Metcalfe, H., Modood, T. and Virdee, S. (1996) *Asian Self-Employment: The Interaction of Culture and Economics in England*. London: Policy Studies Institute.

Michaelas, N., Chittenden, F. and Poutziouris, P. (1996) *Determinants of Capital Structure in Small Privately Held Firms*, The Institute of Small Business Affairs Research Series, Monograph 2.

Miesenbock, K. J. (1988) 'Small business and exporting: a literature review', *International Small Business Journal*, 6 (2), 42–61.

Miller, D. (1987a) *Material Culture and Mass Consumption*. Oxford: Basil Blackwell.

Miller, D. (1987b) 'Strategy making and structure: analysis and implications for performance', *Academy of Management Journal*, 30 (1), 7–32.

Miller, D. and Droge, C. (1986) 'Psychological and traditional determinants of structure', *Administrative Science Quarterly*, 31, 539–60.

Miller, D. and Toulouse, J.-M. (1986) 'Chief executive personality and corporate strategy and structure in small firms', *Management Science*, 32 (11), 1389–1409.

Milward, N. and Stevens, M. (1986) *British Workplace Industrial Relations, 1980–1984*. Aldershot: Gower.

Milward, N., Stevens, M., Smart, D. and Hawes, W. R. (1992) *Workplace Industrial Relations in Transition*. Aldershot: Gower.

Min, P. G. (1991) 'Cultural and economic boundaries of Korean ethnicity: a comparative analysis', *Ethnic and Racial Studies*, 14 (2), 225–41.

Min, P. G. (1993) 'Korean immigrants in Los Angeles', in Light, I. and Bhachu, P. (eds) *Immigration and Entrepreneurship: Culture, Capital and Ethnic Networks*, New Brunswick, NJ: Transaction.

Miner, J. B., Smith, N. R. and Bracker, J. S. (1989) 'Role of entrepreneurial task motivation in the growth of technologically innovative firms', *Journal of Applied Psychology*, 74 (4), 554–60.

Miner, J. B., Smith, N. R. and Bracker, J. S. (1992) 'Predicting firm survival from a knowledge of entrepreneur task motivation', *Entrepreneurship and Regional Development*, 4, 145–53.

Miner, J. B., Crane, D. P. and Vandenberg, R. J. (1994) 'Congruence and fit in professional role motivation theory', *Organization Science*, 5 (1), 86–97.

Mintzberg, H. (1979) *The Structuring of Organisations*. Englewood Cliffs, NJ: Prentice Hall.

Mintzberg, H. (1994) 'Rethinking strategic planning, part I: pitfalls and fallacies', *Long Range Planning*, 27 (3), 12–21.

Mintzberg, H. and Quinn, J. (1991) *The Strategy Process, Concepts, Contexts, Cases*, 2nd edition. Prentice Hall International.

Mintzberg, H. and Waters, J. (1982) 'Tracking strategy in an entrepreneurly firm', *Administrative Science Quarterly*, 25, 465–99.

Mitchell, F., Reid, G. and Terry, N. (1995) 'Post investment demand for accounting information by venture capitalists', *Accounting and Business Research*, vol. 25.

Mitchell, J. C. (1969) 'The concept and use of social networks', in Mitchell, J. C. (ed.) *Social Networks in Urban Situations*. Manchester: University of Manchester Press.

Mitchell, J. C. (1973) 'Networks, norms and institutions', in Boissevain, J. and Mitchell, J. C. (eds) *Network Analysis: Studies in Human Interaction*. London: Mouton and Company.

Mitchell, R. K. and Seawright, K. W. (1995) 'The implication of multiple cultures and entrepreneurial expertise for international public policy', in Bygrave, W. D., Bird, B. J., Birley, S., Churchill, N. C., Hay, M. G., Keeley, R. H., and Wetzel, W. E. J. (eds) *Frontiers of Entrepreneurship Research*, 143–71. Babson Park, MA: Center for Entrepreneurial Studies, Babson College.

Mitra, J., Pawar, K. and Soar, S. (1991) *The Role of TECs and Ethnic Minority SMEs*, 14th National Small Firms Policy and Research Conference.

Mitter, S. (1986) 'Industrial restructuring and manufacturing homework', *Capital and Class*, 27, 37–80.

Mittlestaedt, R. and Peterson, M. (1980) *Franchising and the financing of small business*, Paper in Studies of Small Business Finance series prepared by The Inter-agency Task Force on Small Business Finance.

Modigliani, F. and Miller, M. H. (1958) 'The cost of capital, corporation finance and the theory of finance', *American Economic Review*, June.

Modigliani, F. and Miller, M. H. (1963) 'Taxes and the cost of capital: a correction', *American Economic Review*, June.

Moini, A. H. (1997) 'Barriers inhibiting export performance of small and medium-sized manufacturing firms', *Journal of Global Marketing*, 10 (4), 67–93.

Monck, C. S. P., Quintas, P., Porter, R. B., Storey, D. J. and Wynarczyk, P. (1988) *Science Parks and the Growth of High Technology Firms*. London: Croom Helm.

Mønsted, M. (1993) 'Introduction of information technology to small firms: a network perspective', in *Entrepreneurship and Business Development*, 359–72. Klandt, H. (ed.) Aldershot: Avebury.

Montazemi, A. R. (1987) 'An analysis of information technology assessment and adoption in small business environments', *INFOR – Information Systems and Operational Research*, 25 (4), 327–37.

Montazemi, A. R. (1988) 'Factors affecting information satisfaction in the context of the small business environment', *MIS Quarterly*, 12 (2), 239–56.

Morgan, R. E. and Katsikeas, C. S. (1997) 'Export stimuli: export intention compared with export activity', *International Business Review*, 6 (5), 477–99.

Morris, M. and Ogan, C. (1996) 'The Internet as mass medium', *Journal of Communication*, 46 (1), 39–50.

Morris, M. H. and Trotter, J. D. (1990) 'Institutionalising entrepreneurship in a large company: a case study of AT&T', *Industrial Marketing Management*, 19, 131-9.

Morrison, A. (ed.) (1998) *Entrepreneurship: An International Perspective*. Oxford: Butterworth-Heinemann.

Morrison, A., Rimmington, M. and Williamson, C. (1998) *Entrepreneurship in the Hospitality, Tourism and Leisure Industry*. Oxford: Butterworth-Heinemann.

Morrison, P. and Morrison, P. (1998) 'Wonders – the sum of human knowledge', *Scientific American*, July, 95–7.

Muller, M. (1996) 'Good luck or good management? Multigenerational family control in two Swiss enterprises since the 19th century', *Entreprises et histoire*, 12, 19–48.

Mullins, D. (1979) 'Asian retailing in Croydon', *New Community*, 7, 403–5.

Mumford, A. (1995) 'Learning styles and mentoring', *Industrial and Commercial Training*, 27 (8), 4–7.

Murphy, G. B., Trailer, J. W. and Hill, R. C. (1996) 'Measuring performance in entrepreneurship', *Journal of Business Research*, 36, 15–23.

Murray, C. (1990) *Emerging British Underclass*. London: Economic Affairs Institute.

Murray, G. (1995) 'Third-party equity – the role of the UK venture-capital industry', in Buckland, R. and Davis, E. (eds) *Finance for Growing Firms*. London: Routledge.

Murray, J. A. and O'Gorman, C. (1994) 'Growth strategies for smaller business', *Journal of Strategic Change*, 3, 175–83.

Myers, S. C. (1984) 'The capital structure puzzle', *Journal of Finance*, 34 (3), 575–92.

Namiki, N. (1988) 'Export strategy for small business', *Journal of Small Business Management*, 26 (2), 32–7.

Namiki, N. (1994) 'A taxonomic analysis of export marketing strategy: an exploratory study of U.S. exporters of electronic products', *Journal of Global Marketing*, 8 (1), 27–50.

Nath, R., Akmanligil, M., Hjelm, K., Sakaguchi, T. and Schultz, M. (1998) 'Electronic commerce and the Internet: issues, problems, and perspectives', *International Journal of Information Management* 18 (2), 91–101.

The National Westminster Bank/British Franchise Association Franchise Survey, NatWest Bank/BFA, 1987, 1988, 1989, 1990, 1991, 1993, 1994.

Naylor, J. B. and Williams, J. (1994) 'The successful use of IT in SMEs on Merseyside', *European Journal of Information Systems*, 3 (1), 48–56.

Negroponte, N. (1995) *Being Digital*. New York: Alfred A. Knopf.

Nelson, D. (1975) *Managers and Workers: Origins of the New Factory System in the United States, 1880–1920*. Madison, WI: University of Wisconsin Press.

Newby, H. (1977) *The Deferential Worker*. Harmondsworth: Penguin Books.

Ng, I. and Maki, D. (1993) 'Human resource management in the Canadian manufacturing sector', *International Journal of Human Resource Management*, 4 (4), 897–916.

Nickell, G. S. and Seado, P. C. (1986) 'The impact of attitudes and experience on small business computer use', *American Journal of Small Business*, 10 (4), 37–47.

Nicolescu, O. (1994) 'Opportunities, barriers and factors influencing the success of trading in Romania', *Proceedings of the 23rd European Small Business Conference*, 416–43. Belfast.

Nicoll, A. and Kehoe, L. (1998) 'Warning on Internet security risk', *Financial Times*, 20.3.1998, 2.

Niedleman, L. D. (1979) 'Computer usage by small and medium-sized European firms: an empirical study', *Information Management*, 2 (2), 67–77.

Nilsson, P. (1997) 'Business counselling services directed towards female entrepreneurs – some legitimacy dilemmas', *Entrepreneurship and Regional Development*, 9 (3), 239–58.

Nohria, N. (1992) 'Is a network perspective a useful way of studying organizations?', in Nohria, N. and Eccles, R. G. (eds*) Networks and Organisations: Structure, Form and Action*. Boston, MA: Harvard Business School Press.

Nolan, P. (1989) 'Walking on water? Performance and industrial relations under Thatcher', *Industrial Relations Journal*, 20 (2), 81–92.

Noon, M. and Blyton, P. (1997) *The Realities of Work*. London: Macmillan.

North, D. and Smallbone, D. (1996) 'Small business development in remote rural areas: the example of mature manufacturing firms in northern England', *Journal of Rural Studies*, 12 (2), 151-67.

North, J., Blackburn, R. and Curran, J. (1997) 'Reaching small businesses? Delivering advice and support to small businesses through Trade Bodies', in Ram, M., Deakins, D., and Smallbone, D. (eds) *Small Firms: Enterprising Futures*, pp. 121–35. London: Paul Chapman Publishing.

Norton, E. (1990) 'Similarities and differences in small and large corporation beliefs about capital structure policy', *Small Business Economics*.

Norton, E. (1991a) 'Capital structure and public firms', *Journal of Business Venturing*.

Norton, E. (1991b) 'Capital structure and small growth firms', *Journal of Small Business Finance*, 1 (2).

Notess, G. R. (1997) 'Searching the hidden Internet', *Data Base for Advances in Information Systems*, June/July, 37–40.

Nove, A. (1986) *The Soviet Economic System*, 3rd edition. London: Allen and Unwin.

Nowikowski, S. (1984) 'Snakes and ladders', in Ward, R. and Jenkins, R. (eds) *Ethnic Communities in Business*, 149-65. Cambridge: Cambridge University Press.

Oakey, R. P. (1984) *High Technology Small Firms*. London: Frances Pinter.

Oakey, R. P. (1985) 'British university science parks and high technology small firms: a comment on the potential for sustained industrial growth', *International Small Business Journal*, 4 (1), 58–67.

Oakey, R. P. (1995) *High-Technology New Firms: Variable Barriers to Growth*. London: Paul Chapman.

Oakey, R. P. and Cooper, S. Y. (1989) 'High technology industry, agglomeration and the potential for peripherally sited small firms', *Regional Studies*, 23 (4) 347–60.

Oakey, R. P. and Cooper, S. Y. (1991) 'The relationship between product technology and innovation performance in high technology small firms', *Technovation*, 11 (2), 79-92.

Oakey, R. P., Rothwell, R. and Cooper, S. Y. (1988*) The Management of Innovation in High Technology Small Firms*. London: Pinter Publishers.

Oakey, R. P., Faulkner, W., Cooper, S. Y. and Walsh, V. (1990*) New Firms in the Biotechnology Industry*. London: Pinter Publishers.

Oakey, R. P., Cooper, S. Y. and Biggar, J. (1993) 'Product marketing and sales in high-technology small firms', in Swann, P. (ed.*) New Technologies and the Firm*, 201–22. London: Routledge.

O'Connor, J. and Galvin, E. (1997) *Marketing and Information Technology – The Strategy, Application and Implementation of IT in Marketing*. London: Pitman.

OECD (1986) 'Self-employment in OECD countries', *OECD Employment Outlook*, September. Paris: OECD.

OECD (1997a) *Globalisation and Small and Medium Enterprises (SMEs)*, vol. 1. Paris: OECD.

OECD (1997b) *Information Technology Outlook 1997*. Paris: OECD.

OECD (1998) *Use of Information and Communication Technologies at Work*. Paris: OECD.

O'Farrell, P. N. O. and Hitchens, D. M. W. N. (1988) 'Alternative theories of small firm growth: a critical review', *Environment and Planning. A*. 20, 1365–83.

O'Grady, S. and Lane, H. W. (1996), 'The psychic distance paradox', *Journal of International Business Studies*, 2nd Quarter, 309–33.

Ok Lee, D. (1995) 'Koreatown and Korean small firms in Los Angeles: locating in the ethnic neighbourhoods'. *Professional Geographer*, 47 (2), 184–95.

Olm, K., Carsrud, A. L. and Alvey, L. (1988) 'The role of networks in new venture funding of female entrepreneurs: a continuing analysis', in Kirchhoff, B. A., Long, W. A., McMullan, E., Vesper, K. H. and Wetzel, W. E., Jr (eds) *Frontiers of Entrepreneurship Research*, 658–9. Wellesley, MA: Babson College.

Oman, C. (1984) *New Forms of International Investment in Developing Countries*. Paris: OECD.

Orr, A. (1995) 'Customers for life', *Target Marketing*, 18 (3), March.

Osowska, F. (1996) *Rates of Return to Education and Training for Individuals*. Sheffield: Department for Education and Employment.

Owualah, S. (1987) 'Providing the necessary economic infrastructure for small business: whose responsibility?', *International Small Business Journal*, 6 (1), 10–30.

Ozanne, U. and Hunt, S. (1971) *The Economic Effects of Franchising*. Washington, DC: US Select Committee on Small Business.

Padaki, R. (1994) *Woman and Her Enterprise: A Study of Karnataka State*. Bangalore: The P & P Group.

Padmanabhan, K. (1986) 'Are the franchised businesses less risky than the non-franchised businesses?', *Proceedings of the 1st Conference of the Society of Franchising*, Nebraska, 28–30 January

Painter, J. (1997) 'Regulation, regime, and practice in urban politics', in Lauria, M. (ed.) *Reconstructing Urban Regime Theory: Regulating Urban Politics in a Global Economy*. California: Sage.

Pajaczkowska, C. and Young, L. (1992) 'Racism, representation and psychoanalysis', in Donald, J. and Rattansi, A. (eds) *'Race', Culture and Difference*, 198–219. London: Sage.

Parker, D. (1994) 'Encounters across the counter: young Chinese people in Britain', *New Community*, 20, 621–34.

Parker, K. T. and Vickerstaff, S. (1996) 'TECs, LECs and small firms: differences in provision and performance', *Environment and Planning C: Government and Policy*, 14, 251–67.

Parker, S., Brown, R., Child, J. and Smith, M. (1972) *The Sociology of Industry*. London: George Allen and Unwin.

Parker, S. C. (1997) 'The distribution of self-employment income in the United Kingdom, 1976–1991', *Economic Journal*, 107 (441), pp. 455–66.

Patel, S. (1988) 'Insurance and ethnic community business', *New Community*, 15, 79-89.

Pavitt, K., Robson, M. and Townsend, J. (1987) 'The size distribution of innovating firms in the UK – 1945–83', *Journal of Industrial Economics*, 35 (3), 297–316.

Pavord, W. C. and Bogart, R. G. (1975), 'The dynamics of the decision to export', *Akron Business and Economic Review*, 6, Spring, 6–11.

Peach, C. (1996) 'A question of collar', *Times Higher*, 23 August.

Peacock, P. (1986). 'The influence of risk-taking as a cognitive judgmental behavior of small business success', in Ronstadt, R., Hornaday, J. A., Peterson, R., and Vesper, K. H. (eds) *Frontiers of Entrepreneurship Research*, 110-18. Babson Park, MA: Center for Entrepreneurial Studies, Babson College.

Pearce, I. (1980) 'Reforms for entrepreneurs to serve public policy', *The Prime Mover of Progress: The Entrepreneur in Capitalism and Socialism*. London: The Institute of Economic Affairs.

Pearson, G. J. (1989) 'Promoting entrepreneurship in large companies', *Long Range Planning*, 22 (3), 87–97.

Pearson, P., and Quincy, M. (1992) *Poor Britain, Poverty, Inequality and Low Pay in the 1990s*. London: Low Pay Unit.

Peck, J. (1991) 'Letting the market decide (with public money): Training and Enterprise Councils and the future of labour market programmes', *Critical Social Policy* 5, 4–17.

Peck, J. (1993) 'The trouble with TECs ... A critique of the Training and Enterprise Council initiatives', *Policy and Politics*, 21, 289–305.

Peck, J. and Emmerich, M. (1993) 'TECs: time for change', *Local Economy* 8 (1), 4–21.

Peck, J. and Tickell, A. (1994a) 'Searching for a new institutional fix: the after-Fordist crisis and global-local disorder', in Amin, A. (ed.) *Post-Fordism: A Reader*. Oxford: Blackwell.

Peck, J. and Tickell, A. (1994b) 'Too many partnerships ... The future for regeneration partnerships', *Local Economy* 9 (3), 251–65.

Penrose, E. (1959) *The Theory of the Growth of the Firm*. London: John Wiley.

Perry, C., MacArthur, R., Meredith, G. and Cunnington, B. (1986) 'Need for achievement and locus of control of Australian small business owner-managers and super-entrepreneurs'

International Small Business Journal, 4 (4), 55–64.

Peters, T. and Waterman, R. (1982) *In Search of Excellence*. New York: Harper and Row.

Petrin, T., Prasnikar, J. and Vahcic, A. (1988) *Development strategy of the Commune of Nova Gorica for the period 1988–1998*. Paper presented to the 5th International Conference on the Economics of Self-Management, 6–8 July, Vienna, Austria.

Pettigrew, A., Arthur, M. and Hendry, C. (1990) *Training and Human Resource Management in Small to Medium Sized Enterprises: A Critical Review of the Literature and a Model for Future Research*. Sheffield: Training Agency.

Pfeffer, J. and Leblebici, H. (1977) 'Information technology and organizational structure', *Pacific Sociological Review*, 20 (2), 241–61.

Phillips, B. and Kirchhoff, B. (1989) 'Formation, growth and survival: small firm dynamics in the US economy', *Small Business Economics*, 1 (1), 65–74.

Phizacklea, A. (1990) *Unpacking the Fashion Industry*. London: Routledge.

Phizacklea, A. and Ram, M. (1996) 'Open for business? – Ethnic entrepreneurship in comparative perspective', *Work, Employment and Society*, 10 (2), 319–39.

Pinchot, G. (1986) *Intrapreneuring*. New York: Harper and Row.

Piore, M. and Sabel, C. (1984) *The Second Industrial Divide: Prospects for Prosperity*. New York: Basic Books.

Pollard, C. E. and Hayne, S. C. (1998) 'The changing face of information system issues in small firms', *International Small Business Journal*, 16 (3), 70–87.

Poon, S. and Strom, J. (1997) *Small businesses use of the Internet – some realities*. Paper submitted to the Internet Society 1997 Conference, Kuala Lumpur, Malaysia.

Poon, S. and Swatman, P. M. C. (1997) 'Small business use of the Internet – findings from Australian case studies', *International Marketing Review*, 14 (5), 385–402.

Poon, S. and Swatman, P. M. C. (1998): 'Small business Internet commerce experiences: a longitudinal study', in *10th International BLED Electronic Commerce Conference: 'Global Business in Practice'*. Bled, Slovenia.

Porter, M. E. (1980) *Competitive Strategy – Techniques for Analysing Industries and Competitors*. New York: Free Press.

Porter, M. E. (1985) *Competitive Advantage: Creating and Sustaining Superior Perform-*ance. New York: Free Press.

Porter, M. E. (1990) *The Competitive Advantage of Nations*. London: Macmillan.

Porter, M. E. and Millar, V. E. (1985) 'How information gives you competitive advantage', *Harvard Business Review*, 63 (4), 149–60.

Portes, A. and Bach, R. L. (1985) *Latin Journey: Cuban and Mexican Immigrants in the United States*. Berkeley, CA: University of California Press.

Poutziouris, P. and Chittenden, F. (1996) *Family Businesses or Business Families?* UK Institute for Small Business Affairs Monograph in association with National Westminster Bank, Leeds.

Powell, W. W. (1990) 'Neither market nor hierarchy: new forms of organisation', in Commings, L. L. and Straw, B. M. (eds) *Research in Organizational Behaviour*, 295–336, Greenwich, CT: JAI Press.

Premchander, S. (1994) 'Income generating programmes for rural women – examining the role of NGOs', *Small Enterprise Development*, 5 (1).

Price, S. (1993a) 'Performance of fast-food franchises', in *The UK Fast-Food Industry, 1993, A Market Analysis*, Ch. 4. Cassell.

Price, S. (1993b) 'Performance of fast-food franchises in Britain', *International Journal of Contemporary Hospitality Management*, 5 (3), 10–15.

Pryor, A. K. and Shays, E. M. (1993) 'Growing the business with intrapreneurs', *Business Quarterly*, 57 (3), 43-9.

Pugliese, E. (1993) 'Restructuring of the labour market and the role of Third World migrations in Europe', *Environment and Planning D: Society and Space*, 11, 513–22.

Pyke, F. (1992) *Industrial Development through Small Firm Cooperation*. Geneva: International Labour Office.

Pyke, F. and Sengenberger, W. (eds) (1992) *Industrial Districts and Local Economic Regeneration*. Geneva: ILO.

Quelch, J. A. and Klein, L. R. (1996) 'The Internet and international marketing', *Sloan Management Review*, Spring, 60–75.

Quinn, R. and Cameron, K. (1983) 'Organisational life cycles and shifting criteria of effectiveness', *Management Science*, 29 33–51.

Rai, A., Patnayakuni, R. and Patnayakuni, N. (1997) 'Technology investment and business performance', *Communications of the ACM*, 40 (7), 89–97.

Rainnie, A. (1989) *Industrial Relations in Small Firms, Small Isn't Beautiful.* London: Routledge.

Rainnie, A. (1991) 'Small firms: between the enterprise culture and New Times', in Burrows, R. (ed.) *Deciphering the Enterprise Culture.* London: Routledge.

Rainnie, A. and Scott, M. (1986) 'Industrial relations in the small firm', *International Small Business Journal*, 4 (4), 42–60.

Ram, M. (1991) 'The dynamics of workplace relations in small firms', *International Small Business Journal*, 10 (1).

Ram, M. (1992) 'Coping with racism: Asian employers in the inner city', *Work, Employment and Society*, 6, 601–18.

Ram, M. (1994a) *Managing to Survive: Working Lives in Small Firms.* Oxford: Blackwell.

Ram, M. (1994b) 'Unravelling social networks in ethnic minority firms', *International Small Business Journal*, 12 (3), 42-53.

Ram, M. (1997) 'Supporting ethnic minority enterprise: views from the providers', in Ram, M., Deakins, D. and Smallbone, D. (eds) *Small Firms: Enterprising Futures*, pp. 148-60. London: Paul Chapman Publishing.

Ram, M. (1998) 'Enterprise support and ethnic minority firms', *Journal of Ethnic and Migration Studies*, 21 (1), 143–58.

Ram, M. and Deakins, D. (1995) *African-Caribbean Entrepreneurship in Britain.* Birmingham: University of Central England.

Ram, M. and Deakins, D. (1996) 'African-Caribbean entrepreneurship in Britain', *New Community*, 22 (1), 67–84.

Ram, M. and Holliday, R. (1993) '"Keeping it in the family": family culture in small firms', in Chittenden, F., Robertson, M. and Watkins, D. *(eds) Small Firms: Recession and Recovery.* London: Paul Chapman.

Ram, M. and Jones, T. (1998) *Ethnic Minorities in Business.* Milton Keynes: Open University Press.

Ramachadran, K., Ramnarayam, S. and Sundararajun, P. S. (1993) 'Subcultures and networking patterns: comparison of entrepreneurs from two states of India', in Birley, S. and MacMillan, I. C. (eds) *Entrepreneurship Research: Global Perspectives.* Elsevier Science.

Rath, J. (ed.) (1998) *Immigrant Businesses on the Urban Fringe: A Case for Interdisciplinary Analysis.* Basingstoke: Macmillan.

Ray, D. M. (1986) 'Perceptions of risk and new enterprise formation in Singapore: an exploratory study', in Ronstadt, R., Hornaday, J. A., Peterson, R. and Vesper, K. H. (eds) *Frontiers of Entrepreneurship Research*, 119–45. Wellesley, MA: Babson College.

Ray, D. M. (1994) 'The role of risk-taking in Singapore', *Journal of Business Venturing*, 9, 157–77.

Raymond, L. (1985) 'Organizational characteristics and MIS success in the context of small business', *MIS Quarterly*, 9 (1), 37–52.

Raymond, L. (1987) 'The presence of end-user computing in small business: an exploratory investigation of its distinguishing organisational and information systems context', *INFOR – Information Systems and Operational Research*, 25 (3), 198–213.

Raymond, L. (1989) 'Management information systems: problems and opportunities', *International Small Business Journal*, 7 (4), 44–53.

Raymond, L. (1990) 'Organizational context and IS success: a contingency approach', *Journal of Management Information Systems*, 6 (4), 5–20.

Raymond, L. and Magenat-Thalmann, N. (1982) 'Information systems in small business: are they used in managerial decisions?', *American Journal of Small Business*, 6 (4), 20–6.

Rayport, J. F. and Sviokla, J. J. (1994) 'Managing in the marketspace', *Harvard Business Review*, Nov.–Dec., 141–50.

Rayport, J. F. and Sviokla, J. J. (1995) 'Exploiting the virtual value chain', *Harvard Business Review*, Nov.–Dec., 75–85.

Razin, E. (1993) 'Immigrant entrepreneurs in Israel, Canada and California', in Light, I. and Bhachu, P. (eds) *Immigration and Entrepreneurship.* New Brunswick, NJ: Transaction.

Read, L. (1994*) The financing of women-owned businesses: a review and research agenda.* Venture Finance Working Paper No. 8, University of Southampton, Department of Geography.

Rees, H. and Shah, A. (1986) 'An empirical analysis of self-employment in the UK', *Journal of Applied Econometrics*, 1, 95–108.

Rees, T. (1992) *Women and the Labour Market.* London: Routledge.

Reeves, F. and Ward, R. (1984) 'West Indian business in Britain', in Ward, R. and Jenkins, R. (eds) *Ethnic Communities in Business*, 125–46. Cambridge: Cambridge University Press.

Reid, G. and Jacobsen, L. (1988) *The Small Entrepreneurial Firm*, David Hume Institute. Aberdeen: University Press.

Reid, S. D. (1982) 'The impact of size on export behaviour in small firms', in Czinkota, M. R.

and Tesar, G. (eds) *Export Management: An International Context*, 18–38. New York: Praeger Publishers.

Reid, S. D. (1981) 'The decision-maker and export entry and expansion', *Journal of International Business Studies*, 12 (2), 101–12.

Reid, S. D. (1983a) 'Export research in a crisis', in Czinkota, M. R. (ed.) *Export Promotion, the Public and Private Sector Interaction*, 129–53. New York: Praeger.

Reid, S. D. (1983b) 'Firm internationalisation: transaction cost and strategic choice', *International Marketing Review*, 1 (2), 45–55.

Reid, S. D. (1985) 'Exporting: does sales volume make a difference? – Comment', *Journal of International Business Studies*, Summer, 153–5.

Rex, J. (1982) 'West Indian and Asian youth', in Cashmore, E. and Troyna, B. (eds) *Black Youth in Crisis*, 53–71. London: Routledge and Kegan Paul.

Reynolds, P. and White, S. (1997) *The Entrepreneurial Process: Economic Growth, Men, Women and Minorities*. Westport, CT: Quorum.

Riding, A. L. and Swift, C. S. (1990) 'Women business owners and terms of credit: some empirical findings of the Canadian experience', *Journal of Business Venturing*, 5 (5), 327–40.

Riordan, D. A. and Riordan, M. P. (1993) 'Field theory: an alternative to systems theories in understanding the small family business', *Journal of Small Business Management*, April, 66-78.

Ritchie, D., Asch, D. and Weir, R. (1984) 'The provision of assistance to small firms', *International Small Business Journal*, 3, 62–5.

Ritchie, J. (1991) 'Enterprise cultures: a frame analysis', in Burrows, R. (ed.) *Deciphering the Enterprise Culture – Entrepreneurship, Petty Capitalism and the Restructuring of Britain*. London: Routledge.

Rix, A., Parkinson, R. and Gaunt, R. (1994) *Investors in People – A Qualitative Study of Employers*, DfEE Research Series No. 21. London: HMSO.

Roberts, E. B. (1991) *Entrepreneurs in High Technology*. Oxford: Oxford University Press.

Robertson, M., Swan, J. and Newell, S. (1996a) 'Interorganisational networks and the diffusion process: the case of networks not working', in Kautz, K. and Pries-Heje, J. (eds) *Diffusion and Adoption of Information Technology*, Proceedings of the First IFIP WG 8.6 Working Conference, Oslo, Norway, October 1995, 147–59. London: Chapman and Hall.

Robertson, M., Swan, J. and Newell, S. (1996b) 'The role of networks in the diffusion of technological innovation', *Journal of Management Studies*, 33 (3), May, 333–59.

Robinson, R. and Pearce, J. (1984) 'Research thrusts in small firm strategic planning', *Academy of Management Review*, 9 (1), 128–37.

Robinson, V. and Flintoff, I. (1982) 'Asian retailing in Coventry', *New Community*, 10, 251–8.

Robson, M. (1996a) 'Housing wealth, business creation and dissolution in the UK regions', *Small Business Economics*, 8, 39–48.

Robson, M. (1996b) 'Macroeconomic factors in the birth and death of UK firms: evidence from quarterly VAT registrations', *Manchester School of Economic and Social Studies*, 64 (2), 170–88.

Robson Rhodes (1984) *A Study of Business Financed under the Small Firms Loan Guarantee Scheme*, Department of Trade and Industry. London: HMSO.

Rockart, J. F. and Scott-Morton, M. S. (1984) 'Implications of changes in information technology for corporate strategy', *Interfaces*, 14 (1), 84-95.

Rogers, E. and Kincaid, D. (1981) *Communication Networks*. New York: The Free Press.

Rogers, E. M. (1995) *Diffusion of Innovations*, 4th edition. New York: The Free Press.

Romanelli, E. (1989) 'Environments and strategies of organisation start-up: effects on early survival', *Administrative Science Quarterly*, 34, 369–87.

Rosa, P. (1993) *Gender and small business co-ownership: implications for enterprise training*. Paper presented at INTENT, Stirling University.

Rosa, P. and Hamilton, D. (1994) 'Gender and ownership in UK small firms', *Entrepreneurship Theory and Practice*, 18 (3), 11–25.

Rosa, P., Hamilton, D., Carter, S. and Burns, H. (1994) 'The impact of gender on small business management: preliminary findings of a British study', *International Small Business Journal*, 12 (3), 25–33.

Rosa, P., Carter, S. and Hamilton, D. (1996) 'Gender as a determinant of small business performance: insights from a British study', *Small Business Economics*, 8, 463-78.

Ross, G. C. (1977) 'The determination of financial structure: the incentive signalling approach', *Bell Journal of Economics and Management Science*, Spring.

Rothwell, R. (1986) 'The role of the small firm in technical innovation', in Curran, J. (ed.) *The Survival of the Small Firm*. Aldershot: Gower.

Rothwell, R. (1991) 'External networking and innovation in small and medium-sized manufacturing firms in Europe', *Technovation*, 11 (2), 93–111.

Rothwell, R. and Dodgson, M. (1991) 'External linkages and innovation in small and medium-sized enterprises', *R&D Management*, 21 (2), 125–37.

Rotter, J. B. (1966) 'Generalized expectancies for internal versus external control of reinforcement', *Psychological Monograph*, 80, 1–28.

Rowden, R. (1995) 'The role of human resource development in successful small to mid-sized manufacturing businesses: a comparative case study', *Human Resource Development Quarterly*, 6 (6), 355–73.

Rubenson, G. C. and Gupta, A. K. (1990) 'The founder's disease: a critical re-examination', in *Frontiers of Entrepreneurship Research*, 167–83. Wellesley, MA: Babson Center for Entrepreneurship Research.

Rubin, P. (1978) 'The theory of the firm and the structure of the franchise contract', *Journal of Law and Economics*, 23, 223–33.

Rumelt, R. (1991) 'How much does industry matter?', *Strategic Management Journal*, 12, 167–85.

Sadler, D. and Southern, A. (1995) 'The economic significance of the steel industry to Cleveland: production strategies and supplier linkages', *Northern Economic Review*, 24, Winter, 66–81.

Saga, V. L. and Zmud, R. (1994): 'The nature and determinants of IT acceptance, routinization, and infusion', in Levine, L. (ed.) *Diffusion, Transfer and Implementation of Information Technology*, Proceedings of the IFIP TC8 Working Conference, Pittsburgh, 11-13 October 1993, 67–86. Amsterdam: Elsevier.

Sako, M. (1992) *Prices Quality and Trust: Inter-Firm Relations in Britain and Japan*. Cambridge: Cambridge University Press.

Salaff, J. and Hu, S. M. (1996) 'Working daughters of Hong Kong: filial piety or power in the family', *Asian Thought and Society*, XXI (61), Sept.–Dec., 187–9.

Sandberg, W. and Hofer, C. (1987) 'Improving new venture performance: the role of strategy, industry structure, and the entrepreneur', *Journal of Business Venturing*, 2, 5–28.

Sanders, J. M. and Nee, V. (1996) 'Immigrant self employment: the family as social capital and the value of human capital', *American Sociological Review*, 61 (2), 231–49.

Sassen, S. (1991) *The Global City: New York, London and Tokyo*. Princeton, NJ: Princeton University Press.

Sathe, V. (1989) 'Fostering entrepreneurship in the large, diversified firm', *Organizational Dynamics*, 18 (1), 20–32.

Sawyer, A. (1983) 'Black controlled business in Britain', *New Community*, 11 (1–2), 55–62.

Saxenian, A. L. (1985) 'Silicon Valley and Route 128: regional prototypes or historic exceptions?', in Castels, M. (ed.) *High Technology, Space and Society*. Beverly Hills: Sage.

Saxenian, A. L. (1990) 'Regional networks and the resurgence of Silicon Valley', *Californian Management Review*, 33 (1), 89–112.

Saxenian, A. (1996) *Regional Advantage: Culture and Competition in Silicon Valley and Route 128*, Cambridge, MA: Harvard University Press.

Sayer, A. (1997) 'The dialectic of culture and economy', in Lee, R. and Willis, J. (eds) *Geographies of Economies*. London: Arnold.

SBA (1996) *The State of Small Business 1996*. Washington, DC: Small Business Administration.

Scarman, Lord (1981) *The Brixton Disorders 10–12 April 1981*, Cmnd 8427. London: HMSO.

Scase, R. (1977) *Industrial Society: Class, Cleavage and Control*. London: Allen and Unwin.

Scase, R. (1995) 'Employment relations in small firms', in Edwards, P. (ed.) *Industrial Relations, Theory and Practice in Britain*. Oxford: Blackwell.

Scase, R. (1998a) *Towards the Future: An Agenda for Debate*. London: Office of Science and Technology.

Scase, R. (1998b) 'Employment beyond 2000', *Partnership with People*. London: Institute of Directors.

Scase, R. (1999) *Britain Towards 2010*. London: Office of Science and Technology.

Scase, R. and Goffee, R. (1980) *The Real World of the Small Business Owner*. London: Croom Helm.

Scase, R. and Goffee, R. (1982) *The Entrepreneurial Middle Class*. London: Croom Helm.

Scheré, J. (1982) 'Tolerance of ambiguity as a discriminating variable between entrepreneurs and managers', *Academy of Management Best Papers Proceedings*, 404.

Scherer, F. M. (1980) *Industrial Market Structure and Economic Performance*. Chicago: Rand McNally.

Scherer, R. F., Brodzinski, J. D. and Wiebe, F. A. (1991) 'Examining the relationship between personality and entrepreneurial career preference', *Entrepreneurship and Regional Development*, 3, 195–206.

Scholhammer, H. and Kuriloff, A. (1979) *Entrepreneurship and Small Business Management*. New York: John Wiley.

Schreier, J. (1973) *The Female Entrepreneur: A Pilot Study*. Milwaukee, WI: Center for Venture Management.

Schumacher, E. F. (1974) *Small is Beautiful*, London: Abacus.

Schumpeter, J. (1934) *History of Economic Analysis*. New York: Oxford University Press.

Schwab, B. and Schwab, H. (1997) 'Better risk management: a key to improved performance', *Journal of General Management*, 22 (4), 65–75.

Schwartz, E. B. (1976) 'Entrepreneurship: a new female frontier', *Journal of Contemporary Business*, Winter, 47–76.

Schwengel, H. (1991) 'British enterprise culture and German Kulturgesellschaft', in Keat, R. and Abercrombie, N. (eds.) *Enterprise Culture*. London: Routledge.

Schwenk, C. and Shrader, C. (1993) 'Effects of formal strategic planning on financial performance in small firms: a meta-analysis', *Entrepreneurship Theory & Practice*, Spring, 53–64.

Schwer, R. K. and Yucelt, U. (1984). 'A study of risk-taking propensities among small business entrepreneurs and managers: an empirical evaluation', *American Journal of Small Business*, 8 (3), 31–40.

Scott, M. and Rosa, P. (1997) '"New businesses from old": the role of portfolio entrepreneurs in the start-up and growth of small firms', in Ram, M., Deakins, D. and Smallbone, D. (eds) *Small Firms: Enterprising Futures*, 33–46. London: Paul Chapman.

Scott, M., Roberts, I., Holroyd, G. and Sawbridge, D. (1989) *Management and Industrial Relations in Small Firms*, Research Paper No. 70. London: Department of Employment.

Scottish Enterprise (1993) *Scotland's Business Birth Rate: A National Enquiry*. Glasgow: Scottish Enterprise.

Scottish Enterprise (1995) *P1 to plc*. Glasgow: Scottish Enterprise.

Scottish Enterprise (1997) *Local Heroes*. Glasgow: Scottish Enterprise.

Sear, L. (1996) 'Business Links: the regional story', *Regional Review*, 6 (2), 15–17.

Sear, L. and Agar, J. (1996) *A Survey of Business Link Personal Advisers: Are They Meeting Expectations?* Durham: Durham University Business School.

Sear, L. and Green, H. (1996) 'Small business development and enterprise support', in Haughton, G. and Williams, C. (eds) *Corporate City? Partnership, Participation and Partition in Urban Development in Leeds*. Aldershot: Avebury.

Segal Quince and Partners (1985) *The Cambridge Phenomenon*. Cambridge: Segal Quince and Partners.

Sen, C. and Lee, H. (1994) 'The impact of information technology on the franchise decision', *Proceedings of the 8th Conference of the Society of Franchising*, Nevada, 13–14 February.

Senn, J. A. and Gibson, V. R. (1981) 'Risks of investment in microcomputers for small business management', *Journal of Small Business Management*, 19 (3), 24–32.

Seringhaus, F. H. R. and Rosson, P. J. (1991) 'Export promotion and public organisations: the state of the art', in Seringhaus, R. F. and Rosson, P. J. (eds) *Export Development and Promotion: The Role of Public Organisations*, 3–18. Boston, MA: Kluwer Academic Publishers.

Sethi, V. and King, W. R. (1994) 'Development of measures to assess the extent to which an information technology application provides competitive advantage', *Management Science*, 40 (12), 1601–27.

Sexton, D. L. (1987) 'Advancing small business research: utilizing research from other areas', *American Journal of Small Business*, 11 (3), 25–30.

Sexton, D. L. and Bowman, N. (1985) 'The entrepreneur: a capable executive and more', *Journal of Business Venturing*, 1, 129–40.

Shakeshaft, C. and Nowell, I. (1984) 'Research on themes, concepts and models of organisational behaviour: the influence of gender', *Issues in Education*, 2 (3), 186–203.

Shanklin, W. L. and Ryans, J. K. (1988) 'Organising for high-tech marketing', in Tushman, M. L. and Moore, W. L. (eds) *Readings in the Management of Innovation*, 2nd edition, 487–98. New York: HarperCollins.

Sharma, D. (1993), 'Introduction: industrial networks in marketing', in Cavusgil, S. T. and

Sharma, D. (eds) *Advances in International Marketing*, vol. 5, 1–9. Greenwich: JAI Press.

Sharma, D. and Johanson, J. (1987) 'Technical consultancy in internationalisation', *International Marketing Review*, 4 (4), 20–9.

Shaver, K. G. and Scott, L. R. (1991) 'Person, process, choice: the psychology of new venture creation', *Entrepreneurship Theory and Practice*, 16 (2), 23–45.

Shaw, E. (1997) 'The real networks of small firms', in Deakins, D., Jennings, P. and Mason, C. (eds) *Small Firms: Entrepreneurship in the 1990s*. London: Paul Chapman Publishing.

Shaw, E. (1998) 'Social networks: their impact on the innovative behaviour of small service firms', *International Journal of Innovation Management*, 2 (2) 201–22.

Sillince, J. A. A., MacDonald, S. Lefang, B. and Frost, B. (1998) 'E-mail adoption, diffusion, use and impact within small firms: a survey of UK companies, *International Journal of Information Management*, 18 (4), 231–42.

Sisson, K. (1993) 'In search of HRM', *British Journal of Industrial Relations*, 31 (2), 201–10.

Sjöberg, L. (1993) *Life-Styles and Risk Perception* (14). Stockholm: Center for Risk Research, Stockholm School of Economics.

Small Business Action Update (1998). Department of Trade and Industry, URN98/573.

Small Business Foresight (1996) *Small Business Foresight Digest*, Edition 1.1. Durham: University of Durham.

Small Firm, Big Future, Conservative Party pamphlet, 1983.

Smallbone, D. (1990) 'Success and failure in new businesses', *International Small Business Journal* 8 (2), 34–47.

Smallbone, D. and North, D. (1996) 'Survival, growth and age of SMEs: some implications for regional development', in Danson, M. (ed.) *Small Firm Formation and Regional Economic Development*, 36–64. London: Routledge.

Smallbone, D. and Wyer, P. (1994) SMEs and exporting: developing an analytical framework. Paper presented to Small Business and Enterprise Development Conference, Manchester, 28–9 March.

Smallbone, D. and Wyer, P. (1997) *Export Activities in SMEs: A Strategic Framework*, Working Paper Series, CEEDR Publication No 6. October 1997. Middlesex University: Centre for Enterprise and Economic Development Research.

Smallbone, D., North, D. and Leigh, R. (1992) *Managing Change for Growth and Survival: The Study of Mature Manufacturing Firms in London in the 1980s*, Working Paper No. 3. Planning Research Centre, Middlesex Polytechnic.

Smallbone, D., North, D. and Leigh, R. (1993) 'The growth and survival of mature manufacturing SMEs in the 1980s: an urban–rural comparison', in Curran, J. and Storey, D. (eds) *Small Firms in Urban and Rural Locations*, 8, 79–131. London: Routledge.

Smallbone, D. J., Leigh, R. and North, D. (1995) 'The characteristics and strategies of high growth firms', *International Journal of Entrepreneurial Behaviour and Research*, 1 (3), 44–62.

Smallbone, D., Piasecki, B., Damyanov, A., Labriandis, L. and Venesaar, U. (1998) *Internationalisation, Inter-Firm Linkages and SME Development in Central and Western Europe*, final report to EU Phare (ACE) Committee. London: Centre for Enterprise and Economic Development Research, Middlesex University.

Smith, N. R. (1967) 'The entrepreneur and his firm: the relationship between type of man and type of company'. Occasional Paper, Bureau of Business and Economic Research, Graduate School of Business Administration, Michigan State University, East Lansing, Michigan.

Snyder, M. and Cantor, N. (1998) 'Understanding personality and social behavior: a functionalist strategy', in Gilbert, D. T., Fiske, S. T. and Lindzey, G. (eds) *The Handbook of Social Psychology*, 4th edition, vol. 1, 635-79. Boston, MA: The McGraw-Hill Companies, Inc.

Soh, C., Mah, Q. Y., Gan, F. J., Chew, D. and Reid, E. (1997) 'The use of the Internet for business: the experience of early adopters in Singapore', *Internet Research: Electronic Networking Applications and Policy* 7 (3), 217–28.

Soh, P. P., Yap, C. S. and Raman, K. S. (1992) 'Impact of consultants on computerization success in small businesses', *Information and Management*, 22 (5), 309–19.

Solemn, O. and Stiener, M. (1989) *Factors for success in small manufacturing firms – and with special emphasis on growing firms*. Paper presented at Conference on Small and Medium Sized Enterprises and the Challenges of 1992, Mikkeli, Finland.

Solomon, G. T. and Fernald, L. W. (1988) 'Value profiles of male and female entrepreneurs', *International Small Business Journal*, 6 (3), 24–33.

Soni, S., Tricker, M. and Ward, R. (1987) *Ethnic Minority Business in Leicester*. Birmingham: Aston University.

Sparrow, P. and Marchington, M. (1998) *Human Resource Management: The New Agenda*. London: Financial Times, Pitman.

Spence, J. T. (1985) 'Achievement American style – the rewards and costs of individualism', *American Psychologist*, 40 (12), 1285–95.

Srinavasan, S. (1992) 'The class position of the Asian petite bourgeoisie', *New Community*, 19 (1), 61–74.

Stacey, R. D. (1990) 'Dynamic strategic management', in Armstrong, M. (ed.) *The New Manager's Handbook*, 299–333. London: Kogan Page.

Stacey, R. D. (1996) *Strategic Management & Organisational Dynamics*. London: Pitman.

Stafford, W. (1995) 'Ferdinand Tonnies on gender, women and the family', *History of Political Thought*, XVI (3), Autumn, 391–415.

Stanworth, J. (1977) *A Study of Franchising in Britain: A Research Report*. London: University of Westminster.

Stanworth, J. (1984) *A Study of Power Relationships and their Consequences in Franchise Organisations*. London: University of Westminster.

Stanworth, J. and Curran, J. (1976) 'Growth and the small firm – an alternative view', *Journal of Management Studies* 13, 95–110.

Stanworth, J. and Gray, C. (eds) (1991) *Bolton 20 Years On: The Small Firm in the 1990s*. London: Paul Chapman Publishing.

Stanworth, J. and Purdy, D. (1993) *The Blenheim Group plc/University of Westminster Franchise Survey*, Special Studies Series Paper No. 1, International Franchise Research Centre.

Starr, J. A. and Fondas, N. (1992) 'A model of entrepreneurial socialization and organization formation', *Entrepreneurship Theory and Practice*, 17 (1), 67–76.

Starr, J. A. and Yudkin, M. (1996) *Women Entrepreneurs: A Review of Current Research*. Wellesley, MA: Center for Research on Women, Wellesley College.

Steinmetz, L. L. (1969) 'Critical stages of small business growth', *Business Horizons*, 12 (1), 29–34.

Stern, P. and Stanworth, J. (1994) 'Improving small business survival rates via franchising – the role of banks in Europe', *International Small Business Journal*, 12 (2).

Stevenson, H. and Gumpert, D. (1985) 'The heart of entrepreneurship', *Harvard Business Review*, 63 (2), 85–94.

Stevenson, L. (1983) *An investigation into the entrepreneurial experience of women*. Paper presented to the ASAC Conference, University of British Columbia, Vancouver.

Stimpson, D. V., Robinson, P. B., Waranusuntikule, S. and Zheng, R. (1990) 'Attitudinal characteristics of entrepreneurs and non-entrepreneurs in United States, Korea, Thailand, and the People's Republic of China', *Entrepreneurship and Regional Development*, 2, 49–55.

Stinchcombe, A. L. (1965) 'Social structure and organization', in March, J. G. (ed.) *Handbook of Organizations*, 142–93. Chicago: Rand McNally.

Stokes, D. R. (1997) 'A lesson in entrepreneurial marketing from the public sector', *Marketing Education Review*, 7 (3), Fall.

Stokes, D. R. (1998) *Small Business Management*, 3rd edition. London: Letts Educational.

Stokes, D. R., Fitchew, S. and Blackburn, R. (1997) *Marketing in Small Firms: A Conceptual Approach*, Report to the Royal Mail, Small Business Research Centre, Kingston University.

Stone, M. and Brush, C. (1996) 'Planning in ambiguous contexts: the dilemma of meeting needs for commitment and demands for legitimacy', *Strategic Management Journal*, 17, 633–52.

Stopford, J. M. and Baden-Fuller, C. (1994) 'Creating corporate entrepreneurship', *Strategic Management Journal*, 15 (7) 521–36.

Storey, D. J. (1982) *Entrepreneurship and the Small Firm*. London: Croom Helm.

Storey, D. J. (1992) *Should We Abandon Support to Start-Up Businesses?* Working Paper No. 7. Warwick: Warwick Business School Small and Medium Enterprise Centre.

Storey, D. J. (1993) 'Should we abandon support to start-up businesses?', in Chittenden, F. and Robertson, M. (eds) *Small Firms: Recession and Recovery*. London: Paul Chapman Publishing.

Storey, D. (1994) *Understanding the Small Business Sector*. London: Routledge.

Storey, D. J. and Johnson, S. (1987) *Job Generation and Labour Market Change*. Basingstoke: Macmillan.

Storey, D. J. and Strange, A. (1992) *Entrepreneurship in Cleveland, 1979–1989: A Study of the Effects of the Enterprise Culture*, Employment Department, Research Series No. 3.

Storey, D. and Westhead, P. (1994) *Management Training and Small Firm Performance: A Critical Review*, Working Paper No. 18. Warwick University: SME Centre.

Storey, D. J. and Westhead, P. (1996) 'Management training and small firm performance: why is the link so weak?', *International Small Business Journal*, 14 (4), 13–24.

Storey, D., Keasey, K., Watson, R. and Wynarczyk, P. (1987) *The Performance of Small Firms: Profits, Jobs and Failures*. London: Croom Helm.

Storey, J. (ed.) (1989) *New Perspectives on Human Resource Management*. London: Routledge.

Storey, J. (ed.) (1995) *Human Resource Management: A Critical Text*. London: Routledge.

Strassman, P. A. (1997) '40 years of IT history', *Datamation*, October, 80–90.

Stratos Group (1990) *Strategic Orientations of Small European Businesses*. Aldershot: Gower Publishing.

Styles, C. and Ambler, T. (1997) *The First Step to Export Success*, PAN'AGRA Research Programme, London Business School.

Styles, C. and Ambler, T. (1994) 'Successful export practice: the U.K. experience', *International Marketing Review*, 11 (6).

Sullivan, D. and Bauerschmidt, A. (1990) 'Incremental internationalisation: a test of Johanson and Vahlne's thesis', *Management International Review*, 30 (1), 19–30.

Summon, P. (1998) 'Business Link impact and future challenges', *Small Business and Enterprise Development*, 5 (1), 49–59.

Swanson, C. E., Kopecky, K. J. and Tucker, A. (1997) 'Technology adoption over the life cycle and aggregate technological progress', *Southern Economic Journal*, 63 (4), 872–87.

Swanson, E. B. (1974) 'Management information systems: appreciation and involvement', *Management Science*, 21 (2), 74–85.

Swanson, E. B. (1994) 'Information systems innovation among organizations', *Management Science*, 40 (9), 1069–92.

Swanson, E. B. and Ramiller, N. C. (1993) 'Information systems research thematics: submissions to a new journal, 1987–1992', *Information Systems Research*, 4 (4), 299–330.

Swartz, L. N. (1995) *Worldwide Franchising Statistics: A Study of Worldwide Franchise Associations*. Arthur Andersen, November.

Szajna, B. (1996) 'Empirical evaluation of the revised technology acceptance model', *Management Science*, 42 (1), 85–92.

Szarka, J. (1990) 'Networking and small firms', *International Small Business Journal*, 8 (2), 10–22.

Tacis (1997) *SME-Policy in the European Union*. Brussels: Tacis Services DG1A, European Commission

Tan, W. L. (1998) 'Asia: Singapore', in Morrison, A. (ed.), *Entrepreneurship: An International Perspective*. Oxford: Butterworth-Heinemann.

Tann, J. and Laforet, S. (1998) 'Assuring consultant quality for SMEs: the role of Business Links', *Small Business and Enterprise Development*, 5 (1), 7–18.

Tapscott, D. (1995) *The Digital Economy*. New York: McGraw-Hill.

Tapscott, D. and Caston, A. (1993) *Paradigm Shift: The New Promise of Information Technology*. New York: McGraw-Hill.

Tayeb, M. (1988) *Organisations and National Culture*. London: Sage.

Taylor, A. (1993) 'DTI will talk only to large lobby groups, Heseltine says', *The Financial Times*, 18 June.

Taylor, F. W. (1947) *Scientific Management*. London: Harper and Row.

Taylor, S. E. (1998) 'The social being in social psychology', in Gilbet, D. T., Fiske, S. T. and Lindsey, G. (eds) *The Handbook of Social Psychology*, vol. 1, 58–95. Boston, MA: The McGraw-Hill Companies, Inc.

Tesar, G. and Tarleton, J. S. (1982) 'Comparison of Wisconsin and Virginia small- and medium-sized exporters: aggressive and passive exporters', in Czinkota, M. R. and Tesar, G. (eds) *Export Management: An International Context*, 85–112. New York: Praeger Publishers.

Tesler, L. G. (1995) 'Networked computing in the 1990s', *Scientific American*, Special Issue, 6 (1) 'The Computer in the 21st Century', reprinted from the September 1991 issue, 10–21.

Thomas, H. and Krishnarayan, V. (1993) 'Local authority assistance to ethnic minority-owned small firms: some recent survey evidence from Britain', *Local Economy*, 8, 261–7.

Thompson, G. (1993) 'Network coordination', in Maidment, R. and Thompson, G. (eds) *Managing the United Kingdom*. London: Sage.

Thompson, M. and Wilson, A. (1991) *Wage levels, labour markets and firm size: evidence from six local labour markets*. Paper presented at the 7th ESRC Small Business Initiative, University of Warwick.

Thong, J. Y. L. and Yap, C. S. (1995) 'CEO characteristics, organizational characteristics and information technology adoption in small businesses', *Omega – International Journal of Management Science*, 23 (4), 429–42.

Thong, J. Y. L., Yap, C. S. and Raman, K. S. (1994) 'Engagement of external expertise in information systems implementation', *Journal of Management Information Systems*, 11 (2), 209–31.

Thong, J. Y. L., Yap, C. S. and Raman, K. S. (1996) 'Top management support, external expertise and information systems implementation in small businesses', *Information Systems Research* 7 (2), 248–67.

Tichy, N. (1981) 'Networks in organizations', in Nystrom, P. C. and Starbuck, W. H. (eds) *Handbook of Organisational Design Volume 2: Remodelling Organisations and Their Environments*. Oxford: Oxford University Press.

Tichy, N. M., Tushman, M. L. and Fombrun, C. (1979) 'Social network analysis for organisations', *Academy of Management Review*, 4 (4), 507–19.

Tiebout, C. M. (1957) 'Location theory, empirical evidence, and economic evolution', *Papers and Proceedings of the Regional Science Association*, 3, 74–86.

Timmons, J. A. (1994) *New Venture Creation*, 4th edition. Boston, MA: Irwin.

Towers, B. (1992) *A Handbook of Industrial Relations Practice*. London: Kogan Page.

Training Agency (1989) *Training in Britain*. London: HMSO.

Trompenaars, F. (1993) *Riding the Waves of Culture*. London: The Economist Books.

Trutko, J., Trutko, J. and Kostecka, A. (1993) *Franchising's Growing Role in the U.S. Economy, 1975-2000*. US Small Business Administration.

Tsur, Y., Sternberg, M. and Hochman, E. (1990) 'Dynamic modeling of innovation process adoption with risk aversion and learning', *Oxford Economic Paper*, 42, 336-55.

Turnbull, P. W. (1987) 'A challenge to the stages theory of the internationalisation process', in Rosson, P. J. and Reid, S. D. (eds) *Managing Export Entry and Expansion*, 21–40. New York: Praeger.

Tybejee, T. T. (1994) 'Internationalisation of high tech firms: initial vs. extended involvement', *Journal of Global Marketing*, 7 (4), 59–81.

UK Franchise Directory (1993) 9th edition. Franchise Development Services Limited.

US Department of Commerce (*c.*1997) *India: Marketing U.S. Products and Services* (Country Commercial Guide), undated.

Van Auken, H. E., Gaskill, L. R. and Kao, S. (1993) 'Acquisition of capital by women entrepreneurs: patterns of initial and refinancing capitalization', *Journal of Small Business and Entrepreneurship*, 10 (4), 44–55.

Van der Horst, H. (1996) *The Low Sky: Understanding the Dutch*. Den Haag: Scriptum.

van der Wees, C. and Romijn, H. (1987) *Entrepreneurship and Small Enterprise Development for Women in Developing Countries*. Geneva: ILO Management Development Branch.

Vandermerwe, S. and Birley, S. (1997) 'The corporate entrepreneur: leading organizational transformation', *Long Range Planning*, 30 (3), 345–54.

Venkatraman, N. and Ramanujam, V. (1987) 'Measurement of business economic performance: an examination of method convergence', *Journal of Management*, 13 (1), 109–22.

Vernon-Wortzel, H. and Wortzel, L. (1997) *Strategic Management in a Global Economy*. New York: John Wiley.

Vesper, K. (1990) *New Venture Strategies*. Englewood Cliffs, NJ: Prentice Hall.

Vyakarnaram, S., Jacobs, R. and Handleberg, J. (1997) *The formation and development of entrepreneurial teams in rapid growth businesses*. Paper presented to Babson Entrepreneurship Research Conference, Babson College, Boston.

Waldinger, R. (1995) 'The "other" side of embeddedness: a case study of the interplay of economy and ethnicity', *Ethnic and Racial Studies*, 18 (3), 555–80.

Waldinger, R. and Tseng, T. (1992) 'Divergent diasporas: the Chinese communities of New York and Los Angeles compared', *Revue Européenne des Migrations Internationales*, 8, 91–115.

Waldinger, R., Aldrich, H. and Ward, R. (eds) (1990a) *Ethnic Entrepreneurs*. London: Sage.

Waldinger, R., McEvoy, D. and Aldrich, H. (1990b) 'Spatial dimensions of opportunity structures', in Waldinger, R., Aldrich, H. and Ward, R. (eds) *Ethnic Entrepreneurs*, 106–30. London: Sage.

Walsh, J. and Dewar, R. (1987) 'Formalisation and the organisational life cycle', *Journal of Management Studies*, 24, 215–31.

Wanogho, E. (1997) *Black Women Taking Charge*. London: E.W. International.

Ward, J. L. (1987) *Keeping the Family Business Healthy*. California: Jossey-Bass.

Ward, R. (1991) 'Economic development and ethnic business', in Curran, J. and Blackburn, R. A. (eds) *Paths of Enterprise: The Future of the Small Business*, 51–67. London: Routledge.

Ward, R. and Jenkins, R. (eds) (1984) *Ethnic Communities in Business*. Cambridge: Cambridge University Press.

Watkins, D. S. (1973) 'Technical entrepreneurship; a Cis-Atlantic view', *R&D Management*, 3, 2.

Watkins, J. and Watkins, D. (1984) 'The female entrepreneur: background and determinants of business choice – some British data', *International Small Business Journal*, 2 (4), 21–31.

Watkins, J. and Watkins, D. (1986) 'The female entrepreneur: her background and determinants of business choice – some British data', in Curran, J., Stanworth, J. and Watkins, D. (eds) *The Survival of the Small Firm*, 220–32. Aldershot: Gower.

Weber, M. (1976) *The Protestant Ethic and the Spirit of Capitalism*. London: Allen and Unwin.

Webster, F. E., Jr (1992) 'The changing role of marketing in the organisation', *Journal of Marketing*, 56, October, 1–17.

Weidenbaum, M. (1996) 'The Chinese family business enterprise', *California Management Review*, 38 (4).

Weiner, B. (1985) 'An attributional theory of achievement motivation and emotion', *Psychological Review*, 92 (4), 548–73.

Weiner, B. (1992) *Human Motivation: Metaphors, Theories, and Research*. Newbury Park, CA: Sage Publications, Inc.

Weinrauch, J. D., Mann, K., Robinson, P. A. and Pharr, J. (1991) 'Dealing with limited financial resources: a marketing challenge for small business', *Journal of Small Business Management*, 29 (4), 44–54.

Weiss, L. (1998) *The Myth of the Powerless State: Governing the Economy in a Global Era*. Cambridge: Polity Press.

Welch, L. S. and Luostarinen, R. (1988) 'Internationalisation: evolution of a concept', *Journal of General Management*, 14 (2), 34–55.

Welsch, H. and Young, E. (1993) 'Male and female entrepreneurial characteristics and behaviours: a profile of similarities and differences', *International Small Business Journal*, 2 (4), 11–20.

Welsh, J. A. and White, J. F. (1984) 'A small business is not a little big business', in Gumpert, D. E. (ed.) *Growing Concerns: Building and Managing the Smaller Business*, 149–67. New York: Wiley.

Werbner, P. (1980) 'From rags to riches: Manchester Pakistanis in the garment trade', *New Community*, 9, 84–95.

Werbner, P. (1984) 'Business on trust: Pakistani entrepreneurship in the Manchester garment trade', in Ward, R. and Jenkins, R. (eds) *Ethnic Communities in Business*, 166–88. Cambridge: Cambridge University Press.

Werbner, P. (1990) 'Renewing an industrial past: British Pakistani entrepreneurship in Manchester', *Migration*, 8, 17–41.

West, A. (1988) *A Business Plan*. London: Pitman Publishing.

West, G. M. (1975) 'MIS in small organizations', *Journal of Systems Management*, 26 (4), 10–13.

Westerberg, M. (1998) *Managing in Turbulence: An Empirical Study of Small Firms Operating in a Turbulent Environment*. Luleå, Sweden: Luleå Technological University.

Westhead, P. (1997) 'Ambitions, "external" environment and strategic factor differences between family and non-family companies', *Entrepreneurship and Regional Development*, 19 (2), April–June, 127–57.

Westhead, P. and Birley, S. (1993) *Employment Growth in New Independent Owner-Managed Firms in Great Britain*. Warwick: University of Warwick.

Westhead, P. and Storey, D. (1997) *Training Provision and Development of Small and Medium-Sized Enterprises*, Research Report No. 26. London: HMSO.

Westwood, S. and Bhachu, P. (eds) (1988) *Enterprising Women: Ethnicity, Economy and Gender Relations*. London: Routledge.

Whatmore, S. (1991) *Farming Women: Gender, Work and Family Enterprise*. London: Macmillan.

Wheeldon, P. D. (1969) 'The operation of voluntary associations and personal networks in the political processes of an inter-ethnic community', in Mitchell, J. (ed.) *Social Networks in Urban Situations*, 128–74. Manchester: University of Manchester Press.

Wheelock, J. (1991) 'The flexibility of small business family work strategies', in Caley, K., Chell, E., Chittenden, F. and Mason, C. (eds) *Small Enterprise Development: Policy and Practice in Action*. London: Paul Chapman Publishing.

Whisler, T. L. (1970a) *The Impact of Computers in Organizations*. New York: Praeger.

Whisler, T. L. (1970b) *Information Technology and Organizational Change*. Belmont: Wadsworth.

Wiedersheim-Paul, F., Olson, H. C. and Welch, L. S. (1978) 'Pre-export activity: the first in internationalisation', *Journal of International Business Studies*, 9 (1), 47–58.

Wiklund, J. (1998) *Small Firm Growth and Performance*. Jönköping, Sweden: Jönköping International Business School.

Wiklund, J., Davidsson, P., Delmar, F. and Aronsson, M. (1997) 'Expected consequences of growth and their effects on growth willingness in different samples of small firms', in Reynolds, P. D., Bygrave, W. D., Carter, N. M., Davidsson, P., Gartner, W. B. and McDougall, P. P. (eds) *Frontiers of Entrepreneurship Research 1997*, 1–16. Babson Park, MA: Center for Entrepreneurial Studies, Babson College.

Williamson, O. (1975) *Markets and Hierarchies: Analysis and Antitrust Implications*. New York: The Free Press.

Williamson, O. (1985) *The Economic Institutions of Capitalism*. New York: Free Press.

Williamson, O. (1991) 'Corporate economic organization: the analysis of discrete structural alternatives', *Administrative Science Quarterly*, 36, 269–96.

Williamson, O. (1996) 'Economic organisation: the case for cander', *Academy of Management Review*, 21 (1), 48–57.

Wilson Committee (1979) *The Financing of Small Firms: Interim Report of the Committee to Review the Functioning of the Financial Institutions*, Cmnd 7503. London: HMSO.

Wilson, N., Watson, K. and Summers, B. (1995) *Trading Relationships, Credit Management and Corporate Performance*. The Credit Management Research Group, University of Bradford Management Centre.

Winckles, K. (1986) *The Practice of Successful Business Management*. London: Kogan Page.

Winkler, J. (1977) 'The corporatist economy', in *Industrial Society*, R. Scase (ed.) Industrial Society: Class, Cleavage and Control'. London: Allen and Unwin.

Withey, J. J. (1980), 'Differences between exporters and non-exporters: some hypotheses concerning small manufacturing business', *American Journal of Small Business*, 4 (3), 29–37.

Wojtas, O. (1993), 'Scotland employs best test pilots', *Times Higher Education Supplement*, 8 January.

Woo, C., Cooper, A., Dunkelberg, W., Daellenbach, U. and Dennis, W. (1989) *Determinants of growth for small and large entrepreneurial start ups*. Paper presented at Babson Entrepreneurship Conference, Babson, USA.

Wood, R. and Bandura, A. (1989) 'Social cognitive theory of organizational management', *Academy of Management Review*, 14 (3), 361–84.

Woodward, M. D. (1997) *Black Entrepreneurs in America: Stories of Struggle and Success*. New Brunswick, NJ: Rutgers University Press.

Wortman, M. S. (1994) 'Theoretical foundations for family-owned business: a conceptual and research-based paradigm', *Family Business Review*, 7 (1), Spring, 3–27.

Wright, M. (1988) 'Policy community, policy networks and comparative industrial policies', *Political Studies*, 36, 593–612.

Wyer, P. (1990). *The effects of varying forms and degrees of government intervention upon the effective competitiveness of UK small businesses*. Unpublished PhD thesis. Birmingham: University of Aston.

Wyer, P. (1997) *Small business interaction with the external operating environment – the role of strategic management and planning within the small business*. Paper presented to Small Business and Enterprise Development Conference, Sheffield, 30–31 March 1998.

Wyer, P. and Boocock, G. (1996) *The internationalisation of small and medium sized enterprises: an organisational learning perspective*. Paper presented to the 7th ENDEC World Conference on Entrepreneurship, Singapore, 5–7 December.

Wyer, P. and Mason, J. (1998a) *Recognising the complexity of the small business management task within Malaysia: toward an understanding of 'best management practice'*. Paper presented to the Second Global Change Conference – The Impact of Change in the 21st Century, Manchester, April.

Wyer, P. and Mason, J. (1998b) 'An organisational learning perspective to enhancing understanding of people management in small businesses', *International Journal of Entrepreneurial Behaviour and Research*, 4 (2), 112–28.

Wynarczyk, P. (1993) *The Managerial Labour Markets in Small Firms*. London: Routledge.

Wynarczyk, P., Watson, R., Storey, D. J., Short, H. and Keasey, K. (1993) *The Managerial Labour Market in Small and Medium Sized Enterprises*. London: Routledge.

Yap, C. S. and Thong, J. Y. L. (1997) 'Programme evaluation of a government information technology programme for small businesses', *Journal of Information Technology*, 12 (2), 107–20.

Yap, C. S., Soh, C. P. P. and Raman, K. S. (1992) 'Information systems success factors in small business', *Omega – International Journal of Management Science*, 20 (5/6), 597–609.

Yellow Pages (1993) *The Business Database*. London: British Telecommunications Plc.

Yoffie, D. B. (1997) 'Competing in the age of digital convergence', *California Management Review*, 38 (4), 31–53.

Young, S. (1987) 'Business strategy and the internationalisation of business: recent approaches', *Managerial and Decision Economics*, 8, 31–40.

Young, S. (1990) 'Internationalisation: introduction and overview', *International Marketing Review*, 7 (4).

Young, S., Hamill, J., Wheeler, C. and Davis, J. R. (1989) *International Market Entry and Development*. Hemel Hempstead: Harvester Wheatsheaf.

Zafarullah, M., Ali, M. and Young, S. (1998) 'The internationalisation of the small firm in developing countries – exploratory research from Pakistan', *Journal of Global Marketing*, 11 (3), 21–38.

Zaltman, G., Duncan, R. and Holbek, J. (1973) *Innovations and Organizations*. New York: Wiley & Sons.

Zimmer, C. and Aldrich, H. (1987) 'Resource mobilization through ethnic networks', *Sociology Perspectives*, 30 (4), 422–45.

Zinatelli, N., Cragg, P. B. and Cavaye, A. L. M. (1996) 'End user computing sophistication and success in small firms', *European Journal of Information Systems*, 5 (3), 172–81.

Zmud, R. W. (1984): 'An examination of push-pull theory applied to process innovation in knowledge work', *Management Science*, 30 (6), 727–38.

Zmud, R. W. and Apple, L. E. (1992) 'Measuring technology incorporation/infusion', *Journal of Product Innovation Management*, 9 (2), 148–55.

Index